FARRAR
STRAUS
GIROUX

Independent Spirit

Hubert Butler

INDEPENDENT

SPIRIT

Essays

Farrar, Straus and Giroux

New York

The essays in this edition were originally published in Ireland in the following
books: Escape from the Anthill, The Lilliput Press, in 1985, copyright © 1985,
1986 by Hubert Butler; The Children of Drancy, The Lilliput Press, in 1988,
copyright © 1988 by Hubert Butler; Grandmother and Wolfe Tone, The Lilliput
Press, in 1990, copyright © 1990 by Hubert Butler; In the Land of Nod, The
Lilliput Press, in 1996, copyright © 1996 by Hubert Butler.
Published simultaneously in Canada by HarperCollinsCanadaLtd
Printed in the United States of America
First edition, 1996

Library of Congress Cataloging-in-Publication Data
Butler, Hubert.
Independent spirit : essays / Hubert Butler.
p.   cm.
Includes index.
I. Title.
AC8.B82   1996   824'.914—dc20   95-47240   CIP

Contents

Editor's Preface

Hubert Butler was born in Kilkenny in 1900 and died there in 1991. A writer—historian, translator, amateur archaeologist, essayist—of uncommon grace and power, he was not well known for much of his life except to readers of journals as diverse as *The Irish Army Journal* and *Peace News*, though his essays also appeared in *The Irish Times* and *The Bell* (of which he was briefly review editor) and were broadcast on Radio Éireann and the BBC. Born into an Anglo-Irish family with connections to Kilkenny that went back to the twelfth century, and himself educated in England, Butler decided as a boy—certainly before the Easter Rising of 1916—that his future lay in Ireland. This was a choice that few of his class and culture were making, and once it was made, the imaginative and literary life that followed became, it would seem, effortlessly international.

After Oxford, Butler worked with the Irish County Library movement under the guidance of George Russell (AE) and Horace Plunkett, travelled extensively for a decade and more in Europe and beyond, teaching English in Alexandria in 1927 and Leningrad in 1931, exploring the Baltic and Balkan countries, spending 1934–37 in Zagreb, Belgrade, and Dubrovnik on a scholarship from the School of Slavonic Studies in London. His translations of Leonov's *The Thief* and Chekhov's *The Cherry Orchard* (which he prepared for his brother-in-law Tyrone Guthrie's Old Vic production starring Charles Laughton, and which many consider the best English translation of that masterpiece) appeared in 1931 and 1934. In 1938–39, Butler worked for a Quaker relief organization in Vienna, helping Jews to escape Austria; he returned to Kilkenny upon his father's death in

1941 and remained at his family home, Maidenhall—with sojourns to America, China, and Russia—until his death.

Not until the 1980s, when Antony Farrell of The Lilliput Press collected and published in Ireland the essays Butler had written over the previous half century (104 of them: in *Escape from the Anthill*, 1985; *The Children of Drancy*, 1988; *Grandmother and Wolfe Tone*, 1990; and *In the Land of Nod*, 1996), did his work become known to a larger public. The four books included, it should be noted, several small masterpieces that had never been published anywhere before. A later volume of selected essays appeared in London, with an introduction by Roy Foster; *Independent Spirit* marks effectively Butler's first appearance in the United States.

There are deeper reasons for the obscurity of Butler's career than mere publishing inefficiency or cultural caprice, and they go to the heart of his most valuable strengths and virtues. Butler espoused an Irish republicanism that was hardly congenial to most people in his Anglo-Irish world, and he lived his robust Irish Protestantism throughout a lifetime in fiercely Roman Catholic Eire. He honored Irish history, about which he wrote with keen passion and intensity, yet inveighed against the forces that encouraged banal or sentimental versions of it, set himself against sectarian vehemence, and vigorously opposed the institutions that obscured or deformed the possibilities for a peaceful, united Irish future. His distaste for the genteel hypocrisies of British imperialism, as for Irish bombast, was clear. Thus, in London as in Dublin or Belfast, conventional and mediocre minds marginalized or ignored him.

What Roy Foster has called Butler's "resolute suspicion of established authority stepping in to dictate decisions which should be personal . . . his own skepticism, irony and integrity"—these were qualities that encouraged readers to revere him in his old age, when his books first appeared, but that had made him dangerous to orthodoxy earlier on. As Maurice Craig observed in his foreword to the first of the Butler books, "For all his elegance, Hubert Butler is no belletrist. For him an essay is a projectile, aimed at a particular target and freighted with what it needs to do its work: no more and no less. All his projectiles tend to converge on the same area of moral choice: the responsibilities of the individual to his community and, by implication, those of the community towards him, in the special sphere where belief and conduct, dogma and decency, are so often in conflict."

The essays in *Independent Spirit* give ample proof of Butler's power and effect as a writer who, as Edna Longley put it, "like Orwell fuses moral attitude with prose style." His essay on "The Eggman and the Fairies," the ones on "Boycott Village" and "Abortion," and the haunting long article that concludes this book, "Little K," which centers on issues raised when considering the fate of a grievously and permanently disabled baby—these unforgettably demonstrate his allegiance to principles of lucid charity, scrupulous honesty, moral care; and his deep understanding of the baleful influences of social and government censorship, clerical authority, ancient and comforting prejudices. It is bracing and humbling to remember that Butler wrote these in Ireland at a time when public discussion of sex-related crimes, divorce, abortion, let alone euthanasia, was severely and punitively prohibited. Yet it was an Ireland Butler loved and whose beauties he celebrated; one is reminded, as one is so often in Butler's work, that cruel repression and thoughtless tyranny lurk in the shadows of even the most benign or amiable society. As Dervla Murphy has noted: "Although a resolute crusader for honesty in every area of life, he is tolerant of individuals who have been conditioned by Church or State (or both) to operate within a cocoon of hypocrisy."

Butler's remarkable essays on Yugoslavia, equally, suggest the magnitude of the wrongs he was eager to expose, the complexities he was willing to consider, and his awareness of the many ways that simple prejudices deform public life and discourse. Yet when he publicly discussed the scandals he later wrote about in "The Sub-Prefect Should Have Held His Tongue," "Butler himself hardly anticipated the results of his determined campaign to publicize the forced conversion and eventual massacre of thousands of Orthodox Serbs by the collaborationist regime of 'Independent Croatia' in 1941," as Foster has written. Not only the Papal Nuncio in Dublin was outraged; "most Irish—and Western—opinion saw little beyond Catholic martyrs and Communist tyranny . . . The sad and salient point is that the scandal [forced] Butler out of the localist, intellectual, historically minded, non-sectarian meeting of hearts to which so many of these essays are dedicated."

Butler did not remove himself to England, as other Irish writers in comparable circumstances had done; but his "enforced withdrawal to the life of a country scholar," Foster continues, led him to write in solitude on various aspects of Irish myth and history; this work, "encapsulated in 'Influenza in Aran,' landed him in controversy, albeit academic rather than headline-grabbing, once more." Those essays, too, are of lasting value, and some of them are republished here.

Butler's writing on European affairs demonstrates not only his reportorial gifts and astute intuitions about diverse political cultures but also his formidable linguistic skills; his mastery of Serbo-Croatian, Russian, and other Slavic languages, as well as French and German, was key to his effectiveness in the situations that he was almost alone, in the Anglophone world, to perceive as crucial. For readers who are new to the Balkans, whose interest was aroused only during the recent years of shocking war there, Butler's reports from the 1940s are riveting. Similarly, his consideration of the appeal of fascism, and the easy victories which National Socialists enjoyed over not just Germany but much of Europe's political classes, is still urgently relevant, when today so many people imagine these temptations to be follies of the past, or only of Germans, or only this, or only that. "The Invader Wore Slippers," "Carl von Ossietzky," and "The Children of Drancy" show a grasp of both the courage it takes to oppose tyranny and terror and the slippery, self-deluding dangers in believing oneself immune to political corruption; Butler's wisdom here is as rare and remarkable now as it was when he composed these striking essays decades ago. Joseph Brodsky, a fervent enthusiast of Butler's writing, put it well: "Hubert Butler shows an extraordinarily keen eye and ear for every shade and whisper of demagoguery. The events he happened to witness left him no choice if he wanted to retain his sanity and self-esteem."

Brodsky appreciated, too, that Butler's rootedness in Ireland gave a special strength to his interpreting the "large world eastward, finding its weather, in the 1930s and 1940s especially, quite familiar." To quote again (from Brodsky's introduction to a French edition of some of Butler's essays on European politics): "Make no mistake: Hubert Butler was no Nazi hunter or Protestant crusader against the Vatican: he was a dishonesty hunter. He just happened to know Serbo-Croatian better than the gentlemen in the Roman Curia, and was more aware of the bloody record of some of the Croatian prelates retained by Rome for an otherwise worthy cause. But then, he happened to know several things better than others did, apart from languages. Small wonder that he came to regard the postwar world's ethics as 'dirty-grey.' "

Brodsky especially appreciated Butler's attraction to "Mitteleuropa . . . Our understanding of its present conditions logically stands to benefit from what he depicted half a century ago. A man of immense learning, he was interested in this borderline zone, with its fusion of Latin and Slavic cultures, presumably because he sensed in their interplay the future of European civilization. Born where he was, he couldn't help being concerned with the fate of Christendom, whose natural son he was. It's too bad that he wasn't listened to earlier. And it's too bad that he is not with us now."

But Brodsky also cared about the elegance and music of Butler's writing about Ireland, its landscape and people, its literature and history. He wanted to be sure that "Crossing the Border" and other essays about the unity of Irish culture would be read anew at the end of the century, when the possibilities for a resolution of divisive disputes in Ireland may be within reach. He believed that American readers especially would appreciate how Butler's work starts out in Ireland and ends there, how he goes far afield and yet never leaves the home of his birth. The attention Butler paid to the texture of life in Riga, or the idiosyncratic strengths of Edmund Wilson's prose, or the hopes of Swiss immigrants in eighteenth-century Ireland, or the colorful oddities of Balkan tribal rituals, not to mention the politics of fascism's sympathizers or opponents—these penetrating studies would not have had their delicacy and strength without his deep study of and commitment to his own land.

At the heart of Butler's rousing reappraisals of the heroes of the Irish Rebellion of 1798, one finds a strongly contemporary note of warning about the temptations that the twentieth century's Global Village can put in your way, with its hectic noise, its facile internationalism, its relentless banality. For Butler, the more you are lured into disregarding the vivid realities of your own local life and the more you accept that your well-being or safety or happiness will be determined by forces beyond your control, the more you risk complete loss of identity and the less able you are to understand what goes on beyond the borders of your own country. Also, the more globally interconnected we are, the more important it becomes to know who you really are, in your own setting, to grasp the truth about your own milieu and your own world. This was for Butler certainly a matter of personal moral choice, the ethics of personal commitment, but readers of these essays will see that it became the basis for a subtle, powerful theory about the strengthening of national cultures, the maintenance of cultural identity, and the preservation of real freedom in a homogenizing, mass-media-ized world.

The critics have been virtually unanimous in their appreciation of Butler's prose. W. J. Mc Cormack said that Butler's was "an incisive and yet relaxed English, instinct with shrewdness and generosity," that he was "an essayist in the highest tradition of Swift and Shaw." And Hugh Bredin thought, about Butler's first book, that "opening it was like discovering gold."

They and others quickly appreciated that it was pointless simply to place Butler in the landscape of Irish, or Anglo-Irish, literature. The melodious clarity of his prose, his intellectual virtuosity, the large nature of his concerns about the human condition encourage us to appreciate him as a truly international writer. It has been suggested that certain writers, in this cruel century, emerging from locales both part of yet at the periphery of major national cultures, were gifted with a special angle of oblique vision that allowed them to comprehend truths that were obscure to more centrally placed figures. This is a well-known feature in American literature, of course, and there are notable European examples: Camus in Algiers, Arendt in Königsberg, Kafka in Prague. Butler himself early on perceived what he called the "tilt" of Ireland toward England, and part of his greatness lay in the strength with which he kept his poise and good sense when the world around him was aslant. "Like Milosz from Poland or Holub from Czechoslovakia," John Bayley wrote, "Butler is a true cosmopolitan, and his writing has something of their unruffled astringency and meditative humor."

Again to quote Maurice Craig: "The one great truth which seems to underlie almost everything in these essays is this: that the magnitude of a moral issue, like that of an angle in geometry, is independent of its reach or scope . . .

"Courage, common sense and elegance: and the rarest of these is elegance. Again and again I have been struck, in reading these essays, by the felicitous phrase, the apt metaphor, and the vivid image, as though this prose had been written with the care which poets give to the writing of their verse. And why not? It is, in the end, for his style that an author is read; and what is the use of writing to persuade if you cannot charm your reader and disarm him?

"Hubert Butler is a deceptive writer. Just as we find ourselves sagely nodding agreement with one of his strictures, the knife is deftly slipped between our own ribs and we are transfixed upon his point."

The "Note on Sources," beginning on p. 569, indicates the published sources for all the essays included in *Independent Spirit*. The dates given in the chapter headings are of the original composition or publication, when it is known.

The preparation of this book could not have been accomplished without the astute, essential help of Antony Farrell, whose pioneering publication of Butler's essays cannot be overpraised; of Mrs. Butler, who generously and imaginatively aided in sorting out the material; of Julia Crampton, Hubert Butler's daughter, who offered invaluable information; of Joseph Brodsky, who first brought Butler's work to the attention of Farrar, Straus and Giroux; and of Roger Straus, whose patience and goodwill permitted me the time to edit this book. He and I can only regret that we did not know of this marvelous body of work until after Butler's death, and that we were not able to see this volume into print during the lifetime of the friend who introduced Butler to us.

Elisabeth Sifton

Independent Spirit

Introduction*

1985

These essays are not so heterogeneous as they look. They are all skewered together by a single idea. Or perhaps I should call it an obsession, a mental necessity that turned into a physical one. When I was a boy of fourteen I decided I was going to live in the place where I was born and where my father, grandfather and great-grandfather had lived before me. It seemed then an easy and obvious thing to do, since I was my father's eldest son and he had a house and farm in Kilkenny. There was also another reason, which influenced me, even when I knew how insubstantial it was. Though we have long been unimportant people, the Butlers, of whom my family is a junior branch, had ruled the neighbourhood since the fourteenth century, and there is scarcely a parish in Tipperary or Kilkenny that does not bear some trace of our sometimes arrogant, sometimes kindly interference. Could I not interfere too?

It was some time before I grasped how difficult this was going to be and noticed that not only was all my education slanted away from Ireland but that the whole island was tilted eastwards. It was very hard to stand upright unsupported on this precipitous slope, for as many people were pushing me from the west as were pulling me to the east. And ambition was tugging me vigorously the whole time towards the land of opportunity. And in fact, in a strongly centripetal world, staying at home is scarcely even respectable; certainly no one thinks it public-spirited. The man who does it can surely have no feeling for "broad horizons" and mighty enterprises, for the unity of

*Originally published as the introduction to *Escape from the Anthill*.—ed.

mankind and the exploration of the universe? Even in a manual worker it can be a discreditable thing to do, for our economists often moralize now about the need to make labour more "mobile" so that it can be drafted to those spots where it is most needed. It is perverse and selfish to resist.

And if living in one's own neighbourhood is difficult, to write about it is harder still. Who, anyway, are our neighbours? Our real neighbours, both of the spirit and of the flesh, both those we know and those we don't, seldom live near us nowadays. We keep contact with them by telephone and plane and car, or else we have one-sided commerce with them through books and television screens. In spite of that, though the familiar hills and rivers seldom now enclose a stable or self-sufficient community, I think they are only waiting to recover their plundered significance. The canals that once diverted the rivers are all choked and after five generations the railway cuttings that ravaged the hills are collapsing. Why should the great dams at Ardnacrusha and Poulaphouca, or the television mast on Mount Leinster, or the huge roads that level out villages and raths and esker ridges, prove more enduring? They are all linked with certain ways of life and thought, and ideas have never been as ephemeral as in the twentieth century.

But to look ahead like this is not very comforting to the beleaguered country dweller. At eighty-four I am, like everybody else, very disillusioned but only averagely discontented. Fundamentally I think as I always did. The post to which I am willingly tethered still holds firm and I have grazed around it in a sufficiently wide circle. Close-cropped grass comes up again fresh and sweet, and whoever comes along next may find my patch slightly improved.

So even when these essays appear to be about Russia or Greece or Spain or Yugoslavia, they are really about Ireland. We choose some of our experiences and others are forced on us, but they have little meaning till they are related to some central focus of ideas and this focus for me has never varied. Many of the irrelevant things that have happened to me have been boring or nasty, but not all of them. For example, like many Europeans, I have exchanged a couple of dull sentences with Chou En-lai and seen the Great Wall of China, but I have no idea how to profit by this fascinating adventure, for I think we Westerners can mostly only sense the sweetness of China, we can bring nothing home with us. We are like honeybees which can get nectar from white clover but not from red, because their sucking apparatus is too short. And I do not believe that we should be spiritually impoverished if for a century or more we were excluded from all Asia and all Africa beyond the shores of the Mediterranean.

But nowadays can we exclude ourselves from anything? Can the ant ever escape from his anthill? Even the most sedentary and home-bound person is obliged to roam the world in spirit ten or twenty times a day. The newspapers and the radio and television release a million images of remote places and people. They settle like butter-flies on the brain till every cell is clogged with the larvae from their unwanted eggs. How can one protect oneself from the ravages of secondhand experience? Here and there perhaps one can replace this predigested stuff with experiences of one's own. But to most people this seems an affectation, like the quest for free-range eggs or vege-tables from "organic" farms.

While we are more or less committed to mass travel and to in-formation that is canalized for press conferences, the experiences that nourish us are individual, not collective. Few of us have been of use to any Indian, Negro or Chinaman, and the regard we have for them is unmixed with personal gratitude; yet many generations of vicarious involvement have caused us to think we are necessary to each other, and it will take as many more to unlearn this.

When this happens we shall recognize again that within a few square miles we should have everything which we can possibly need. Here in Kilkenny the earth is fruitful and the neighbours are intelli-gent, imaginative and kind; their minds are well adapted to poetry and jokes and the propounding and solving of problems. Though it is not easy to be independent of tinned pineapples and the Dublin dailies, we could be, at a price. But even the tinkers and the retired colonial administrators are more restless and discontented than they used to be. The colonials, travelling round the earth, have lost the countryman's acquiescence in seemingly immutable things like tem-perature and rainfall and local prejudices. It is now easy to avoid what one cannot change, so they move about. And though our tin-kers come back every summer to the same lanes and clearings, the last ones who came here had spent the winter washing dishes in the Cumberland Hotel at Marble Arch. They play the familiar tricks with a touch of urban sophistication, and it is hard to see them as neigh-bours whom it is one's duty to love.

All this sounds misleadingly nostalgic. In fact nothing has hap-pened that cannot be reversed if it is accurately recorded. That is the purpose of these essays, in which I try to show that the countryside, where mean and silly things happen because energy and intelligence have been drained away, is an essential part of the world pattern which too few have studied. In "Boycott Village," for example, I complain that no one has investigated why ordinary people with nice intentions and neighbourly instincts proved to be such incompetent guardians of freedom. I do not know what the answer is but, if we relate the facts as we see them, posterity will perhaps handle them less clumsily than we have done.

I grew up before the great emigration of the Anglo-Irish in the 1920s had begun, when some of the pioneers of the Irish Literary Revival were still alive and active, and through *The Irish Statesman* AE was still confidently elaborating his plans for a cooperative Ireland. These were dreams with reality and achievement behind them, but they could not stand up to the Gaelic dream of Patrick Pearse, for it had been sanctified in blood. Now that dream too has faded, though the blood sacrifice still goes on, like the fire that smoulders slowly towards the forest when the picnic is over.

Now there are no dreams left to sustain us and all we have is a ragbag of tangled notions and prejudices. I do not doubt that a new generation, with fresh ideas and the vigour to carry them through, will solve some of our problems, and yet in times of troubled peace like ours, when the old idealisms have lost their magic, the future, I believe, lies with the solitary individual of whom Chekhov used to write. I quote from one of his letters:

I see that our salvation will come from solitary personalities, scattered here and there over Russia, sometimes educated, sometimes peasant. Power is in their hands even though there are few of them. No man is a prophet in his own country and these solitary individuals, of which I speak, play an imperceptible role in society; they do not dominate it but their work is visible.

It was in the same way that Vershinin reassured the three sisters that knowledge and intelligence were never wasted. He said there was no town so boring and dead that three people of intellect and education could not make a faint impression; they would get swallowed up, of course, by the dark masses, but not without leaving some slight influence, and after them there would be six, then twelve, till at last they would be in a majority. "In two or three hundred years life would be unspeakably, amazingly lovely."

Yet now something has happened to thrust this future loveliness even farther away. Vershinin had not foreseen that as culture, under official patronage, became increasingly centripetal, Feeny, Meany and Sweeney, the three people of intellect and education, would fall under the irresistible techno-cultural influence of the capital. Long before the three had propagated six and the six twelve, each nourishing his successors with the rich decay of his talents, the tempter would address himself seductively to them. Feeny and Meany would persuade themselves that they could serve their little town best from outside. Feeny would get a plum of a job as adviser to Channel 3 on South-Eastern Regional Culture, and Meany, no longer his ally but his rival, would draw a smaller income from his Friday afternoon talks on rural problems; Sweeney would stay behind, a new element, jealousy, penetrating his loneliness and distorting his judgment.

And what of the dark masses? They would be just as dark as before but with no trouble to themselves they would be given extension lectures and loan exhibitions, so that even Sweeney in his unpopular enthusiasms would seem superfluous and the task of swallowing him up would be greatly eased.

It is in fact a problem of men, not methods, and we can hope for little from the clever educational gadgets with which we try to irrigate the intellectual deserts. The soil that has been robbed of its natural creativity cannot be restored to health by fertilizing chemicals. Make it possible for Feeny, Meany and Sweeney, the "solitary individuals," to live in their own homes, for nature has planted them there like antibodies in a diseased constitution. Only they have power to regenerate it.

This, of course, is contrary to all current notions. Everything that is seminal or germinative in the way of ideas is thought to develop in the great centres of culture, where intellectuals congregate. It is in the press, the theatres, the clubs of the metropolis that revolutionary ideas are expressed and challenged. Things are openly said that could scarcely be thought in a provincial town. Yet there is something self-destructive about these great congestions of originality. A sense of doom hangs over them as over the exuberant freedom of the Weimar Republic.

Here is one of the reasons. In a vast society like ours, "the man of intellect and education," as Chekhov saw him, is one among several thousands, a natural solitary, in fact. His function is to be the pinch of bread-soda in the dough, and not to foregather with other ex-solitaries and form a bread-soda pudding. Yet an Irishman sees this happening every year. Feeny and Meany, drawn away from their solitude, bring with them to the city their instinct to defy. They gather together with other ex-solitaries; then they are no longer solitary and what is more they find they are no longer original. Their insights and perceptions, which surprised and often vexed their fellow citizens, are banal and irrelevant among the exuberant heterodoxies of their new community. In place of the known neighbours whom it was their duty to challenge, there are faceless strangers who can only be met with abstractions. To get attention in such circles, the ex-solitary may have to turn in his tracks, to sacrifice the particular to the general, and to accept as valid some mass-produced consensus whose insufficiency he would quickly have detected among the familiar diversities of his native town. In this way the cities acquire fanatics at the same rate as the provinces lose their solitary individuals.

Am I exaggerating? Probably, but there is evidence from Russia and Italy and Germany that totalitarian beliefs spread from the cities to the provinces where sharp antagonisms had been held in check by a long history of neighbourly interdependence.

So I go on believing that the strength to live comes from an understanding of ourselves and our neighbours or the diaspora that has replaced them. If we could focus on them all the curiosity and wisdom that we disperse round the world, as we focus all the rays of the sun through a burning glass on a pile of dead leaves, there is no limit to the warmth and life we could generate. It is easier of course to collect the dead leaves than to make the sparks to kindle them. Yet I believe the life which Chekhov prophesied, "unspeakably, amazingly lovely," is not out of our reach, though it may now be a century or two farther away than he calculated.

For the most part these essays are unaltered from their first publication though a few of them deal with problems that appear to have been solved or episodes that have long been forgotten. We have lived though two world wars and, in Ireland, rebellion and civil war. Yet the basic things remain the same. When I was a boy of ten the Ulster Unionists were saying Home Rule is Rome Rule and civil war was threatened. Now I am eighty-four and the Ulster Unionists are saying Home Rule is Rome Rule and civil war does not seem immeasurably far away. It is as though we were on a scenic railway in a fun fair. We pass through towering cardboard mountains and over raging torrents and come to rest in the same well-trodden field from which we got on board.

I have lived for long periods at home, and my garden, with its vegetables and raspberry canes, its orchard and neglected flower beds, has had to take the place of people and events. Thirty-three years ago my life of active involvement in enthusiasms which I shared with my neighbours ended abruptly. I have described how this came about in "The Sub-Prefect Should Have Held His Tongue." I shall not refer to this again, as my affection for my neighbours has not changed. We were all of us victims of events beyond our control. Ireland was caught in the backwash of a tremendous religious struggle in Central and Eastern Europe, which we did not understand and for which we were unprepared. It was inevitable that there should be casualties.

Are we here in Ireland any nearer to that eighteenth-century dream "to unite the whole people of Ireland, to abolish the memory of past dissensions, and to substitute the common name of Irishman in place of the denomination of Protestant, Catholic and Dissenter"?

The idea of a religious war is so abhorrent and disgraceful that many prefer to think that it is for loyalty to the British Crown that Ulstermen will fight. They are wrong, because Ulster loyalty is to a Protestant monarch and would not survive if the monarch became a Roman Catholic. In fact it is the old insoluble conflict between authority and private judgment. Though all of us sometimes defer to authority, sometimes judge for ourselves, the moment we cease to act as individuals and think collectively, what was a matter of choice becomes a matter of principle and a clash between Catholic and Protestant is likely.

Can ecumenism help? In Ireland 160 years ago there was a vigorous ecumenical movement. The circumstances were more favourable then than now but it ended in a deadlock. I have told the story in the following pages.

In "The Eggman and the Fairies" the Captains and the Kings have all but gone and taken with them their sophistication and learning, their love of their home and their self-knowledge by means of which what looked irremediable might have been remedied. The Clearys in their cruel innocence and isolation could only escape from poverty and ignorance into fairyland.

Most of the other Irish pieces are self-explanatory.

When I was thirty-one and Soviet Russia was fifteen years old I taught English for a term in Leningrad. I was very happy there and would like to have stayed longer but the pull of my home and those I loved was too strong for me. I came back with as little understanding of Marxism and Communism as I went but I made many friends whom I still remember with affection. There was a multitude of small misunderstandings and difficulties but they all counted for nothing compared with the imaginative kindness with which I was welcomed. In "Peter's Window" I tell the story of that time.

Men and women are surely more important than the systems in which they imprison themselves. Yet it is not easy to disentangle ourselves and to commit ourselves unreservedly to personal relations. Organized religion cannot liberate us, for it is a system too, and there is nothing more bitter than the conflict of two religious systems, as I have found both in my own country and in the foreign country I know best, Yugoslavia.

Three years after I returned from Russia I went to teach in Zagreb in the Anglo-American-Yugoslav Society. It had been founded by my friend Dr. Milan Churchin, editor of *Nova Europa*, the leading liberal journal of Central Europe, and by Dr. Georgievitch, the Orthodox Bishop of Dalmatia. I also had a small scholarship from the School of Slavonic Studies in London.

Yugoslavia had been born in 1918 after the defeat of Austria-Hungary and the rise of the Succession States. For the southern Slavs it was the fulfilment of an ancient dream of harmony between four neighbouring and kindred peoples. I was at Oxford then and there was springtime in the air. There were Serbs, Croats and Czechs, there were Irish too, all rejoicing in their newfound freedom. We all had minority problems and I was surprised that Ireland, least scarred by war, did not identify herself with the other small new states more warmly, share experiences and take the lead for which she was qualified. The Croats knew about Ulster and some of them talked of Croatia, ruefully, as "the Ulster of Yugoslavia." This needed a readjustment of roles, but one knew what they meant. They were Catholics, and to them Zagreb, the Croatian capital, was "a little Vienna." They wondered how they would fare in union with the more primitive Serbian Orthodox, who had fought for freedom while they had mostly fought for Austria-Hungary.

The day we arrived in Zagreb, 9 October 1934, news had just come that King Alexander, a Serb, had, with Barthou, the French Foreign Minister, been assassinated in Marseilles by agents of the separatist Croat leader Pavelitch. Zagreb was plunged in well-organized mourning with portraits of the king surrounded by black crape in the shopwindows and black bows on the funnels of the railway engines. Two days later the king's body arrived from Split, where it had been shipped from Marseilles on its way to Belgrade. It lay for a couple of hours, surrounded by pot plants, in the first-class waiting room at the station, where it was visited by mile-long processions. One of those who prayed beside the royal coffin was Archbishop Bauer, the Catholic Primate, accompanied by his Auxiliary, Monsignor Stepinac.

During our time in Yugoslavia the shadow of the assassination hung over the whole country. Hitler had come to power in Germany and Jewish refugees were flocking to the Dalmatian coast. In Italy and Hungary, Pavelitch and his helper, Artukovitch, were training the army of the Croat rebels who were, in 1941, to sweep into Yugoslavia with the Nazis and proclaim the Independent State of Croatia.

And yet my recollections are of peace and beauty. There was almost no traffic in Yelachitch Trg, the central square. Fat amethyst pigeons strutted through the market stalls looking for pickings and panicking when the church bells rang. The scent of mimosa and wood smoke, holy candles and freshly tanned leather drowned the faint whiff of petrol. On Sunday, we walked up Slijeme Mountain, where wild cyclamen and hellebore grew through the beech woods. In our room I rooted oleander cuttings in bottles between the double windows. And when my pupils were on holiday I wrote down the story of Mr. Pfeffer.

Zagreb, in the 1930s, was a very cultivated little town; it had an opera house and theatres, and there were still remnants of an Austrianized aristocracy in the leafy suburbs. Dalmatia was Italianate and Belgrade was still largely Turkish in character. When one went south and penetrated to Montenegro, one seemed to pass from our cruel, complicated century to an earlier one, just as cruel, where each man was responsible to his neighbours for his crimes and where organized twentieth-century barbarity had not yet emerged. Possibly in "The Last *Izmirenje*" I have idealized what I saw. To know what Montenegro was really like you must read Djilas' superb autobiography, *Land Without Justice* (1958).

The war came and Yugoslavia was carved up by Germany and her allies. Croatia, which had not resisted the Nazis, was rewarded with her independent state under the rule of Pavelitch, King Alexander's convicted murderer.

Then in Zagreb an Aeschylean tragedy was enacted. The same young priest who had stood beside the coffin of his murdered king, reappeared before his countrymen as Archbishop at the right hand of his king's assassin, helpless in the face of Pavelitch's resolve to exterminate the Orthodox by expulsion, massacre or forced conversion. Unhappy but icily correct, Stepinac considered himself to be the servant of a power that is higher than the king or his murderer, and one that has rules for every occasion. His conscience was clear.

Violence came a second time to the city. Caring for neither king nor priest nor pope nor assassin, the Communists swept in, resolved to make all things new. I have written about this period in my two essays "The Sub-Prefect Should Have Held His Tongue" and "The Artukovitch File," yet I would like here to recall the historical background to the events I have described. There are three great sources of power and influence in Eastern and Central Europe: Roman Catholicism, Byzantine Orthodoxy and Communism. Orthodoxy, which broke away from Rome five centuries before the Protestant Reformation, was once, with its Patriarch magnificently enthroned at Constantinople, the rival of Rome in power and splendour. Now the Orthodox Church is a shadow of its former self. With St. Sophia a secular museum, the Patriarch lives on sufferance from the Turks in a small quarter of Istanbul. Since the Russian Revolution the other Patriarchs over whom he reigns as *primus inter pares* are weak and scattered. Communist Moscow threatens them from the East and the Catholic powers from the West. Those Russian Orthodox who survived beyond the borders of Tsarist Russia and later the Soviet state, have had to fight for their faith and culture against the politico-religious scheming of Austria-Hungary and her successors, Czechoslovakia and Poland.

A powerful instrument in this little-known stuggle is the Uniat Church, devised by King Sigismund III of Poland and the Pope in the sixteenth century to attract the peasants of the eastern borderlands away from Orthodoxy. The Orthodox received into this church retained their ritual and their married clergy but Rome, not Moscow, became the focus of their obedience.

This Uniat Church has been used many times in our century by the Western Powers for political purposes. At the beginning of the war in 1914, when the Austrians were advancing against the Russian Ukraine, a detailed memorandum about its occupation was formulated by the Uniat Archbishop, Count Szepticky of Lemberg, in Austrian Galicia. Apart from the military and juridical arrangements, the Orthodox Church in the new Protectorate was to be detached from the Moscow Patriarchate and subjected to Szepticky himself, as Uniat Metropolitan. Prayers for the Tsar were to be forbidden and prayers for the Emperor substituted. The Muscovite saints were to be eliminated from the calendar. The new Prince of the Ukraine was to be Archduke Wilhelm, who had changed his name to Vasily, learned

Ukrainian and wore an embroidered Ukrainian tunic. But the Russians struck back, occupied Lemberg, arrested the Archbishop and published the memorandum in the Petrograd papers. Soon after this the Revolution occurred.

In the Second World War the Uniat Church was active in Croatia; in 1941–42, Dr. Shimrak, the Uniat Bishop, played a notable part in the campaign for the conversion of the Orthodox.

For many years the Czechs and Slovaks used the Uniats to secure and, if possible, extend their eastern frontier, where Carpatho-Russian Orthodox were settled along the Ukrainian border. They revived for themselves the old Austro-Hungarian dream of a vast Ukrainian protectorate and for this purpose rechristened Carpatho-Russia "Carpatho-Ukraine" and supported the Uniats against the Orthodox. The story of this often violent struggle has been told month by month in *Svobodnoye Slovo* (*Free Word*), the organ of the many émigré Carpatho-Russian Orthodox in the United States.

In Europe it is now only in Greece that a free Orthodox Church survives. When in 1964 there was a friendly meeting in the Holy Land between the Pope and the titular head of the Orthodox Church (the Patriarch in Constantinople), Chrysostom, the Primate of Greece, and his bishops refused to participate and even asked for the dissolution of the Uniat Church. The world was shocked that when all Christendom is craving for unity the Primate of Greece could be so intransigent, yet it is intelligible enough. The Greeks are the countrymen of Aesop, who wrote so many fables about small animals to whom large ones made friendly overtures. It is natural for them to dread the Uniat embrace.

Should we involve ourselves with complex happenings in far countries? Sometimes we have to, but we misinterpret them at our peril.

On May Day 1949 a crowd of 150,000, said to be the largest ever seen in Dublin, assembled in O'Connell Street to protest against the imprisonment of Archbishop Stepinac of Yugoslavia and the Hungarian Cardinal Mindszenty. There were bands, speeches, telegrams, women fainted and a young man, wrongly suspected of distributing Communist leaflets, was struck on the head and taken to hospital.

In America there were even greater demonstrations and many thought that with so righteous a cause, and Russia still weak after the Nazi invasion, the moment for a third world war had arrived.

I know nothing about Cardinal Mindszenty but I knew that the struggle in which Stepinac was involved was totally misconceived. It was a pre-Communist and inter-Christian one. As in Ireland, race and religion go together, Catholic Croat confronted Orthodox Serb and Hitler's war had triggered off a massacre of the Orthodox by the Catholics. Hugh Seton-Watson, the well-known historian of Central Europe, wrote in 1945: "The Communists saved Yugoslavia from a bloody civil war on racial lines, which would have been inevitable if Mihailovitch [the Serbian Orthodox general] had come to power."* This is something which in Ireland we would be reluctant to believe. Who could wish a Communist solution to our own racial and religious problems?

We live and think under a nuclear cloud and stretch our brains, built for solving human problems, into thinking cosmically. If sooner or later they fail us, friend and enemy will be destroyed together. How soon can we return to being men, not human adjuncts to machines, and handle again man-sized problems? How soon can we escape from the anthill which we have built round ourselves?

*Hugh Seton-Watson, *Nationalism and Communism* (London, 1945), p. 90.

A Fragment
of Autobiography

1987

My father farmed about six hundred acres, half of them at Burn-church farm, near Bennettsbridge, and half at Drumherin, some six miles northeast of Kilkenny City. From the time I was eight I used to bicycle with him to Drumherin, where the two Phelan brothers, Johnnie, who was enormously fat, and Paddy, who was thin, were stewards. It is, I believe, the wild country where John Banim placed his story "Crohoore of the Billhook." For a long way the road to Ballyfoyle was lined with tall beech trees soaring above the banks on which moss, eight inches deep, half smothered the primroses and ferns within it. There was a big lake on the farm, the Kilkenny res-ervoir, which my father had sold to the Corporation. He and Paddy and Johnnie went round the fields prodding the bullocks. Paddy had a stick which he dipped in cow dung and slapped on the back of those which were to go to the fair. My father must have hoped I would make some interested comment, but I was always thinking of something else and never did.

Burnchurch farm, where a third brother, Joe Phelan, was the steward, is only half a mile away from Maidenhall and is beside Burnchurch rectory, which my great-grandfather had built for himself five miles from Burnchurch church. He was a portly pre-Disestablishment rector and a friend of the Bishop, who pressed on him a second parish, that of Trim in Co. Meath. He persuaded his son, Richard, who was at Balliol, to come home and be rector of Trim. Richard, whose memory I revere, was a distinguished archae-ologist who lived out the rest of his life in Trim and published with the local printer a still valuable history of the town, republished in

1978 by the Meath Archaeological Society. He was married to Harriet, the liveliest of Maria Edgeworth's many half sisters.*

To his eldest son, James, my great-grandfather gave Priestown, the small family home near Dunboyne in Meath which had been Butler property since the time of Edward II. After his father's death, when the remarkable twelfth Baron Dunboyne had died, my great-uncle James was one of several distant cousins who claimed to succeed him. He failed. The twelfth Baron was the Roman Catholic Bishop of Cork, and, sooner than be succeeded by remote Protestant relations, he had defied the Pope and married, hoping to rear a son whom he would bring up in the Catholic faith. But he had no son, and he got an appalling denunciation in Latin from Pius VI for "living in foul concubinage with a heretic woman."

Though we live in Kilkenny we are only distantly related to the Butlers of Ormonde, who had lived in Kilkenny Castle since 1391. Since they are gone and their memory is fading, in 1967 I formed the Butler Society with the present Lord Dunboyne so that a large and once powerful family should not lose its place in history. I only rarely met my Priestown cousins but I had very many English cousins through my English grandmother. Till I went to school my father taught us maths, my grandmother taught us history and my mother taught us French and English and at the same time managed to run the dairy and keep ducks and hens. She used to send them, wrapped up in butter paper, to relations in England, in particular to my cousin Alice Graves, who in return sent me the suits that her two sons, Cecil and Adrian, had outgrown. They were at school in Berkshire and I was appalled one day to learn that I was to follow them to Bigshotte Rayles. It was in the prep school belt of the Home Counties, a land of pine trees and heather and chalk and golf courses.

It was so extraordinary to be dumped in this strange place that I thought my parents had given me away. My first few weeks I wandered round in a swoon and when anyone asked a question I gaped at them. When one day Miss Reeve, the headmaster's sister, took my temperature (two boys had measles and lived behind a flapping carbolic sheet) I bit the thermometer in half; she tried again and I bit the second one.

I have forgotten the names of thousands of former acquaintances but I remember the names and faces of all the boys at Bigshotte. I remember all the shrubs between the pavvy and the swimming bath.

*On Maria Edgeworth, see below, pp. 244–53.

Hundreds of episodes present themselves in heavy type. Everything else since is in italics. It is said of prep schools "that they rub the corners off." This agonizing process was applied to me, and it could not have been more painful and irreversible were it done with a pincers and a file. I was well fed and never beaten or much bullied. Indeed, I was the favorite pupil of Mr. Reeve, the headmaster, and he cast a blight over one Easter holiday by coming to stay. He was an excellent teacher and, thanks to him, I got the top mathematical scholarship to Charterhouse.

My enthusiasm for mathematics started when I got to trigonometry and discovered there was an abstract world which ran parallel to the treacherous concrete one and could not be reached from it. I had stopped believing in Heaven and everything I had been told about it soon after I got to Bigshotte. (How could Mr. Reeve or anyone else possibly know?) I was proud that, when the prayer bell rang, I began my second prayer, the one my mother taught me, "Lord God, if thou existest . . ." Here in trigonometry was an escape route I could believe in.

Ronnie Huggard and I were to sit for scholarships to Charterhouse, and when the other boys had drunk their cocoa and gone to bed Mr. Reeve set us problems (he called them "riders") to do in the empty classroom. It was wonderfully peaceful. We could hear Mr. Reeve reading aloud to Miss Reeve on the Private Side, the flames flickering in the dying fire, Rex, the school dog, snoring, and upstairs Matron saying "Lights out!" It was a magical hour. At half-term Ronnie and I went up to Charterhouse and some weeks later the news came that I had got my scholarship. There was a whole holiday to celebrate my victory and it was spent playing cricket, though I would much rather have spent it indoors doing riders with Ronnie. But Ronnie was weeping bitterly. He had yearned to go to Charterhouse but without a scholarship his father could not afford to send him.

Mr. Reeve made me Head Boy early on. Since all I wanted was to get away this did not mean much to me. It was announced at Evening Prayers and this time I heard the sound of Bernie Cooper snuffling piteously behind me as we knelt. He had thought he was going to be Head Boy.

Years later an unpleasant idea occurred to me. Perhaps Mr. Reeve favoured me not because he thought me interesting and clever but because Cousin Alice Graves was Sir Edward Grey's sister and he was English Foreign Secretary at the time. Their mother and my

English grandmother were sisters. I only knew of him because Granny used to write him disapproving letters about his commitment to Home Rule.

About Charterhouse there is no need to say much, as Robert Graves, who was a nephew of Cousin Alice, has said it all in *Goodbye to All That*. He reports a conversation he had with Nevill Barbour, who became a friend of mine at Oxford. It wouldn't be enough, they agreed, to dismiss the whole school and staff and start all over again. No. "The school buildings were so impregnated with what was called the public school spirit, but what we felt as fundamental badness, that they would have to be demolished and the school rebuilt elsewhere and its name changed."

At Charterhouse, except in class, there was no mixing between the houses, and the scholars sat together at a small table in Upper Long. There were two other scholars at Verites but I found them both uncongenial and there was no escape from them. As for the masters, all the younger ones were at war and old ones were rescued from retirement to replace them. A. H. Tod, my dreadful one-eyed housemaster, must have been one of these.

My love affair with trigonometry ended during my first term, when in broad daylight Mr. Tuckey, a Cambridge Wrangler, told us all about Functions in a crowded classroom in the Science Building. It was no longer numinous and mystical and I scarcely minded not understanding. Next term the headmaster Frank Fletcher (he was called Fifi and his wife Mimi) shifted me over to Greek. I caught up on it fairly quickly. Mr. Dames Longworth, the fifth-form master, was a tweedy Irish gentleman from Co. Westmeath. He swaggered about the room twirling his moustache and swaying his shoulders dramatically as he recited Greek iambics in a booming voice. "And old crocks for Studio?" he used to exclaim when the drawing master poked his head round the door to collect two pupils who were excused for the OTC (Officers' Training Corps) once a week. He was wealthy and had made himself irremovable by presenting the school with a racquets court. He and A. H. Tod had together compiled a famous book, *Tod and Longworth's Unseen Passages of Greek and Latin Translation*, which circulated round all the public schools of Britain. Tod's other distinction was that years before, drilling the OTC in Founder's Court, he had stepped back into the fountain. In the New Bugs exam at Verites every examinee was expected to know this.

As a housemaster Tod was a disaster. He was becoming senile

and he never knew my name. Once he stopped me and said, "Heh, Butler, send Butler to me!" My happiest day at Verites was when it caught fire and we had to toss all Tod's furniture and his collection of brass horse ornaments out of the window. I was the school swot and I sat in my study poring over Virgil and Homer but without real enjoyment, because Tod and Longworth seemed to lie between. I climbed very quickly to the top of the sixth and my mother was worried that I was not Head Boy or even a School Monitor. It was their privilege to stroll round Founder's Court, hands in pockets and coat swept behind them, in a special manner. I did not mind. As at Bigshotte, all I wanted was to be away.

At the end of the summer term in 1918 my moment came. I got all the five scholarships and prizes that were available in the classical sixth. Since my academic career ended disastrously and since they may still exist, I do not think it is boastful to give their names. I got the Talbot Scholarship and Medal for Greek, the Thackeray Prize for English Literature (Thackeray had been at Charterhouse), the Petilleau Prize for French and the top leaving scholarship. For many terms I had got the Form Prize, but as the war was on all prize money was given to the Red Cross and we got slips to stick into the books we already had, and I think most of the money for the Petilleau Prize went to the Red Cross, too, because I was given *Princess Mary's Book of France*, which I had no use for, and there was no money for a second prize. When M. Petilleau, who lived in Godalming, heard this, he was very much distressed and went to his bookshelves and took down the complete works of Molière, bound in calf, and gave it as second prize. I was very good at Latin verse, which seems to me now the most futile of accomplishments, and, on the strength of a translation of part of Shelley's *Adonais* into Lucretian hexameters, Fifi decided to send me up for the scholarship at Balliol, where he had been himself.

I failed but got the top scholarship at St. John's. Fifi called me into his study to tell me. I was too old to cry like Ronnie Huggard but I had been humiliated and wanted to leave in a blaze of glory, so I did cry. Fifi patted me on the shoulder and said something about the Southern Irish temperament and that I wanted to be *"aut Caesar aut nullus."* There were still two terms to put in before Oxford but I told my parents I was leaving. It was an unheard-of thing, as the war was over, but I got them to agree.

My mother had wanted me to go into the Foreign Office, as she thought Edward Grey might take an interest in me, but my father still hoped I might be a farmer, so it was agreed I should take an agricultural course at Reading University, where William de Burgh, an Irishman, a cousin through the Greys, was professor of philosophy, and he and his family became lifelong friends. Eric Dodds was lecturing there, too, a stage in his progress from teaching at Kilkenny College to being Regius Professor of Greek at Oxford. In his autobiography *Missing Persons* (1977) he has written a charming account of de Burgh. I was happy and free for the first time. I learned no agriculture and I do not believe that the demobilized officers for whom the course was planned learnt any either. It had been hastily put together by experts on soil and pasture, bookkeeping and the building of pigsties and cow sheds (for this we started at the beginning with slides of Doric and Ionic columns), but the farm was some distance away and we only rarely cast a glance at cows and crops. Yet there was something conclusive about it. I had a younger brother, and nature clearly did not want me to be a farmer.

When I was fifteen I had passed through Dublin, still smoking after the Easter Rebellion, and I had decided I was an Irish Nationalist. This led to constant quarreling with my family, which became worse when I found an ancient copy of *Robert Elsmere* by Mrs. Humphry Ward at home and became a "Free Thinker." This was an exciting new phase for me and I felt proud that unknown to myself I had been one at Bigshotte three years before and had never felt, like Elsmere, "a castaway on a shoreless sea." On the contrary, it had opened up to me the new abstract world of trigonometry and helped me to get my scholarship to Charterhouse. Elsmere's friend Henry Grey said to him consolingly: "The parting with the Christian mythology is the rending asunder of bones and marrow. It means parting with half the confidence and joy of life. But have trust! Reason is God's like all the rest. Trust it. I trust Him. The leading strings of the past are dropping away from you; they are dropping from all the world." I found this intoxicating, but who could I talk to about it? I had to go to Mr. Tod with the two other scholars to be prepared for confirmation. But how could I tell that dreadful old man in the armchair that the leading strings of the past had dropped away from me and that I did not wish to be confirmed? No, I couldn't, not possibly, and so the Bishop of Winchester laid his hands on me and asked God that I should daily increase in the Holy Spirit more and more.

I consoled myself with the thought that when I got to Oxford all would be well again, but I found when I got there that Mrs.

Humphry Ward had become a sort of joke and nobody agonized about their doubts as Elsmere had done. Religion had become a subject, like Philosophy or Physics. You either took it or you didn't.

Yet in the lovely relaxed atmosphere I was no longer bored and I ceased to be a compulsive swot. Instead I was distracted by all that was new to hear and read and see.

There was still Plato and Thucydides and all the others, and Caesar and Virgil the third time round, but I could no longer concentrate. I never replaced my large Liddell & Scott's *Greek Lexicon*, which had got burnt in the Verites fire. For me only Lucretius survived the lecture room and I still sometimes read him in an unscholarly way. It seems to me that if the atomic physicists who succeeded him two thousand years later had written in verse as he did, they would have seen that knowledge is only the beginning of wisdom. It is not safe in the hands of those who are not sensitive, as he was, to the beauty of the earth and the fragility of all we value.

I saw *John Bull's Other Island* and read *The Irish Statesman* and learnt about my own country, which I had previously only known from ground level. In the long vac. I met Sir Horace Plunkett and visited him at Kilteragh, the house he built for himself at Foxrock, which he had made a meeting place for all those who were interested in their country and, aided by his secretary, Gerald Heard, for all the leading writers of the day. It would be pointless to mention all the eminent people I met there, as I was too inexperienced and shy to talk to them. Lennox Robinson took me to one of Yeats's evening parties and I went to AE's also, and a world unknown in Bennettsbridge opened up for me.

All my thoughts and hopes were about Ireland and I only got a second in Mods. But all the same two of the dons at St. John's, Last and Costin, told me I was being considered for a Fellowship. I listened politely, with my mind elsewhere. I knew that I would disappoint them in Greats.

Two years later I was back in Ireland with a bad degree, a third, or to be more precise no degree, because from what I took to be principle, but must have looked like pique, I refused to go through the ceremony. I cannot defend myself, as I gave offence to many who had nothing but goodwill towards me.

My brother-in-law Tyrone Guthrie, who was at St. John's with me, got a fourth but he had already found his vocation in the theatre and quickly recovered.

Cannot some alternative be found to exams in which ten people are bruised for every one who is exalted? One is not consulted when one's feet are put on the bottom rung of a ladder, and the higher you go the more painful the fall.

At home I found that the new world I had discovered was closing in again. The civil war had started, soon Kilteragh was to be burnt because Sir Horace was a senator, and AE was to die in England. Yet before this happened Plunkett urged me to join the County Libraries. He had used his influence with the Carnegie Trust to persuade it to start them in Ireland. To AE in the cooperative village the library was to have been the intellectual centre, while the creamery was the economic one. It was he who sent me to learn the trade in Ballymena, the headquarters of the Co. Antrim libraries. The organizing librarian in Dublin was Lennox Robinson, the playwright.

The libraries were a cultural bridge between north and south, and I believe a great opportunity was lost in Ireland when, owing to an unhappy episode at the Dublin headquarters, their control, while they were still in embryo, was transferred to Dunfermline in Scotland. This is how it happened. In August 1924 a short-lived periodical, *To-morrow*, published a story by Lennox Robinson called "The Madonna of Slieve Dun," which the clerical members of the governing body considered blasphemous. They called for Robinson's resignation. The Carnegie Trust was informed and, unwilling to take sides in such a sensitive issue, they abolished the central organization in Dublin and resumed control from Dunfermline. From then on each County Library had to work on its own and the happy days, when all the librarians north and south of the border knew each other and visited each other and sought for advice in Dublin, were over. Till then writers had been in charge of all the County Libraries. There was Lennox Robinson and his assistant, Tom MacGreevy, a poet, in Dublin; Robert Wilson, a poet, in Co. Sligo; and Geoffrey Phibbs, a poet, and his wife, the artist Norah McGuinness, in Co. Wicklow; Frank O'Connor in Cork; Helen Roe, an archaeologist, in Co. Leix. Frank O'Connor has written of this period, his apprenticeship, in *My Father's Son*, first in Sligo and then in Wicklow with Geoffrey Phibbs, of whom he has given a delightful account.

I have always blamed Lennox Robinson for the breakup of our little community. His story was unimportant and sooner than take his stand for "intellectual freedom," which is always at risk in Ireland, he should have resigned and so ensured that the central organization survived in Dublin. Soon after this I left the libraries.

Dublin had been in the past, and should be in the future, the cultural if not the political centre of Ireland.

I had a motor bicycle and through my years in the County Libraries I discovered the varied beauties of my country and the rich diversity of its people. Why is it that now we look at the beauty mainly as something we can sell to tourists, and the diversity of its people, their faith and their loyalties, not as an enrichment but a source of bitter antagonism?

I believe it was from AE that I learnt to be an Utopian. He recalled that it was in the small states of Greece, each scarcely bigger than an Irish county, that all our arts and sciences were first developed. What happened once can happen again, and he saw the future of Ireland as a union of small cooperative communities. There is no trace of this now, but we have only to wait. The great metropolitan civilization, which has sucked all the vision and enterprise from the provinces, is already under threat. It has armed the ignorant, and two embattled mouse-brained dinosaurs, one in the east, one in the west, confront each other. Will they both perish without progeny or will we find some way of liberating ourselves from our machines so that once more as men we can handle man-sized problems?

When my father died in 1941 I came home with my wife, Peggy, to live in Bennettsbridge. I brought home with me some refugees from Vienna, where after the Anschluss I had been working with the Quakers at the Freundeszentrum in Singerstrasse, and I soon found friends in Kilkenny. There was James Delehanty, who ran *The Kilkenny Magazine*, to which many later well-known writers contributed. There was the Kilkenny Archaeological Society, which with friends I revived in Kilkenny after a coma of fifty years. It is still thriving. There was also the Kilkenny Arts Society, through which in 1952 we started the first Kilkenny Debate. It was on Partition. There were protests in Stormont and fury in Kilkenny and extra guards were drafted into the town. James Douglas, Secretary of the Unionist Council, and Colonel Topping, the Chief Whip, debated Partition with Sean MacBride and Eoin O'Mahony. Myles Dillon was in the Chair. That was the first of nine or ten peacefully contentious occasions. The debate on Neutrality with Basil Liddell Hart, the great military expert, and Brigadier Dorman O'Gowan would still be relevant today. I believe passionately in Irish neutrality, not an ignoble one as in Hitler's war, but one in which each citizen was on a war footing, a war for peace. Three Irishmen have thought in that direction: AE, Paddy Kavanagh and Bernard Shaw, and a plan for civil conscription has been sketched by AE in *The National Being*.

Then there was the Kilkenny Art Gallery Society, which after the death of the founder, George Pennefeather, fell on evil times. It had a new and splendid revival when Lord Ormonde gave Kilkenny Castle to the nation on 12 August 1967 and a spacious, well-planned art gallery was developed from the kitchen premises on the lower ground floor. My wife, Peggy, is its secretary.

I believe that it is in the first twenty-five years of our lives that our characters are shaped and our tastes are formed, and that the rest of our lives are spent either deploying our education, if we are at peace with it, or, if we are at war with it, making some compromise between what is congenital and what is acquired. I was at war with mine on an unremarkable battlefield and I have told in my essays whatever seems to have had slightly more interest than if, like satisfied people, I had had a nine-to-five life with a pension at sixty.

Like all my family I have loved growing things. My father was a skilled gardener and strawberries and sea kale went in quantities to the Dublin market. He had a gardener and was able to draft extra help as well as manure from the farm, when he needed it. He planted espalier trees round the four quarters of the walled garden. It is over an acre and most of the espaliers are now gone except for a huge and prolific Bramley Seedling that has lost all but three of its eight arms. Till recently we were able to send in fruit and vegetables to the weekly country market, which, now that the creameries are gone, seems with its many branches to be the last trace of Plunkett's and AE's cooperative Ireland.

My greenhouses are now tumbling down and I use only a quarter of the garden; with reduced household and elderly appetites it is enough. But gardens, unlike houses, are easily restored and I see nothing final about this.

Can one write in the country far away from publishers and editors? It's difficult but not impossible. I published my first book, *Ten Thousand Saints* (1972), whose argument I still stand over, in Freshford, Co. Kilkenny; my present publisher lives at Gigginstown in Co. Westmeath; and I had a long connection with Irish and English journals till they mostly died, and also with Radio Éireann and the BBC Third Programme.

I take comfort from the fact that two centuries ago, Richard and Elizabeth Griffith, who lived here at Maidenhall, ran a flax mill on the river Nore and became well-known writers in England in their day.

All culture was not then as now focussed on the capital, yet everything changes with incredible rapidity, and no one can predict what the future holds.

Henry and Frances

1950

One afternoon fourteen or fifteen years ago we were cataloguing the library of our neighbour, Miss Power of Kilfane. It is a long beautiful room with tall windows between the bookcases looking onto a sweep of green lawn and beyond it a classically planted park. The library with its great fire was a delightful place in which to work or shirk work and we found ourselves too often sinking into luxurious arm-chairs and reading the books we were supposed to be cataloguing. Most of them were collected in the eighteenth and early nineteenth century and the family had two ruling passions, Art and Sport. The Kilkenny Theatre and the Kilkenny Hunt were their creations, but the first of their two enthusiasms evaporated when the Theatre closed its doors in 1819 and when soon afterwards its founder, Richard Power, died. John Power's hunt still flourishes but the literature of hunting is not large and only a few books appear to have been added to the shelves in Victorian times. In his day, Richard Power filled his bookshelves not only with a unique collection of plays; he had also a fine store of essays, biographies and political pamphlets. I was cat-aloguing these books when, on one occasion, I took down four small volumes dated 1770. They were called *A Series of Genuine Letters between Henry and Frances*, but they had no author's name and I searched the pages for a clue. Some of the letters were dated from Kilfane and some from Farmley, where Henry Flood, the orator, lived; I exclaimed aloud when I discovered that many of the letters were dated from my own home, six miles away. Maidenhall is a small unpretentious Georgian house and I knew nothing of its history in the eighteenth century, for my great-grandfather did not come to the district till 1800 or later, but to the best of my knowledge it was built about 1745. Then I remembered having seen the name Griffith on an old title deed. I borrowed the books to compare dates and make what inferences I could from the letters themselves. I was fascinated by the supple and often witty prose and successfully placed the authors, for there were two of them, Richard Griffith (Henry) and his wife, Elizabeth (Frances), who lived here and built this house over two hundred years ago.

The letters are disappointingly meagre about the ordinary social life of Bennettsbridge and Kilkenny; they mainly deal with the complicated, uneasy love affair of Henry and Frances. The Griffiths were a learned and cultivated couple, who, for some reason to which they only allude mysteriously, had first to delay, then to conceal their marriage for several years. Possibly delays and dissimulations were caused by money difficulties or a disapproving relative, but I think it more likely that Frances' pride was the hindrance. Henry did not consider it necessary to be faithful to her and wrote to her about his infidelities in an aloof, philosophical way. For example, he had told her how his maid Nancy had had to be dismissed because she made such a scene about being supplanted in his affections by Sally. Frances tried to reply with equal philosophy but probably her heart was not in it:

As for the affair of Nancy and Sally, it is of no farther consequence to me than if James and the Coachman had been the Disputants. Nor did I mention my Opinion of Sally with any Design; for you may easily conceive that it is a matter of Indifference to me whether your present favourite was called Sarah or Anne; for while I am in possession of the Jewel that is lodged within I care not who holds the Casket.

> O free for ever be his eye,
> Whose heart to me is always true.

Her biographer, Miss Tomkins, has discovered an ingenious sentence in Frances' novel *The History of Lady Barton* which suggests a different outlook and may throw light on the postponement of the marriage. "There is something extremely indelicate in professing a Passion for a virtuous Woman before we have undergone a sufficient Quarantine after the Contagion of an abandoned one, and Man in such a Situation resembles a Centaur, half-human and half-brute."

Perhaps she was waiting till Henry had been purged by time of all those earlier contagions before she would acknowledge him as her husband.

Henry lived at Maidenhall, farming and building a flax mill; Frances stayed with her old aunt at Abbey Street, Dublin, and later in lodgings in Chapelizod. Now and again, heavily chaperoned, she paid visits to her husband at Maidenhall. Before they published their letters they must have pruned them drastically, because though they are certainly genuine letters they contain very few of those trivial accounts of everyday life which the originals must certainly have had and which we would today find so enthralling. In the first edition the Irish place names had been changed to English, so that the polite eye should not be offended by our barbarous nomenclature. Though frank about his morals he is fastidiously evasive about his occupation and finances, and it is only by inference and reference to other works that we find why he paid visits to country houses round Kilkenny and what happened to his flax mills.

He was doing some electioneering work, though for whom he was canvassing I do not know; as for the flax mills, he had got a grant from Parliament for starting linen manufacture on the Nore and in the expectation of a larger one he had built his factory and the house of Maidenhall. Then to set it going he had mortgaged it all. But very soon times changed for the worse, the second grant was withheld and Henry was ruined. It was soon after this that he and his wife decided to publish their letters to see if they could earn by literature what they had lost on linen. They succeeded and she became an immensely popular novelist and the first English translator of Voltaire; he too earned a living by his novels and his philosophical reflections. Most of their original work except the *Letters* is today unreadable but it charmed their contemporaries. Fanny Burney, after she had been reading *The Letters of Henry and Frances*, took up *The Vicar of Wakefield* by a new writer, Oliver Goldsmith, but she tells us she nearly threw it aside after reading a few pages, so disgusted was she with its coarse, indelicate outlook on life and in particular on matrimony; it was a cruel contrast to the "so elegantly natural, so unassumingly rational" tone of the Griffith *Letters*. In London the Griffiths became well known in the circle of Garrick and Johnson; their little boy, Harry, who in the days of their poverty had to be brought up by his grandmother at Portarlington, became a nabob in India. He returned to Ireland, bought the estate of Millicent in Co. Kildare and played an influential part in Grattan's Parliament.* He was the father of Sir Richard John Griffith, the distinguished geologist and civil engineer.

Last year I got a letter from a lady in an American university, enquiring about the Griffiths, on whom she was writing a thesis. Americans are well known for their choice of recondite subjects for theses, but I was ashamed that this learned couple should be the object of careful researches in Alabama, while I, who lived in their house, knew so little about them. I found that an excellent biographical sketch of them had been published in 1938 by the Cambridge University Press by Miss J. M. S. Tompkins, who had collected much new material from English sources. Naturally it was their late London career that interested her most; for me these few troubled years they spent in Bennettsbridge have by far the greatest appeal.

In those days it was possible for country gentlemen to see their lives in terms of classical analogy and imagery. It was easy enough for Irish landlords who left their latifundia to be administered by agents to picture their estates as "rural retreats" to which they retired like Horace or Cicero from the cares of state to plant trees and study philosophy. They reflected on the vicissitudes of life, its inequalities and injustices, with a freedom that would have seemed to a later generation subversive and disloyal to their class. Henry Flood regarded his substantial estate nearby at Farmley, as "Tusculum," where he relaxed from toil. He had amateur theatricals and lent his support to the revival of interest in the Celtic past. Griffith, though only an unsuccessful mill owner with a bare six-hundred acres, modelled himself naturally on these philosophical grandees, calling his tours around his Bennettsbridge farm his "Ambarvalia."

Henry used to attend the Kilkenny assizes and watch with philosophical melancholy the procession of the condemned to the gallows. His contempt for worldly values was of a rather static and literary kind but there are many letters which show him to have been a kindly and original character. He had a peculiar variety of colic, which he treated with opium and horseradish emetic and once or twice with the "Hygean waves of Scarborough." When on a journey his agonies used to arouse so much exasperation and compassion in his fellow passengers that he forced himself to fast. Once at an inn he had three gingerbread nuts and a pint of white

*Henry Grattan (1746–1820) was the dominant figure in the Irish Parliament of 1792–1800.—ed.

wine and the landlord presented him with a bill for the full dinner. Griffith retaliated by going into the street and calling in an old beggar woman, to whom he insisted that the dinner which he had paid for but not eaten, should be served. "She is my stomach," he told the furious landlord.

Henry scarcely mentioned his employees or his factory. Before he purchased his machinery he paid a visit of inspection to Smyth's Linen Factory at Waterford and, for Frances' benefit, he tried to assimilate this revolutionary spectacle into his rational philosophy. In the mid-eighteenth century Chartism was still far off and machinery seemed capable of liberating Rational Man, a noble and exalted being, from his dependence on other living creatures. The animal nature, unlike machinery, "through Caprice is capable of disappointing the Ends of its Creation." Rational Man, Henry thought, would be made free to contemplate Truth and Beauty and to practise Morality and Religion. "The Vulgar Herd, who are insensible to these advantages, I take to be more imperfect instruments than a Windmill or a Loom."

There is no evidence that Henry and Frances were snobbish or insensitive employers. Henry at least was by no means fastidious in his intimacies. But it seemed to them that the higher pleasures were the fruits of the cultivated understanding, and those to whom fortune had denied cultivation were of necessity barren and therefore uninteresting. We hear almost nothing about them.

Last autumn, watching a reaper and binder going round one of his fields with a couple of men accompanying it, I remembered how Henry used to sit among the stooks in a barley field, writing to Frances and reading Pliny's *Letters*. Watching the binders and stackers, he counted forty-seven women and fourteen men. Yet their lives were more remote from him than the lives of the ancient Romans. When his son was born, he wrote to Frances that if it *had* to be called Pliny he would prefer it to be named after the Younger Pliny than Pliny the Elder, since he would wish it endowed with liveliness rather than learning. Frances too liked to clothe her jokes and reflections in classical dress.

They had great skill in descriptive writing. How could the following account by Henry of a painted ceiling be bettered? "A Fricassy of Cherubims with here a Head and there a Leg or an Arm, peeping through the Clouds, which look like a good, rich thick Sauce poured about them."

They were wholly unpolitical people. I doubt whether it ever occurred to them that happiness could be brought about by social legislation. Happiness depended on the right ordering of life, on the enjoyment of rational delights, and the consolations afforded by wisdom and learning. In this system religion had an important function since it gave warmth to life, and Henry and Frances tinker with it experimentally like a pair of amateurs trying to coax heat out of an old-fashioned boiler. The principle on which it worked, they were aware, was Belief in God. This, Henry thought, was accessible to Protestants only. "The popes of Rome," he declared, "by assuming to themselves the powers of Binding and Releasing, have long since superseded their God." And at the request of a friend of his Henry wrote a strong letter denouncing the Errors of Rome and the Foulness of its Superstitions, its idle Forms and useless Ceremonies.

The occasion for this letter is remarkable. A Roman Catholic neighbour of Henry's had changed his religion in order to receive an estate valued at £700 per annum. He had been crushed by a letter "all fire and brimstone" from a brother, who was a priest at Bordeaux, and he had asked Henry to compose a reply for him. Henry reproduces his reply, of which he was evidently proud. It could only have been written in the Age of Reason, when a Rational Argument was a weapon which could be adapted to every circumstance. It can justify apostasy for £700 per annum and is equally formidable whether it comes from the brain of the apostate or the friend who impersonates him. Henry was too volatile to be called a humbug; he could not deceive himself for long. He was an experimentalist and would quickly have revolted against his own arguments if anyone had imposed them on him as dogma.

"Our Religion," Henry wrote, "is deduced from the plain Text of the Scriptures, yours from the sophistical Comments of the Priests. When a Priest once asked a Protestant, where his Religion was before Luther, he answered humorously but not less justly by asking him where was his Face before it was washed?"

He was as satisfied when his speculations led him to an orthodox conclusion as a patience player when his patience comes out. Riding, once, towards the Castlecomer hills from Maidenhall, he saw the horizon flushed with fire, so that he thought the coal seams were ablaze and that the whole earth was burning. He learnt from a passerby that it was some natural exhalation of the healthy soil, but he fell to meditating on the Last Conflagration which is prophesied in the Scriptures. At last it seemed to him that he had found a way of reconciling Religion and the Philosophy of Nature. His explanation is ingenious rather than convincing. It concerns the extra weight of the earth due to God's Creation of Living Things. Bodies attract in proportion to the weight of matter in them. The centripetal by degrees overcomes the centrifugal and the earth rushes into the sun. Hence the conflagration. About this argument Henry said rather smugly, "As I am not quite orthodox, on some points, I own that I heartily rejoice when I can make amends on others."

Henry believed in resurrection of the body, but he elaborated this sombre belief with private fancies of his own. He often meditated how his body could best be disposed of so that its elements could be converted into some other animate being or beings with the greatest speed and economy. Mummification he held in horror. "I could not bear the Thought of lying a moment Idle, alive or dead." Burning he could tolerate, provided it were not in an "Asbesto Shroud." But best of all, he said, "I would choose to be devoured by Beasts, as by that means, I should more immediately become Part of Living Animals." He preferred dogs and among dogs he chose a mastiff for its courage, a hound for its sagacity and a spaniel for its fidelity.

Even before his financial crash they were finding life in the countryside lonely and unsatisfying. When Frances was away, he now had no friend to console him for his absence at Maidenhall, save a "low-spirited cat" called Sultana Puss. "Her nerves," he said, "are so weak (which I attribute to her drinking tea in a morning without Eating), that the least loud Word sets her trembling; so that I dare not chide an awkward Housemaid for fear of putting Madam into her Hysterics."

On his visits to country houses, Henry was continually affronted by the spectacle of "bookless, sauntering Youth." "Before this century shall be closed," he wrote, "it is not impossible that anyone who can commit a Speech or a Sentence to Writing will pass for a Conjurer, who can paint his Thoughts on Paper." And to Frances he wrote: "Your Sense, your Principle and your Taste are thrown away upon the Deaf Adder and the very Seeds of them all stifled in the Growth or buried like a bad Ploughman's Grain by Clods of Earth laid over them." In another letter he compares her writings "to certain rich Essences which only affect the finest Capillaries." Their neighbours were sociable enough but without fine capillaries and, thinking of their tedious visits, Henry said, "Momus very justly found fault with the Construction of a House, because it had no Wheels to be moved by when the Situation became uneasy."

At last Henry gave up Maidenhall, which he had loved so much. He told Frances how riding home from Dublin, when his decision was made, his impatience to see it grew at every mile. "The thoughts of quitting it have the more attendered me towards it. If I thought there was a Naiad or a Dryad in the Place who would lament my absence, I should sacrifice my Interests to my Superstition; but my Religion teaches me that wherever we go our Guardian Angel accompanies us. I think I but obey its Call whenever I change my Situation to my Advantage."

The Griffiths often indulged romantic dreams but they held them under control, submitting themselves constantly to calm and ruthless examination. It is rumoured that their marriage ended in separation, but, even if this were true, I doubt whether either of them would have considered it an ill-advised marriage. Continually at every stage they had tested the flavour of their relationship and found it good. It can only have been the dregs that they jettisoned.

But his marriage was still recent and wholly satisfying when Henry left Maidenhall. He must have felt that a turning point in his life had been reached and that a rather more solemn self-analysis than he had hitherto attempted should be undertaken. On leaving the house he made a will in favour of Frances and her infant son and wrote upon the wrapper the reasons for his marriage and his theological beliefs.

I was not overreached into this Match by Art nor hurried into it by Passion, but, from long experience of her Sense and Worth, I reasoned myself into it. . . . I found that I had so engaged her Affections that no other Man could make her happy and so dallied with her Character, that only myself could repair it. . . . I am in my Religion a Christian; but of the Arian heresy as it is stiled by bigotted Councils. I was for many years a Deist, till Dr. Clayton, Bishop of Clogher, his Essay on Spirit and subsequent Writings on the same Subject had reconciled the doctrine of the Trinity to human reason and metaphysical science.

> *Humanum est errare et nescire;*
> *Ens Entium, misere mei.*

Last year the Nore flooded, as it so often does, and flattened out the remaining wall of Griffith's flax mill, which has been used for some generations as a boundary fence. The millstream has long been choked up and it was only quite lately that poking about on the banks of the river I found traces of its stone-built sides. The cottages that housed the mill hands as well as the sixty-one harvesters have gone without trace, but the elm trees which Henry planted are still standing. As for Maidenhall, it has not changed very much; its successive owners have always been poor and never had the money to make many of those lavish improvements which were admired in Victorian times.

Beside the Nore

1984

I have lived for most of my life on the Nore and own three fields upon its banks, some miles before it turns to the southeast and forces its way under Brandon Hill to join the Barrow above New Ross. In sixty years it has changed remarkably little. From a top window, looking across the river towards Blackstairs and Mount Leinster, I can still see the same stretch of cornfields, nut groves and mountain slopes. Beside the woods of Summerhill and Kilfane I can spot the round tower of Tullaherin and Kilbline, the sixteenth-century castle of the Shortalls. There is only one new cottage in sight.

This does not mean that we stagnate. The landscape is domestic and life is mainly prosperous but it has edged away from the rivers. The Nore, which traverses the county of Kilkenny and passes through the city, and the Barrow, which skirts its eastern border, and all their tributaries gave up work and took to an easy life about a century ago. The mill wheels stopped turning and the roofs fell in on the mill workers' cottages, flags and duckweed and kingcups choked the millrace and there is so much tranquil beauty around that some hope and many fear that the tourist agencies will soon discover us.

A century ago there were twenty-two flour mills, three large distilleries and four breweries on the Nore between Durrow and Inistioge. But industry had left the rivers long before I was born, and as children we were constantly driving donkey carts down little lanes to riverside ruins beside which we bathed and fished and picnicked. And every ruin had its story and the tradition that these stories are worth recording, correcting, analysing has never died out.

Our riverside ruins are mostly not depressing, for many of their founders were original and complex men, whose lives gave evidence that vision and ingenuity can flourish here. Some of their industries did not survive them for long. They subsided gracefully after a generation or two but, like the flowers of summer, were fertile in their decay. Various economic causes can be alleged for their failure but often there is nothing to be said except that men grow old and have bored or stupid sons and that today there are many prosperous industries which would be more admirable as ruins covered with valerian and wild wallflowers.

One of our favourite picnic places was Annamult Woollen Factory, a very stylish and spacious ruin on the King's River just before it joins the Nore. Before the kingcups and the bullocks took over, it was in 1814 one of the most progressive factories in the British Isles. Its owners, Messrs. Shaw and Nowlan, rivalled Robert Owen, the utopian industrialist, in their concern for their four hundred workpeople. The children all had free schooling and lesson books, their fathers and mothers had health-insurance cards, and every Sunday they danced to the fiddle in the large courtyard. George Shaw and Timothy Nowlan were stern but just, and rather quizzical. (Shaw was, I believe, a great-great-uncle to George Bernard.) Employees who misbehaved were punished but not sacked. Sometimes the offender, dressed in a yellow jacket, was obliged to roll a stone round the courtyard in full view of the Sunday merrymakers. The factory, while it lasted, was hugely successful. The Prince Regent and all the employees of the Royal Dublin Society dressed themselves in its woollens, and the fields around Annamult were white with a flock of six hundred Merino sheep, vast bundles of wool with tiny faces, which the Prims, a famous Kilkenny family with Spanish relations, had imported from Spain.

The marble works at Maddoxtown, below Kilkenny, is another beautiful spot with proud memories. Children still hunt about among the loosestrife and the willow herb for polished slabs, green Connemara, pink Midleton and Kilkenny which is black with white flecks. William Colles, who invented special machinery for cutting and polishing by waterpower, was so clever that his neighbours thought him a necromancer. He almost succeeded in making dogs weave linen by turning wheels, and he invented an instrument, like an Aeolian harp, which played tunes as it floated down the Nore. His house and his manager's house, which face each other across the Bennettsbridge road, are still among the pleasantest of the old houses that decorate the banks of the Nore. Colles was a philosophical man; he wrote tragedies, and to remind himself of the "lapse of time" he had his portrait painted every seven years. His business had prospered in adversity, for it was during the Napoleonic Wars, when foreign marble ceased to be imported, that he was able to flood the English market with his chimneypieces, punch bowls, buffets and vases. Then metal mantelpieces arrived and a few years ago all the blocks of marble that littered the riverbank were bought by a firm which pounded them into a variegated paste, from which ten chimneypieces could be made as easily as Colles made one.

Maidenhall lies between Annamult and the marble works. There are many beautiful little towns along the Nore, but since "each man kills the thing he loves" it is perhaps unsafe to admire them. Their beauty depends on humpbacked bridges and winding streets and large trees, all of which obstruct the motorist in his race to progress. The curves of the bridge are now being straightened with cement but often you can see the great stone slabs of the parapet jutting out of the stream below the bridge.

All these little towns should have had their chroniclers, for one chronicler attracts another and a village, conscious of its history, can resist the tyranny of the government official. The Nore has not been as lucky as the Barrow. I am sure that it was the O'Learys, hereditary scribes and bakers of Graiguenamanagh on the Barrow, who attracted Sean O'Faolain to the village in 1945. As editor of *The Bell*,* he stayed there for a week and studied the town as a good teacher studies a child. How did it begin, how was it going to develop? He found that it had been started by Wiltshire monks planted there by the Normans. For generations they had adhered to their English ways but had finally become assimilated. At the time of the Reformation the last Abbot was one of the Kavanaghs and their descendants still own the beautiful woods along the riverbank at Borris. O'Faolain made a transparent map of the town, marking all its shops and dwellings and offices, and laid it over an outline map of the old Cistercian Abbey. You can see how O'Leary's Bak-

---

*O'Faolain founded *The Bell* in 1940. It published the best in Irish fiction, poetry and journalism, and led the struggle against censorship. With a break from April 1948 to November 1950, it continued publication until 1955. Contributors included Peadar O'Donnell (editor from 1946), Austin Clarke, Elizabeth Bowen, Oliver St. John Gogarty, Patrick Kavanagh and Flann O'Brien. Hubert Butler was review editor under O'Donnell's editorship. See below, pp. 85–90.—ed.

ery crept over the cloisters, how the refectory became a corn store, and Denny's Pig Scales took over the monks' cemetery. Everything changes, yet there is a core of continuity. O'Faolain traces how the very same processes which eliminated typhus in Graig and gave fresh water, sanitation and medical care, also almost destroyed the town. When the railways brought "civilization," the bargees, the canal workers and the local craftsmen all became superfluous and got on the trains themselves. In 1841 there were 2,248 inhabitants, and in 1945 there were 844. And now? Are charabancs likely to be more beneficent than the railways?

If Inistioge on the Nore is one of the loveliest of Irish villages, much of the credit is due to William Tighe of Woodstock, the large house whose ruins lay till recently on the hill above it. For anyone who wants to know about the Nore and the Barrow, his work *A Statistical Survey of the County Kilkenny, 1802* is still indispensable. It has never been surpassed and never will be, because the tribe to which he and Colles and Griffith belonged, the rural polymaths, is now extinct. Tighe was a classical scholar, an archaeologist, an economist, a sociologist, a politician (a passionate opponent of the Union). He knew the names of all the flowers and all the fish of the two valleys of the Nore and the Barrow, in English, Irish and Latin, and the price of potatoes in Goresbridge in 1798 and how many "unlicensed tippling houses" there were in Inistioge in 1800 (twenty-eight). He was a humane man and soberly recalls how melons and pineapples could be bought in Kilkenny while the poor children of Iverk went to school "almost naked."

He wrote a poem in four cantos called "The Plants" about the Oak, the Rose, the Palm and the Vine. In the manner of Virgil's *Georgics* it is intended to be diverting as well as instructive. There are 150 pages of notes in Greek, Latin, Hebrew, French and Italian, and he lists thirty-nine species of oak. He was specially interested in the oaks of Mamre, where Abraham, Isaac and Jacob were buried, and he built a small house near Woodstock in an oak grove and called it Mamre, the name by which it is still known.

His eighteenth-century archaeology once collided sensationally with the less adventurous kind which grew out of it. On Tory Hill, in south Kilkenny, there was a large stone slab inscribed with words which he copied scrupulously on a page of his *Statistical Survey* and interpreted as BELI DIVOSE.

(ƐLI ꞒIVO)Ǝ

He deduced from this that Baal and Dionysus were worshipped in early Ireland. Nearly a generation later John O'Donovan, who was working on the Ordnance Survey, came up with a different explanation. He found people alive in Mullinavat who remembered hearing of Ned Connick, the carpenter, and how he had climbed up Tory Hill and carved his name on an ancient block of stone which had later been turned over.

Tighe had copied the inscription so conscientiously that it is only necessary to turn his page upside down and, making allowances for the roughness of the stone and Ned Connick's illiteracy, you can easily read:

E C O N I C 1731

William Tighe's sister-in-law, Mary Tighe, whose effigy by Flaxman is housed behind the church at Inistioge, wrote a long poem called "Psyche," or the Legend of Love. She died young but, published after her death, "Psyche" received considerable critical admiration. It is based on the story of Apuleius about the love of Cupid and Psyche.

The burning of Woodstock House, the home of poetry and learning, in 1922, was one of the saddest of Ireland's tragedies. But the beautiful plantations survived and there is scarcely in all Ireland a more charming walk than that which runs below the ruins along the Nore. On one side the river with its swans and water lilies, on the other the wooded cliffs and mossy glades sprinkled with ferns and frochans and foxgloves.

When I was young there were plenty of river picnics and neighbours visited each other by cot (long flat-bottomed boats which were used for net fishing). It was every boy and girl's dream to take a cot to Inistioge, where the river becomes tidal. My brother and I once got as far as Thomastown and then our patience ran out and we walked to Inistioge and spent the night at a small hotel. There was a large stuffed white rabbit on a chest of drawers and at dawn we awoke scratching and observed two columns of insects advancing on us from the rabbit.

The hotel turned into a pub and small shops have come and gone, but Inistioge is still the most beautiful and peaceful of villages. Not long ago I was sitting on a bench beside the bridge waiting for my grandchildren to come down the river by canoe from Maidenhall. I remember the red valerian, a broad bank of colour reflected on the dappled current. In such a place time stands still. The past comes close in disconnected fragments and I was thinking of the days when we were children and had dancing classes with the young Tighes at the Noreview Hotel in Thomastown; their mother, with my Aunt Harriet, used to run a Christian Science Reading Room opposite the Castle in Kilkenny, two spiders into whose web no fly ever came; and I remember when we went to Woodstock a sidecar used to meet us at Thomastown station and the branches of the trees brushed our faces as we drove along.

The Tighes were friendly charming people who did not deserve the misfortunes that happened to them. When the war broke out Captain Tighe took his family to London, where he met his death in an accident that has never fully been explained. I do not believe they ever returned. In the spring of 1920 the Black and Tans took over Woodstock and patrolled the country at breakneck speed in their Crossley tenders. Then the Treaty came and they left as rapidly as they had come.* It was an empty, undefended house that was finally destroyed.

Later in the afternoon an old man came and sat beside me, and I asked him what it was like when the Tans were in Woodstock. He was very ready to talk and afterwards I wrote down what he told me.

They were in the village too [he said] and we had them in the house next door to us. They weren't too bad. They made us have a notice on all the doors with the names of the people in the house. I remember there was a young chap, Ned Brennan, maybe eight or nine, and they stuck him up on the pub counter and asked him to sing, and he sang "Wrap the Green Flag Around Me"! He was a young chap, you see, and it was one of the songs he'd learnt. But the Tans just laughed and filled his pockets with pennies. When he came home his mother was very angry and said it was "blood money" and wouldn't let him keep it.

The Tans had two spies going round the village [he went on] and didn't fourteen of our chaps chase after them so that the two jumped into the river. And our chaps shot one of them and the other got out and ran back to Woodstock to tell the Tans. And after that didn't the Tans burn Hanrahan's farm, oh, a big place with cow sheds and barns and hayricks. And they did nothing to save old Mrs. Hanrahan from burning, till Mrs. Newport of Ballygallon—she was an Englishwoman—came and blamed them for not getting her out, and they got her out and she took her to her own place.

---

*The Black and Tans were British reinforcements sent to help suppress the Sinn Féin movement; they departed after the Treaty of 6 December 1920 that granted Ireland Dominion status as the Irish Free State.—ed.

I have always believed that local history is more important than national history. There should be an archive in every village, where stories such as the old man told me are recorded. Where life is fully and consciously lived in our own neighbourhood, we are cushioned a little from the impact of great far-off events which should be of only marginal concern to us.

Aunt Harriet

1987

When she got old and ill my grandmother grew frightened of being
buried alive and she constantly asked for assurance that she would
be given an autopsy. It was a persistent fear. "She's going on about
old Topsy again," my mother said once, when coming out of her
room. My mother was under great strain and I was no use to her.

I was at Oxford and found it a place of such abundance that
Ireland and everyone in it, particularly my relations, were diminished.
I was incessantly carping at them. In England we were nobody, while
in Ireland, I maintained, if we gave it our first loyalty we could be
somebody.

When Aunt Harriet, my father's sister, died, I went with my
parents to keep Aunt Florence company at Lavistown. It is a small
Georgian house with white Venetian blinds, built for the manager of
the marble works by the founder, William Colles. The marble works
were still functioning in a desultory way just below Lavistown on
the banks of the Nore. My father and mother slept in the big room
over the dining room where the coffin was laid on two chairs under
the window. I slept in the small dressing room off it.

Lavistown, which was four miles away from Maidenhall, was
almost a second home to us; we were often there. I was very fond
of Aunt Harriet, who superintended the cooking and the cook, Ellen,
while Aunt Florence looked after the garden and the gardener, Donovan. We used to see more of Aunt Harriet because she had a bicycle,
while Aunt Florence had to get Donovan to harness Maureen, the
fat white pony. Aunt Harriet usually bicycled over with a cake in the
basket on the handlebars and *The Christian Science Monitor* under
it, for she was both a Christian Scientist and a Gaelic Leaguer. "Well,

chickabiddies!" she exclaimed when she saw us. The cake she gave to my mother, *The Christian Science Monitor* to us children, ostensibly because of the children's page, but I'm sure she thought some effluence of her faith might reach us through it. The stories were usually about dressed-up rabbits, mice, bluebottles, more moral than Beatrix Potter but less entertaining. Any message they contained was lost on us, but I was offended on Aunt Harriet's behalf when my mother said, "Anyway, it's good thick paper; wonderful for packing eggs."

My mother said Aunt Harriet became a Christian Scientist because a certain Dr. Davis had failed to meet her under the clock on the platform at Kingsbridge Station in Dublin. She became a Gaelic Leaguer, I expect, because of the Cuffes, who lived at Sheestown, a small house the other side of the Nore. Otway Cuffe was the brother and heir of the Earl of Desart, who lived at Desart Court about ten miles to the west. Mrs. Cuffe was the daughter of a Cornish nobleman and they had thrown all their hereditary prestige, which in those days was considerable, into the Gaelic Revival, the development of a unique Irish civilization independent of politics. His sister-in-law, Lady Desart, put her vast wealth largely at Otway Cuffe's disposal for the development of local industries. Though the bulk of the Unionists were sceptical, the Cuffes had many disciples. The Gaelic movement interested Aunt Harriet, while Aunt Florence was absorbed by home industries and craftwork, and they had a large framed photograph of Otway Cuffe in the dining room at Lavistown.

All this might seem irrelevant to the story I have to tell about Aunt Harriet. It is a very brief story but nothing at all if I do not convey the closeness I felt to that body in the box. Love? Affection? Admiration? I think absolute involvement is the right phrase. She must have suspected in me, when I was quite small, some germ of heterodoxy of the kind she had nursed in herself. One day, when I was playing on the gravel at Lavistown, I fell and scraped my leg. I pointed out to Aunt Harriet that it was bleeding. "It's nothing," she said and put a piece of stamp paper on it. I pulled it off the moment she was out of sight and never told my mother, who would have been angry; Christian Science was unpopular in those days because a co-religionist of Aunt Harriet's, Mrs. Tighe of Woodstock, refused to have a doctor for her son and he died.

My two aunts went on sketching holidays every spring to Vernet les Bains, but one summer Aunt Harriet went to Boston for some special celebration of Mary Baker Eddy, the great prophetess and heresiarch of Christian Science. My mother thought she might marry an elderly Christian Scientist there and feared for our prospects. We had always held that money that you inherit, unlike money that you earn, belongs to the family. We had forebears called Kingston who owned a shipyard in Cork and, when it closed, retained the ground rents of the buildings that went up on the quays beside the Lee. The ground rents passed on to their descendants, getting less and less with each generation, together with some good miniatures of themselves in a blue velvet frame by Frederick Buck of Cork. We got the miniatures and my aunts the ground rents.

Aunt Harriet came back much invigorated from Boston. She had been also to the Niagara Falls. Mrs. Eddy was dead at the time but she had seen her house and I think the cradle where she had been a baby. She had worshipped in the Mother Church of Christ Scientist and had not brought back a Christian Scientist husband. She would like to have told us more about Boston but everybody fidgetted uncomfortably when she started to talk of Mrs. Eddy and asked her feverishly about the Niagara Falls.

Aunt Harriet was the strictest sort of Christian Scientist. She never admitted to any illness. She never went to a dentist but let her teeth fall out so that her cheeks contracted round three or four solitary tusks. This did nothing for her appearance. Aunt Florence had frequent small illnesses and many visits from the doctor. There must have been some snappishness between the sisters but we children never heard a word of it. We squabbled as much as most families do, but confronted by the outside world we were loyal to each other.

In those days, the Sinn Féiners were in the habit of visiting people, two by two and often by night, asking them for money for "dependents of the Irish Republicans." They went to Lavistown one night and Aunt Harriet looked out of her bedroom window and said reproachfully that she would give them nothing, that she had given up the Gaelic League when it had become political and when the Sinn Féiners had started a campaign of violence. After this little lecture they went away.

I told this to a friend of my own age who lived nearby. "I don't wonder," she said, "the Shinners got a shock and went off when Old Harriet poked her face out at them." I took offence and told her she had no right to talk like that. She said pacifically, "You should see my Aunt Eileen."

I have left Aunt Harriet in her coffin a long way behind, but I am thinking of the memories she took with her; they were all unimportant, but the past is a mosaic of tiny pieces, a fragment of a larger picture, Ireland in the 1920s and the last days of the Anglo-Irish, and I will continue with more minutiae.

In the days before the war and the 1916 Rising, the more enlightened of the Anglo-Irish were trying desperately to identify themselves with Ireland. Aunt Harriet organized the first local Feis, an ancient festival of song and dance and miscellaneous junketting which centuries before took place at Tara. At the Kilkenny Feis there were competitions for Irish dancing and singing, lace making, cake, jam, section honey and craftwork. When it was all over Aunt Harriet was presented by the committee with a Tara brooch, a richly ornamented safety pin with which the ancient Irish held their clothes together, mass-produced from originals in the National Museum.

The Gaelic League was not "political" in those days and even the British saw nothing against it. When Lady Aberdeen, Ireland's all but last Vice-Reine, came down to open our local concert hall, she defied the ridicule of the Anglo-Irish neighbours by dressing herself and the ladies of the party in emerald green with Tara brooches. She and her husband were very Scottish; he wore the Gordon tartan and they wrote a book called *We Twa*. They bred Aberdeen terriers and were Aberdonianly thrifty, and it was one of their aims to show how very Scottish one could be and yet loyal to the Crown. Why could not the Irish be the same? She entertained very little in the Vice-Regal Lodge, but started a campaign against tuberculosis with no political overtones, and motored all over Ireland trying with some success to introduce village nurses into every community.

Despite all this they were unpopular with both the more orthodox Gaels and ordinary Unionists; they were suspected of "liberalism," which in Ireland was anathema to the traditional Unionist, and one of our neighbours wrote a poem about them of which I can only remember one line: "They cut the penny buns in half when Larkin came to tea." (Larkin was a celebrated labour leader.)

The Cuffes and Aunt Florence and my mother all threw themselves into the crusade against tuberculosis (Aunt Harriet believed it was a delusion of the mind) and I think the Bennettsbridge village nurse was among the first in Ireland.

When Lord Aberdeen retired in 1915 he was made a Marquess and, conscious of his work for Ireland, he chose the title of Aberdeen and Tara, but the use of this most famous of all Irish place names by a Scottish peer gave great offence. On leaving they sent photographs of themselves with an Aberdeen terrier beside them and one of the recipients wrote a letter which got great publicity: "Thank you very much for the beautiful photograph of yourselves and your little dog Tara." They changed Tara to Temair, which is a more ancient version of Tara but, as few knew this, no one objected.

Behind Lavistown is a big house, Leyrath, where Sir Charles Wheeler Cuffe, a distant relative of the Desarts, lived with his cousin Baroness Prochaska, an Austrianized Czech who was full of enthusiasm for home industries and handicrafts. She was very plain with projecting eyes and teeth and a gobbly Central European voice. I expect she knew the Czech language but only spoke it to her inferiors. She must have considered that the Anglo-Irish were a little like the Austro-Czechs, whose doom like theirs was only a few years away. She took up beekeeping vigorously and prevailed on the County Council to appoint a beekeeping instructor. She had a row of hives at Leyrath with names like Peace, Love, Harmony. I don't know whether it was she or Otway Cuffe who was responsible for the carpentry instructor who travelled round the country villages. In Bennettsbridge he gave instruction to some twenty local boys in my father's barn once a week. I was taught with the other boys of my own age to make a small bracket on which to put a Holy Lamp. I was eight at the time and very class-conscious but had never learnt to say, "Please, sir, can I leave the room?" And something awful happened that made the other boys titter and the instructor pause to give me good advice. I thought of it with shame for months and months. This is the first time I've ever mentioned it.

The Baroness bought a horse-drawn coffee van and got up every fair day at 6 a.m. and, joined sometimes by Aunt Florence, sometimes by Aunt Harriet or my elder sister, brought it to James's Green, where the Kilkenny Fair was held. There they sold, very cheaply, tea, coffee and buns to the farmers, drovers and cattle dealers. There was always a lot of money round the town on fair days, the pubs were crowded and there were men with plum-coloured faces walking unsteadily in the street. The coffee van had an unacknowledged relevance to this. This went on for twenty years but the Baroness got ill and went to Auteven Cottage Hospital (this was one of Lady Desart's gifts to Kilkenny), and one day soon after that a lady who was deputizing for her, and had a less dominating character, was stopped, by order of the Corporation, and was not allowed in. The public-house keepers and other traders in Walkin Street, which led to the fair green, had put pressure on the Corporation. They claimed that they had a right to give drinks or proper breakfasts to drovers and that the coffee van was depriving them of their livelihood. They said that the farmers were supporting the coffee van because they were too mean to give their men the money for a proper breakfast.

Word of all this came to the Kilkenny Farmers' Union, an organization on which the Anglo-Irish landowners were well represented. A special meeting was held and they were all on the side of the Baroness and her coffee van. And it was resolved that a message should be sent to her in hospital thanking her for her tireless work over the years and wishing her a speedy recovery. At the same time pressure was put on the Corporation to withdraw the veto on the coffee van which the public-house keepers had forced them to make. The coffee van continued as long as the Baroness lived, but when she died it died with her.

I used to bicycle in with my father very early on the day of the Kilkenny Fair and we found the cattle from his two farms at Burnchurch and Drumherin waiting for us there, so it is not very difficult to revive all these memories, some of which are recorded in Aunt Florence's scrapbook. It only slowly and sadly became apparent to my father that nature did not intend me to be a farmer. It was my younger brother, a small child then, who took over.

The Kilkenny Fair and the Kilkenny Farmers' Union ended long ago, as did the instructors for beekeeping and carpentry, Lady Aberdeen's locally appointed nurse and her Women's National Health Association. I dare say they are not missed very much and have been replaced by something just as good, but some faculty of independent initiative, of overcoming apathy with an idea, has become rarer.

While Aunt Florence went to church in St. Canice's Cathedral, Kilkenny, Aunt Harriet stayed at home praying and reading Mrs. Eddy's *Science and Health with a Key to the Scriptures*. Aunt Florence must have come back full of chat about the neighbours and their hats and the bishop's sermon. Did she have to suppress it all or did Aunt Harriet welcome this contact with the outside world?

I felt for her because at this time I was a very earnest Free Thinker, although I discovered at Oxford that my particular earnestness was twenty years out of date. I had the old nursery at the top of the house as my study, and from there I could see my father and mother and two sisters setting off in the wagonette to Ennisnag church. I saw them turn down the avenue and eight minutes later I could see the top hat of old Egan the coachman (he sat on the box) appearing and disappearing and reappearing between the chestnut trees along the road, and when it finally vanished I felt lonely but unyielding. Solitude was the price Aunt Harriet and I had to pay for our convictions. I did not change much but the world changed. In England people slipped out of faith and into indifference without mental or spiritual struggling. Earnest rationalism like Lecky's and Bury's is the natural child of Irish Protestantism. It is the Catholic majority that keeps most of us defiantly Protestant.

Because of this, like a jelly that has stiffened inside its jelly mould and slid out intact, I found myself accepting the Protestant ethos and bothering less about its dogma and mythology. We respect individualism and in particular "the sacred right of private judgment," as Grattan called it at the Convention of Dungannon in 1782.* In Ireland it has played the same part in the life of the Irish Protestant as Authority has in the life of the Irish Catholic. It is frequently under attack and I have always done my best to defend it.

What was Lavistown like in January 1925? The house is still there but it has changed, and I have to resurrect it by conjecture and present experience, not memory. The aconites might have been just out under the shelter of the big cypress tree that fell down many years ago, and a few tight buds of snowdrops perhaps, but the mauve crocuses, the small ones that seeded themselves under all the deciduous trees that lined the path to the garden and the back avenue, would only just have poked above the leaf mould.

The pony Maureen would have been there, but would Ellen, the cook? The tennis court would have been there and properly mown, and not the flat shaggy rectangle that survives still beside so many Irish country houses, recalling the days before 1922 when there were often tennis parties at different houses six days a week.

I remember the inside of the house better. Aunt Florence took in *The Queen* and used to enjoy discussing with us the Social Problem page. Aunt Harriet had a row of Irish books and Dinneen's Irish dictionary, and when I was sixteen she gave me William James's *Varieties of Religious Experience*, which did not interest me very much because I was proud to have no religious experience. It wasn't until years later that I discovered she had left a yellow ribbon in a chapter called "The Religion of Healthy Mindedness" with a subsection on "Mind Cure."

---

*The Volunteer Convention at Dungannon, Co. Tyrone, which negotiated with the English. See below, p. 133.

I must come back to that night of 25 January 1925. We had a quiet low-voiced supper in the drawing room opposite to the dining room in which Aunt Harriet lay, and then we went to bed. I went first because I was in the little dressing room. It was only the second time I had been in a house with a dead person (Granny had died the year before) and I took a long time to go to sleep, thinking of Aunt Harriet and all the things that had happened and not happened between us. It was a long chronicle of trivialities, letters I had not answered, copies of the *Monitor* with marked passages that I had not acknowledged, little openings for thoughtful conversations which I had gently closed.

Perhaps Aunt Harriet had access to some peace of mind, some freedom from pain which she had spent her life trying to share with us. But it was very difficult to think like this. It was another hour before I slept and at about four I was roused by a tapping sound. It came from the room below. It is only because my elder relations are all dead and I am an old man now, soon to go into a box myself, that I can write like this. Perhaps I should not, for I have nothing interesting to relate, only what happened in my mind, and that is discreditable but not exciting.

If I could have gone downstairs directly from my room I know I would have, but to get down I had to go through my parents' room. They would certainly wake and I would put into their minds a horrifying thought, which it was my duty to confirm before expressing.

I spent the rest of the night wrestling with this problem even after the tapping had stopped. What worried me was the thought that in some supreme effort of faith she had half conquered death, which like a wave in an ebbing tide had left her stranded half alive on the foreshore.

I recalled Granny's fear of being buried alive. Would Aunt Harriet have woken up and not known whether she was already buried? And what could we do? Would I have to get Mr. Lewis the undertaker? Where did he live? Was there a hammer and a chisel in the house?

I got up as soon as I could and as I passed through my parents' room my mother said to my father, "Did you hear that rapping in the night? It must have been the knob of the blind cord tapping on the windowpane. There was a bit of wind." "Yes, I expect so," my father said indifferently. When I got down, all was quiet and the blind cord did have a knob at the end of it but the wind had stopped and I could not convince myself that my mother's explanation was the correct one. She had never believed in Aunt Harriet's faith healing. "She could have saved herself with something quite simple like cascara," she had said. I seldom think of that night now, though I once used often to do so. It was not a question of being right or wrong in what I thought. I had envisaged a possibility and at all costs I should have tested it. It was the first of ten or fifteen grave mistakes that I think over in the wakeful nights. I wrote a poem about them, and then found that Yeats had written some lines that were more apposite.

> Things said or done long years ago,
> Or things I did not do or say
> But thought that I might say or do,
> Weigh me down, and not a day
> But something is recalled,
> My conscience or my vanity appalled.*

In the daylight, common sense prevailed. Aunt Harriet was self-effacing and considerate. She would sooner have gone through the ordeal of death a second time than be resurrected in a blaze of newspaper publicity. Very quickly the night vision of hands battering helplessly at unyielding wood was submerged. Mr. Lewis, the undertaker, arrived with the hearse, and we took Aunt Florence with us to lunch at home and afterwards we met the hearse at Danesfort Cross and followed it to Burnchurch church, where my great-grandfather, once rector there, and all his family were buried. My mother said she had tried to find if there was some special Christian Science burial service and some special minister to perform it. Now it seems to me we did not try hard enough and that we should have urged her fellow believers to come down and do honour to their dead sister, who in a lonely way had been loyal to their principles.

Later still I felt that in view of the Cork ground rents it had been mean of us not to give my two aunts a tombstone to themselves. Instead we added their names as postscripts on the base of the tall cross put up to my Uncle Richard, who had caught cold and died after a tennis party in 1877 at the age of nineteen.

Forty years later, when I was in Boston, because of Aunt Harriet I went to the Mother Church of Christ Scientist and in a Christian Science Reading Room I found Mrs. Eddy's *Science and Health with*

---

*From "Vacillation," in *The Winding Stair and Other Poems* (1933).

a Key to the Scriptures. I was astonished. Mrs. Eddy took the offensive against philology.

"The dissection and definition of words," she wrote, "aside from their metaphysical content is not scientific." Extracting the "metaphysical" content from the name Adam, she writes: "Divide it in half and it reads A dam, as the obstacle which the serpent Sin would impose between Man and his Creator," and elsewhere she writes: "Adam and his race are a dream of mortal mind because Cain went to live in the Land of Nod, the land of dreams and illusions."

Was this the way Aunt Harriet and thousands of others reasoned? And yet I had to acknowledge that, as newspapers go, *The Christian Science Monitor* has many merits.

I learnt in Boston that Mary Baker Eddy had many enemies and critics there. One of them has related that some of the more ardent of her disciples thought she had conquered death as well as pain and that, when she proved to be mortal after all, one of them impersonated her and drove round Boston for several days in her well-known carriage till the faithful were ready to accept the truth.

Goodness often blossoms like roses on very rickety trelliswork, and beauty can grow out of nonsense. There are no grounds for supposing that one can live a life without pain and sadness, but is it wrong to believe that somehow, somewhere, this is possible?

Two years after Aunt Harriet, Aunt Florence eased herself out of life slowly and securely by many small illnesses. I got the Cork ground rents, but after a few years the Post Office bought half the buildings on the site of the Kingston shipyard and claimed to be exempt from ground rents. My two sisters got Lavistown. The gate lodge on the back avenue, where Donovan lived, belongs to my niece, who sold Lavistown to friends, who have made it a study centre. Students come there to learn about the flora and fauna of the Nore Valley. The cows there produce special cheeses and the pigs special sausages. It is still a place where it is easier to believe in happiness than in pain.

The Auction

1957

I am not quite sure how soon after Otway Cuffe's death, in 1912, Mrs. Cuffe gave up Sheestown and went to live in Kerry, but I was already a public schoolboy, a Carthusian,* and ripe to be embarrassed when my relations made scenes publicly, and there had been just such a scene at the Sheestown auction to which I had gone with my mother in the pony trap. Mr. McCreery, the auctioneer, had offered for sale a large wooden hut and my mother, who needed a new henhouse, rather tremulously bid it up to £17. It was knocked down to her, and she was walking away, appalled at her own audacity, when someone remarked how kind the Cuffes had always been to the poor of Kilkenny. Not one tuberculous slum child but several had passed successive summers in that hut in a leafy glade by the Nore. Tuberculosis! My mother for a couple of seconds was frozen with horror, and then she was gesticulating frantically across the crowd to Mr. McCreery and to Aunt Harriet, who stood within reach of him. "Tell him! Stop him!" I felt a frisson of sympathy and dismay. Tuberculosis! Tuberculous poultry! Tuberculous eggs! A quiver like an electric current ran through all the better-dressed bosoms in front of me, because Lady Aberdeen, the Lord Lieutenant's wife, had started a crusade against tuberculosis—it was a word that was on everybody's lips, particularly Unionist lips. I must here permit myself a digression about tuberculosis.

It was one of those rare and blessed battle cries, like cooperative creameries and village halls, which appeared to have no political or

---

*A student at Charterhouse, in England.—ed.

religious implications. Indeed it was better than either, for often a priest wanted to consecrate a village hall or put a crucifix instead of a clock above the rostrum, and there were rumours that the creameries were used for political agitation when the farmers' boys for miles around, having taken their milk churns from their donkey carts, had leisure for exchanging views. But nobody could say anything of the kind about tuberculosis. When my mother had started a branch of the Women's National Health Association in Bennettsbridge, Lady Aberdeen had come down and talked to the Association and driven round the neighbourhood. My sister had sat on one side of her and Miss Foley, the priest's sister, on the other, and Mrs. Cuffe beside the chauffeur. It was an immensely amiable, nonpolitical nonreligious occasion. Tuberculosis acted like a love potion, and at the end of it we children had distinctly heard Miss Foley say, "A thousand thanks, Countess, for my most delightful drive." With the savage snobbery of children, learning for the first time the exciting art of speaking in inverted commas, we had pestered each other for months and months with poor Miss Foley's over-unctuous gratitude. So now tuberculosis, which had once seemed a sordid, almost shameful secret between the doctors and the dying, was invested with dignity and importance. Now that it was made everybody's business, it attracted to itself not only the tender and the charitable but also the ambitious and the interfering and the timid, who saw that sympathy for the sick might be interposed as a fluffy bolster between themselves and Home Rule, which they saw irrevocably approaching. But because I found it all a bore when I was in my teens, I am likely to underestimate the self-denial and unrewarded service of those who, like my mother, spent endless hours with ledgers, petty-cash books, subscription lists, committees. My mother, unlike the Cuffes, had never been sustained by any golden dream of a new era in Ireland, but simply by a Victorian sense of duty to the poor and her own humorous curiosity about other people's lives.

For a moment or two I felt rather proud of the effect that my mother had caused in the large crowd with the magical word "tuberculosis." All the expected responses could be seen, and even Aunt Harriet, who as a Christian Scientist considered tuberculosis "a form of false thinking," had leant over loyally and, seizing Mr. McCreery by the sleeve, had whispered some agitated remarks into his ear. But quickly the mystical moment passed, the auctioneer and the public began to get impatient, and at my elbow I heard the curate of St. John's, Kilkenny, say sourly to his neighbour, "I don't wonder she wants to get out of it. Seventeen pounds! Ridiculous! Why, I could knock it up myself for seven pounds. As for tuberculosis, all that's needed is a little disinfectant." I was greatly mortified on my mother's behalf and scarcely noticed how the episode ended. (I think she decided to write herself to Mrs. Cuffe.)

I wriggled unhappily out of the crowd in the yard and walked down past Cuffe's Model Dairy to the river, which for a mile or two upstream above Sheestown Weir flows under park trees through the small demesnes of Sheestown and Kilfera on its western banks. It is full of trout and salmon, and all the way from Durrow in Co. Leix to New Ross in Co. Wexford there are meadows of rich grass on each bank, the Scotch firs and larches grow straight and thick, and every now and then, south of Kilkenny town, beeches spread themselves out extravagantly over bluebells and wood sorrel. Through them you can see the hindquarters of a fat pony, the sparkle of a tomato house, the corner of a tennis net and, less frequently, a real exotic like a contented Jersey cow or a disconsolate but still defiant cricket pavilion. Surely this valley had everything in the world that anyone could wish for, the raw material for every variety of happiness? Why is the manufactured article so rare? Why, at sixteen, were my parents convinced that I would never be able to live here? Has any river in the world carried so many cargoes of nostalgia and bittersweet memories to the sea, for one could cover an acre with faded newsprint about the Nore, sad simple verse composed in Tasmania or Bangkok or Pittsburgh, and sent home to Kilkenny? If the Nore ends one line you will know infallibly that a succeeding line will end with "days of yore," "distant shore," "never more," "long years before," "memory's door," "parting sore." The answer to my last question is no doubt that all the rivers of Ireland are the same.

In fact, though, I don't want an answer, because the answer is obvious. I want an admission. Living in social harmony is a most difficult art; the most absolute concentration is required, and perfect equilibrium. Our island is dangerously tilted towards England and towards Rome, good places in themselves but best seen on the level. Everybody is rolling off it and those that remain, struggling hard for a foothold, drag each other down. But it is not necessary to argue, it is only necessary to look.

Sheestown is divided from Kilfera by a small rocky glen in which St. Fiachra's Well is situated, and beyond it across smooth lawns, a tennis court and a high embankment built above the rapids of the Nore, you can see the Norman castle of the Forrestals now incor-

porated into Kilfera House. There is also the ruined church of Sheestown in which the Forrestals and Shees are buried, and the small
cemetery of Kilfera where the roots of the beech trees have tilted or
flattened half the tombs. A headless statue of a medieval ecclesiastic
is propped against the railings of the Victorian table-tomb of Mr.
Kenny Purcell, "One-time Clerk of the Peace Kilkenny" and a former
owner of Kilfera. It is said locally to be St. Fiachra himself, that
much-travelled saint, who in Kilkenny gave his name to Kilfera and
in Paris gave it to the "fiacre," because there was a cabstand beneath
his church; but the statue is a thousand years later than Fiachra's
time and is probably an abbot from some dissolved medieval monastery, Jerpoint perhaps, or Kells. A small stone building, said to be
his hermit cell, had to be removed when Mr. Kenny Purcell went to
his rest in 1869, but he too has been disrespectfully treated because
the marble walls of his sepulchre are gaping apart. My toes were just
small enough to get a foothold between the iron bars and I could see
a couple of stones and a tin can, but no trace of the Clerk of the
Peace.

You get all the confusion of Irish history in a few acres. First St.
Fiachra, then the Norman Forrestals, then, overshadowing them, the
Shees, English you would suppose. But no, they are Irish Uí Seaghdha
from Kerry, who anglicized their name and their habits with immense
rapidity and success in Tudor times. Robert Shee had allied himself
with Piers Butler, eighth Earl of Ormonde, and had been killed in
1493 in Tipperary fighting against the O'Briens of Munster at the
head of a hundred Kilkennymen. The Shees were one of the ten great
merchant families of Kilkenny, the other nine all being English.
Robert Shee's son, Richard, became Sovereign of Kilkenny; his grandson, Sir Richard, was educated at Gray's Inn, became legal adviser
to Queen Elizabeth's friend Black Tom Butler, the tenth Earl of Ormonde, and when Ormonde became Lord Treasurer of Ireland, was
made Deputy Treasurer. He and his family acquired great wealth and
many houses in Kilkenny town and county and built the Alms House
in which Standish O'Grady had established his knitting industry and
permanent craft exhibition.* Sir Richard's son, Lucas, married the
daughter of Lord Mountgarret, whose other daughter married the
eleventh Earl of Ormonde. Lucas's son, Robert, when the Civil War
broke out, persuaded his uncle Mountgarret to accept the presidency
of the Confederation. The royalist Parliament was held in the Shee

*See below, "The Deserted Sun Palace."

mansion in Parliament Street, which till 1865 stood where the gates of the Market now are.

The Shees were an urbane and cultivated family who wrote for each other long epitaphs in elegiacs and hexameters which are more pagan than Christian. "*Homo bulla* . . . (Man is a bubble) . . .":

> *Nec genus antiquum nec honesta opulentia rerum*
> *Nec necis imperium lingua diserta fugit*
> *Nec fidei fervor nec religionis avitae*
> *Cultus ab extremo liberat ense nihil.*

> (Neither ancient lineage, nor honourably
> amassed wealth nor eloquence can evade the
> stern summons of death, nor can fervent faith
> and the practice of the religion of our fathers
> reprieve us from the sword of doom.)

Then a prayer is asked for a speedy passage to Heaven, supposing, that is to say, Heaven exists:

> *Si tamen haec mors est transitus ad superos . . .*

Elias Shee, from whose tomb in St. Mary's, Kilkenny, I have taken these five lines, is described by Richard Stanihurst* as "born in Kilkenny, sometime scholar of Oxford, a gentleman of passing good wit, a pleasing conceited companion, full of mirth without gall. He wrote in English divers sonnets." I do not think the Shees or the nine other Kilkenny merchant families, all Catholics, all dispossessed by Cromwell, could be considered "priest-ridden." Had fate treated them more kindly, would they, like the wealthy Flemish burghers, have become patrons of the arts and sciences; would they have produced their own Erasmus and formed eventually the nucleus of a proud and independent Anglo-Irish civilization? Elias Shee was described by his sorrowing relatives as "*orbi Britannico lumen*," a light to the British world, because of his wit, his learning, his breeding, but his family remained conscious of their Irish descent, calling themselves after Cromwellian times O'Shee, when more prudent families were dropping their O's and Mac's.

Yet I cannot feel very confident of any such Anglo-Irish development in the seventeenth century. Is there, perhaps, as AE suggested,

---

*A sixteenth-century historian of Ireland.—ed.

"some sorcery in the Irish mind" rebelling against any peaceful and prosperous fusion, some intense pride of race?

When I got back to Sheestown I found that my mother had bought me a bookcaseful of Otway Cuffe's books. She was looking at them apprehensively, wondering whether she was not infecting me with something more virulent than tuberculosis, and, when we were driving home, she tried to counteract any possible bad effects by telling me how Cuffe's heart had been broken by ingratitude and that, when a couple of years before he had invited the Cave Hill Players from Belfast to act in a play of O'Grady's about Red Hugh O'Donnell* at Sheestown, a couple of thousand spectators had streamed out from Kilkenny. They had trampled down some rare shrubs, and stolen and broken teacups. She also said that O'Grady's play was very bad, and that she had had to laugh at Otway Cuffe in a saffron kilt reciting a roistering rebel Irish ballad in a refined English voice. Manager after manager had cheated Cuffe at the woollen mills and woodworks. And she said that all the intelligent people had emigrated. Her own brothers, Etonians, Harrovians, Carthusians, had all gone, except Uncle Charlie at Graiguenoe, and were British officers or Indian civilians. Ireland was an exhausted country. "Look how stupid X is!" and she mentioned one of my father's oldest friends.

Everything she said was true, yet I knew that she herself would never grudge her teacups or her shrubs where her own ideals and affections were involved, and that she was trying to inoculate me against the terrible virus of nationalism. My responses cannot have satisfied her, for a few days later I found that she had torn out from some of the books the blank page on which Cuffe had written his name, and had used upon the title page the little machine for stamping notepaper with our address, Maidenhall, Bennettsbridge, Co. Kilkenny. I diverted some of the annoyance I felt with my mother to the little machine, which I ever afterwards regarded with abhorrence. I could remember our excitement when it had arrived ten years before and we had won countless pennies for the League of Pity by stamping notepaper for my mother and father with it.

My mother bought a large red book called *Careers for Our Boys* and tried vainly to engage me in conversation about the British consular and diplomatic services. She suspected rightly that I was not

*A leader of the Irish against the English invasions during the reign of Queen Elizabeth I.—ed.

merely indifferent but hostile: she trembled for me because the 1914–18 war was on and all the heresies which had seemed so venial a couple of years earlier now carried on them the mark of Cain. Our bishop, Dr. d'Arcy, the successor of Dr. Crozier, a mild and scholarly commentator on the Pauline Epistles, had himself a few years before, as Bishop of Down, consecrated Unionist machine guns to be used against Home Rulers, and sometimes Kipling's poem on Ulster was quoted. I remember only one verse:

> We know the war declared
> On every peaceful home,
> We know the Hell prepared
> For those who serve not Rome.

It would have been social suicide to question that God and the Empire were indissolubly allied. My mother was not herself given to adamantine loyalties; there were few of them which she could not have adjusted in our interests. She was not a Roman matron like my grandmother, who would have sacrificed us all upon the altar of God or Empire, but she saw that we, unlike the Cuffes and Lady Desart, were not in the income group which could afford to be unorthodox. My father belonged to the minor Anglo-Irish gentry and, except for remote kinship of blood, had no link with the two or three noble Butler dynasties which still reigned nearby, and which we were to survive in Kilkenny. And if ever I made some heretical remark about the Easter Rebellion, she would look at me not with indignation but with loving anxiety, as though I had coughed up a spot of blood onto my handkerchief. There was no precedent for it in my upbringing or my heredity. Nothing like it had been seen in her own family; in my father's there had been Aunt Harriet, but when the Gaelic League had become "political" Aunt Harriet had shut her Dinneen* forever and become a disciple of Mrs. Eddy. It could not, therefore, be a congenital disorder, it must have been acquired by contagion, and looking round in a wide sweep for possible "carriers," she fixed on my distant cousin Theobald Fitzwalter Butler, who had been head boy at Charterhouse a term or two before I had gone there and who had visited us several times and had made contentious remarks at mealtimes. "He's got it off Theo," I often heard her murmur dis-

---

*Rev. Patrick Dinneen (1860–1934), Gaelic Revivalist and Jesuit scholar, compiled the standard Irish-English dictionary. It was first published in 1904 as *Foclóir Gaedhilge agus Béarla*, and rewritten in 1927.

mally, desperately to my father, after some evening of unprofitable disagreements.

Theo and his friend Eric Dodds had done relief work in Serbia before conscription had come and then, dissociating themselves from the war, had returned to their own country. Theo had taught at a school in Co. Down, Dodds at Kilkenny College. One day Dodds, a stocky independent fellow, walked out to tea from Kilkenny and inflamed my grandmother by his pacifism and his defence of Irish sedition. Theo told us that Dodds had won "The Craven Scholarship." Ritual Irish jokes, one part mirth, three parts gall, were later made about the Craven, though not by my grandmother, who was too deeply shocked and too fastidious, in the well-bred English way, for puns. Dodds did not come again. But nonetheless, almost as much as Theo (who was thought more insidious because he was more ingratiating), he was supposed to have corrupted me and perhaps, indeed, he did leave behind a stimulating breeze of heterodoxy for which I should be grateful, though it would have needed a hurricane to do more than ruffle our settled Anglo-Irish loyalties.

I wish I had seen more of them, since they could have helped me to a less inhibited introverted patriotism, with facts and external contacts; had I had more confidence and been less dependent on my family, I could have been pleasanter to them. I could have acknowledged, I think, that my mother's powerful intuitions were often right, even when they were irrelevant. Of Dodds and Theo she said, "They're great Irish patriots now, but when the war is over they'll take jobs in England." And so indeed it happened. They are both of them now, like Elias Shee, "*orbi Britannico lumina,*" since Dodds is Regius Professor of Greek at Oxford and Theo a legal luminary at the Inner Temple. Yet I cannot regard either of them as backsliders. Though it seems to me to be man's duty to work in and for the community which he acknowledges to be his own, we also have a duty to develop our faculties to their fullest extent. Often these two duties cannot be reconciled and we have to choose between spiritual and intellectual frustration. So long as we do not accept our mutilated destiny with levity or resignation, we cannot be condemned as dodgers.

My mother's intuition about Cuffe's books was also sound. Among those from which she removed Cuffe's name was Edward Martyn's *The Heather Field*. This now almost unreadable play, which George Moore declared to be "the first play written in English inspired by the example of Ibsen," has not yet lost its magic for me, but forty years ago I found it overwhelming. Is it sentimental, morbid, is the dialogue forced and preposterous, are the characters overdrawn? I am still blind to all its defects; it seems to me the most poetic expression I know of the terrifying intellectual isolation of Ireland, its power to breed ideas, ideals and emotions in rich abundance, its incapacity to nourish them or defend them from the venomous dislike of the "niddys" (I got that word from Standish O'Grady) and the professionally virtuous. It shows how isolation, in time, breeds isolationism, driving poetry into suicidal extravagance and generating in sane and sober people every variety of arrogance and eccentricity. Carden Tyrell, who tried to reclaim a heather field with grants from the Board of Works, is a tragic figure, a symbol of the incompatibility of poetry and practical life. The drainage of the heather field swamps the land below it and that necessitates more loans from the Board of Works and "a vast ramification of drains" to carry the water away to the sea. Carden is hypnotized by the magnitude of the enterprise, the huge tract of luxuriant pasture which will take the place of swamp and heather. But it is the vast expenditure that appals his wife and her worldly friends, and she tries to get Carden certified as insane. Carden becomes more and more the slave of his dreams, till one day his little son comes in joyously with a posy of purple flowers. Then Carden does, in fact, enter the dream world of the insane, a world of happy hallucination, in which reality is a passing nightmare and the rainbow fantasies of his boyhood alone are permanent. Everyone is bewildered with the wild and witless poetry of his remarks, till his friend Barry Ussher solves the mystery with the curtain line: "The wild heath has broken out again in the heather field."

That line could almost act also as an epitaph on O'Grady's work in Kilkenny, on Cuffe's, on Lady Desart's, on the work of the scores of poetical social reformers who flourished in Ireland in the first quarter of the century. In every case the wild heath has broken out again in the heather field, and the memory of those who tried to eradicate it by "modern" methods has failed. Yet the urbane nihilism of the Shees belongs to a more prosperous age. "HOMO BULLA. *Vita quid est hominis gracilis nisi spuma, quid ipse? Nil nisi bulla.*"

I don't suppose anyone, for example, will write about old Albinia Broderick, the sister of Lord Midleton, the leader of the southern Unionists, who conceived it her mission to atone for the sins of her ancestors, exacting landlords of the southwest; she dressed as an old Irish countrywoman and ran a village shop, while behind her on a stony Dunkerron promontory rose the shell of a large hospital which she had built for the sick poor of Kerry, but which, because of its unsuitable though romantic site, had remained empty and unused.* There is a labyrinthine story of idealism, obstinacy, perversity, social conscience, medicine, family, behind this empty structure. The man who could unravel it would be diagnosing the spiritual sickness of Ireland, and diagnosis is the first step to a cure. It might be a more worthwhile task than the hospital, had it come into being, could ever have performed. But that task belongs to Kerry, not Kilkenny.

Here, I want to find out what happened to Otway Cuffe. This implies a rejection of that mystical interpretation of Irish dreaming which Shaw has expressed so memorably through the mouth of Larry Doyle:

Here [in England], if the life is dull, you can be dull too, and no great harm done. But your wits can't thicken in that soft moist air, on those white springy roads, in those misty rushes and brown bogs, on those hillsides of granite rocks and magenta heather. You've no such colours in the sky, no such lure in the distances, no such sadness in the evenings. Oh, the dreaming! the dreaming! the torturing, heart-scalding, never satisfying dreaming, dreaming, dreaming, dreaming! No debauchery that ever coarsened and brutalized an Englishman can take the worth and usefulness out of him like that dreaming.

Shaw, the great realist, had nothing but a fatalistic philosophy of abdication to offer the Irish: "Leave Ireland." It was the same philosophy which my parents, rejecting it for themselves, offered to their children, and, rejecting it for myself, I have not yet anything better to offer mine. Yet malaria has not always existed in marshes and can now be expelled from them, and frustration and melancholy are not ineradicable in any corner of the world.

Looking at my own family history, I was unable to trace a single one of my paternal ancestors who had lived out of Ireland since the thirteenth century, when they came here: why should our island in my generation suddenly become uninhabitable for us? I could not and I cannot accept that there is anything inevitable about this, or that misty rushes and magenta heather inevitably debauch the intelligence.

Seen against the backcloth of a lunatic world, Irish lunacy is an

---

*She has been briefly written about in M. Ward, *Unmanageable Revolutionaries: Women and Irish Nationalism* (London, 1983). Under her Gaelicized name of Gobnait ní Bruadair she remained a strong Republican presence on Kerry County Council and in Sinn Féin, whose newspaper, *Irish Freedom*, she owned. In 1933 she seceded from the women's organization Cumann na mBan and formed Mna na Poblachta, dedicated to preserving the pure Republican conscience.

ephemeral and contingent disorder. Sometimes cosmic lunacy dwarfs and counteracts the regional kind. Hitler's war stopped the importation of foreign timber and building materials to Ireland. They became costly rarities and Miss Broderick's chimerical hospital turned under demolition into a profitable business investment, I have been told. In a less crude way projects doomed to failure, like Carden Tyrell's, are not unprofitable if the apparent waste of energy and enthusiasm can be scrupulously recorded. Perhaps Cuffe would have been more of a Carden Tyrell than he was if O'Grady had not published two of Edward Martyn's other plays that were in the Nore Library in Kilkenny, and if *The Heather Field* had not been in that bookcase at Sheestown.

The Deserted Sun Palace

1978

The empty but still imposing shell of Desart Court stands at a cross-roads a few miles from Callan in Co. Kilkenny. This noble Georgian house was burnt in 1923, rebuilt and finally dismantled a few years ago. The Land Commission is prepared to make the shell safe and sound if any established society will take charge of it. The guardianship would be for many years to come a negligible responsibility, yet at present there is no association, either local or metropolitan, able to undertake it. A century ago the old Kilkenny Archaeological Society took abbeys and castles under its protection with the most matter-of-fact assurance, but nowadays we who live in the country, partly from modesty, partly from habit, look to Dublin for guidance and Dublin societies mostly have their hands full and can help us little. There is a danger that this fine fabric will disappear into road material.

Desart Court in its present form covers only a small plot of land and harms no one. Its avenues have been turned into roads which cross beside the house, and the huge brick-walled garden which faces it has reverted painlessly into an enclosed field and orchard. Its woods have been thinned but not devastated and are still lovely. The whole scene might be allowed to stay as it is for a few generations at least, like a rather dim but adequate illustration in a textbook of local history, recent as well as remote, for the Cuffes of Desart, who are now all gone, were active till the last.

They had been in Ireland before Cromwell, but one Joseph Cuffe distinguished himself in the service of the Protector and obtained lands that had previously belonged to the Norman family of Comerford, which had backed the royalist and Catholic side. The Cuffe history for a generation was true to pattern. They were successful opportunists, turning from republicans to monarchists, from Stuarts to Hanoverians, when the suitable moment arrived. The Comerfords, who had been more consistent, were never allowed to interfere with them. Their only rivals were the Flood family of Farmley, from whom Henry Flood the orator was descended. With them they had a feud, which led to duels and lawsuits and even murders about the political representation of the borough of Callan.

Yet very early on the Cuffes showed signs of a generous, independent outlook and within the narrow limits of class loyalty they did their best. When the refugees from a tyrannical government in Geneva decided to build a town on the Waterford coast which was to become a centre of liberty, industry and enlightenment, a Cuffe was one of the principal Irish promoters of the scheme. But on second thoughts the British government of the time suddenly decided that it would be unwise to introduce rebellious and republican Genevans into this disaffected region. After Cuffe had superintended the laying of the foundation stone, the plan was shelved and the Genevans stayed at home.*

There is much about the life of the Cuffes in the late eighteenth century in Dorothea Herbert's fascinating reminiscences. Her visits from Carrick to her uncle and aunt at Desart brought her into touch with the lively society which existed for some twenty years in Kilkenny during and before the Napoleonic Wars. The Desarts were highly temperamental. You can read how Lord Desart's daughter, Mrs. Cooke, mourning for her husband, painted all the flowerpots black, reupholstered the furniture in sable and tarred the stables, turning an elderly visitor's white horse piebald, for which he flogged the yard boy. I wonder if the ill-omened portrait of John, Lord Desart, was burnt in 1923? According to Miss Herbert it was painted with poisonous paint and the artist lost his sight, and Lord Desart and the three pets who were portrayed with him all succumbed to different diseases. His Lordship died of a violent fever, the two dogs also perished and his fine horse was never any good after this fatal picture was painted. Lord Desart's end was so sudden and so much deplored that his funeral procession lasted for three miles.

They went in for high-spirited and rather callous practical jokes in those days.

---

*See below, "New Geneva in Waterford."

One day at Desart, Mr. Hamilton Cuffe, who was teazingly nice dressed, took the Parson's Nose of a Duck for himself and she, my cousin Lucy, knowing his foible, laid her finger on it. A fit of romping took place, which ended in a serious Quarrel and violent Hystericks on her part. This was no sooner over than my Uncles affronted me by recommending Mrs. Jephson as a Stepmother, if anything happened to my Mother. This threw Mama and her daughter into Hystericks and all the Servants in the House were dispatched for remedies before our Sobs could be abated. Many freaks passed at Desart that time which I now forget.

There is or was in Desart woods a famous oak claiming, like many others, to be the oldest in Ireland and it may well have been part of the ancient Irish forests. The woods have never been better described than by Humphrey O'Sullivan, the Callan schoolmaster, who wrote a diary in Irish twenty years after Dorothea's time when Desart woods were being replanted.

I went to Desart by the same roads which I took on Easter Friday. We walked through dark evergreen pinewoods, through fine lane-ways, now crooked, now straight, shaded from the face of the sun, listening to the fluting of the lark in the way-side meadows. We went through Derrymore, through the Lord's Plantations, skipping like goats through Derreen to the fish-ponds of Desart. The landscape from this beautiful sun-palace is exquisite: a gaseous exhalation came from the sun, the mountains to the south were dark blue. Ballykeefe Hill near us to the north was newly planted and so was Knocknarah and all around us sheltering oak and ash and meadows smooth as silk and green as corn grass. . . . The sky was cloudless save for one cloudlet adding to its beauty as a dimple to a damsel's chin. . . . Slieve na man cloudless, Mount Leinster and the other mountains to the east reclining on a couch of fog, raising their heads and nodding to the sun like a gentle young bride to her husband. It is in the heart of this valley that the head-mound and capital city of Ireland ought to be.

There seems to have been an unbridgeable gulf between the accomplished and benevolent Cuffes and the people of whom Humphrey O'Sullivan was the informative and sensitive interpreter. He is a remarkable figure with his homemade education and his passionate loyalty to the last remnants of the Irish traditions and language which he knew to be dying. Much of O'Sullivan's huge diary is uninteresting and repetitive, yet it is easy to believe that he had in him some seed of truth, some zest for life, which in a less unhappy and divided society would have flowered into poetry and prose of a high order.
Yet a deep pessimism undermined and discoloured all his

thoughts. Everything he wrote was perishable, for the language in which he wrote it was rapidly being outlawed. Little by little he had to renounce that dim hope which sustains the solitary writer, of being understood at least by posterity. It is not unnatural that he should often break into bitter railing, finding his sole consolation in the thought that rich and poor, oppressor and oppressed, are all equally doomed.

He may have been thinking of Desart Court, "that beautiful sun-palace," when he wrote:

What is the good of repining? The bright walled castles will disappear and the glittering sun-palaces, the earth form elemental, the entire universe like a wisp-blaze. Will it be long till this Irish language in which I am writing goes too? Fine big school houses are daily being built to teach in them this new language, the Saxon tongue. But, alas, no attention is being paid to the fine smooth Irish tongue, except by wretched Swaddlers, who are trying to see whether they can wheedle away the children of the Gael to their accursed new religion.*

The Swaddlers to whom he refers were a group of earnest Evangelicals who appeared in Kilkenny at this time and made war simultaneously on what they considered the frivolity of the Protestants and the idolatry of the Catholics. They learnt the Irish language and to propagate their views they tried to interrupt the Kilkenny theatre season and were denounced by the Protestant bishop.

O'Sullivan would certainly have been surprised if he had known that when the fate which he foresaw had overtaken the Irish language in Kilkenny, it would be one of the Cuffes of Desart who would try to revive it. The story of Otway Cuffe and his sister-in-law ought to be told because of its interest as well as its sadness. Though it happened for the most part only a generation ago, it already seems to be of another age. Yet it belongs, like the shell of Desart Court, to the shifting pattern of Irish history, and should not be forgotten.

Lately, an exhibition, organized by the National Museum, paused for a short spell in Kilkenny Castle. It was called "the Landed

---

*Some have compared this to Prospero's monologue in *The Tempest*:
> Our revels now are ended . . .
> The cloud-capped towers, the gorgeous palaces,
> The solemn temples, the great globe itself,
> Yea, all which it inherit, shall dissolve
> And, like this insubstantial pageant faded,
> Leave not a rack behind. We are such stuff
> As dreams are made on, and our little life
> Is rounded with a sleep.

Gentry" and in Dublin it was advertised by a poster of a smart lady in a top hat and hunting kit* jumping over a bill of eviction. The show was full of fascinating items, orders for footmen's livery and for the stocking of wine cellars, and imperious instructions to farm labourers and tenants on the great estates. In order to be fair, reports of Clothing Funds were included and a note that Daniel O'Connell was also a landowner with an estate of 30,000 acres. Yet the general impression was created that the Anglo-Irish had been, contrary to what Yeats had said, a Petty People, whose main concern had been horses and rents.

There were a few mistakes (e.g., Sheestown, a small estate near Kilkenny, where Otway Cuffe had lived, was wrongly located in Co. Waterford), but it represented well enough the skeletal structure of a civilization outwardly as dead in Ireland as that of the Hapsburgs in Bohemia. If there had been more than a spark of life left today, surely some voice of protest would have spoken of the Grattans, Floods, Edgeworths, Parnells, Plunketts and a thousand others, who had built that Anglo-Irish civilization, which is still, battered and hiding behind a Eurocratic façade with neo-Gaelic trimmings, unchangingly ours. It is only the heirs of those who created it who are doomed. J. C. Beckett, in his fine book *The Anglo-Irish Tradition*, declared that in the Anglo-Irish community even the will to survive appeared to be fading and predicted that, before the end of the century, Protestantism, their prevailing religion, would be virtually extinct in the Republic.

In the exhibition there was a photograph of the fourth Earl of Desart and his Countess, who lived at Desart Court near Kilkenny. It was taken from a London illustrated paper and the caption under Lady Desart's picture explained that she had "a good seat on a horse" and tackled "Pat's fences" with the same grace with which she rode in Rotten Row. There followed a humorous story of how she tricked "Land-Leaguer Pat," who had thrown stones at the foxhounds, into playing "God Save the Queen" on his harmonica.

I knew Lady Desart when I was young and she was old and she was not in the least like that. She was a plump and plain little Jewess with high intelligence and spirit, a guttural voice and very strong

---

*In fact, a photograph of Lady Clonbrock, best known as organizer of the Clonbrock and Castlegar Poultry Cooperative, which with associated home industries and crafts, outlasted all similar rural cooperatives and only died in 1952. See Patrick Bolger, *The Irish Cooperative Movement*, for a different photograph of her.

pince-nez. She would have looked ridiculous on a horse, though she may have pretended to like them because her husband, whom she loved, was master of foxhounds and had even written a novel called *The Honourable Ella of Foxshire.* He died in 1898 and was succeeded by his brother, a distinguished London barrister, and there was then no longer any need for his widow to model herself on the Honourable Ella. As she was very rich, she felt free to follow her own ideas or rather those of her youngest brother-in-law, Otway Cuffe, who was a disciple of a well-known writer, Standish O'Grady. Cuffe had led a wandering life outside Ireland, but when he realized that he was likely to succeed his brother as sixth Earl of Desart, he had, under O'Grady's influence, begun to take very seriously his responsibility to his country.

Of O'Grady, whom the Cuffes had brought to Kilkenny, W. B. Yeats was later to write: "Whatever should come out of Ireland in the future will owe itself to two books, O'Grady's *Bardic History of Ireland* and Ferguson's *Poems.*" The *Bardic History*, in George Dangerfield's words,

released Cuchullain and the other heroes of the Ulster Cycle from the grip of a scholarship, which had preserved the Irish myth, like a splendid fly in a kind of philological amber.

"In O'Grady's writings," said AE, "the submerged river of national culture rose up again, a shining torrent. It was he who made me conscious and proud of my country . . . He was the last champion of the Irish aristocracy and spoke to them of their duty to the nation as a fearless prophet might speak to a council of degenerate princes."

When in 1898 Cuffe urged O'Grady to take over *The Kilkenny Moderator*, the Unionist and Protestant weekly, from Mr. Lawlor, the editor, who had to look after a sick brother in Bournemouth, nobody but he could guess the storms this dynamic character might precipitate in a stagnant community. All that Mr. Lawlor knew of O'Grady was reassuring. He wrote in his valedictory editorial, "Mr. O'Grady is among the first rank of the Irish gentry; he is first cousin to Lord Gort, second cousin to the present Viscount Guillamore and near relation to the Persses of Roxborough, the Wallers of Castletown Waller. . . ." Then followed more names of distinguished families all of which have long disappeared and a list of medals and other distinctions he had won at Trinity. "Furthermore, Professor Lecky of Trinity and Lord Castletown of Upper Ossory have subscribed to bring over an eminent artist from England to paint his picture." What could be more reassuring than this? In fact, the portrait was by an Irishman, John Butler Yeats, W. B.'s father, and O'Grady, though a fervent champion of the "Landed Gentry," was also one of their most savage critics.

In one of his books which few in Ireland could have read, he had addressed the leaders of Anglo-Ireland in the manner of Carlyle.

Your ancestors who raised the noble classical buildings of Dublin loved a classical quotation, but could one in twenty of you translate the most hackneyed Latin tag in a newspaper? Christ save us all! You read nothing, you know nothing. You are totally resourceless and stupid . . . England has kept you like Strasburg geese which are kept until they can hardly stand without support and so slow and sleepy that they are scarcely aware when they are killed. As I write, the Protestant Anglo-Irish, who once owned all Ireland from the centre to the sea, is rotting from the land in the most dismal farce-tragedy of all time, without one brave deed, without one brave word.

He predicted that unless they could "reshape themselves in a heroic mould there would be anarchy and civil war, which might end in a shabby, sordid Irish Republic, ruled by corrupt politicians and the ignoble rich," and he told them that they gibed at Ireland and everything Irish:

What native, I ask you, with the spirit of a rabbit would bear forever such an aristocracy as ours? . . . Yet bad as you are you are still the best class we have. You are individually brave and honourable men and do not deserve the doom which even the blindest can see approaching.

You are hated to an extent you can only dimly conceive. The nation is united against you. In your hands the Irish nation once lay like soft wax ready to take any impression you chose and out of it you have moulded a Frankenstein which will destroy you.*

As editor of *The Kilkenny Moderator*, with Otway Cuffe and Lady Desart behind him, he maintained for two years a highly original provincial newspaper. Mr. Lawlor, like most provincial editors, had flattered his readers. O'Grady challenged them.

He looked to the Ormondes for a lead, for in one of his books he had recalled the centuries of struggle during which they had built up their princedom.

*From *Toryism and the Tory Democracy* (1886), first published as a broadside and then reprinted in *Selected Essays and Passages* (n.d.).

Love, labour, sorrow and fighting, consultations many with the wise, close intense study of the characters of men, recruitments and dismissals innumerable before a Butler could write the proud title "Capitanus Suae Nationis," have a nation of which to be captain and a territory on which to sustain his nation.

And he asserted that only by dedication like this could the Anglo-Irish recover the authority which was their due. Only under their guidance could Ireland be true to her history, part Gaelic, part Norse, part Norman, part Scottish, part English, but distinctively Irish and united. He was supported by all those writers, most of them Anglo-Irish, who had created the Abbey Theatre and the Literary Revival and by the Gaelic League, at that time a nonpolitical and nonsectarian body, whose president and founder, Douglas Hyde, was, like Standish O'Grady, a rector's son. Many of them wrote for the *Moderator*.

When O'Grady came to Kilkenny the landed gentry were still outwardly at least immensely influential. The Ormonde supremacy was securely based on history. In the muniment room of Kilkenny Castle one of the greatest collections of historical documents in the British Isles still survived. In drawers and pigeonholes were charters heavy with the wax seals of the Plantagenets, the title deeds of monasteries that had long been dissolved and of kindred families that had been dispossessed by Cromwell or William of Orange. There were still Van Dycks, Lelys and Knellers in the Gallery.

The Ormondes had never seemed more splendid. The third Marquess and his wife had just been visited by the Duke and Duchess of York (later George V and Mary) and were shortly to receive Edward VII and Alexandra; they had been to Potsdam and the Kaiser had given Lord Ormonde the Order of the Crown of Prussia, First Class. Socially the Desarts ran them close, for the fifth Countess was later to be sister-in-law to the Princess Royal. They were all good landlords and because of the Irish love of sport they seemed to be very popular, and even though the genius of the first Duke (1610–88) and his capable son may have trickled away in Hanoverian times down obscure branches, the Ormondes still brought a breath of majesty and feudalism to puppy shows and agricultural gatherings. They had it in their power to drape ordinariness, even their own, with some of the glamour of the Middle Ages. It is unlikely that any of these people had ever heard of O'Grady.

His first year in Kilkenny was the centenary of the 1798 rebellion, and there were processions to commemorate a Wexford man called Hammond who had been executed in the town for manufacturing pikes. In demolishing an old house a pike was found in the wainscoting. It was regarded as an omen and it was urged that it be put in the Tholsel (townhall) in place of Gladstone's bust. But O'Grady maintained, in the *Moderator*, that the date to celebrate was not 1798 but 1782, for it was then that the Volunteers had assembled at Dungannon in Ulster and had extorted from England those concessions which had made Grattan's Parliament possible. The Commander-in-Chief of the Volunteers had been an Ulsterman, "the Good Lord Charlemont," and Irishmen of all creeds and classes had, for the first time, been united for a single purpose.

Now, O'Grady maintained, an analogous situation had developed. In 1782 the Volunteers had seized their opportunity, because England was at war with France and welcomed their offer to defend the Irish shores. In 1898 England was at war with the Boers. O'Grady, in the *Moderator*, refused to speak on the moral aspect of this war; all he saw in it was an opportunity for raising a new national army. If such a force were mustered now, the two opposing factions in Ireland could unite for the defence of Ireland, and Dublin would quickly take the lead from Kilkenny as once it had taken it from Dungannon. Thirty thousand British troops, which were garrisoning Ireland, could be relieved for service in the Cape.*

O'Grady, looking round Kilkenny for some military potential uncommitted to Boer or Briton, had to overlook the Kilkenny Militia and the local branch of the Irish Brigade, who were drilling to fight each other in the Transvaal; he could see nothing but those two embryonic armies the Catholic Boys Brigade and the Protestant Church Lads Brigade, and that phantom of a cavalry force the Kilkenny Foxhounds. He managed to collect recruits from the two boys' brigades and got Otway Cuffe, a former army officer and equerry to the king, to drill them. He said prophetically, "If we do not act now, a very dangerous class of men will take over the drill financed from the other side of the Atlantic. Our natural leaders, the Irish Gentry, must step forward and lead."

O'Grady saw another way in which the Irish people could rally round those whom they had formerly revered. The Childers Re-

*On the eve of the First World War, Sir Horace Plunkett made a similar proposal for the conversion of the two private armies of the North and South into units of a Territorial Army.

port had revealed that since 1880 Ireland had been overtaxed by £250,000,000 and it was calculated that of this sum Kilkenny County had been annually overtaxed by £135,000. A Financial Relations Committee had been formed with a Kilkenny branch under the leadership of Lord Ormonde. They had met in the courthouse and O'Grady had declared that if the Anglo-Irish headed the crusade for financial justice, they could once more become the legitimate representatives of the people. Men of education and breeding could still, as in the past, influence the destinies of their country. There must be no delay.

But the committee members had other things to attend to and in the autumn O'Grady wrote: "Of the sixty Kilkenny gentlemen, who trotted down High Street en route for Knockroe last Monday, every man is a member of the Financial Relations Committee, yet it has never met since its appointment eleven months ago. What artillery can ever penetrate our subterhuman torpor?"* Yet O'Grady and Cuffe were not discouraged. To advertise and pay for their new volunteers they started a gymnasium and club, and there were frequent concerts at which Irish songs and dances alternated with gymnastic displays.

O'Grady believed in reviving in each county all the old cultural societies and industrial enterprises which had been killed by the centralizing policy that had followed the Union. He was proud that *The Kilkenny Moderator*, Protestant, Conservative, Anglo-Irish, was the first significant Irish paper to print a weekly Irish lesson. Soon they started in Kilkenny a branch of the Gaelic League with Cuffe as President.† Douglas Hyde, invited down to address the Gaelic League, told his audience that no Act of Parliament could bring them a national identity. They themselves must create a cultural uniqueness

*Yeats explained in his autobiography their strange apathy: "Landlord committees were formed in every county and Lord Castletown made a famous speech declaring that Ireland must imitate the Colonists who flung the tea into Boston Harbour. Protestant Ireland had immense prestige, almost every name sung in modern song had been Protestant. Yet they lacked hereditary passion and whatever corporate action was attempted, the show however gallant it seemed, was soon over."
†They were following in an old local tradition, for Henry Flood of Farmley, near Desart Court, the great orator of Grattan's Parliament, had in his will left most of his fortune for the foundation at Trinity College of a chair in Irish history and language and the purchase of all Irish manuscripts. The Kilkenny Archaeological Society, whose aims were even broader, was founded in 1848 and rapidly became the most famous provincial archaeological society in the British Isles. The founders were the Rector of Ennisnag, a Kilkenny parish priest and a predecessor of O'Grady's as editor of the local Unionist paper. It was a disaster for Ireland that Flood's relations successfully contested his will.

strong enough to resist the pull of sectarian and political fanaticism and to rescue them from the "ocean of vulgarity" in which the English press was submerging them.

Lady Desart here interposed that her own people, the Jews, had revived a forgotten language and were using it to bind together the disparate branches of her race.

Cuffe referred to the ancient Irish system, which was patriarchal, regional, communal. Though primitive, it contained in itself the germ of a society happier than ours. To help our neighbour should not be a duty but a love: "As for myself, if I devoted all my thoughts and hopes to my near surroundings the field would still be far larger than I could cover. Yet I could do more for my country if I kept to this field than spread myself over the universe."

It was a time of excitement and hope, which was suddenly arrested by what was called the County Scandal, a war between the Ormondes and the Desarts. This became of more interest to the Kilkenny citizens than the Boer War itself and, maybe, it had more significance for them.

Here is the story: The Colonel of the Kilkenny Militia, the popular and sporting Charlie Gore (this is not his real name), had been the fourth Earl of Desart's agent and it had been discovered on Lord Desart's death that he had appropriated £6,000 belonging to the family. Charlie Gore's family, a much respected one, had paid what was owing and Charlie, though dismissed, was not taken to court. Then, as time passed, he saw an opportunity of clearing his name. The missing money, he said, had really been owed to him by Lord Desart, an unpaid racing debt. To save Lord Desart's reputation he had adjusted the matter himself.

Lady Desart and her two brothers-in-law reacted strongly. Not being litigious people, they persuaded their friend O'Grady to print a letter telling the true facts in the *Moderator*. In this letter Ellen, Lady Desart, called the Colonel a "thief" and challenged him to sue her for libel. The Colonel, after a long delay, contemptuously replied that the matter had been settled up long ago by reference to the Lord Chancellor, the Commander of the Forces and the Marquess of Ormonde. The fifth Lord Desart then replied that the Lord Chancellor had assured him that he had made no enquiry at all and, if the Marquess and the Commander of the Forces had given a decision, they had done so without reference to a single member of the family against whom the offence had been committed. The Cuffes demanded that the Colonel be relieved of his responsibilities as a magistrate and the command of the Kilkenny Militia.

O'Grady accompanied the letter with an angry editorial and Lord Ormonde, already enraged that this upstart journalist had dared to reprove him and his friends for their neglect of the Financial Relations Committee, decided to reinstate the Colonel as publicly as he could.

When the Bishop, Dr. Crozier, asked Lord Ormonde as Lieutenant of the County to review the Church Lads Brigade in the large grounds behind the palace, he had brought the Colonel with him as aide-de-camp and at a suitable moment asked the Colonel to step forward and address the boys. The Colonel spoke and the Bishop replied, "in terms," wrote O'Grady, "of eulogy and approbation." (The Bishop was later to say that he was not addressing the Man but the Office and that he had not invited the Colonel to the Palace.)

O'Grady was beside himself. All the pillars of society which he had hoped to strengthen, the Church, the aristocracy, the army and, worst of all, the Butlers, appeared to be collapsing. He rushed to his desk and wrote a scorching editorial. He concluded:

Now for this blazing scandal I do not blame the poor Colonel, whose weak good nature may have led him into these courses. I blame the bad and dishonourable men, who, out of sheer perversity and worse motives, backed him up in the maintenance of his commission and have undertaken to see him safely through this affair. Those men who have betrayed the honour of the county are the Marquess of Ormonde, the Protestant Bishop of Ossory and the Master of the Kilkenny Hounds.

How the third of them, Sir Hercules Langrishe, comes into the story I do not know. But in the next editorial O'Grady focused all his fury on Lord Ormonde, who had disappointed him most. He began:

We are not at war with the Bishop, but with the great and dominant social power in our midst, reaching up to the Throne and down to the smallest Kilkenny huxter, a power which has almost obliterated a sense of honour and public morality in the minds of the few and dulled and paralysed the conscience of the community who had weakly followed the line of least resistance and afforded support to a stained reputation.

After that he printed a detailed summary of what had happened and sent copies of the *Moderator* to the colonels of all the regiments on Salisbury Plain and one to the Duke of Connaught. The Kilkenny

Militia was at that time on manoeuvres in North Kilkenny and it is said that he urged them to mutiny.

In a very short time a writ for libel came from the Bishop. He asked for £2,000 and engaged "six eminent counsels." Further writs were reported to be on the way from the Marquess of Ormonde and Sir Hercules Langrishe, who were yachting at Cowes, and from others, whom O'Grady had accused of shielding the Colonel. At a special meeting of the Kilkenny Club, of which Lord Ormonde was President, O'Grady was asked to resign.

It would take too much space to carry on this story to the end of the Boer War, to O'Grady's departure from Kilkenny, saddened but not discouraged. Yet there were many fascinating incidents. I should like to tell how the Kilkenny Militia, in their red tunics, spiked helmets and snowy bandoliers, set off a thousand strong, to embark at Waterford for training on Salisbury Plain. At their head was Colonel Charlie, on their heels a straggling Kilkenny mob, screaming, "Hurrah for Kruger and Lady Desart!" and throwing stones and bits of coal. "Nature abhors a vacuum," O'Grady wrote. "If the leaders of society betray their trust, new centres of influence will arise."

O'Grady left and Mr. M. W. Lawlor returned from Bournemouth and took over the *Moderator* again. For many months he wooed back its affronted subscribers among the gentry with philippics against O'Grady and his "wanton, wicked and libellous attacks against one of the most exalted, popular and esteemed Peers of the Realm, whose popularity in the hunting fields of Kilkenny and in yachting circles in England and America is so well known. He brought about a state of things," he declared, "which should bring a blush of shame to the face of even a strolling play-actor, if such a person were capable of blushing." He spoke of his "slanderous wagging tongue" and his "Silly-Billy publication, the vehicle of idiotic drivel." He revealed that O'Grady was only "collaterally" related to the Gorts and Guillamores and that a lot of kitchen utensils had been sold at his auction, which had never been paid for. "A man of failure," he summed it all up, "at everything he touched." Finally he sent him a bill for printer's ink and another writ.

It was the Cuffes' letter to the *Moderator* that destroyed O'Grady's paper and so I have no doubt that it was Ellen, Lady Desart, who rescued him from financial disaster. She and Otway Cuffe continued vigorously the work which he had inspired and started. The list of their enterprises is scarcely believable. They built a theatre, a hospital, a model village with a woodworkers' factory at

Talbot's Inch, a public library, a recreation hall, a woollen mill, a tobacco farm and many other small cooperative ventures. There was a little bridge across the Nore to link Talbot's Inch with the woollen mill. Cuffe became Mayor of Kilkenny and you will see his name carved on John's Bridge, which was rebuilt in his mayoralty, underneath that of his forebear the Earl of Desart, who was mayor when the previous bridge was erected. They were trying to domesticate and regionalize the dragon of international industrialism, at a time when almost everyone was directly or indirectly in the pay of the dragon.

The story of the slow decay of all these enterprises, one by one, through strikes, fraud, arson and under the unchanging pressure of politics, religion and social jealousy, would have value as a small-scale model of a universal phenomenon. Trouble started almost immediately.

In the Kilkenny woodworkers' factory they needed a cabinet-maker, and Cuffe after long advertisement had to accept a non-trade-union worker from Glasgow. Thereupon 18 men out of 100 went on strike. The Glasgow man was a Jew and this incensed the strikers still more. They struck him and chanted in chorus, "Clear out, Ikie!"

None of the strikers, the Kilkenny papers defiantly declared, were Kilkennymen and they underlined the mean ingratitude to Cuffe and Ellen Desart, the Jewess, who had poured money into the Kilkenny industries, regardless of profit. The English trade union officials backed up the strikers. There came a sharp letter from Alexander Gossip, general secretary of the National Amalgamated Furnishing Trades Association of Finsbury Pavement. He said he was "not prepared to tolerate unnecessary grievances of kind indicated." He trusted that Cuffe "would at once see that end was put to same." Representatives were sent to Kilkenny but Cuffe refused to see them, and answered all their letters with haughtiness. The interference from England, the flare-up of anti-Semitism and the threat to that community, which Cuffe was trying to build up not upon impersonal officialism and scheduled rights but on personal relations, all this cut him to the quick. He refused all mediation and started to replace the strikers with men from outside. He knew they might be stopped by picketers at Kilkenny station, so he had them met at the station before it, Gowran. One morning a little man called Flanagan got out of the train at Gowran with his trunk and found the draughtsman there with a jennet trap. They set off together, when suddenly a side-car loaded with strikers lurched down on them. "That's your game, is it?" they screamed. "Get out, you white-livered little scamp!" "I'm only doing my duty," said little Flanagan, but he was dragged out of the trap and the box flung on the road. Finally box and Flanagan were hoisted onto the sidecar and cantered off to Kilkenny. A procession of tradesmen and a piper met them in John Street and with the piper playing a victory march and the tradesmen cheering, they drove their bewildered captive and his trunk through the town. That was the first of a series of disasters.

When after years of disappointment, Cuffe died in Australia, all the shops in Kilkenny were closed and the flag on the Tholsel was flown at half-mast. He had seen the doom that was approaching and had tried to reverse it, but it was too late. Meanwhile O'Grady in Dublin continued a journal, *The All-Ireland Review*, which he had started in Kilkenny and in which, as always, he tried to reconcile the old ascendancy with those who were groping towards the recovery of a national identity. He never retreated from his Anglo-Irish and Protestant background. In one of his novels his hero was an Irish Protestant who fought for William of Orange. From its legendary past to its confused present, Irish history was to be seen as a unity based on diversity.

Few of his disciples understood this. He had brought a new theme to Anglo-Irish literature, and new ideas, like sparks in a time of drought, can purge or destroy. Patrick Pearse and Thomas MacDonagh, who were executed in 1916, produced at their school, St. Enda's, one of O'Grady's Ulster plays. Cuffe organized another at Sheestown; it was acted by the Cave Hill Players from Belfast. Both were well attended.

Could anyone have guessed at the explosive force of poetry and ideas? Why does it so rarely happen that those who lay the fire are allowed to light it? Yeats had said, "O'Grady's *History of Ireland* had been the start of it all," and George Dangerfield observed that the book was "somewhere at the heart of the Easter Rising in 1916. Cuchullain was one of the shadowy heroes who fought side by side with the living in the General Post Office." Yeats in his old age never ceased to wonder at the effect of his own poetry.

> Did that play of mine send out
> Certain men the English shot?*

O'Grady's health broke down soon after the Rebellion and he left Ireland to join his son in an English rectory. Then came the Black

*From "The Man and the Echo," in *Last Poems, 1936–1939.*

and Tans and the Treaty, and early in 1922 the British Army left Kilkenny in trains with "Back to Blighty" chalked on them, as the crowds cheered and the church bells rang. The soldiers added to the noise by ringing from the carriage windows the large bells which they had used on the Crossley tenders.

Many of the Anglo-Irish who accepted the new Government, as did Ellen, Lady Desart, took office in the new Senate, and when the civil war broke out they became the target for the Republicans, who rejected the compromise of a Free State from which most of Ulster was excluded. The houses of three Senators were burnt and one night in February masked men broke into Desart Court, hacked the furniture and the doors with axes and, making a huge pile, sprinkled it with petrol. Some furniture survived in an untouched wing. It was sent by van to Kilkenny, but it too was stopped on the way and burnt. Presumably this was to punish Senator Lady Desart, who was not in fact the owner. Between January 1922 and March of the following year 139 country houses were destroyed, many of them treasure houses of great beauty, with fine libraries, whose owners had shaped Irish history. When on 28 June, the Four Courts, where the archives of centuries had been stored, was bombed, it was like the end of a civilization. In May 1922 Kilkenny Castle was taken by the Republicans and relieved after a few days by the Free Staters.* Thirteen years later all the contents were sold and for thirty years the dry-rot invaded room after empty room.

But no purely cultural impoverishment could matter so much as the withdrawal of a whole historic class. Though O'Grady had called them degenerate, outworn and effete, and had prophesied with accuracy what would happen to them, they were stupid and defenceless simply because since the Union they had exported all their brightest and their bravest to England. They had generalled her armies, governed her provinces, dominated her newspapers and her theatres, written her plays. Many of those who remained behind had been educated in England and knew nothing of Ireland's problems.† Waterloo may or may not have been won on the playing fields of Eton, but Ireland was certainly lost there.

---

*The fifth Marquess of Ormonde has told the story in the *Journal of the Butler Society*, Vol. 1, No.4.
†Characteristically those who defended Anglo-Irish values most vigorously after the Treaty were those who had previously criticized them most severely. When a bill was brought in to repeal the right of divorce, which England had introduced, Yeats in the Senate gave his famous No Petty People speech and Lady Desart supported him.

AE wrote of O'Grady:

When a man is in advance of his age, a generation, unborn when he speaks, is born in due time and finds in him its inspiration. O'Grady may have failed in his appeal to the aristocracy of his own time but he may yet create an aristocracy of intellect and character in Ireland.

A Visit to Hesse and
Some Thoughts About Princes

1968

The Butler Society started in 1967 when the sixth Marquess of Ormonde entrusted Kilkenny Castle to a local committee for its preservation. Ours was an attempt to isolate out of world history one small corner, a family, its kinsmen, its neighbours. It soon became clear that the Butlers were no better than any other family, but their records had been well kept, and it was possible to find kinsmen in France and Germany, in America and Australasia.

Our test-tube approach to the study of the human family has not, perhaps, come up with any startling discoveries. The mere problem of survival of a voluntary community in a world which has become increasingly regimented and officialized, has absorbed much of our energies. Yet our Society is still young and we know that our approach is the right one. All round us men are rebelling against the civilization of the anthill and wish to be individuals, not units, humans not machines, and are juggling in different ways with the old human constants which are under threat, neighbourhoods, kinships, beliefs, skills, traditions.

This is an old story in Ireland. When I was young I was a disciple of Sir Horace Plunkett, who with George Russell (AE) covered Ireland with creameries which were to be the nuclei of a new society, cooperative and regional. AE recalled how all the arts and sciences had started in small Greek city-states the size of an Irish county. But he was an Ulsterman and his visions were anchored pragmatically to agricultural credit banks and the marketing of butter and eggs. Then Patrick Pearse, a visionary without the ballast of dairy products, translated AE's dream into Gaelic and taught his pupils at St. Enda's about an Irish society that was patriarchal, aristocratic and heroic. His nationalism tottered on the brink of racism.

Douglas Hyde, our first president, tried to mediate between the two groups. He had started the Gaelic League* as a sort of purge by which the Irish could be freed from their worship of the secondhand and from that "ocean of vulgarity in which the British Press is submerging us." He was nonpolitical and said that no Act of Parliament could recover our nationality for us. "Ours is the least reading and most unlettered of peoples, our art is distinguished above all others by its hideousness. Unless we can act as Irishmen we shall become the Japanese of Europe, capable only of imitation."

There is nothing sadder than the failure of a dream, but few have capsized so totally as the Sinn Féin dream of the 1916 Rebellion. Sinn Féin means "Ourselves" and implied that, if necessary by blood sacrifice, our Irish cultural identity must be preserved. Now, as I write, seventy-eight Japanese businessmen are in Dublin to teach us how to imitate their imitations and as an earnest of their concern for us have bought a million pounds' worth of pork.

Sadly I move from Ireland to Germany, where the Butler Society spent one of its happiest and most successful rallies in August 1968. To me it was deeply interesting, for here was a family society that had gone on for eighty years and still showed no signs of failing, where old families, despite wars and revolution, still live in family homes. I observed how all these German houses seemed to reach out towards posterity with an assurance which we have mostly lost. It is this that gives to the least pretentious of them a dignity combined with domesticity that is becoming everywhere rarer. I believe that the continuity of a country's culture rests with families, not with governments and county councils, and that it is Ireland's loss that of all the many hundreds of Butler castles (to mention one historic family alone), all but one are ruins, waiting patiently for the bulldozer.

Could one reason for Anglo-Irish apathy be that great empires act centripetally on their subjects and that the German empire was not old enough to overcome those family and regional loyalties which keep a national identity alive?

I was in the archives room of several castles and mansions of the von Buttlars of Hesse, who claim kinship with the Irish and English Butlers. At Markershausen they have a unique portrait of the fifth Earl of Ormonde, who was beheaded in the Wars of the Roses,

*In 1893.—ed.

and Horst von Buttlar-Brandenfels had made a small museum to illustrate family history, German, English and Irish. In Schloss Elber-
berg there are trunks full of letters, diaries, records of the part played
by the von Buttlars in the Thirty Years' War.

The von Buttlars, a large and once-powerful family, who since
the thirteenth century have lived in the wooded hills that border Thu-
ringia and East Germany, have had their regular *Familientag* for several generations and they still keep in touch with members of their
family now divided from them by political barriers. One day they
took us to Oberkaufungen, where we saw the council chamber,
church and administrative offices of the Althessische Ritterschaft.
When the Landgrave of Hesse still reigned in Cassel, there must have
been here a busy centre of authority; thirty of the noble families of
Hesse still survive and I believe that, like the von Buttlars, they still
have their own *Familientag* and a sense of family solidarity that has
long since died out in Ireland and England.

In the church, Vetter Adolf von Buttlar-Stiedenrode laid a wreath
on the war memorial in memory of all the Butlers who died on either
side in two world wars. The Ritterschaft, though politically powerless, still owns corporately the medieval settlement with its assembly
rooms, stables, coach houses and vast surrounding forests of Oberkaufungen. There is a well-preserved skeleton here of an organization
that was once active and powerful. What was it like in its prime?

Now that everywhere power has passed to oil companies and
steel corporations, and the Volkswagen factory at Cassel could no
doubt buy out the Landgrave of Hesse and all his nobility, one can
consider objectively the German principalities and their courts. Is
there anything at all to be said for small-scale paternalism (a neutral
word, for fathers can be bad as well as good)?

Liberal historians would agree with H. A. L. Fisher, who called the
German princes "the idlest and most selfish aristocracy in Europe."
They were powerful, too. When the Landgrave Philip of Hesse espoused Protestantism, all his subjects had to follow suit and, when
he divorced his wife, Luther himself was obliged to find in the Bible
a justification for polygamy.

A later Landgrave sold Hessian soldiers to the British Government to fight against the American rebels in 1780 and the Irish rebels
in 1798. About half of them were killed and he spent the sale price
of three million pounds on science, literature, the arts and the adorn-
ment of his capital. I am told that the large Hercules building in
Wilhelms Hohe with its maze of fountains and terraces and its *Was-*

servexierungsportplatz (you invite your friends into a grotto and put ten pfennigs into a slot machine and they are "water-vexed" from many little jets in the rock) was paid for by selling tall Hessians to Frederick the Great, who collected them for a special regiment.

How very wicked! But the arts thrived in Cassel. The Landgraves bought nineteen Rembrandts for the gallery and took pride in those clever citizens who invented the first logarithmic tables, the first theodolite, the first German commercial bank, the first herbarium, steam engine and chime of bells. The brothers Grimm initiated there the science of philology, and their famous fairy tales laid the foundations of folklore. And now when a prosperous city of two hundred thousand inhabitants has been erected on the ruins left by Hitler's war, it is to the surviving achievements of the Landgraves and their nobility that the sightseer and foreign tourist are almost exclusively directed.

Could one say that, as nurseries of talent and the arts, these tiny states surpassed the great ones that gobbled them up? About this, German genius is divided. Schiller constantly satirized their pompous little courts, but he judged them by his own experiences, which by our standards were not very terrible at all. The Duke of Württemberg arrested him because he gave up his medical studies to write plays and left Stuttgart without permission. But he escaped to another duke, got a pension from a third, and ended his life with Goethe and Herder at the court of Weimar.

In Weimar, Karl August the duke had put Goethe in charge of the mines, the roads, the treasury, the university of the little state; he directed its theatre. His life overflowed with rich and varied small-scale experiences, and it was in these years that he wrote his greatest works, made his remarkable discoveries in botany and anatomy, and became a European figure.

There is reason in this. An independent mind is always feared and detested, but the stupider princes were too capricious and jealous of each other to gang up effectively against it. If some gifted rebel like Luther or Schiller fell out with his prince, there were a dozen other rival states in which he could find asylum; he did not, like Einstein or Thomas Mann, have to leave Germany altogether. If censorship is to be effective, a high degree of social coordination and a loyal civil service is necessary. These were nineteenth-century achievements, and because of them, German genius, which stagnated under Bismarck and Kaiser Wilhelm, was extinguished in the days of *Ein Volk, Ein Reich, Ein Führer.*

The princes were, of course, very ordinary people, operating in a familiar social cycle. Were the petty princes of Italy during the Renaissance very different? Robbers became robber barons, who became barons, who became victims of robbers, who became . . . Irish history makes the process well known to us. There was in the nineteenth century a delusion that the amalgamation of robber families into robber states would arrest the cycle or make it more humane, civilized, creative. The reverse has happened.

In the days when genius flourished in Hesse the most publicized event was when the coopers of Cassel made an enormous barrel upon the surface of the frozen Fulda River and brought it in a gay procession as a present for the Landgrave. Much later, Bismarck, in the process of unifying Germany, deposed the Landgrave and annexed Hesse to Prussia. Everyone, including the Hessians, thought this was progress. Cassel became a vast railway and road junction; then a huge factory for the making of machine tools appeared. The Volkswagen factory and Henschel works followed. Cassel grew and grew till in the late war it became an obvious target for the British Air Force, which by persistent bombing over many weeks destroyed the entire city, old and new. The huge fires could be seen at Göttingen, fifty miles away, and did worse then expunge the city. They seem to have sterilized the soil in which it was built. Anyone who has made a bonfire in a field knows that for a long time only nettles and thistles will thrive where the grass roots have been scorched.

The new Cassel, though prosperous, is like any other big modern city. Everything in its shops, its theatres, its cinemas, is mass-produced, derivative. It is a faceless, joyless place. Apart from its German shop signs, it might be in Kansas or Lancashire. When it attracts another bomb, bigger and better, there will, apart from men and women, be only a vast and smothered spiritual potential to regret. Or is it possible that before then, by the study of the past, some new way of realizing the great and generous German genius will be discovered?

The Bell:
An Anglo-Irish View

1976

In my generation we have had several good Irish journals, but two whose influence surpassed that of all the others. When I was growing up, there was *The Irish Statesman*, which led me and many others out of the Anglo-Irish ghetto in which we had been brought up and reminded us that we were Irishmen. For our parents of the ascendancy it was easy and obvious to live in Ireland, but we of the "descendancy" were surrounded in the 1920s by the burnt houses of our friends and relations. England beckoned us and only an odd obstinate young person would wish to stay at home.

In fact, we who stayed were rather odd. I had met AE and Sir Horace Plunkett and had been enchanted by them. I had seen W. B. Yeats prancing up and down the floor of the Oxford Union, declaiming against English politicians. Empires were crashing all round us and Oxford was full of scheming young students from the new resurgent nations. I was proud that I belonged to one of them. I was, however, too young and inexperienced to know that Plunkett and AE and the other older men who ran *The Irish Statesman* were already tired and disillusioned, although the final insult to Plunkett—the burning of Kilteragh—had not yet happened. But many of their creameries had already been destroyed by the Black and Tans, who believed that the farmers hatched sedition over their milk churns. It was round the creameries that AE's new Ireland was supposed to develop: a community of spirit was to grow organically from the cooperative marketing of eggs, beef and butter.

In 1923 Plunkett persuaded me to join the Irish County Libraries, and in them I found many like-minded people, such as Lennox

Robinson, Thomas MacGreevy, Geoffrey Taylor, Robert Wilson the poet, Frank O'Connor and Helen Roe. It was the writers who brought calamity on the libraries, as one can read in Lady Gregory's journals, when they collided with Irish piety and prudery. The result was that the central organization moved to Dunfermline in Scotland and we all dispersed. In 1927 I went off as a teacher to Egypt, then to Russia and to Yugoslavia, and returned to Ireland only in 1938. *The Irish Statesman* was gone. Plunkett and AE had left for England, with the result that we remnants of the Anglo-Irish "intelligentsia" would have been nobody's children had Sean O'Faolain's *The Bell* not taken us under its wing.

There were in fact quite a few of us. There were survivors from the days when Irish writing had been focused on Coole Park—Joseph Hone, Lennox Robinson and the Yeats brothers; there were those who had made their name in England—Cecil Day Lewis, L. A. G. Strong, Elizabeth Bowen; there were Northerners—Louis MacNeice and W. R. Rodgers; and there were my own contemporaries—Geoffrey Taylor, Arland Ussher, Denis Johnston, Monk Gibbon, Harry Craig, Arthur Power, all of us rather odd and not finding it easy to put Ireland first.

Taylor became literary editor of *The Bell*, later on I became its review editor. We both knew the country as a whole. We had organized new libraries in the North, in Derry and Antrim, and knew the truth of what O'Faolain had written in an editorial for one of his Ulster numbers. Partition, he declared, had resulted from the stupid rivalry between the "hypernationalism" of the South and the "hyperinternationalism" of the North. The Ulsterman, cut off from his roots, was being suffocated by the indiscriminate flood of news and views that poured in on him from overseas, as we were in the South by our intense introversion. In my Coleraine library I had also learnt a little about Ulster intransigence, although I met more Anglo-Irish nationalists there than in Kilkenny.

O'Faolain's attitude to Ulster was generous and imaginative and he met with a generous response. In the pages of *The Bell* the Dean of Belfast defended the Ulster Protestant with firmness and courtesy, as did Frederick Leahy, a northern clergyman. Others took part in the dialogue. Leahy maintained that the Ulsterman fears "principles," not people, that his Protestant faith is very dear to him, that his loyalty to the English monarch is dependent on the Protestant succession and that his religion is rooted in Ulster, whereas the creed of the South is international and must be judged not in Ireland alone but by what happened all over the world, in Spain, South America and Canada. Yet he ended as follows: "North and South we both love Ireland. May God yet unite us peaceably and securely!" Thomas Carnduff, an Ulster poet, wrote in the same way: "We Belfastmen love Ireland. Every sod and stone and mountain and lake is part of us. . . . Yet the Orange movement began with the people, it has remained with the people. . . . The sneers and gibes at Orangeism have only strengthened its hold upon the Ulstermen."

A symposium of "the five strains," which omitted the Scottish strain, provoked a memorable letter from James Auchmuty which possibly has relevance today. He said, just as Leahy had, that the northern Presbyterian looks to Scotland as his spiritual home. "He is sprung from the same Gaelic granite as his fellow-countrymen and moulded to a different pattern." I believe that for the truth about Ulster you must still look to *The Bell* and not to the sensationalism of the contemporary press. But as I reread Auchmuty, I remember a prophecy which I read not long ago in a Dublin daily by a Belfast sociologist, A. E. Spencer: that, after many vicissitudes and much bloodshed, Ulster might become a part of a new self-governing Scotland, enriched by oil and federated with England. Ulster had once been the bridgehead between two branches of the Gael; in this way history would only be repeating itself. That indeed would be the end of a dream that many of us believed in, but I can conceive of worse endings.

The Bell pealed out its invitation to all those who loved the Irish language and loathed the way that the politicians, the pedagogues, the urbanized peasants had sucked the life and beauty from it. Those who inherited it as a mother tongue used it to pass examinations and get jobs in Dublin. The East Gael used it to oust the West Briton who here and there still administered the institutions his ancestors had built up.

The true lovers of the language, O'Faolain himself, Daniel Binchy or Myles Dillon, bitterly turned on those who by compulsion had made it something to be shirked and scorned. To Arland Ussher, an Anglo-Irishman, it had been "his first love in languages, abounding in a beauty and expression of phrase of which the Irish-English of Synge alone could give some idea." "It was," he wrote,

the great language of conversation, of quips, hyperboles, cajoleries, lamentations, blessings, cursings, endearments, tirades. Its unsuspected rhythm had even given an intimate and personal quality to the great Irish writers of English. It was the winged word in its flight that was beautiful. Stuffed and mounted on the page of a school book, it stank.

I have quoted Ussher more fully than others, because the Irish National Movement, like the Gaelic League and the Literary Revival, has often been attributed to a rebel faction of the Anglo-Irish who, like Ussher, were tired of "broad horizons" and empire building but found at home a promise of warmth, stability and intimacy in which the shyer, more complex talents might expand. Once in 1941 O'Faolain looked back forty years and thought of those who "had kept the air vibrant with their patronage, curiosity, optimism and width of interest." Now that Anglo-Ireland seems all but dead and the defence of Protestantism left to the northerners, there can be no chauvinism in recalling that more than half of those he mentioned were Anglo-Irish Protestants. As O'Faolain said, they were national, not "nationalistic," and in the pages of *The Bell* you will observe how difficult was the task that confronted them. The old strands of affection and loyalty had to be unravelled and woven tenderly into a new pattern. There was British imperialism and Catholic univer-salism; there was Irish and English racialism; and there was the many-sided dissent of Protestantism.

Michael Lennon described in two articles how, years before, Douglas Hyde steered the Gaelic League past all these rocks and shoals and whirlpools. For example, because Lord Castletown, who was proud of his Gaelic ancestry, was serving in South Africa, Hyde discouraged pro-Boer demonstrations.

In the very first number of *The Bell*, Elizabeth Bowen, still teth-ered to Ireland by her home and many family ties, considered what role, if any, the Big House could still play. It no longer carried priv-ilege with it, but loneliness, isolation, expense. Yet one held on. Old houses crumble, but the vigour and resolution that built them takes a long time to die. Elizabeth Bowen mentioned the strength that these houses impart, the great feeling of independence:

One lives by one's own standards, makes one's own laws and does not care within fairly wide limits what anybody outside the demesne wall thinks. . . . The purpose of our big rooms was social. "Cannot we," they seem to ask, "be as never before social? Cannot we scrap the past with its bitterness and barriers and all meet, throwing in what we have?" . . . The doors of the big houses stand open all day. The stranger is welcome just as much as the friend . . . in fact he is the friend, if he does not show himself otherwise. But who ever walks in? Is it suspicion, hostility, irony, that keeps so much of Ireland away from the big house door? If this lasts, we impoverish life all round.

She wrote and reviewed fairly frequently for *The Bell* and it was there, I think, rather than at her own front door that she met Catholic Nationalist Ireland. Yet her book *Bowen's Court*, which celebrating one Anglo-Irish family and one dearly loved region in effect celebrated them all, was written behind demesne walls and by its rare independence of spirit might seem to justify them. Yet her grandmother's house in Tipperary, which was my grandfather's, kindly but traditional people, had been burnt in 1923 and Elizabeth Bowen well knew that the ghosts of the ascendancy haunted these long avenues and scared away all but those realists to whom O'Faolain appealed. She filled Bowen's Court for many summers with English writers and the few Irish ones that sought her out. But then her husband died and *The Bell* died and finally she allowed Bowen's Court itself to die. When I last met her in Co. Kilkenny, just before her own death, she spoke of Ireland with such bitterness that I have tried to persuade myself that it was her last illness that was speaking and not her utter disillusionment.

A few years after O'Faolain had left *The Bell*, something happened which brought him to my defence in its pages and earned him my deep gratitude. I had given great offence by supporting the Serbian Orthodox against the Croat Catholics and was publicly denounced in Dublin and Kilkenny.* I had long before published the relevant facts in *The Church of Ireland Gazette*, but apart from Elizabeth and my brother-in-law Tyrone Guthrie, who wrote a letter to *The Irish Times* which was not printed, the only prominent people who dared suggest that there might be truth in what I had said and that I was right to say it were Sean O'Casey in *Sunset and Evening Star* and Sean O'Faolain, who wrote at length in the February 1953 issue of *The Bell*.

The Bell had a special quality about which I have not spoken. No doubt they used rejection slips in plenty, but in its early days Frank O'Connor, as poetry editor, and Geoffrey Taylor treated their contributors as friends, explaining their refusals with comments and advice and sometimes in a friendly foreword criticizing what they printed. O'Faolain too worked as though he were not merely making a magazine but shaping a literature or calling it into being. Given

*See below, pp. 452ff.

time, that is what *The Bell* might have done. Peadar O'Donnell carried on worthily for six or seven years after O'Faolain retired; then he too found the strain too much and increasingly withdrew from it. I never learnt why *The Bell* died. Slowly it began to sag like a balloon from which the air is escaping. Some strong puff of passionate conviction might have inflated it again, but none came. For a while it had kept hope alive; for a while O'Faolain's enthusiastic vision kept it going. "When the will of Ireland," he wrote, "becomes intense again, Romantic Ireland will return. When the will of the world, now barely hanging by its finger nails, becomes intense again, romance will warm life all over the globe."

Crossing the Border[*]

1955

The Bridge is thrown across the border because something of the kind is needed. It is manufactured in southern Ireland, assembled for publisher's reasons in the North. It is quite a small bridge and cannot take much traffic, but all who sincerely want to see the other side are invited to use it. It is a movable bridge and when we have had some experience with the border we'll try it across some other chasms and obstacles as well.

At present the border is more of an obsession than it need be. Those small sheds which extend from Pettigo to Ravensdale are not, in fact, supposed to stop ideas, but only cattle, clocks, silk stockings and so on. Yet they have an inhibiting effect on the writer. We have been hypnotized into thinking that there is a real barrier there, and, like those neurotic hens which can be kept from straying by drawing a chalk ring round them, we do not venture across. The editors of *The Bridge* intend to ignore the border till they bruise their noses against it. They intend to bring as many and varied ideas backwards and forwards as they dare, because they believe that, in that respect, demand and supply are complementary.

Political union when it is enforced has never of itself brought happiness, and ours is not, in the political sense, an anti-partition paper. We believe that free and friendly intercourse is an essential

---

*This was a draft editorial for a projected literary magazine to be called *The Bridge*, written after the closure of *The Bell* in December 1954. Geoffrey Taylor was interested in Butler's scheme; Peadar O'Donnell suggested that £2,000 would be needed to float the new venture. But *The Bridge* never appeared.—ed.

preliminary to happy union. Without that a united Ireland might prove a disappointing place when we reached it, a mere atomic cushion whose unity results from the decay of regional loyalties and the displacement of small rivalries by large ones. A pessimistic Ulsterman once told me that there were not enough borders and that in his opinion we should make a few more down South. A period of appalling cosmic boredom was ahead of us and the only hope was to diversify it a bit by interposing frontiers. They might delay the passage of the mass-produced standardized ideas and emotions with which we are being overwhelmed.

I think he was wrong. Borders do not keep out vulgarity and stupidity. The only way of holding them at bay is to have an intelligent and vigorous public opinion. At present there is, south and north of the border, an almost unbelievable spiritual stagnation. A dumb, stupid antagonism breaks into an occasional muffled snarl or jeer. Where there is disagreement, there should, at least, be the stimulus of conflict. It is from challenge and response that civilizations have arisen in the past. Why are our differences so unfruitful?

Here is one reason. Too many people would sooner be silent or untruthful than disloyal to their side. From cowardice they keep their private opinions suppressed till they have a chance of becoming public ones. Then they burst out with the force of an explosion. What should be said is blurted. There are clarion calls and crusades and political landslides and united fronts, but the art of free controversy was never so neglected.

Timid or stupid people often enjoy times of crisis. They can suspend, for the country or the cause, those careful discriminations, which tire the brain and do no good to the career. "Now," they cry, "is not time for academic straw-splitting and parlour theorizing. Close the ranks! He that is not with me is against me!" And so there is always a drift towards crisis, a gentle, persistent pressure towards some simple alignment of Good and Evil, Friend and Enemy. Even the churches are drifting slothfully towards a crude Manichaeism of Darkness and Light and away from Christ, who said so inscrutably that we should love our enemies.

Some think we can solve all our problems by saying there is only one problem, Communism, and only one border, that which runs from Stettin to Trieste. Destiny, at first, often plays unfairly into the hands of such people and appears to justify their cynicism. Arguments like theirs once seemed to unite and invigorate Italy and Germany. A crusade against Bolshevism was proclaimed and, as if by a miracle, we saw harmony and industry and uniformity instead of chaos, and all by suppressing "destructive thought." Now Italy and Germany are spiritually prostrate. Bolshevism, more triumphant than ever before, has started a counter-crusade in Eastern and Central Europe and produced there a semblance of uniformity, federation and strength, again by suppressing "destructive thought."

No, you cannot exorcise the lesser bogeys by conjuring up a larger bogey to scare them away. There is nothing so flattering and encouraging to a bogey as to fear him. Moreover the solidarity, which is based on hate and fear, when it cracks, cracks irreparably.

What effort is being made here to resist totalitarian thinking? Our newspapers and clergy and public men should always be ruffling the surface of unanimity, stirring it round to keep it from boiling over. Too often they are doing exactly the opposite, lending their sanction to easy sweeping statements and collective damnations. Instead, we ought always to be looking for evidence of the variety and complexity of men and labelling them with caution. A label may give the clue to one man's whole personality, of another it may describe only a vague tendency or passing impulse. Think how hard it is to say what an Irishman is! Some say it depends on his passport and domicile. At other times there is talk of Faith and Fatherland and it is said that an Irishman must be a Catholic. But nationalism is not always in vogue among Irish Catholics and often, as today, you will read in Catholic papers that the idea of an Irish nation is a Protestant one and a bad one at that, the product of humanitarian liberalism and the hatred of Catholic universalism. Grattan and his colleagues would probably have agreed to much of this and it is worth arguing that those who have accepted the Irish label with fewest reservations have been Protestants. In fact, we cannot refuse it to anyone who feels a concern for this country and is ready to put its interests first.

We shall aim at being serious without being self-important, and we shall not be in the least afraid of being thought provincial. We live in a small country but its problems are complex and interesting enough for the most ambitious intelligence. We all know those weighty sentences which begin: "The fate of Europe for the next two generations may well depend on the decision which is made at X— next Tuesday week." We shall try to avoid them because I do not think our fate depends on these things. For example, God made Mr. Trueman an unimportant person and, therefore, whatever he decides is unimportant or decided already or soon to be reversed. The important events are those which result from our own energy or enthusiasm.

All the same we are Europeans, and England does not now stand between us and Europe. Other small nations have been crushed and planted and half obliterated. They have had minority and ascendancy problems. They have had partitions and language revivals. It is possible to trace a general human pattern. Those who deny that there are laws of social development are usually most enslaved by them and here in Ireland we seem innocently to be falling into traps from which others have just laboriously extricated themselves. We are stupidly, snobbishly uninterested in other small nations, yet we have more to learn from them than from the large ones. For example, the culture of the United States of America is now something which we absorb with our mother's milk. It is so ubiquitous that we swallow it without even recognizing it. Even less does it stimulate us to creation.

As for England, she is no longer, as she used to be, the oppressor of Irish culture. She is more subtly dangerous. She is like one of those rich kind aunties who undermine the family by indulging and then adopting the pretty nieces and the clever nephews. The old parents are left behind with the plain, stupid ones and home life is poisoned with envy, loneliness and a sense of inferiority.

Perhaps Ulster suffers more than we do from the kind aunty, because she has been more dearly loved and has sacrificed more clever nephews. Surely even the most loyal subjects of King George must be aware of what is happening. They must have guessed that the more formidable of Ulster's enemies are those who keep quiet. "Time is on our side," they are saying. "We breed faster than they do, and Ulstermen with imperial responsibilities are leaving Ulster or neglecting it. The Province has the artificial vitality of the garrison town and no organic life. If ever the pipeline were cut, it would perish. Fermoy is ours today, Enniskillen will be ours tomorrow." That, no doubt, is how the Britons exulted when, after the Romans left and for a few short years before the Saxons came, they surged back into Verulam and Caerleon. It is an argument as sound as it is hateful. Yet few southern Irishmen would wish to absorb Ulster like greenfly invading a neglected tree, like Poles pouring into German Silesia or Czechs into the Sudetenland. Ulster would no longer be of value to Ireland if she were robbed of her rich history, her varied traditions. If she gives up these, which link her to the rest of Ireland, and becomes a mere imperial outpost, she will deserve the fate of Breslau and Fiume and Königsberg, arrogant and alien towns ultimately overwhelmed by the unsophisticated countryside which they had dominated. On the other hand, if she keeps her Irish character the border will slowly cease to be a menace and an anxiety. Either it will become meaningless and will drop off painlessly like a strip of sticking plaster from a wound that has healed, or else it will survive in some modified form as a definition which distinguishes but does not divide. It will not be the policy of *The Bridge* to minimize or deny any distinctions of culture or history or traditions that are real, but sometimes fictitious distinctions have been introduced irrelevantly and maliciously where they do not belong. I do not think that Ulstermen will say we are violating their frontiers if we choose to ignore them.

Divided Loyalties

1984

In 1984 Ireland is so deeply divided that few now talk of a *modus vivendi* between Unionist and Nationalist, between Catholic and Protestant. You never read that ancient newspaper cliché about a "Union of Hearts," or think as I did when I was a boy, and read AE's *The Irish Statesman*, that Ireland might become the central focus of our love and loyalty.

Nobody ever investigates how these ethnic and religious love affairs, which occasionally occur, are conducted. It is obvious, though, that while they can be easily frustrated, they can only very warily and deviously be promoted.

Opposites often attract each other but the attraction seldom lasts if the full extent of the opposition is ignored. It is as neighbours, full of ineradicable prejudices, that we must love each other, not as fortuitously "separated brethren."

I became an Irish nationalist when I was very young. I had to return to school at Charterhouse some days after the Easter Week rebellion and to pass barricades near O'Connell Bridge. I had to show a pass signed by the sergeant of the Royal Irish Constabulary in Kilkenny. There were still wisps of smoke coming from Sackville Street, the names of Pearse and Connolly meant nothing to me but I felt it was my war in a way that the war in which I was being prepared to fight in the Charterhouse Officers' Training Corps was not. When I came home for the holidays I argued ignorantly with my parents about it. Most of our Protestant neighbours, diminished in numbers and in spirit by the everlasting brain drain to England, were solidly Unionist. They got their little jokes about Ireland from *Punch* and *The Morning Post*.

As far as I was concerned, the first crucial discussion occurred when my slightly older cousin, Theobald Butler, came to stay. He had been head boy at Charterhouse but had become an Irish nationalist and, refusing to fight in an imperialist war, had taken a job in a school in Co. Down. He had first done relief work in Serbia with a friend, Eric Dodds, who for the same reason was teaching at Kilkenny College. Dodds had won the famous Craven scholarship at Oxford. There were heated arguments when they came to lunch. Sometimes after this, if I made a nationalist remark, my mother said, "Oh, you got that off Theo and Dodds. They'll scuttle back to England the moment the war is over." And that indeed is what they did, for England has a magnetism for the Anglo-Irish intellectual that very few can resist. Sometimes even a few acres of Irish soil can give us an unreasoning obstinacy and the illusion of security, but Theo and Dodds had not an acre between them. Before he died Theo had a full inch of London legal achievements after his name in *Burke's Peerage*, and Dodds became Regius Professor of Greek at Oxford. In his autobiography, *Missing Persons* (1977), he has described the missing person, the Irish nationalist he once was, and the disillusionment endured by all Anglo-Irishmen who had given their first love to Ireland. "The birth of a terrible beauty has ended with the establishment of a grocers' republic," he wrote.

But, if you are heir to some trees and fields and buildings and a riverbank, your love for your country can be more enduring. It is a not too blameworthy extension of self-love; you feel qualified to influence its destiny on a small scale and you are not content, as so many of the Irish are, to radiate goodwill to Ireland from across the sea. We were minor gentry and our activities were all minor, but my father had brought the village creamery to Bennettsbridge and was the committee's president, and my mother ran a Boot-and-Coal Fund and a committee connected with tuberculosis, both subsidized by annual jumble sales and concerts. My aunt had founded the Kilkenny Horticultural Society and used to drive a fat pony round the country judging cottage gardens; I used to think she judged the cottagers as well as their gardens. She had a bossy manner and this seemed to me suitable enough.

AE had believed that, as the cooperative movement developed in Ireland, a real village community would grow round every creamery and that the principle of sharing would extend into every branch of life, spiritual, economic, cultural. The communal marketing of eggs and butter would lead to more intimate and domestic forms of sharing. AE saw the hedges planted with apple trees and gooseberry bushes, as in Germany, and gymnasiums and libraries, picture galleries and village halls, to which each man or woman made his contribution according to his powers, so that each village became a focus of activity and debate. Sixty years ago, an ingenuous young person could really believe this would happen. There, anyway, was the new creamery on the edge of the village and it stood till 1983, when it was bulldozed away. To make all these creameries AE travelled hundreds of miles on his bicycle, and Plunkett, a sick man kept alive by his burning zeal, made these long journeys which he recorded in his diaries: "A two hours crawl in the Major's brougham to Longford. Did good I think but, oh, how boring and tiring! Two long speeches to two small meetings. My thoughts germinate in other brains and when the brains are attached to the proper physique the enthusiasm works."

When I told my mother about the gooseberry bushes, she said "Stuff and nonsense! Those trees that the Kilkenny Corporation planted along the canal walk were all slashed down in a week. When O'Grady and Otway Cuffe gave that Irish play at Sheestown the crowds all strolled out from Kilkenny and pulled up all the shrubs and broke the teacups."

When I suggested to my sister, who organized the village concerts, that they should do a Synge play or a Lady Gregory or at least a George Shiels, she said, "Oh, they'd hate that sentimental Irish stuff," and as usual, she sent for a bunch of one-act farces from Messrs. French in London, and she was quite right. They vastly preferred them.

And it always happened like that. When it was rumoured in the Kildare Street Club that the creameries had become social centres where the farmers discussed sedition over their milk churns, and when the Black and Tans started burning them, many members congratulated themselves on the hostility they had shown to Plunkett. The rest of the story runs along familiar lines.

AE and Plunkett died disillusioned, in England. Kilteragh, Plunkett's house in Foxrock, which had been the meeting place for the Anglo-Irish who were concerned about their country, was burned to the ground in the civil war, because he had become a senator.

I was young at the time and did not realize that I was living at the end of a relatively humane and sensible era and at the beginning of a cruel and chaotic one: Ireland had her freedom and Europe had her League of Nations. I enjoyed my holidays at home, the raids and rumours, the "battle of Kilkenny" and the three-day siege of Kilkenny Castle, and I believe there were many young people as silly as myself.

Compared to other counties, Kilkenny was peaceful and gentle. Apart from the burning of three famous and beautiful houses, Woodstock, Desart Court and Bessborough, life went on as usual with rare interruptions.

One night, at 3 a.m., we were woken by loud knocking at the front door. My sister and I went down and found two unknown men there. We were elated rather than scared. Here was real life at last. One of the men said they wanted money for the "dependents of the Irish Republic." I said, "We've no guns in the house; if you're just common thieves we can't stop you taking what you want." He replied, "Ah, we're not that sort of chap at all," and they went away.

Another afternoon two of them came again, asking as before for money. My mother and I were in the porch and she danced about with fury. "I know who you are," she said to one of them. "You're Jim Connell. Take your cigarette out of your mouth when you're talking to me." He took it out and I began to scold my mother for interrupting what might have been a revealing conversation. It was only the second time I had seen a Republican, and when I went back to Oxford I wanted at least to say what they were like and what their plans were. My mother answered me sharply and we started an angry argument. The two men looked at each other in embarrassment and slunk politely away.

The third occasion was an episode that found its way into J. G. Farrell's *Troubles*. My sisters and I were on our way with two friends to the St. George's dance at Kilrush, seven or eight miles beyond Kilkenny. It was a period when everyone had to have a permit signed by the police for his car, and all those who were legally on the road could be thought of as the enemy. When we got to Troyeswood, a mile outside Kilkenny, we found a wall built across the road. In front of it stood two men with long white beards, which proved, when we got closer, to be white scarves veiling their faces; they had revolvers. Behind them lay three or four cars turned upside down in the middle of the road. They turned us out of the car and led us across the hedge into the field where already a dozen of our friends were grouped with another muffled figure guarding them. When three or four more cars had been turned over and their occupants ushered into the field, we were told, "At the expiration of half an hour you may proceed to your destinations."

We walked back in our evening clothes across Kilkenny. Some

stayed at the Club House Hotel. I tramped back home to tell my family.

Far worse things happened in Tipperary. One night in March 1923, Graiguenoe Park, my mother's home at Holycross, was burnt. We shared her sadness, for we had spent many happy days with our cousins there. It was between thirty and forty miles away, but when we were children we thought of it as in another country, much wilder, less ordinary. My sister and I used to get up early and start off with our night things on our bicycle carriers and the dew still on the grass. As soon as we crossed the Tipperary border the smell of turf, unknown to us in Kilkenny, prepared us to expect everything strange and new. Leaving behind us the familiar woods of Farmley and Desart Court, we crossed Slieveardagh and, turning aside after Littleton bog, we made for Killough hill and, when it came in sight, we knew we had arrived.

The little bridge across the Suir at the approach to Holycross had been rebuilt by an ancestor of my father, James Butler, twelfth Baron Dunboyne, and his wife, Lady Margaret O'Brien, in 1624. There is a Latin inscription on it and an appeal in verse to the passerby:

> Dic, precor, ante abitum,
> verbo non amplius uno,
> evadat Stygios
> auctor uterque lacus.

> Pray, traveller, before you pass,
> offer one prayer only,
> that the two builders may
> escape the Stygian lakes.

This interesting pagan fancy has been Christianized in the Tourist Board translation into "Hell."

James Butler gave a miraculous statue of the Virgin Mary to the Abbot of Holycross. It had come from a wrecked Spanish galleon and was said to cure toothache and keep rats from the grain.

Even Graiguenoe itself, a large early Victorian house built by my great-grandfather beyond the ruins of Holycross Abbey, had romance and mystery for us. My uncle had been boycotted in 1910 and there was a police barracks on his property and for a time a general store. His farmworkers had stood by him and could buy their food there when the shopkeepers in Thurles, intimidated by the Land Leaguers,* refused to supply them.

Some years ago there was a dramatic dynamiting of the ruins of Graiguenoe in the presence of a photographer from *The Tipperary Star*, and the stones were used in the reconstruction of Holycross Abbey. When I went there soon after, there was no trace of the house except for a broad band of daisies that wound through the field where the avenue had been. Tom Nolan, the coachman's grandson, still lived in the lodge and I found that the new proprietor farmed a thousand acres more than Uncle Charlie had done.

Some twenty houses of the Anglo-Irish were burnt at this time in Tipperary. Most of them vanished without record, but many letters must have been written like the one which follows. It is from the housekeeper at Graiguenoe to my aunt, who was in London at the time.

31 March 1923

From Mrs. A. Good, Housekeeper, Graiguenoe Park, Holycross, Co. Tipperary, to Mrs. Charles Clarke.

Madam,

By now you know the bad news how Graiguenoe is burned down. Oh it was terrible to see it blazing away!

Just at 5 past 12 on Wednesday night the bell was rung. I was only just in bed, so I jumped up and called the girls and went to Nolan; but he was up. They never stopped ringing till Nolan and I went to the hall door; and there were two men with revolvers and demanded to know why we did not open before and come out; so I said, "Surely you will give us time to get our things." He said, "Yes, if we were not too long." He wanted to know how many there were in the house. I said, "Three girls more." He wanted to know who were all those inside there. I said, "That is yourself in the mirror." He thought (when he saw our reflections in the glass) that a lot of people were there. So we all got our things put together as quick as we could, but all of us had to leave a lot of things as they kept asking, "Are ye ready, as we are in a hurry," so we got out. Nolan saved three pictures out of the dining room and your dressing case and a small case under the bed and Mr. Clarke's dressing bag, but they did not want him to take anything only his things. He also saved the harness; he worked like a nigger but he could do nothing more. He also tried to save the harness room by throwing buckets of water on the inside and the roof; but no use. The fire

*The Land League, founded in Dublin in 1879, spearheaded a mass movement for land reform and home rule in Ireland.—ed.

got too firm a hold on everything before those demons left. They had petrol, straw and hay so they made a good job of it. The only place not burned out is the scullery and Mrs. Curtin's room. We were in the coach house watching it blazing. The flames were very high but the wind was in our favour, or the outhouses would also be in flames.

The Laundry Basket (Dublin) was in the passage and the man asked us was it ours and I said Yes, so he let us take it; also there is a basket at Thurles laundry, which I expect will come back on Monday. Will the things be sent to you? They could be packed in a box. Also we managed to grab some coats off the rack in the dark. They turned out to be your grey coat and the brown. Will I send them on also? There were about seven or eight men through the house but they told us not to stir from where we were for at least half an hour as the house was surrounded and we may be shot. They left before one o'clock so you see we got no time. We stayed all night.

It was heartbreaking to see the house burning where we were living so long. But we were thankful Mr. Clarke was not there for the story was bad enough and he may be shot. They asked several times where was the Boss. We all came up to Mrs. Hilton's at 7 o'clock in the morning. Bridget has gone home, also Maggie and Josie. I am staying here with Mrs. Hilton for the present. I will never forget the sight and experiences of Wednesday night. I feel sorry for you and Mr. Clarke, but I'm thinking there will be no gentlemen's places soon.

Hoping you and Mr. Clarke are well,

I am, Madam, yours respectfully,

A. Good

I can't find a pen so please excuse pencil.

Did the Anglo-Irish deserve the fate which was so often predicted for them? Wolfe Tone* wrote: "They have disdained to occupy the station they might have held among the people and which the people would have been glad to see them fill. They see Ireland only in their rent rolls, their places, their patronage, their pensions. They shall perish like their own dung. Those that have seen them will say, 'Where are they?' "

The Anglo-Irish could have dodged their fate if their interest in Ireland, let alone their love, had been more than marginal. They recognized a duty certainly to their neighbourhood and this duty was usually intelligently fulfilled, but it only rarely happened that, like Plunkett and a few of their contemporaries, they could give their first love to their country. I believe that in a generation or two, had there

---

*See the next essay, "Wolfe Tone and the Common Name of Irishman."—ed.

been no 1914 war, no rebellion and no civil war, this duty might have turned itself into love as it often had in the eighteenth century.

Then, for a brief period, they had been able to represent something very precious. Only they could give Irishmen a sense of historical continuity and of identity. It was to be found in their bookshelves, when those who remained no longer read books, in their estate maps when they no longer had estates, in their memories when they no longer had the leisure or literary skill to write them down. The Irishmen who burnt down those Tipperary houses were sawing away the branch on which they were sitting. Clamouring that they were a distinctive people, they obliterated much of the heritage that distinguished them. The burning of the Four Courts, which swept away the records of eight centuries, was only one episode in this tale of self-destruction.

A new and more suffocating ascendancy, that of international commerce, was on the way; many of those ruined houses would have been strongholds of resistance to it, and the Anglo-Irish, with their easygoing pragmatic Christianity, would certainly have tempered the religious and political passions of our northern countrymen.

Wolfe Tone and the Common Name of Irishman

1963

Preface
1985

This talk was given on 24 September 1963, the bicentenary of Wolfe Tone's birth. Much has altered since then, but I believe that my argument has not been affected by the passage of time and that it is pointless to restate it in the terms of 1985 rather than those of 1963.

Yet in the meantime certain things have happened that cannot be ignored. The New Ireland Forum made a valiant attempt peacefully to revive "the common name of Irishman" and to arrest the spiralling violence which threatens to overwhelm us all, North and South, from which without help we shall never recover. And our history tells us that outside helpers usually come to stay.

The Forum failed of its effect but left a lingering sweetness in the air. The desire for unity and harmony is something like the desire for sleep. Sleep is chased away by too eager a pursuit. It slips in unbidden and unobserved when its time has come, the scarcely valued by-product of some more significant harmony, whose source is elsewhere. "A healthy nation," wrote Bernard Shaw, "is as unconscious of its nationality as a healthy man is of his bones."

The authors of the Forum Report believe that in the New Ireland "the cultural and linguistic diversity of the north and south" could be "a source of enrichment and vitality" and they believe it could be politically guaranteed. Yet how can a government guarantee anything so elusive as the cross-fertilization of cultures? It happens spontaneously or not at all.

Cultural diversity was honoured more than now in the days of

Douglas Hyde and his Gaelic League, of Yeats and his colleagues of the Abbey Theatre. They received no government support or encouragement but they proved that the blending of English and Irish temperaments and talent can be a rich and fruitful one.

The Irish with the defeat and flight of their ruling classes became a peasant people ashamed of their native language, which they associated with subjection and poverty. It was the nineteenth-century scholars and writers, mainly men of Anglo-Irish stock, who first gave it dignity and honour. If unity in diversity is ever again to be achieved, it must be done not by governments but by individuals of both English and Irish loyalties. And, in fact, unperceived there is already a slow but steady move in that direction.

There have been "pairings" of towns and villages in the six counties and the twenty-six. Unrecorded by the press there have been many cultural exchanges, theatrical, literary or merely social. In this neighbourhood, for example, the Northern Ireland Project was started in the Christian Brothers School in Carrick-on-Suir. Accompanied by pupils from Kilkenny College, a Protestant foundation, its students visited Ballymena Academy in their Easter holidays and their visit was returned. This has happened for five years now.

Multiply these enterprises by a hundred or a thousand and wait for ten or twenty years, and the dreams of the New Ireland Forum will for the most part be realized. Will there be a United Ireland? Who knows? But the common name of Irishmen will have abolished the memory of past dissensions.

THEOBALD WOLFE TONE 1763–98

I regretted, when it was too late, the rather foolish title I had chosen for this talk, "The Ideology of Tone," for, of course, what made Tone great was that he had no ideology. It was he who first used the famous phrase "the common name of Irishman," a name with which he hoped to supersede all the ideologies with which the Ireland of his day was divided. Well known as they are, I shan't apologize for repeating his exact words; it was his ambition, he wrote, "to unite the whole people of Ireland, to abolish the memory of all past dissensions and to substitute the common name of Irishman in place of the denominations of Protestant, Catholic and Dissenter."

Is Tone a completely out-of-date figure or do his ideas still have something to say to us? What I want in particular to discuss is this notion of a "common name of Irishman." For Tone it was full of gunpowder. He expected to overthrow with it the Irish Parliament, to break the connection with England and, with the aid of revolutionary France, to establish an independent Irish Republic. Well, the *explosion* did happen, and appalling havoc was wrought and, though it appeared to many of his contemporaries that all the wrong things were blown up and Irish freedom postponed for some generations and then mutilated, plainly there was dynamism in the idea of "the common name of Irishman." At least about *that* Tone had not been deceived. Like a great inventor who blows up himself and his friends with the thing he invents, he had discovered something which nobody had observed before. He was the father of Irish Republicanism and also, I think, of Irish nationalism, and since such ideas are very contagious, he was probably answerable in some indirect way for Garibaldi and Kossuth and a dozen national heroes who handled, after him and more effectually, the same explosive material. In most cases their problems were easier than his, for Ireland was more deeply divided than any other country in Europe. Garibaldi and the others wanted to bring freedom to some oppressed but more or less homogeneous and like-minded people, Italian, Polish, Hungarian, Czech. Tone had to invent a nation out of a native majority and a powerful minority which had strong loyalties and affinities outside Ireland. The two parts were linked together by little but a common history and the encircling sea. Even now many people are more impressed by the disaster that befell the United Irishmen than by Tone's discovery that such hostile groups could ever unite under a common name.

In unity they had slowly come to the decision that the Irish government was the worst of all possible governments and that the English and Protestant domination, which it represented, must be overthrown. Tone, a Protestant himself of English descent, decided that this could not be achieved without violence and the help of revolutionary France.

Tone's rebellion, as we know, was an utter calamity and ushered in one of the worst of Irish centuries. The Irish Parliament, corrupt and unrepresentative but at least Irish, was dissolved; the Orange Order, seeing no tyranny but Popish tyranny, swept away the last traces of that Protestant Republicanism of the North on which Tone had based his hopes of a United Ireland. The Catholic Church in Ireland became increasingly segregationist, and it was considered godless for a Catholic Irishman to be educated alongside his Protestant compatriots. The Irish people, whose distinctive character the eighteenth century had taken for granted, lost its language and, after the Famine, many of its traditions. A period of industrial expansion was followed by one of poverty and emigration. Finally, the partition of Ireland in the 1920s set an official seal on all the historical divisions of our country, racial and cultural and religious, which Tone had striven to abolish.

You might think that all this would have utterly discredited Tone's attempt to link us together under a common name. Yet it has had no such result, though no one since him has ever achieved even his small success in uniting us.

What dynamism is still left in this old idea of nationalism, and in particular of Irish nationalism? Is it just a faded bit of sentimentality left over from the past, something concerned with shamrocks and Patrick's Day processions and seasonal conviviality? Or has it still the power which Tone discovered in it to supersede a dozen different loyalties, political, racial, material, spiritual, and to unite people who are otherwise disunited in many of their most intimate beliefs?

Is it possible for such an idea to survive into the space age, and, if it has lost all its vigour, should we try to revive it and if so how?

To Tone, of course, as to Grattan and all their contemporaries, Ireland meant the whole of Ireland, North and South, and the dissensions they hoped to abolish had no geographical frontier. The common name of Irishman would have been meaningless to them if applied to the twenty-six counties only.

There is another factor that was very important. In Tone's day the majority of Irishmen still lived in Ireland, while today by far the most of the Irish people live outside our island. Two centuries ago, when Tone was born, the idea of a widespread Irish race was not a very significant one, and there was no tincture of *racialism* in Tone's idea of an independent Irish nation. When he was in Philadelphia intriguing with the representatives of revolutionary France about Irish independence, he met many Irish settlers, but though he felt warmly towards them, he did not consider that they had much bearing on the problems of Ireland. *Effective* Irishmen lived in Ireland, which was the Irish nation, and the sentimental ties, which now bind the foreign emigrant to his motherland, were then very weak. That is to say racialism, which in Europe has often since usurped the place of nationalism, hardly existed.

Tone's remarks about the American Irish in Pennsylvania, as about all the European immigrants there, are caustic. He had the view that oppression degrades men, and he tended, as did most of the revolutionaries of his time, to look for leadership among those who had escaped it. Of the Pennsylvania Irish he had a low opinion: after denouncing the ignorant boorishness of the Germans and the uncouthness of the Quakers, he wrote:

of all the people I have met here the Irish are incontestably the most offensive. If you meet a confirmed blackguard you may be sure he is Irish; you will, of course, observe I speak of the lower orders. As they have ten times more animal spirits than the Germans and Quakers they are much more actively troublesome. After all I do not wonder at it, nor am I angry with them. They are corrupted by their own ignorant government at home and, when they land here and are treated like human creatures, fed and clothed and paid for their labour and no longer flying from the sight of any fellow who is able to purchase a velvet collar to his coat, I do not wonder if the heads of the unfortunate devils are turned with such an unexpected change in their fortunes and if their new gotten liberty breaks out as it too often does into pettiness and insolence. For all this it is perhaps not fair to blame them.

So when we examine Tone's common name of Irishman to see whether it still has validity and power we have to recognize that it concerns our country and not our blood. For him the English or Scots whose ancestors had settled in Ireland and who made Ireland rather than England the focus of their loyalties and the centre of their interests, became Irish. An Irishman who went to England or America and acted analogously became English or American.

I think this rather obvious and platitudinous point is worth stressing because "nationalism" as a whole has fallen into some disrepute in our century. It is regarded, by liberal Englishmen, for example, as a sort of petty obstruction in the way of some great brotherhood of mankind, a clot in the bloodstream of universal concord that is to encircle the earth. But if you discuss the matter with them, you will find that they are still obsessed and horrified with the racialist fantasies of the Fascists and Nazis thirty years ago. In fact what they call German nationalism and Italian nationalism were the antithesis of the nationalism of Wolfe Tone. So-called Italian and German nationalists of thirty years ago were racialist and anti-nationalist. Hundreds and thousands of men, who lived for centuries under the same hills, beside the same lakes, were all at once told that they were aliens. In their thousands, Germans were ejected from the Tyrol and Slavs from northern Italy. What had this to do with nationalism, which is comprehensive and based on neighbourliness and shared experiences and a common devotion to the land in which you live? It has nothing to do with racial origins. Tone, the father of Irish nationalism, was of English descent and it is absurd that there should ever be any doubts on this matter.

But if you look into the matter more closely you will see how this delusion that racialism was nationalism came about and how it found a very fertile soil in our complicated scientific age, though it is really a very primitive idea. Speed of communications and the growth of worldwide enterprises have made it possible now for people to live in one country and have major loyalties outside it. All over Europe and in Ireland too there are pockets of foreigners who do not need or wish to be assimilated. You've all read, I am sure, of those vegetable diseases which used to die on the long sea voyage across the Atlantic but now after a swift and comfortable air flight arrive in full vigour and ready to ravage a whole continent. It is the same, I think, with "the memory of past dissensions," to use Tone's phrase. Our prejudices arrive intact wherever they are exported and it is not as easy as it used to be to eradicate them. We can keep in touch with like-minded people by post in disregard of the person next door; we can get all the support we want for our views by turning a knob on the radio. That is why nationalism, as Tone conceived it, that is to say a concentration of affection for the land in which you live and the people with whom you share it, has become in our day a delicate and fragile plant. It implies an intercourse with your neighbours which is direct and personal, whereas nowadays we need not bother with our neighbours, particularly if, as most people do, we live in cities; there are a dozen impersonal, indirect ways of bypassing our neighbours and being adherents of some remote community.

I remember reading how, under Mussolini, Italian schoolchildren in Boston used to send their exam papers to be corrected in Italy. But obviously we Irish have been immune from the worst excesses of racialism which we have seen in Europe. And for this surely Tone and those many Irish nationalists of mixed descent and no racial prejudices must have much of the credit. Yet today nationalism everywhere is sick and discredited. And in the North of Ireland, which was once the seedbed of republican ideas, the province from which most of the leaders of the United Irishmen derived and from which Tone hoped for the most vigorous support for his movement for national unity and independence, in the North nationalism is very sick indeed. The question is: Can it be revived and should it be revived? And if so, from what direction will revival come?

Before I discuss this, it occurs to me that I have misinterpreted Tone a little and talked of the common name of Irishman as though this was to him an end and not a means. In fact he thought of it as a weapon by which, in his words, "to subvert the tyranny of our execrable government and to break the connection with England, the never-failing source of all our political evils."

None of this has much relevance today. If the idea of belonging to a small united nation did recover some of the dignity and power that it had for Tone and his contemporaries, that is not how it could be used. Possibly the connection with England is still an evil in that it is draining away our population and our energy and perhaps implicating us in quarrels and enterprises that should not concern us, but for this England is not to blame, since every year our immigrants leave Ireland for England in huge numbers of their own accord. Many join her army, and fighting against England or the North we should be fighting against our own people with a bitterly divided mind.

In fact, of course, in our very complex and impersonal space world, our enemies are not people or races any longer but ideas and moods and attitudes of mind; and persuasion and understanding are the only effective weapons against these things. The English are not our enemies nor the Russians nor the Chinese. If we think in military terms, which were valid for Tone, we get into a hopeless impasse. We would not wish to weaken English democracy against Russian Communism. We would not wish to weaken the Russian Communists against the more intransigent and numerous Chinese. Behind every spectre we see a worse one looming from which the first spectre appears to be protecting us, so we had better not see spectres at all but concentrate on the real world, small, personal and concrete, into which we were born. And in this particular sphere the weapon "the common name of Irishman," which Tone forged so successfully and used so unsuccessfully, may still have the same power which it always had.

But how are we to re-forge it and against what are we to use it? We have a feeling that everything is wrong but at any moment it is easy to present ourselves with a pleasant and reassuring picture of all being well. In Tone's time it was far easier to diagnose what was wrong, for there were extremes of poverty and wealth and glaring injustice. But in his time too one cannot forget that there were plenty of people to paint rosy pictures and to point to the expanding trade, the growing wealth of the country under Grattan's Parliament, and to argue that it was best to leave things as they were. Perhaps it would have been, but we can only stand still in a society where there are no Tones, no men with quick sympathies and passionate convictions and the power to see below the surface. Such a society would perhaps be a tranquil one, but it would be a dead one and Ireland in the 1790s, unlike Ireland today, was very much alive.

A visitor from the 1790s to Ireland today would, of course, be favourably impressed by many things he saw. Three-quarters of the things that Tone fought for have already been achieved and seemingly not by the romantic radicalism which he espoused, but by the slow and irresistible permeation of liberal ideas, by science, enlightenment, commerce and good communications. Wealth is more evenly distributed, and the religious and political and social discriminations about which we complain in the North and in the South, would seem to this visitor very trifling. Most of them lack legal sanction and are best described in terms of prejudice or ignorance rather than persecution. Look out of any town window and you will see hundreds of television masts, arguing not only growing prosperity but also broadening horizons, a wider knowledge of the world and its problems, a more educated and contented people. What have we to grumble about?

This visitor, if he were Wolfe Tone himself, would probably look for some spirit of revolt seething below the calm surface, but he would fail to find it. In the 1790s Ireland had been in turmoil. Belfast and the North surged with excitement and hope, delighted with the American Revolution and still watching the progress of the French Revolution with passionate interest; in the South there was a great deal of dull and inarticulate misery but among the Protestants there was still the exhilarating memory of the Convention of Dungannon and, with the foundation of the Volunteer Movement, the assertion of Irish independence. In the Irish Parliament violently opposing views were expressed with eloquence and force. It was a very corrupt and unjust society, but not at all a dead one.

In the 1960s political excitement is subdued, our hopes moderate and, though we are often dull, we can usually articulate our grievances or else escape them. We can go on strike or write a book—and, if all else fails, we can emigrate. It is natural enough that we should be rather low-geared in the expression of our hopes and convictions. Europe has had a whole generation of visions and visionaries. They seem mostly to have ended badly. We have become everywhere, not only in Ireland, very sceptical and we value the man most who has few feelings and no ideas or convictions that are not shared by the passive majority. In fact Ireland today and all Europe is a paradise for the bureaucrat and the Laodicean.

Tone was neither of these and he would have been in no way reassured by the absence of violent discord, the appearance of prosperity. He would have noticed our huge and constant emigration and deduced from it some deep discontent, for how can a man express his dissatisfaction with his country and his despair for its future more emphatically and finally than by leaving it? He would have seen that in 150 years Ireland had become immensely unimportant, unimportant even to herself, and he would probably have argued as before that this was due to her connection with England, which the Act of Union had made more complete. And certainly he would have been staggered by the alteration in their relationship. When he died, Ireland had been in some sort of parity with England, that is to say its population was about half that of England, and Dublin was the second city in the empire. Tone's rebellion was not, like the 1916 rebellion, a wild gesture of defiance, without hope of success. It really might have succeeded. Holland, as the historian Lecky explained, had been no larger when she defied Louis XIV, nor had Prussia when Frederick the Great had turned her into a great power, nor had the United States when she flung off the English yoke. In addition there were far more men of exceptional ability in Ireland than in Holland or Prussia or even the American colonies. The Protestant gentry had in the Volunteer Movement shown their independent spirit, while the revolutionary doctrines had spread through the industrial North and the Irish Republic would have met with warm support in France and the United States.

I don't think Tone would have been particularly dazzled by the various scientific improvements on which we pride ourselves. He would have observed that, despite them, our society was not the vigorous creative polemical one for which he had worked but stagnant and shrinking. I think he would have noticed in the republic what an Irish priest from Donegal recently called "the gathering lethargy in rural Ireland." Father McDyer has more intimate knowledge than most of us, so he will forgive me quoting him. He found that apathy and despair had decimated the population and left ruined homesteads behind it.

Many of the fires that are still sending up smoke are only tended by the enfeebled hands of an aged couple, whose children have gone elsewhere. . . . What an eloquent commentary [he went on] this was on our age and times. What pillage, persecution and the battering ram failed to achieve, the lure of far-away urban life and the lack of initiative, cooperation and patriotism at home were fast accomplishing.

He had seen thousands of good acres going to loss and he prophesied, "If we stood by and watched the people flee the land and their houses one after another falling into ruin, all Ireland's struggles will be in vain and the friendly lovable populous Ireland which has existed for centuries would cease to be."

I repeat this melancholy forecast, because Father McDyer is obviously not a melancholy person; these calamities have acted on him as a challenge. I only wish some Irishman of English descent would face as candidly the far more sensational decay of the other part of the Irish people, Wolfe Tone's people, the Anglo-Irish, and would have as wise and astringent advice to give them. Perhaps he could tell them how they could block their ears to the song of the same siren that has depopulated the West. For of course it is "the lure of far-away urban life," sometimes called "broader horizons," that has emptied all the houses where once great decisions about Ireland were made, bold ideas canvassed and the first rough outlines of a great civilization, half English, half Gaelic but wholly Irish, planned.

Tone was a generous-minded man and I don't think that if he returned to Ireland today he would be at all elated by the complete accuracy with which his sad predictions had been fulfilled. In the last year of his life, when he was aware that the allies upon whom he had counted to make the revolution bloodless had fallen away and that the rebellion on which he was embarking would be hideous and the chances of success very small, he prophesied that his people, the Anglo-Irish of the ascendancy, would disappear, because, he said, they refused to identify themselves with their neighbours, to accept, in fact, "the common name of Irishman." They have "disdained," he said,

to occupy the station they might have held among the People, and which the People would have been glad to see them fill. They see Ireland only in their rent rolls, their places, their patronage, their pensions. They shall perish like their own dung. Those who have seen them shall say, "Where are they?"

This was an astonishing prediction to have made in 1798 about so numerous, wealthy and powerful and also enlightened a body as the

Anglo-Irish ascendancy, but if he returned today he would find it three-quarters fulfilled.

It is the disunity of our country, of course, that is responsible, in part at least, for the stagnation and emigration which one can observe North and South. It has disturbed that equilibrium of opposing forces which is necessary to a country's happiness. Without the Protestant North we have become lopsided. We lack that vigorous and rebellious northern element which in the eighteenth century was responsible for both our nationalism and our republicanism. And without the South the North has become smug and has succumbed to what ought to be the most discredited of all contemporary delusions, the lure of broad horizons and all the rest of it.

But let us consider, anyway, the reasons why the North holds aloof. The most important of them is what I've just called Broad Horizons, that is to say the fear of leaving a large worldwide community and becoming attached to a small and insignificant one. The other reasons are all subordinate to this one but I'd better mention a couple of them, both well known.

The northerners fear that the principles of religious freedom for which their ancestors have fought will be jeopardized under an authoritarian Church.

They speak of loyalty to Britain and its monarchy and to the Anglo-Saxon culture with its great literature and traditions.

Now there is real substance in number two and number three, particularly number two, the authoritarian Church. When Ireland was still united we wrangled about these two things, and, when she is reunited, we shall continue to do so. I'll try to show later that our disputes about these matters, which are sterile in a divided Ireland, would become fruitful in a united one. But I don't believe that at present these disputes are the real source of division.

It is a matter of Broad Horizons and, since we are almost as much hypnotized by them as the Ulstermen are, that is what we have chiefly to consider. All our minds are ranging constantly over the whole world and we are thinking of worldwide opportunities, of international responsibilities, of the exploration of space. The problems of Ireland north and south have begun to seem very puny.

The other day Captain O'Neill, Premier of Northern Ireland, taking a world view of Ireland in the contemporary manner, said this:

The prosperity of Ulster largely depends upon the development of the whole British economy and this in turn hangs upon events in the wider world outside. We must always remember that our future may depend as much upon a decision in Geneva or a pay rise in Japan as upon what we decide at Stormont.

Now what astonishes me about this statement is that it is not expressed as a wail of impotent despair, a lament that the art of government had come to an end and that we are all of us now creatures of almost blind chance. But Captain O'Neill said this with what was obviously a certain proud satisfaction. He and, I suppose, most Ulstermen have adapted themselves to this extraordinary world in which what occurs in Tokyo can be as significant to an Ulsterman as what happens in Limavady or Coleraine. They have come to accept it as something perfectly natural and even rather inflating to their local dignity that they should be linked up so closely with this mighty scheme of affairs, that they are tiny specks on an almost infinite horizon. In the time of Wolfe Tone, Belfast was in a constant ferment of intellectual and political excitement. In its ideal it was closer to Philadelphia than to Westminster; it had perhaps a slightly exaggerated view of its importance and some of its admirers even called it the Athens of the North. My point is not that it was at all like Athens but that it wanted to be; today I am sure it does not. The idea of vastness has submerged every national ambition. Ulstermen would be content if the whole of Ireland was the Ballymoney of the Empire or the Cullybackey, the less than Cullybackey of the Universe.

Now this seems to me a disease of the mind which cannot be treated economically or politically. It seems to me related to the fact that for a century or more Belfast, which once teemed with intellectual vitality, has been sterile and indistinguishable from a thousand other British cities. Not a single new idea has come out of it, whereas Dublin in its most rebellious and discontented period fifty years ago was amazingly prolific in genius.

One can think of a dozen names of European distinction and they all derived from the cross-fertilization of Irish and Anglo-Irish, of Catholic and Protestant culture. In the South, this flowering of genius came to an end when the Anglo-Irish Protestants, who accepted Ireland as their native land, gradually disappeared. It is obvious that the two halves of Ireland need each other and that the Ulster rejection of the South has damaged her as much as it has us.

Yet I do not see how it is any good addressing such arguments to the North while this mood of megalomania, which has affected us too, prevails. It should really, though, be called minimomania, for it means seeing ourselves as a tiny dot on a vast panorama of world events, seeing ourselves unable to communicate with our next-door neighbour or influence him except through some great central sorting house, where ideas are collected and redistributed.

While this mood prevails, with us as with them, it's no good offering compromises to the North by which their religious liberties are guaranteed or their loyalties to the British monarch or anything else. We have to rediscover first the pattern of the small world and find that our neighbours really are the people next door and not the wage earners in Japan or some delegates in Geneva. We have to recover some lost arrogance and recognize that we are in fact just as much masters in our own countries as we are masters in our own homes and these remote peoples and conferences need scarcely matter at all. We live in such complex days that it is immensely difficult to prove the obvious. How can one convince Captain O'Neill that the neighbours of the people in Strabane are not the Japanese but the people in Lifford, and that if Newry was on good terms with Dundalk it would not much matter what was thought in Geneva? Perhaps we shall have to be shocked out of these obsessions.

I got a small but helpful shock not long ago. I heard a Belfast man in a pub ask his neighbour, "Who is Parnell?" He was an intelligent-looking man who probably had a television set and had read all about the Profumo case and knew about the riots in Alabama and about the Buddhist priests who had burnt themselves in Vietnam, but he did not know who Parnell was.

In fact he had such broad horizons, the range of his interests was so wide, that his own place in history had become obscure and unimportant to him. He was befogged and benighted like someone trying to find his way home by a map of the world.

None of this of course would matter if we were, with our increased span of knowledge, developing a new race of human being, immune from vulgar prejudice and petty jealousy. But in fact we are just as small as we ever were and our minds are just the same size. But some of the best minds are so stuffed with world affairs as to be almost stupefied, immobilized by the great burden of irrelevance that they have to carry round with them. Naturally there is not room for Parnell or indeed for any Irish history, yet the story of Parnell is still supremely relevant to us. All our traditional squabbles about land and property and divorce and morals and nonconformity and democracy, it is all there to be seen and studied in Irish terms and not in Japanese. We cannot afford to cut ourselves off from our history, or from the people and the ideas and the traditions which shaped it, just because we live north of Carlingford Lough. An Irishman *must* know about Parnell, even if it means knowing rather less about Vietnam and Japanese labour conditions.

That is why many are sceptical about our allegedly broadening horizons. When we see a vast forest of television aerials rising over a city we like to think of enlightenment, a deeper understanding of the great world pouring down on us all from the heavens; but does it? Perhaps sometimes it really does. But you can also think of all these masts as ten thousand hypodermic syringes thrust down into our minds to stupefy us and give us the pleasant illusion of participating in remote horrors, with no responsibility for them, and that this enlarged world about which we are always talking is only a sort of drug addict's hallucination. And that when we wake from it, we shall have lost the power to focus so that we confuse what is real and immediate with what is distant and unimportant. In such a mood we are easily scared by these bogeys from Geneva and Japan.

You may think I have put this rather fancifully, so I'll quote to you the same idea, as it was expressed much better than I have done in Wolfe Tone's day by Lord Charlemont. A great Ulster landlord, he never considered Ulster as anything but an integral and vital part of Ireland. And I don't think the problem of reconciling remote loyalties with near ones was ever stated more clearly than he has done.

Let it not be said that Ireland can be served in England. It never was. It is the nature of man to assimilate himself to those with whom he lives. . . . The Irishman in London, long before he has lost his brogue, loses or casts away all Irish ideas, and from the natural wish to obtain the goodwill of those with whom he associates, becomes in effect a partial Englishman, perhaps more partial than the English themselves. . . . Let us love our fellow-subjects as brethren, but let not the younger brother leave his family to riot with his wealthier elder. . . . Where is the English party that is not more or less hostile to the constitutional and commercial interests of Ireland? But Ireland must be served in Ireland. . . . It is the unnatural son who profusely assists in the luxurious maintenance of a beloved alien at the expense of his mother's jointure.

Reasoning like this—and Charlemont was the most reasonable Irishman of his day—we would argue that the Irish Protestant genius in Ulster as in the South was evaporating in the service of England and that to their cost they are neglecting for the maintenance of "the beloved alien" their duty not only to their Anglo-Irish brothers in the

South but their duty to all their Irish compatriots, Protestant and Catholic.

While I'm convinced that this business of Broad Horizons is what is really drawing the North away from us, there are other grounds for dissent, for instance the British Crown and our religious differences. I don't think the disagreement about the Crown is very deep-seated. Catholic scholars who disapprove of nationalism are perfectly correct in tracing the republican and separatist spirit to Protestant origins and in particular to Ulster. Five out of six of the United Irishmen were Protestants. The Protestant gentry who in 1782 assembled in the church of Dungannon were fully prepared to make the Duke of Leinster King of Ireland if the royal assent had been refused to their demand for an independent legislature. The American revolt was enthusiastically greeted in the North. There were bonfires in Belfast and riots when dragoons tried to cut down the emblems of Washington. On the other hand the leaders of the southern Catholics disapproved and sent an address to the king proclaiming "their abhorrence of the unnatural rebellion" and laying at His Majesty's feet "two millions of loyal, faithful and affectionate hearts and hands . . . zealous in defence of His Majesty's most sacred person and Government."

There is scarcely a Protestant in the South who had not among his forebears a Cromwellian, whose son would gladly have had Charles II decapitated as well as Charles I if any serious effort had been made to restore to the royalists their expropriated lands. And many of them were republicans from principle and not merely from self-interest.

I am saying this not to decry royalism and praise the republic but merely to suggest that North and South there is no ancient and inviolable tradition in favour of one or the other and that to associate the Anglo-Irish with monarchy and the Gaelic-Irish with republicanism is a fantastic misreading of history. If we dropped these hyphens and assumed the common name of Irishman, the question could easily be discussed on its merits.

The religious differences that have divided Ireland are of course more fundamental. Except under Grattan's Parliament and in particular by Tone, little attempt has been made to solve them in the only way they can be solved, that is to say by the common name of Irishman. In those days there was a warmth of generosity based on a sudden realization of neighbourliness and a common home. For a short time it succeeded in thawing the rigid frozen barriers of race and creed that divided the Irish. This did not mean any pretence of common blood nor did it mean that doctrinal differences had lessened. Tone was an extreme Protestant, but as secretary of the Catholic Committee he had urgently pressed for full Catholic emancipation forty years before it was grudgingly conceded. Leaf through his diary and on one page you will find him rejoicing over the calamities that had befallen the Pope through the French Revolution, on the next page he is vigorously defending Catholic liberties against Protestant oppression. He saw the barriers all right but some warm buoyancy of spirit enabled him to leap them.

What is happening today? I can only offer a very superficial and untheological view, but that is the plane on which most of us pass most of our lives, so it is perhaps not irrelevant. The churches are no closer doctrinally than they were in the days of Tone but there is a supposition that new harmony will come from adjustments in dogma and friendly exchanges between ecclesiastics at various conferences in Europe and in America and that this harmony will spread by degrees to distant lands where different religions confront each other, to the frontiers of Catholicism and Orthodoxy in Central Europe, to the frontiers of Protestantism and Catholicism in Ireland. I hope this is so, of course, and that it is not one of these large-scale ecumenical delusions, but I still think that Tone's way is best. The fact is that difference of dogma has never been a great source of friction in itself and the disappearance of these differences may not bring the brotherhood for which we hope.

Ireland was conquered and anglicized at a time when the English and the Irish shared the same faith. The Orthodox-Catholic friction in Eastern Europe derives not from differences of dogma, which are few, but from the old rivalry between the Austro-Hungarian Empire and Tsarist Russia, between warring cultures, in fact. That particular friction still continues and, though it is considered indiscreet to mention this, it has in our day caused immeasurable persecution and slaughter.* On the other hand, as you know, many hundreds of Protestant sects are now at peace with each other without in the least agreeing. They have reached this by conceding to each other the "right of private judgment," or, as it could often be called, the "right to be wrong." This arrangement has worked very well and one of the Founding Fathers of the United States, James Madison, even de-

*See below, pp. 181–88 passim.—ed.

clared that American religious harmony was based on a multiplicity of sects, all of them disagreeing with each other.

The right of private judgment for Irish Catholics as well as for Irish Protestants was vigorously sustained by the Volunteers in a proclamation from Dungannon in 1782. It ran:

> that we hold the right of private judgment in matters of religion to be equally sacred in others as ourselves. Therefore that as men, as Irishmen, as Christians and as Protestants we rejoice in the relaxation of the Penal Laws against our Roman Catholic fellow-subjects and that we conceive the measure to be fraught with the happiest consequences to the union and to the prosperity of the people of Ireland.

There was a difficulty, of course; it was not clear how the centralized and authoritarian Catholic Church could ever reciprocate by conceding to Protestants the right to be wrong. Because of this doubt, Charlemont, the head of the Volunteers, and Henry Flood, both of them good Irishmen and in no way bigoted, withdrew their support of full Catholic emancipation. Their dilemma was surely a real one and it is useless to reproach the Ulstermen with bigotry because fifty years ago they resisted Home Rule on religious grounds and because the same objections were repeated at the time of Partition.

We must find some way of living together, and I think Tone's way, the way of generous inconsistency, is still the best. After all, we all of us respect the two opposing principles of authority and private judgment. Everyone in the world regulates his conduct by both, deferring sometimes to traditional authority, sometimes to his own rebellious sense of fitness, or, as some Protestants say, his inner light. The Catholic Church is held by us in Ireland to be the principal guardian of authority and the churches of the Reformation are held to be the guardians of private judgment. This of course is only a rough approximation to the truth, since many post-Reformation sects, the Mormons, for example, are authoritarian. But it is reasonable to think that social harmony in a united Ireland would be based on an equilibrium of these two opposing forces, an equilibrium which Partition has disastrously disturbed. Opposition is inevitable, since we are all differently constituted and, if the clash of opposites was muffled or arrested, society would come to a standstill like a clock whose pendulum had ceased to swing. We may even come to be grateful for sharp expressions of opposition and only disturbed when, as in totalitarian countries, dissent is dead and every emphatic "Yes!" does not meet its equally emphatic "No!"

If Ulstermen started arguing about these matters again, it would, I believe, be a hopeful sign. It would mean that they were returning from the world of broad horizons, where such disagreements are subordinated to salesmanship, to the small and stable personal world, where we do disagree about important things but the common name of Irishman has power to reconcile us. Let me repeat that broad horizons are all right for Standard Oil or for the export of sewing machines, but for the ordinary man, with limited sensibilities and limited intellectual capacities, they are best avoided. In the long run it means the export of men and women who are much more important than oil. A child could see that the reason why Captain O'Neill feels himself to be imprisoned in Stormont by the Japanese is because, for 150 years, we have been exporting all the brains and all the energy through which these not very difficult problems could be solved.

You will probably think my arguments specious and in fact we will possibly not recoil from broad horizons till we have suffered from them ourselves. We make plenty of jokes about the inefficiency of international bureaucracy but we have not yet seen for ourselves its heartless cruelty.

In 1942 the French Catholic writer François Mauriac saw something at a Paris railway terminus which caused him to say that an era had ended. That dream of progress through enlightenment and science, which men had conceived in the eighteenth century, had collapsed for ever.

What he had seen in Paris was a lot of small boys and girls between the ages of two and fifteen crowded into cattle waggons. He did not know at the time that there were more than four thousand of them and that they were going to be killed and burnt in Poland.* Very few people did really know this, for it was one of those vast impersonal bureaucratic enterprises in which everyone, engine drivers, policemen, typists, civil servants, everyone did his duty and delegated responsibility to someone else and no one felt qualified to intervene. Mauriac did not condemn the French or the Germans or their allies, but the whole modern world of centralized and scientific bureaucracy. And surely he was right.

Remember, for example, that in Nazi-controlled Europe the strongest resistance to those deportations, which have made our century the most barbarous in history, came not from the great imperial

---

*See below, "The Children of Drancy."—ed.

peoples but from some small ones like the Danes and the Bulgarians. They assumed in others the same attachment to their native land which they felt themselves—and they resisted.

So I don't think that Tone is a back number at all, or that his pattern of small-scale loyalties has been superseded by the march of history and the increasing unity of mankind and all the rest. All that is empty newspaper talk. There is nothing sentimental or self-loving about Tone's ideal of "the common Name of Irishman," and it still has potential dynamism. If we think anything else, we have misunderstood Tone, a practical, adventurous, much-travelled man, who sentimentalized nothing and nobody and had no very inflated idea of himself or his country or his countrymen. All the dangerous and sentimental dreams nowadays are international, and imperial and ecumenical. It is because of these dreams that we talk about masses and classes, about inferior and superior races, about the white man's burden and the black man's rights, about cosmic clashes between truth and error. These dreams have caused extraordinary convulsions and are likely to cause more. Tone had no international or ecumenical ideas at all and though he was a revolutionary and a rebel he did not idealize either the "toiling masses" or the Irish race. He was simply an Irishman, at a time when the existence of such a phenomenon was widely disputed.

Tone travelled to Europe and America by means of sails and horses, yet I think he had just as good an understanding of what men are like as we have, who go by jet. *His* was still a very personal world; there was no such thing as a public relations officer, so the son of the bankrupt coach maker from Bodenstown interviewed the heads of governments and the generals of armies. He promoted two invasions of Ireland and accompanied them himself. Perhaps he acted foolishly, but at least he acted for himself and took full responsibility for his actions. He was not like some modern conscript warrior, whose enemies are all chosen for him by some distant authority, and who, because of that, expects to be excused for the crimes which he commits, explaining that he did them under orders in association with 20,000 others.

Has this personal world of Tone gone beyond recall? Are we totally committed to the impersonal world in which we do everything through our representatives and nothing by ourselves? Let us anyway be quite clear what sort of society ours is. It is one of which the Paris episode I related is so typical that it has escaped comment. Possibly we don't talk about these things because men don't talk about maladies which they believe to be incurable. Subconsciously perhaps we think that our world would be better blown up and that is why the great powers are making such strenuous efforts to do so and the small ones are offering such feeble resistance.

But I can't see that the situation is incurable or that the personal world in which we are responsible for our own actions and our neighbour is the man next door has irrevocably gone. Here in Ireland the fabric of this old personal world, though it has been split in half, is still, both sides of the border, fairly sound, and I think we could maintain it.

I think we shall extricate ourselves from the world of broad horizons before we are blown up. The disentangling process will of course be very long, but as other nations, as soon as they realize what is happening, will be engaged in it too, it will be a cooperative undertaking.

I ought to end with a quotation from Tone himself, but he was a warm impulsive man who broke into history simply because the reflective men had failed. I don't think there is an opening yet for impulsive men like him and I'd prefer to quote again from Charlemont, the reflective Ulsterman, whom Tone pushed aside.

Like circles raised in the water by the impulse of a heavy body, our social duties as they expand grow fainter, and lose in efficacy what they gain in extent. . . . The love and service of our country is perhaps the widest circle in which we can hope to display an active benevolence. . . . If every man were to devote his powers to the service of his country, mankind would be universally served.

I don't think this is just a piece of eighteenth-century rhetoric. I am sure it has the universal validity of a geometrical formula. If we assumed the common name of Irishman and acted within the narrow circle of our capacities, there would be no need for campaigning or crusading about the border. North and South we would apply ourselves to a thousand urgent problems, social and material and personal, which since the death of Tone we have been taught to regard as parochial and beneath our dignity and which we have neglected for 150 years. One day we should find that almost without our knowing it the border had gone.

Grandmother and

Wolfe Tone

1962

Brian Inglis, former editor of *The Spectator*, is one of the most articulate of living Anglo-Irishmen. This is not saying much, for that
once-voluble people seems now to be stricken with aphasia. The title
of his book, *West Briton*,* was a name which, in their late prime,
attached itself to the more corrupted of the Anglo-Irish. As their
fortunes declined, they tried to shed it but it had stuck and in the
days of their collapse it was flung as a taunt at the whole community.
Now Mr. Inglis, a sophisticated, guilt-ridden exile, wears it as a sort
of comic hat. His swan song of the West Britons in Malahide† is first-
class. He is amusing, impartial, compassionate, and his book is as
cheering to the remnant that still hangs on in its native land as a nice
cup of Ovaltine to the victim of disseminated sclerosis.

I read *West Briton* on the Barcelona express but was not sure
what was wrong with it till I picked up a discarded French literary
magazine from the seat, and read an article, "Où sont les polémi-
cistes?" The writer complained that paralysis has overtaken us all
because we have made an idol of "objectivity." No educated man
now dares take up a cause till he has mastered 90 percent of the facts
and all the background. "Would Zola ever have defended Dreyfus if
he had been objective? No, he would have waited till he could examine all the files at the French War Office." It seems we cannot

*London 1962.
†A salubrious, prosperous satellite town on the coast north of Dublin, once the heartland
of conservative Anglo-Irishry; a byword in the 1960s for decayed gentility and class-bound,
snobbish Protestant provinciality.—ed.

move without a professional lead, so we wait for an academic to lose his temper. But an academic is ex officio never angry. He is paid to be objective. While he is being scrupulously fair to the Romans and making allowances for the Jews and balancing the claims of law and order against those of charity, the thirty pieces tinkle unnoticed and unneeded in his letter box. Then, this sour Frenchman continues, Professor Iscariot, Ph.D., gives his trifling windfall to the Save the Children Fund and settles down with relish to a fait accompli. Once more he has facts and dates to handle instead of the chaos of unregulated passion through which the rest of us must pick our way by the flickering light of indignation or sympathy.

While reading this engagingly objective book, I listened for the familiar tinkle and heard it once or twice. Inglis does not betray a country or a cause, but has he not sometimes consciously and frankly betrayed himself? Let's leave that till later and begin by repeating that the Malahide story could not have been better done. In that prosperous little Dublin suburb they talked of Fairyhouse and the Fitzwilliam Lawn Tennis Club and Gilbert and Sullivan, and reached for Ireland through George Birmingham and Percy French. They were proud of the width of Carlisle Bridge, the size of Phoenix Park and the world supremacy of Guinness. They disapproved strongly of the Black and Tans. But Grandmother told the children how a despicable gang of cowards and cutthroats had shot policemen in the back and driven away Uncle So-and-so, who had always been so good to his employees. Consequently they cheered madly for the English Army Riders at the Horse Show and jerked the hats off the seditious who did not stand up for "God Save the King." They prided themselves that the word "Dunleary" never crossed their lips and made jokes about "Erse" and "Telefón" and "Aerphort." What dull provincial jokes they were! Surely the Anglo-Irish could have found a place for these sad cinders of a once-blazing enthusiasm in the overflowing ashpit into which whole centuries of their own misdirected idealism had been thrown? For whereas the Irish nationalists had been wrong about most things, the Irish Unionists had been wrong about everything. Had they any option, a defeatist might argue, except to fade away—or become editor of *The Spectator*?

No whisper of self-criticism was ever heard in this tight little society and characteristically it was when he was studying the Irish famine for an Oxford essay prize that Inglis first became aware that Kingstown had been called Dunleary till George IV set foot in it and millions had in fact died and emigrated through English incompetence so gross that recent English historians have had to explain it as the genocidal yearnings of the subconscious mind.

Family loyalty and class loyalty are not so obsessive as we grow older. For an Irish Protestant, national loyalty is a difficult and fragile growth. It may bolt into useless flowers like a summer lettuce or it may germinate hardly at all. Brian Inglis cherished his nationalism, once he had discovered it. His pages on "The Sham Squire" show what a good historian he can be and, though what he says of Galway and the Irish countryside could have been written by any English tourist after a summer holiday (the Little People, Grace O'Malley and so forth), his account of working on *The Irish Times* is unique.

His analysis of the slow social transformation of Malahide is also fascinating. He describes how the West British of the Pale got "mixed" and how it came about that natives slid into the cavities of its decaying golf clubs. Impeccably wellborn Britons, fleeing from the Labour government and unconscious of the gradations of Irish society, had swept into all the social sanctuaries, carrying with them in the backwash of their wealth so many people who were "not our sort" that "we" had become hopelessly contaminated. The rot had set in.

Having apparently vomited up Malahide, Inglis found that he had exchanged a firm loyalty for a wobbly one and that life is full of strain and misunderstanding and frustration for the hybrid, who works in Westmoreland Street and is expected to call it West Moreland Street. (In fact, of course, West Moreland Street is just as ignorant a solecism as Drogheeda or Yoggle!*) If he is a defeatist, he at least earned the right to be one by fighting his battles on Irish soil. I think he is a defeatist, because he once wrote in *The Twentieth Century* that, even if the Anglo-Irish were to vanish from Ireland, it would not greatly matter so long as the important contribution which they made to London journalism was sustained. I do not think he wrote this because he is an important London journalist, but because if he were to justify his retreat to himself, it was comforting to look "objectively" at the handful of old country crocks, retired British servicemen, civil servants and suburban car salesmen in whom the spirit of Anglo-Ireland has its contemporary incarnation, and to assume that it would die with them. With an odd mixture of modesty and arrogance, he is oppressed by the lofty superiority of the dedi-

*Droghedar, pronounced Drawda, and Youghal, pronounced Yawl.

cated romantic heroes of Protestant nationalism, Fitzgerald, Emmet, Parnell, but tries to bring Wolfe Tone, whom he finds the most congenial, "within his reach" by lowering his stature a little. He suggests that Tone's Irish patriotism derived from pique with Pitt for ignoring his scheme for colonizing some Pacific islands, that like Inglis himself he tried to get a job in England, that he drank more Burgundy than was good for him and made a messy, unsuccessful attempt to dodge hanging by cutting his throat. But he misses the whole grandeur of Tone. Tone never allowed himself to be paralyzed by "objectivity" but forged a philosophy for himself out of the confused and conflicting aspirations of his day, out of his own untidy impulses and selfish ambitions, and having forged it, adhered to it and died for it.

Tone would remain great even if it were proved that his ill-success had delayed Catholic emancipation and precipitated the Union. The only extenuation for the feebleness of the Anglo-Irish today is that no strong challenge is ever presented to them. Mr. Inglis' account of his experiences in "the real army," as Grandmother called it, illustrates this. When he was training for the RAF in Rhodesia, he decided that supposing the British invaded Ireland to recover the ports, he would present himself for internment as an untrustworthy alien. But was he really untrustworthy? Would he ever have used his aeroplane to bomb the British out of Spike Island? If he had been interned there would have been so much gentlemanly understanding about it that the distance between Theobald Wolfe Tone and Brian Inglis could be measured only in light-years.

Clearly Inglis accepts in a general way Tone's social philosophy. Tone's political ideals are now largely realized and would inflame nobody; his unorthodox Protestantism is that of most British intellectuals today. Yet in that one direction where Tone's leadership is still needed, Inglis and most of his compatriots hang back as though they were paralyzed. Obviously Tone, who had seen the American Revolution and its consequences, would have been in favour of the absolute separation of church and state, which for the first time brought religious tolerance to America and made the United States possible. Can one doubt that every Protestant revolutionary nationalist who has ever lived, Emmet, Fitzgerald, Davis, Parnell, would have favoured it? In our century, Horace Plunkett and Yeats and the Protestant rebels of 1916 would have agreed that it was the only way to end partition and annihilate bigotry, both Catholic and Protestant.

I think that Inglis believes this too, for he says that "the future relationship of Church and State is sooner or later going to become the most serious issue in Ireland," and he hints at the possibility of future bloodshed if the problem is not solved. And anticipating his own departure from Ireland he says: "What else was there to retain our interest in politics if the subject of the future of Church and State was barred?"

Why should the subject be barred? There appear to be two reasons according to Inglis. Irish Protestants have lost their stamina and no Protestant or Anglo-Irishman, being an outsider, can help solve the church-state relationship: "Irish Catholicism must be left to come to terms with itself." He does not see that the principal evidence that the Irish Protestants have lost their stamina is that they so constantly reiterate this paltry excuse for apathy.

Irish Protestants constitute 25 percent of the population of Ireland, North and South, yet those of the Republic enjoy telling each other and being told either that they have no stamina or that they would "only do harm by interfering." In this way they can free their minds from the unglamorous complications of Ireland and the dreary forms of bloodshed which they foresee. They have an excuse for whatever form of disengagement may be comfortable and for devoting themselves agreeably to what they call "wider issues" in a larger society. But for a small historic community can there be any issue wider than survival and the prevention of bloodshed?

"Outsiders only make things worse by intervening." Chicago gangsters have grown fat on this repulsive old sophistry . . . moral cowardice dressing herself up in a diplomat's bemedalled frock coat. The great Protestant nationalists did and said what they thought to be right and never argued that they could help their friends best by withholding their support from them. Nor did they consider themselves "outsiders."

The argument for nonintervention is ignorant as well as base. Jefferson and the Founding Fathers who introduced the separation of church and state did so in an atmosphere of tense religious rivalry. They could have been called "outsiders," for Jefferson and John Adams, at least, were Unitarians, but if they had left it to the orthodox and the respectable to compose their differences nothing would have happened and America would be a more deeply divided country than Ireland is today.

Nor could a move to separate church and state be called sectarian if the Anglo-Irish supported it, for hundreds of Protestant ecclesiastics, North and South, would oppose it passionately, as did their colleagues in America. Nor would it lead to "irreligion." Of all the great powers the United States has the highest percentage of church-goers.

There are in fact only two forms of escape from the dilemma of the Anglo-Irish who wish to express themselves freely. One is that chosen by Mr. Inglis: "Go to England!" The unpopular alternative still remains: "Go back to Wolfe Tone!"

Mr. Inglis rightly places a great deal of blame for our dilemma on Grandmother, a totem figure beside every Protestant hearth. She would have detested Wolfe Tone, who stabbed the real army in the back and chose a messy, unchristian death. But Inglis takes the wrong way of exorcising her since it ends in disengagement. He follows the will-o'-the-wisp of objectivity, saying: "How could we Irish Protestants blame our fellow countrymen for bigotry? We had taught them how." This argument which appears to lead to unity and brotherly love really leads to London.

Besides, it is false. Grandmother with the real army behind her had, as a Catholic, oppressed the Irish for four centuries; as a Protestant she had oppressed them for only three. When Inglis says that, because of the penal laws, Irish Protestants can never give disinterested advice he is only searching for an excuse for not sticking his neck out. If Tone and Emmet and all the others did not by dying close that chapter, what profit is there in Mr. Inglis' cosy penitence? And where does "objectivity" begin? Where does it stop? The Catholic Church prides itself on its universality so it must be judged by its universal and not by its local activities. Why not say the penal laws started not in Ireland in 1688 but rather in France three years earlier, when after the Revocation of the Edict of Nantes several hundred thousand Lost Sheep were bayoneted back into the Fold? Why not recall that at the Battle of the Boyne William III had eleven hundred Huguenot officers with him, fugitives from a Catholic persecution which unlike the relatively tolerant affair which he instituted was genuinely annihilating? Why not admit that scarcely twenty years ago countless Lost Sheep of Central Europe were driven back into the Fold with a Belsen-model crook and that their sufferings, though briefer, far surpassed those of the Huguenots or the Irish Catholics? Mr. Inglis has seen the reports of their leaders; he knows them to be true, but considers it "injudicious" to publish them.

All these facts prove is that collectively even kind and intelligent men are always ready to put pressure on their neighbours to make them conform, that Catholics and their "separated brethren" still have excellent reasons for fearing each other not as individuals but as organized groups, and that real danger only arises when the state also ranges itself on the side of conformity.

There is only one way out, the way of Jefferson and Tone. In the North the Protestant Parliament for the Protestant people must go, and in the South the separation of church and state must be introduced and adhered to absolutely. Through not recognizing this, Inglis wandered down many strange bypaths before he admitted himself lost. He was a rebel without a cause, since, rejecting all those offered him by the Malahide Golf Club, he could find none in his warm, honest heart. So he window-gazed in Ireland in a discriminating way, but in the late 1940s each exhibit seemed more shop-soiled than the last. Yet Ireland still offers opportunities to the countrymen of Tone. On the way to them there is a rich crop of slights and misunderstandings to be harvested, but it is better to be arrogant like Yeats and to stay than to be deprecating like Inglis and to go. As Yeats knew, Irish independence, like American, was primarily the notion of a small Protestant minority. It is in stark opposition to the imperialist universalism of the English and to the Catholic universalism of the Irish and derives from a handful of unpopular Trinity students and a few Belfast radicals. Similarly, American independence was principally the work of some unorthodox Anglicans from Virginia, some unorthodox nonconformists from Massachusetts and Thomas Paine, a renegade English Quaker. The two groups made contact in revolutionary France and their affinity has often been underlined. When, for example, the American War of Independence broke out, Belfast Protestants lit bonfires and sent congratulations to George Washington while Dublin Catholics sent loyal messages to George III. Ireland might not be the dull, divided little island which it is today if those groups, North and South, to whom the idea of national independence is chiefly due, had played a greater part in its realization.

But the longer Inglis stayed in Ireland, the further he strayed from his hero, Wolfe Tone. One of the causes which he adopted on behalf of the Civil Liberty Association, that of Baillie Stewart, is intelligible only as a hysterical comeback at dead, defeated Grandmother. When Irish liberals campaign on behalf of the illiberal and secure an Irish passport for Artukovitch (as Foreign Minister he introduced gas chambers into Yugoslavia) and country refuges for Skorzeny and sympathy for Lord Haw-Haw and Amery and Baillie Stewart (Inglis thinks that all these three were badly treated), they have started to sell their freedom and it will not be long now before Grandmother is called back from the shades and, heavily shrouded by NATO or the Common Market, once more takes things in hand.

Fortunately for Inglis, deliverance from all this came in the shape of the managing director of Associated Newspapers, who enabled him to transfer from a good Irish newspaper, *The Irish Times*, to a bad English one, *The Sketch*. *The Sketch* was a low rung on a lofty ladder, which led to a distinguished editorial chair and to the view that the Anglo-Irish, except for export purposes, are as good as dead.

The last words but six in this sad and honest book are "an assured monthly cheque." They are deliberately ironical.

New Geneva in Waterford

1947

The little fishing village of Passage lies on the west bank of the Suir, between Dunmore East and Waterford. It still retains a rather special air of antiquity and distinction, but I do not think that many of those who live around it realize how near it once was to becoming the centre of a large and flourishing city with academies of sciences and the arts and many thriving industries. The city was a dream of the late eighteenth century, but a dream that came very near to realization. In Ireland itself very little if anything has been written upon this project, but here in Geneva, the mother city of this future town, I have found much of interest in the archives of the Hôtel de Ville, where the records of the city council and many documents relating to its history are scrupulously preserved. There are minutes and letters and biographies; there is even a plan of the New Geneva on the Suir.

Why was the plan conceived, why did it fail? I will try to compress into a few paragraphs a complicated story which is woven out of the troubled history of two small states.

In the last decade but one of the eighteenth century the city of Geneva was in ferment. It had a conservative aristocracy and also a prosperous and ambitious middle class which had been deeply affected by the liberal ideas of the time. Rousseau himself had been a citizen of Geneva, and Voltaire at Ferney had lived only a few miles away. Geneva was a hotbed of humanitarian thinking, very disquieting to its rulers and also to its neighbours in the kingdoms of France and Savoy. In 1768, at a time of similar commotion in Geneva, Rousseau had given the following advice:

There is a last course left for you to take. Instead of staining your hands with the blood of your compatriots, you can abandon these walls, which should have been the refuge of liberty and now are to become the resort of tyrants. All, all together, in the broad daylight, you may leave the town, your wives and your children in your midst, and, since men must wear chains, you can go and wear the chains of a great Prince, rather than the hateful and unbearable yoke of your equals.

In 1782 the troubles culminated in a small but bloodless revolution: the middle-class *représentants* overthrew and imprisoned the aristocratic council. But in a very short time the council was restored to power by a joint invasion of the armies of France, Savoy and the canton of Berne. The disciples of Rousseau and the advocates of democratic ideas were thrown into despair . . . they decided that the only hope for their afflicted city was for the democrats to emigrate in a body bearing with them the crafts and craftsmen, chief among whom were the watchmakers. On them the prosperity of Geneva was based.

In those days, in so many ways wiser than ours, refugees were welcomed, and invitations to the Genevan rebels came from many of the princes of Europe, from the Grand Duke of Tuscany, and the Elector Palatine, from the Landgrave of Hesse-Homburg, and finally, through the medium of an English republican and great friend of Geneva, Lord Mahon, from George III of England. I believe it was the Genevans themselves who pressed that their colony should be in Ireland rather than in England. In England they feared the jealousy of the English watchmakers, also the competitive claims on English sympathies of the loyalist refugees from the War of Independence in America. Moreover, Ireland was at that time also entering a period of generous idealism and enthusiasm. It was the year of the Convention of Dungannon, when the Volunteer Army was formed which extorted from England those concessions which made Grattan's Parliament possible. On 3 October the Dublin Volunteers (commanded by Lieutenant General Henry Grattan) assembled at the Royal Exchange and passed resolutions to the effect that

Irishmen armed for the defence of their constitution and liberties ought naturally to be attached to every country or body of men, armed for the defence of a like glorious cause . . . Therefore, the virtuous Genevese had the most lively claim on their pity . . . and should be received among them as brothers and friends.

The Duke of Leinster, the commander of the Southern Branch of the Volunteers, himself offered two thousand acres to the Genevans, and accommodation for one hundred in Leinster Lodge till their houses had been built. Lord Ely, offering them land in Wexford, explained that he was quite disintererested.

I am already extremely rich . . . I wish to benefit the most enlightened people in the universe, the first Protestant colony on earth. When I am called to leave this earth, I shall repose with the serenity worthy of a man who knows that in giving happiness to you, he has reared a monument more durable than marble and shaped by the most able artist.

The newspapers of the time and the speeches of the Volunteers were filled with eulogies of the "virtuous Genevese" who had "stood up like Catos against Tyrants." Some of them were given honorary rank in the Volunteer regiments. However, it was not the Duke of Leinster's land near Athy which was ultimately chosen, but some confiscated property near Waterford Harbour which belonged to the British government. Lord Temple, the Viceroy, favoured the project, and a grant of £50,000 as well as 11,000 acres, including the town of Passage, was decreed. From this sum the transport of the citizens' families from Geneva was to be paid and the building of the town was to be started.

There is no need to question the sincerity of the Volunteers, but on the generous motives of the British government Swiss writers have cast a doubt. The county of Waterford was at that time disturbed by the activities of the White Boys (*les enfants blancs*), and the sinister John Beresford, one of the architects of the Union, was not only a large landowner in the district but also a member of the commission of the Genevan settlement. Lord Temple himself, in a letter to a friend, explains why a southern rather than a northern site was chosen. "I wished to remove them from the Northern Republicans and to place them where they might make an essential reform in the religion, industry and manners of the south." The Genevans interpreted their role differently. "We must not overlook the need to conciliate the poor, who cultivate the soil that is offered to us," wrote Clavière, one of the Genevan commissioners.

The greed and harshness of the great landowners have made the tenants violent and irritable. That is the reason for the disorders of which you have heard. They are in revolt against treachery and abominable outrage. If we behave well we shall gain their confidence.

A group of Genevans arrived in Ireland and rapid progress was made. An engineer visited the site and made plans for a water supply and a cotton factory and a laundry. At the start there were to be fifty houses, a communal bakery and an inn; there were to be a tannery and a paper factory. There was to be a big square in which was to stand a university which it was hoped would attract, like the Academy of Sciences at Geneva, scholars from all over Europe. It was to have forty-four professors and assistants and to cost £4,554 per annum. In the plan of the settlement, a dotted line runs from Passage to the base of the Creden Head, including nearly a thousand acres of tidal land described as *"sables à conquérir sur la mer."* Today the tide still sweeps in as it has always done, across the great curve of Woodstown Strand, but Swiss engineers were celebrated even then and it is possible that their ambitious project would have been realized.

One of the Genevan members of the commission, Ami Melly, went back to rally the refugees who were assembled at Neuchâtel and to summon the disaffected watchmakers to emigrate. Four of the principal watchmakers employed two thousand workmen, and their displacement would naturally be a serious blow to the city. Melly had taken the precaution of securing Irish citizenship, but even so he was clapped into gaol by the rulers of Geneva. He was tried, and despite the protests of the British government and the personal support of two Irishmen—James Butler, Lord Cahir, and another—he was sentenced to a long term of imprisonment. However, he escaped on a rope of knotted sheets and rejoined the refugees at Neuchâtel. The warder who looked after Melly was arrested. It is characteristic of Swiss scrupulousness and attention to detail that he was punished not only for conniving at Melly's escape but also for stealing two of his shirts.

There is a long poem of the period dealing with the escape and describing how Melly was led out of prison by an angel. Though there was a "Nouvelle Genève" printing press at Waterford, which published some French poems, I think this one is more likely to have been printed at Neuchâtel than in Ireland. The poet, not a very good one, exhorts the Genevan craftsmen and scholars to follow Melly to Waterford.

> Pour vous, pour vos enfants une ville s'élève,
> Déjà l'on voit bâtir la Nouvelle Genève!
> C'est là que le bonheur, que la prosperité

Vous attendent sans doute avec la liberté,
Aux bords da Suir en Cook, Dublin vous favorise.
Par differens moyens Georges vous est propice.

Readers will be puzzled to know what Cook had to do with it till it is recalled that the old Templars' Castle of Crook was included in the land granted to the Genevans.

Melly had had a discouraging reception from the watchmakers. They were beginning to get used to the new regime, and to dread the hazards of the journey to Ireland. The outlook for New Geneva was not so promising. All the same, in July 1784 Mr. Cuffe, an Irish enthusiast, laid the foundation stone of the projected city. On it was a bronze plaque inscribed with the date and the reason for the settlement. In a large tent over the spot where a statue of Lord Temple was to be erected, a fete was given to the burgesses of Waterford.

Six weeks later both the government and the Genevan representatives had decided to abandon the plan—New Geneva never came into being. A few Genevan settlers remained in Waterford, but the majority scattered over Europe waiting for better times to return to their city. The watchmakers never stirred.

Why did the plan collapse? The Genevans attributed it to a change of Viceroy and government policy. The serious Lord Temple had sponsored the scheme but "the virtuous Genevese" were not to the liking of the gay Duke of Rutland. Moreover, George III began to distrust the Genevan rebels. The aristocratic party at Geneva had a capable representative in London, M. Saladin, a connection by marriage of an English earl. He managed to persuade the government that Melly, though he might be an Irish citizen, had a wife and family in Geneva as well as a house and shop. His attempt to cause a widespread emigration of wealth and skill from his native town could not be overlooked. George III, recovering from his momentary sympathy with the Genevan rebels, for which Charles James Fox had been principally responsible, exchanged courtly compliments in royal Latin with their oppressors: "*Pacem tandem recuperavisse,*" he wrote, "*atque sublata anarchia vestram administrationem stabilivise lubenter intelleximus.*" And he signed himself "*Vester bonus amicus, Georgius R.*"

Louis XVI's agents were working hard to frustrate the emigration. As for the local magnates of Waterford, they found that the Genevans were expecting a far more liberal system of franchise than was current in Ireland. In a very short time, if it was granted, the safe seats of the landlords would be in peril. To others it appeared unwise to establish a body of foreign republicans at the mouth of the Waterford river right opposite Duncannon Fort. Could they be relied on in the event of invasion?

To add to their difficulties, the idealistic leaders in Neuchâtel and in Ireland were beginning to quarrel among themselves, and the Genevan merchants were less and less inclined to give up their comfortable homes and businesses and venture into the unknown. Some time before they had all reopened their shops. Jean Gosse, the bookseller, had written to his son, who was a refugee dreaming of Ireland: "The troops whose drumming I could not endure do not now seem such devils after all." Another of the *représentants*, Etienne Dumont, whose name is still borne by one of the streets in old Geneva, wrote: *"Il faudrait pour ranimer notre zèle quelques nouvelles décisions sur notre chère Irlande."* Worse than all this, a solicitor, Richards, came back from Ireland to Geneva "cruelly deceived in his hopes" and begging for bread for his seven children.

Pensions and jobs were found for some of the disappointed refugees. Of the leaders, several were later to make a considerable mark in history, and it cannot be too much emphasized that they represented the real intellectual elite of Geneva. Their boast that they could transfer the intellectual life of Geneva to Ireland was not an idle one. H. A. Gosse, one of those interested, was the founder of the Academy of Natural Sciences, and his bust now stands outside Geneva University. Etienne Dumont played a prominent part in French politics before the Revolution, and assisted Mirabeau with his speeches. Clavière, whose words I have quoted, became a Girondin leader and took his life to avoid the guillotine. D'Ivernois, the leader of the emigration, later succeeded in interesting Jefferson in the project of transferring the Genevan Academy to the United States. Here, too, he failed, but he was later, as Sir Francis d'Ivernois, to play a significant part in British diplomacy.

Ami Melly was the leader of the watchmaking as opposed to the intellectual branch of the emigration. When Ireland failed him, he obtained the consent of the liberal Emperor Joseph II to set up a colony of Genevan watchmakers in the city of Constance. The interesting story of this refugee settlement is told in M. Chapuisat's *Figures et choses d'autrefois* (1920). Du Roveray, Gasc, Ringler are well-known names in Genevan history, which are also associated with the emigration to Waterford. There is a list of the emigrants in the archives of the Château de Crans, near Geneva, the home of the Saladin family, but it is not at present accessible.

Other books and papers in which the emigration is discussed

are: *Sir Francis d'Ivernois* by O. Kamin; *Henri-Albert Gosse* by M'lle. Plan; *La Prise d'Armes de 1782* by E. Chapuisat; *Lettres de Jean Roget à Samuel Romily* (1911); and Rivoire, 2530: *Pièces relatives à l'asyle offerte aux Genevois en Irlande.*

For many years blocks of stone lay about on the abandoned site. It was proposed to colonize it with American loyalists. Finally, the New Geneva, which was to have been an example to Ireland of the triumph of freedom and democracy, became a prison for Irish patriots.

New Geneva may have dropped out of Irish history, but its name is familiar to all in the old song "The Croppy Boy."

However mixed may have been the motives of the British and Irish governments in encouraging the Genevan colony, it is hard not to regret its failure. The new city was to lie on the very edge of Co. Wexford, where sixteen years later, in 1798, Irish rebels were to fight a last desperate battle. Those sober and thrifty disciples of Rousseau and champions of liberty would surely have exercised a moderating influence on the fierce passion aroused by the struggle. In all their dealings they spoke and wrote with friendliness and understanding of the Irish people among whom they were to settle.

In telling this story I have used only such material as I have found in the archives at Geneva, and also the work of an eighteenth-century German traveller, Kütter, *Briefe über Irland*, in the National Library, Dublin. A closer investigation of Irish sources would certainly throw fresh light on the sad catastrophe that befell the New Geneva.

Down the Parade

1950

The other day I saw an advertisement in one of our Kilkenny papers about a new building site in the castle gardens. Any of you who have been to Kilkenny will remember the broad avenue, the Parade, shaded with lime trees, that leads into the town from the Thomastown road. There are benches at intervals under the trees, stone drinking troughs and fine cut-stone archways; in the morning this is where nursemaids wheel their prams, and in the evening lovers walk here. The castle gardens lie behind the wall upon the west side, and when I read the advertisement, I instantly began to wonder whether the wall would have to come down and what about the lovely lime trees? I am an amateur archaeologist, and we're a conservative unpractical lot. The prospect filled me with horror. Yet there must surely be some very sound reason why this beauty must be defiled while the centre of Kilkenny has various derelict sites covered with nothing but nettles and tin cans. No doubt I am prejudiced. I was born to the southeast of Kilkenny city, and so it has always seemed to me that the Parade, with its lime trees and quiet spaciousness, was an elegant front door to the town. It would be unbecoming to turn it into a waste of villas like the roads to Castlecomer and Freshford—like the exits of a thousand other Irish towns.

I feel more than a shadow of uneasiness. When you destroy a landmark which no longer serves a useful purpose, are you, like a wise surgeon, removing an appendix, a useless organ which nobody needs? Possibly, but I haven't often heard of this being done till it was threatening trouble. Just the opposite—I have heard of a patient who successfully sued his doctor for removing it without permission in the course of another operation. Apparently the patient liked his appendix; he'd had it since he was a baby and it had never done him any harm. He got heavy damages. Yes, if I wanted to show our town to a stranger I would consider the Parade the front door even if I lived in Freshford instead of Bennettsbridge. It may be an anachronism like an appendix but it has most certainly never done anybody any harm.

Only the other day I found out for the first time how the Parade got its name. The second Duke of Ormonde as a young man had a fancy for exercising his troops there. He was a problem child, and his grandfather, the great Duke, who was devoted to him, used to indulge any whim that was not actually harmful.* Parading soldiers up and down was one of them. The great Duke spent much of his time in exile in France because of his loyalty to Charles I, and, when he returned and became Viceroy of Ireland, he brought various Frenchified notions home to Kilkenny. He put conical caps and ducal crowns like those he had seen in the châteaux of France on the rough mediaeval bastions of the castle. The entrance to the town from Bennettsbridge had been smashed about by Cromwell. He repaired the damage as best he could by judicious tree planting and landscape gardening. Somewhere behind the walls and the lime trees, where now there is nothing but shaggy grass or old apple trees, there was once a splendid summer house. It contained a banqueting hall with a sky-blue ceiling on which angels floated, and attached to it was a most startling innovation: a contemporary visitor describes it as "an engine of curious device, which with the help of one horse supplied the house with the watery element." The watery element finished up in style—after shooting out of a fountain of the famous black Kilkenny marble it broke in spray over a ducal crown!

But these are not really the days which the Parade evokes for me. It was during the Napoleonic Wars that I think the Parade really came into its own. At that time Kilkenny had its brilliant theatrical season, once and sometimes twice in a year, and fashionable visitors from all over the British Isles sauntered up and down, under the lime trees, greeting their friends to the strains of a military band which was playing under the castle walls. I picture them slipping out in twos and threes in the summer evening during the intervals from the theatre, that square Georgian building opposite the castle. I hate to tell you, but it is now the income tax office. These phantom figures

*On the first Duke of Ormonde, see above, p. 70.

have programmes in their hands—I saw a programme the other day and a very charming little pink sheet it was and beautifully printed—standing in groups they seem to discuss the acting or they stroll about showing off their fine dresses. It was not a democratic age, and I see a crowd of ragged, hungry beggars crowding round to gape at the beauties and the beaux and to make racy comments in Irish. There are linkboys shouting and sedan chairs jostling. The only shadow on this merrymaking is cast by a curious evangelical body called the New Light Group who strongly disapprove of playacting and sinful gaieties. They do their best to be spoilsports but the mass of the crowd is not hostile. For Richard Power, the patron and creator of the Kilkenny amateur theatre, is known to be a friend of the poor as well as of the arts. It is his genius that has brought all these wealthy people to Kilkenny, and for close on a generation kindled the love of poetry and drama in the most unlikely breasts. For a few weeks every year the Kilkenny tradesmen line their pockets by day and by night crowd in to hear the plays of Shakespeare and Sheridan and Goldsmith and scores of lesser-known dramatists. Those too poor to get in content themselves with the thought that every penny earned by the players will be spent on the relief of poverty. In some years more than a thousand pounds, a vast sum in those days, was distributed in this way.

The Kilkenny Theatre is now scarcely recognizable; its roof has been lowered and the stage and auditorium divided up into small dens for the tax collectors. I saw at a local auction the architect's plan of the theatre, which was surprisingly elaborate and handsome in design. There was also a souvenir fan of the period with a picture on it of the great O'Neill in all her charms. She was the famous Drury Lane actress who was persuaded on several occasions to leave her London triumphs and act in Kilkenny for charity with amateurs. It must have been one of the players, Sir William Becher, who persuaded her, for in the end he induced her to marry him. Becher not only acted but, like the other local gentry, entertained on a magnificent scale during those weeks; so that it came to be said by the mothers of marriageable daughters that Kilkenny was next best to Bath as a venue for suitors. Once Becher gave a ball in the Club House, which is now a nice, comfortable old-fashioned hotel. He pulled down the wall of the adjoining building to enlarge his dancing floor—those were the days! There were routs at the castle and in the Assembly Rooms, at the Tighes, of Woodstock and at the Wandefords' of Castlecomer House. According to the season there were meets of the Kilkenny Hounds and river picnics on the Nore. There was a prologue at the beginning of every season, written and recited by one of the players. One or two of them we owe to Tom Moore, who also came often to Kilkenny and indeed found his wife, Bessy, there. He saw her, I believe, one day through the windows of Rice's Hotel in Patrick Street, where he was staying, and lost his heart to her for ever. The Bryans of Jenkinstown were patrons of the plays and it was while he was visiting them in the late autumn that he saw the last rose of summer blooming alone in the Jenkinstown garden. When a few years ago the Land Commission took over Jenkinstown, its former owner made cuttings from the rose bush and so the descendants of this celebrated plant still bloom in Kilkenny gardens.

I could go on gossiping like this, but I think it will be best if I let the players speak for themselves. Did they act well? I wonder. I don't know. The Kilkenny papers said they were the marvels of the age. On the other hand Charles Kendall Bushe said that he admired the prompter more than all the others. "Because," he said, "I declare to you, I heard the most and saw the least of him." But Bushe was the father of one of the players and likely to be disrespectful. I think that four of the players, at least, were of outstanding capacity and would have made their mark upon any stage. The verse of the prologues is unpretentious but it has vigour and charm. The players were not afraid of blowing their own trumpets. Here is how, one of them, Sir Robert Langrishe, spoke of the plays:

> The capital once elegant and gay
> Now own our revels of superior sway.
> Each vapid man of fashion in the streets
> Thus coldly greets the brother fop he meets.
> What? Still in town? They tell me nowadays
> That we must go to those Kilkenny plays.
> The Colonel's gone. Tomorrow I leave town.
> Come and I'll draw you in the dog-cart down.
> There will be room enough for you, you'll find.
> For I shall leave the pointers all behind.

Most of the players belonged, like Charles Kendall Bushe, to families that had vigorously opposed the Union, which they saw would bring about the destruction of Anglo-Irish culture and shift the focus of social and cultural life from Ireland to London. They tried in Kilkenny to make a rallying point for native talent and enthusiasm and to resist the overpowering pull of England. Here is how young Bushe chastised some of those who went to England to better themselves:

> But some I miss who say that little worth
> Attend these sports, for they're of Irish birth.
> Can Mrs. Coolan in these ranks be found,
> Once known by Coghlan's more Hibernian sound?
> For twice ten years in Clonakilty known,
> She spent last season full six weeks in town.
> Returned to Admiring friends I heard her say,
> Readin the peepers while she tests her tay.
> "Kilkinny plays, O what a name I hear!
> How harsh, how barbare to a travelled ear.
> Things low like these with me are ne'er in vogue,
> Who cant unfortoonate endeuer the brogue"!
> And then with conscious simper wonders tells,
> O' th Lord Mayor's Balls, Vauxhall and Sadlers Wells.
> Her brother too not here? but he is undone.
> Alas he made a grand debut in London.
> Arrayd in recent spoils observe the booby!
> Allan for coats he owes, for half-boot, Hoby.
> And still with frequent eye he looks behind,
> Lest some rude Tipstaff bring the debt to mind.
> In proud preeminence behold him strut
> Raised to a peer's buffoon or witling's butt.
> What triumphs does St. James lounge afford.
> He walks with and is laughed at by a Lord.
> But sad misfortune should he chance to meet,
> Some good old friend, some kinsman in the street.

And the following year there was a cut at the snobs who found Ireland unfashionable:

> Lord! the wild Irish, they in hosts come down,
> And leave their native bogs to take the town.
> Oh! What a bore and yet they're right, believe it,
> To quit that country who have means to leave it.
> Where e'r he turns, contending cares invade,
> Ashamed to own them and to cut afraid.
> Perplexed, his secret hand behind bestowd,
> His half averted gives the unwilling nod,

Thro meanness thus at fashion makes the attempt,
And most contemptible to shun contempt.

Kilfane House, where Richard Power lived, and Kilmurry House, the home of the Bushes, still stand near Thomastown. In Kilfane, preserved by the loving care of its owner, the spirit of the Kilkenny Players still lingers, in the beautiful but lonely park, in the long library where the Kilkenny prompt books, with Power's annotations in the margins, still line the bookshelves. In the dining room there is his portrait in the role of Hamlet, a tall, dark, sad man. Beside him is Creevy, the diarist, who stayed at Kilfane and admired the unusual combination which prevailed there—the love of art and the love of sport. Over the mantelpiece is Sir John Power, Richard's brother, who started the Kilkenny Hounds. The Hounds have survived till today, though the Kilkenny Players with whom they were so closely associated lasted only twenty years.

The last years were the most festive. William Lamb, the future Lord Melbourne, Queen Victoria's first Prime Minister, came with his wife, Lady Caroline, in a last attempt to cure her by a trip to Ireland of her infatuation for Lord Byron. Grattan and Moore, of course, were habitués and Maria Edgeworth and father, as well as the members of the Vice-Regal court. I believe that Maria brought Sir Walter Scott on one occasion.

The theatre closed in 1819 and it was more than the plays that ended. One of the Kilkenny gentry, writing to the papers long afterwards, said it was the last time they had acted as a group on behalf of their country and felt themselves first and foremost as Irishmen. Whatever they did after that, good or bad, they did as isolated individuals.

The castle today is a derelict place. At the end of the war the army, which was garrisoned there, quitted it, and now it stands in the Parade, a huge, empty, patient-looking colossus. What has the future in store for it? Some think that, if its owner agreed, it should become a museum of Norman Ireland, as it was for so many centuries the centre of Anglo-Norman civilization in the southeast. In Kilkenny we pride ourselves on our interest in history, the town once possessed the first and finest of our provincial museums, and today it still has a flourishing Archaeological Society. We could make there an inspiring historical record of the growth of the Irish nation and the fusion of all the different racial strains that make up the Irish people. In Kilkenny you are always very conscious of this mixture. In the Ormonde Deeds, which were housed in the castle, you will find a record of the great Catholic families, Norman and English, whom Cromwell dispossessed and turned adrift. Many, perhaps most of them, crept back after a time from their exile in Connaught or Leix. Often they wore under their shirts the title deeds of their lost estates and were looked after tenderly by their former tenants. Sometimes they took to the hills and waged war on the Cromwellian settlers who occupied their lands. They were called Tories, and it must have been from one of these returned exiles that the Tory Hill gets its name—that small hill which rises behind Mullinavat on the east of the Waterford road and seems twice the size because of the flatness of the surrounding countryside. The blood and names of these evicted Anglo-Normans are still widely diffused through the country—Purcell, Shortall, Comerford, Cody and Tobin and the rest of them.

In the 1940s the Ormonde Deeds were moved to Dublin. We were sad about this but undoubtedly they are safer and more accessible to students in the National Museum. But I would like to think that we could one day get photostats of these incredible documents back in Kilkenny. There were drawers full of manuscripts in Latin and Norman French. Below them dangled the wax seals of Plantagenet Kings, Lord Deputies and Justiciars. Parchment is very tough, and many of them look as bright and clean as when they were written in exquisite spidery calligraphy.

But talking about calligraphy, there was hardly anything in the castle muniment room to equal the diaries of the Ladies of Llangollen. It was a very small book in handwriting so minute that a magnifying glass is necessary to read it with any comfort. Eleanor Butler and Sara Ponsonby were two old ladies who had spent their childhood at the castle and at Inistioge. They had been very unhappy and at last had made a plot to escape together from their families. They lived for the rest of their lives in a cottage in Wales, at Llangollen, on the coach route between London and Holyhead, and distinguished travellers seem invariably to have stopped on the way to enjoy the hospitality of these learned and in those days startlingly unconventional friends.

Opposite the castle a row of small, demure Georgian houses stretches from the castle stables to the Bank of Ireland. By degrees, like their fellows in Dublin, they are being turned into offices. Once upon a time they were cosy family residences and Kilkenny, like other county towns of Ireland, had a gay and sociable winter season. In the *Diaries of Dorothea Herbert* you can read how lively life might be in a small county town, in her case Cashel and Carrick on Suir, and I think that it is possible that still in old houses, in solicitors' and newspaper offices, records of this vanished life exist. But every year nowadays we have to live in a more cramped and impermanent way. Very few families stay in the same place for long or can afford to keep old papers that are not of immediate interest. There is no room for ancient trunks and unvisited attics, and we cover up our traces far more quickly than our ancestors did. There should be county archives and museums, public repositories, in every county to replace all those private storehouses that have had to be abandoned. Without them we are developing as crude and simple an outlook as if we had been born in a trading post in the Prairies and all the lessons of history are lost on us. We are often baffled nowadays by problems that are as old as the hills and we cannot profit by the mistakes and successes of those who went before us.

That is why it is sad when a landmark that is unique and traditional and our very own disappears. Even when it has to go we should mourn it a bit, because it reminded us of the continuity of history. It made us aware that the strange days through which we are passing are no stranger than those which our ancestors lived through. In every small forgotten town in Ireland there have, many times, been upheavals and excitements as startling as any we have experienced.

Three Friends

There is still every year a commemorative service and a dinner in Dublin for Eoin O'Mahony. He was known to everyone from his school days onward as "the Pope," but why this was so no one knew. He was a great Irishman whose greatness lay in a field that he had made peculiarly his own.

When he died in 1970 I wrote an appreciation of him in *The Irish Times* and, as he is still remembered, I will repeat it here. I had a special reason for admiring him which I did not express at the time. He had seen in the extended family a blueprint for what life might one day be like. Perhaps some generations or centuries from now groups of people, linked together maybe as kinsmen, maybe as neighbours, will feel a special responsibility for each other, based on a closer knowledge and affection than is possible in our faceless and centralized society.

In forming the O'Mahony Society, Eoin was following an ancient pattern. The O'Mahonys had been a closely knit Irish clan, which history had dispersed. In contrast the Butlers were merely a group of families, sometimes closely, sometimes remotely, sometimes not at all related. Yet when the Butler Society was formed we discovered for ourselves French and German cousins, and there were intermarriages. We had the advantage of the O'Mahonys in the abundance of our historic records, which reach back to the first coming of the Normans. The Butler Society started when the sixth Marquess of Ormonde gave Kilkenny Castle to the Irish nation, the O'Mahony Society much earlier. Yet despite all their differences the two societies developed along parallel lines. We felt we were exploring the past in order to illuminate the future. Eoin wanted to restore richness and variety and friendship to lives that our civilization has sterilized and, within the compass of one man's powers, he succeeded.

Eoin never had any great triumphs or disasters and yet he liked pomp and ceremony and relished life's vicissitudes. But he kept his celebrations small and personal and on a do-it-yourself scale, and he used pomp and ceremony not to magnify the great but to make ordinary people interesting. If one went to one of his gatherings or one of those dead parties which he brought to life by attending, nobody was a spectator, everyone was a participant. Nobody came away feeling he had surrendered to mass banality, as can happen at those public functions where everything proceeds smoothly towards a well-regulated climax. At any event that Eoin organized, the Organization Man, whom American sociologists rightly regarded as the Satan of the 1960s, was sure to be routed ignominiously, and the Natural Man would take over. Eoin had such faith in him that he could make the sketchiest of plans, change them at the last moment and sweep on, not to the anticipated conclusion, but to an even better one.

I only attended one O'Mahony rally, but it had a wild spontaneity, a happy, confident chaos that must have had years of practice, megatons of spiritual buoyancy, behind it. Only a great artist in social intercourse could have brought it off.

Eoin had issued hundreds of gold-embossed invitations to the O'Mahony rally at Dunmanus Castle in the name of the Vicomte and Vicomtesse de O'Mahony, a nice young barrister and his wife, who live at Orléans. The Vicomte was the elected chieftain of the clan, and probably owed his election to Eoin, who did not bother to tell him about the invitations.

A shower of them fell on Fleet Street and a reporter from the *Daily Express*, attracted by the idea of an invitation from a vicomtesse to dance in an ancient castle on a remote promontory in West Cork (he swore that the word "Dancing" was written in the left-hand bottom corner), had packed his white tie and tails and, taking a day off his holidays and a ticket to Cork, had arrived at Dunmanus at the same time as ourselves. An English family with a tent and a caravan were encamped within the castle ruins and had just before been astounded by the arrival of an advance detachment of clansmen, bearing on long staves the banners of the O'Mahonys and of all the nations that had given them refuge in the days of their exile.

They planted their flags all around the caravan, and very soon a thousand other O'Mahonys followed them and the small alien encampment, amazed but entertained, had been politely and totally submerged. Soon Eoin was in the thick of it all, booming eloquently in three languages, kissing continental hands, explaining and introducing. The O'Mahony rank and file and their friends were then planted on one side of a broken-down moat and the Vicomte stood on the other with Eoin beside him to interpret.

"I have to apologize," began the Vicomte in high good humour and in French, "that this is not my castle, and that it has not any roof, and that we are not able to dance in it, and that it wasn't I who sent out that invitation." Eoin translated all this jovially, and then we quickly passed on to serious matters, the long history of the O'Mahonys of Carbery and Kinelmeaky, their kinship and rivalries with the O'Sullivans and MacCarthys. Only the journalist sulked. When there was a pause in the narrative, he went up to Eoin and said, "I understood there was to be a dance."

"Well," said Eoin, "there's an excellent hotel in Skibbereen. Very nice people indeed, and, if you tell them you want to dance, I am sure they'll be delighted." Eoin was then swept away by his kinsmen, and the journalist went and sulked on a lump of fallen masonry. He grumbled to some bystanders that he had been brought to West Cork on false pretences, that this was his holiday, not a job. But soon he observed that the O'Mahonys were entertained rather than touched by his misadventure. They were pointing him out to each other— "Do you see that fella? Did you hear what he has in his suitcase?"— and he saw that he was becoming a stock character in a new version of a traditional Irish story, the innocent Englishman who had never heard of Pope O'Mahony.

So he moved off to Skibbereen and, drinking himself into a good humour in the hotel, wrote a charming account of the rally for the London daily.

That was a typical O'Mahony occasion. It was an everyday setting, the ruined castle, the rocky shore, the drifts of bog asphodel, the gorse, the pools of water lilies white as well as orange. And there were everyday people there. There were solicitors from Cork and a garage proprietor from Killarney and hospital nurses and a camp counsellor from Massachusetts. More notable was Rev. Jeremiah O'Mahony from Palm Beach, who was President Kennedy's chaplain and pronounced his name O'Mahóney. The most surprising clansman from America was coal-black. Or could he have been, like myself, a mere O'Mahonyphile?

Without the magic of Pope O'Mahony to fuse us and transmute us, it would have been the dullest of seaside outings. But like a watchful cook stirring the jam, Eoin was introducing them all to each other the whole time. He could glamorize even the dullest. This one's aunt had swum the Channel, that one's brother had been in the San Francisco earthquake or as a girl she had known Fanny Parnell. Sometimes a stray sentence expanded into an immense anecdote, breeding other anecdotes, startling and complex but never malicious. If one of them were to end sadly like "Then the poor fellow took to drink and fell down a lift shaft in Las Vegas," it was like a wreath laid on a tomb. To be remembered by Eoin was to be honoured.

His great genius was to use the splendid in the service of the simple. Once I made myself hugely unpopular by flouting received opinion and became a local pariah. My friends rallied to me, but Eoin's support was the warmest and characteristic of him. He packed a shirt the next day (I think it was a shirt, not pyjamas, in that small, odd brown paper parcel), bussed to Naas, and hitchhiked the rest of the way. He came out from Kilkenny on a creamery lorry, whose driver, he found, was a distant cousin of his. I do not think that we talked about the row at all. He was not much interested whether I was right or wrong. As with the prisoners whom he was always trying to release, he had his own way of judging matters and always liked official verdicts to be reversed and personal ones substituted. The next morning he spent at a table in the porch writing about thirty letters on notepaper headed with the address of a smart Dublin hotel, at which he often entertained his friends. For even if it meant starving himself later he liked to be hospitable in the grand manner.

One, I observed, was to a Cardinal, one to Her Serene Highness Somebody. He was asking them no doubt to use their influence, either for the prisoners or for building a bridge to Valentia Island, and some may have been letters of introduction for friends going abroad. (He once gave me a package of eleven.) Then he put the letters in the brown paper parcel and hitchhiked back to Dublin. A day or two later an announcement appeared at the very top of the Social and Personal section of The Irish Times: "Mr. Eoin O'Mahony, B.L., K.M., has been staying with Mr. Hubert Butler, B.A., in Kilkenny." He probably sent it to the London Times as well. I have never before or since appeared in that illustrious column, and I have always made a special thing of not being a B.A. But I immediately saw the point. Eoin was showing his solidarity, not with my opinions, but with me, in the most public and ceremonious way he could contrive.

I have just been listening to the Radio Éireann recording of an earlier O'Mahony rally at Castlemore Castle. It was so clear and characteristic, it was almost as though Eoin and his wonderful personality had been embalmed for eternity. But ten years from now, how would it sound to those who never knew him? I think, though he left so little published writing, Eoin may wear better than most of us. For the Faceless Organization Man, whom Eoin combated, though he looks so vigorous, is really already a deader. Very soon we shall be searching for the scraps of the human personalities which he has pounded juggernaut-wise into the dust, and trying to piece them together. That is where Eoin and those he influenced will come into their own again. The seeds he sowed will begin to germinate in the vast and mouldering technological rubbish heap.

Being proud of him, we can be proud of Ireland too, for it is one of the few countries in which so eccentric a genius could be so warmly appreciated and so deeply regretted.

OWEN SHEEHY-SKEFFINGTON*
1971

I have known Owen for thirty years and more. Dublin, of course, was the main focus of his activities but his influence was nationwide. Much has been written about his work in the Senate and in Trinity and elsewhere, but living in the country I and many others have admired him chiefly as the champion not of lost causes but of causes that are bound to be won long after those who made victory certain are dead. Such causes don't attract the impatient or the self-seeking; they owe everything to the dedicated lives of a few, who have a clear vision of the future and know how we can shape it. Owen had absolute faith that what *should* be finally *will* be, however long we must wait. He had a buoyancy of spirit that made him the most inspiring friend and teacher.

And of course he was a great teacher, not only in the scholastic sense, for he was loved and respected by thousands of unacademic people whom he first taught to think for themselves. Inevitably we in the country know him best through the reports of his speeches in the press, through his letters and articles, and we may have got a rather unbalanced view of Owen as primarily a superb and fearless

*The text is of a speech Butler gave at a memorial meeting in the Examination Hall, Trinity College, Dublin, 11 June 1971.—ed.

controversialist. But, in fact, those newspaper battles were his way of defending his life's work, much of which, though known to his friends, neighbours, colleagues, was of that disinterested kind that never gets into the press.

There was nothing pedantic or doctrinaire about Owen's great campaigns. They arose out of deep feeling. For example, when he fought for the abolition of corporal punishment in schools, he was well aware of the difficult lives of Irish schoolteachers, their over-crowded classes, out-of-date curricula and all the things that strain the nerves and spoil the temper. But even if cruelty and stupidity derived from defects in our social system, they had to be noted and denounced, or that system would never be altered. Owen had the law of the land as well as the evidence of a thousand books, educational, medical, psychological, behind him. But the books had never got off the bookshelves into the classroom and the infiltration of any new idea is extraordinarily slow. One man with strong enlightened con-victions is worth many books. And in Ireland that man was Owen.

Owen, of course, followed a star, but it would be hard to give that star a name. He was a humanist, as we know, and he once engaged in what must have been the longest newspaper war ever waged in Ireland in defence of the liberal ethic, but liberalism and humanism are too narrow, almost sectarian, words in which to de-scribe what Owen did and was. I think he was one of the greatest of Tone's men, for he gave to others what he claimed for himself, "the common name of Irishman."

I don't believe Owen ever expressed himself more forcibly than in that celebrated after-dinner speech which he gave a few months before he died. Malcolm Muggeridge, who might be considered the leading crusader against the liberal ethic in England, had come over for the launching of his new book. He had had an intellectual back-ground not unlike Owen's, but had arrived at diametrically opposite conclusions. Muggeridge had been born of humanist parents but had lost all faith in the socialist future for which they had been working. He had not been able to shake off their disbelief in the Christian story but had allied his total scepticism with a social despair which he and his followers considered to be Christian. Owen quoted him: "All human hopes are fraudulent and their realization in purely hu-man terms must always prove deceptive. . . . A passion to change the world and make it nearer the heart's desire automatically excludes God."

He has propagated these views with great wit and charm and a superb mastery of all the mass media, so that in sceptical, agnostic England he has made thousands of disciples. You can easily see how. What can be more soothing for an easygoing people who are often visited by pangs of social conscience than to be told that the world is a priori evil and that it is almost blasphemy to try to change it?

We can see how Owen was likely to react to such a creed:

I have read Mr. Muggeridge quite a lot. I am reminded how Zola, talking to the youth of his day, says that one of the precepts he would suggest to them is that "they should not be able to read a newspaper without growing pale with anger." Well, I find that the reading of what Malcolm Muggeridge says as a rule enables me to live up to this precept. Not that he is not at times extremely witty and, though somewhat sourly, amusing and entertaining, contemptuous of all who try here below to lessen unnecessary misery and to improve the lot of man. A favourite sneer-word of his is the adjective "utopian." He forgets that the word "utopia" was first used by a saint of the Church, St. Thomas, referring not to something immediately, or perhaps ever, realizable but to a better state towards which humanity might legitimately aspire.

Mr. Muggeridge derides the welfare state and Oxfam also, which endeavours to ease the lot of many on this earth and he talks of "that earnest open Oxfam face shining like a morning sun with all the glories flesh is heir to."

He reminds me of a character in a fine novel by Romain Gary. The character, Orsini, has a deep contempt for himself and his aim is to convince himself and others that all his fellow-humans are as contemptible as he is or even more so. I believe that the searing contempt that Mr. Muggeridge keeps displaying for the rest of humanity and, in particular, for anybody who tries to do any good here below, derives from a deep inner contempt for himself.

Owen was criticized later for attacking the guest of honour at a dinner, which Muggeridge's publishers had given to celebrate the launching of his new book, *Jesus Rediscovered.* Yet Owen was always courteous and fair. He was attacking not a clever journalist but a noisome and contagious way of thinking. It must have astonished the publisher that, in Ireland of all places, the fashionable new devotion should meet its fiercest challenge. Owen's speech was printed in *Hibernia* and Muggeridge replied to it in the following issue, 5 December 1969.

Was Owen anti-Christian? I think his life gave the answer. If he now and then dissociated himself from Christianity, it was because the word was being made disgraceful. He believed in, and practised, all the Christian virtues; he was a great fighter but he was also humble. He liked to quote Herbert Spencer: "What I must realize is how infinitesimal is the importance of anything I do, and how infinitely important it is that I should do it."

Owen never wrote any books, so he is not well known outside Ireland, but here we all know him. The purpose of these annual lectures is to ensure that he will be remembered in perpetuity by the community for which he spent himself so selflessly.*

ELIZABETH BOWEN†
1979

I know that our posterity will be grateful to those who helped keep this little church alive. Many will say that it is neither notable nor beautiful and that Elizabeth Bowen's real monument is her books. I wonder about this. Her books are brilliantly perceptive, witty and, despite an underlying sadness, full of happiness, as she was. Are they, though, *aere perennius*, more enduring than bronze? The Roman poet who made this proud and justified claim for his works over two thousand years ago lived in times that he thought disturbed, but they were calm and peaceful compared to ours. In our day, events succeed each other very rapidly, books are often out of date before they are published and whole epochs of history can end, as in eastern Europe, and leave scarcely a trace behind. People and places are far easier to expunge than they ever were before. And Elizabeth's talent (perhaps one could call it genius) was gentle, secretive, undemonstrative and closely linked to a way of life, a class, a community that is quickly disappearing. I have heard her described as the last of the Anglo-Irish novelists, though I do not think she herself would have accepted that. At the end of *Bowen's Court*, that wonderful book of social and family history, she reflects that the Anglo-Irish are tougher than they appear; they have, she thought, an independence of mind which, though it is sometimes based on "isolation, egotism and lack of culture" (she was thinking in particular of her own Cromwellian ancestors), may help them to survive.

Also, too, I think we underestimate the extent to which our remembrance of people, families, classes and even races is linked with bricks and mortar. It ought not to be so, but it is. It is impossible

---

*Sadly, owing to some confusion, the lectures were not continued, but the Scholarship for French Studies founded in Owen's memory is still regularly awarded.

†Spoken at the erection of a memorial tablet to Elizabeth Bowen in Farahy Church, 18 October 1979.—ed.

not still to be moved by the sight of Voltaire's house at Ferney, Tolstoy's home at Yasnaya Polyana, though history has swept past them both in violent revolution. It is hard for an Anglo-Irishman not to regret the virtual destruction of Edgeworthstown, the total destruction of Moore Hall and Coole Park and, finally, just beside this church, of Bowen's Court itself, and not to suspect that our indifference was a foretaste of the neglect and distortion that whole centuries of Anglo-Irish history may have to suffer in the future. These four houses had all, in their day, given shelter to an attempt to blend two traditions, the imagination and poetry of the Gael with the intellectual vitality and administrative ability of the colonist. And though this mingling of loyalties frequently did happen, each generation found it not easier but harder to create for Ireland some common culture which all its citizens could share.

In Elizabeth's day the whole weight of Ireland's long resentment against England fell upon the Anglo-Irish, the very people who, at different periods and in different places, had eagerly awaited this mingling and worked for it. Elizabeth was aware of all the difficulties. Since she was twenty she had constantly thought of the burning of Bowen's Court. My grandfather's house in Tipperary, which was the home of her grandmother Elizabeth Jane Clarke, whose memorial tablet you see there on the wall, had been burned to the ground in the early 1920s and so had the houses of many of her neighbours, some fellow worshippers in this church. Yet when she inherited Bowen's Court from her father, she set herself to keep the house going though it was against all the dictates of common sense and self-interest and even her own English upbringing.

She had to forge an Irish literary personality for herself, for though her father and all his brothers and sisters were superficially more Irish than herself, warmhearted people with Irish voices and long humorous Irish anecdotes about relations and County Cork neighbours, they were mostly unliterary and unintellectual, and when they had lived in Dublin even her father, a learned man, was unaware of the Abbey Theatre and the cultural revival which had accompanied it. Yet Elizabeth, knowing well the debt she owed to England, felt passionately Irish and often explored what this Irish feeling was. Was it sometimes, perhaps, little more than the imaginative understanding, the empathy which a sensitive writer has for those whom circumstances or the craft of letters has brought within her orbit? Possibly, yet she felt that her three-hundred-year-old Irishness was as good as anyone else's and committed her to her country.

She had a special feeling for James Joyce, though she described him as a Catholic-born city-bred man, everything in fact that *she* was not. "In Ireland," she wrote, "we breed the finest natures and then by our ignorance, our prejudice and our cruelty, we drive them from our shores. . . . We have given to Europe and lost to Europe her greatest writer of prose."

We had all assumed that because she was so hospitable, so generous and so celebrated a writer, she must be rich. She was too proud to admit to prolonged financial worries. Surely, if all those to whom Bowen's Court had been an oasis of friendliness and lively thinking in a dreary world had known the truth, they would have done something to assure its future.*

The purpose of this tablet is not only to honour a great writer and a friend; it is also to honour the probing mind, the scrupulous observation and the truthful vision of which we stand in such desperate need today.

---

*In 1960 when Elizabeth sold Bowen's Court, a large grey eighteenth-century house under the Ballyhoura Hills, she was persuaded that the new owners would live there and preserve it, but hardly a year later it was demolished and today it is difficult to find even where it stood. Farahy Church, whose services Elizabeth and Alan, her husband, used to attend, lies on a small steep hill just inside the gates of Bowen's Court on the road between Mitchelstown and Mallow, and is the last physical reminder of the Bowens in Ireland. It was in a state of disrepair and there was talk of pulling it down, but it was saved by the efforts of the Rev. Robert McCarthy and the painter Derek Hill, an old friend of Elizabeth. An annual service of commemoration is held there and the church is maintained by contributions from its congregation and donations from the many summer visitors, who sign their names in the visitors' book and are welcomed to Farahy by Mrs. Hannon, occupant of the Bowen's Court gate lodge.

Boycott Village

1958

Fethard-on-Sea is a small village of about a hundred houses on the Wexford coast. It is not a seaside resort, for the muddy creek which brings the houses to an end can surely only be called "the sea" to distinguish the village from the less notorious Fethard in Tipperary. The ancient hotel near the creek is now Mr. Leslie Gardiner's General Stores, but neither he nor Miss Betty Cooper, who sells cornflakes, sweets and newspapers on the opposite side of the street, expects much from the seaside visitors. Tourists, of course, pass through, but they are mainly the self-sufficient kind with picnic baskets in the boot. They are bound for Baginbun, a short distance away, where there is a charming secluded shore, rock pools lined with emerald seaweed and, on most days, no one else. It was at Baginbun that the Normans first landed in Ireland eight centuries ago. They had been invited by Dermot Mac Morrogh, the great chieftain to whom all Wexford belonged. He had stolen another chieftain's wife. There had been unpleasantness and reprisals as a result and so he had asked for English help. The English came and they stayed. So much so that today men of English blood predominate in Wexford.

And now there has been turmoil there again about another truant wife and things have happened that have shocked all Ireland, North and South, and made the hope of unity recede still further. It is not a parochial squabble; it is not exclusively an Irish one. It is a collision between human nature and the "immutable" principles of the Roman Catholic Church. Such collisions happen somewhere every day, but this one has been watched with such breathless interest because in Ireland we still have the primitive power of focusing our minds like burning glasses on tiny patches. Just as bird-watchers go to the Saltees, those three uninhabited islands which lie off Baginbun, so men-watchers should come to Ireland to see how men, not yet trapped in the mental zoo of the television set and the Sunday press, still think and act in a natural untamed state.

In the spring of 1957 Eileen Cloney had reached the age of six. She lived with her parents and her baby sister in a bald grey castle just outside Fethard. It is six hundred years old but it has been liberally renovated with concrete and has rather new-looking battlements and a turret. There is a huge barn beside it, whose corrugated-iron roof has grown rusty in the salty air. There are elm trees and sprawling hedges, where in late June, when I first saw Dungulph, the blackberries were beginning to flower, the last bells were still clinging to the tips of the foxgloves and the first ones climbing up some stray mulleins. It seemed an enchanted place in which to be six years old. But Eileen Cloney had reached school age, and Father Allen and his curate, Father Stafford, were insistent that there must be no further delay. She must go to school. They were emphatic about this, because Mrs. Cloney, a strong-minded woman, showed signs of wanting to send Eileen to the small Protestant school, where there were twelve other pupils, children of local farmers and of Leslie Gardiner. Though her husband was a Catholic, Mrs. Cloney was the daughter of a Protestant stockbreeder of Fethard. I have never met Sean Cloney or his wife, Sheila, but they seem to be a likeable pair and their marriage appeared to be a happy one. The sudden split, which occurred in the middle of April, arose out of Eileen's schooling. It is disagreeable to discuss the characters and lives of quiet modest people like the Cloneys, who have never courted publicity, but circumstances and, in particular, Father Allen and Father Stafford, have decreed that their private lives are no longer their own. Sean Cloney, in his press photographs, looks a pleasant, good-looking, easygoing young man. He has that amused, cynical, shoulder-shrugging appearance that is common enough in Ireland. Sheila Cloney, who has hitherto escaped the press photographer, seems to have been more vigorous and dominating. Immediately after her marriage she started to make the 116-acre farm at Dungulph pay, wrestling herself with the tractor and the accounts and achieving such success that last year they bought a combine harvester. She was as devoted to her own church as to her home and, when she came in from the fields, she often went with broom and scrubbing brush to the Protestant church of Fethard. It was being redecorated this spring and she was among the most tireless of the volunteers who every night tidied away the builders' debris.

It was on 13 May that the squabble became public property, but it is not yet clear who was squabbling with whom. Was Sheila at war with Sean or was she warring with Father Allen and Father Stafford, while Sean, shrugging his shoulders, looked on? Certain it is that Sheila on 27 April took the car and the children to Wexford, where later it was found abandoned in the street. Three days later a barrister came from Belfast with "terms of settlement." They were drastic terms, suggesting an extreme state of feminine exasperation. Sean was to sell Dungulph Castle and they were to emigrate together to Canada or Australia, where the children were to be brought up as Protestants. "No one influenced her in her decision," Sean declared to a reporter. "Once Sheila gets an idea into her head, a regiment of soldiers wouldn't change her."

The news was received with consternation in Fethard. There was a thunderous pronouncement from the altar, and the next day a boycott started of all the Protestants in the neighbourhood. There was a Catholic teacher in the Protestant school, a Catholic sexton in the Protestant church; they both resigned. The elderly music teacher, Miss Knipe, lost eleven of her twelve pupils, Mr. Gardiner's General Stores and Miss Cooper's more modest emporium were rigorously boycotted. So were the Protestant farmers who sold milk, and from one of them a Catholic farmhand walked away. The boycott, the priests declared, would continue till Mrs. Cloney brought back the children.

For the first week the better-disciplined Catholics refused to greet or to look at their Protestant neighbours, but here and there a rebellious one gave a furtive smile when no one was looking. At the end of the week, either because a breath of Christian charity forced its way through some crack in the united front or because it was better to abate the rigour of the boycott rather than betray any lack of unanimity, the boycotters began to smile and nod. But there was no relaxation of economic pressure.

By this time the newspapers of Dublin and Belfast were headlining the news from Fethard. It was anticipated that very soon a word from the local Catholic bishop, the Bishop of Ferns, would put an end to what was becoming a national scandal. But the ecclesiastical intervention, when it came, was more astounding than what had preceded. On Saturday, 30 June, the Annual Congress of the Catholic Truth Society was being held in Wexford, and at the Church of the

Immaculate Conception, Cardinal D'Alton was received by the
Bishop of Ferns. In front of them and five other bishops of the Roman
Church, including the Archbishop of Dublin, the Bishop of Galway
preached a sermon defending the boycott.

There seems [he said] to be a concerted campaign to entice or kidnap Catholic
children and deprive them of their faith. Non-Catholics with one or two honourable exceptions do not protest against the crime of conspiring to steal the
children of a Catholic father. But they try to make political capital when a
Catholic people make a peaceful and moderate protest.

In the same newspaper which reported this apology for a "peaceful and moderate protest," we read that two of Mrs. Cloney's brothers in Fethard had been obliged to seek police protection because a
shot had been fired at one of them near his home. At the same time
a young Protestant teacher from Trinity College arrived to take
charge of the Protestant school, which had been closed since the
teacher had abandoned her pupils. He found a warning nailed onto
the school door:

SCABS!
BEWARE OF THE LEAD
IN BOYCOTT VILLAGE!

No prominent Catholic had come forward to condemn the boycott except a barrister, Mr. Donal Barrington, who in his address to
a Catholic social study conference in Dublin said that the boycott
was doing damage to the cause of Catholicism. "It is," he said, "the
most terrible thing that has happened in this part of the country since
the Civil War," and he went on to say that he was only echoing the
opinion of all the intelligent Catholics, laymen and priests, with
whom he had discussed the matter. But their opinion had been given
in private and he felt it his duty to speak publicly. "There is a time
in the affairs of people when nothing is necessary for the triumph of
evil but that good men should maintain what is called a discreet
silence."

No other Catholic made so bold a comment, till a week later
Mr. de Valera himself declared in the Dáil:

If, as head of the Government, I must speak, I can only say from what has
appeared in public that I regard this boycott as ill-conceived, ill-considered and
futile for the achievement of the purpose for which it seems to have been intended, that I regard it as unjust and cruel to confound the innocent with the

guilty, that I repudiate any suggestion that this boycott is typical of the attitude or conduct of our people, that I am convinced that ninety percent of them look on this matter as I do and that I beg of all who have regard for the fair name, good repute and well-being of our nation, to use their influence to bring this deplorable affair to a speedy end.

Mr. de Valera was right. The Irish are not by nature bullying or ungenerous; they are indulgent to human weaknesses and disinclined to totalitarian judgments. This essay, therefore, is not about bigotry, but about the ineffectuality of ordinary people with nice intentions and neighbourly instincts. This has often been demonstrated before in totalitarian countries, but only the last stage in the suppression of the amiable, when they are being finished off by threats and violence, has been closely observed. The earlier stages of coercion by "peaceful and moderate protest" have never had the same attention, yet they are more important. For the handful of free spirits, who in any community are the last-ditch guardians of freedom, are not defenceless till the amiable majority, which forms an inert but not easily negotiable obstacle in the path of tyranny, has first been neutralized. How is this done? It is not difficult. The events in Fethard show how eagerly the amiable will cooperate in their own extinction.

It is now fifty years since the *Ne Temere* decree,* which condemns the Irish nation to live in two mutually distrustful camps, was first applied to Ireland. It has broken up many homes besides the Cloneys' and brought an element of hypocrisy or perjury into every marriage between Irish people of different faith. Yet never till now did the whole Irish nation observe and deplore the cruel tensions which it has created. It is doubtful whether de Valera lost a single vote by championing the boycotted. For the Church of Ireland† is much more than a vast complex of emptying palaces, rectories, cathedrals. In Ireland it is still the spearhead of the Reformation and few people are ready to renounce the liberties won at the Reformation, even when they repudiate the reformers. Father Stafford and his anathemas are as much an anachronism in Ireland as the Anglo-Irish ascendancy.

Yet this time the Protestant hierarchy made a scapegoat of Mrs. Cloney and did not reiterate those protests against *Ne Temere* which our primate made long ago and more recently republished. He and

---

*Issued on 2 August 1907 by Pope Pius X, the *Ne Temere* decree declared marriages between Roman Catholics and Protestants null and void unless performed in a Catholic church, and required that the children of such marriages be raised in the Roman Catholic faith.—ed.
†Meaning of course the Protestant Church of Ireland.—ed.

others had denied the validity of a promise "extorted under pressure," and such denials undoubtedly influenced Mrs. Cloney in her decision. Weakened perhaps by the emigration of vigour and intelligence, our clergy counselled appeasement and that "discreet silence" which Mr. Barrington saw as the prelude to the triumph of evil. By inference they accepted the *Ne Temere* promises as valid; they deprecated excessive newspaper publicity, condemned any lay attempt to organize aid for the boycotted Protestants as "senseless retaliation" and, in our diocesan magazine, gave retrospective approval to a strange undertaking given by Mrs. Cloney's father, Mr. Kelly. Speaking "on behalf of the Church of Ireland community," he had pledged it to do all it could to bring back his grandchildren to Fethard, and published this promise in the Irish papers. Tactfully he said nothing about the boycott, which is known locally as "Parish Cooperation" and was described by Father Stafford in the press as "this grand, dignified, legal profession of our Faith." By implication Protestants were committed to act as watchdogs for the observance of a decree directed against themselves. It was assumed that, as a quid pro quo, the boycott would be called off, but the Church of Ireland bit the dust in vain. The boycott continued and our clergy, returning from their Munich, gave themselves over to exhortation against mixed marriages and the social intercourse that might lead to them. Canute, rebuking the waves, was not less profitably engaged. In the countryside we have dwindled to 2 or 3 percent of the population (the rector of Fethard controls five amalgamated parishes); if we are to mix exclusively with ourselves, we are condemned to social isolation, celibacy, inbreeding or dreary marriages of convenience. But can we really believe that our duty to our neighbour is to avoid him socially, lest we love him as ourselves and forget the dangerous contagion of his faith? For that is the way in which the gospel precepts appear to have been revised.

This ecclesiastical advice will not of course be followed, but nor will it be repudiated, for, as in the early days of the Brown Shirts in Germany, respectable people put their faith in the healing properties of time. We like to think that, left to themselves, our difficulties will all "blow over," "peter out," "die down." There is a rich range of synonyms for the spontaneous disappearance of evil and we seldom commit the folly of sticking out our necks or poking in our noses. And, in fact, if we only have patience, the victim of injustice will probably emigrate and cease to embarrass us with his tedious lamentations.

Irish Protestants are generally "broad-minded" about belief. They tend to judge other religions as they judge their own, by its social consequences. Having sometimes a hereditary interest in property, they are impressed by the Catholic defence of property. A true instinct also informs them that the Catholic Church is basically as unsympathetic to Irish nationalism as is the average Irish Protestant and might at any moment barter its support of the Irish Republic for a favoured position in the Commonwealth. This emerged clearly at Fethard. The Bishop of Galway, in his Wexford address, deliberately gave arguments to the northerners against the abolition of Partition and cannot have been dismayed by the repercussions in Belfast. A united Ireland, in which there would be a 25 percent heretical minority, might seem to present the Church of Rome with problems insoluble, except in the vast dilution of the Commonwealth. But to declaim against Irish unity would be unpopular; the Orangemen could safely be left to do all the declaiming, for Ulster eyes are dim with gazing on far-off imperial horizons and cannot focus clearly on what goes on under the nose. A fund was raised for the boycotted Protestants and a northern MP sent to distribute it. On 12 July* not a single Orange orator failed to mention Fethard, but, as interest on the large "political capital" derived from the boycott, the dividend that went to Fethard was small.

Some weeks ago Father Allen bought some cigarettes at Gardiner's. This momentous act did not mean the end of the boycott, but it has cast a rose-pink veil over its origins and the responsibility for its continuance. An irreverent person, peering through the veil, would see that the boycott can never now end. The lost customers have found other tradesmen, eager to supply their needs, a new newsagent bicycles round with the papers to Miss Cooper's former clients, a new milkman goes the rounds and the old schoolteacher and the old sextoness will never return. Nor will Miss Knipe's pupils. To end the boycott more unpleasantness and fresh dislocations would be necessary, and these are things which in Ireland we always avoid if we possibly can.

Postscript I
1978

In the past years there have been some verbal concessions about the *Ne Temere* decree but very little effective change. Yet I am confident

---

*Orangeman's Day, a holiday commemorating the Battle of Boyne (1690), in which the forces of King William III of England, Prince of Orange, defeated those of James II, at the Boyne River, is the traditional occasion for oratory and display on behalf of Ulster Protestantism.—ed.

that had Protestants listened to Primate Gregg's "Resistance in God's Name is the Duty of us all" and acted with courage and unity, they would have caused the total abolition of the decree in 1958.

At that time we were doing up our house in Co. Kilkenny, which was fifty miles away, and we bought all our putty, paint and as much else as we could at Gardiner's General Stores and Miss Cooper's Fancy Goods Shop. In two journeys we spent twenty or thirty pounds and I wrote to *The Irish Times* suggesting that if all the Protestants within fifty miles of Fethard did all their shopping there, the boycott would be over in a week. I wrote anonymously, as one often did in the 1950s.

However, our bishop, Dr. Phair, wrote in reply that this would be "senseless provocation" and that was the end of my campaign. As he had always been friendly to me, I might have forestalled this had I the wit to sign my name.

Ne Temere came up in *The Irish Times* fifteen years later, when the Rev. R. C. Johnston declared that Fethard had been a turning point in our history and that Protestants in their spinelessness had left the defence of their liberties to liberal Catholics like Noel Browne and humanists like Owen Skeffington. In reply I recalled Gregg's words and insisted that had Dr. Phair encouraged us rather than the reverse, there would have been such an avalanche of Protestants from Wexford, Waterford and Kilkenny as would have kept all the boycotted in plenty for the rest of their lives and secured the repeal of *Ne Temere*.

Dr. Phair was dead but his widow was much hurt; she wrote to me privately and said that those who suffered were aware of their prayers and that £1,754.10.4 had been subscribed to the Fethard Relief Fund in the Bank of Ireland and that his behaviour had met with general approval. I am sure it did but it seemed to me as though the Protestant leaders were trying to buy us off our duty with cheques and as though the welfare of some shopkeepers and dairy farmers was at stake and not our children's freedom and the Protestant right of private judgment.

A great common gesture would have given us courage and confidence and arrested the sad, slow Protestant decline. It would have reminded the northern Protestants that we belong together and that they belong to Ireland.

Success would have been inevitable, for the decree, only imposed on England and Ireland in 1908 and not extended to Germany, was in no way infallible. It could, in Gregg's words, be "withdrawn at any time or thrust into the capacious wastepaper basket kept at Rome for the reception of Papal utterances that have miscarried."

Here is the conclusion of the statement made by the House of Bishops of the Church of Ireland soon after the application of *Ne Temere* to Ireland in 1908: "We, the archbishops and bishops of the Church of Ireland, appeal on behalf of the oppressed and helpless to all lovers of justice and liberty to do their utmost by all lawful means for the redressing of a grievous wrong."

Postscript II
1984

In the past six years Irish Protestants, faced with a real possibility of extinction before the end of the century, have reacted more vigorously than before to the demands of the dominant majority.

In November 1983 the Irish Catholic hierarchy issued a new "directory" about mixed marriages. Couched in conciliatory terms, it left the situation much as it was before, except that the promises made by the Catholic parent to bring up the children as Catholics could be oral and not written. The House of Bishops of the Church of Ireland was deeply dissatisfied; in their view a promise is a promise, whether written or spoken. The Protestant bishops also complained that "God's Law" was being invoked to support the Catholic claim: "We do not know where in God's Law there is support for a promise to ensure the Roman Catholic upbringing of all the children." The directory claimed that in some areas of Ireland the Protestant spouse was frequently only nominally so and therefore had no difficulty in agreeing to the Catholic ruling. The Church of Ireland reply was that in other areas the reverse was true. They were surprised, too, that whereas the directory regarded the Protestant attitude to divorce as an impediment to mixed marriages, an exception was made for the Orthodox Church, which also recognized divorce. I would suggest that the reason for this is practical not spiritual; since the Russian Revolution the Orthodox Church has been so weakened and divided that it presents a tempting mission field. There was every reason to be conciliatory.

There had been an earlier confrontation on a different issue. The Constitutional Amendment of 1983, whose intention was to guarantee beyond all possibility of change the existing law against abortion, was passed by a majority, which was deceptive, as only half the electorate voted. It split the country as it had seldom been split before.* The Protestant churches, galvanized by Dean Griffin of St.

*See below, pp. 187–89.—ed.

Patrick's Cathedral, took a prominent part in the resistance. Accepting that abortion is an evil, they still saw no necessity of copper-fastening a law whose observation it was impossible to guarantee. Many felt that the publicity given to the Amendment would be counterproductive. The evidence that between three thousand and five thousand women were going annually to England to have abortions revealed how easily the law could be defied. Many, too, asked themselves what advice they would give if someone dear to them was raped or told by her doctor that she would bear a hopelessly handicapped child or was forced by circumstances to give her fatherless child to others to rear. To them it seemed that the Amendment was the negation of the Protestant right of private judgment.

There is some truth in the directory's argument about nominal Protestantism. Although there is far less vocal "unbelief" today than a century ago, when it was based on biblical criticism and caused heartbreak and alienation, there is widespread indifference in both churches. On the other hand there are many who long for spiritual guidance but cannot accept it in the form in which it is offered. They see how in our materialistic and deeply divided society the churches have lost their mediatory power. There are sectarian murders, which have nothing to do with a conflict of principle. Great blocks of hereditary conformities, which owe nothing to the movement of the individual mind, jostle each other in inflexible hostility. The arguments of the ecumenists at no point touch these embattled certainties. The leaders of rival churches have come together and, forgetting their differences, have preached against violence. Their united voices have had no effect. They are addressing themselves to a small but powerful body of men, superbly armed and subsidized from many sources, who are confident that, if they crush their adversaries, and win, they will ultimately be accepted. History, they know, is on their side; in country after country coups d'état, brought about by violence, have later received ecclesiastical sanction.

The only future for the churches in a time of mounting violence is to forget all their dogmatic differences and the supernatural claims with which mass unanimity is cemented and to concentrate on the Christian teaching of brotherly love, which applies to all our neighbours and all our countrymen, whatever their faith. This is the only catalyst that can break down every consensus which has outlived its day and free that teaching from sectarian overtones.

Christianity was born in a small community and it was to small communities, no bigger for the most part than Fethard-on-Sea, that

St. Paul wrote his epistles. The New Testament precept "Thou shalt love thy neighbour as thyself" was not purely allegorical. It was not impossible then to identify oneself with those with whom one associated and to feel a deep concern for them.

Today the idea of neighbourly love has been diluted till it covers all humanity. We grieve for distant events and people with sympathy as thin and ephemeral as the newspaper in which we read about them. We suffer from a disease so widespread as to seem incurable. Yet where the diagnosis is obvious, the cure cannot be for ever beyond our reach.

Is it possible that in some far-off day Christian society, responding to human needs, will gradually be structurally transformed?

The Eggman and the Fairies

1960

You can see Slievenaman from my fields, though it is across the
Tipperary border, a pale blue hump with the soft, rounded contours
of ancient hills whose roughnesses have been smoothed away by
time. Starting after lunch you can climb to the tip and be back by
summer daylight, though it is more than two thousand feet high. It
can be seen from five or six southern counties and is one of the three
or four most famous of Irish hills. Finn MacCool lived there and so
did Oisin and Oscar, and fifty beautiful maidens, who give it its
name, "The Mountain of Women," embroidered garments for them
there, or so they say. The top of the mountain to within a couple of
hundred feet of the cairn of stones is bare except for an odd patch
of sphagnum moss and heather. Below it there is more heather, well
grazed by sheep, and a few frochan clumps, but except for some piles
of stones that might once have been a house and a rough track for
carting turf, there is not much sign of human traffic.

I had always supposed that the Clearys' house had been in one
of these ruined stone heaps upon the mountainside, because I could
not associate their uncanny story with the prosperous and populous plain below. But one day I went to look for Ballyvadlea, where
they lived at the foot of the mountain. A hurling match was being
broadcast from Dublin and the cottagers came reluctantly from their
wireless sets to direct me to the "fairy house." It was almost indistinguishable from their own, except that it was bare and without
flowers or shrubs, an ugly cement building rather smaller than the
county council houses of today but of the same type. It was only a
couple of hundred yards from a main road and, though it suggested

poverty, it did not suggest mystery, remoteness, primaeval superstition. Farmers and gentry driving past the door to Fethard or Clonmel in 1895 have been talking of Dreyfus and Cecil Rhodes and some of these, who took part in the Ballyvadlea tragedy, may be still alive. They belong to our age and clime. The fairies are, if not exactly at the bottom of the garden, at least only a few fields and a few years away.

It is not very easy to build up a consecutive story out of a court case, for the end is always told before the beginning, and the central episode, seen differently by different witnesses, is often blurred like a negative several times exposed. But roughly this is how it happened.

In the spring of 1895 the Clearys were living at Ballyvadlea below Slievenaman. Michael Cleary was a labourer and his young wife, Bridget, was the daughter of a neighbour, Patrick Boland. Michael and Bridget were fond of each other and never quarrelled. They were religious people believing in the mysteries of the Catholic Church. But they also believed in the fairies and Michael was persuaded that, many years before, his mother had changed her nature. A fairy had entered into her body and once she had disappeared for two nights and it was known that she had spent them on the fairy-haunted rath at Kilnagranagh. It lay above John Dunne's cottage on the low road, and when Bridget too began to talk, like his mother, of Kilnagranagh and often to walk towards it of an evening on the low road, the old dread took shape in Michael's twilit mind. And some contagion of his fears spread to all his neighbours and all his relations, the Kennedys, the Bolands, the Dunnes, the Ahearns and Burkes, paralyzing their wills and dulling their sensibilities. A whole community seemed to be bound with the spells of fairyland and powerless to extricate themselves. They appealed to the priests and the peelers* to save them from themselves, but no external power was stronger than their obsessions. "It's not my wife I have," Michael told John Dunne, "she's too fine a woman for my wife. She's two inches taller than my wife." And even Bridget Cleary herself talked to her cousin, Mary Kennedy, as though she were bound with spells. "I've a pain in my head," she said, "he's making a fairy of me now and an emergency. He thought to burn me three months ago." She began to suffer from nerves, and her illness was to Michael yet stronger proof that she was possessed. Dr. Creary, the local doctor, declared it was due to dyspepsia, but he carried no conviction, and Michael went to Denis

*Policemen.—ed.

Guiney, the herb doctor, who prescribed a decoction of herbs and milk to be cooked in a saucepan and fed to the possessed woman.

But Michael had not much faith, either, in this innocent herbal remedy. He was convinced that there was only one way in which his Bridget could be restored to him. The fairy must be burnt out of her and then he would go to Kilnagranagh, and he would find the real Bridget there. She'd come out of the rath, riding a white horse and bound by cords to the saddle. He'd have to cut the ropes and then, if he was able to keep her, she'd stay with him.

But I should have mentioned that Michael Cleary once casually told his cousin John that Bridget on her evening walks to the fairy rath sometimes met an eggman on the low road. He used to go the rounds of the Tipperary farmsteads with his cart, collecting eggs for a wholesale distributor in Clonmel. When the story was all told in the Clonmel courthouse the eggman was mentioned only once and never again by judge, jury, witnesses or prisoners. For all the relevance he appeared to have to the story he and his cart might well have been swallowed up into the fairy mound. Yet these oblique and tenderhearted people had a habit of hiding their thoughts from themselves, and perhaps they sometimes thrust upon the fairies the guilt for desires and jealousies whose crudities they shrank from facing. It is possible that Michael suspected his wife of a tenderness for the eggman and just as a grain of grit will provoke an oyster to secrete a pearl, so the eggman from Clonmel unlocked the door to fairyland.

When Michael Cleary's father died he was waked in a house eleven miles from Ballyvadlea, and on their way to the wake, the neighbours assembled the evening before in Michael's house. Patrick Boland, Bridget's father, was there and the Kennedy cousins including William, aged sixteen, and William Ahearn and several others. Bridget's cousin, Hannah Burke, was still washing some shirts that were needed for the wake, and Mary Kennedy, young William's mother, went off to feed their hens, but when the others started to walk off for the wake, Michael Cleary stopped them. He said he would not leave his wife's sickbed and that "he did not care the devil about his father whether he was alive or dead." "No and ye won't go either," he said to them, "until I give her a little of the business I have to give her. Wait, boys, till you see her, till you see what I'll put out the door. I haven't Bridgie here these six weeks."

So they did not leave for the wake, but stood about till midnight watching with mild exclamations while Michael tried to drive the fairy out of Bridget's body. Her father, Patrick Boland, raised some objections which Michael dealt with impatiently. "Haven't you any faith?" he said. "Don't you know it's with an old witch I'm sleeping." "You are not," said Patrick Boland, "you are sleeping with my daughter." And telling about it later in the Clonmel courts, he, like the other witnesses, preserved a trance-like calm, as though he were watching a tragedy in which he was doomed to be a spectator, knowing the truth and yet powerless to intervene.

It is Hannah Burke who gives us the most coherent account of it all. She came back from washing the shirts about 7 p.m. on this first day of fairy exorcism, 14 March 1895. She found the Clearys' door locked and two neighbours called Simpson standing outside unable to get in. Through the window they could hear a voice saying, "Take it, you witch or you bitch!" And when the three of them were at last let in she found the three Kennedys and John Dunne holding Bridget down on the bed, while Michael tried to give her herbs boiled in new milk from a spoon. Mary Kennedy, returned from feeding the hens, had brought some wine with her, and Michael threw it over Bridget's face and breast, exclaiming "Are you Bridget Boland, in the name of God?" while her father echoed, "Are you Bridget Boland, in the name of God, the daughter of Patrick Boland?" But Bridget was exhausted and speechless and the liquid was pouring down her chemise. So, while the Rosary was recited, the men raised her out of the bed and put her onto the fire. It was John Dunne's suggestion. "We raised her over it," he exclaimed to the courts, "I thought it belonged to the cure." Hannah had just been putting sticks on the fire to make them a cup of tea and when Bridget, in the men's arms, saw her, she exclaimed in a mournful voice, "Oh, Han, Han!" She was wearing, Hannah recollected, a red petticoat and navy-blue flannel dress, green stays and navy-blue cashmere jacket, and Hannah, a conscientious witness, said of her later: "When she was taken out, she looked like one that was silly, she looked wild and deranged and had not her own appearance. She looked different. She looked worse when she was taken out of bed than when I went into the room." She was just "tipping the bars" and her father and Michael Cleary were questioning her urgently in the name of God. It was too much for Hannah, she shouted out, "Burn her away, but let me out and I'll go for the peelers." She got out, but she did not go for the peelers.

That was the first night of burning; though there had been thirteen people in the house, we do not know much else about the remaining five hours before the visitors walked off to the funeral, except for what Patrick Boland told the court. About the first night he was very reassuring. "Indeed," he said, "the fire wouldn't do anything the first night, 'twas no fire I might say." He had left with the others at midnight and returning with them from the wake the following day, he had found nothing to complain of in Bridget's condition. "She was grand then when I came back from Michael's father's wake, and the next night after that she was grand and the night after that she was grand until we were all taking a cup of tea." At this point the old man broke off in tears; he tried to tell what happened on the third night in a few disjointed phrases. It appeared that Michael had gone to his wife with the dish of herbs and milk and said, "I'll make you take it, you old witch! I have herbs that there's nine cures in. It will be very hard to make her take these." He struggled to explain what followed but failing to articulate, wound up: "I had to run away from the smell. So 'tis all the way to make a long story short he burnt her."

The witnesses all rambled incoherently backwards and forwards between the two nights of burning, lingering over what seems to us trivial, suppressing what appears to be relevant. They lived in a fairy-haunted world, whose thoughts and feelings can be measured by no ordinary rule. The poet is apt to overestimate its charm, the moralist its cruelty. The mere chronicler is exasperated by his powerlessness to sort out the events of the successive nights. Of all the witnesses Hannah Burke is the most easy to follow. The peelers to her were almost as real as the fairies, she had actually thought of going to fetch them, and her chronology is the same as ours. After Bridget had been on the fire the first night, Hannah Burke had returned and put on her a fresh nightdress, which she had been airing for her and she had examined her body. Like Patrick Boland, she agreed that Bridget was "grand." "I saw no marks on her except the size of a pin and a little blister on her hip not the size of sixpence, and a couple of little spots of burns on her chemise and a red spot under her chin. I thought it might be from the pin in her chemise, so I put a safety pin there instead." She stayed on with Bridget after the men had left for the wake and gave her some new milk, whey and claret wine, but when she left at 2 a.m. Bridget was still awake.

Hannah came the next morning with the fresh milk and her daughter Katey for company. She laid the milk on the window, and Michael gave her a shilling for it. But he said that Bridget had taken the shilling back from Hannah and, putting it under the blanket, had rubbed it against her thigh, a fairy trick, before returning it to Hannah. But when Michael had accused her of doing this, she had denied it. "No, I am not a pishogue." Yet she was aware how easily one might become a fairy, and for her, too, the borderland between fact and fantasy was very ill defined. "Your mother gave two nights with the fairies," she argued gently, "that's why you think I'm one."

Michael Cleary then went to the parish priest, Father Ryan, and asked him to come and say Mass for his wife. We know that in health she was "grand," so it was surely because she was a fairy and had rubbed the shilling on her thigh that he appealed to him. But Father Ryan, doing his duty, appeared to have no inkling of the turmoil that was going on in the hearts of his parishioners. The court seemed to think it strange that he should know so little, and it is difficult not to feel that Father Ryan, depending on the time-honoured formulae and ceremonies of his Church, felt excused from those simple movements of the mind and heart which might have saved the Clearys. Michael told the courts that Bridget, when she had received the sacrament, had removed the wafer from her mouth, refusing, fairy that she was, to swallow it.

To this Father Ryan replied reproachfully, "I wish to add that if any Catholic saw Bridget Cleary remove the Blessed Sacrament from her mouth, he would be strictly bound to tell me at once so as to enable me to save the Sacred Species from profanation." I cannot altogether blame the Clearys if it was only the supernatural claims of Father Ryan which impressed them. They appealed to him as a magician, whose magic had worldwide power and authority to reinforce it, to stand up against a more ancient magic whose power was waning. And they were deeply disappointed in his failure. The fairy failed to come out of Bridget and they were thrown back again on their own resources.

The next evening Michael tried Bridget once more with the herbs and boiled milk. He was very resolute this time. Hannah had made them cups of tea and the fire was blazing brightly. Young William Kennedy held the candle for Michael to work by, an oil lamp stood on the dresser, and Patrick Boland and all the neighbours were there as on the former night, all of them distressed and friendly and solicitous. There was bread and jam and claret wine as well as cups of tea. Bridget kept saying that she was not a pishogue and that she was not turning into a fairy like Michael's mother, and her father and husband kept appealing to her in the name of God to say whether she was Bridget Boland or not. And once she asked for Tom Smith and David Hogan, "two honest men," and she said she'd do anything they said. Smith and Hogan appear to have come and gone without altering the situation very much. And once, shifting inexpertly to the everyday world of crime and detection, she said, "The peelers are at the window. Let ye mind ye now!" But everyone knew they were not and the observation had no consequences.

It was midnight and young William Kennedy had gone to sleep in the back room with his brother James, but they were roused by a sudden hullabaloo in the front room. Michael had taken from under the bed what was called in the Clonmel courthouse "a certain utensil" and poured the contents over his wife, then, seizing a burning log from the grate, he had forced her to lap up the herbs and milk from the saucepan, while young William once more held the candle by the bedside. Then Michael forced bread and jam down her throat, crying out all the while, "Are you Bridget Cleary, my wife, in the name of the Father, the Son and the Holy Ghost?" while Mary Kennedy demurred, saying, "Leave her alone, Mike, don't you see it's Bridgie as is in it?" Then Michael locked the door so that no one could leave and put the key in his pocket. Then he put Bridget on the floor and threw the lamp on her and some oil from a half-gallon oil can from between the table and the dresser, so that Bridget was in a blaze of fire and the house suffocated with smoke. All the neighbours stampeded to the door and tried to break it down, so great was their dismay, but Michael told them they were not to leave till he had got his wife back. "Are you Bridget Boland in the name of the Father, and Son and the Holy Ghost?" shouted Michael once more. "Hold her over the fire and she'll soon answer!" Someone seemed then to have found the key in Michael's pocket and Patrick Boland escaped. William, a delicate boy, dropped the candle and fell down "in a weakness," and his mother threw Easter water over him. There were signs of renewed disapproval from the neighbours, but Michael silenced them, saying, "Hold your tongues! It isn't Bridget I'm burning. You'll soon see her go up the chimney!" Reassured by this, some of the neighbours came forward to help him and, in the words of Hannah Burke, "They placed Mrs. Cleary in a kind of sitting position on the kitchen fire, her body resting on the bars. The fire was a slow one. Mrs. Cleary's appearance was greatly changed."

After that there is mention of a large sack-bag with a dirty sheet in it, which Michael laid on the floor. Knowing what he had to do, he laid what was left of Bridget on it, on her back with her feet bent up. "It's not Bridget," he repeated. "As I couldn't drive the devil out through the chimney, I'll drive her through the door." He asked Pat Kennedy to help bury her somewhere till she could be put by her mother's side. At first he said "No," but then he agreed and at 2 a.m. Michael and Pat went out and buried the body. Michael had lost his confidence now: "She's burned now," he said, "and God knows I didn't intend to do it. It's Jack Dunne I may thank for it all."

Mary Kennedy went round to the Clearys' cottage the next morning and found a little group of neighbours already assembled. Hannah was there and old Pat Boland, Bridget's father, was on his knees, lamenting. "Now that my child is dead," he said, "there is no use in saying anything about it, but God help me in the latter end of my days!" Michael was wearing the same light suit of clothes he had worn when Bridget was being burnt and it was badly marked. He had stayed back from work to clean it. "I saw him," said Hannah, "scraping the stains like of grease off the ends of his trousers, and says he to me, 'Oh, God, Hannah, there is the substance of poor Bridget's body.' " But he still considered that it was her body only, for he told them again that his wife had gone to Kilnagranagh to see the fairies and that they were to come there that evening and help him lift her from the white horse and cut the ropes that bound her to it and persuade her to stay with him. And in fact that evening and later evenings, till he was arrested, a crowd of people did go with him to the rath. He carried a bread knife in his hand to cut the ropes. But fewer and fewer went, and John Dunne, declaring now that it was "all moonshine," urged him to go to the priest.

Michael's mother, she who had given two nights to the fairies, also gave evidence. When she reached his cottage she had found him, she said, still scraping himself, "scraping the juice of the poor creature off his clothes." "Mike," said I to him, "if you were scraping your clothes for ever and if you cut them off you, God would never let the stains go out of your clothes, the stains of your poor wife." And then she had said, "Acorrah, go down to the police barracks and tell them what you have done."

"No, Mother," he had answered, "because people would be calling you a prosecutor."

Michael asked them then to come and help him bury Bridget and one of the Kennedys said he'd come and help if she was to be buried in consecrated ground, but Michael had gone away, and without him to direct them, the neighbours wandered round the kitchen garden, hunting for the body.

Michael Cleary was at confession. Kneeling at the altar, he had torn his hair and cried would he ever be forgiven?

When the priest came out into the chapel yard, John Dunne, he who had helped to lift Bridget onto the fire because he thought it "belonged to the cure," accosted him. "They burnt her to death last night, Father," he said, "and I have been asking them all the morning to take her up and give her a Christian burial."

Hannah Burke ended her evidence abruptly: "That's all I have to say and sorry I am."

Michael from the dock said, "You did that well, Han."

"I did so, Mick."

"I hope you will do it in Heaven as well as that."

"I will with the help of God, Mick."

When the nine prisoners from Ballyvadlea were taken for trial in Clonmel, there were demonstrations in the streets and in particular against Denis Guiney, the herb doctor. They received, however, a merciful sentence, and commentators on the case in the Dublin and London periodicals were on the whole more tolerant than the Clonmel neighbours. The reaction against Victorian rationalism had started and there was a new reverence for the supernatural when it had a respectable ancient tradition behind it. Folklore had become a science, and in Ireland Standish O'Grady, by his poetical reconstruction of the Irish past, had prepared the way for Yeats and AE and the Celtic Twilight. I do not think that the fairies suffered any serious setback by the happenings at Ballyvadlea.

In *The Nineteenth Century* E. F. Benson wrote an essay on the trial, which was typical of the period in that he covered a great deal of ground with very thin speculation. He drew analogies from the Hottentots, who try to shake out the spirit of disease from the dying, and the Zulus, who believe in Amatongos, or ancestor spirits, and he offered the Clearys a respectable place in the *Encyclopaedia of Primitive Superstition*. But to those who live around Slievenaman such a diagnosis seems as inadequate as it is pretentious. There is no need to call in Zulus and Hottentots. A woman had been burnt to death for witchcraft in Kilkenny in 1324 on the instigation of the bishop, an English Franciscan, the only known instance of such burning in Ireland. Such catastrophes often happen when reason is in bondage to Fear of the Unknown, even when such Fear calls itself Faith.

In fact the Ballyvadlea tragedy had quite a sophisticated and civilized background. Everyone was perfectly familiar with priests and peelers, doctors and prosecutors, and for many centuries they had been subject to the laws of England and the faith of Rome. Nor were they altogether outside the current of world affairs. Some years before in the little village of Mullinahone, where the Clearys did their shopping, twenty-eight volunteers had set off to defend the Papal States against Garibaldi and had returned from Sardinian prisons to a welcome with bonfires on the mountain and triumphal arches.

All the Clearys and their neighbours lived in that perilous region of half-belief which the sophisticated find charming because they are more acquainted with its tenderness than its cruelty. It is a no-man's-land of the imagination, in which fantasy, running wild, easily turns into falsehood and ruthlessness. It has still in the twentieth century its appeal and highly civilized people, as well as simple ones, claim access to it.

In the past in Ireland both the churches and the Anglo-Normans often tried to harness the fairies to their ecclesiastical and political designs, and the results were often so delightful that the guard upon the frontiers of fairyland has sometimes been unwisely relaxed.

In an old Irish poem about Slievenaman, St. Patrick raised Oisin, the famous hunter, from the dead and said to him:

> Oisin, sweet is thy voice.
> Tell us how many deer fell upon Slievenaman?

And Oisin answered:

> We killed six thousand deer
> In the glen which lay in the mountain,
> O cleric of the clerks and bells!
> A thousand hounds with their collars of gold
> Fell before noon by one hundred hogs.

In fact St. Patrick did not dispel the spirits of the mountain but became one of them himself. The fairy goldsmiths made chalices and fonts for Patrick and the saints as readily as they made collars for the hounds of the Fianna. The result is that cultivated Irishmen will often have the same ironical, indulgent smile for the mysteries of their faith as for the legends of Fionn. And simple people, like the Clearys, not so skilled at walking the tightrope between belief and disbelief, are at the mercy of some temporary spasm of credulity. None of them consistently believed that Bridget was a fairy. Even now and then the voice of reason insisted: "Don't you see it's Bridgie as is in it?" But reason could make no headway against Michael's passionate conviction, whose origins Michael himself maybe did not rightly understand.

The great Norman castles on the flanks of Slievenaman, Kilcash and Kiltinan and the others, have long ago fallen into ruin or decay, and the noble lords whose horses and hounds evoked memories of the Fianna have vanished. Life has been drab and poor for many generations and poets like to transfigure it with the myth and magic of fairyland. A couple of centuries ago a native of Slievenaman, Father Lalor, wrote a charming and sophisticated elegy in Irish on the death of his friend Archdeacon Kavanagh. He saw the Archdeacon, like St. Patrick, among the fairies on Slievenaman, and the fact that these two solitary priests did not believe in the fairies makes their need of them more poignant. The poem starts gaily:

> As I one time was travelling the province
> Airily, cheerfully spending my youth;
> Some time to gamble I bestowed and to drinking,
> And a small, short time I devoted to knowledge.

Then Father Lalor describes his visit to the fairy palace on Slievenaman, the wines and the clothes and the servants, and how he asked the fairy queen why the mist had swept up from the Nore enveloping Dunane and Barnan-Ely, "What makes the side of Carnduff impenetrable to the sun?" And the fairy queen had replied that it was because

> A steady pillar of the church has died
> Who was the friend of the poor and needy . . .
> The friend of idiots without reason's light,
> Who in the Lord's vineyard laboriously toiled.
> He was an example to the whole diocese,
> He never spent his time on lands or flocks,
> He never raised the price of land by bidding against the labouring classes.
> Now the white hand which distributed the sacrament
> Is stretched without the power of motion by his side, alas!

Then the damsel had vanished and the splendid palace with her and there was nothing left on the mountainside but the mist, the gorse and the heather.

I doubt whether Archdeacon Kavanagh was quite so good as they thought him on Slievenaman, or Bridget Cleary so bad, or Oisin so splendid a hunter. A great deal of Irish poetry and romance is born of isolation and the nostalgia of those who escape it. Eyes that are dim with tears are not particularly perceptive; focused on the fairies, they never give the eggman his due. Indeed I have read

through hundreds of verses about Slievenaman without finding a single reference to him. And as for the Clearys, nobody, of course, since
E. F. Benson, has mentioned them at all; though they were poetical
people, they are out of harmony with what the poets tell us of that
fairy-haunted mountain.

> In purple robes old Slievenaman
>   Towers monarch of the mountains,
> The first to catch the smiles of dawn
>   With all his woods and fountains . . .
> There gallant men, for freedom born,
>   With friendly grasp will meet you;
> There lovely maids as bright as morn
>   With sunny smiles will greet you
> And there they strove the Red above
>   To raise Green Ireland's banner—
> There yet its fold they'll see unrolled
>   Upon the banks of Anner.

Abortion

1956

The 1956 trial of an abortionist in Dublin was reported in only one newspaper.* I imagine that the reticence of the greater part of the press is to be explained by the plausible theory that reading about other people's sins, even when they have been chastised, is a doubtful incentive to virtue, and that if a sinner has been adequately punished, he should be spared the extra humiliation of publicity.

The Irish Times took a contrary view, justifying its publication of the facts on the grounds of public morals. Society must be made aware of its frailties before it can correct them. There may have been a further motive which was not avowed lest it be misconstrued as sympathy for the criminals. The interpreters of the law are, in a democratic country, responsible to the people and the people have a right to judge for themselves how this trust is fulfilled.

This sharp distinction of policy does not depend on editorial caprice, it runs through our whole social existence and particularly the insufficiently explored danger zone of sexual morals. Even when we condemn the same thing, we condemn it from such different standpoints that the unanimity of our wrath seems precarious and

*A nurse, Mary Ann Cadden, was arrested on 28 April 1956 in Dublin and charged with the murder of Helen O'Reilly, a young married woman from Ballyragget, Co. Kilkenny. At her trial, which opened at the Four Courts on 22 October 1956, ninety-four witnesses were called, eighty-eight for the prosecution and six for defence. Although evidence was largely circumstantial, on 1 November (at the time of the Suez Crisis) she was found guilty and sentenced to death by hanging three weeks after the trial. As the judge pronounced sentence, bidding the Lord to have mercy on the defendant's soul, Nurse Cadden interrupted him saying, "I'm not a Catholic—take that!" Her sentence was commuted to life imprisonment.

accidental. The angel that stands at the gate of the garden is attentive to Catholic doctrine, but his sword, the law, came from a noted Protestant workshop. Time has blunted it a little and he wields it with more ferocity than skill.

Unanimity, even of disapproval, is so rare and valuable that it is necessary to examine carefully the points at which it is threatened.

Abortion is in Ireland universally condemned. Even those who believe most in the Protestant right of private judgment would not wish the laws against it repealed. Private judgment on moral problems has in their eyes had too little training here to be trusted with so heavy a responsibility. Reflection, therefore, may lead us to rebel against the application of the law but not against the law itself.

The impact of the law has not seldom been diverted by such reflection and justice has not suffered. When men commit offences against themselves, they are often liable to be punished as though it were against others they had offended; yet embarrassment is usually shown in imposing the penalty. The man who attempts to take his own life is often treated with pity and comprehension. Excuses are sought for him in mental or physical breakdown, or if he be a hunger-striker or a defeated general, in patriotism or principle. The convicted abortionist who tried to kill himself was not therefore considered to have aggravated his guilt.

There are other unnatural offences which the law has always been disinclined to punish. Origen, putting a strange interpretation on an utterance of Christ's (Matt. 19:12*), deprived himself of the hope of posterity. Such an act was a breach of the civil law of Rome, but his contemporaries recognized the purity as well as the perversity of his intention. It was not till many years later that a jealous rival sought to have him condemned for a "monstrous act." He failed.

In Romania there is a sect of Christians of high moral character whose men have for generations, from mistaken piety, committed the sin of Origen. As far as I know, the Romanian government has not taken proceedings against them.

Suicide and self-mutilation lie within the same range of unnatural acts as contraception or abortion, and raise the same moral problems as state sterilization and euthanasia. Non–Roman Catholics can dis-

---

*"For there are some eunuchs which were so born from their mother's womb: and there are some eunuchs which were made eunuchs of men: and there be eunuchs which have made themselves eunuchs for the kingdom of heaven's sake. He that is able to receive it, let him receive it."—ed.

cuss them from the standpoint of social expediency without disrespect to the moral order. In their interpretation of natural law and its adjustments to society they are more sensitive to humanitarian than to doctrinal considerations, and their principles are as likely to carry them to extremes of ruthlessness as of indulgence. For example, Bernard Shaw, who was brought up an Irish Protestant, in a letter to *The Irish Times*, advocated "involuntary euthanasia" but was himself opposed, on principle, to imprisonment and punishment. Very few Irish Protestants would follow him far in either direction along this road, but it is one on which our thoughts, if they move at all, travel easily, while Catholic thinking has long diverged from it. Shaw is not, I believe, further away from contemporary Protestant orthodoxy than was John Milton when *Areopagitica*, the gospel of free speech, and the *Doctrine of Divorce* were written. The *Doctrine* was more than two centuries ahead of its time; *Areopagitica* is, in Ireland at least, still poignantly topical. Two fortresses of Protestant opinion, captured with difficulty, have been abandoned with hardly a struggle. Only Yeats, like Milton the greatest poet of his age, defended them with passion.

The Protestant toleration of contraception is often treated as a symptom of newfangled self-indulgence and degeneration. In fact it is in line with the Great Puritan's distrust of that

fugitive and cloistered virtue . . . whose whiteness is but an excremental whiteness. There would be little work left for preaching if law and contemplation should grow so fast upon these things which heretofore were governed only by exhortation.

Abortion, on the other hand, is in most Protestant as well as Catholic countries still strongly condemned. Liberal thinking has not yet discovered for it a place in that sphere of exhortation to which the prophets of science will soon, in all likelihood, relegate it. Yet already the law can only grasp it by the tail. The bird escapes the table and grace is solemnly pronounced over a handful of dirty feathers. The recent trials reveal with what hypocrisy and confusion of thought the topic is inevitably attended.

Abortion often comes within reach of the law solely because in a number of cases it still cannot be achieved without a skilled accomplice, who charges black market prices. This person can be caught and punished.

Yet is not this accomplice, who is made to bear the full weight of the punishment and retribution for the unnatural act, a mere incident in its achievement? The will to withhold life or to destroy it unborn will already have expressed itself in action before, as a last and terrible resort, the technician's aid is invoked. The originators of the unwanted life will first have exhausted all the resources of the drugstores and their own invention. By Roman Catholic teaching, that will is evil from the moment it enters the heart, but except for the ban on the import and sale of contraceptives, no attempt has been made to incorporate this doctrine in our country's laws. First, it would be impossible; secondly, in the eyes of the law and in actual fact, we are not all of us Roman Catholics. It is only the last phase of this destructive endeavour which the law can recognize, and blackmail or bribery or professional jealousy or incompetence and physical suffering are the unvarying routes by which detection travels.

The Roman Catholic has been trained to respect as sacrosanct our natural reverence for the body and the fruits of the body. It would be impertinent for a non–Roman Catholic to guess how far the sanctions of such a faith, unsupported by the law, can govern behaviour. But outside the Roman Catholic Church this powerful instinct is, for the most part, allowed to take its own course, a congenital revulsion against all that impairs the body or its functions. It is not without the blessings of religion, but there are few anathemas to guarantee it. It admits, therefore, a strong counterpoise in an equally potent inhibition, deriving from nature but refined by civilization. I mean that strong revulsion against encroachment upon the physical intimacies of others, or the secrecies of passion. Only prurience or deep moral indignation can override it.

The power of imaginative withdrawal from the privacies of other men's lives is surely an important element in morality which the moralist too often disregards or disposes of with a glib quotation: "To the pure all things are pure." He asks us to infer that this aloofness is a rare privilege of holiness. On the contrary, it is one of the mind's most precious resources, an aspect not of acquired saintliness, but of uncorrupted human nature, reflected daily in our lives and in our legislation and in our complex and incalculable reaction to moral problems.

The repugnance which the abortion trials inspired sprang, I believe, not only from the nature of the offence but also from the manner of its exposure. Two taboos, not one, had been violated. An unnatural act had been committed and a more than unnatural searchlight focused on it. We revolted against looking in the direction in which the searchlight pointed. It was as if we feared that, if we explored those recesses of the erring soul, we might find more than we bargained for: faithfulness, perhaps, or tender forethought; anyway a confusion of tortured but normal emotions from which it would be hard and hateful to disentangle the guilty impulse. We turned with relief to the outer fringe of light, where abortionists and procurers were momentarily illuminated. No taboo protected them. Some advertised, most took money, all courted a moderate publicity. Other offences seemed likely. In such a setting the dingiest sin looked scarlet. Here were the obvious *corpora vilia* for the moral demonstration.

Since taboos are often in conflict, it is sometimes impossible without the selectiveness of faith to regard them as inviolable. A taboo can be brought under the control of reason and yet survive undiminished. The dissection of corpses was condemned by the Church in the Middle Ages (as was inoculation in the eighteenth and anaesthetics at childbirth in the nineteenth centuries). The abortionist, to the common man, for long remained as evil a figure as his parasite, the body snatcher. Today the dissection of the dead is as repulsive to our senses as it was to our ancestors; yet we accept it with our intellects, which have power to control our senses.

The arguments by which taboos are manipulated are not always as good as the humanitarian arguments of medicine. Two, at least, in common use at abortion trials seem crude and disingenuous.

It is assumed that the desire of gain is the only motive which can induce a man to assist at these illegal operations. If he tried to palliate his offence by asserting that he believes, as Protestants believe of contraception, that it is a matter for private judgment, he would not be credited with sincerity. Therefore, he seldom does. Even when his charges for a delicate and often risky operation are less than a third of his defending counsel's it is still he who is the bloodsucker, drawing his wages from the panic and distress of his client. Is this true? I am not thinking of Dublin personalities; I am merely recalling that almost all European countries where laws against abortion exist have free and open debate about the consideration and modification of that law. In some countries these modifications have been adopted by the state. I am not qualified to say whether the state was right in so doing, but I refuse to believe that all these would-be reformers were influenced by the profits to be drawn from abortion or would indeed have tolerated them. Clearly, in fact, the baser type of abortionist and his ally, the blackmailer, will thrive and do the best business where his trade is regarded as most dangerous and nefarious, and tariffs can, in consequence, be highest.

There is a second argument. With constant use, the element of truth in it has been worn down like the surface of a matchbox. Roughly the thesis is that private moral practices have far-reaching social effects. To challenge it seems to be condoning immorality, so it has escaped the analysis it deserves. I can do no more here than suggest grounds for supposing that it is firstly highly dangerous, secondly untrue.

To associate the welfare of the state with private morals is only to open the door to a materialistic eugenics equally repugnant to Protestant and to Roman Catholic. It was through that door that state-licensed abortion came in Russia, and in Germany the laws for the sterilization of the unfit and the annulment of the *Misch-Ehe.* * It is useless to deny that these innovations occurred at a time of social invigoration or that moral purges are seldom effected without the aid of some corrupt fanaticism, racial, political, religious. Except with a stupid or a servile people is there any point in employing such a clumsy and two-edged instrument of control? It can be used as easily to attack the domestic virtues as to defend them. Personal morality must be built upon the natural impulses of loyalty, love and disinterested affection, without appeal to that general well-being of the state around which controversy will always rage.

Secondly, there is evidence enough that men are, like certain other mammals, by nature monogamous, philoprogenitive, child-loving, and that contrary impulses either depend on congenital idiosyncrasy or are the symptoms not the causes of social decline. Rationalist historians argued that the decay of Roman civilization was accelerated by the withdrawal of the best and most intelligent to monasticism and celibacy. Christian propagandists are constantly guilty of a similar inversion of the facts. We were used, for instance, to hearing that the decline of France in the political world was due to the overthrow of moral standards. If that is so, what is the explanation of the fabulous growth of Russian power and influence? At a time when the marriage laws were so loose that divorce could be achieved in a few hours and abortion clinics were distributed over the whole country, the population was expanding rapidly. Though five great states had been carved out of imperial Russia, in a very few years Lenin had as many subjects as the Tsar. When the time comes for a nation to expand, the abortionist cannot stop it; in a

---

* "Mixed" marriages, ie., between Jews and non-Jews.—ed.

time of decay or uncertainty his popularity has the significance of a symptom, not a cause.

There is little connection between morality and the birth rate, and even less between the birth rate and national pre-eminence. Do nations make their chief contribution to civilization at the time of their greatest fertility and expansion? Jews, Greeks and Southern Slavs increased enormously in numbers but not in repute after they had suffered defeat and degradation. Negroes and Red Indians multiplied like cattle when they were treated like cattle. Our own period of greatest expansion was in the ignoble decades before the Famine. When Ireland was Christianizing Europe our population would have fitted into one of our great cities. If there is any connection between spiritual superiority and birth rate it would be as easy and as profitless to say it was an inverse one. The more conscious we are of our responsibilities to those who come after us (and such consciousness must be one of the tests of civilization), the more attentive we shall be to the conditions of their birth, the less ready to give nature her head. These misgivings are not proof of health and wisdom, but they most often assail those who lack the armour of ignorance or apathy. They may lead men to neurotic thoughts and acts and yet be neither base nor self-indulgent.

Finally, does any doctor seriously believe that science, which is every hour perfecting new ways of destroying life swiftly and anonymously, which has succeeded in reproducing animal life without intercourse, will be for long baffled by the problems of destroying unborn life? It is possible that before our abortionists have served their sentence, inventions will be accessible to all which will throw the professional out of business. In that case the law would abdicate a control it could no longer exercise and bequeath it to the sanctions of the Roman Catholic faith, the Protestant private judgment, and, if he could help, the customs officer.

In the meantime the law stands and must be enforced and the abortionist is the obvious scapegoat for the public abhorrence of abortion. If he acts in accordance with principles, he must be prepared to suffer for them; if he is a mere blackmailer few will regret his condition. Sometimes the same man doubles the part of blackmailer and abortionist, and blackmail is seen as a secondary attribute of his crime. In fact, blackmail is bred not of abortion but of the law against abortion, and it is necessary that the law should take rigorous and public measures to disavow it. This does not always happen.

The sentence pronounced on the offender should be in accordance with enlightened opinion, not with popular sentiment which is readily misinterpreted or exploited. Men gladly "compound for sins they have a mind to by damning those they're not inclined to." Moral indignation can be stimulated by loose or foolish words, but it is today too precious a commodity to be abused or squandered.

The offence was likened to murder, which is thereby belittled, and the savage penalty accorded with this interpretation. The analogy is false and cannot be defended without callousness or casuistry. We live at a time when widespread homicide is organized by states and condoned by churches. Inside the state itself, society, mobilized for war, can exert upon its incompatibles a pressure for which there is no precedent. Thousands have chosen unsanctified modes of escape for themselves and their progeny.

The names of only the more eminent of these criminals are known. About them all the moralist is forced to be as reticent as the statistician. We have not the data either to count or to condemn. One thing, however, is sure. Only the very inexperienced can now maintain that every attack upon the living or the about to live which the state has not authorized is necessarily occasioned by murderous impulses. Our vehement and implacable feelings about the taking of unborn life, if they are genuine, may derive as easily from ignorance and good fortune as from morality.

But are they genuine? There is a simple test which we can practice upon ourselves. Let us suppose that behind that flamboyant doorway in Merrion Square we knew that children were being not prevented but ill treated. How would we have reacted? Would we not have burst through it ourselves, had the law delayed intervention? Instead, for years we have passed it by, laymen and professionals, with at most a disapproving shrug, a cynical observation. True feeling expresses itself otherwise.

THE REFERENDUM*
1983

I believe the proposed Amendment to be religiously divisive, but if all these discussions help us to understand each other, these months of complicated argument won't have been spent uselessly.

---

*A referendum was proposed on a "Pro-Life Amendment to the Irish Constitution," aiming to strengthen the existing law against abortion. The proposed Amendment was: "Article 40.3.3: 'The State acknowledges the right to life of the unborn and, with due regard to

There are many Protestant sects, but most of them attach weight to private judgment and we hesitate to force our own convictions on others, especially when we do not fully understand the other person's world.

Yet I am speaking for myself alone when I say that we have no right, as outsiders, to put pressure on others to bear children against their will, against their judgment and maybe against their consciences. Abortion is always an evil but best seen as a symptom of a far greater evil, the total uncaringness of our society. The child belongs to its father as much as to its mother and he, no less than she, may be unwilling to launch into the world a child which for some reason he cannot acknowledge and to which he cannot give a father's love and care.

What happens to these unwanted children that are born to a single parent? I suspect that a great many of them find their way into institutions, or are advertised around for adoption. Many of them never lack the sense of being unloved and deprived, and few parents will ever lack a sense of guilt towards them. It is a human dilemma which the Amendment will in no way help us to solve. It will merely give to those who vote for it a totally barren and unjustified sense of a duty accomplished.

For it is not just a moral issue but a practical one as well. If through our easy, unreflecting votes an increased number of unwanted children are brought into the world, are we going to shoulder our responsibility towards them? We may persuade ourselves we will be able for it—but stop and think! What have we done in the past year for an unmarried mother or an unwanted child? Answering for myself I should say "precious little." What are we likely to do in the future? Ask yourselves about that too. And indeed what can you do? The world in which the unwanted child is born today is a very cruel one. It is no longer one of settled families, settled neighbourhoods, long-standing, hereditary friendships and obligations. Each man has to fend for himself much more than ever before.

For us to talk passionately about the killing of the unborn is sanctimonious and hypocritical. Who gives unqualified respect now to the commandment "Thou shalt not kill"? In every country in time

---

the equal right to life of the mother, guarantees in its laws to respect, and, as far as practicable, by its laws to defend and vindicate that right.' " Butler made these remarks at an anti-Amendment meeting in Kilkenny on 18 May 1983. On 7 September, the vote was 66.45 percent Yes, 32.8 percent No. There was a turnout of 53.67 percent; those in the majority represented 35.66 of the overall electorate.—ed.

of war or civil disturbance such as exist today all over the world, killing is regarded not only as venial but even as heroic, though it leaves behind broken families and fatherless children. What are armies and navies for, except for killing? What else is the object of our stupendous armaments? Let us not add hypocrisy to callousness. When we go in a few weeks' time to vote, let us in full confidence vote against the Amendment.

Saints, Scholars and
Civil Servants

1954

Every now and then small books on local antiquities are published in the provinces, reviewed enthusiastically in the local press, and bought conscientiously by the local clergy and intelligentsia. They make no impact on Dublin scholarship, no one reads them there or pays them the more valuable tribute of seriously criticizing them. They are not usually very good and yet they have a charm and an authenticity that is their own. The writers have visited what they describe again and again, they have scrubbed old tomb slabs with bunches of wild carrot, barked their shins climbing locked gates and waited patiently while the village antiquary fetches some treasure for their inspection and pricing. It is perhaps a Chinese calendar found by his brother after the earthquake of San Francisco. However austere the writer's intentions, he seldom manages altogether to exclude the traces of the sunlight and the fields and long desultory conversations in farmyards. Here he is vague and skimpy because it began to rain, here there is excess of detail because he wanted to stretch to its uttermost some hawthorn-scented evening.

These books were once lush and gossiping. Now they are rather prim and scared, as though some official of the Board of Works was watching with ironic smile. They do not digress very much now and that is a pity because it is in digressions that we provincials have the advantage. A Dublin guess as to who built the Giant's Grave is as good as ours, but only we know who stole the Corporation mace. In one respect the books have not changed at all: there are plenty of misprints. Mr. O'Kelly's book on the place

names of Co. Kilkenny* belongs to the new "austere" school of
country lore. Mr. Brandon's† is at a slight tangent to it, but they
both illustrate so well the obstacles in the path of those who study
the Irish past that they can be considered together.

Mr. O'Kelly is an accomplished Irish scholar, and in a small way
he has done for Kilkenny what Canon Power did for Waterford.
Expanded and improved, this book might rival Power's in importance. But first of all every Kilkenny person should buy it, read it
and, most urgent of all, criticize it and send their criticisms to Mr.
O'Kelly. Even those who are not Irish scholars are entitled to comment, for Mr. O'Kelly, like many other topographers, has had to
wrestle with that demon of unreality which the Gaelic League begat
upon the Post Office. I wish, for instance, he could have liberated
the citizens of Bennettsbridge from that Civil Service conceit Baile Ui
Cheochain, by which their village has been rechristened, for it has
been known as Bennettsbridge or Pons Sancti Benedicti since the
fourteenth century. Though the new address may recall a forgotten
townland, no local person has ever used it or even heard of it. Even
the Ormonde Deeds do not record it. How did we come by it? Often
I've wondered whether it has not some origin like the Slovene mountain which is mapped "No-thank-you-I-don't-smoke." The Italian
cartographer from Milan was in a hurry. He had waved his cigarette
case enquiringly at the mountain and had been misunderstood by the
natives.

Local history is bedevilled by these metropolitan intrusions. Irish
place names are a slow indigenous growth. Many of them come and
go with the tribes and families that cultivated the fields. As they fade
they carry a little history away from everyday speech, but a sediment
remains in the printed record. What can be stupider than to falsify
this record?

For example, did the lips of man ever utter Mr. O'Kelly's phrase
"Garran an Chraimirigh"? Did they not always say "Cramersgrove"?
Or just "Cramers" or "the Grove"? Two generations ago the Miss
Cramer-Roberts were known to many. I have photographs of them.
Their tennis racquets had very long handles and there were buttons
all down the front of their black bodices. They would have looked
at you in blank amazement if you had talked to them about Garran
an Chraimirigh. They were harmless people: they ought to be allowed

*Eoghan Ó Ceallaigh, *Place-names of Co. Kilkenny* (Kilkenny People, 1954).
†Rev. E. A. Brandon, *To Whom We Dedicated* (Dundalgan Press, W. Tempest, 1954).

the luxury of knowing best about their own name. For a similar reason Wallslough should not be called Loch an Fhaltaigh. It derives from the Norman family of De Valle. They may have been aliens but they came to Ireland before the potato. Ought not the same courtesy to be extended to them as is shown to "Kerr's Pink" and even "British Queen"? A generation ago local Irish scholars such as Canon Carrigan, the historian of Ossory, would never have made these mistakes.

As one explores more ancient names the need for unprejudiced common sense becomes more and more apparent. Mr. O'Kelly's pages, like those of every similar book in Ireland, are peppered with the names of saints whose hallowed, featureless figures are used to stop the gaps in our knowledge of the past, gaps through which the salubrious breeze of free inquiry might otherwise be blowing. On page 54 three of these saints, of whom history has no record, follow one after the other: St. Lamraighe of Killamery, St. Sheallacham of Kiltallaghan, St. Teresa of Kiltrassy. Now the first two of these saints Mr. O'Kelly has invented and the third he has imported from Spain. Canon Carrigan gives no authority for any of them. Killamery derives from the Lamraighe tribe, which is also to be traced in Munster and in Monaghan.

Mr. Brandon's little book concerns the saints, principally Irish, to whom the Irish Protestant churches are dedicated. It appeared first in instalments in the *Church of Ireland Gazette*. It was an excellent idea but badly executed. Such a book cannot easily be written if one has not caught some infection from Dr. Plummer's scholarship, Father Shearman's enthusiasm or Canon O'Hanlon's gigantic industry. It is true that Plummir (*sic*) is listed tersely just after F. (*sic*) Gibbon's *Decline and Fall* (two [*sic*] volumes), but one looks as vainly for the learned credulity of Plummer as for the learned scepticism of Gibbon. This is very depressing because the book makes its appearance with some pomp, a foreword by a bishop and another by a lord, and acknowledgments to a dozen church dignitaries.

The decline in Irish book production is so acute that now, as with an infants' class, the critic has first of all to give marks for tidiness before approaching the question of knowledge. Mr. Brandon and his printers start at the very bottom of the class. From the National Muesum (*sic*) on the first page to Wedon, alias Weedon, Northamptonshire, and St. Ethelbreada, alias St. Etheldreda of Ely, on the last, the printers have added on every page a philological puzzle of their own to all those that the student of hagiography must encounter. The *Gazette* is an admirable paper, but those who know it will conjecture sadly that this tornado of misprints originated in Middle Abbey Street rather than in Dundalk. For did not the *Gazette* recently publish an excellent article in which simultaneous homage was paid to W. B. Yeates, the poet, and J. B. Yates, the painter?

I have calculated that between them and their printers, Mr. O'Kelly and Mr. Brandon have in a single year added seven or eight new saints to the calendar. Does not this floodlight one of the methods by which in even less literate centuries the hosts of Heaven were recruited? The Irish saints, over six thousand of them, live in a seldom-traversed reserve into which, for some generations now, no unsurpliced scholar had ventured very far. One hundred and fifty years ago the clergy themselves were more enterprising. Ledwich, a canon of St. Canice's, Kilkenny, dared to say that the Irish saints mostly never existed. He said that St. Coemgen was a mountain, St. Senan a river, and St. Domangart was just Co. Down.

Let the impious and foolish tales of ignorant and superstitious ecclesiastics warn us of that miserable degradation of the human mind, which alone could give them currency and credit.... To believe that a barbarous people, naked and ignorant as American Indians, should have preserved the pedigree of St. Kevin is too much for the most stupid credulity.

This is very rude as well as unjust, and Ledwich made it worse by exhorting the "Hibernians" that their hearts "must overflow with gratitude to the Author of all Blessings" because of the "fostering care of Britain," which had led them to polite manners. It is refreshing, nonetheless, to hear a scholar say just what he thinks, even when candour is easy, as it was for Ledwich in 1804. National consciousness cannot have been as sensitive then as it later became, for John, Earl of Upper Ossory, of the royal line of Ossory kings, accepted the dedication of Ledwich's book. Nor did any rumour of tithe wars or disestablishment disturb the peace of Aghaboe Rectory in those pre-Victorian days.

I do not think that his outburst did any harm. It provoked a long and lively discussion and out of the commotion several of the great figures of Victorian scholarship emerged—Petrie, O'Donovan, O'Curry, Graves, some of them "Ascendancy Irish," some native. The new archaeology was more neighbourly as well as more cautious than the old.

Though Ledwich's valuable essay on the history of Kilkenny certainly paved the way for the Kilkenny Archaeological Society, that Society, which for nearly a hundred years exercised a great influence on the study of the Irish past, was swayed much more by Petrie, a Protestant champion of the Irish saints, than by Ledwich; as the century went on, less and less was said against St. Kevin and his fellows, and as the Anglo-Irish and their church began to feel the draught of doom, a reticence which had originated in courtesy continued in discretion.

For the middle years of the *Journal of the Royal Society of Antiquaries of Ireland*, as this Kilkenny organ was later to call itself, the Irish saints became the unchallenged property of Father Shearman, a delightful writer to whom the saints and their complicated family ramifications were as real as his own parishioners. His work is of lasting value, for, even if the people, places and events, which he coordinates so ingeniously, belong not to this world but to fairyland, the texture of his argument is sound, his learning and industry beyond praise.

The Prince Consort was invited to be Patron of the Society and he sent £25. By many delicate adjustments the harmony of the Society was maintained. I am sure that no one was so crude as to say, "You be nice about our royal family and we'll be nice about your saints," but the scandal of Ledwich was never repeated and in one of Father Shearman's genealogical trees it can be seen that both St. Mochop of Kilchop and St. Aedhan the Leper were distant cousins of Queen Victoria.

All that is long ago. Reading Mr. Brandon's book I felt convinced that the reaction against Ledwich had now gone far enough and that the movement for the rehabilitation of the Celtic saints, which had begun in chivalry, had ended in sterility. It is not only that Ledwich wrote much better than his more orthodox successors, but his ideas acted like leaven even on those who disagreed with him, while Mr. Brandon's little book could only have been published in a society in which the last bubble of intellectual ferment had long ago died down.

One would not wish a return to the rolling periods of Ledwich, but Mr. Brandon's periods wobble so at the joints that it is often a miracle that they reach the end of a paragraph without a collapse: "It is to be regretted that the church has not used the name of this saint more widespread," or "His chief claim to fame is due to the mentioning of him by St. Augustine."

Sometimes he risks a conjecture of his own. "He [St. Fethlimidh] was known as 'the Small,' which seems to imply that he was a person of diminutive proportions," but he is not often so daring. His only aim seems to be to prove that we are no upstart garrison church, or, as he puts it, that "the historicity of our church is constantly emphasized by our dedications." At no point does he show any of that concern, which Ledwich expressed so tactlessly, for the "human mind" and its possible degradation by believing things that are not true, and yet if his church and mine has claims for survival in Ireland, is not that concern for truth one of the strongest?

He is very careless, though accuracy is surely an important element of truth, even when you give it an ecclesiastical capital. The Synod of Drumceatt, which he spells differently in different places, was not held in Co. Meath but near Limavady. No saint was ever called St. Molna or St. Finntian Munnu, and St. Laserian was not called Lamliss, though he had a cave at Lamlash on the Isle of Arran. What does Mr. Brandon mean by saying that "St. Ibor, an obscure fifth-century saint, probably had Danish origins"? The Danes were not in Ireland in the fifth century. To say that St. Moling was also called St. Tighmulling is like saying that Mr. Brandon is also called Mr. Celbridge-Rectory.

But it is poor fun criticizing Mr. Brandon like this, for his book is far better than no book. No Irishman who is sensitive to the numinous quality of our civilization can afford to ignore the Irish saints. Mr. Brandon can reflect that if he wrote a book in a more sceptical vein, he would have to meet a volley of abuse greater than Ledwich ever encountered.

But why should it be undermining to our morals or bruising to our national pride if one were to argue that the Irish saints were many of them the tribal gods of a gentle and intelligent people, whose racial origins retreat so far into history that to use national terms for them, Celt, Iberian, Gaulish, would not be easy? I was brought up in the diocese of St. Canice, but the less I believed in him, the more I was fascinated by him. He covered five Irish counties and as many Scottish and Welsh ones with his churches and miracles. He left his crozier in Iona, the little toe of his right foot in northern Italy, and, standing on one leg, was fed by seagulls in the Gower Peninsula.* He is a link between the mediaeval world and one that is immemorially old. Those who treat him as a monastic fiction are as wrong as Cardinal Moran, who saw him in his own image as a busy Irish

---

*In Wales.—ed.

prelate with widespread diocesan responsibilities. The lives of the Irish saints reflect an ingenious innocence, a primaeval charity, that links them with Greek legend and the beginnings of poetry. For example, when St. Ailbe, travelling in Italy, resurrected two horses and their groom, who had been killed by lions, he took pity on the hungry, disappointed carnivores and arranged for a suitable meal (an *aptum prandium*) to come down from Heaven for them on a cloud.

St. Coemgen was not, I am sure, as Ledwich maintained, a mountain, but St. Senan has undoubtedly a very queer relationship with the Shannon, as though the same tribe had left its name with saint and river. And Coemgen's pedigree is quite as odd as Ledwich declared. He is said to have got his name because he was beautiful, *caem*. But his father was Caemlug, his grandfather Caemfid, his mother Caemell, his brothers Caeman and Nathcaem, his sisters were similarly called and they were almost all of them saints. Though there are several lives of Coemgen we are told nothing more convincing about him than that he gathered apples off willow trees and that a bird nested in his outstretched hand. Surely his life requires a more cold-blooded Ledwichian analysis than that given him by (say) Mr. Liam Price in his learned and excellent surveys of Co. Wicklow.

The only really repulsive saint in Mr. Brandon's collection is not Irish but Norse, and has, alas, some claims to "historicity." St. Olaf the Holy, also called St. Olaf the Fat, who has a church in Waterford, is a figure from Belsen. At his orders those who rejected the Gospel had their hands or feet cut off, had their eyes gouged out, were crucified or strangled. Mr. Brandon is very terse about him and even the charitable Canon O'Hanlon is at loss to account for these excesses "in so just and humane a king." "A zealot in his endeavours to establish Christianity," he declares, "Olaf seems often to have wanted prudence." In his case it is a relief to learn that his toenails grew for thirty-six years after his death, that there was in Norway an annual ceremony of cutting them, and that when his unbelieving brother had him burnt alive (one may ask how did he have toenails if he was burnt alive), a dragon issued from his ashes and destroyed the brother. These anecdotes are reassuring because they permit us to be sceptical of what without them might be plausible. There is hope that St. Olaf was quite an ordinary man like the rest of us and that his "imprudences" as well as his virtues have been exaggerated.

Since archaeology became a state-supported profession, first audacity went and then integrity, and there is today in Ireland no room for any but the pundit and the puppet, and a curious parasitical entente has been established between them. I have heard distinguished scholars discoursing at Glendalough and Clonmacnoise, evading the central issues and revealing their real thoughts only in giggling asides. There is the same falsity in this as in the pseudo-democratic brogue which Victorian noblemen used for the gardener or the joviality of headmistresses on Parents' Day. Only the stupid are deceived but it is to them that this homage is paid.

Professional scholars will be indulgent to Mr. Brandon because he does not seriously challenge their authority, but let some Ledwich of our meagre days, shorn of his imperial arrogance, raise his head from a country rectory to write a serious but sceptical investigation of Coemgen and there would be a sally from all the fortresses of learning. What a brandishing there would be of monophthongs and cranial indices and marginal glosses! The wretched Ledwich junior would fly for his life and only the most experienced student of academic footnotes would be able to detect that the scholars in their hearts had sympathy for the heresies that had been uttered but resented that the diplomatic truce should be breached by an outsider.

If you turn to the country publications of a hundred years ago and compare them with those of today, you will be stunned by the utter decay of that lively and daring spirit of inquiry which once gave rise to the Kilkenny Archaeological Society and was nourished by it for many years. Where did it go to and what are the inhibitions that prevent its return? The first stage in their detection is to recognize that they exist. As the scholar bends over his manuscript, a shadow falls on his page, and then a second shadow and a third. Who is it that has tiptoed behind him? Is it the minister of finance, calculating the cost of university chairs and the grants for excavation? Is it the president of the Gaelic League or the secretary of the Tourist Board, watching over our cultural and spiritual exports and imports? Is it St. Olaf brandishing his imprudent crozier? Is it . . . ?

But the shadows fall so thick and fast on my own page that I cannot see to write. I shall write no more.

Boucher de Perthes:
The Father of Prehistory

1986

Some years ago I was looking at the earliest records of the old Kilkenny Archaeological Society, which I had recently revived in our neighbourhood. It had been started in 1848 by our rector, Mr. Graves, with the help of some doctors, newspapermen and country gentlemen. Though it was later to attract the antiquaries of Dublin and finally to be absorbed by them and moved to the capital as the Royal Society of Antiquaries of Ireland, these first journals belonged to its obscure and rustic infancy. I was surprised therefore to find that two years after its foundation the Society had already captured the interest of a Frenchman. He was given the title of Honorary Foreign Corresponding Member and his name was M. Jacques Boucher de Crèvecoeur de Perthes, president of the Société d'Emulation at Abbeville (near the coast some 135 kilometres north of Paris).

Boucher de Perthes (1788–1868) was the son of aristocratic parents from Abbeville. His father, liberal enough to keep his post as a director of customs throughout the Revolution, was an enthusiastic botanist and the founder of the scientific society of which his son was to be president; his mother's family claimed descent from that of Joan of Arc. Boucher de Perthes adopted his father's profession and was made director of customs at Abbeville in 1825. Becoming interested in the geological strata of a local gravel pit, he gradually collected a large number of hand axes and other flint tools, undoubtedly man-made, of the kind known later as Abbevillois. These artefacts were present, with the bones of extinct animals, in strata described by the geologists as Antediluvian (before the Flood). From 1838 onwards he sought to convince the scientific world that man had existed thousands of years earlier than anyone had supposed: he had in fact discovered the Old Stone Age. He was met with the same total indifference as was later to be the lot of Mendel when he approached the leading specialists of his generation. He did receive some encouragement from the great Danish archaeologist Worsaae, and eventually one of his leading detractors, Rigollet of Amiens, excavated the gravel pits of St. Acheul in order to refute him but discovered the tools now called Acheulian, and in 1854 published findings in agreement with Boucher's. However, it was not until 1859, more than twenty years after he began to publicize his discovery, that the antiquity of man and the work of Boucher de Perthes himself finally received the stamp of official scientific approval.

In France he is honoured today as the Father of Prehistory, but in 1850, though he had already published the volume of *Antiquités Celtiques et Antédiluviennes* (1847) in which his great discovery was announced, almost no one had read it. He was still regarded by the pundits of London and Paris as a ridiculous old provincial bore. For many years he had been pestering them to visit Abbeville and sending them parcels of flint implements and bones and books. Some of the implements seemed fakes and the accompanying diagrams were very unprofessional. How could anyone believe this tedious person when he said he had discovered the implements beside the bones of extinct animals during the digging of a canal near Abbeville?

And how had it come about that our obscure Society had been the first of all the learned bodies in the British Isles to honour M. de Perthes? Were there perhaps, I speculated, champions of Antediluvian Man in Kilkenny? I looked up the *Journal* of 1859 for evidence of their triumph, for in the spring of that year Sir John Evans and Dr. Prestwich had at last visited Abbeville and a month later communicated to the Royal Society their official recognition of Antediluvian Man. The old gentleman, after years of arduous campaigning, had been gloriously vindicated.

I found nothing of all this in the *Journal* for 1859. When after his victory the Honorary Foreign Corresponding Member visited Ireland, he did not come to Kilkenny. So I concluded that it was as the president of an exemplary regional society and not as the Father of Prehistory that he had been co-opted. His father had founded the Société d'Emulation in the Revolutionary year VI (1795) and he himself had revived it, when it was almost moribund, in 1825. To the Kilkenny Archaeological Society it must have appeared as a model, for both groups gloried in being provincial and were proud to have created in two intellectually decaying corners of Europe two lively, critical and fearlessly speculative associations.

It may have been Boucher who took the initiative. I found in the appendix of an early *Journal* a list of donations which included one of Boucher's famous parcels. It must have caused some surprise in the Irish Society but it was characteristic of Boucher and throws light upon the birth of a science. It contained, besides the momentous work on Antediluvian Man, samples of Boucher's philosophy, poetry and folklore, and even a satirical comedy called *La Marquise de Montalle*. The Kilkenny Society was by no means as austere as it later became and must still have been conscious of its own origins in local sentiment and belles lettres. Evidently they did not laugh at M. de Perthes (but nor, I suspect, did they read him). Without comment, they co-opted him.

It is curious that even today the Father of Prehistory continues to irritate his spiritual children. It seems to them intolerable that fate should have selected this discursive old dilettante, who grew prize pears, wrote poems and plays, organized a swimming bath and, though a customs official, advocated free trade, to carry through a major revolution in geology and anthropology. Had they not dedicated their entire lives to these pursuits? And since collective jealousy is more potent than the individual kind, being laced with professional esprit de corps, some have almost managed to delude themselves that Boucher de Perthes never existed. When I looked him up in my *Chambers Encyclopaedia* (1935) I found that everything was forgotten about him except the jawbone of Moulin Quignon, which he found in 1863 and which is now regarded as a trick played on him by his workmen. For many scholars the science of prehistory did not open till 1859, when tardily and condescendingly Dr. Prestwich and Sir John Evans accepted the invitation of Boucher to Abbeville. For those who might consider this English chronology as odd as that of the Old Testament, which the prehistorians overthrew, Miss Joan Evans, daughter of Sir John, explained in a long article on Boucher de Perthes (*Antiquity*, 1949): "Belief indeed became possible when it was an experienced geologist, and not Boucher de Perthes, who presented the case." In other words, truth has no status till it is endorsed by an "expert."

Miss Evans' article is the most agile exhibition of professional solidarity and filial piety I have ever seen. She deplores Boucher's "horrid little outline plates" with which he tried to convince the sceptics, and, following the Parisian critic Aufrère, she says that Boucher in his autobiography rewrote his own early correspondence so as to antedate by some decades his theory of prehistory. On a lower plane, she says that when he offered his collection of antique Picardy furniture to the museum at Cluny, "it was to secure for himself more consideration in the city" and to get an excise post in Paris, a marble plaque and a gallery bearing his name. When he suggested that a local painter should paint a picture of all the celebrities of Abbeville, "he doubtless expected to find himself in the front row." When he claimed to have visited practically every excavation near Abbeville in the past ten years, "the claim may be well-founded for he was an idle man and a good walker."

Some of this is partly true, yet all is wholly false. Certainly Boucher's discursiveness could be irritating, but only in our dullest moments do we pursue knowledge for its own sake. "Science," he wrote, "helps us to prove but prevents us understanding." In the Age of Science many scholars wear their learning as a well-trained carriage horse wears his blinkers. As an archaeologist Boucher was remarkably modest and open-minded. It seemed to him that it was just because he had a rather vagrant mind that he hit upon the truth, which seldom frequents the highways. "I know about as much science as a donkey does of music," he wrote. That meant that he had fewer misconceptions to eradicate. "Ignorance," he wrote, "is a field in which the nettle and the thistle never took root, so they do not have to be grubbed up."

Boucher fully grasped that the knowledge to which he aspired could not be deep if it was to be wide. "My science," he wrote, "is only foresight," a form of intuition based on wide-ranging reflection and experiment in a dozen arts and sciences, and his triumph was perhaps the last and the greatest of the old polymathic humanism. He took it very lightly indeed: "This victory proves that often it is good to be obstinate and that conviction, united to perseverance, can take the place of knowledge."

Boucher gloried in being an autodidact, an attitude that sometimes reduced his critics to helpless exasperation. Aufrère comments on the scientific innocence of Boucher's five-volume *De La Création*, but he does not quote this extraordinary passage from the introduction.

Perhaps what I am writing is a repetition of what has already been said, for I am completely ignorant of all that has been published on the matter. No scholar has talked to me about it and I have not read the relevant books.

Boucher claimed later that in these volumes he anticipated the discovery of Antediluvian Man, but Aufrère cannot trace him there. In fact the concept of Antediluvian Man was not the child of geology but was hatched in a densely woven cocoon of miscellaneous speculation. In the same way the idea of evolution is thrown off casually in a footnote to Vol. II, p. 362, of *Antiquités*, where, two years before the publication of *The Origin of Species*, Boucher suggests that as the sea retreated, marine animals may have modified their shape by jumping with their flippers. But, as a humanist, Boucher was more concerned with the implications of his theories than with the theories themselves. He sometimes called himself a Pythagorean, for he believed that the power of God is manifest in every living thing, moulding transitory forms and then discarding them: "The creative power is great, for it is that of God himself." This consciousness of divinity is present in every being, so that there can be no such thing as an atheist. The word is meaningless.

As for *De La Création*, Boucher said that only ten people besides himself ever finished reading it and that he never gave it to his friends so that the obligation of reading it should not weigh upon their minds. Yet Aufrère says that Victor Hugo and Lamennais had drawn inspiration from it without acknowledgment, and that it had delighted the followers of the socialist writer Fourier.

Though she gives it an individual twist, Miss Evans gets most of her disparaging comments on Boucher from Aufrère, who is in his own right an interesting character. Obliged to work for some years in Boucher's museum at Abbeville, and impatient with the traditional idolatries of the little town, he scrutinized all the drawers and cabinets in which the old bachelor had stored the debris of eighty years. In the end the Father of Prehistory came to fascinate him more than prehistory itself. He read all his novels, plays, philosophy, folklore and travel. He compared the rough drafts of letters with their published variants. He collated the labels on the exhibits with the records of their discovery. He proved (and no one can now disagree, because everything was destroyed in a bombardment of May 1940) that Boucher, in the cause of prehistory, cheated quite a bit. "In order to get the truth accepted, he was often less than truthful himself."

At the bottom of a drawer M. Aufrère found, ticketed as carefully as a mammoth's bones, a tooth and a chestnut curl. The curl was in a metal frame, embossed with the arms of the de Perthes and the de Crèvecoeurs, and was inscribed: "hair of M. de Boucher de Perthes, April 1853." Beside it was a tooth in a little box labelled:

"last molar extracted from upper jaw by the dentist, M. Catel, March 2, 1855." Combining this with the evidence of the novels, Aufrère deduced a strong vein of narcissism or at least a preoccupation with self which was hardly normal. He found too that Boucher's early novels were inspired by a love affair, real or fanciful, with Napoleon's sister, Princess Pauline Borghese, and he has commemorated this in the reconstructed museum at Abbeville. In the middle of a case full of Boucher's antediluvian artefacts, Aufrère has set a plaster model of the Princess's hand. This is meant, I suppose, to symbolize the intimate association of science and sentiment in Boucher's lifework. I value it more as evidence that Aufrère too was, like Boucher, an ingrained original and hence capable of appreciating the unique blend of obstinacy, clowning and ecstatic vision in which the science of prehistory was born. Aufrère does justice to Boucher, the prophet-scientist, when he writes:

Making a discovery is not just making a lucky find, it is being susceptible to the splendour of an idea. That was what he was, for his thought is rich in resonances. It was through ruminating and writing on the history of man, his arts and sciences, that Boucher had pushed back the frontiers of human history.

But does Aufrère make sufficient allowances for the pathological quirks which may be induced in us by decades of unmerited neglect? Also something more than ordinary vanity is needed to make a man keep and label a decayed molar. What was it? If we knew, we might come to understand better the long solitary life from which prehistory was born and Boucher's Pythagorean belief that the body was the transient lodging of the eternal spirit, which moulded it and would discard it. For his beliefs and his discoveries and the shape of his life were not dictated by his birth and circumstances. He was sociable, rich and vigorous. He had been handsome. He longed to marry, to see his plays staged, to live in Paris. But some irresistible introversion rooted him to Abbeville and to womb-like speculations, which he could share with few.

And is not the learned resistance to prehistory also very interesting psychologically? A congress of scientists had been held at Laon, only a couple of hours by train east of Abbeville. Boucher had as usual bombarded them with parcels and invitations to his gravel pits. They had discussed Antediluvian Man and rejected him, without inspecting the gravel pits, reading Boucher's books or visiting his collections.

I am far from considering myself a savant [he wrote] or even a very clever man, but I am not blind. What seems to me ten times worse than criticism is this obstinate refusal to look at the facts and to say "It's impossible!" without going to see for themselves.

But many times he wrote about it more passionately and surely justifiably: "Hate and persecution at least offer you a chance . . . but indifference is a wall between you and the light, it burns you alive. I'd sooner an enemy who flung Truth back into her well and crashed the bucket down on her head."

The English geologists, Falconer, Prestwich, Evans and many others, who came to Abbeville after 1850 to pay their respects to Antediluvian Man and to the Father of Prehistory, were all of them pleasant, well-educated men, as their long letters to Boucher which have survived the bombardments testify. Yet they would all have agreed that, when you have a revelation of the truth and wish busy experts to accept it, you must draft your propositions in a brief business-like way. Prestwich, announcing Boucher's discovery to the Royal Society, explained his failure to convince them earlier "as politely as he could." This phrase is Miss Evans', but none of them would have thought it inappropriate. The contrast of their busy lives and Boucher's leisured dilettantism is one on which Miss Evans loved to dwell. When Falconer at last accepted Boucher's invitation to Abbeville, he was a day later than he said; the house was all shut up and Boucher himself was sitting in his carriage ready to drive away to the country. Instantly the Father of Prehistory leapt out, cancelled his visit to the country, had his house opened up again and laid himself out to make a convert of Falconer. He succeeded; and a few weeks later Prestwich and Evans, urged on by Falconer, were at Abbeville too. Boucher was at their hotel soon after 7 a.m., and when they returned, converted, from the gravel pits, he gave them what Miss Evans calls "a sumptuous fork lunch." This sounds excessive, almost vulgar. In contrast Prestwich, displaying Boucher's implements and expounding Boucher's discovery to a distinguished gathering in London eight days later, "entertained them with his legendary sherry." For busy men this was just right.

Hugh Falconer in a letter to Prestwich strikes the precise note of amused condescension with which the learned world allowed itself to be convinced by a donkey!

I have a charming letter from M. Boucher de Perthes, full of gratitude to *perfide Albion* for helping him to assured immortality and giving him a lift, when his countrymen of the Institute left him in the gutter. He radiates a benignant smile from his lofty pinnacle on you and me—surprised that the treacherous Leopard should have behaved so well.

Yet it was just the fantastic element in Boucher's character which, allied to his practical earnestness, made him assert the impossible and maintain it doggedly against the experts. Falconer, Evans and Prestwich could have spent a lifetime classifying their tertiary pebbles and sipping their legendary sherry, but they could never have taken that great leap into the inconceivable that the customs officer of Abbeville accomplished with bravado and relish. If they had been capable of such a leap they would have taken it years before, for they had all the evidence beside them. In 1797 John Frere had reported the same combination of artefacts and antediluvian bones in Suffolk, and a dozen other such discoveries had in the intervening years been recorded. The geologists were responsible, gregarious people; industrialists consulted them about seams and measures. Probably they instinctively shied away from that solitude in which subversive discoveries are made. And deep in their subconscious there may have been some apprehension of the explosions that could be triggered off by Antediluvian Man. First there was the War with Moses, as Boucher called it, and round the corner they might have caught a glimpse of evolution and "godless" materialism, and the sinister pseudoscience of social "Darwinism." These premonitions cannot have been clearly defined, but they may have clouded that zone of sensibility that Boucher was trying to inflame, and decided them against opening the door to Antediluvian Man. Boucher himself was not at all frightened by him; there had long been a comfortable place prepared for him in his many-chambered humanist philosophy.

One could find dozens of passages in which Boucher tried to placate the professional scientists; but his main offence was that he had been right, so the more he abased himself and called himself a donkey, the worse it became. If it proved that a scientific revolution could be introduced by a donkey, all the academies in Europe would totter.

Undoubtedly many of Aufrère's semi-genial assaults on Boucher's integrity are unfair. He complains that Boucher tendentiously "edited" the correspondence from which, as an old man, he composed his eight-volume autobiography. But, in fact, he explained in his preface that he had rewritten from memory such letters as he had not copied or could not recover. The bulk of the letters are as they were written, and give a charming picture of the life of a scholarly eccentric in a provincial town. They are fertile in imagination and invention, and French scholars still glean ideas from them. Lately, for example, M. Roger Agache used a long and detailed letter from Boucher, written 150 years ago, to illustrate a thesis about the "crop marks" visible from the air in northern France.*

Miss Evans insists that the man who really introduced prehistory was not Boucher but his dead friend Dr. Picard. "He wore Picard's mantle," she writes, "with such dramatic effect that he soon forgot it had not always been his own."

Yet all the evidence for this comes from Boucher himself via Aufrère, and I do not believe that Miss Evans could have distilled so much poison from Aufrère's book if that distinguished work had been wholly sweet-tempered. Are there perhaps traces in it of the old jealousy between the paid scholar, who lacks freedom, and the independent one, who lacks status? Certainly Boucher's great friend and disciple Dr. Picard had taken the first steps towards the discovery of prehistory, but it is from Boucher himself, who gave Picard every encouragement till his early death in 1841, that we draw most of our information about the young doctor. It was Boucher's Society which printed his theories and gave him a forum for discussing them. In the first draft of his *Antiquités*, composed in 1844, Boucher had written a page attributing everything to Picard, of whom he claimed to be no more than an inadequate interpreter. "He was starting his career when I was ending mine." Why did he later leave out all but a sentence of this touching tribute? He was getting on for seventy. Recognition seemed far away and maybe he felt that by his obstinacy he had earned the greater part of such applause as his book might gain. In fact it gained none. Less than a hundred copies were sold of the book which ushered in the new science of prehistory. The booksellers begged him to take back their stock. He sighed not only for his masterpiece but also for the fine-quality paper which had had to go to "the writers' cemetery, the butter merchant."

Moreover, in the third volume of *Antiquités* he gave ample justice to all those who had preceded Picard and himself, John Frere of Hoxney, Father McEnergy, Schmerling and many others. "I abase myself before labours like these. All that I can say for myself is that I have been the most obstinate."

Revue Archaeologique de-l'Est, 42, 1962.

Miss Evans asserts that after his victory Boucher was "more anxious for his own reputation than for the scientific implications of his discoveries." Yet if you read the letters he wrote in the triumphant year of 1859, you will see how little his reputation was bothering him. When in 1908 the Abbevillois erected a statue to him, they inscribed on the base: PALAIONTOLOGUE ET PHILANTHROPE, but in 1859 the Philanthrope was in the ascendant. There are long, painstaking letters about the cure for drunkenness, the rescue of horses from burning stables, and the agricultural use of a freshwater mussel which he had discovered in the Somme.

Boucher was a great giver of prizes and medals. He offered awards for exemplary working women in a dozen towns in Picardy, dispensing in this way during his lifetime 100,000 francs, and bequeathing after his death a further 150,000 francs. It would have been strange if he had not accepted medals and prizes himself, but he took this casually enough. He once wrote: "They wanted to make me a municipal councillor . . . and even a deputy, but I was like that old soldier who was taken prisoner by the Turks. He said, 'They offered me all the offices, Bey, Pasha, Vizier, . . . even Eunuch, but I refused them all.' "

In 1860 Boucher set off for the British Isles. He describes his visit in one of his travel books, which cover all of Europe and some of Africa. He writes as unaffectedly as he must have conversed. For an old gentleman who had recently extended human history by many millennia, he was on this journey remarkably unassuming; he expected and received no acclamation whatever.

When he reached London his distinguished friends were as kind to him as if he had been their old uncle just up from the country. Prestwich asked him to supper to meet his sister and Falconer gave him lunch at the Colonial Club and took him to the Zoo. At the Athenaeum, to which he had sent one of his parcels, he met "M. Th. Huxlevy" (he seldom got any English name right) and was given a month's membership. Most of the time he wandered round by himself, as he had done in Kiev and Belgrade and Algiers. He visited "Kesington," "Pale Male" and "Hyde Parck." He changed his linen twice a day because of the dirt and, watching rain from a hotel window, he composed one of his sad rhymes, about London cutthroats and pickpockets (he had seen one of their victims running and shrieking "Policy! Policy!"), and a young prostitute, who was killed by a resurrectionist. His happiest day was when he went to "Escher" for a memorial service to Louis Philippe, who had always been kind to him (the Comte de Paris had accepted Antediluvian Man). The train at Esher was two hours late; he had left his overcoat on the wrong platform and, in retrieving it, was nearly run over by the train. Aufrère says of him that he was "a man of great gaiety, with no luck!" Boucher describes these episodes with so much humour, zest and philosophical comment that the loneliness in which prehistory was conceived can only be guessed at.

Miss Evans cannot bear to agree with Aufrère that Boucher wrote extremely well and that it was often his fearless championship of liberal causes that prevented his plays, which were usually satirical, from being performed. She dismisses them with scorn and in his other writings she grudgingly allows him "facility" and "a capacity for eloquence, not uncommon in men brought up on the windy rhetoric of the revolution." Yet Aufrère says of his plays, "They had verve and observation and had a happy turn of phrase. And if he had not been dogged by ill-luck, he would have made his mark as a playwright." And he relates how the greatest of French comedians, Potier, was an ardent champion of Boucher's plays against the censor.

In fact, in an easy unpretentious way Boucher was an admirable writer fully deserving Aufrère's many comments on his excellent French and the graceful purity of his style. The problems to which he addressed himself sometimes no longer puzzle us, but his books are not all period pieces. In 1961 his *Petit Glossaire*, a satirical attack on the French administration, was republished in paperback 126 years after its original appearance. A delightful anthology could still be made from his autobiographical volumes and his travel books.

Archaeology in 1850 was still considered to be a bridge between humanism and the physical sciences. Boucher planted prehistory at the humanist end of this bridge and defended it against all aggressors. The bridge has long ago been blown up and prehistory has been built into the fortress of science. It flourishes there but disturbing things have happened which would not, perhaps, have occurred in the old days of provincial humanism.

Boucher had greatness because he was a crusader for the unity of knowledge in an age when its fragmentation was already far advanced. His appears to be a lost cause but it is one that will always have adherents. Fighting his own battles, he was fighting for others too, the individualists, the provincial, the scholar who refuses to specialize. As that ill-organized community cannot now even recognize its own champions, it is good that in Abbeville, at least, the Father of Prehistory is still greatly honoured.

The Decay of Archaeology*

1963

Kilkenny has a claim to be considered one of the earliest and greatest centres of archaeology not only in Ireland but in the British Isles, and the man who set it going was James Graves of Ennisnag Rectory in our parish. It is exhilarating to speak of that period, the middle years of the last century, and I shall do so later, but I am going to start with the reflection that provincial archaeology, which I consider to be the most important branch of it, is at a low ebb and has to contend with forces that seem almost insuperable.

Some weeks ago I was at Kilfane, which, for a variety of reasons, is one of the focal points of this story. In the 1840s three young Kilkennymen, John Prim, who was later editor of *The Kilkenny Moderator*, James Lecky, a poet and a relation of the great historian, and a novelist called Paris Anderson, wandered together around the county, exploring the ruins of the past and later writing novels, poems and essays in the romantic mood of the time about local history and traditions. On one of these expeditions they came to Kilfane and found the crusader Cantwell Fada covered in rubble and ruins, which they carefully removed. It had been a Protestant schoolhouse before, and Long Cantwell had lain in one corner of it, and naughty children used to be told to kiss him on the lips as a horrifying form of punishment. Then the roof had fallen in and nettles had grown up, and by the time the three romantics arrived he was completely submerged. They put the crusader on end and leant him against the rear

*Text of an address to a meeting of the clergy of the Diocese of Ossory at Kells Rectory, 15 November 1963.

wall, where till a few years ago he remained, a majestic figure, the most beautiful stone effigy in Ireland—far more impressive confronting the visitor at the end of the long roofless church than he now is in profile as the Office of Public Works have set him halfway up the church.

Developments followed quickly; in the 1840s the same enthusiasm that had caused John Prim to help in the resurrection of the crusader caused him to collaborate with James Graves in the establishment of the Kilkenny Archaeological Society, and in connection with it they published a poem about Cantwell Fada by James Lecky. It is not a very good poem, but it is important because it recalls the mood and motives of those who were responsible for this great intellectual renaissance in the Irish provinces. It was expressed in sentimental terms that are unfashionable today but it was hugely dynamic. Lecky's sonnet on Cantwell Fada, written before they had cleaned him up, ends:

> "Ah me!" said I, "men's hearts are hard and cold;
> Else would they move the rubbish gathered round;
> And cherish this the piety of old."

After Cantwell Fada had been cleaned up, four plaster casts of him were made. Two were sent to Cork and Dublin, one was sent to the Irish Exhibition of 1853, another was housed in the Kilkenny Museum. A period of enormous bustle and intellectual activity ensued in Kilkenny, but it all emerged from the challenge to men's hearts more than to their heads, and the first archaeologists were clergymen, poets, novelists, editors, amateurs, a word that comes from *amo*, I love.

But I must leave this cheerful period of dogcarts and strong boots and come back to an autumn afternoon in 1963 when I took three Dublin friends to see Cantwell Fada. Our first surprise came at the entrance gate, for he is to be found in the old fortified church in the back avenue of Kilfane House. Till the trees were cut and nettles grew over the stumps it had been a beautiful place and remained accessible. But we found the entrance gate and the side gate both securely locked and made unclimbable with thick coils of barbed wire; or almost unclimbable, I should say, for we put our coats over the spikes and the barbs and after a considerable struggle and only a few tears in our trousers we got across. The crusader and the old church are vested in the Office of Public Works, which has put up threatening notices about defacement of their property, but it was plain that though middle-aged antiquarians might be deterred by the barbed wire, it had acted as a challenge to the small boys of the neighbourhood. Not only had the threatening notice about defacement itself been defaced. That goes without saying; they always are and perhaps they deserve to be. The old Kilkenny Archaeological Society sought to "cherish this the piety of old" by trying to arouse interest and affection around the countryside and not by fines and intimidation. No, the defacement that mattered came from stones thrown at the crusader himself; the expression of his face had altered because minute chips had been knocked off from his eyelids and elsewhere.

And I had confirmation of this from an odd source the following week. Two antique dealers from Manchester turned up, two pleasant and highly educated vultures who were attracted across the sea by the smell of social decay. They said they had just been visiting Cantwell Fada and that they were appalled at the deterioration he had suffered. Why had he not been put under shelter? Did we not realize how easily Kilkenny limestone weathers? But it was what one of them said next that really appalled me. "Oh, I had one of the bitterest disappointments of my life when I was here last. I came to buy the crusader and I was prepared to offer as much as five thousand pounds for it, but I found that the old lady, would you believe it, had given it to the Office of Public Works just a fortnight before. Oh, wasn't that bad luck!"

This story shows how official archaeology has had to fill the gap left by the old voluntary society, and how, try as it might, it is an impossible task. The metropolitan experts are hardly to be blamed, because about a generation ago the amateurs created the experts rather as Frankenstein created his monster, by endowing chairs and agitating for laws and state control; then they themselves became fewer and feebler and more fainthearted, and finally abdicated to their salaried creatures all the control they had once freely exercised over their own neighbourhood.

In the days of Prim and Graves no one would ever have dared contemplate selling Cantwell Fada to Manchester, nor would the expert have ventured to change his position without consulting those in Kilkenny who were interested.

My father could just remember Mr. Graves of Ennisnag, a hideous old man with a sallow complexion, a bothered expression and buckteeth. He grew elaborate ferns on the riverbank at the rectory and tried to scare small boys away from his orchard with a notice board: BEWARE! SCOLOPENDRIA SET HERE! He was a true amateur archaeologist: polymathic, independent, touchy and truculent. (He was a kinsman of Robert Graves, who has something of the same temperament.) He was far more widely educated, as were the other amateurs of the time, than the average archaeological specialist is today. I use amateur here and throughout in the old-fashioned sense of unpaid. He was a dedicated man, and when offered his travelling expenses for an archaeological outing to Truro, he refused almost huffily. Nobody offered him a chair or lectureship—there were not any—and his zeal if anything hindered his promotion. The government regarded the study of Ireland's past with some mistrust. A survey of Irish antiquities, parish by parish, had been initiated by the state and entrusted to Petrie, O'Donovan and O'Curry, but after a parish in Co. Derry had been completed, it was abruptly suspended. It was feared that by stirring up memories of ancient history the work might cause disaffection.

Yet the amateurs were pugnacious and confident and the Kilkenny Archaeological Society grew famous. Its aims were quite different to those of present-day official archaeology. They were expressed best in the sentences from Camden's *Britannia* with which all the early issues of the *Journal* began: "If any there be which are desirous to be strangers in their owne soile, and forrainers in their owne citie, they may so continue, and therein flatter themselves. For such like I have not written these lines nor taken these paines." They really believed that the wounds of history might be staunched by accurate knowledge properly applied. Local history was the core of the matter, the centre from which one worked outwards, and for a very long time expert knowledge was thought of as something to be used in the interests of the community and not as metropolitan knowledge was to become, an end in itself. This was widely understood and the membership of the Society grew; in its first years, for example, while it was still the local Society of the southeast of Ireland, it had as many as 106 clergy, Protestant and Catholic, as members. After the focus of the Society had shifted to Dublin and it became the Royal Society of Antiquaries, this membership rapidly declined, and when I revived the Society locally in 1945 the total Kilkenny membership was three or four.

The first journal of the Society, that of 1848–52, is now almost impossible to obtain, and I once asked the secretary of the RSAI to help us with a reissue, which at that time could have been cheaply edited. He said he saw no point since there was nothing that was of any consequence in these early journals. As a matter of fact they are in every way more important and interesting than the current ones since they show the sudden upsurge of the scholarly, enquiring spirit in a more or less dead country area. Graves and Prim and their colleagues were pioneers, throwing out new ideas in every direction; since then there have been individual scholars, but never a whole movement which infected masses of people and not just some select students. The editor of *The Kilkenny Moderator* himself reported the exploration of Dunbell rath in 1848. Defective as it was, it remained until 1928 one of the best and most serious archaeological investigations of its kind in the country. There were no further excavations in Kilkenny until a highly professional one was undertaken on Freestone Hill on the Dublin road by my friend Professor Bersu of Frankfurt, when I was secretary of the revived Society. This excavation was financed through the Irish government, but Professor Bersu had been brought to Kilkenny by myself (he was a Jew and life had been made impossible for him in the Institute of Archaeology in Frankfurt), and the site had been found for him by members of our Society. He had given us lectures both at Dunbell rath and elsewhere, for which we paid him small sums. Nonetheless we felt that the Dublin authorities were rather surprised, perhaps even annoyed—so low had the prestige of the regional societies sunk—when this very distinguished scholar published the results of his excavations in our local journal. We were regarded as very parochial. The fact that the whole archaeology of Ireland had been shaped by the enlightened parochialism of James Graves, and that this was something basic, was soon forgotten when the Society moved to Dublin.

But I must go back to the 1850s, when Kilkenny was still a great centre of Irish and British archaeology. A museum and library was opened in Butler House, the Ormonde dower house in Patrick Street, and later sited in an archway across the same. Many donations came from the Ormonde family, the castle and its muniments room was always at the disposal of local scholars, and several papers were written from the Ormonde Deeds. In these early journals a clear picture of mediaeval Kilkenny and its slow change into modern times can be constructed. Lord Ormonde himself, the second marquis, was president of the Society and a great enthusiast. He edited the *Life of St.*

Canice (from whom Kilkenny took its name) from the Salamanca Codex and made a gift of a free copy to all the Society members.

In 1856 the Society acquired a remarkable new member, M. Boucher de Perthes of Abbeville in France, who is known as the Father of Prehistory.* He never came to Kilkenny, but until his death his name was annexed at the end of the Society's membership lists as the Honorary Foreign Corresponding Member. In this way our Society, without realizing what it was doing, became the first archaeological society in the British Isles to give an honorary membership to one of the great figures of European archaeology.

It was actually the material success of the Kilkenny Archaeological Society that at last ruined it. They wove their own splendid winding sheet. As more and more members poured in from all over Ireland, it was inevitable that they should begin to think on a national scale and not on a purely provincial one. On the proposal of Graves, the committee forwarded a petition to the Board of Education that the Irish language be introduced as an optional subject in all Irish schools. It was curtly refused. They were right, of course, in most of their national projects but slowly and perhaps inevitably the centre of gravity of the Society shifted to Dublin, local interest waned and local membership fell off. A project of Graves's for sending questionnaires about local antiquities to all the clergy, teachers and scholars of the county was abandoned, the subscriptions were raised to metropolitan standards, and the whole character of the Society changed. Very soon it became tiresome for the widely scattered members to go down to Kilkenny for their meetings, so instead the quarterly meetings were held in Kilkenny, Cork, Dublin and Belfast. Finally this too became annoying to the Dublin people, so for the past generation council meetings have all been held in Dublin. The library was transferred to Dublin and housed in Merrion Square, and the museum was moved up in 1910 and loaned to the National Museum. There was a strong case for doing this, of course, because the library and museum were constantly being pilfered and neglected. In the old journals you will find long lists of books and periodicals stolen and lost. It is said that one day a large and celebrated ogham stone, accompanied by smaller antiquities, walked out of the door and has never been seen since. Kilkenny people were of course blamed, but I don't think that was wholly fair. The lifeblood of the

*See above, pp. 198–208.—ed.

Society had been drawn away from the town and it was inevitable that both museum and library should die of inanition.

The Kilkenny period of the Society lasted almost to the turn of the century, when the original motives of the founders were still understood, when it was still a voluntary body, and when the salaried expert was considered the assistant of the disinterested enthusiasts. He was their representative and not their indulgent mentor, as he later became. Of course the process was not specifically Irish but universal. It developed out of the worldwide acquiescence in specialization, but its results were more disastrous in Ireland than elsewhere.

As mentioned, I revived the Society in 1945; it still survives and is, I believe, the largest and most prosperous provincial society in Ireland. I had to sever my connection with it in 1952,* but I still wish it well and am delighted and proud that it is still there. But I want you to understand how much circumstances have altered since the days of James Graves, and how much all these local ventures need the disinterested integrity and unpaid enthusiasm which the 106 clergy of those early journals afforded to those pioneers.

In October, for instance, an extraordinary thing happened, which will probably go unrecorded in our Kilkenny papers and excite not a ripple of interest in the county. As you know the Society has at last, with the aid of the Office of Public Works, got under way a project for which we were long working, that is to say, the restoration of the Rothe House in Parliament Street. They have ideas of forming a museum there and in the meantime they wrote to the RSAI, the former Kilkenny Archaeological Society (I don't know whether it should be called a parent society or a daughter society), asking that they should be allowed some Rothe relics belonging to the old Society to put in their restored house. The RSAI is now dominated by officials from the various Dublin institutes, including the National Museum. They have no confidence in provincial societies, believing that they will quickly dissolve and their collections disappear. So the council of the RSAI, moved to action by the letter from the Kilkenny Society, summoned a meeting and unanimously handed over as a gift to the National Museum the contents of the Kilkenny Museum which had been loaned to it in 1910. An official of the museum then wrote that the Rothe House could have what it wanted but strictly as a loan.

*Because of the controversy described below, pp. 452ff.—ed.

The Rothe Stone, which the KAS had asked for, had been lying in the vaults of the museum for fifty years, and if you examine the original constitution of the Society you will see that the RSAI's hasty vote, at which none of the council members understood the issue, was totally illegal. You will see the reports of the years 1850 and 1851 concerning the museum collection: "All such objects are, by the Constitution of the Society, merely held as deposits entrusted to its care" (by their owners). You will also see that by Rule 21 of the Revised Rules (1911) the council has no right to dispose of the collection without prior sanction being obtained from the Society.

Yet we are all now so dependent on state institutions for our cultural ventures that nobody will dare question the legality of this move. And I understood why it happened. The contents of the old Kilkenny Museum had been dumped in the National Museum and partially incorporated, and even when the objects had not been lost the labels had; it would be now almost impossible to identify what belongs to us were we to make a row and claim them back. So we are to get back our own property as a loan. Remember these things had been given to the Kilkenny Society largely by Kilkenny people such as the Ormondes and Graves and Prim, without any idea that they would one day be permanently alienated from the town. I don't question that we have in the country districts become immensely careless of our property, but this carelessness comes from the feeling that to look after these things is now a public not a private responsibility as it appeared to Graves—but the answer to our problems is very definitely not to hand them over to Dublin.

There are two principal reasons for this: first, the hazards of fire and violence make it wise that our antiquities should be dispersed rather than concentrated in a capital. A generation or two ago (you will know these facts better than I) it was felt that the local parishes were not taking proper care of their ancient records, so they were moved to the Four Courts. Then the Four Courts was burnt when it was seized by the Republicans in the Civil War after the Treaty, and in a few hours Ireland, which had been one of the countries richest in local history, became one of the poorest. So my view is that on the whole it is safer for something to be neglected in the place of its origin, where there is a faint hope that it may excite the interest of some native, as Cantwell Fada in his decay roused the interest of Prim and Lecky and Graves and inspired the old Society. For in our day capital cities and bureaucratic institutions can offer only a precarious asylum for these valuables. And often things that mean much to us here mean little in the capital, where there is a superfluity of records of every kind. So they are lost or jumbled like the contents of the Kilkenny Museum when it was housed in the National Museum.

My second reason may shock you. It may sound ungenerous to say so, but the salaried expert cannot afford to be as strenuous a defender of our antiquities and our right to free speculation as the amateurs of a hundred years ago. Archaeology, by becoming a profession out of which you support a family and/or an academic reputation, often becomes very timorous and self-important. Also the paid expert does not have to try to convert others to his enthusiasms—an ardent enquirer, if he is not a pupil, may seem just another ingenuous bore. Graves and Prim had to try to communicate their enthusiasm to others because at the lowest they wanted the subscriptions in order to publish their journals, at the highest they were trying to educate a whole neighbourhood and perhaps change its view of the past and the present.

I noticed this particularly when the Irish government gave one of our Kilkenny treasures to President Kennedy on his recent visit. It was a fourteenth-century treaty between James, Earl of Ormonde, and the O'Kennedys of north Tipperary, one of the many Irish branches of the Kennedys (to which there is no evidence that President Kennedy's family belonged). It no more concerned the family of the President, of whom we are rightly proud, than it concerned about a million other Kennedys and Butlers throughout America and the British Empire, and the gift was an example of the way in which archaeology has to capitulate to political sentiment when it accepts state support and state control. The history of these O'Kennedys was discussed in the first issue of the *Kilkenny Archaeological Journal* (that one which is unobtainable because the RSAI did not consider it worth reissuing) and the document was recognized as one of the great treasures of the muniments room in the castle, where it stayed secure for six centuries. Now this document is launched into the void. It will, of course, be carefully treasured by the Kennedys. But what will happen when their heirs are no longer millionaires and the American equivalents of those two gentlemen from Manchester approach them? Where will it end up?

I found the sequel to the donation of this document very interesting. When I wrote to *The Irish Times* in protest I got a great deal of support, public and private, and no official scholar defended the government action, but no official scholar attacked it either. All the more formidable attacks in *The Irish Times* came from retired scholars with pensions; from Galway University, a retired speaker of the senate, a retired comptroller and auditor-general for Northern Ireland, and so on. Nobody wrote officially from any of the universities, academies, libraries or museums, though they contacted me privately. No one wrote even from the Society of Antiquaries, which had owed so much in its early days in Kilkenny to the Ormonde Deeds. One of the letters I received was from an old friend who is a principal librarian in Trinity.* He explained that he had written to *The Irish Times* in my support, urging that the whole transaction was quite illegal, and, in the words of the auditor-general, "a misappropriation of public assets," which could only be legalized by a bill in the Dáil. But he said, "I wrote from my private address, as a private person, and I suppose that is why they did not print my letter. But I couldn't very well write as a librarian of Trinity because we're expecting £400,000 from the government for the new Trinity Library and we couldn't risk offending them too much." Now I hope you'll understand why James Graves of Ennisnag would not accept his expenses for that archaeological trip to Truro.

Through an accident of history the Communists in Russia have preserved the record of the tsarist days, the ascendancy both of rank and of intellect, more carefully than we have preserved the records of the eight centuries of Anglo-Irish domination here. The reason for this is, I think, that after the peasants had murdered the landlords in Russia they looted only the things that were useful to them; and the government, when it came round to confiscating what remained, often found all the most valuable things, the documents, the pictures, the books, more or less intact, and from them vast collections have been formed. In the freer atmosphere of Ireland the Anglo-Irish owners survived to sell many of our records. The same applies to buildings: whereas Kilkenny Castle fell into ruin after 1934 and is being laboriously restored, many great palaces in Russia like the Yussupov Palace in Leningrad are still surviving as museums with the furniture of the period, or else converted to old people's homes or schools.

This also applies in a more marked degree to the way we have treated the memory of our great writers of Anglo-Irish stock. Contrast the fate of Edgeworthstown House and Coole Park and Moore Hall with that of the houses of Tolstoy and Chekhov and many other

*Trinity College, Dublin.—ed.

non-Communist writers. Tolstoy's country house near Tula and his town house in Moscow survive almost as he left them. The same applies to Chekhov's house in Moscow, his villa at Yalta, his little farm at Melikhovo south of Moscow, and, I think, his birthplace at Taganrog. In the early period of the Revolution an attempt was made to do propaganda through these survivals from the past, and the guides sometimes still do a little, but in general these places are allowed to speak for themselves and they do so very dramatically. The Russians of the future, whether they are Communist or something different, will have an opportunity of observing this evidence of historical continuity which our children may lack. In 1956 I visited in the same year Tolstoy's home, Yasnaya Polyana, in Russia, and what is left of Edgeworthstown House in Longford, and afterwards I gave a talk on the Russian service of the BBC in which I compared these two famous houses as centres of enlightenment in their day. I felt too ashamed to say how much better Yasnaya Polyana had fared, or to recall that when some forty years ago Edgeworthstown House had been put up for sale, no effort had been made to preserve it or its contents as a record of Maria and her famous father and the great influence they had exercised from there.

In 1945, to commemorate the bicentenary of Jonathan Swift's death, the Russians printed 100,000 copies of *Gulliver's Travels*. The Irish did nothing at all. I don't believe the Russian way of preserving the records of the past is the best one. That would mean evicting Major Briggs-Swifte, confiscating his property, Swifte's Heath, for the state and installing an expert Swift scholar comparable to the learned Tolstoyan they have at Yasnaya Polyana. I am convinced that James Graves's way of ensuring that we are not "strangers in our owne soile" is a far better way, which has to be applied with vigour.

To begin with, state-paid scholars should be delegated to voluntary societies. With a little experience we would come to do this better because we know our own neighbourhood, its needs and traditions. The case of Cantwell Fada is typical: without consulting us he has been moved from the position where James Graves set him, but he has been left more inaccessible to us than he ever was before. When the same thing happened after the Office of Public Works had done some restoration work at Kells and Kilree some sixteen years ago, they left both places equally inaccessible. There was a locked gate with a bull behind to deter visitors from Kells priory, and an impassable barrier of thorns and barbed wire at the Kilree round tower. I discovered that the county council had power to co-opt a

Monuments Committee and was authorized to carry out its decisions. We formed a committee of three members from the KAS and I persuaded them to set aside £25 to build the present gateways and stiles at Kilree and Kells. I also got the county council to unearth the thirteenth-century effigy of Johannes filius Galfridi at Ennisnag. In 1952 the county council held a special meeting to turn me off the Monuments Committee,* which died soon after, but the point is that we have power through the county councils to do a great deal for our antiquities, even in our churchyards, without applying to Dublin. And I found the county council, when I worked with it, generous and efficient.

The work done by the Board of Public Works at Kells and Kilree came about in rather an odd way. Mr. O. G. S. Crawford was staying with me. He was an original man, as you can tell from his autobiography, one of the principal archaeologists in Britain and the first to make use of air photography for the discovery of ancient sites. He founded and edited *Antiquity*, which was the leading archaeological journal in England, and as an official in the Ordnance Survey at Southampton did much valuable mapping of English, British and Roman antiquities. He was a self-sufficient old bachelor, not at all officially minded but not society-minded either, and I totally failed to interest him in the KAS. His first reason for visiting me was to put an order with a Kilkenny butcher for a weekly supply of meat, as, after the war, he did not consider the meat he got in Southampton adequate.

While he wandered up High Street and Rose Inn Street pinching meat and comparing prices he was struck by the beauty of Kilkenny, and he said he would come back later and make a photographic survey. In the meantime I took him to a couple of our archaeological outings; at the first one he looked hugely bored and irritated, at the second one he fell asleep. Then he went to Dublin for a few days and he found the meetings of the Society of Antiquaries equally dreary and soporific. He regarded all our efforts as moribund and our societies dead beyond hope of revival. When he returned I took him to Kells. It was at that time covered with ivy and some of the walls were in danger of collapsing, so on his advice we reported the matter to the Board of Works. Mr. Crawford's name had a magical effect, and the next summer very extensive work was done on both Kells and Kilree. They spent £1,000 and made an admirable job of

*Again, because of the controversy described on pp. 452ff.—ed.

it, but something happened which revealed to me what an impassable gulf yawned between the ideals of James Graves and the archaeologists of our century. One of the officials from the Board who came to visit me was a learned and charming man. He found my efforts to revive the KAS vaguely commendable but not necessary. After all it had been superseded by the RSAI. Why multiply societies? I found it difficult to explain to him that local interest was now almost stone-dead and that we were trying to revive it. We had had several meetings of our Society at Kells. We had sent out invitations to the local people and asked the teacher to bring his pupils. They had responded, taken part in our discussions and obviously been interested.

So when the work at Kells was nearly completed, I was astounded when one day he said to me at lunch, "Oh, I've told the workmen that just three days before we clear out they are to pull down the handball court in the chancel. If they do it quickly enough there'll be no trouble."

Now the handball court should never have been built on the property of the Office of Public Works, but it had been there for many years and Dublin had connived at it. Very recently £800 had been collected round Kells and spent on it. The surest way to alienate the Kells people was to destroy their handball court. I suggested, therefore, that we collect a fund to build a handball court somewhere else, but we were still a young Society and did not move with sufficient confidence. The matter ended in the worst possible way. The demolition plan leaked out, probably through the workmen, before we got the fund under way. The Kells people immediately sent a deputation to the Ministry and the Minister intervened and stopped the plan. We were suspected of letting the cat out of the bag and both in Dublin and in Kells our Society suffered a setback. And for many succeeding years the happy feet of the handball players trod down the noses of the abbots on the thirteenth-century slabs.

All this is very small beer, but we live in a small community in which such small things are deeply important. I hope I have not suggested that we were constantly at war with Dublin. We were not. The representatives of the museums and libraries and Office of Public Works and the RSAI were very generous to us. For example, when I organized a Kilkenny exhibition in the Tholsel, the National Library gave us photostats of a huge number of Kilkenny documents and pictures which I located and we have always had help when we asked for it. Our problem was how to resist the centralizing tendencies of the day and recover something of the originality and independence of the old Society. It was difficult and unfair to expect help from the highly centralized organizations of Dublin in doing this. Yet every year I became more conscious that this decentralization was urgently necessary and that only we ourselves could bring it about.

At this time a very pleasant and satisfactory thing happened. Mr. Crawford did return to Kilkenny, as he had promised me, to make his Kilkenny Survey. He lodged in the Club House Hotel and got up between six and seven o'clock every morning, because he said that it was at that hour that the light was right for photographing certain buildings. They had often to be photographed from the top windows of the building opposite and, as he believed that everyone should share his disinterested admiration of Georgian fanlights, a great many people in Kilkenny had reluctantly to get up early too in order to show him into their attics. He is the only person I know who penetrated that small wooden or plaster pepper pot which used to stand on top of the Monster House. The view which he took from it of the turret on the Tholsel I used for the cover of our first bound copy of *The Old Kilkenny Review*. In a couple of years this photograph became unique. The eighteenth-century turret was replaced by a copper one and the whole roof of the Tholsel altered at the time when the interior was gutted and the horrible winding butterscotch staircase was put in to replace the broad and dignified old one. Crawford took about two hundred photographs and as Kilkenny was soon after to recover from the shortages of the war and the shopkeepers were able to put up smart chromium fronts to replace the Georgian ones, Crawford's two volumes are already a valuable record of a period of Kilkenny that is slowly disappearing. Crawford did all this work free. He charged only for the printing of the photographs, which he insisted must be done by the only capable man in England, who lived in Wiltshire. So I sold the negatives to the National Library for £34, deducted the printing costs and lodged the balance to the Kilkenny Archaeological Society. And we sent him in return the largest Christmas turkey we could find in the Kilkenny shops.

With Crawford's agreement, I held on to the two volumes myself. I felt doubt arising about the Society and Crawford had never believed in it at all. He had all the disinterested love of learning that Graves had and he was just as cantankerous and individualistic, but he was typical of the modern expert in that he could not be bothered with people who were not as sophisticated as himself. And the members of our Society were mostly very innocent and some of them had complacency added to innocence, which, as you know, converts it into ignorance. Graves and his colleagues never despised innocence, but often went out of their way to meet ignorance and deflate it or chastise it.

I have said that official archaeology has turned its back on its own origins and betrayed them. Now I am going to suggest, on the basis of my own experience in Kilkenny, that this divorce from its original raison d'être has at times made it something dangerous and politically evil. I read recently an archaeological book in which our Irish government was commended because in its first years it had abandoned the narrow parochialism of the past and in 1934 had appointed an eminent Austrian archaeologist as the director of our National Museum. Well, I met Dr. Adolf Mahr once or twice, and possibly the rumour was untrue that he was to be our cultural *Gauleiter* if Hitler occupied Ireland. But he certainly scorned the Irish as much as he scorned the Czechs (it was at the time of Hitler's victory over the Czechs that I first met him). He was a good Nazi and just before the war broke out he went back to Vienna, but the Irish government, I suppose to emphasize our neutrality, kept his place open for him and, till the war ended, sent him his salary to Vienna.

Towards the end of the war a very detailed collection of information about Ireland, *Militärgeographische Angaben über Irland*, was discovered in Brussels, and it was reported that the principal contributor was Dr. Adolf Mahr.

I have had confirmation of this from Dublin scholars. It appears that our government was determined to be rid of him before 1939 but dared not risk offending the Germans by a direct dismissal. Therefore an Irish agent in Austria sent him a bogus official message summoning him home. It was learnt that on reaching Vienna he was very coolly received by the authorities, who wished him to remain at his observation post in Ireland through the war, protected by the prestige and the immunity that is claimed by salaried archaeology.

It was said that the assistant to him as cultural *Gauleiter* in Ireland was to have been a scholar called Hartmann, working on Irish folklore. He was a well-liked person who went home of his own accord before the war broke out, but there is no reason to suppose that he would have refused the important post to be assigned to him.

I need not stress how difficult this prostitution of learning would have been if archaeology had been, as it used to be, decentralized and without an official or professional character, and if even a small attempt had been made to revive in the provinces the pugnacious integrity of the old Kilkenny Archaeological Society.

While he was in Ireland, Mahr was in charge of James Graves's collection, so you can judge how far archaeology had travelled from Ennisnag when it became a science. James Graves had believed that its object was to prevent a man becoming "a stranger in his owne soile, a forrainer in his owne citie," and that it was a duty for which no man should accept payment (remember that trip to Truro), and here we were paying a "forrainer" a salary in the name of archaeology when he was no longer even on our "soile" but intriguing with those who despised us in order to take it away from us.

Another thing happened in the succeeding years which convinced me that the state-supported science of archaeology was a far inferior branch of learning to that championed by James Graves and Boucher de Perthes. It concerns Dr. Bersu, the celebrated German-Jewish prehistorian, who, as I mentioned, came to Kilkenny first in about 1950. He was the director of the Institute of Archaeology at Frankfurt and at the outbreak of the war had been excavating in the south of England. His reason for staying on was the same as Dr. Mahr's for returning to Austria, only upside down. Dr. Mahr was a Nazi and Dr. Bersu was a Jew. Though Bersu and his wife are very old friends of ours, I cannot tell you this story without saying things about him that he would prefer to have suppressed. Yet I can never speak unkindly of a German Jew, for we none of us know how we would react if we were told that our race was inferior and should be exterminated. An Irish republican told me lately that in his opinion the Irish had never recovered psychologically from being told for centuries that they were inferior, and of course for the Jews it has been far worse. Dr. Bersu never liked to admit he was a Jew and I never once heard him express any solidarity with Jews. And since none of his friends wished to wound him, we never mentioned it.

It was the extra-special torment of many German Jews that they had given up their Jewish faith and traditions and immersed themselves so deeply in German life that they could not face the fact that they were anything but German. It was, of course, in part the absence of this sense of solidarity among themselves that made them such an easy prey to Hitler. So since Dr. Bersu had left Germany before the war of his own accord he did not consider himself a refugee; he found that the archaeologists of other countries, such as Mr. Crawford, accepted him into the fellowship of international archaeology, and this fellowship was a sort of temporary substitute for his German citizenship. But he did not want to abandon being a German and therefore preferred to be interned on the Isle of Man with other German nationals. But since he was of known eminence he was allowed, with his fellow internees, to direct excavations in the raths and ring forts of the Isle of Man. He was a very meticulous excavator and his wife did the mapping and charting for him. He discovered that in many of the Manx forts traces could be found of concentric rings of postholes, and he deduced from this that our raths had once been roofed over.

At the end of the war things were difficult for him. His position in Frankfurt had been filled and he was not sure he could recover it. Crawford suggested to me that he come to Kilkenny while he explored possibilities in Ireland, and that is how he came to be associated with our Society. De Valera proved very sympathetic and personally secured him a salary, and we found him a site to excavate, the Iron Age fort of Freestone Hill near Gowran.

I had hoped that he would encourage some of our members to help with the dig so that ultimately they would learn how to do it with modern methods. Dr. Bersu was extraordinarily friendly and sympathetic and demonstrated to us several times the progress of the work. While Dr. Bersu and his helpers, his workpeople and students, were in Freestone Hill, and reporting progress to us, we all felt things were moving and that we had assisted in a small way in the uncovering of our past. He was still working there in the summer of 1948 when the centenary of the foundation of the Kilkenny Archaeological Society was celebrated. For this occasion the RSAI had invited twelve leading archaeologists from Europe, England and America. They were to spend three days in Dublin and then they were to come to Kilkenny for another three days. With Lord Ormonde's permission we invited them and the accompanying members of the RSAI to a party in the Picture Gallery of Kilkenny Castle, where the old Society had been entertained so often before by the Ormondes when it was still inhabited.

Some of our members were asked by the RSAI to put up the visiting scholars in our homes and my guests were to be Professor Sprockhoff, a leading German prehistorian, and a Spanish professor whose name I've forgotten. I was very pleased because we do not often see such eminent people in Kilkenny and I thought it would be stimulating to us all, so I gladly agreed and I told Bersu.

His reaction was astonishing. I had never seen him so moved. In tones of the deepest resentment he said, "No! No! You cannot have Sprockhoff. Oh, if you have Sprockhoff, I can never come here again. It was he who prevented me from even reading in the archaeological library [even then I don't think Bersu mentioned the word 'Jew'].

Himmler, who was, as you know, a great patron of archaeology, sent him to Norway and he worked on excavations under Vidkun Quisling. They liked his excavations, because Himmler linked them up with his theories of the Aryan origins of the Germanic people. I don't mind about the Spaniard being a Fascist and Francoite. After all, the Reds killed his sister and he has some excuse—but Sprockhoff, no, no!!"

So I wrote straight off to the RSAI saying that I had to change my mind and would like to have the Spaniard but I could not have Sprockhoff, and I explained why.

And the RSAI secretary wrote back in a friendly way. He understood my objections and said that the English scholars who had been invited had refused to come for the same reason. One of them was, I think, Sir Cyril Fox. And in fact no English scholar attended the centenary celebrations, though there were delegates from America (a McCarthyite archaeologist), Spain, Belgium, Germany, Norway and several other European countries. This struck me as very astonishing. Had all the Anglo-Irish, whose forebears had built the Society and formed 80 percent of its membership, lost interest or influence, or had they become Naziphile? I've never discovered.

After my refusal no further hospitality was sought for Sprockhoff and he was put up at the Club House Hotel. The Spaniard was sent to keep him company, so, to my disappointment, I had nobody.

The RSAI was of course aware that there was a difficulty about Sprockhoff and Bersu. To settle it they used the smooth tactics that officially organized bodies invariably adopt. There was to be a special lunch for the visitors and the Kilkenny natives at the Club House Hotel; Professor Boe, the great folklore expert from Norway, was put in the chair; and a list of the officials of the KAS to whom he was to express gratitude in his after-dinner speech was given to him. But anyone who had been tiresome about Sprockhoff, including myself, the secretary and founder, was omitted from the list. Bersu, the distinguished Jew, who had shown such kindness to our Kilkenny Society, was not invited at all. He was very wounded about this and urged me not on any account to mention it to his wife, Maria: "She will be so upset." But I was annoyed at what had happened and, though I was secretary, boycotted all the country meetings that took place afterwards. Because of this it was from Bersu that I learnt what occurred on Freestone Hill. The RSAI had taken the whole party, Sprockhoff included, to see the excavations, and Sprockhoff had walked out into the middle of the ring fort and complimented Bersu on the excellence of his excavations and the interesting nature of his discoveries. This was important to Bersu, for the Irish archaeologists had all belittled the significance of his postholes. "It is all right about Sprockhoff," Bersu told me afterwards, "he was very nice."

There was so much to say about this that I said nothing at all, though I have often met Bersu since. I was aware that something sad and wicked and all too human had happened, and that Bersu and Sprockhoff and the RSAI and, in our ignorance, our Society too had become implicated in it. It seemed to me that prehistory, by becoming a science, had lost the dignity and integrity with which it had been born at Abbeville. A trade union of professionals had taken it over, agreeing that even crime which conduced to the "Advancement of Learning" was excusable. Bersu had had a legitimate grievance against Sprockhoff because he had made him feel that, as a German Jew, he was "a stranger in his owne soile and a forrainer in his owne citie" and because he had worked for Quisling and Himmler. But all this was forgiven when Sprockhoff had been pleasant about the postholes.

Yet the reputed postholes which our ancestors made maybe three thousand years ago are merely a nuisance if, in order to investigate them, we must blur the record of what happened twenty years ago. Nearly a thousand German Jews who had escaped to Norway had been rounded up while Sprockhoff was excavating Aryans for Quisling, and if Bersu had escaped to Norway neither Boe nor Sprockhoff would have been able to prevent him and Maria from being burnt at Auschwitz.

I looked up Sprockhoff's works in the British Museum to find out if he was as wicked a man as Bersu said. Unfortunately they had not the book on Norway which he wrote when he was working for Quisling, but from the other works I saw he appeared to be a gifted and conscientious scholar, and probably quite a kindly one. He had simply felt he owed allegiance to the government which sponsored his researches.

Among the Sprockhoff books in the British Museum one that interested me most was a Festschrift compiled by scholars in Europe to congratulate him on his sixtieth birthday in 1952. Four years earlier no English archaeologist would attend the Kilkenny meeting because of Sprockhoff. Now they all contributed eulogistic articles or signed their names to the foreword, whether they were Communist or Tory, German or Jew. And Bersu's name was there too.

It seems to me that the archaeology of James Graves and Prim is a far finer thing than that of Sprockhoff and, if it is to survive, the RSAI must be restored to its old country basis and turned into a federation of county societies, all proud and tenacious of their amateur status.

For the implementation of such schemes we must depend on the old voluntary spirit. Only amateurs can build up vigorous and independent societies, holding to the old principles of free speculation and to the conviction that the purpose of archaeology is to prevent us from becoming "strangers in our owne soile, forrainers in our owne citie" and not just to add one more science to the dangerous superabundance of sciences. These were the ideas that were born a couple of miles from here over a century ago, and I don't believe they are yet obsolete.

Postscript
1989

This was compiled and read twenty-six years ago. Many of those I spoke of or spoke to are dead; personalities, places, institutions have changed or lost their significance; I was middle-aged and now am old. Yet I think it is worth reproducing, for I still believe that archaeology should be treated not as a science or profession but as a voluntary pursuit. It is far better to return to the largely extinct county archaeological societies of the last century and to know your country far and wide, as few people do now, and to be able to decipher the traces that history has left upon it.

In this decade science has thrown the metal detector into the hands of the amateur, and that is how the Derrynaflan hoard of eighth-century altar vessels became the greatest discovery of recent times. The hoard was discovered on 17 February 1980 by an Englishman, Mr. Webb, and his son, using metal detectors, and caused a great sensation that rippled through the newspapers for a year or two before it was forgotten. It was said to be worth over £5 million, and as no specific legislation about treasure trove had been introduced since the founding of the state, in 1986 a High Court Dublin judge pronounced that it was the property of Mr. Webb.

This was, of course, disputed, and in 1987 a Supreme Court ruling declared the vessels to be objects of national heritage and they passed into state ownership. They are now on view in the National Museum, where Mr. Webb had originally brought them. Except for Derrynaflan Church being in the custody of the Board of Works and governed by the law of trespass, and the use of metal detectors being forbidden, those are restrictions that are impossible to enforce. Mr. Webb behaved honestly, reporting the find as soon as it was made.

For the future it has been suggested that a Monuments Inspector should be appointed for every three or four counties to watch over their antiquities. This seems to me a characteristically expert opinion. How could one person control the use of metal detectors in three or four counties? Some years back, my grandson as a small boy camped with a friend in a wood a couple of hundred yards from my house and found a large grove of cannabis, with bags of fertilizer and gardening tools. A dozen treasure hunters with metal detectors could have wandered through it unobserved, and if they chose their time judiciously there is scarcely a spot in the hills and fields and woods of Ireland that they could not explore.

People like responsibility, and I believe many societies would spring into existence if they could be given the exclusive right of authority over the use of metal detectors on a known project. A county committee is usually drawn from a wide area and a network of close observation would form itself automatically. With thirty-two related county societies and museums (or thirty-three to cover Tipperary north and south), the Derrynaflan Chalice would belong to the North Tipperary Museum and would have been found long ago if someone authorized by the local society had explored the old churches of Tipperary with a metal detector. I suggest that the revival of the old county archaeological societies would be the best method of controlling and containing the threat and potential of mechanized archaeology.

Influenza in Aran

1987

When I arrived in Aran in 1963 by the *Naomh Éanna* at Kilronan I was sneezing, and by the time I had raced to St. Enda's church at Killeany and seen the stone on which he had floated in from Connemara I was feverish and coughing. I spent the rest of my time in bed reading the only two books on Aran and its saints which I could find, a big one by Mr. Ó Síocháin and a small one by Father Scantlebury.* I also studied Irish with my landlady's daughter, a little girl of four called Teresa. These lessons started when she had her hands behind her back and said, "You can't see my fingers!" I said, "No more I can! But say it in Irish!" She replied immediately, "Ní féidir leat mo mhéaranna a fheiceáil!" And so it went on. She was as instantaneous as an interpreter at the United Nations General Assembly and she asked no salary. She taught and I learned with pleasure and indeed joy. This is how Irish should have been. Yet in 1987 forty thousand Irish are leaving Ireland every year, cursing their elders who forced them to learn Irish instead of something "useful" like business management or word processing or nuclear physics.

But to come back to those two books: Father Scantlebury is cautious and a little dry, Mr. Ó Síocháin is exuberant and daring. He says that Aran might well be the tail end of Hy Brasil, the wonderful island which, like Plato's Atlantis, is lost beneath the sea. He adds that Aran was once "the greatest spiritual storehouse the world has ever known." When the Celts first settled there, they had a

*P. A. Ó Síocháin, *Aran Islands of Legend* (Dublin, 1962); C. Scantlebury, S. J., *Saints and Shrines of Aran Mór* (Dublin, 1926).

mighty empire in Europe behind them and "centuries of civilization of the highest order." Of St. Enda, the doyen of the spiritual storehouse, Mr. Ó Síocháin says, "He was probably one of the greatest teachers the Church has ever known." Father Scantlebury says the same thing more cautiously. There is much of interest in both these books. Mr. Ó Síocháin writes perceptively of John Synge's brief but memorable sojourn in Aran, and of the many owners who collected rents from the islands but never visited them.

I too am tempted to use the language of hyperbole about Aran. It seems to me one of the most enchanting and interesting spots in Europe, since it has held on to a precarious beauty and simplicity which the rest of the world is disastrously discarding. But it is St. Enda and the spiritual storehouse that chiefly arouse my curiosity. When my friend Dr. Simpson came out from Galway to visit me on the Whitmonday excursion, I hoped to communicate some of my enthusiasm to him but I failed miserably. He dismissed Ó Síocháin scornfully and Scantlebury patronizingly, and talked to me in terms of the Latin *Life of Enda*, of conflations, collations, recensions. After a glance or two he slapped both my books down on the counterpane. "I see they repeat that old error, which Zimmer exposed, of Conall Derg being the father of Enda. Conall was a purely fabulous person."

"Of course," I agreed, "he was the wicked King of Clogher, who brought the poisoned ox to St. Lassar on Devenish Island." (I should explain that I enjoy the ancient Irish habit of explaining with an entertaining anecdote any proper name that puzzles them, as so many do. Devenish [Damh Inis] on Loch Erne, means Ox Island.)

"But surely," I added, "even if it were a different Enda who was son of Conall Derg and spent his youth burning churches and plotting to murder his grandfather, did the real Enda of Aran ever do or say anything that we would recognize as even faintly Christian? Weren't he and all the other saints of Aran merely very successful magicians?"

He dodged this and talked instead of folklore and comparative religion and then his voice tapered away into something about the charm of innocence. We both of us began to yawn and after a bit he got up to catch his boat.

He left me with the impression that Enda is sliding gently out of history on the heels of Conall Derg and that the whole spiritual storehouse is in danger of collapsing. Just as Enda had much in common with his church-burning namesake, so many of the other saints of Aran had either a sinful past or a sinful namesake. Moreover, they are almost all Enda's relations and so are the saints of Wales, Cornwall, Scotland and Brittany. Three generations ago Father Shearman accommodated all the most important ones into three or four intertwined family trees. If one goes, and there are many hundreds of them, they all go. For they support each other like a house of cards in which no single card can stand alone or can safely be pulled away, and if Enda, the greatest teacher in the greatest spiritual storehouse, were to go, a hundred spiritual storehouses would collapse with him, leaving a forest of interrogation marks behind.

For different reasons, romantic, religious, academic, tourist, no one wants this to happen. If Enda and his storehouse were to disintegrate, they would do so without any sort of explosion. No tremors would be recorded on Aran. *Naomh Éanna* would not sink or have to be renamed. Nor would Dr. Simpson bother to force his new perceptions on Father Scantlebury or Mr. Ó Síocháin.

This absence of explosion is a proof that learning, which in Ireland has always flourished best in the country, is dead. It has not transplanted well to the universities. Real learning is dynamic, dangerous, exhilarating. It is built on curiosity, not on knowledge. When it explodes, someone feels liberated, someone else is hurt. At present in place of curiosity there is textual criticism, and philology and scientific excavations, which are all highly skilled crafts like agriculture and hairdressing. No bombs are thrown at Atlantis or the spiritual storehouse, but there is much silent and salaried sneering.

Dr. Simpson and the textual critics are at present working on Enda. When they have amputated what is fabulous or corrupt, there will be almost nothing left of the great teacher and saint. But because of their fine finicky methods, his will be an almost painless extinction. Every sentence is analyzed separately and any attempt to judge truth by everyday criteria is deemed amateurish.

Mr. Ó Síocháin argues like this too but more artlessly. He relates how Enda in his warlike, church-burning phase had tried to abduct a virgin from his sister St. Fainche's convent and how the virgin, on a hint from Fainche, had said she would prefer to be the bride of Christ and had composed herself on a couch and died. Mr. Ó Síocháin finds this too extreme and says that it was a clever little trick of Fainche's to make Enda repent. The girl was not really dead; her deathly pallor was due to shock and the dim conventual light. In fact he euhemerizes her, as Dr. Simpson would say. Enda repented and built his sister a church in Co. Louth, which, rather oddly, he called after himself, Killany. He built several such churches.

Were Enda and his colleagues just "folklore," the unmotivated fabrication of country people? I do not think so. The travels of the saints, their friendships and quarrels, their kinships, their prophesies and cursings, have a close-woven consistency in which a pattern is dimly discernible. They cannot be the product of local and arbitrary fantasy. Behind the fiction lies truth of some kind. What is it?

I have a rough idea of what happened and Enda, like the others, offers clues. His story, though odd, is not chaotic. It is like the agitated and mysterious shadow thrown by a tree on a windy, moonlit night. In the daytime the mystery disperses; the tree is seen to be earthbound and all its movements occur in a prescribed orbit. Our predecessors wrote history in a primitive picture language. How is one to interpret it? My guess would be that the saints were the fabulous pre-Christian ancestors of pre-Celtic and proto-Celtic tribes and amalgamations of tribes, and that in their pilgrimages and pedigrees and in the multiplicity of their names, nicknames, cult centres, we can read the true story of the wanderings of tribes. But since on this early pattern of history writing later patterns have been superimposed, we have a palimpsest that is very hard to decipher.

Was Enda or Enna, as he is often called, an ancestor? And if so, can one guess what his tribe was? Before the Celts came to Gaul and it was populated by Iberians, Ligurians, Illyrians, who knows what tribes invaded Ireland? After the Celts, it was the Eneti-Veneti who had easiest access to Ireland.

Thomas O'Rahilly, speculating in a Rhys lecture on how the Q-Celts came to Ireland, since he knew of none in Gaul, suggested that in the mass migration of the Q-Celtic Helvetii from Switzerland, which Caesar had arrested with immense slaughter, a remnant might have escaped to Ireland, ferried across by the Veneti.

In this many-tiered conjecture what interested me was that so distinguished a scholar accepted the travels of the Veneti to Ireland quite casually. However, in his book *Early Irish History and Mythology* he took it all back, acknowledging that the Helvetii were not Q- but P-Celts and that there *were* Q-Celts, the Quariates, in Gaul. His manner of saying "I was wrong" is interesting. "My suggestion," he wrote, "had the fatal merit of picturesqueness, which impressed itself on people who were not in a position to appreciate my arguments." If his lecture were reprinted, he said, he would relegate it all to a footnote, "in the hope of preventing the less experienced reader from drawing lopsided conclusions." But if the Helvetii were not, as he thought, Q-Celts, why mention them at all?

If the Veneti, who were also called Eneti, never came to Ireland and had nothing to do with Fintan and Enda, well, I was wrong and I apologize for my lopsided conclusion, but a few years later they did have a better reason for coming than transporting the Helvetii. They lived on the coast of Brittany, leaving their name at Vannes. They were the most accomplished navigators in Gaul. They had a fleet of over two hundred ships and, when Julius Caesar attacked them, they were able to summon allies from Britain and all the maritime tribes of northern Gaul. They felt themselves to be invincible and dared to imprison the two ambassadors that the Romans sent. This was an unforgivable outrage and, when Caesar had built a more formidable navy than theirs at Bordeaux and defeated them, none was spared. In his words (he always writes in the third person):

Caesar thought that punishment should be inflicted the more severely, in order that for the future rights of ambassadors might be more carefully respected by barbarians. Having, therefore, put to death all their senate, he sold the rest for slaves.

So he says, but there were many thousands of Veneti and I do not doubt that many escaped to Britain and to Ireland. Gwynedd in Wales is supposed to owe its name to them, and some have suggested Fenit in Kerry and Fanad in Donegal.

Early tribes had eponymous ancestors: the Moabites had Moab, the Hittites had Heth, the Ionians had Ion, the Persians Perseus, and we do not doubt that the Gaulish tribes had them too, though the Romans, intending that Roman Gaul should be unified, aimed at the suppression of all the old tribal loyalties, in which the Romans showed no interest at all. Caesar did not view the Celts as Mr. Ó Síocháin does. The Gauls to him were all just "barbarians."

Yet we know that the Esuvii had Esus as ancestor, the Lepontii had Lepontius, the Salassi had Salassus. Who was the ancestor of the Eneti-Veneti? Surely someone like Enetus or Venetus. But we know these proper names only in their Romanized form where the singular ended in -us, the plural in -i. The Gaulish form could easily have been, or become after several generations in Ireland, something like Enna or Enda and Fintan.

When St. Enda arrived on his stone in Aran he found a very wicked King Corban in control. When St. Enda approached, Corban's subjects all fled in wonder and horror to the coast of Clare, "for the sun cannot abide with darkness nor heathendom with the light of the Gospel." Only Corban himself stood his ground, "a second Pharaoh, *obduratus in malicia*," but finally even he was convinced by a miracle and Enda took over the island. He divided it at first among nine other saints but then, to their anger, decided to keep half for himself. This and some other questions about procedure were settled by two doves flying from Rome. One dropped a missal into St. Enda's lap, the other flung a cape over his shoulders to indicate his primacy. Only St. Brecan at the Kilmurvey end of the island disputed this.

A different story is told of the division of the island between St. Enda and St. Brecan. They agreed to start Mass at the same time, one at Cill Éanna, the other at Teampall Bhreacáin. They were then to walk towards each other and where they met the island was to be divided between them. But St. Brecan cheated and began Mass before St. Enda and so was able to start sooner. However, St. Enda quickly caught on to the deception and prayed to the Lord. As a result, when St. Brecan and his disciples reached the sea at Kilmurvey their feet stuck fast in the sand and Enda came up to them and so got his fair share of Aran.

Who was this Brecan who held on to his corner of Aranmore when Enda routed Corban and his followers? The late Anne O'Sullivan, my dear friend Neans, edited a poem put into the mouth of a supposed Brecan of Aran.* He was pictured as an old bishop dictating his life story to a young man with special reference to the dues owed by the various families, especially the O'Muldowneys and O'Hallorans, to him and his successors. He relates how his original name was Bresal and his first mission was to Aran, where he at once destroyed the reigning idol, Brecan, and himself took his name.

The story delights me, for I have always maintained that the Irish saints were tribal ancestors Christianized, and here we see it actually happening.

The newly sanctified Brecan had said, "The fierce Brecan was in Aran before me; I undertook to expel him and I sanctified his place."

Anne O'Sullivan suggests that the "fierce Brecan" was "an idol," but in the pre-Christian saga there is little talk of idols and much of ancestors. St. Brecan and St. Enda, competing for territory with Corban and his flock, are behaving like tribes, not like individuals, and in historical retrospect the ancestor, a revered figure, symbolizes the tribe, and when in time the tribe dissolves, the ancestor, still a revered figure but without a vocation, easily turns into a saint. In Gaul the

---

Celtica, Vol. XX, p. 28.

ancestor, losing his tribe under the Romans, became a god. Thus the god Esus was ancestor of the Esuvii of Normandy, while the goddess Nantosvelta was surely the amalgamated ancestress of the Nantuates and Svelteri of southeast Gaul.

Another inmate of the spiritual storehouse was St. Grigóir of Aran. The great Celtic scholar Rudolf Thurneysen was baffled by an ancient prophecy that Pope Gregory the Great would be descended from the tribe of Curoi Mac Daire, the famous chieftain of the Dingle Peninsula in Kerry: "*Wie der Verfasser auf diesen Gedanken gekommen ist, ist unbekannt,*" he wrote. It is not, however, unknown. Father Shearman, a Victorian country scholar, knew all about it and wrote at length in 1876 in the *Kilkenny Archaeological Journal.*

He writes that there was an Irish St. Grigóir or Gregory, a native of the Blasket Islands opposite the Dingle Peninsula, who went with another saint, Faelcu, to Rome; he dismisses as idle talk the story that while in Rome the pontiff died and a dove settled on Faelcu's head and he was offered the papacy, but he believes that on return they settled in Inishmaan in the Aran Islands, where as canons regular they founded Cill na Cannanach, or the Church of the Canons.

It was natural, he thinks, that because of this visit to Rome the Aran islanders should confound their St. Gregory with Gregory the Great, and make him share a feast day, 12 March, with the great pope. And it was not surprising that they should call after him Gregory's Sound, the strait between Inishmore and Inishmaan, through which he and Faelcu passed on their return from Rome. And he says that in 1876, when he wrote, the fishermen who voyaged down the sound on their way to Galway still lowered their sails in homage to the Irish pope.

Father Shearman thinks it quite natural that in Kerry, Grigóir's native land, the strait between the Blasket Islands and the Dingle Peninsula should also be called Gregory's Sound and that St. Gregory the Great should be given the Kerry pedigree of his Irish namesake.*

Father Shearman has done better than Thurneysen but his argument should be carried a little farther into regions where he would be unwilling to follow me. Opposite Aran on the Clare coast were the Grecraige or Gregraige, with one ancestor called Grecus and another called Grec mac Aarod. There are Grecraige on Lough Gara in Co. Sligo and their territory is called the Gregories, so obviously

---

*You will find the great pope's Kerry pedigree in Shearman's *Loca Patriciana*, p. 273.

Grecraige turns easily into Gregory and makes St. Grigóir-Gregory look like a Christian incarnation of the pagan ancestor Grecus.

But to learn more about St. Grigóir-Gregory I must go back to Kerry, his native land, and the southern Gregory's Sound. At the base of the Dingle Peninsula is Castle Gregory, and inevitably I would claim it for St. Gregory, but an Anglo-Norman family called Hoare once lived nearby and it is alleged that one of their number was called Gregory. Yet St. Gregory's claim is stronger because he was patron of a church at Glenbeigh in the next barony of Iveragh and in Father Shearman's time his feast day was observed there on 12 March. But even here, like mocking spirits from the pre-Celtic and pre-Christian past, the Grecraige are recorded in Inis Grecraige or Beare Island, a few miles off in Bantry Bay.

The Grecraige appear in many forms in many parts of Ireland with many ancestors and heroes and saints. To mention one of each, there were Gracraige in Munster with Grac as their ancestor, as hero, there was King Grig of Scotland, the ancestor of the Macgregors, who was also confused with Gregory the Great; there was St. Colman Grec of Fermoy, whom Canon Power, the historian of the Decies in Co. Waterford, thought at first must be a Greek but then decided was one of the Grecraige.

I made it my duty to hunt them all down, but I must come back to Aran and the spiritual storehouse.

St. Cybi (also called Cuby) was a Cornishman who founded several churches in Cornwall and Wales and then went to Ireland, where he spent four years in Aran. He took with him two disciples, Maelóg (31 December), the son of Caw, and Cyngar (7 November), an elderly relation of failing health who could take no food but milk, so St. Cuby brought a cow and a calf with him.

They straightaway fell out with an irascible saint called Fintan. Maelóg quarrelled with him initially by digging the ground outside his house and they had to get Enda to make peace between them.

Then Cyngar's calf strayed into Fintan's cornfield and Fintan's people tied it to a great tree. Cuby sent one of his disciples to beg Fintan for the return of the calf but Fintan refused. Then St. Cuby prayed that the calf should return to its mother, for without it the cow would not give milk and old Cyngar would die. The Lord heard his prayer and the calf returned to the cow dragging the great tree by the roots behind it. Fintan then prayed to the Lord that he would drive away Cuby from Aran and an angel of the Lord came to Cuby as he slept, advising him to go eastward. And Cuby answered, "May

God destroy Fintan from the island!" And the angel said, "So shall it be."

Then Cuby went eastward to Meath and on the way he built three churches; the third was the great church of Mochop. But Fintan pursued him farther east till he reached the sea and Fintan said, "Cuby, go beyond the sea." And Cuby turned on him and said, "All thy churches are so much deserted that there are scarcely three to be found in the whole island of Ireland where there is singing at the altar."

So Cuby and his disciples built a boat and Fintan said to prove he was a saint he must cross the sea without covering the planks with hide. The Lord aided Cuby and he crossed in a skinless currach to Anglesea. His adventures in Wales and back to Cornwall were many and varied. To commemorate his Welsh activities, there are Caergybi at Holyhead, Llangybi in Caernarvonshire and Llangybi in Monmouth.

Two aspects of this are interesting. Another version of the story describes Fintan not as a saint but as a rich landowner. Secondly, one of the churches which Cybi built while he was fleeing from St. Fintan was called Kilmore Mo Cop, that is to say "the big church of St. Mo Cop" (for "mo" [my] is said to be a prefix of affectionate respect "My Cop"). Now St. Mo Cop has an Irish pedigree and is culted three days later than St. Cybi, and it is very strange that a church which the great St. Cybi founded should be called after an insignificant successor. The fact is that both St. Cybi and St. Mo Cop clearly belong to the great family of Goban saints, who are very difficult to distinguish from each other, and several of whom are called Mo Coppoc or Mo Goppoc Artifex.

St. Gobban or Goban is usually thought the most fabulous of the Irish saints, although he only behaves as all the others do. The critics of his sanctity connect him with Goibniu, the Celtic god of smithcraft. This god had a Welsh counterpart, Goibnenn or Gwydion, who was responsible for Abergavenny, became St. Govan in Pembroke and Sir Gawain of the Round Table. The critics believe that god and saint and knight developed out of the Irish word "goba," a smith. There was a St. Goban in Suffolk and a St. Gobain in Picardy. In Aran, St. Cybi, St. Goban and the virgin saint Gobnait of Inishere made a family party, for Cybi's first cousin, St. David, had a sister Magna, who lived in the Galtees and was Goban's mother, and Gobnait was culted the same day as a St. Goban. If they could be distinguished from each other there must have been about

twenty of these Goban saints. They were mostly craftsmen and builders, and Petrie has fused them all into one real architect who built
the round towers of Antrim, Ferns, Kilmacduagh and Killala. But
even remote Gobans, like St. Gobain of Laon, built their own
churches, as did St. Cybi. Order comes into this confusion only if we
assume an ordinary tribal ancestor, whose name incidentally suggested smithcraft. What was the tribe?

I suggest they were the Cubi of the Upper Loira, a primitive tribe
overrun by the Bituriges, who gave their name to Bourges and were
the only Celtic tribe in Aquitania.

Further, I suggest that in Ireland the Cubi were hard pressed by
the Veneti, as in Gaul they were pressed by the Bituriges. I cannot
otherwise explain why the Fintan saints treated the Goban saints so
badly. St. Fintan of Clonenagh once exposed his disciple, Presbyter
Goban, as an appalling sinner at the very moment when he was
celebrating Mass. He was ejected and died miserably and in sin.

Another Goban saint was chased away by a St. Fintan in Wexford and many other saints treated them harshly or displaced them.
St. Abban blinded Goban, his church builder, for overcharging. Another Goban was such an ignorant man that he had to have his hands
blessed by St. Maedoc before he could build.

All the Aran saints had lives as adventurous as Enda's. I must
write of St. Ceannfionnán, or Concannon, because Concannon was
Teresa's name. His name means Whitehead and his sister Ceanndearg
or Redhead is also culted in Aran, but Mr. Ó Síocháin thinks she
must have been a male because no nun could be called Redhead. St.
Ceannfionnán was the son of a king and, like three other saints of
Aran, went to Rome and was offered the papacy.

Ceannfionnán was beheaded in Connemara, the only Irish martyr; many Irish heroes with "ceann" (head) in their names had an
adventure with their head. I should mention too a lake near Kilmurvey once called Stagnum Genanni or Ceannfionnán. (The Gen-
nani, an ancient tribe, once lived in the west.) It has not been
connected, though, with St. Ceannfionná or the Concannons, but
with a white-headed cow of St. Enda's. It turned round three times
in honour of the Trinity and disappeared into the lake.

Was Ceannfionnán a saint or a cow? I suspect he was neither
but as no tribal ancestors come to mind perhaps someone else will
take up the question.

Who was the wicked Corban who was turned out of Aran by
Enda? He and his people were surely some scattered half-forgotten

community. For example, in the midlands St. Ciarán of Saighir also had trouble with a wicked king called Corban or Cobran, who had an evil eye. St. Ciarán and his mother, St. Liadán, who lived nearby, had two erring disciples called respectively Gobran and Cerpan, who died miserably. St. Ciarán dealt with them all as Enda would have done. King Corban or Cobran was struck blind at Rathdowney in Co. Leix, where he gave himself and his property to St. Ciarán; Gobran was redeemed from Hell and Cerpan was revived. It is natural to say that Corban, Cobran, Gobran and Cerpan never lived and their names are four regional variations of the same name. It is harder to say that they were invented, for there is still at Rathdowney a place called Killcoran or the church of St. Cobran. There is a large rath round the ruins of a church and a mound beside it was removed a hundred years ago and found to contain a mass of human bones. Did a saint or wicked king ever live there? Surely it is more probable that it was a settlement of an ancient, widespread tribe, submerged by later invaders, the Corban tribe in fact. Was there any known primitive tribe whom they represented? To speculate about that would take me far away from Aran.

Let us go back to Aran and St. Caradoc Garb, who left his name at Cowragh and Port Caradoc between Kilronan and Kilmurvey. I know only one Caradoc saint and he was Welsh and twelfth century and possibly real. Many saints and heroes have been called "Garb," which means rough. In a saint, Canon O'Hanlon suggested that it meant he was "somewhat abrupt in his manner of rebuking sin," but the early hagiographers had far odder explanations. For example, St. Enda's sister, St. Fainche Garb, is said to have got her nickname because she swam under Loch Erne to avoid a suitor and St. Diarmaid, seeing her emerging with shells and pondweed clinging to her skin, said, "That is rough." In fact no one knows, or has ever known, what "garb" really meant and the reason is that it meant nothing; it was a tribal element applied to the ancestor or ancestress of the tribe by his or her descendants. There were two saints and a pagan hero called Senach Garb and the mountain in Kerry, which is called after the latter, had three other heroes called Senach Garb on it and a river Garb nearby. But the proof that it was tribal is offered by a Scottish hero, Fergna Garb, who was the eponymous ancestor of the Garbraige tribe. Now, however rough his manners or his skin may have been, a whole tribe would not be called "the rough" on his account. So we must ask not "What does 'garb' mean?" but "Who were the Garb-folk originally?" Since a certain hero Garb was also called Car-pad, the best guess I can make at the moment is that they derive from the Carpetani, a very large Iberian tribe of the Upper Tagus.

I wrote, of course, most of all this when I got home. I worked out my general theory about Enda and his colleagues in Aran itself but developed it when I got back to my library in Kilkenny. The book which I have used most and enjoyed most is *Silva Gadelica* by Standish Hayes O'Grady, published in 1892. It is a collection of ancient Irish tales in two volumes, the first in Irish, the second in translation.

Till recently, I had not read his introduction and realized what a highly idiosyncratic and independent-minded man he was. His biography has never been written but I have heard that, a great Celtic scholar, he lived in London and worked in the British Museum. Here is a short passage from the introduction:

This work is far from being exclusively or even primarily designed for the omniscient impeccable leviathans of science that headlong sound the linguistic ocean to its most horrid depths, and (in the intervals of ramming each other) ply their flukes on such audacious small fry as even on the mere surface will venture within their danger. Rather is it adapted to the use of those weaker brethren who, not blindly persisting in their hitherto blissful ignorance, may be disposed to learn, if but a little, of an out of the way and curious branch of literature.

It would be no less instructive than easy to point out how and where lordly Cetaceans of philology, enviously invading shallows in which the humble Celtic whitebait sports at ease, lie stranded (as Milton has it) "many a rood in length."

He calls himself "a humble quarryman" who brings up the raw material for the "Keltologues" and "philologists," the folklorists and others: "Personally, I cannot boast of being anything that ends in either -logue or -ist."

Did he have some grievance against them? I don't think so. The other Standish O'Grady had a vision of a society which in our century and here in Ireland was governed by intellectual aristocrats. Standish Hayes O'Grady believed that Irish scholarship could be liberated from the combination of the -logues and -ists and that the impeccable omniscient leviathans of science should work fraternally with those who merely rescue the past without bothering themselves unduly about the language within which it is recorded; the whale would disport itself with the whitebait.

I believe O'Grady might, had he lived, have seen O'Rahilly as "a lordly Cetacean lying stranded in the shallows." As a humble whitebait he might have had sympathy for me.

I started this investigation in Aran, so I shall end it in Aran. I decided that, when I passed through Galway on my way home, I would try and goad Dr. Simpson into some interest in all this. He was very friendly but nothing came of it. I was embarrassed by not being sure how to pronounce Fainche and finding that he had scarcely heard of her or, for that matter, the Carpetani. They were gate-crashers, like myself, at a party to which only the Celts and Celticists were welcomed.

"I gather," he said, "that you are saying that toponyms are frequently tribal in origin. That of course has been allowed for. But certainly the systematic study of onomastics has often been helped on by freewheeling methods like yours. Splendid! But see that they don't degenerate into uncontrolled folk philosophizing like poor Ó Síocháin's. Names have no more generality of behaviour than the pertinent dimensions of the specific culture of which they form a part."

Simpson always expresses himself with great lucidity, but he has a curiously numbing effect on me. He paralyzes the curiosity on which my confidence is based. My convictions do not seem wrong but in the wrong place. Corban may have felt like that when the fierce light of the gospel beat down on him, but he may have stammered out a few unpleasant things before he disappeared.

"But what about the spiritual storehouse?" I said.

"My dear fellow," he answered a little irritably, "all that you are arguing is really very old stuff. You'll find that Jorgensen of Wisconsin noted the chronological difficulties about Enda and others in *Gelehrte Anzeigen* fully forty years ago. As for Gobban, I wrote only last week for the Bollandists that it is no doubt a hypocoristic form of 'goba,' smith, with geminated *b*."

"Then Ó Síocháin is wrong?" I persisted. "There weren't really any saints?"

"Ó Síocháin!" he snorted. "What in the world does he know about anything? Ó Síocháin is utterly unimportant."

"Well," I answered, "about a thousand copies of his book are sold to one of yours. Would yours have been published at all without a university subsidy?"

He looked very much hurt and so I did not finish what I was going to say, that country scholarship had deteriorated hugely since archaeology was professionalized.

Neither of us wanted to quarrel, so he did the only thing he could do, which was to pour me out a geminated whiskey and say that I must look after my cold.

As I walked to the bus, I reflected that Jorgensen and his colleagues had made a vast gulf between life and scholarship, between living and knowing, and that it would take a generation or two to fill it in. Educated Irishmen are now bored with the saints, who intrigued so intensely the sceptical antiquarians of our great-grandfathers' day. The question "Who were the saints?" had aroused curiosity then. There were theories and counter-theories and local societies had grown up as arenas in which fierce battles could be fought about them. Now all is still and dead, and the saints have been laid away in lavender in a bottom drawer. And curiosity has no status unless it is paid.

Yet for the Irish people to forget the saints is for them to forget their childhood. We are emotionally and intellectually committed to them. They beckon us along a private road that leads not only to the Irish past but to the past of Europe. It is through them that we can learn about the youth of the world and the infancy of religion. Whether they really lived or not, they belong to us more than to anybody else.

Maria Edgeworth

1954

There are some Irish writers who are so precariously balanced between England and Ireland that an Irishman often has to do a bit of special pleading in order to claim them for Ireland at all. If I had felt that Maria Edgeworth was one of these borderline cases, I might have been tempted to concentrate on her Irish stories, *Castle Rackrent, The Absentee* and *Ormond*, and to treat her other work, her educational tales and English novels, as in some way secondary. But in fact from the time she was fifteen and returned to Edgeworthstown with her father, Ireland became her home and Irish life her major preoccupation. Yet though she lived in Ireland, she was far less provincial than many of her great English contemporaries; she was accepted on the Continent as a European in a way that Jane Austen, a much greater novelist, never was. The Edgeworth Way of Life, expounded by her father and herself, found them disciples far and wide. Friends in Paris once urged them to set up a salon there in rivalry to Mme. de Staël, for it was thought that the Edgeworths and their philosophy of rational conduct would be a wholesome antidote to the brilliant romanticism of the de Staël circle.

All this led Maria to speak condescendingly of Jane Austen, who had found all the material for her art ready to hand in a Hampshire village and whose novels never touched on the social problems which agitated the Edgeworths. "One gets tired," said Maria of Jane, "of milk and water, even when the milk is of the sweetest and the water the purest."

One cannot wholly blame Maria for this undervaluation or for the havoc the once-fashionable Edgeworth notions made of her own talents as a novelist. Ireland in those days offered a challenge to the heart as well as to the head, and in warmhearted intelligent people like Maria and her father it was bound to stimulate ideas of justice and reform. The Edgeworths found arrogance on one side and poverty and ignorance beyond belief upon the other, and a deep social fissure which it seemed to them only education and mutual trust could bridge. They had a passion for social justice and they could not be content to be chroniclers of country manners like Jane or like Maria herself in *Castle Rackrent*.

In her old age Maria recognized clearly what had happened. She admitted that her best-conceived characters were those, like Sir Condy of *Castle Rackrent* and Thady Quirk, which she had created with a minimum of what she called "philosophical construction." "Where I least aimed at drawing character," she wrote, "I succeeded best." She would like to have gone on writing about Ireland but she said that passions were too high and there was no place for a writer who wished to hold the mirror up to nature. The people would smash the mirror and that would be the end.

If she was often very didactic it was because she was an invincible optimist, believing that there was no evil to which experience and self-knowledge could not discover a cure. In this she was no mere echo of her father, dominating character as he was. R. L. Edgeworth was certainly dynamic. He invented springs for carriages, "macadamized" roads and early types of bicycles and telegraphs. He was an enthusiast for education and domesticity, which his twenty-two children and five wives did not succeed in quenching. As a young man he had been a disciple of Rousseau and for a time had brought up his eldest son as a child of nature. But the more he saw of the miseries of Ireland, the less respect he had for primitive simplicity and for Rousseau, who had sung its praises. When the Edgeworth philosophy took its final form, I think it could be summarized in three words: "Learn by experience," or perhaps "Think for yourself." That was the refrain that recurred through scores of Edgeworth novels and tales.

Perhaps it is easier for us than it was for our parents to understand how such a chilly platitude could become a slogan in a crusade. For if there is any truth in the theory that history repeats itself in cycles, have we not come round again to the problems of the Edgeworths and their friends? Then, just as now, civilization had rocked and men were slowly recovering from the intoxication of tremendous dreams. The magic of the dreams had faded but they had not relaxed their hold upon the mind. Men of opposing factions were mobilized to think in blocs and there was a stigma of treachery attached to those who chose to be independent. Edgeworth was one of those whose pride it was to think for himself into whatever eccentricities this might lead him, and Maria had inherited some of her father's uncompromisingly experimental spirit. The Edgeworths and their circle despised nothing so much as intellectual timidity. If you had a belief you must also have the courage to practise it. Maria's brother-in-law, Dr. Beddoes, for example, a well-known physician, used to terrorize the landladies of Bristol by driving cows upstairs to his patients' bedrooms. Why? Simply because the doctor was convinced that in pulmonary complaints nothing was so wholesome for an invalid as a cow breathing on him. And is not health more important than stair carpets?

Her father was more cautiously experimental than this and the success of his methods was to be read in his well-run estate, his contented tenantry and his happy children. The large plain house in the Irish midlands became famous in Europe and a focus of pilgrimage almost like Mme. de Staël's house at Coppet or Tolstoy's at Yasnaya Polyana.

If you think I exaggerate, look up the Edgeworthstown chapter in Mr. and Mrs. Hall's famous *Travels in Ireland* and you will find those two quite hard-boiled pilgrims almost inarticulate with emotion. They seem to be on tiptoe from the moment they enter Co. Longford, fearful to violate this sanctuary of family happiness but at the same time anxious to draw from their visit and share with the world all the enlightenment they could:

For from this mansion has issued so much practical good to Ireland and not alone to Ireland but to the whole civilized world. It has been for long the residence of high intellect, well directed genius, industry and virtue. It is a place that perhaps possesses larger moral interest than any other in the kingdom.

Mr. and Mrs. Hall, like so many others, saw Maria working at her stories in the general living room, children in and out the whole time, for in addition to some dozen brothers and sisters there were nephews and nieces, but her mind was so attuned to domesticity that they did not disturb her. Indeed in one of her letters she writes that she was taking her writing desk into her sister Lucy's room, for Lucy, while in bed, liked to hear the sound of Maria's pencil. In most modern writers distraction like that would be almost unintelligible but with Maria it was no affectation. Affection for her family and friends was the fuel which kept her mind in motion.

Maria and her father, much more than Rousseau or Montessori or anyone else, were the progenitors of the progressive school with its educational toys and uninhibited ethic. And it was as an educational reformer that Maria first acquired a European reputation. I wonder if it is her fault or ours that no modern child has an appetite for the sort of story she wrote. This may be an accident of fashion, for though to us her stories seem steeped in the most austere morality, the Victorians did not find them moral enough. Or rather they complained that the Edgeworths used all the wrong arguments for inculcating virtue, basing it on neighbourliness and reason and common sense rather than the Ten Commandments. They did not, like Charlotte M. Yonge, the Victorian favourite, link virtue to the eternal verities. Indeed *The Quarterly Review* printed what her friend Dumont called "an infamous and calumnious attack" on Maria. The writer complained of "the deplorable omission of expressions of devoutness, which from its persistence it is impossible to believe to be accidental." Elsewhere the Rev. R. Hall wrote: "Her books are the most irreligious I have ever read. She does not attack religion but makes it appear unnecessary by exhibiting perfect virtue without it. No works ever produced so bad an effect on my mind as hers."

But what our children miss is fantasy. The Edgeworths had no use for it. Maria's stories about little Rosamond are crisp and logical, like a proposition in Euclid. There are no fairies, pirates or bunny rabbits' tea parties. Particularly about rabbits was Rosamond very rational. She discussed with her mama the idea that it was wrong to kill and eat rabbits, but rejected it as unreasonable. And when a rabbit nibbled a shrub that her mother had given her, her brother made her a humane and ingenious rabbit trap. I haven't a doubt that if Rosamond's mother lived today she would blame myxomatosis on Peter Rabbit. She would argue like this: "If you grant to animals false feelings that they have not, you will finally forget the true feelings which they have."

How can one explain the immense appeal that these uncompromising stories had for the children of 150 years ago? Maria tried to give a plain unadorned view of society and its obligations, scaling it down to a child's vision. She never bluffed or condescended. Children felt they were being initiated into the secrets of the grown-up world, its taboos and dangers, and perhaps this was as thrilling to them as mystery and adventure are to children today.

"Rosamond and the Purple Jar" is the best known of these stories. It exemplifies so well the remorseless but benevolent Edgeworth logic that I'll relate the plot.

Rosamond, going out shopping with her mama and a servant to carry the parcels, inevitably wanted to buy almost everything she saw in the fascinating shops, but her mama countered all her excited suggestions with cool prim logic.

"Nay, Rosamond, I have a pair of buckles, I do not want any more," or "Yes, Rosamond, the jewels are pretty but what use are pretty baubles to me? . . . You say I would discover a use, but I would rather find out the use before buying."

And then they come to a chemist's shop and Rosamond can scarcely be drawn away from the delirious contemplation of a purple jar in the window.

"Oh, mama, but it would be useful. We could put flowers in it."

"You have a flower-pot, Rosamond, and that is not a flower-pot."

"But I could use it as a flower-pot, mama."

"Perhaps, if you were to examine it closer, Rosamond, you would be disappointed."

"No, indeed, mama, I am sure I shouldn't."

A little later Rosamond starts to limp on the pavement. "Oh, mama, there is a great hole in my shoe and a stone is got in. My shoes are quite worn out. I wish you would be so very good as to buy me another pair."

"Nay, Rosamond, I have money but not enough to buy shoes, buckles, pretty baubles and purple jars."

But the limp becomes worse, really cruel, and they have to go into a shoe shop, dark and smelling horribly of new leather, but they find a pair of shoes that exactly fits. And Rosamond is given her choice. She may have the shoes or she may have the purple jar and wait till the end of the month for the shoes.

After reflection she decides, "Oh, mama, I *think* I can wear the bad shoes till the end of the month. I would *prefer* the flower-pot if you will not think me very silly."

"Why, I cannot promise not to think you silly, Rosamond. But when you have to judge for yourself, you should choose what will make you happy and then it will not signify who thinks you silly."

"Then, mama, I am sure the flower-pot will make me happy."

You will remember or can guess the rest. When the servant arrives with the purple jar, Rosamond finds to her dismay that it is just a plain glass jar full of nasty purple liquid. And every day her shoes get worse and worse so that she can't jump or dance or run. She offered to exchange the jar with her mother for a pair of shoes, but the calm logical answer came back, "Nay, Rosamond, you must abide by your choice."

Rosamond's mama would be attacked from a dozen different angles today. A woman, we'd say, who could afford a servant to carry her parcels, should be ashamed to let her child hobble round in broken-down shoes and there would be medical talk about permanent injury to the instep and so on. But the key to the Edgeworth doctrine surely lies in the mother's remark: "What does it signify who thinks you silly, if you choose what will make you happy?" The Edgeworthian parents never, like the Victorian paterfamilias, put themselves on pedestals. They seldom preached and never punished. But nor did they hasten headlong, as we should do, to protect their children from the educative consequences of an unwise choice.

The stories themselves don't sufficiently explain the little world of mutual solicitude and patience which Maria assumed as a necessary background to these chastening adventures. Mr. Edgeworth's letters and, much more so, Maria's make things clearer. For instance, there is his letter to Maria about little Fanny, who had asked him what a section was when he was busy. He tells Maria to buy a lemon for her and get a small cylinder of wood turned. Then Maria is to demonstrate with a knife what a transverse section is and then what a longitudinal section is. The Edgeworth educational system demanded a warm and constant intimacy between elders and children. Boarding schools were regarded as an easy, inadequate way out. It was only because Mr. Edgeworth was dead and Maria old that the youngest of the brood was sent to Charterhouse.

Many little sisters—there were ten of them—went to the making of Rosamond. And that rather abstract little girl becomes more intelligible if we set the reality beside the fiction. It is a little daunting to read of Maria's young sister Harriet coming in before breakfast at 8 a.m. every morning to read her Mme. de Sévigné, but turn a page or two and you will find Maria taking Harriet and Fanny to visit Sir Walter Scott at Abbotsford or to Mme. de Genlis, Lord Edward's mother-in-law, decaying in a Parisian garret. Or dressing them up for a dance at Almacks. And then coming home again and helping Maria make a gutter in the main street at Edgeworthstown, her own idea, her own plans and "twenty men," Maria claims proudly, "employed for three weeks." Those returns to Edgeworthstown were always happy. "We look to our dear home for permanent happiness," wrote Maria. "We return without a regret for anything we have left behind except our friends."

A few days pass and we read of Harriet again. She is taking the part of a fire-eater in a charade and devouring lighted spills; "she only burnt her lips a little." Or listen how the children organized a *fête champêtre* at Edgeworthstown in 1805 to celebrate old Mr. Edgeworth's birthday. First of all they contrived to get their elders and the babies out of the way for the afternoon.

I had little Lucy in my arms [wrote Maria] and, after the chaise, on horseback came rosy Charlotte all smiles, and Henry with eyes brilliant with pleasure. We came home with no suspicion of what was prepared, when our ears were suddenly struck with the sound of music and as if by enchantment a fairy festival appeared upon the green. An amphitheatre of verdant festoons suspended from white staffs with scarlet streamers. Youths and maidens in white, their heads adorned with flowers, were dancing while their mothers and little children were seated on benches round the amphitheatre. William danced a reel with Harriet and baby Sophie, and Kitty served cakes and syllabus and then William at present in the height of his electrical enthusiasm proposed to the dancers a few electrical sparks to complete the joys of the day. Everybody flocked after him to the study and shrieks of surprise and terror mixed with the laughter. And when we came out the grass-plat was lit up by boys waving flambeaux, illuminating the beauty of green boughs and flowers.

You see it was part of the theory that when Rosamond had learnt to reason for herself and had discovered that purple jars might not be purple, she should use her intelligence and daring to its utmost limits. Not only could she play with fire, she could swallow it if she chose. So you can understand Maria's indignation when Mme. de Staël gibed at the *triste utilité* of the Edgeworth educational system. There was no evidence that it produced either prigs or pedants.

Their educational schemes had of course their setbacks. Maria's brother Lovell put into practice an old dream of his father's, and with the support of the Catholic priest and the Protestant rector of Edgeworthstown started an interdenominational school there. This experiment, a unique one in those days, went well for ten years. But Lovell's business capacity was not equal to his educational zeal. He bankrupted the estate and Maria had to take it over and run it herself from her literary earnings.

It would be hard certainly to claim that even in her novels Maria was not excessively didactic. The book of hers which I prefer, *The Absentee*, is more propagandist even than *Uncle Tom's Cabin*. It is like the most entertaining sermon that was ever written. All the characters are tilted slightly from the plane of reality towards the central argument of the book: "An Irish landlord must live among the people from whom he draws his subsistence." Because they neglect this principle, Lady Clonbrony lives beyond her income, trying to buy her way into fashionable London society, while fashionable London merely laughs at her provinciality and vulgar Irishisms. For the same reason Lord Clonbrony is *désoeuvré* and feebly resentful. He exaggerates his Irishness from defiance. Meanwhile in Ireland, unknown to the absentee landlord, the bad agent of the Clonbrony property prospers, the good agent is squeezed out by intrigue. And among the humble tenants, we see virtue discouraged and vice triumphant all because of the canker of absenteeism.

But fortunately the young lord shares many of Mr. Edgeworth's views about estate management. He travels to the family estates incognito. There is a superb account of social life in Dublin and the provinces in the years after the Union. The young lord reveals himself and establishes the rule of reason and order. And the earl and countess drive home to Clonbrony Castle to the cheers of their tenantry.

Maria's plots are complicated and ingenious as is fitting in an inventor's daughter. Sometimes one seems to hear the pulleys creak and the ropes strain as virtue is hoisted onto her pedestal. One recalls Mr. Edgeworth raising by a new device his patent metal spire on Edgeworthstown church and how a bugle blew when the hoisting started and when at last the golden weathercock settled into position, a flag flew and the congregation cheered. And how that did not prevent a murmuring among the devout: "Yes, but is Mr. Edgeworth really orthodox?" Maria's enthusiasm and ingenuity are no answer either to a parallel question: "Is Miss Edgeworth really a novelist?" Compared to Jane Austen, I don't think she is, but she was a writer of great and significant books, and her integrity if not her art should secure her a place among the immortals.

Her last book, *Helen*, caused her much misgiving. It was rewritten several times and is as far removed as possible from the spontaneous ease of *Castle Rackrent*. Her father had been dead seventeen years, during which she had written little, and those who blame him for turning her from an artist into a moralist have to explain why the book which she wrote without any encouragement from him should blaze with such moral fervour. Maria had a horror of half-lies, of innuendo and evasion, and the plot of *Helen* hinges on a very charming lady's inability to make an awkward admission. Little lies breed big lies, and at last the truth can only be vindicated by a lady as downright and disagreeable as Rosamond's mama. This lady hears the whole slanderous story from her dentist, as she sits in the dental chair. Such is her indignation that she bites his finger, and, with her toothache still raging, sets off to expose the falsehood.

These last novels seem today very archaic in construction but I think they have the same importance as some of Mr. Edgeworth's mechanical contrivances, those dim foreshadowings of the bicycle and the telephone whose debris were found not long ago in an outhouse at Edgeworthstown. They were experiments which, had he not been so preoccupied with moral problems and perhaps with Ireland, he might have brought to perfection. I don't mean by this that either he or his daughter failed in what they attempted, but that their proudest achievements must be looked for in their lives rather than in their art.

Maria Edgeworth was a brilliant and sociable personality who gave only half her genius to her art. As with her father, her ambition was as much to change society as to observe it. And though she left little imprint upon public life, who can set a limit in space or time to the influence of a happy and dynamic personality? Scott and Turgenev recorded their debt in print, for they said that it was *Castle Rackrent* that first inspired them to write as they did about Scotland and about Russia. But how many others had no opportunity of acknowledging what they owed to Maria! One debt to her, as a writer of children's stories, was paid in a way that delighted her. When the great famine was at its height and Maria, an old woman of eighty, was launching appeals on behalf of the stricken people of Edgeworthstown, a present arrived for Miss Edgeworth to distribute, 150 barrels of wheat and rice from the children of Boston, who had loved the stories of Rosamond and Harry and Frank.

Maria was a great family woman, so I can't do better than finish with a family tribute. In the home circle one is most likely to get impartiality from one's in-laws, and Richard Butler, the dean of Clonmacnois, a scholar and antiquarian, was married to Maria's sister Harriet. Here is what he wrote to a friend after Maria, in the last years of her life, had paid them her annual visit.

We have just had Maria Edgeworth with us, as cheerful and as fresh as ever. Having her is like having the sunshine always about you and I think she is more in her element and puts out all herself more in strictly domestic life than any other. Her constant flow of gaiety is one of the most surprising things in nature. Neither sadness nor malice nor anything very bad can stand long in her presence.

Irish Literature*

1956

What does one mean by Irish literature? All the literature emanating from Ireland with which you in Moscow are familiar is written in the English tongue and much of it, perhaps most of it, by men of Anglo-Irish descent, not by members of that Celtic stock which forms the majority of the population of Ireland. How did this come about? It is a paradox for which there are many analogies all over Europe. When the English conquered Ireland in the twelfth century, Celtic civilization was already in decline, and early Irish literature—fabulous, fantastic sagas of gods and heroes, akin but, I think, superior in imagination and antiquity to the other epic literature of the North—had passed its creative period. It could not hold out against the dominant Anglo-Irish culture and civilization. All the same, poetry and prose continued to be written in the Irish language, but it was a literature of protest, nostalgia and rebellion, handicapped by poverty and isolation. It was hopelessly cut off from the mainstream of European culture.

So Irish literature, in the form which Europe came to know it, became Anglo-Irish literature. But it remained a distinctive thing all the same; it never quite became English literature, and even today, when it is hard for small national cultures to resist absorption by their more powerful and sophisticated neighbours, there is still such

---

*Butler was invited to a meeting of the Union of Writers in Moscow in October 1956 and was told they would pay his fare to Leningrad, which he wished to visit the next day, if he gave them a talk on Irish literature. He shut himself up in his hotel bedroom, wrote this and delivered it the same afternoon to a handful of assembled writers.—ed.

a thing as Irish literature. For the Irish temperament and the Irish environment are so distinctive that they leave their mark on everything that is written in Ireland in the English language.

A few years ago, I remember, you celebrated the bicentenary of Jonathan Swift. He was one of the earliest and certainly the greatest of those Irishmen of English descent who took the Irish side against English oppression and arrogance. He was born in Ireland and lived a large part of his life in Ireland, and I think it is fair to consider him an Irish writer, because it was the Irish social conditions which roused his indignation and made him one of the world's greatest satirists. Berkeley, the great philosopher of idealism, was another Irish writer of English descent of the eighteenth century. There were many others, but most of them were controversialists, essayists, politicians, theologians. Ireland was the background to their studies: it furnished them with arguments and analogies. But it was not till the beginning of the nineteenth century that any writer of significance attempted, as Maria Edgeworth did, to give an imaginative picture of Ireland, and make it the principal subject of her art. I have overlooked Oliver Goldsmith, of course, but though his *She Stoops to Conquer* and perhaps much of *The Vicar of Wakefield* were based on Irish experiences, Goldsmith (whose own name is probably an anglicization of an Irish one) anglicized all his Irish experiences, in the manner of all polite eighteenth-century writers. Ireland was considered too barbarous a land to be a fit subject for the craft of letters.

With Maria Edgeworth, everything changed. She was the first incontrovertibly Irish writer of all these writers of Anglo-Irish stock. Walter Scott was her admirer and claimed to be her disciple. He wanted, he said, to do for Scotland what Maria had done for Ireland: to give such a picture of his Scottish countrymen, their strength and their weaknesses, as Maria had done for the Irish in *Castle Rackrent* and other novels. Maria had the support in all this of her father, R. L. Edgeworth, a remarkable man of very independent views and inventive talent. Their country estate, Edgeworthstown, became in Ireland in the early nineteenth century as famous as Yasnaya Polyana was in Russia later. They were Utilitarians and Materialists of the school of Bentham. They were in contact with many distinguished thinkers in Europe, and every man of note who came to Ireland from abroad stayed at Edgeworthstown. R. L. Edgeworth, at the outbreak of the French Revolution, had been elected a member of their National Assembly. The question of socialism scarcely arose in those days in Ireland. The Irish peasantry, illiterate and ill-fed, had no leaders but their priests, who were often as ignorant at they were themselves, and the more generous-minded of the Irish landowners, who, like the Edgeworths, took up their cause. The most the Edgeworths could do was to run schools of their own, as Tolstoy and Chekhov did here, and try to improve the health and the agricultural methods of their neighbours. This they did, and they became model landowners all over Ireland.

I am trying to tell you about Irish literature, not Irish social conditions, but the two themes are often closely related and I could not avoid this digression. I think we must look along these lines for the explanation of the fact that, although the Irish are an extremely quick-witted, poetical, imaginative people, with a remarkable gift for fluent self-expression, nonetheless they have been, in European literature right down to our own day, extraordinarily inarticulate. The Irish writers of whom you heard will have been almost all of them émigrés or of Anglo-Irish stock. In this way very many of the great names in English drama are Irish or Anglo-Irish—Goldsmith, Congreve, Sheridan, Farquhar, Oscar Wilde. In our own day, Bernard Shaw and Sean O'Casey both emigrated to England. The greatest of English political orators and writers of political prose was Edmund Burke, an Anglo-Irishman—and the same picture is to be seen all along the line. Why did the Irish Catholic, the man of the majority (for all these I have mentioned were Protestants), fail to take the place which was his due in European letters—long after the old religious and political disabilities had been removed and national independence achieved?

Some would say it was a question of temperament: the Irish mind is often volatile, fantastic, paradoxical, and except when allied to the sturdy practical English temperament it cannot express itself. Others would say that the subjection of Ireland had lasted too long, the best brains had wasted themselves on political resistance, the spirit of the others had been broken. Perhaps there is something in this. Chekhov wrote somewhere—I cannot quote him accurately—that, himself the descendant of serfs, he had spent his life, little by little, squeezing the slave out of his own mind. And our James Joyce, who was of Irish Catholic stock, refers, but in the bitterness of defeat and without Chekhov's optimism, to the slave-soul of Ireland.

A third reason that could be given is the exaggerated power and claims of the Catholic Church, which increased rather than diminished after Ireland obtained her freedom in 1922. The fate of Edgeworthstown House, which I have compared as a centre of enlightenment and free speculation to Yasnaya Polyana, might be taken as a symbol of this development. The Edgeworths' own people, the Anglo-Irish, made no effort to preserve it; it owes its survival today to a community of Catholic nuns. The unhealthy predominance of the Catholic priest in Ireland happened because in the Irish rebellions of the seventeenth century, the English destroyed the Irish Catholic ruling classes and the priesthood stepped into their places as spokesmen and leaders of the Irish people. The Irish talent is naturally critical, subversive, satirical—Swift, Shaw, Joyce, Wilde are typical Irish writers—and the atmosphere of Catholicism, rigid, disciplined, orthodox, is stifling to it.

You will see what I mean if you compare two great Irish writers, both of them rebels against the Catholic Church but one of them an Irish Catholic, the other an Irish Protestant: I am thinking of James Joyce and Bernard Shaw. James Joyce is a deeply pessimistic, introverted writer. His great genius cannot escape into the open, but he turns it destructively on everything he loves. He is almost a nihilist, while Shaw has none of this slave despondency about the Catholic Church or any human institution. Even when his judgments were very foolish, and they often were, he wrote as a man who was his own master; the Catholic Church was an oppressor, whose powers ordinary human effort could control.

It was at the turn of the century, 1890–1910, that Ireland perhaps experienced the greatest flowering of literature. The inspiration of this movement was the Celtic past, but once again the pioneers— the playwrights, the poets—were of Anglo-Irish and Protestant stock. The movement started with the renewal of interest in the great Irish epics of the past by Standish O'Grady, the son of an Irish Protestant clergyman, and it was followed up by the foundation of the Abbey Theatre, with which almost all the Irish writers of the last generation were directly or indirectly associated. The biggest name, of course, was the great poet W. B. Yeats, like Shaw a Nobel Prize winner. Other names were Lady Gregory, J. M. Synge, Lennox Robinson, Edward Martyn, George Moore the novelist, and Bernard Shaw, who also wrote plays for the Abbey Theatre. *John Bull's Other Island*, which Shaw wrote about Ireland, was written for the Abbey and is, in my view, one of his very best plays. There were many writers. The whole history of this movement is described, in a rather caustic vein, in George Moore's brilliant trilogy of recollections, *Ave atque Vale*.

All these men and women were Irish patriots, and the movement they founded was immensely fruitful and productive. They were linked in many ways with the leaders of the Irish Rebellion of 1916, many of whom were also poets and playwrights. But when independence was achieved, the Abbey Theatre and the group which had created it, were disastrously eclipsed.

Two new factors had introduced themselves to complicate the already complicated lives of Irish writers. The second was the language. The Irish language had been virtually dead, except in the far western regions, for a century, but the romantics of 1916 wished to revive it, and we have now had for nearly forty years an aggressive campaign against the English language which has weakened the prestige of Anglo-Irish literature, far and away the noblest part of our cultural heritage; at the same time the attempt to revive the Irish language has totally failed in all its objectives. It is spoken even less than it was spoken fifty years ago, and in writing, it has made no impact whatever on Irish literature. Yet some strange, romantic, and unrealistic inhibitions in the Irish character prevent the acknowledgment of failure. The expensive and useless machinery of the whole country to it is entirely cynical.

You will not be surprised, therefore, if I say that we are now passing through a bad period in our history. Anglo-Irish literature is scanty and unpopular, and after 1922 there was a big emigration of the Anglo-Irish to England, to be followed twenty years later by a greater emigration of the unhyphenated Irish. There is much talent among the younger Irish Catholic writers, but there is the usual lack of stability, solidity, independence of mind. Some of our best Irish writers, in a mood of despondency, have drifted over to England in the wake of Sean O'Casey. But I must mention a few names of those who remain among the older generation: Sean O'Faolain, the founder and for long the editor of our monthly *The Bell*, has written good novels of Irish peasant and middle-class life; Frank O'Connor is widely known for his very caustic and witty short stories; there is Austin Clarke, a good poet and outstanding literary critic; there is Francis Macmanus, with a long series of novels of country life, of which perhaps *Watergate* appeals to me most. Then, there is Mervyn Wall, whose *Leaves for the Burning* is a delightfully satirical account of a group of literary friends who journey across Ireland to the funeral of W. B. Yeats. On their way, they stop at many villages for drinks, and in their discussions and their adventures, a brilliant picture of the Ireland of the 1940s, with its dreams and disillusionments, is revealed.

I could mention many other names but I have spoken to you for long enough and they would be names only. I would only like to add one observation. I have said much about Irish emigration, and you might assume from that that we were a people without strong ties to our country. It is quite the reverse; whether we are of Irish Catholic or Anglo-Irish descent, our country is usually an obsession to us. We can never escape the hold it has on our affections.

For example, James Joyce left Ireland as a young man and returned only once, for a few weeks. He lived the greater part of his life in Trieste, as a teacher of English, and in Zurich and Paris, but Trieste, Zurich and Paris are never mentioned in his books. There is nothing there but Dublin and Ireland. *Ulysses*, his eccentric masterpiece, is a vast volume describing the events of a single day in Dublin in 1904. His other works all have a similar setting.

And somehow, when we stray away from that theme, we often seem to lose our grip, as though we could only write about things we knew intimately, in our bones. O'Casey's great plays *Juno and the Paycock* and *The Shadow of a Gunman* seem to me incomparably finer than anything he wrote as an émigré in England.

I cannot find any ready explanation for this. Perhaps you can find parallels for it in Russian literature. But I am certain this love of our country and our people always has been, and perhaps always will be, a dominant feature in our literature.

Topical Thoughts on Shaw

1976

Shaw died a quarter of a century ago last November, but his anniversary has been celebrated more warmly in England than in Ireland.
Yet few Irish writers have been more generous to their native land.
Most people know of his benefactions to the National Gallery, but
is there a street named after him or a tablet to his memory in Carlow
to which he left all the Irish property he possessed? Were his plays
ever performed there? How many of those who apply for help in
some cultural venture to Fóras Éireann know how much they owe
to Mrs. Shaw? The wording of her bequest gave offence because it
implied that we needed to be taught the arts of social intercourse. If
by this she meant good manners, maybe she was not far out.

Shaw had a lasting loyalty to Ireland. As Michael Lennon once
pointed out, his was the first and most powerful voice that was raised
in Britain against the execution of the Easter Week leaders. In *The
Manchester Guardian* he defended the right of Reggie Dunn, the
murderer of Sir Henry Wilson, to make his speech from the dock. In
the Second World War he defended Irish neutrality. Yet, when in
1946 the BBC had a Shaw night in honour of his birthday, Radio
Éireann was silent.

It is in *John Bull's Other Island* that Shaw, a much-inhibited
man, revealed most of himself and traced the pattern of his involvement with Ireland. The play is now seventy years old, but though the
jokes have worn thin with constant borrowing, history has not yet
overtaken his quick mind.

Larry Doyle, the Irish emigrant, is chosen as the mouthpiece of
Shaw's views on Ireland; in Tom Broadbent, English liberalism, with

which Shaw was so closely connected, is ironically personified, but it is Father Keegan, the lonely ineffectual outcast, who is the hero of the play. It is he who is allowed the last word, interrupted by Broadbent's "foolish dream of efficiency," his own visionary commonwealth, "when these islands shall live by the quality of their men rather than by the abundance of their minerals." Doyle has decided to dedicate himself to Broadbent's dream, whose foolishness he recognizes in his heart, and he turns on Keegan as he would upon the Tempter. Larry has found happiness and occupation in London and a refuge from the "torturing, heart-scalding, never satisfied dreaming" of Ireland, its sneering envy and derision. Yet he still acknowledges and dreads its irresistible appeal.

John Bull's Other Island was written in 1904 for the Abbey Theatre in Dublin but was rejected, and it played to huge crowds at the Court Theatre in London. Writing his preface some years later, Shaw said that it had been intended for an Irish audience and its lesson, which in Ireland would have been salutary, was in England "demoralizingly superfluous." Its critical but friendly picture of Tom Broadbent merely fed English vanity, whereas it was intended to chasten Irish pride. Broadbent, though he might be intellectually ludicrous and a self-deceiver, was concentrated, purposeful and serious. His qualities were complementary, not antithetical, to Irish qualities.

Shaw does not refer to Father Keegan in his preface. It is as though he felt that Keegan's uncomfortable logic would be unintelligible anywhere outside Ireland and was doomed to be ineffectual. The fate of his play had perhaps proved to him that Ireland would always grudge him a direct channel for his ideas. He never tried again to interpret his country to his countrymen, and if we omit Father Keegan from the play as well as the preface, its "lesson" seems to be that the best thing for an intelligent Irishman like Larry to do is to emigrate.

Yet there is much evidence that Shaw suppressed Father Keegan in his mind but never quite exorcised him from his heart. If he had a second time addressed himself privately to the Irish ear with a renewed hope of being listened to (this would have been a supreme tour de force for a world-famous dramatist but not beyond Shaw's capacity to surprise), he could scarcely have silenced the insistent voice of Father Keegan or commended so confidently to Larry the easy escape of emigration from his dilemma.

Shaw, in his preface, despite its evasions, says many acute things and commits himself to a number of optimistic predictions about the fate of Ireland under Home Rule. It is hard to quarrel with his facts. Why have his prophesies proved so utterly, so ludicrously wrong? Before examining them in detail, let us show how his prophesies and his philosophy were in sharp conflict.

In 1904 Shaw saw an Ireland from which the Larry Doyles were emigrating and to which the Haffigans and Dorans were confined by poverty and sloth, the Father Keegans by some mystical loyalty. "Ireland, sir, for good or evil, is like no other place under heaven and no man can touch its sod or breathe its air without becoming better or worse." Shaw found nothing in his individualist ethic to detain the Larry Doyles or to bring them back to their country. Let them go with his blessing! For nationalism, according to Shaw, is a disease that comes from foreign rule and will vanish with it. The free spirit is immune from it. Yet obviously such a selective emigration would affect Ireland far more radically than Home Rule or any other social or political reform, for history is made by men and not by measures. Shaw made no allowance for this shift of population, a significant one surely. How could it not lead to an Ireland that was both mean and mystical, given over to the extremes of self-denial and self-seeking?

This miscalculation was particularly unfortunate in his predictions about Protestant Ireland. His analysis of Irish Protestantism is brilliantly true; his prophesies about its influence under a native government, which seem so plausible, show no sign yet of being fulfilled. It was as though for some useful purpose he had estimated the capacities of a tank and was indifferent to the fact that there was a large leak in it.

What were his data and conclusions? Shaw called himself "violently and arrogantly Protestant by family tradition," and he contrasted Irish Protestantism with the Church of England, "a reformed Anglican Catholic Anti-Protestant Church." "We are Protestants," he said, "to the extremist, practicable degree of individualism. . . . The Protestant is theoretically an anarchist, as far as anarchism is practicable in human society, that is to say he is an individualist, a freethinker, a self-helper, a Whig, a Liberal, a mistruster and vilifier of the state, a rebel." There is some truth in all this, even though when our extravagances are denounced in Roman Catholic pulpits we so often try to disavow them instead of proudly acknowledging them. If Lecky and Yeats and Shaw were Irish Protestants—and our Church has honoured and accepted them in life and death—we are plainly not rigid in matters of doctrine. We often show a scandalous readiness to discuss freely and sympathetically outrageous subjects, not only divorce and pacifism and contraceptives, but euthanasia and Communism and disbelief in the supernatural. From the extremes of scepticism to the extremes of credulity, our most fundamental common trait is our dislike of spiritual tyranny. This is closely allied to our individualism and where it has been upheld, has proved a strong safeguard against totalitarian tyranny. Totalitarianism has made little headway in Protestant and democratic countries. Shaw was right.

But Shaw thought that the true nature of Irish Protestantism had become distorted into conservatism and conformity by its association with an ascendancy class. Paradoxically it had come about that rebellion and separatism and republicanism had proceeded in Ireland, despite our Pantheon of Protestant rebels, not from Protestantism, their natural source, but from Catholicism, which is dogmatically opposed to all these things. He believed that under Home Rule the natural order of things would be restored. The Irish Protestants would, after the first shock had subsided, fling themselves vigorously into the national government, "which would be sorely in need of parliamentary and official forces independent of Rome. . . . They would be in the vanguard of Irish nationalism and democracy as against Romanism and sacerdotalism, for an Irish Catholic, by himself, would be unable to struggle against his priests."

Nonetheless he thought that finally, when the struggle against England, which was exhausting all the strength of the Roman Catholic laity, was over, they would at last have leisure to shake off. The Roman Church would become the official Irish church and the Irish Parliament would insist on a voice in the promotion of churchmen.

The Roman Catholic Church, against which Dublin Castle is powerless, would meet the one force on earth which can cope with it victoriously. That force on earth which can cope with it victoriously, that force is democracy, a thing far more Catholic than itself. Until that force is let loose against it, the Protestant garrison can do nothing to the priesthood except consolidate it and drive the people to rally round it in defence of their altars against the foreigner and the heretic. When it is let loose, the Catholic laity will make as short work of sacerdotal tyranny in Ireland as it has done in France and in Italy. . . . Home Rule will herald the day when the Vatican will go the way of Dublin Castle and the Island of Saints assume the headship of its own Church.

Splendidly argued and absolutely wrong. Protestants today play scarcely any overt part in the government of the Republic. As a body, they were not even very active in resisting the invasion of their liberties by the Catholic majority. For example, it was left mainly to the professional writers, Catholics mostly, to fight the censorship bill. The average Protestant was far more deeply roused by sentimental, class-bound issues like the question of prayers for the king or for the state.

Protestant values have been defended, but by exceptional and isolated men, like W. B. Yeats, who, almost alone in the Senate, stood up for the right of divorce, which exists in Protestant England. He was supported ardently by a Jewish countess, tepidly by a Quaker, and opposed by a Protestant bishop. Yeats was an individualist, a Whig, a Liberal and a freethinker. In fact, he was everything that Shaw said a Protestant should be, but he was the last of his tribe, it seemed, not the forerunner of the revived Protestantism which Shaw anticipated.

What was the reason for the failure of Shaw's predictions? I have referred to the major cause, the emigration of the Larry Doyles, Protestant and Catholic, who could have been retained in Ireland only by some derivative of Father Keegan's mystical loyalty which Shaw reverenced but dreaded and repudiated. A secondary reason was partition, which Shaw did not, perhaps could not, anticipate. It reduced the Protestants of the South to political helplessness. The majority clutched nostalgically at the shadows of vanished things, at property and privilege and ancient political loyalties. Imperceptibly they became not more Protestant, as Shaw anticipated they would, but less. Sometimes they seemed not to live in Ireland at all but in a little cocoon woven of ancient prejudices. Their land was turned into land bonds, their libraries into library subscriptions and wireless sets. They were able to live restricted but self-contained lives, with only an accidental dependence on the organism in which they were encysted. They evolved a portable Protestantism, which their children could take with them to Toronto or Singapore and which for its correct functioning depended for nothing on the Irish environment. Therefore, they were not bothered by the encroachments of Catholicism in Ireland. Seen against an imperial background, Catholicism did not threaten them: it was an ally against revolution, in no way an enemy.

Shaw, who satirized so vigorously the pettiness of Irish nationalism, was blind to the danger of its opposite, which might be called pseudo-cosmic thinking. Those who practise it are like men in a submarine who scan the ships but ignore the sharks and the swordfish, the coral and the anemones a few yards away from them. Yeats had protected himself from this disease by an inoculation of nationalism. He had been associated with what Shaw called "that quaint little offshoot of English pre-Raphaelitism, the Gaelic League," but which was, in fact, quite a valuable sprout of national self-sufficiency which had grown crooked and straggling through mismanagement.

There was another reason, closely allied to this, why Shaw's optimistic predictions about Irish Protestantism were not fulfilled. The heaviest losses in emigration were endured by its upper strata, the favoured breeding ground of the cultivated heretic and liberal and rebel, the Leckys and Burys, Plunketts and Shaws, as well as the Parnells and Casements and scores of others. They are disappearing fast and it looks as though the Protestant remnant will be of an altogether different calibre. Respectability is the most disintegrating force that Protestantism has to fear, its slow suffocation in the Dublin suburbs among foreign missions and poppy days. A dozen different strands of Protestantism were once held together by the ascendancy class but now they are drifting impotently apart.

It is of course possible that Shaw's predictions will still come true, if a new consolidation of Protestant thinking were to occur. This can only happen by a recall to the principles of the Reformation, the parent of so many scattered communities. This might mean a vigorous and perhaps combative reassertion of opposition to the church of the majority. Severed from the bitterness of ascendancy politics, such an assertion would not be nationally disintegrating. It would be just the reverse, for a more vigorously defined spiritual frontier would cross and recross the political border and ultimately make nonsense of it. And those who defend spiritual frontiers know that prejudice and manufactured hatred are the worst of weapons.

I think that Shaw's peculiar inhibitions had much to do with his misinterpretation of Ireland, so I am justified in returning to them. He wrote once that he never thought of the English as his countrymen, and I think he cherished his Irishness as a sort of alibi. He was glad of any excuse for not revealing his feelings, grateful even for this transparent mask of foreignness. Compare how H. G. Wells, a fellow socialist, abandoned himself to his characters, withholding none of the self-knowledge, self-disgust, self-love that could give life and body to his characters. I don't think Shaw ever conceded more of himself to any of his characters than he did to the mincing or fastidious Larry Doyle, the man who feared passion whether for Norah Reilly or for Ireland. There is little doubt that emotionally Shaw was *au dessus de la mêlée* and thereby perhaps able to bring a new freshness and detachment to the study of human relations. He understood a great deal that had never been understood before about the lesser insincerities, hypocrisies, inadequacies that distort and obscure the major passions from which he was immune. He had the unflinching but unnatural vision of those who look at the sun through smoked glass. I don't think anyone who had ever loved passionately could have written that playlet about love's periphery, "How he lied to her 'husband.' " It is a poor play, but here as elsewhere, his characters are sharply differentiated and closely observed (he is often wrongly accused of not being able to observe human beings). They are real people, whose prime preoccupation, love, was one to which Shaw was blind, as a bee is said to be blind to certain primary colours though sensitive to colours outside our human spectrum. This abnormality led him to emphasize the importance of frailties and fancies which tend to be overlooked. For example, Teddy Bompas is very vain about his wife's sex appeal and is furious with her young admirer when, from discretion, he pretends that he is not in love with her. Tom Broadbent falls in love at first sight not with Norah Reilly but with his own conception of an Irish colleen. Instances could be multiplied. Shaw never had to shrink from obvious emotionalism. He was not susceptible to it.

It is a queer paradox that Shaw, whose international influence was greater than that of any other European writer, was yet incapable of international thinking. His tributes to Hitler, Mussolini, Stalin, his defence of the Italian invasion of Abyssinia, are appalling in their tasteless frivolity, unless one thinks of Shaw as a genius shaped like Joyce by a small community to be its gadfly but pitchforked by fate into being a World Figure. He was denationalized, a very different thing from being international; that is to say, he had no passionate regard for any particular land or people, so that there was no untranslatable residue which an intelligent foreigner could not assimilate. Hence he was popular abroad and yet had no understanding of foreign countries. He seems to have seen the Balkans, for example, through the eyes of Antony Hope.

I suppose it is idle to wonder what would have happened to Shaw had he never left Ireland. No doubt his genius would have been suffocated or cruelly cramped. And yet he carried to the end some of the stigmata of the *déraciné*, and latterly he suffered badly from the pseudo-cosmic disease. That crusade for reformed spelling, for example, has surely a rootless, expatriated sound, like Joyce's learned gibberish, O'Casey's staccato Stalinism and Yeats's intercourse with Yogis. Were these really serious experiments in literature, art, politics or religion? Or were they just the symptoms of a wild, nervous recoil from the narrow loyalties of a country which criminally failed to give nourishment to these tremendous talents?

Do Shaw's predictions look more or less probable in the laicized, permissive, ecumenical climate of today? What has happened to the "violent and arrogant" Protestantism of eighty years ago, its individualism and its distrust of the Anglican compromise? We certainly have a politer vocabulary and we have even been heard to call ourselves "Anglican." But I doubt whether anything has happened that cannot be explained by partition and falling numbers. We have always been laicized, we were more permissive in the eighteenth century and far more ecumenical in the 1820s, when Doyle, Catholic Bishop of Kildare, and Magee, Protestant Archbishop of Dublin, and many other leading ecclesiastics discussed the union of our churches and pulpits were freely exchanged.

Shaw, a child of the Church of Ireland, educated by Wesleyans, was proud of the friendly Protestant umbrella which sheltered so many Christian heterodoxies. Till quite recently his distrust of the word "Anglican" was shared. In the late 1950s a proposal that it be used as our official designation was rejected in the General Synod by a large majority. A couple of generations earlier, Lord Plunket, that Archbishop of Dublin whose statue stands in Kildare Street, thought that the word turned us into a garrison church. "We are not," he declared, "as some would represent us, the English Church in Ireland. Let the word 'Anglican,' as describing our faith and morals, be banished from our vocabulary!"

Why has the word come back? Is it because in our decline we find comfort in belonging to a large community outside Ireland? (When surrounded by Moslems, the Orthodox of Montenegro used to boast, "We and the Russians are two hundred million!") Or is it because we wish to dissociate ourselves from the aggressive Bible Christians of Ulster? Or is it Tom Broadbent at work again? Have his grandchildren, still dedicated to his "foolish dream," imported to Ireland the spiritual lubricant best suited to the machinery of their industrial efficiency?

In fact, in the realm of ideas, nothing has changed. It is still only Father Keegan's vision—of an Ireland living by the quality of its men rather than by the abundance of its minerals, the dream of Horace Plunkett and AE and their once-strong following—that could reconcile our shattered community. But who takes such a possibility seriously nowadays?

Leavis on Lawrence

1976

F. R. Leavis is a writer of note. Some find him "the most powerful literary critic of our time" and "an interpreter of wonderful delicacy and rare courage." This book* is irascible and donnish and smells of mortarboards and beta-minuses and provokes me into saying that "interpretive," one of his favourite words, does not exist.† Nonetheless, I am sure that in his hero worship of D. H. Lawrence he is right and courageous, and maybe only an academic can nowadays effectively draw the teeth of academism.

Leavis believes that Lawrence was the last creative writer of the twentieth century, a proposition that first left me gasping and then curiously rejuvenated. Fifty years ago I read everything he wrote and, through my friendship with his biographer, Catherine Carswell, was on the outermost periphery of his adoring circle. It was not at all an excluding one, but generous and warm. Cathie showered introductions on me to Frieda's mother in Baden Baden, to Ivy Litvinov‡ in Moscow and others that lay dormant for years. When, much later, I was staying with friends in New Mexico, I made a point of exchanging six words with Dorothy Brett in a café, six lines with Witter Bynner, who was away, and nostalgically observed Mabel Dodge Luhan's Red Indian husband speeding past in an expensive car.

Yet by then I had given up reading Lawrence. The eager, pas-

---

*F. R. Leavis, *Thought, Words and Creativity: Art and Thought in Lawrence* (London and New York, 1976).

†See Fowler's *Modern English Usage* (1952), p. 281.

‡An English novelist and wife of the Soviet diplomat Maxim Litvinov.—ed.

sionately interested and experimental world which he addressed had vanished, and the mere fact that his defence should rest with Dr. Leavis shows how much the world has changed. Leavis does not suggest warmth, whereas the genius of Lawrence lay in his uninhibited spontaneity, his ebullience. Wheat and tares poured out together and you were expected to sift them for yourself. I used to grumble about this, like everybody else, and still note priggishly that in one of his best stories, "England, My England," he refers twice to Mater Dolorata and a few pages on writes of Lachesis as the Fate that cuts the thread. I used to take it for granted that he had initiated a uniquely bold and perceptive study of human relations that more sophisticated writers would continue.

But they did not. And that is the theme of Leavis' book. After Lawrence's death, England lost its "educated public." "The utterly undistinguished Kingsley Martin became an intellectual power in England to be matched by Auden as a major poet." Egalitarianism became the modern religion and "the technological Benthamite spirit had its supreme anti-human triumph." As evidence of this degradation of letters, Leavis mentions that to balance the Minister for Sport there is now a Minister for Arts, who has set up an Arts Council to foster "creative productivity." There are societies with "advisory panels to promote fiction in Britain, to enable publishers to increase their print runs and to bring down the price of good new novels."

Is Leavis right? I think so. The "creative productivity" campaign has had some appalling results and it is easy to foresee that under EEC we may have an Art and Letters mountain to match the tomatoes and cucumbers. In Grand Central Station I saw a whole stall devoted to the sale of *Sons and Lovers* under a broad banner: BY THE AUTHOR OF LADY CHATTERLEY'S LOVER. It is as a pornographer that he has enabled publishers to "increase their print runs." He wrote: "I, who loathe sexuality so deeply, am considered a lurid sexuality specialist."

I am sure this is true. To Lawrence, sex was a fascinating mystery, causing in men and women infinitely various patterns of behaviour, which those to whom sex is an all-effacing obsession will never see. Lawrence, as Leavis observes, loathed whatever turned the individual into the unit, whatever classified him by race or sex or class or profession, levelling out what was unique in him and binding men and women together in defence of "their rights." One can of course be indifferent to "rights" from dullness or egoism, but Lawrence's stormy life was spent in trying to dynamite the categories and not to dodge them.

It is only in small groups that men and women can resist the classifying disease, and Lawrence's repeated attempts to form them in various parts of Europe and America were only failures in a practical way. He was, to use a phrase of Leavis's, "a centre of radiant potency" which "even in the age of Social Studies may survive as a force of life bursting through the hard surface." I witnessed how it could beat even against the walls of the Kremlin. When we called on Ivy Litvinov, one of his earliest admirers, her first words to us were: "Now I hope you're not going to ask me the usual questions about 'the Great Experiment.' I've got nothing to say about it. I'm just a middle-class English woman who happens to live in Russia. Let's talk about D. H. Lawrence." And that is what we did. Marx and Lenin dropped easily into their places. I have often wondered what form Misha Litvinov's deviations took. If he was at all like his grandmother, they would be interestingly different from those of, say, Solzhenitsyn.

After Lawrence and the Bloomsbury writers, English literature was dominated by witty, embittered public schoolboys—Connolly, Spender, Auden, Huxley, Orwell, Greene, Waugh, Isherwood, the Sitwells. They satirized the Establishment but more or less reluctantly accepted its values and its rewards, using it as a comic backcloth to their political, religious, social somersaults. None of them had Lawrence's vision of a different and a happier world to which sects and parties can contribute nothing but a writer must dedicate his whole life.

Huxley, belonging to one of the great English intellectual dynasties, understood Lawrence best. He wrote of the coal miner's son: "Of the most eminent people I have met I feel that at any rate I belong to the same species as they do. But this man has something different and superior in kind, not degree."

Dr. Leavis's book is a chapter-by-chapter commentary on several of Lawrence's major writings. He does not minimize the frequent tediousness, silliness, inconsistency that sometimes makes him hard to read. Yet he certainly believes that Lawrence, as a man and as a writer, was something different from and superior in kind to those who succeeded him.

Two Critics

1952

E. M. Forster is rather an isolated figure in English letters, whose high standards of intellectual integrity have resisted the assaults of the modern world better than anyone else's. Edmund Wilson's recent collection of essays, a literary chronicle of the 1940s, show him to be an American counterpart of the great English writer.*

Superficially they are poles apart. Wilson is robust and pugnacious as a reviewer; the shoddy, the sentimental, the commercial come in for very rough handling, and as a writer of fiction he has no inhibitions; all that is human is material for his art. Forster is very different in temperament and tactics. His hatred of the second-rate and the fraudulent is as deadly and his claims for the writer are as sweeping, but his blows are aimed with shrewdness rather than force. Even obtuse people will be on the alert to man the defences of Philistia when Wilson thunders by, but Forster is more likely to slip past the frontier guards and plant his time bomb in the citadel.

But no less than temperament, history and geography have influenced their tactics. As a novelist, Mr. Forster's claims on posterity are evident to us in these islands, where the classics are still reread and quiet voices are resonant beyond the grave. He can afford to wait; in America, Mr. Wilson has to hurry. Ignorance brays louder and more confidently, and every new mechanical invention widens her range. In England the worst that Forster can say of science is that she has renounced her right to rule and "plays the subservient

---

*E. M. Forster, *Two Cheers for Democracy* (1951); Edmund Wilson, *Classics and Commercials* (1951).

pimp," but in America she has a far greater power to override and distort the creative instinct in man. Wilson's indictment is incidental to his criticism, but it recurs again and again in casual epitaphs on murdered talents. In Hollywood he sees "an intractable magnetic mountain, which twists American fiction askew." Of Scott Fitzgerald and Nathanael West he says, "Their failure to get the best out of their best years may certainly be laid partly on Hollywood with its already appalling record of talent depraved and wasted." Of another once-promising writer, Louis Bromfield, he synopsizes an appalling story. What can he say of it, he asks, since it is subliterary, it is proto-film. In a postscript he quotes a gushing review of it from the *New York Herald Tribune*. The weeds are all watered, the flowers left to die. He finds proto-films also in Steinbeck and Hemingway and Kay Boyle. His characters, he says of one reputable novelist, are blank spaces like the figures on billboards before the faces have been painted in. When their features are finally supplied, they will be the features of popular actors.

In the better-class newspapers he finds "ineptitude and cynicism masked by competence of presentation." The writer has been reduced by the speed and volume of communication to the subhuman role of digestion and abridgment. Speaking of *Time*, he says that the thoughts of the men who put it together "appear to have been mashed down and to figure in what they print only as blurred streaks of coloration that blot the machine-finished surface."

In revenge these poor human appendages of the printing press tinge everything they touch "with a peculiar kind of jeering rancour . . . which makes the whole human race hateful."

In 1943 he wrote:

The Socialists are now, for the most part, simply patriots as they inevitably become in time of war; the Communists are Russian nationalists, who would not recognize a thought of Lenin if they happened by some mistake to see one; the liberal weeklies are not merely dull shades of the luminous spirits they once were but false phantoms, whose non-incandescence is partly due to an alien mixture of the gases of propaganda, injected by the Stalinists and the British.

This appalling position of the writer in the United States is masked by the huge apparatus of learning, the academies and the libraries, which to Wilson often appear as more subtle agencies of talent-wrecking. *Finnegans Wake*, he mourns, is not a literary issue but a subject of academic research. It went straight from the hands of Joyce to the hands of the college professor. Young men, who should be challenging and appraising what is new and unfamiliar, have been diverted by the universities to the safer work of exposition and research. Wilson reverts several times to this academic blight. The scholar sees the writer not as a comrade or a teacher, but as the raw material for a thesis, "a means of raising his status in the hierarchy of the academic world."

It is evidence of the vigour and vitality of the liberal tradition in letters that Forster and Wilson can record such melancholy facts and yet produce books that are stimulating and combative and without despair. After all, misunderstanding has always been the lot of the genuine writer, who is often a provocative person. Wilson angrily challenges a professor who argued that Dr. Johnson had exaggerated the hardships of his youth. Nonsense, Johnson knew what he was talking about when he recited the miseries of the writer's life: "Toil, envy, want, the patron and the jail." Society changes its methods of redress and the critic's task is to reconnoitre on behalf of literature, finding out from which direction the counterattack is coming and giving the alarm. The writer of integrity does not suffer more today than before, but the instruments of seduction have been so perfected that the uglier forms of coercion have been discarded except in the more backward countries. This makes the critic's task more complex; he must look for danger and hope in unlikely quarters by devious routes.

Mr. Wilson has even to be gratified by the huge popularity (seven and a half million readers in the United States) of a badly written, pietistic novel called *The Robe*, "an almost unrivalled fabric of old clichés." For the book has a certain purity of intention and differs from the usual frankly faked, specially flavoured publisher's goods in being long and tedious. "It demonstrates that the ordinary reader, even in our ghastly time, does long for moral light and that he cannot live by bilge alone."

Edmund Wilson's is a noble, lonely head bobbing above the bilge water and only occasionally subsiding beneath it. He is a stern critic of prose style and sometimes appears to look on literary precision as one of the guarantees of freedom. I think he would agree with Forster and George Orwell that "bureaucrats, who want to destroy liberty, tend to write and speak badly." They hide their meaning in woolly or portmanteau phrases. Wilson is deadly serious, slashing at Faulkner for his syntax and his indifference to the dictionary. "This is no coining but groping," he says justly of "regurg," "dismatchment" and "perspicuant." He chastises Maugham for his beclichéd obscurity and he offers appalling samples of slop from his best-selling American contemporaries. Few distinguished critics can have read so much bad literature with such well-disciplined revulsion. Though his patient précis of best-sellers, which intellectuals are supposed to ignore, the detective stories to which they are supposed to be indulgent, is very entertaining, entertainment is not his aim. There is permanent value in these conscientious essays, small test tubes, sealed and labelled, containing samples of the bilge water in which the American genius is drowning.

Yet Wilson has his own dreadful lapses, which show how hard it is to think clearly in a land where muddle is mechanized. In his affectionately commemorative essay on Paul Rosenfeld, a victim of American philistinism, one reads: "The first time I ever saw him I had not yet met him," and "His taking the Andersons to Europe is an example that happened to be known of the kind of thing he liked to do," and of Katherine Porter he writes: "Somewhere behind her stories there is a conception of a natural human spirit in terms of their bearing on which all the other forces are appraised." And every now and then his possessives and relatives coagulate in diseased bunches. It is not mere human carelessness, it is how a top-quality robot would write if his plugs needed cleaning. But can you blame him? To write clearly in America is like trying to take a country walk on an autostrada.

Reading these essays one is grateful for all the cultural rifts in the English-speaking world. American and British writers can scrutinize each other with a detachment that would be embarrassing between intimates. I don't mean, of course, that a critic such as E. M. Forster would ever be tempted to the grosser forms of partiality, but there are friendly reticences and decencies of intercourse among British writers which sometimes act as a windbreak to the salutary breeze of criticism. For example, Mr. Wilson's assault on Harold Nicolson has a barbarian effrontery that is refreshing and without malice. He reminds me of the Gaul who tweaked the beard of the musing Senator, perhaps some bland, accomplished precursor of Atticus or Maecenas. Nicolson is one of the most civilized people in England. He is more polished and witty than Wilson, he writes better and has a more ordered and agile mind. E. M. Forster, who deals so trenchantly with Mrs. Miniver, locating her in the top drawer but one, "moral masquerading as social distinction," is too close to Nicolson to focus him. Even if they are unknown to each other, a hundred shared ideals and inhibitions will deter Forster from a cold-blooded analysis of top-drawer Miniverism. (Nicolson, like the celebrated lady, has learnt "the defensive value of honesty," they are both disarmingly truthful and modest about little things.) If Anglo-Irish writers had not been starved out by the Gael so that they had to sell themselves to the English for porridge, they could have dealt with every grade of Miniverism from here. It is not an Irish vice, and it is at the right range for potshots. Curiously enough, it is on an Anglo-Irish theme, his *Life of Hamilton Rowan*, that Wilson first engages Nicolson.

Nicolson to Wilson is the "good little governing-class boy, whose real country is neither England nor Europe but the British Foreign Office," whose "coy and sly humour . . . almost always works in the conventional direction." In literature he feels a fascination for "the more scandalous type of poet . . . but he is forced in a reflex action to detach himself socially from their company by a quiet but well-placed accent of amusement, disapproval and disdain." Wilson points out how Nicolson talks of Hamilton Rowan's "really deplorable career," and is "fascinated, indulgent, alarmed, disapproving." Nicolson does, in fact, betray towards revolutionary enthusiasm that kiss-and-tell attitude which is common to so many of the children of light, to the scores of subtle intellects which have been governessed by the British Foreign Office and her flighty nursemaids, the BBC and the British Council.

I think that Wilson, with his transatlantic detachment, is right in general about official England, though often wrong in detail. He works from American analogies of copybook clarity. American ambassadorial prose is archetypal in its awfulness, its mindlessness and pomposity, if we are to judge from Wilson's essay on Joseph E. Davis ("the greatest master of official bad English since the late President Harding"), who, through the filming of his *Mission to Moscow* by Warner Brothers, has become the symbol of the plain, rugged American businessman. On a more intellectual plane there is Archibald MacLeish, the Librarian of Congress, who in a sermon to writers in 1940 warned them that "perhaps writers, having so great a responsibility to the future, must not weaken the validity of the Word, even when the deceptions of the Word have injured them." Mr. Wilson interprets this (correctly, one judges from the context) as a reminder to writers never to weaken authority by exposing the falsity of its official propaganda.

E. M. Forster is a more urbane critic than Edmund Wilson; the iron hand is seldom out of the velvet glove and sometimes it seems unnecessarily well upholstered. I like him best when he is being serious rather than playful, least when, as in his wartime broadcasts, he becomes a public figure and talks of "what we are fighting for," and so on. All the recognizable features are there, but the picture is dwarfed and distorted by its frame, as though he had been snapped on the pier with his mild, serious face sticking up above the plywood torso of an alderman. All that he says is true enough, but the best truths are homemade, and here with what I suppose is loyal self-effacement we find him handing out high-quality factory stuff.

Contrast a prewar point of view with a wartime utterance of 1940. First 1939:

I hate the idea of causes and, if I had to choose between betraying my country and betraying my friend, I hope I should have the guts to betray my country. . . . There is a terror and a hardness in this creed of personal relationships, urbane and mild though it sounds. Love and loyalty to an individual can run counter to the claims of the State. When they do, "Down with the State!" say I, which means that the State would down me.

Then 1940:

This being so, I think we have got to go on with this hideous fight. I cannot see how we are to make terms with Hitler, much as I long for peace. For one thing, he never keeps his word, for another he tolerates no way of looking at life but his own way.

Maybe there is nothing in practice irreconcilable in these two statements, because for one who is not a German it can only rarely happen that absolute resistance to Hitler runs counter to absolute loyalty to one's friends. Yet, to a German, such a conflict of loyalties must often have occurred, and Forster in 1939 was trying to speak as a human being, not as an Englishman. He was surely going too fast in 1939, too slow in 1940. It would be better never to have divulged his belief in a creed of personal relations *à l'outrance*, if he was going to repudiate it a few months later. What is the use of professing a faith which in time of war splinters along the familiar fissures of race or class? Forster in 1939 simplified the issue for himself artificially by talking of "betraying my country." For "our duty to our country" now says less than it did to subtle minds. Imperialism has stretched it till it is flimsy and transparent as gauze, and science has frayed its once sharp edges, making distinctions of culture and blood appear arbitrary and unreal. Some have seen the mirage of world unity, so we are prepared to sacrifice our country on a number of different altars, but they are usually very private altars and when we tell about them, as Mr. Forster does, it is in a tone of bravado or jesting. And till we catch some approving eyes (there must be a quorum of them) we don't admit we are serious. If Forster had got his quorum I don't think he would have moved to the microphone and spoken as if he accepted the BBC alignment of loyalties, the "we's" and the "they's." He would not have said "we," knowing that "we" meant the Turtons and Pembertons, as well as the negligible handful who accepted his creed of personal relations, and that "they" meant the German equivalents of Turtons and Pembertons, and also the small handful of German independents. He would have recognized that Hitlerism is only a wild German fantasia on the theme of complacency and self-deception. There is also a Russian variation. All the respectable Germans of the Turton-Pemberton class accepted Hitlerism with mental reservations that counted for little. The same class in England would have adjusted its conscience to something equally cruel. How otherwise would they feel so tolerantly now towards Rommel and Manstein and Weizsäcker and all the other respectable people, who travelled so far in fellowship with the Nazis?

As I read on, I reflected that these are Mr. Forster's thoughts all right, but triturated and put through a sieve so that the muscle and bone of his thinking are no longer there. How limp is his prophecy that in regard to English culture the Germans, if victorious, would use the methods adopted in Poland and Czechoslovakia . . . and with the maximum of brutality! The statement is not exactly false. On the lips of a stupid person it would even be true, for the imperceptive can only judge from the evidence they observe, and it was not apparent to everybody that the Westerners were to be bribed and the Slavs to be bullied. But Mr. Forster could only have accepted a simplification of the truth if his mind had been processed in some way, not violently distorted by a magnetic mountain, but conditioned, like Nicolson's, to respond to varying temperatures. For brains can be retarded or forced nowadays just like bulbs (it is a matter of moving them at the right moment from obscurity to sunlight). And these wartime broadcasts have, in fact, the fragrance and colour we should expect from Mr. Forster, but it is as though he had been kept in a cupboard for a long time, then given a drink and taken to decorate a political platform.

Forster's articles on war and the arts raise many questions that can only be touched on here. To what extent should writers associate themselves, as writers, with programmes of national defence? As men, they have the normal responsibilities to their neighbours and their consciences. But are they not falsifying facts if they claim that creative art, man's power to express himself about the world, is linked inextricably with libraries and publishing houses, and all the institutions which dictators love to pervert? Learned establishments have crushed as much originality as they have liberated and are often more fecundating in their decay. We are tired of hearing how Constantinople, when it fell, fertilized Europe for the Renaissance with its debris. Forster, who has often acknowledged his debt to Cambridge, suggests that today it would be better to raze her to the ground than turn her into a technical finishing school. (He will not get his quorum of approving eyes here, so he is resolutely playful.) "She would survive as a memory then. And a memory can do more than either a mummy or a travesty towards civilizing the world." It would be rash, of course, to invoke Moslems and dynamite on behalf of the arts, but writers should not be bamboozled into laying down their lives for libraries or for law and order. How many masterpieces have been produced in the interstices of chaos when there were no professors to liquidate, or printing presses to enslave! If we must die altruistically, let us follow Forster's 1939 advice and die for our friends.

Alternating Wilson's essays with Forster's we can observe how rich and varied is the liberal, individualistic spirit. Forster, who often makes donnish little jokes and is fastidious in speech to the point of primness, is, perhaps, the more subversive of the two. We are misled by his cosy, tea-and-crumpets vocabulary, "plucky," "perky," "mushy," "stodgy," "stuffy," "Sunday-schoolish," "a bit of a rip," phrases which are the printed equivalents of "mischievous" twinkles. Nor does he handle very skilfully those dangerous weapons, paradox and overstatement. To the Americans he suggested in a lecture that man's best chance of harmony . . . might lie in "apathy, uninventiveness and inertia." I have extracted this remark unfairly from its context, but it has already been still more ruthlessly excised and misrepresented in print. Plainly, it is as unwise to use the language of personal relations on a public platform as to leave one's purse on the dressing table of a hotel bedroom, as one does at home. Forster surely meant that the energy and zest and taste, which should have gone to the study and ennoblement of human relations, is being wasted on harmful inventions and mechanized enthusiasms. "The more highly public life is organized, the lower does its morality sink."

What is the source of the optimism which is still vigorous and tonic in both these writers? It does not lie in religion, though they are both traditionalists, often tracing back American and English culture to the Christian faith, which was once its principal nourishment. In Forster's eyes Christianity has little left of its old spiritual force and, if it is still a power to be reckoned with, it is on a material plane of money and political influence. "The indwelling spirit will have to be restated, if it is to calm the waters again, and probably restated in a non-Christian form." But he finds scattered through all the nations and classes, political and religious communities, "an aristocracy of the sensitive, the considerate and the plucky," between whom there is a secret understanding, whenever they meet. No new gospel is required, but a new technique to make effective the good will and the good temper, which are already existing. And individualism is unconquerable. "The dictator can order men to merge, he can incite them to mass antics, but they are obliged to be born separately and to die separately and, owing to these unavoidable termini, will always be running off the totalitarian rails."

It is for "Love, the Beloved Republic" that Forster reserved these three cheers for which democracy is unworthy. If Wilson used a battle slogan, I think it would be intellectual integrity. He would classify Communism with institutional Christianity among "the dogmatisms of unsure people." His essay on the Soviet writer Leonid Leonov is perceptive. He recognizes the talent, the subtlety, the apparent liberalism, but I think he diagnoses incorrectly the paralysis of orthodoxy in which Leonov's ingenious plots subside. Direct coercion over literature exists, of course, in Russia, but in the main literature is shaped, as in the United States, by popular taste, for corruption has for some time made coercion superfluous. Leonov writes like that because he thinks like that, not because Zhdanov* ordered him. Why does he think like that? That is a harder question, but I believe the best answer could be given in cultural and social terms, bypassing politics.

Wilson deals firmly with a characteristic attempt to treat Baudelaire as a Christian penitent, a move in that withdrawal towards traditional religion which is habitual in times of political disillusionment. He follows Anatole France in his diagnosis: "In his arrogance Baudelaire wished to believe that everything he did was important, even his little impurities, so that he wanted them all to be sins that would interest heaven and hell."

---

*A. A. Zhdanov (1896–1948), a Politburo member from 1939, figured prominently in Soviet cultural politics under Stalin. As overseer of ideological affairs from 1944, he pursued a hard-line policy designed to stamp out signs of Western influence, especially in Soviet literature and music.—ed.

"Are Baudelaire's angels religion?" he asks. "Aren't they rather the literary devices of uncomfortable Rationalists, who, disgusted by the dullness of democracy, the vulgarity of revolution, have resorted for protection against them to the mythology and animism of childhood?"

Wilson's "Dissenting View about Kafka" is another admirable antidote to the higher defeatism. Kafka has been given a cosmic significance which his great talents do not deserve. "The plights of his abject heroes" are taken to be "parables of the human condition." Wilson recalls with common sense that Kafka was psychologically crippled. At the age of thirty-six (he died at forty-one) he wrote a long letter to his father, a bustling Jew in the wholesale women's wear trade, blaming him for his failure in life, and all his life he was wrestling with the concrete banalities and squalor of his private destiny. Too feeble to throw off his father's well-intentioned dictatorship, he chose to see his fate symbolically: Man, submitting to endless frustration from a mysterious, bureaucratic Being, unpetitionable (this nasty word is Wilson's) and inscrutable. Under Wilson's analysis, Kafka, a superb chronicler of realistic nightmares, of the comedy and pathos of futile effort, survives, but Kafka the moral guide, the interpreter of God's ways to men, is expertly demolished.

Wilson had no piety but much pietas, the sense of continuity with the past. Some of his essays commemorate forgotten authors, like Octave Mirbeau, a warmhearted, quixotic playwright of second rank, who was overshadowed by successful imitators; others are tributes to contemporaries of his own, Whipple and Rosenberg and Eastman, who seem through some uncompromising individuality of temperament to have eluded the recognition that was their due. Here he seems very close to Forster, who writes of obscure people not from a love of the recondite or to placate the shades of the neglected dead, but from a deeper understanding of the sources of creation. Literature is not an orderly march-past of great writers but a procession of waves, whose crests have no existence apart from the deep disturbed waters on which they appear to ride.

Ernest Renan:
The Statue and the Calvary

1950

Very few people are interested in Renan now. Perhaps his brand of scepticism, which was eager and voluble, is out of date. In the West, religious disbelief is so widespread that it seldom has to be defiant or even articulate. You do not have to repudiate ideas to which you are indifferent. Only in the remote or very conservative parts of Europe, where the old orthodoxies survive unchallenged, can you startle people by disbelieving. But in most other places, particularly in England, religious controversy is tame and gentlemanly.

Renan was born in Brittany and came back there in his old age. Spiritually he never left it. He could never dissociate himself from the simple, unquestioning faith which he had challenged. That challenge had been the Open Sesame to a magic world, where truth, complex and progressively revealed, was adored with all the devotion that the Bretons gave to myth and pious legend. Renan was almost fanatical in his pursuit of the truth. He asked that DILEXI VERITATEM (I loved the truth) be written on his tombstone. Truth, as he saw it, was friendly, not hostile, to the imagination; it was only ruthless to those fabrications which had grown inflexible with age and were cramping to the intelligence and the will. He saw danger and cruelty in them.

I think that Renan differed from other great sceptics like Voltaire and Lucretius by his sensitive, unscornful handling of the ideas which he had rejected. He was neither a revolutionary nor a self-sufficient scholar. He was a Celt whose emotions were swayed by memories and personal loyalties. He loved the Church to which he owed the learning and the dialectical skill which he later turned against it. His childhood and the childhood of his race and all the villages and institutions of his native Brittany had developed under its care. He was bound with a cord which was precious to him; its knots and tangles had to be untied and not cut.

Renan believed that the faith of his childhood must be transcended, not simply bypassed. But the leaders of his Church preferred that their faith should be ignored rather than tampered with; they dreaded heresy more than infidelity. And that, I think, explains the fury and the fervent love which the memory of Renan can still rouse in his native Brittany, and the indifference with which he is regarded in the wider world where there are no strong tensions because there is no strong faith.

His clear and careful prose is today found sentimental and unctuous. The devout find him insidious, the sceptics find him insinuating. They do not understand what Renan was trying to do. He believed that Christianity is a still-living faith, but, if it is to survive, a delicate and skilful operation must be performed on it. Renan had once operated on his own soul, amputating many passionately held convictions. After the torment of his young manhood he had reached happiness, unclouded by doubt or regret, a measured confidence in the powers of the human mind that was proof against disillusionment and catastrophe. He believed that Christianity could survive the loss of all its supernatural accretions.

I think it was partly because of this confidence that he decided to live among the Bretons, to match their fervour with his own and prove to himself that he had not broken with his past but fulfilled it. That is why, as an old man, a scholar of international repute, he chose to settle on the Breton coast, near Tréguier, where he was born and studied for the priesthood. And though Renan died nearly a century ago, he is still loved and hated there. He is a figure of controversy and a dynamic force. When, as happens every now and then, there is a celebration in his honour, it is hard to tell whether it is a challenge to the living or an act of homage to the dead.

Tréguier is a small sleepy town, but it was one of the great early Christian centres of Brittany. It was founded by the legendary half-Druidic St. Tudwal, who in Saxon times led a group of refugees out of Wales. The celebrated St. Yves was born there some seven centuries later. And all around there are innumerable Breton saints of marked individuality and doubtful orthodoxy. Renan himself belonged to the family of one of the most eccentric of them, St. Ronan or Renan. Renan, despite his assault on the supernatural, had a tenderness for these cantankerous Breton saints whose cult had been for centuries the focus of local pieties. What he feared was not the credulity of the simple in which so often true history is enshrined, but its manipulation in the interests of orthodoxy and uniformity. When he was visited by Rhys, the great Welsh archaeologist, he sadly told him how the old statue of St. Budoc had been defaced and the curate had collected a subscription of forty francs to replace it with a Virgin of Lourdes, *ce triste miracle moderne*, to the dismay of the pious, conservative villagers. In many ways Renan, the revolutionary thinker, had a greater love for tradition than the ecclesiastics themselves.

While denying the divinity of Christ, Renan believed in the Christian traditions of brotherhood, selflessness and conscience. He believed that the Reformation of the sixteenth century had once safeguarded these by eliminating much that was idolatrous and heathen. Yet he thought that a yet greater reformation was needed which would embrace the whole of Christianity. "The spirit of reformation," he declared, "is being rapidly overtaken by rationalism, which knows nothing and which will destroy all that which awaits reformation before it has been reformed." "The reformers," he added, "could only save Christianity by attaining to absolute rationalism themselves and joining hands with all the emancipated spirits, who will accept the Sermon on the Mount as the code of conduct."

You can imagine what consternation these opinions caused in the Church. Long after Renan's death the battle was still being fought. And in Tréguier itself the clash of wills is immortalized in stone. Outside the church door in the centre of the square Renan's statue was erected in 1903 in the presence of Anatole France and many other leading intellectuals of France. It was a challenge which could not be ignored. A group of country people had agreed to come in and stop the unveiling, but they were prevented by a tremendous downpour of rain. A few years later, in protest against the statue, a great monument was erected called the "expiatory Calvary." It stands at the base of the rue Ernest Renan, within a stone's throw of the house where Renan was born and his mother kept a small grocer's shop. Below it is inscribed: *Vere hic homo filius Dei est* (Truly this man is the son of God). In front of it, with other saints, the stone figures of St. Tudwal and St. Yves stand on guard. Renan's house had been a museum for a long time and some years ago it was reorganized. There was a ceremonial opening with M. Herriot from Paris, the mayor, a naval band and a banquet for seven hundred guests. Belief and disbelief in the supernatural are in France still real issues, dividing men's minds. Evasiveness and compromise are not honoured. If this is responsible for bitterness and deep social fissures, it is also surely the source of France's cultural and intellectual pre-eminence.

Through long experience the antagonists have learnt to make graceful contact across the abyss. They can be courteous even when intransigent. I am thinking in particular of the letter Renan wrote on his first return to Tréguier, asking to be allowed to visit his old seminary and his teachers, whose favourite pupil he had once been. It is a masterpiece of delicacy and tact. But in the Principal's reply, a refusal, there is sweetness, too, as well as firmness. Perhaps the worst quarrels occur on the fringes of conviction. Renan and his teachers were not so much hostile to each other as completely unintelligible.

Renan was, of course, attacked as well as defended in an uncivilized way. He had indiscreet champions. But I think his bitterest enemies were those who never came within range of his happy, serious, friendly personality. Renan made himself loved by his Breton neighbours. He was a good man and a good Christian; on that point, their intuition was sound. But beyond the friendly circle there was no understanding or sympathy with his work. It needs generosity as well as genius to cut across the current of your age. Renan advanced fiercely unpopular opinions and yet remained smiling and unperturbed, though he was regarded by many as Antichrist and the Incarnation of Evil. I only know of one occasion when Renan lost his temper. He was asked to use his influence on behalf of the son of some Breton cousins of his. He paid a visit but learnt afterwards that the armchair on which he had sat had been sprinkled carefully with holy water by the boy's mother. She sent him, however, a present of some oysters. Renan had the oysters very conspicuously thrown on the manure heap.

Renan, old as he was and declining in health, by his mere physical presence in that remote corner of Brittany gave courage and confidence to many, and in particular to that small band of Breton scholars and poets who had urged him to come home to live. He had loved Brittany and the Celtic peoples and in spite of his unpopular theology there were many there to welcome him. He was the greatest Breton of his age. A heretic? Yes, but hadn't there been plenty of Breton heretics before him? Pelagius, perhaps, and Abelard and Lammenais certainly. The faith of the Bretons, he declared, had always been detached from books and forms, orthodoxy had been imposed through French bishops and concordats made with the French. For centuries there had been no Breton-speaking bishop. The Reformation had once taken a firm hold on the Bretons and it was only an accident of politics that they had not, like their kinsmen in Wales, remained under its sway.

Renan was looking in Brittany for some affinity of spirit that did not rest on scholarship, and, if one is to judge by the small public demonstrations that were made in his honour, I think he must have found it. Once when he was so crippled that he could not walk, he was entertained on the island of Bréhat; as usual on these occasions in France, there was a canon and a mayor and a naval band, a fleet of little painted boats and a banquet and lots of little girls dressed in white with bunches of flowers. When their boat reached the shore he found that a victoria, the first carriage ever seen on the island, had been ferried across the night before to receive him. With the simplicity of genius Renan spoke to the gathering of his father, the sailor, of his neighbours and friends of his childhood. Renan would like to have felt as at home in Brittany as in the Collège de France. He believed in the natural pieties of home and fatherland. "The memory of our native land is for each of us," he said, "a part of our morality." He believed in the power of natural goodness, which can in time replace that precarious goodness, as he would have considered it, which requires the support of a supernatural system. Was he anticlerical? It is not so simple as that. "Fatherland," he said, "and family are the two great natural forms of human association. Both are essential, but they cannot suffice of themselves. Side by side with them must be maintained an institution in which the soul can be nurtured and receive consolation and counsel, in which charity may be organized and spiritual masters and directors found."

Though Renan was isolated and frustrated, yet he had confidence. He thought that one day he would be justified. Though Christianity appeared inseparable from forms and ceremonies, from established hierarchies and supernatural beliefs, these things belong to the childhood of reason, while we are accustoming ourselves to the naked truth. One day we shall dispense with them. What did he mean, though, by the "institution for nurturing the soul," or "the spiritual directors and masters"? In what respect would these differ from the Church and its ministers? It is a point that Renan has not made clear. I think he would say that certain men have a clearer vision than others of the truth and can walk undazzled in the light of it. They are the true spiritual directors, whose task it would be to nurture the soul. But the Church will have none of them. They are feared and hated. It is even asserted that the Christian virtues themselves would collapse if the supernatural origin of the Church was repudiated. Renan denied this.

In fact Renan's enemies gave constant proof of the precariousness of this supernaturally fortified goodness. When his body was laid to rest in the Pantheon, and later, when his statue was erected at Tréguier, a flood of malice poured from the press. I can think of one book, similar to many, whose author dwelt with satisfaction on the last painful months of Renan's illness. "It was proof," he said, "that God had deserted him, as he deserted Voltaire and Arius the Heresiarch," who died of a haemorrhage in a privy at the moment of his triumph, an answer to the prayers of the pious bishop Alexander. "The apostate," says the writer, "was hustled away to die in the grim fortress of the Collège de France, so that he might be out of reach of the pious Bretons, whose faith he had assailed and whose conviction it was that he had been devoured by lice." And he perfects the parallel with Arius: "The apostate," he says, "was a humiliating spectacle in an old coat like a soutane and a sort of ecclesiastical hat tottering in the garden, coughing, spitting, puffing, groaning, trembling, crying like a soul in pain. Two valets followed him bearing a commode shaped like an armchair."

So the statue of Renan at Tréguier was, in a sense, expiatory like the Calvary. In the words of the French Minister at the unveiling: it was to "repair the unjust ostracism to which the apostle of toleration had so long been submitted on the soil of his native Brittany." The mayor of Tréguier declared in 1903, "This statue proclaims in the face of the whole world that our old province has not been absolutely abandoned to fanaticism. To attack this statue will be to attack the glory of France and to do a deep injury to the dignity of human thought."

But the statue has never been attacked. It is as safe as the Calvary in this civilized little town. The citizens are deeply divided in their loyalties, but they can cherish their differences with dignity. Renan, according to one of his biographers, will never attract followers. To have disciples is the destiny of those who *"croient lourdement,"* like Paul and Luther and Wesley. All the same I think that the picture of Renan, the smiling sceptic, aloof, ineffectual, impregnable, has been overdrawn. Renan the fearless enquirer, the fighter for the truth, has been underestimated. He followed the truth without misgiving as to where it would lead him. He saw that what he had written would bring release to some, but pain and bewilderment to others. Would the ill-disposed profit by what he, in good faith, had said? He did not ask.

Renan's faith in human destiny was a very individual, almost aristocratic one. It was proof against the disillusionment that may overtake all our democratic enthusiasm. "Idealists like us," he said, "must approach these fires with precaution. The chances are that we'll lose our head or our wings in them!" And he remarked on that strange magnetism which plays between the opposite poles of religious and socialistic orthodoxy. "How often," he said, "it happens that when a man abandons the Church, he will search for the lost absolute, the lost comfort of believing friends and colleagues, in a fanatical political faith!" And the converse happens too.

Is there something rather smug about Renan's practical sobriety? Sometimes admittedly there is. I think it was not always wisdom so much as a certain physical timidity that prevented him from dissipating his energies in unprofitable idealism, but, whatever the reason, the clarity of his vision was seldom dimmed by passion or prejudice. He believed that truth must be pursued without any reservation. He thought that man, through advancing knowledge, would acquire the power to extricate himself from the difficulties in which his too great confidence might plunge him. In one of his last writings he foretold how Caliban would turn Prospero out of his kingdom, and wisdom and goodness would have to be cherished in exile and in secret. But he thought that it would be better to endure Caliban for a space than to have Prospero restored by the forces of clerical reaction. "Far from being a Renaissance," he said, "that would be in our circumstances annihilation. Let us keep Caliban." These lines were quoted by Anatole France at the unveiling of the statue. I am sorry that he did not quote further, for Renan believed that Ariel, the spirit of religion, would survive all these vicissitudes and adapt himself to changed circumstances.

In fact Renan was convinced that Christ's teaching had a validity that needed no supernatural sanction. He thought it was only obscured by arguments based on historical facts that would always be disputed. You might entice millions into conformity by an elaborate system of beliefs and duties and catechismal phrases, but you would alienate thereby the handful of Christians who loved the truth unreservedly and were ardent and expert in the pursuit of it. Time would prove that they and no others were the best advocates of Christian love and charity.

It is nearly ninety years now since the statue was put up but I discovered in the 1950s that the Breton scholar who had first appealed for its erection was still alive and still capable of inspiring and infuriating his countrymen. He was the founder of one of the leading Breton nationalist associations and, though old and half blind, was unjustly sentenced to a short imprisonment for his political opinions.

What would Renan have thought of Breton separatism? I think, like Matthew Arnold, another philo-Celt, he would have regretted that it was the lowest gifts of the Celtic peoples, and not the highest, for which the modern world could find a use. Political revolt would have seemed to him merely the physical symptoms of a spiritual disequilibrium. There was no place today in the world for those excellences which the Celt had once contributed to European civilization, their gifts of imagination and of poetry, their defiance of the orthodox in thought and feeling. It would be natural that the Celts should wish to rebel against a civilization which claimed to be able to dispense with these qualities. I think here too Renan would have proved a prophet of reconciliation. For he himself had found no conflict between his love of France and his loyalty to his native land.

Peter and Paul

1976

Some years ago we heard a good deal about "the Crisis of Belief" and "the Death of God," and a little heat of a journalistic kind was generated through the rediscovery of God by some lapsed Communists like Malcolm Muggeridge and by defectors from the tepid orthodoxies of the reformed churches. But the fire soon died down.

In fact, the real Crisis of Belief happened some ninety years ago, when in much agony of the spirit, high-minded Anglican clergy and Oxbridge dons, "losing their faith," threw up their pleasant rectories, their stipends and their fellowships, and devoted themselves selflessly to a variety of humanitarian causes. At present what we are suffering from is a Crisis of Unbelief. It does not seem to matter whether we believe or not and most humanitarian enterprises are sponsored by the state. As for "Faith," so many millions have in our century, as Dr. Grant observes, dedicated themselves unquestioningly to such appalling creeds that "faith has gained an equivocal reputation." We are most of us Christians, but like Provost Mahaffy, "not offensively so."

God is no longer an issue (atheism is a word without meaning), but Jesus and Paul can still rouse real love and anger and contention, and these two books,* written from different angles, recall to us how much is imperishable in our Christian heritage. To Canon Phillips the Christ of the Gospels is everything. In Dr. Grant's account of St. Paul He is a vision of Absolute Goodness that arose in Paul's mind after he had heard His story and persecuted His disciples; "Paul,"

---

*Michael Grant, *Saint Paul* (1976), and J. B. Phillips, *Peter's Portrait of Jesus* (1976).

290 : Hubert Butler

says Dr. Grant, "shows an almost complete lack of interest in the words and acts of Jesus." Despite the evidence of The Acts, which are written much later than The Epistles and lack their authenticity, St. Paul never went near the other apostles for three years after his conversion and then saw only Peter and James, the brother of Jesus. The story of Jesus dying upon the Cross fell upon his mind not like a seed that germinates on stony ground but like a grain of pollen dust that fertilizes the flower of a different tree. It was not Jesus the great teacher whom Paul revered but Jesus the Son of God, who was crucified, rose from the dead and ascended to Heaven, Jesus the Redeemer, who sacrificed Himself for us and through whose intervention with the Father our sins will be forgiven.

For Paul and the generation that succeeded him, the crucifixion had transformed the whole world. The Son of God had been delivered to a death of utter degradation and nothing could be the same again. Dr. Grant recalls that the idea of the One dying for the Many was a fairly familiar one in Jewish antiquity. You find it in the story of the Maccabean revolt and in Isaiah and elsewhere. But, for the Western world, Paul with his burning belief restated it in a form that looked as if it would endure for ever! "By means of his life and letters," writes Dr. Grant, "he has left a greater imprint on the human race than any other man." A man of great intellectual power, he addressed himself mainly to humble and uneducated seaports like Ephesus and Corinth; he must have encountered much the same audiences that a travelling preacher would meet in the small towns of Kansas, the great cities of the Californian seaboard—bewildered, questing, fascinated by someone who addressed them not as citizens but as brothers and friends. It cannot have been his arguments (which were complex and often contradictory) that gripped his audience but his passionate belief.

It is now only by his letters that we can judge him, and these are not always easy to construe. Like Jesus, he spoke of neighbourly love but gave it a depth of meaning it had never had before. In the famous Letter to the Corinthians, Love has been mistranslated as Charity, an easy virtue which Paul almost dismisses. Without Love, we may bestow all our goods on the poor, we may have all knowledge and faith that can move mountains, but if we have not Love it profits us nothing. Paul was only trying to restate in new terms a very old message, familiar to the Jews from Leviticus, Tobit and the Rabbi Hillel, one that is hard to fulfill and even to express.

Is Dr. Grant right in saying that Paul told us to "love ALL other men and women"? Can one reconcile such a command with the teaching of Jesus or with Paul's own missionary travels? "Broad horizons" and concern for "the welfare of mankind" seem blessedly absent from the teaching of Jesus, who seldom strayed beyond the frontier of a tiny community. Paul, too, seems to have known personally most of those whom he addressed in his Epistles. The neighbours whom we are enjoined to love, whether in Capernaum or Ephesus, are those with whom we make personal contact. Since we no longer believe in demons to be exorcised or in an imminent Second Coming, neighbourly love is that part of the Christian message that today seems central, yet even Paul himself found it difficult. Believing that his interpretation of Jesus was the only true one, he was prompted "to utter" a never-ceasing stream of denunciations of rival views within Christianity itself . . . thus setting a tragic precedent for the secular persecutors of later centuries who transmuted his hostile words into repressive deeds.

"Rival views" arose at the very start between Paul, the apostle to the gentiles, and the other apostles, whose mission was to the Jews. It was not long before ecclesiastical diplomacy raised its ugly head. There had always been dormant anti-Semitism in the great imperial cities like Alexandria, and after the heroic revolt of the Jews (A.D. 66–73) the Christian communities throughout the Roman world were anxious to save their faces, to exonerate the Romans from the death of Jesus and to blame the Jews alone. In this way the Christian Jews, who had first received Christ's message from the apostles and had once been the most numerous and authoritative of His disciples, were attacked by Jew and Roman and Gentile-Christian alike, so that they rapidly dwindled and disappeared.

Jesus had often spoken to them against the law and the priests, against the Pharisees and the Sadducees, but his followers remained Jews at heart. That is why they called him the Son of Man, a term that had been used for the Messiah. And though to the Jewish patriots the Messiah was to come in his glory to rescue Israel, it was the Christian-Jews who first broke with tradition. The Chosen One was to die ignobly on the Cross and win for them a great victory that was not material but spiritual.

Paul, preferring to talk of Jesus as the Son of God, liberated Him from all national associations and at the same time deeply affronted the monotheism of the Jews by proclaiming Christ as the Second Person of the Trinity. A breach was made between Jew and Gentile that was never healed: the religion of brotherly love that was first preached in Palestine received the first setback there, too. Throughout the New Testament, this conflict of Jew and Gentile ebbs and flows. John makes Jesus say to the Jews: "Your Father is the Devil," but the writer of The Acts tries to minimize this conflict.

Paul, as mediator between the tiny subversive community in which Christianity was born and the world empire which carried it to the ends of the earth, saw the futility of everything on which institutional religion depends. Faith without Love is nothing, knowledge without Love vanishes away. Love cannot vaunt itself or be puffed up. And yet, though there were no church buildings till two hundred years after his time, it was Paul who, by overriding all rival views, established the idea of a universal Church. From the Crucifixion till the present day, Christian theology has been a ceaseless endeavour to strike a right balance between the humanity and the divinity of Jesus, and it was out of this struggle that accusations of heresy and most of the religious wars arose.

Why did Paul say so little about the life and words of Jesus? Dr. Grant suggests that the Gospel stories, which were written nearly twenty years after the Epistles, had not been "invented" then. To Canon Phillips, the writer of *Peter's Portrait of Jesus*, this blunt term would surely give offence. He translates, very readably, the Gospel, which he believes Mark had heard from Peter, but his comments are not always helpful. The vision of perfect goodness which the Galilean peasants had seen was to them beyond all ordinary expression; it could only be written in picture language, in myth. Time has turned the prose of the Authorized Version into poetry, and Canon Phillips, bringing it back again to everyday prose, feels obliged to look for everyday explanations. Why did Jesus expel the demons from the lunatic at Gerasa at the cost of two thousand pigs? The Canon suggests that, waving his arms in the convulsions of recovery, the man stampeded the pigs over cliffs. Surely this interpretation loses the truth of poetry and is prosy without being probable. He is equally puzzled by the two stories of the miraculous feedings near Bethsaida. I do not find the explanation of some German Hebrew scholars offensive: they remarked that in the Septuagint the word *saida* is always translated by the Greek word *epistmos* or "feeding." That is to say, Bethsaida would be "the house of feeding." The pun is a humble relation of the parable and the poem; simple people, encountering what they saw to be indescribable goodness, might choose to link it permanently with a place name which, in the small intimate Jewish world, was on everybody's lips.

Canon Phillips observes that everything altered "as the churches grew from small and simple communities to larger and more complex organizations." In its new surroundings neighbourly concern, a village virtue, once nursed with village parable, is more slow than ever to ripen into love.

Materialism Without Marx:
A Study of Chekhov

1948

Chekhov is, I suppose, sure of eternal fame, but his popularity has its seasonal ebb and flow. He is not a writer for periods of great optimism or pessimism or violent agitation, but when the human spirit is convalescing from some orgy of emotion, Chekhov is the perfect companion and counsellor; he is reasonable, scrupulous and gently astringent. That is why a reviving interest in Chekhov is a hopeful sign of spiritual recovery.

But not everyone thinks this of Chekhov. He is too great a figure not to have his enemies and is constantly misinterpreted. His friend Gorki said that he described the vilenesses and banalities of life so well that most of his readers could not see beyond the superb crafts-manship. They did not notice the inner meaning full of bitter reproach. When Chekhov died, Gorki saw in the chorus of conventional regret and praise the "cold and smelly breath of banality rejoicing over the death of an enemy."

I wasn't surprised to hear an old Russian émigré growling about Anton Chekhov the other day. "A Chekhov revival is always sinister," he said, "we associate him with the degenerate, hopeless days before the Revolution. How he was adored then! Now we'd sooner read even the Soviet writers than him. We prefer something definite." And Communist critics have written about Chekhov just as stupidly. They have applauded his materialism, his gentle but ruthless dissection of the bourgeois soul, but they are angry with him for refusing to trace the defects of the individual to the defects of society and to say that both could be cured by Marxist surgery.

Even in his lifetime Chekhov was attacked on both flanks. He was a decadent and dreamy indifferentist, said the liberals; he was a decadent and soulless materialist, said the conservatives. But I think the real reason for their irritation was that in his pages they saw not their opinions but themselves and it wasn't a pleasant sight. Still, read him they did, and he is still read in Russia.

Chekhov certainly had a philosophy, but for the greater part of his life it was implicit in his art and unformulated. It was only when he was teased by the misinterpretations of his critics or shaken out of his creative calm by the spectacle of cruelty or injustice that he tried to make his philosophy explicit. I think he would object to the word "philosophy." Materialism was not in his view a school or movement, it was a necessity. "Thinking men," he said, "are inevitably materialists and so are animals, savages and Moscow merchants. To forbid a man the materialistic conception is to forbid him seeking the truth." As for his art, he thought of it as an extension of his medical science. From the diagnosis of bodily ailments he could not see that there was any abrupt transition to the diagnosis of spiritual and social ones. Psychical phenomena are so strikingly like physical ones that one must refuse, he said, to draw a distinction between soul and body.

This avowal of his materialism was called forth from Chekhov by his friend Suvorin, with whom he differed about almost everything except their liking for one another. Suvorin was, outside his own family, the most important person in Chekhov's life. Immensely wealthy and influential, he was also imaginative, educated, charming. He was one of the first to recognize and foster Chekhov's talent, and he never relaxed in his kindness to him. Yet to many of Chekhov's contemporaries—the great liberal writer Mikhailovsky, for example—Suvorin seemed the incarnation of evil. His paper, *Novoye Vremya*, was considered the mouthpiece of all those reactionary forces that were keeping Russia in darkness and slavery. Chekhov seemed to have sold himself to reaction by accepting Suvorin's patronage and publishing his stories in his paper.

Yet it was not quite the hackneyed story of the penniless writer prostituting his talents for the powerful newspaper proprietor. Chekhov was jealous of his independence and Suvorin respected it. Though as a businessman he was ready for any shabby trick or lying propaganda, Suvorin had a true feeling for art and an admiration for Chekhov. I suppose he had a dual nature and it was this made him talk so constantly of matter and spirit, art and science, and to see conflicts where Chekhov refused to see them. Suvorin once provoked

Chekhov into a passionate defence of his materialism by writing, "I've nothing against the scientists and their universal matter, provided they leave us just a cranny to shelter in from it."

Evidently Suvorin thought of "the life of the spirit" as existing apart from everyday business, a bit like the literary supplement to *Novoye Vremya* in which he published Chekhov's stories. It was in his supplement too that Suvorin championed that crusade against materialism and the scientific view of life in which some romantic writers of the time were engaged. But Chekhov believed that Suvorin's obsession about materialism was a subjective disease, the result of an inner discord. (He did, in fact, keep his life in two compartments, and wished to adapt his philosophy to duality. There was a spiritually minded Suvorin, a dramatist and a patron of artists and writers, and a materially minded Suvorin, who made a success of his vast journalistic enterprises by giving his readers their own vulgar opinions, and condoning reaction, repression and even pogroms.)

Chekhov said that when something is wrong inside us, "we look for causes outside," and very vigorously he attacked two of Suvorin's favourite authors, Bourget and Sienkiewicz, crusaders both of them. In their novels, which were held to be deeply spiritual, the arrogant materialist who sets out to know the unknowable and refuse to humble himself before the infinite is eloquently chastised. To Chekhov, Sienkiewicz was a vulgar impostor who had captivated the Russian public with his facile sentimentalism. Chekhov said he felt uncomfortable after reading him as if he'd received a slobbery kiss. "Sienkiewicz," he said, "aimed at lulling the bourgeois in its golden dreams. Be true to your wife. Pray with her from the prayer book, make money, love, sport, and all will be well with you in this world and in the world to come." But Chekhov thought Bourget by far the more insidious of the two, because he was clever and witty and easily fascinated Russian writers whose lives and thoughts were so much less rich and varied. "A Russian writer lives in the gutter and eats wood lice, knows nothing of history or geography or the natural sciences. In a word, compared with Bourget he's a web-footed goose." It was all too easy to enlist the Russian writer in these pretentious crusades which only bring purposeless confusion into the province of thought.

Chekhov believed for long that if he was outspoken with Suvorin in this way their friendship and collaboration would be justified. To his brother he wrote:

I speak my mind quite openly with Suvorin every time I see him and I am sure it does some good. Just to say "I don't like it" is enough in itself to show one's independence, and it's probably useful too. If one pounds away at it every day in the end one's pounding will do some good to the Suvorin gang and get under their skin.

But, of course, to say "I don't like it" now and again is not a satisfactory form of offensive. At last, Suvorin did something that Chekhov could no longer forgive. He had been publishing Zola without paying him in his literary supplement, but when Zola had dared to defend Dreyfus, Suvorin, in Chekhov's words, "poured hogwash" over him in other parts of the paper and gave free rein to his virulent anti-Semitism. Chekhov wrote to Suvorin reproachfully, defending Zola's action with passion. "No question of politics, no state interest," he said, "should deflect the writer from his duty. Great writers and artists engage in politics only insofar as it is necessary to defend people against politics." Chekhov did not again write for *Novoye Vremya*. The experiment of pounding away at the Suvorin gang had failed. "*Novoye Vremya*," Chekhov wrote, "is not a paper. It's a ravening beast, it's a herd of famished jackals, gnawing each other by the tails, the devil only knows what it is!" The breach with Suvorin never quite healed.

Chekhov's indignation has been misunderstood even by his biographers. "How could he break with an old and tried friend," one of them asks, "on account of persons strange to them both? It seems as though deep feelings of personal friendship were impossible to this limp soul." Suvorin was healthy and strong, Chekhov sick and nervous? That surely, is the cold and smelly breath of banality again. In fact, of course, it was Suvorin who was the weakling, bending before the rich and powerful; it was Chekhov who was strong, and who refused to let even old friendship stand in the path of what he thought was just and true.

It was only when he was provoked into defending his art that Chekhov talked of materialism. It was not a gospel to preach or enforce. He fancied he was stating the obvious. He thought that the morality which made men try to love each other and to avoid stealing, lying, talebearing came with the slow unfolding of their natures, existed before the churches and did not require them. He said that he was always perplexed when he met a writer who was religious. Yet in his tales some of the most sympathetically studied characters were devout people, priests and laymen; in his village of Melikhovo he built a belfry for the church because the peasants needed one. It was the crusades and campaigns of the sophisticated that he regarded with animosity. They were distracting us from the sober consideration of human problems. "To believe in God," he said, "is not difficult. The inquisitors and our Biron and Arakcheyev [two notorious Russians] believed in Him. No, believe in man! . . . We are higher creatures and if we were to realize the whole power of the genius of man, we should become like Gods."

And as regards his own craft, the interpretation of man to himself, Chekhov was a materialist, disbelieving in orthodox definitions. There was no limit to our knowledge of ourselves save those imposed by ignorance, ill health, sloth or misfortune. Beneath the most commonplace human encounter, the artist could perceive and lay bare a subtle pattern and beneath it a still more exquisite one if his eye was trained to perceive it.

But Chekhov's materialism has disconcerted his Soviet critics because he allied it with a passionate individualism, and it was to the individual and not to the masses or the revolutionary group that he looked for the salvation of society. In one of his letters he wrote:

I believe in the solitary individual and I see that our salvation will come from solitary personalities scattered here and there over Russia, sometimes peasants. Power is in their hands, even though there are few of them. No man is a prophet in his own country and these solitary individuals of which I speak play an imperceptible role in society. They do not dominate it but their work is visible.

The same idea is more familiar to most of us through *The Three Sisters*, where Vershinin encourages Astrov to go on hoping and working. He told him that there was no town so dead and boring that three men of intelligence and education in a population of 100,000 could not make a faint impression. They would get swallowed up, of course, by the dark masses but not without leaving some slight influence and after them there would be six, then twelve, till at last they'd be the majority. "In two or three hundred years, life will be unspeakably, amazingly lovely."

Marxists have accused Chekhov of deluding himself and his reader with dreams of a happy future to which he did not know the way and in which he scarcely believed. Certainly compared with theirs his directions are vague and tentative. He saw a vast expanse of what he called "Eskimos and tundras" stretching between hope and its fulfilment. His faith is so soberly expressed as to be proof against all disillusionment. Rereading Chekhov in 1948 you will feel that the glow of hope which comes from it has not been extinguished by two generations of disaster. Chekhov had pledged himself to no creed and to no fashionable prophet. He described literature for the people and theatre for the people as "all silliness and candy." He believed deeply in Tolstoy and in Ibsen, but he did not believe in Tolstoyanism or Ibsenism. He said he had no faith in vegetarianism, Ukrainian nationalism or psychiatry. When he said that he was a Marxist, he meant that he published his works with a man called Marx who lived in Gogol Street. He would not idealize the peasant: "Muzhik blood flows in my veins," he said, "and you can't astonish me with muzhik virtues."

He thought that writers had a great part to play as interpreters of life. "The best of them," he wrote, "describe life as it is, but in such a way that every line is penetrated, as it were, with a juice, with the consciousness of an aim. Apart from life as it is, you feel also that other life as it ought to be and it bewitches you."

Chekhov was not, as liberal critics like Mikhailovsky have claimed, and since them the Marxists, indifferent to social reform, but he did not believe that this could be brought about in the way that the politicians prescribed, by movements, revolutions, societies, committees. He carried his aversion to organized philanthropy to almost absurd lengths. He said he got suffocated by phrases like "unity," "common interests," "associations," "the solidarity of young writers" and the like. He understood solidarity when applied to politics or the stock exchange or religious sects, but in regard to young writers it was meaningless. If young writers wanted to associate solidly with each other, all they had to do was to behave well to each other as they would to anyone else and neither gossip nor lie nor be jealous. But professional associations lead to mutual suspicion and spying interference from above just as if we were Jesuits. A man like this could be a Marxist even less than a Jesuit. Today it seems as if he had gained rather than lost by his aloofness from creeds and movements, his tenacious belief in the individual. He has not suffered as Tolstoy did from the Tolstoyans, or Marx from the Marxians.

If you were not aware of Chekhov's belief in the solitary individual, you might find something arrogant, eccentric or perhaps childish about some of his enterprises. With his own efforts he wished to make even a physical mark on the soil of Russia. At his little settlement of Melikhovo, with his eyes like Astrov's fixed on some remote country, he planted trees, made a house for the fire engine, a school, some wells, and put fishes in them.

From this standpoint, we can understand Chekhov's sudden visit to Sakhalin, the convict island on the Pacific coast, in 1890. It perplexed all his friends and caused Suvorin to call him a raving lunatic. There were many prison reform societies to which Chekhov could have subscribed and then stayed at home getting on with his stories, but no, this call to Sakhalin was more urgent than his art. He could not be seduced away from it by the protests of his friends or the snubs of civil servants. Except for his medical training and a few weeks in a library, Chekhov was utterly unqualified to investigate the state of convicts in Siberia. He was in delicate health and had travelled little, and in addition he went without any official introduction or facilities. He went as Anton Chekhov, a writer, whose fame was only of two years' standing, an utter amateur, who was not afraid of being thought an intrusive busybody. His book *Sakhalin Island*, the result of this journey, has only recently been translated, because it is in conflict with the accepted Chekhov legend. It is not wistful, resigned and full of subdued melancholy. It is blazing with certainty and indignation, and because of that, in spite of its tragic contents it is perhaps the most hopeful and optimistic of all his writings. He believed that it was worthwhile to be passionately indignant about remediable injustice and that to remedy injustice was not the task of the statistician, the trained welfare officer, the experienced committeemen, it was the task of every man of sensibility and integrity. Before he went, he wrote to Suvorin:

Sakhalin is a place of unendurable suffering such as only man, free or enslaved, can cause. It is clear that we have condemned millions of men to rot in prisons, we have condemned them at random, without reflection, barbarously, we have driven men through the cold in chains, tens of thousands of miles, we have infected them with syphilis, debauched them, multiplied criminals and we have thrown the blame for all this on the red-nosed prison superintendent. To-day all civilized Europe knows that it is not the superintendents but all of us who are guilty.

This, I suppose, was one of Chekhov's "I don't like it" letters to Suvorin, but more was necessary. He went himself to Sakhalin. There was no Trans-Siberian Railway in those days and he was eight months away. He travelled three thousand versts by horse over the remote savage island. He made a complete investigation of the convict system and studied also with sympathy the primitive tribes, the Ainus and Gilyaks, who lived on the island. He returned one December afternoon from this long journey, accompanied by two mongooses, a palm civet* and a flat-faced, hairless Buryat priest, all of whom were to be accommodated in the tiny Chekhov flat in Moscow. The Buryat priest did not stay long, but the palm civet darted under a bookcase, from which it never again emerged except by night to forage for food and bite the legs of sleepers. The mongooses, on the other hand, led a sociable life, tearing off the wallpaper to look for bugs, making messes in visitors' hats and turning their gloves inside out. Chekhov meanwhile wrote his book; it had some considerable effect on the prison system in Russia, but I do not think that it is by that that we should judge it. It was the protest of the individual soul which is never wasted. I think this book on Sakhalin is a refutation of the familiar Chekhov legend of "the limp soul," "the chronicler of drabness and frustration."

*A carnivorous quadruped, between fox and weasel in size and look.

Leonid Leonov

1946

Leonid Leonov presents a problem to the Western reader. It is difficult either to ignore him or to appreciate him as he deserves. Probably our trouble is that he ignores us. In former times eminent writers tried, often with success, to transcend with their books the frontiers of their state or society. In the greatest of their creations we were always reassured that the pattern which they followed was universal, even though it was worked out in regional material. In Leonov's writing, there is abundant evidence of talent and even genius, but this vital reassurance is missing. At least ten translators and as many publishers have, in England, been attracted by him in turn, but they have none of them remained faithful beyond a single book. It is impossible to be faithful to someone, however fascinating, who is persistently looking in the opposite direction and thinking of something else.

As the first of these ten translators, I still go on hoping unreasonably that he will write some masterpiece that will not vanish, like fairy gold, in translation. A visit to him in Moscow in 1931 was not very reassuring. He was a thickset, very self-sufficient young man with country features and friendly but careful manners. He was not at all interested in Western writers and Western ways, and I doubt if he would admit that he has been influenced by them. We Westerners like to think that intelligent Russians suffer from claustrophobia because they do not often meet us, but this deprivation has never cost Leonov a pang. We are irrelevant. We are not, as we persuade ourselves, out of bounds, for Leonov has several times walked confidently out of bounds. Through *The Thief* there runs a strong current of Christian mysticism. In *Sot*, too, a major and respected character, a Tsarist officer turned monk, advances Christian views without being satisfactorily refuted. More dangerously heretical, he inveighs against the machine age and prophesies its end. A less confident writer would have avoided the delicate theme of *The Badgers*, the widespread resistance of the peasantry to the forcible collection of grain by the Soviets. Leonov is a Soviet writer from the bottom of his heart, and because of that he permits himself, and is permitted, considerable liberties. He handles explosives with assurance.

It was characteristic of him that when he said goodbye to me, he should have handed me, with a small bow, a fine icon-like painting of John the Baptist on a heavy wooden shutter. He was unhelpful about brown paper. It was a queer present to give to a foreign bourgeois who was to travel through Russia on crowded Soviet trains, but plainly he was not interested in the impact of Russians and foreigners and the subtleties of intercourse.

I am sorry that Hilda Kazanina does not give an introductory explanation of *The Badgers** and its author. Leonov wrote it as a young man twenty-two years ago; it is his first full-length novel and is marred by many immaturities. Undoubtedly he was inspired by his father, also a writer, who, like the hero, Semyon, was removed as a boy from a country village to Zaradiye, the Moscow quarter of pedlars and hucksters, which is here admirably described. The elder Leonov, one of the *samouchke* or "self-taught" writers who were defended by the established men of letters and persecuted by the Tsar, was imprisoned and banished to Archangel. He exhorted his son Leonid, in simple country verse, never to forget the poor and the peasants. Am I right in thinking that Leonov's revolutionary faith is still based on sentiment and romantic loyalties, so firmly based that he has no need of brittle theories to reinforce it?

Leonov's writing is steeped in religious feeling but of a kind that must surely be as unconventional in Russia as it would be in these islands. Woods and hills, marshes and villages, are saturated with a significance that cannot be stated in economic or social terms. One could call him a pantheist, so deep is his sense of the authority and influence that natural objects exercise over man. He seems continually to hint that the bitter struggles of our time, which we interpret so variously, are merely transient aspects of a profounder cleavage. The civilization of the pavement and the clerk is at war with the civilization of the corn land and the herdsman. Over the richest part

*Kazanina's translation of *The Badgers* was published in London in 1947.—ed.

of western Europe the countryside has long ago capitulated, but in Russia the issue is still undecided.

Leonov watches the struggle with a sinking heart and deeply divided loyalties. There is a striking similarity between the plot of *The Badgers* and of the next novel, *The Thief*, for both deal with transplanted countryfolk and the plot shifts to and fro between the pavement and the fields. The city is in the most literal sense an encumbrance on the land. Leonov's nostalgic countryfolk tread its streets always conscious of the grass, the rye, the bushes struggling under their feet to throw off the cobblestones and disintegrate the great stone buildings. The habits and thoughts of the countryside survive in the same starved vestigial way under the burden of urban convention. "The town eats you up. It takes out your vitals and puts in a lot of tripe in their place." In the teeming alleys of Zaradiye two worlds are perpetually at grips. The Badgers are a group of peasants from the village of Vori who revolt against the Soviet officials and murder the grain collectors. They withdraw to the woods and make themselves dugouts like badgers, putting themselves under the leadership of a Vori man returned from Zaradiye. The Soviet officials are also, some of them, recruited to this urban colony of Vori; some come from the neighbouring village of Gussaki, which because of an ancient rivalry is enthusiastic for the Communists. One or two discontented idealists on either side apprehend the wider issues at stake, and Leonov holds the balance evenly between them. The victory of the Soviets is the outcome of a collision between two sets of personal and social animosities. Whether or not it is the triumph of the right, it is the triumph of the inevitable.

If there is any particular message, it is a sad one, and not novel. The civilization of the cities is almost irresistible, and it is best for the peasants to make as good terms with it as they can. "Why, even books come from the city," reflects one of the Badgers, and without books the peasants are defenceless against their oppressors. Used to the easy victories and bloodless devastations of Fleet Street and Hollywood and the City, we are shocked when we hear of the last peasants in Europe fighting for their liberties with scythes and hay forks. But it is not hypocritical to pretend that we are really, like Tolstoy and William Morris, on the side of the peasants? Without the grain collectors and their ruthless methods the cities of Russia would have starved. In Russia, Leonov allows us to infer, there is still a faint hope of a compromise between city and country.

Those who read *The Badgers* will find a candid and dramatic account of the peasant revolt against the Soviets. Journalists have always told us that these facts lay behind an iron curtain which only they could lift, yet this book was written in 1925. In literature, at least, the curtain is in part of our own making, woven from certain inevitable antipathies and opacities. Unlike his predecessors, the Russian writer of today writes of the Russian majority, and their lives have always been monotonous, moving very slowly between crude climaxes. We like our plots to be swift and complex. We like Somerset Maugham; they have banned him. We are worlds apart, and Leonov is insultingly satisfied with his own world.

In his writing, Leonov is a law unto himself and the terror of the translator. Often he writes with great distinction and subtlety, but he delights in elaborate images which he develops with childlike obstinacy. Thus he will say that a house is like a soldier or an old woman and will carry on some often arch and ponderous conceit through several pages, till at last it is not clear whether we are dealing with real soldiers and women or figurative ones. Another of his tricks is to apostrophize his characters, in the Victorian way, at the crises of their careers. "Ah, what homely joys and cares will brighten the dull monotony of your days, Yegor Ivanich!" This is how Dean Farrar used to address Eric. Yet, in the Russian of the Soviets, the ancient idiom, associated with different pieties, is not altogether flat. I have noticed too that once launched into the main current of his story he sweeps clear of these obstructions and his style becomes swift and free. I advise the reader, therefore, to persevere through the early awkward pages of *The Badgers* and not to blame Hilda Kazanina, who has done a difficult job very competently.

Leonov has been awarded the Order of Lenin and was chosen to give a victory speech from the watchtower of the Kremlin upon Victory Day. Straining to see beyond the familiar horizon, he spoke rather more thoughtfully than is usual on such occasions. Western writers, on tiptoe for the same purpose, would say, I think, that his vision, from their standpoint, was only slightly askew. He said that obsessions about exclusive missions of individual nations never led to any good. Atomic energy entered human society with a veiled face, a benefactor or a murderer of all alike. Scientific innovations went hand in hand with mankind only at such a time as people were completely prepared for their acceptance. This time Nature had put her trust in Man's reason, determined at once to lighten the sufferings that came from famine and war.

The world that lay at the feet of the young men of the earth was an excellent world, but they should remember it was a mined world, where everything exploded if handled without experience. They must be on their guard especially in this century. The earth was becoming the abode of a single family. A new patriotism, looking ahead into the future, was becoming the foundation of social and international ethics. In the common stream of humanity, nations would retain their peculiar features; there would be an industrious China, a noisy, business-like America, a merry and wise England and a little country of Lebanon, no worse than the others merely because it had a bad transport service.

These in any land would be valuable and easily damaged ideas and for safety's sake he packed them in well on either side with soft woolly talk of a popular nature. Here, we pack with a different wool, but if we put Lithuania instead of Lebanon, few would quarrel with these ideas issuing from the top of the Kremlin.

Today there are spiritual barriers that the best-intentioned writers on either side cannot surmount by direct assault. If they make contact it will be by some devious, roundabout route. It is not easy for us to see in what direction Soviet writers are leading. Yet Leonov, for one, is obviously a man of vision and courage. If he, like the others, seldom turns his full face to the world outside Russia, he possibly has his reasons. In the meantime his books are not very companionable but they cannot be disregarded.

Riga Strand in 1930

1930

Once a week in the summer months, a pleasure steamer berths in
Reval harbour and for a few hours troops of excited English tourists
swoop down on the town, swarm up the hill and penetrate in charabancs as far as Pirita and St. Brigid's Abbey. It is a charming spot;
the views, the churches, the crooked narrow streets, compact,
accessible and picturesque, are just what is required. Though they
straggle off unshepherded in fifty different directions, they meet each
other in a few minutes with glad cries in antique shops and cathedrals
where everybody speaks English. When the hooter calls them back
to the ship they have seen everything and yet are not exhausted.

The same ship wisely seldom stops at Riga. Riga is big and
sprawling and new-looking; it has clean, cosmopolitan boulevards,
public parks, and large exhausting museums; the few tourists have a
harried look and the hours pass in catching trams, changing money
and haggling with droshky drivers. There are, it is true, a great many
English people in Riga, but they are a serious, residential tribe, the
complete reverse of the sightseers of Reval or Helsingfors. The Riga
Britons are homesick and resentful businessmen who have come to
buy timber and find that the Letts don't want to sell it, or bored and
studious soldiers who have come to learn Russian and find that the
Letts don't want to teach it. Their subsequent stories of Riga and
Latvia are naturally coloured by their experiences. The timber merchants are confronted with the petty officialdom of a young nation,
proud of its new independence and snatching at all opportunities of
asserting it. The officers are met with blank surprise; their shy, stum-
bling sentences get no encouraging response from the Letts, for Rus-

sian is out of favour and they find their society restricted to the English Club and a few embittered Russian aristocrats to whom Latvia is only a rebellious province, governed by the lower orders. No wonder then that officers and merchants have no rosy memories of Riga; grudgingly perhaps they repeat the legend that the Riga air is very good and that Schwarz's is the best café between Berlin and Tokyo, though they've never been to Tokyo and Schwarz's is very much like other cafés; they bring home amber necklaces and caviar and polished birchwood cigarette cases, but they don't conceal that they are thankful to be out of Riga and would gladly never return.

All the same Riga Strand must have a fascination for more leisured visitors, who have time to be interested in the past and the future of the small republics which rose from the ruins of the Russian Empire. It is the holiday ground not only for Letts but for all the newly liberated peoples of the Baltic. There one may meet Estonians and Finns, Lithuanians and Poles, bathing side by side with Germans, Russians and Swedes, who were once their masters.

Of all the Baltic nations perhaps the Letts have suffered the most, yet their story is typical. Their nationality and their language have survived a double conquest and many centuries of foreign rule. From the west came the Teutonic Knights bearing with them a German culture and occupying the ancient territories of Lett and Lithuanian and Estonian, as far as the Finnish marshes and the empire of the Tsars. Russia too was expanding. Peter the Great was casting covetous eyes upon the Baltic, and at last the "Baltic Barons" in their turn, and all their possessions, passed under the Russian eagles. The Letts now found that they had not one master but two, for the Russians respected the Barons for their solidity and thrift and good husbandry, and confirmed them in their possessions, giving them in return for their loyalty high places at court and in the army. Ever since Peter the Great had first turned the eye of Russia westward, German culture and methods had been admired and imitated. Catherine the Great was a German, and she and her successors often chose advisers from their German subjects. The Baltic Barons found that they lost nothing by their incorporation in the Russian Empire.

If the Barons were the most privileged of the Tsar's subjects, the Letts whom they oppressed were the most wretched . . . their very existence denied, the name of Latvia abandoned, and the Baltic lands divided into Russian provinces in which the racial differences were carefully ignored. The Letts had no appeal from the caprice of their

masters; an early law limited flogging to thirty-six strokes, but humane legislation did not go much further and the Letts remained all
but serfs till late on in the last century. Lettish schools were closed
and Lettish newspapers prohibited, even old songs and customs that
might remind them of their national past were suppressed. Every year
in the old days there had been a great festival of song, the rallying
point of national feeling, and every town and village had its band of
singers. But the rulers recognized that a song can be more dangerous
than a sword and the festival was rigorously suppressed.

Many Letts joined revolutionary organizations and, when the
Revolution of 1905 broke out, the great rehearsal for the Revolution
of 1917, there was an abortive revolt in Riga. A Lettish Republic
was declared and for a few days maintained. The Tsar was alarmed,
concessions were promised, and, when all danger was averted, forgotten: the Barons, momentarily panic-stricken, recovered their composure. But the Letts persevered, their time had not yet come, and
the Great War found them still trusting in the clemency of the Tsar.
It was an occasion when all the subject races must be rallied to the
Russian cause, and the Baltic peoples, who were disaffected and lived
upon the frontiers of the enemy, must at all costs be conciliated. The
German emperor had promised to establish a Lettish Republic, and
the Barons, who took this with a grain of salt, were many of them
ready to welcome a German invasion. The moment was propitious
for a generous gesture from Nicolas II. He agreed to grant a request
hitherto persistently refused: henceforward the Letts might serve under their own officers as a separate Lettish unit. Lettish regiments
were formed and graciously permitted to defend their fatherland and
promised that when they had beaten the enemy they would enjoy
equal rights with the Barons. There were rejoicings in Riga, and the
credulous Letts believed that at last the day of their deliverance was
at hand; but those who were more discerning guessed that whoever
won, the Letts would be the losers, the Barons would not be shifted
and the emperors would find good reasons for forgetting their solemn
pledges. But as often occurs the most discerning were wrong. The
unexpected, the impossible happened: both sides were defeated, Kaiser Wilhelm lost his throne and the line of Peter the Great came to
a tragic end at Ekaterinburg. Yet at first it seemed as if Latvia would
merely be smothered in the collapse of the two empires. By the Treaty
of Brest-Litovsk, Russia treacherously abandoned Latvia to Germany
and after the Armistice the Allies allowed the Germans to remain in
Riga to keep the country safe from Bolsheviks.

Then followed eighteen months of terrible suffering for Latvia. The Letts drove out the Bolsheviks in the east only to find the Germans in their rear, and a third enemy appeared suddenly, for an army of White Russian exiles, mobilized in Berlin, tried to conquer Latvia as a base for an attack on Russia. White and Red and Balt and German alternately ravaged the land, for their landlord Barons made common cause against the Letts. But the Letts fought like tigers. At last, after foreign intervention and unheard-of struggles, peace was restored, boundaries were traced by English colonels and professors and the Latvian Republic was proclaimed.

Now at last the Letts are masters of Riga Strand, and on a June morning the sands are alive with holidaymakers. Where do they all come from? Outside Riga the pinewoods and the wastelands stretch empty and interminable, dotted here and there only with a few ramshackle wooden huts, and Riga itself does not suggest an unlimited supply of pleasure-seekers. Granted that some of them come from abroad, the answer is that a seaside holiday is not so much a luxury in Latvia as a necessity. There is scarcely a clerk or artisan in Riga too humble not to have a rickety wooden dacha for his family during the summer months, and from there he commutes daily.

A great broad shore fringed with pine woods sweeps round the Gulf of Riga as far as the eye can see: the sea is almost tideless and yet the beach is always deep and soft and clean, for the wind blows away the bus tickets and the paper bags and buries orange peels and matchboxes deep in the sand. Then during the long winters the snow and the frost scavenge round the shuttered dachas, there are mountains of ice and the whole gulf is frozen over, so that a year or two ago two men skated forty miles across the sea to the small island of Runo, but when they got there they did not recognize it, for it too was covered with ice.

June when it comes finds the scene completely changed: the syringas are in blossom, the railway is opened and the post office and the postmistress are established; there are bands and cinemas and charabancs, and people run about the shady streets in dressing gowns. Riga Strand is awake again. It is an annual metamorphosis, a conspiracy between man and nature that has started afresh every season since the first dacha went up in the pine woods. There is a story that it belonged to a Scottish merchant and that he called it Edinburga, thus giving its name to one of the seven villages of Riga Strand. Another of the villages is called Dubbelin though the Irish merchant who founded it is only a legend. In any case the villages bear little resemblance to their namesakes. Behind them, parallel to the shore, flows the broad river Aar; in front of them stretches the coastline. There is nothing to interrupt the long monotonous shore; one may walk and walk and still the landmarks keep the same place upon the horizon. There are no rock pools or seaweeds or shells or birds; sea and land meet each other with a minimum of detail and complication. One might walk to Lithuania and meet scarcely anything but water and sand and trees and sky.

There are three sandbanks that stretch round the whole of the Latvian coast as if to grade the depths for bathers; children can splash about in front of the first, while their parents sleep contentedly on the shore, but only the most intrepid swimmers venture beyond the third. In general, though, the Letts are very well used to the sea and the attendants have placed the long line of basket chairs with their backs to the waves, so that the occupants can watch the stream of people passing by under the restaurants in striped Turkish dressing gowns and bathing dresses far too modish to bathe in. The serious bathers do not wear bathing dresses at all, for the beach belongs to the men till eight o'clock in the morning, when they must give place to the women, who have it to themselves till midday.

The villages themselves are scattered among the trees, long grassy tracks run parallel to each other, crisscrossed by others and fringed with wooden dachas. Here and there is an outcrop of cinemas and dance halls. There are more pretentious buildings too with archways and gardens; they are empty and dilapidated but not with age, for carved in the stone doorways one can often read 1905 or 1908 or 1912. Those were the great days of Riga Strand, when wealthy merchants from Moscow and St. Petersburg or noblemen who did not despise Russian resorts came here with their families. Mineral springs and mud baths were discovered and exploited; though Riga Strand was not beautiful like Finland yet it was close at hand and it was not as expensive or as exclusive as the Crimea; at least it only excluded the Jews and they were excluded as a matter of course from every chic imperial resort. There was an imperial decree forbidding them to Riga Strand.

For a decade or more all went well; new wings were constructed, new gardens laid out, fashionable specialists built up practices, more and more medicinal baths were opened—then all at once the same fate overtook the villages of Riga Strand that extinguished all the pleasure resorts of western Europe. But the Great War, which cast only a passing blight upon the others, eclipsed for ever the brief splendours of the Latvian shore. The Baltic lands fell out of favour with the Russians, the Barons were suspected of intriguing with the enemy; for years it was discovered they had been employing German spies as their foresters, and now from being courted they were shunned.

Then began the long campaign among the swamps and forests of northern Europe . . . slowly the Russians fell back and their armies melted away; Bolshevik and German and White Russian swept over the land and devastated it. In Riga telegraph wires were pulled down; rope had run short but there were still men to hang.

Riga Strand has emerged from the terror now and there are visitors there once more, but the clients for whom the casinos and the dance halls and the rickety palaces of 1910 were built are gone for ever. Where now are her wealthy St. Petersburg patrons, where is St. Petersburg itself? Even if they wished to come, there are barbed-wire entanglements six feet high, manned by armed sentries, that can be crossed only with a stack of passports. The Japanese garden with its little bridges and artificial jungles is knee-deep in groundsel and toadstools; there are trenches still and tangles of rusty barbed wire round the sulphur springs at Kemmeri, and the fashionable specialists have no prodigal Caucasian princes to diet in their sanatoria, they have to haggle with Jewesses about mud baths and superfluous fat. The disinherited have come into their own, the Jews have descended like locusts on Riga Strand . . . for them it has the fascination of a forbidden land. Synagogues begin to oust the gleaming onion towers, and Assari, the farthest of the resorts, has almost become a Jewish village. Jewish ladies emerge with blonde curls from the hairdressers, for there are two or three *frisetavas* in every street and Lettish gentlemen prefer blondes. But the Jews have still to mind their step, for the Letts have inherited many of the prejudices of their masters; they too fear and despise the Jews, just as they themselves were despised by the Russians.

In the afternoon the sun beats down scorchingly on Riga Strand, the pine trees are too far away to lend their shade and even beneath them the sand is parched and burning. There are a few boatmen, a few bathers, some ladies stretched in deck chairs under the shady walls of a sanatorium, and in the long coarse grass between the pine woods and the sand the day-trippers lie like logs. It is so quiet that one can hear a baby crying in the next village, the hoot of a steamer on the Aar, a man knocking the sand out of his shoe upon an upturned boat. It is nearly five o'clock, and soon the bells begin to ring for tea in all the pensions and lodging houses along the beach. The sanatorium bell clangs like a fire engine, the ladies in the deck chairs clap their hands to their ears and scream at the matron, but she has been preparing the tea while they were sleeping and swings it all the harder.

After tea the beach becomes awake again, the dacha residents come out with watering cans and make puddles in the grey powder of their flower beds. The earth has forgotten how to drink and for a moment the water sits in a curved bubble on the surface or forms little pellets with the sand. In any case a garden in Latvia is an unnatural thing . . . the flowers in the dachas are tenants for the season like their owners. None of them looks permanent or settled; geraniums and petunias flush up a dizzy scarlet or purple for a month or two like a local inflammation, and die down the moment the owner and his watering can have departed. The big restaurants do not even bother about bedding plants but on a gala night, the night for instance of the firemen's ball, a cart arrives from the country piled high with branches and in half an hour the café is embedded in a luxuriant forest and flowers and shrubs have sprung up out of the dry sand. There are no gardens in the country either; sometimes someone will stick a peony or a dahlia into the grass, but if it does not look after itself, no one else will—and its life is usually a prolonged battle.

As the night falls more people stream out onto the strand, for the air is cool and the sinking sun has spilt a pink light across the shore. It is the hour for the evening stroll, and from dacha and sanatorium the same familiar figures emerge. There are three robust Finnish ladies, the wives of foresters, a German financier and a Lithuanian governess. There is an Estonian gentleman who is very popular with many different ladies in turn; he has friendly charming manners and is always beautifully dressed and carries a cane. He varies the ladies not because he is fickle but because sooner or later they each of them discover that he is stupid almost to mental deficiency. There is a Swedish lady who has come over to cure her pale small son from vomiting. She has a jealous husband who condemns her yearly to dull provincial watering places, and Riga, she thinks, is the dullest of them all. She has a new dress for every meal but her evening parties with kisses for forfeits are not well attended. She started to have English lessons from a British officer and amid shrieks of merry badinage learned "I luv you so" and "keessmequeek" and then she got bored again. All the upper classes are bored on Riga

Strand. "Ochen skoochno!" "Sehr langweilig!" "I'm bored stiff!" It is only good form to be bored.

A more independent type is the Russian lady who lives with her widowed mother in a dacha up the strand. She is severe, uncompromising. Every morning she does Catherine wheels, nude, on the beach for the good of her figure and in the afternoons she mortifies herself by giving Russian lessons to French and English officers. It is a degrading occupation for an aristocrat, and she slaps down her instructions with callous, disdainful efficiency. They want to study Bolshevik idioms and the new alphabet and she has forced herself to master even that. In the back room she stows away her lonely garrulous old mother and the Lettish husband whom she married to get out of Russia, and sometimes when she is late for a lesson, the old mother slips out and gossips with the pupils. What revelations! What merry undignified chuckles! She is delighted to have someone to talk to but suddenly she hears her terrifying daughter outside and slips back shamefacedly into her room.

There are many other Russians on Riga Strand, the remnants of the wealthy patrons of former days. All that they could save from the Revolution they have brought with them but they have no homes or estates to return to; they have to be thankful for a refuge from their own countrymen among a people they have always despised, and to get jobs in Latvia they set themselves to learning Lettish, a language they have always regarded as a servant patois. Life is very hard but they contrive often to be gay and self-confident and outrageous. They still take shortcuts across flower beds if they belong to Jews, and are condescending to Letts at tea parties. They are ingenious at finding ways to restore their self-respect.

There is also a Soviet commissar holidaying on Riga Strand, but it is unlikely that he will join the crowd that watches the sunset in the evening. He is neither gay nor sociable. Even at meals he talks to no one but gazes intently at his plate of food, frightened to look up in case he should intercept a glance of hate. He is pale with enthusiasm or undernourishment, and he obviously enjoys the fleshpots of Riga Strand.

As the evening grows colder the strand empties, and a group of boys come out of the pine woods where they have been collecting sticks and build a bonfire on the shore. The rest of the sand sinks back into the night and they are islanded in the firelight. As the flames burn higher it is easier to see their keen Jewish faces. They have not yet lost the colours of the Mediterranean, though it may be many generations since their ancestors travelled up from Palestine to the shores of the Baltic. The leaders are a woman with loose black hair and a Messianic youth of seventeen. Are they making speeches or telling stories? The eyes of twenty boys are fixed, black and burning in the firelight, on the woman as she cries passionately to them in Yiddish. Three or four boys reply to her and they sing strange, un-homely Eastern tunes. Only a few yards away are the cafés and the sanatoria, but in the darkness the sand seems to stretch away inter-minably and the Jewish scouts seem to be the only creatures alive on the shore, a nomad tribe camping in the desert. They are of the same race, the same families perhaps, as the predatory blondes in the beach costumes, but the spirit that fills them now is alien from Riga or from Europe. Persecution has hardened them and given them strength to survive war and revolution and even to profit by them and direct them. Perhaps it is they in the end who will decide the future of Riga Strand.

At last the fire dies down, the boys make ready for sleep, and once more the small, scarcely audible sounds of the waves break upon the silence.

Peter's Window

1946, 1984

No. 59 Chernishev Pereulok was a large plum-coloured block of bourgeois flats near the Yekaterinsky Sad (the Catherine Gardens), and the Archangelskys' flat was on the fifth floor. The lift had not worked since 1917 and sat in the well of the staircase, full of tram tickets and old newspapers. There was still a large gilt mirror on their landing, though all the others had been removed by the Jacht, or house committee. Darya Andreyevna, the former owner of the flat and its "responsible tenant," set great store by all these traces of former grandeur and the Jacht had yielded before her fury when the mirror was threatened.

When my wife, Peggy, and I and our friend Archie Lyall first came to Leningrad in 1931 on the *Alexei Rykov*, a tourist ship, the Archangelskys had made a special effort to welcome us. We brought news of Nikolai Mihalitch's old friends in England with whom he had had no contact since his wife, Connie, and baby son had left. They had gone home three years before, when the NEP period had given place to the rigours of the Five-Year Plan and milk and baby foods became scarce. We got the introduction to Nikolai Mihalitch through my cousin, Willy de Burgh, professor of philosophy at Reading University. Nikolai's father had been a priest in Tiflis and they had fled from the Bolsheviks to the Crimea (for a short time in White Russian hands). There, his sister had married an Englishman, an officer in the British interventionist forces whose home was in Reading. When the Bolsheviks seized the Crimea, Nikolai was sent to England and became one of the most brilliant of de Burgh's pupils. It was there that, later, he married Connie, a fellow student, and influenced by the left-wing intellectualism of the time, they became Communists and decided to join his widowed mother in Leningrad.

When we first called there were biscuits and tea with hot milk, and strawberry jam in saucers, and his mother was in a state of collapse compounded of hospitality and suspicion. Nikolai had asked a friend of his, Major Tihomirov, a teacher in the Military Academy, to meet us, and a colleague of his own, Baroness Garatinsky, was anxiously awaited. Nikolai Mihalitch had told me her story. She had been an old revolutionary, and in 1917 her peasants, who had taken over her estates in central Russia, had made her their manager. Five years later her position had become impossible and she was now teaching languages in Leningrad. Through the open window we saw her limping slowly up the street, pausing and glancing up and down to see that it was empty before she turned in. "It isn't very safe for us to visit each other," he said; "in any case she doesn't like the stairs with her lame leg, but this is a special occasion." He told me that because of her origins, she was suspect politically. She had a daughter in exile in Siberia and a son in Solovietski Island. In Goskurs, the Polytechnic where she taught, she was the victim of petty persecution. "Women are the worst," he said, and he was explaining how in Leningrad an arts education was more accessible to the female than to the male bourgeois when the baroness walked in. She paused in the doorway, leaning on her stick, and diverted with a smile his mother's effort to introduce us and give her a chair. "Later, later, Nina Gavrilovna." To us she said, "Women are allowed a bit more licence, because even here they aren't taken seriously. Masculine unreliability matters more."

She had a sharp, rather cantankerous manner but spoke English well in a beautifully clear voice. She always talked rapidly and provocatively when she was manoeuvring into chairs or difficult positions, as if to distract attention. She looked coldly into people's eyes when she talked to them. She herself had a lack of personal inquisitiveness that was almost unfriendly. It was as if she could only argue or disagree and did not waste time in liking or disliking.

Nina Gavrilovna was a crushed, dark little woman. She followed our English talk anxiously with her bright black eyes, interrupting her son with nudges and murmurs, when she could: "Kolya, ask the lady after the professor's wife's health!" "Kolya, you are talking so much you have not noticed the lady has nothing on her plate!" (Only Nikolai's mother called him Kolya, as I will for brevity, but actually everybody in the flat was very formal and used patronymics. Even his closest friends called him Nikolai Mihalitch.)

She guessed correctly that her son was being indiscreet but could never learn that it made him worse to interrupt. The baroness, seeing her agitation, said to me, "You mustn't think that because we have much to complain of, we are enemies of the Revolution. The Revolution had to happen, it was the result of generations of suffering and plotting. All the great Russians of the past have played a part in it. It is a historical fact, a great convulsion of human nature. If we are to go on living we must accept it, and I have always done so gladly."

Before we could reply Tihomirov succeeded in changing the conversation. He spoke English in the genteel, mincing way of some educated Russians. He had gold teeth and a moist, glinting smile.

As we left, Kolya said to me, "When you come back from Rostov, you must stay with me. I will get you a job teaching." He translated this to his mother, who gave a glance of agony. "But there is no bed. What will Darya Andreyevna say?" He ignored her. "I will arrange. I will get you a bed. You must stay a term."

We went down the Volga and visited Moscow and Rostov. Archie Lyall wrote a book on our experiences, *Russian Roundabout*, which became a classic for all earlier travellers by Intourist. I came back fearing that Kolya's mother would have dissuaded him from inviting me to stay on. I was wrong. We spent a few days in Leningrad before the *Rykov* sailed back, and it was plain Kolya counted on my staying. Smiling and bowing, Alexander Ivanitch Tihomirov came to our hotel and together we went to the military stores, where, under his guidance, I bought myself a camp bed for forty roubles. The next day the *Rykov* sailed. Kolya, Tihomirov and I went to the docks to see off Peggy and Archie. It was a strange departure, for there was a young woman among the passengers who had had a nervous breakdown. She had been recommended a "complete change" and she and her parents could think of nothing better than a trip to Russia. While there she had gone mad and had to be dragged aboard kicking and struggling and finally lifted up the gangway, screaming.

That afternoon I installed myself in Chernishev Pereulok. It was the name day of all the Sonias and Nadezhdas, and their friends were hurrying up and down the streets carrying bunches of overblown dahlias. A few foreigners were still bathing on the broad strand by the Peter and Paul fortress, but the melon pips, which had started to sprout by the water's rim, had been nipped by an early frost. Work-men were wrapping up the heads of delicate shrubs in the Summer Garden in balloons of paper and taking in the cactuses and coleuses which ornamented the lawns with hammers and sickles.

In the Archangelskys' flat the Jacht had sent a chimney sweep to clean the flue. Everything I saw was coloured and penetrated for me by the thought of the Revolution. Even commonplace or inevitable things had a bloom of special significance because they had matured at such a time and in such a place.

I pitched my camp bed between the stove and the window in the room where we had had our tea party in the summer. Kolya had a divan covered with drab fusty material in the opposite corner. Every-thing in the room was shabby and dark. There were large patches on the wall where his son, Misha, a couple of years before had peeled off the wallpaper and scribbled on the plaster. Over the whole flat there was that sweetish, musty smell of black bread and benzine and scent and galoshes that Russians seem to carry with them, even into exile. I felt lonely and ill at ease. Nina Gavrilovna plainly did not want me there. She refused to believe that, being foreign, I could understand anything unless she shouted at me with plentiful gestic-ulations. Her bed was in a widening of the passage, which was screened off by a dark curtain. Beyond that were two rooms where invisible factory workers lived. To the left was the room of Darya Andreyevna and her husband. In the dark passage outside our room near the front door, Lyubotchka, the Archangelskys' maid, used to sleep on her trunk. Till I had practice I stumbled over her every time I came to bed late. At the far end of the passage was the kitchen, where each tenant had his private Primus, and off that there were two windowless cupboards, the bathroom and the WC. Darya had asserted her authority in these two rooms by pinning up the pictures that decorated the flat when it had been hers, "Stags at Bay," "The Imperial Palace at Gatchina," family groups. They bulged out from their drawing pins with all the fluff and dust that had accumulated behind them. No one dared to remove them, but during the paper shortage hard-pressed tenants had torn jagged strips from them and from their cardboard mounts.

Kolya had exchanged his Russian white summer suit for a Nor-folk jacket and grey flannel trousers. Before, he was like an Italian, but now he was like a Bloomsbury Asiatic. He had a dark, thin fanatical face and abrupt, vehement movements. He did not like to explain or to have his explanations questioned.

My first day I spent alone in the flat writing letters and examining Kolya's books. They were neatly shelved on a pair of skis that he was storing for his elder brother, an engineer. I saw F. H. Bradley, Hegel, Bertrand Russell, Aldous Huxley, D. H. Lawrence. Of Russian writers he had only Lenin and his commentators.

I was interrupted constantly by the telephone. His mother would slip in and answer it, looking at me through the corners of her eyes. "*Ne doma,*" she would say bitterly. "*Ne znaioo!*" "He's not at home." "I don't know!" This happened two or three times. Then she took out her basket and went marketing, and I was left to answer the next call myself three-quarters of an hour later. It was a lady. "Where is Nikolai Mihalitch?" From my way of answering she guessed I was English and she went on in English. "Where can he be? He was due to give his lesson here half an hour ago, and I rang up Techmass, but he hadn't given his class there, and at Goskurs it was the same." I couldn't enlighten her.

At six o'clock his mother let him in and there was a voluble conversation in the passage. He came into the room without greeting me. He looked completely exhausted. "It is arranged," he said, but hearing his mother at the door he leapt up and seized a plate of overcooked vegetable marrow from her. "Isn't your mother going to eat here?" I asked. "No, it would be better not. She does not understand the English." Even when it was irrelevant, I made a point of saying I was Irish not English. I made things worse by saying once that the de Burghs were Irish too. It was as a visitor from England, where he had been so happy, that Kolya was welcoming me. For years he had been waiting for an opportunity to return the kindness which had been shown him. Even for his mother the syllables Dee Buggs had some mystic significance. He did not want to be put off by details.

"What is arranged?" I asked, when he seemed ready for a question.

"Your classes are arranged," he said. "You will have four classes every evening from eight till midnight. I've made out the list. You will be a member of our brigade. Then there is Olga Kulgachev two hours and Engineer Stavrogin three hours in a decade, and you're already fixed up with Alexander Ivanitch. They will start next week." A decade, which sounded to me an eternity, meant ten days. Brigades were groups of friends who shared out pupils or jobs between each other. There were other brigades for house decoration, theatre craft, translating and all the more specialized arts and crafts. "But did you spend all this time looking for work for me? You must have missed all your classes."

"That is of no importance."

For the next few days he once more gave up all his classes in spite of my protests, and we tramped and trammed from one end of Leningrad to the other, interviewing passport officials, professors, pupils.

One day as we were queuing up outside the offices of the Lensoviet, he tried to explain himself to me: "I am a Caucasian from Georgia, like Stalin, with the same theological background. He was a theological student. He believes like the Manichaeans that there is Good and Evil, Black and White, a dichotomy. All this which he thinks Good is Evil." He waved his hand at the Lensoviet and the long queue.

"Why do you like the English so much then? They are not Manichaean. They play down all the major issues of good and evil. They are loyal to small obligations, not big ones. I can't imagine an English teacher neglecting all his classes to help the friend of friends who were once very good to him."

He looked hurt, as if I had accused him of being un-English. But I had meant it as a compliment and I could not let the subject drop. I argued that social organization works better in England, simply because the English only made superficial impact on each other. They glide about, cannoning off each other like billiard balls. They can calculate each other's reactions accurately, because they hardly ever impinge. Perhaps the reason why the Russians are difficult to organize is because they make real contact. It's like playing billiards with bull's eyes.

"You forget I am a Caucasian. That's what I hate about the Russians, always prying and enquiring about each other."

I found his claim to be Caucasian as irritating as he found my claim to be Irish: "I don't think Russians could ever be detached in the tepid, unemphatic English way. You would merely isolate yourselves."

After a pause, he said, "Darya Andreyevna was catechizing my mother about you today. She thinks you are a spy and wants the house committee to turn you out. She has been to the Upravdom [the president of the house committee]. Lyubotchka did her best for you. She said she thought you were a harmless idiot because you smile when you talk to her."

"I only meant to be friendly."

"Yes, but real Russians only smile at jokes."

I had no way of paying for my lodgings, so I suggested that Peggy should pay Connie in Eastbourne every week. He refused indignantly. I was his guest. I accepted this but asked Peggy to send suitable things to Connie instead.

But we were to have other complications that evening. Lyubotchka, the maid, came from Karelia near Finland, where not much was known about plumbing. She had broken one of Connie's wedding-present teacups, and, fearing to admit it, had thrown it down the WC and pulled the plug. Darya Andreyevna a little later found the WC choked and, groping with her hand, discovered a piece of Connie's china. With me there without her permission, it was too much for her. Sobbing with rage, she burst through the door and flung the horrible handful on the floor.

In the fury about the teacup my problem was forgotten. Nobody ever again thought I was a spy. But after that, Darya and Kolya never went to see each other. They communicated, when they had to, by telephone. When our door was open, we could hear Darya Andreyevna's real voice through the passage wall almost as clearly as her telephone voice. Though she lived in the next room for many months, I never saw her again, nor did I ever see her husband, though we were incessantly aware of each other.

Darya's husband had been a colonel in the Tsar's army, a very tyrannical one, Kolya told me, and his wife had been an opera singer and quite famous. After the Revolution she had sung Soviet songs and had been awarded the rank of *naoochnaya rabotnitsa*, or scientific worker. Because of this she had first-category food rations and the right to a certain floor space in her old flat. In relation to the Jacht she became "the responsible tenant." With her food tickets she could get, among other things, macaroni. Nina Gavrilovna could never forgive her this. A Tsarist colonel's wife got macaroni, while her son, a Marxist professor and Privat Dozent at the Oriental Institute, had to live on vegetable marrow. Incessantly nagging Kolya about this, she had made it psychologically impossible for him ever to get a first-category food ticket. All that was necessary was for him to fill in a few forms, but nothing would induce him to do so. Whenever macaroni was mentioned, his face went dead and cold and Manichean.

Soon after this my classes began. The last tourists had disappeared from the streets and I felt like a privileged member of the audience who goes home with the actors after the play. Stacks of logs were being piled in the courtyards and back streets and one heard the whine of saws. The streets got emptier and footsteps echoed. Everyone except Kolya sealed up his double windows with gummed paper and closed the *phortochka*, the little ventilating window by which they were pierced. Everyone bought galoshes, for the pavements were like troughs and held water.

I had no winter clothes and clothing became an obsession, for my arms were too long for everything I could afford. Kolya lent me an old coat, and I wedged a pair of undersize galoshes onto my shoes. I could never get them off again, so I used to take off shoes and all at my classes and hide my feet under the desk. Later on I put my galoshes on my indoor shoes, but I had to walk sedately or the galoshes dragged them off again.

One day, as I was walking to my classes in the twilight, I saw a large leather-coated figure lying on the pavement. He had an open dispatch case beside him with papers scattered about. He was snoring. A woman came from the far side of the Moika River to help me lift him up. "What a shame," she exclaimed, "to see such a beautiful coat lying in the mud!" We examined it together. "I bet he's a commissar!" she said. "One can only get a coat like that with *valuta*." We dragged him to the Mariinski Theatre and propped him up, sitting against one of the columns of the portico. I told her I had *valuta* and needed a coat, so she took a pencil and piece of paper out of his dispatch case and wrote the name of the place where I could get one like it.

Next day I went there. There was only one possible coat but it was still too short in the sleeves. Nina Gavrilovna did not seem to like my wearing Kolya's coat, so I went back several times but could not make up my mind to spend so much money on a coat that did not fit.

Kolya had brought back from England an obsession about fresh air, and was proud that he was the only man among his acquaintances who kept his *phortochka* open day and night. Alexander Ivanitch Tihomirov told me that Max Müller had once come to Petersburg to lecture on Fresh Air but had to postpone his lecture because he had lost his voice. My experience was the same. I always woke up with a sore throat, but it was a point of honour with Kolya not to close the *phortochka*.

Kolya had two other friends who taught English, besides Tihomirov and Vera Garatinsky. Both of them, Yegunov and Lihachev, came of wealthy families who had governesses. Yegunov had had a Scottish governess whose Glasgow accents reproduced themselves in all his pupils. Lihachev was in the navy and settled in Leningrad only during the winter, when he taught at the Marine Academy. His English was the strangest and the most fluent. Onto a precise bookish English he had grafted a cosmopolitan sailor's slang derived from conversations in the lingua franca at Baltic ports. He was never at a loss for a word. We only got two roubles an hour for our classes and big deductions were made for holidays. There were also "voluntary" contributions, which were compulsory; only Kolya did not pay them, as he disapproved on principle.

Alexander Ivanitch, in those days, was a bachelor with close-cropped hair and a smart military appearance. He had been a Tsarist officer. He was courtly and considerate. He described himself to my wife as "very Victorian." But when he deplored the new ways, he did not mean Bolshevism, but fox-trots, red fingernails, James Joyce. The Revolution had been such an overwhelming experience that I doubt if he ever criticized it, even to himself. All the same, to save his self-respect, he permitted himself some tiny heresies, about women in public life, for example. In most totalitarian creeds there is an unimportant corner, like a game reserve, retained for harmless scepticism and good-humoured satire. Alexander Ivanitch knew his way about it perfectly and for some time appeared to me to be a highly emancipated person.

He had learnt English by the "Williamson Method" and used to compare his face in a looking glass with a series of enlarged coloured pictures of the mouth and tongue. He was very conscientious and wished to capture the spirit of the language as well as the idiom. In addition to the mouth pictures he had a collection of English political speeches on gramophone records. Also he recited to me once a week a leader from *The Manchester Guardian*, which as an officer in the army he was permitted to take in.

He had other military privileges regarding rations of food and clothing, which he shared generously with his friends and the two devoted old ladies who looked after him. He lived in a stuffy room above a tailor's shop. It smelt of pot plants and leather and kvass. He used to put on a record just before my lesson, so as to get his ear into training. One unseasonably warm afternoon I walked with Lihachev towards his house. The loudspeakers on the street corners, which bawled out the feats of shock workers, were silent as if exhausted by the heat, and I was astounded to hear a cultured and fruity English voice echoing unchallenged through the narrow empty street. The voice came from Alexander Ivanitch's open window; it was Mr. Asquith addressing a meeting in Edinburgh seventeen years before: "We shall not sheathe the sword," he was declaiming, "till Belgium has recovered in full measure all and more than all that she has lost, till France . . ."

"It is rare and pleasant," said Lihachev, "to hear someone praise liberty who has dined well."

Alexander Ivanitch was revising a pre-revolutionary grammar of English conversation. The questions of the new Russian tourist, instead of being inquisitive and pleasure-seeking, became didactic and uncompromising. He enquired about wages and factories instead of theatres and laundries. The rigours of his catechism were tempered by a strange jauntiness, in which Alexander Ivanitch took a special pride. "Is a sportlike way of asking the time to say 'What do you make the time?' " he enquired, "and can one use the phrase 'oneish twoish' without a preposition?"

I gave him his lessons under seal of secrecy, lest it should get about among rival teachers that he still had anything to learn. Slavs are too logical to value modesty or self-depreciation. "If you yourself," they argue, "think poorly of your faculties, they must be poor indeed."

One day he told me to be very careful what I said to Nikolai Mihalitch. He was unreliable, he explained, and indiscreet. I did not mention that Kolya had given me similar warnings about him. I gathered that Alexander Ivanitch was in touch with the GPU (the Gaypayoo was the current name in 1931 for the secret police). In the end I came to the conclusion that almost all those whom I was able to see constantly had obtained the consent of the GPU and were under obligation to report my movements. I was flattered that they liked my company enough to go to this trouble, but I am sure that Alexander Ivanitch alone attempted a conscientious record of my unmemorable sayings and doings.

He was, in fact, the ideal spy. It was a disinterested pleasure to him to gossip, and it was a bonus for him to feel patriotic. He never did us any harm. Indeed, hovering on the edge of our little group, he was a kind of insurance that we should not be molested. He liked his lessons and wished us well. He once publicly refuted a rival teacher's allegation that I had "a terrible Irish accent."

Kolya had made out the curriculum for English literature in Techmass and Goskurs. It was very impressive. Every English writer who had written anything vaguely subversive was included. There were Kingsley's *Alton Locke*, Mrs. Gaskell's *Mary Barton*, Charlotte Brontë's *Shirley*. Were these about the industrial revolution perhaps? But why Virginia Woolf, Aldous Huxley and E. M. Forster? Copies of the list were typed and I handed them round to my classes and asked them to bring what books they could. About twelve books came: some Byrons, Wildes, Galsworthys, and a book, author unknown, called *A Fairy Sits upon My Knee*. A little Jewess, who, I had been told, was a political spy, brought in and insisted on reading a book by Mildred Cram about a man who marries above himself in London society and does not know that you have to eat asparagus with your fingers. His wife tries to stifle the artistic side of his nature and eventually he flings it all up and returns to his old simple life. No other books could be found. As a result, most classes had to be improvised, and though my pupils were friendly and interested, there was no interval between the four classes, so by midnight I was often nearly speechless from exhaustion.

That winter the fortieth anniversary of Gorki's "creative work" was being celebrated. Nizhni Novgorod was being rechristened Gorki, and a bombing aeroplane had been dedicated to him. Though we never talked of politics, we sometimes discussed "ideology." A woman said that Gorki was "a gumanist" (our "h" is "g" in Russian) and that a bombing aeroplane would not please him much. I asked them to define "gumanism." A man said in English, "It is what you say 'namby-pamby.'" The woman was not satisfied and began to protest. It appeared that about half the class thought namby-pambiness a good thing, but the political spy, a kind of woman who did not want trouble, proposed we go on with Mildred Cram.

The classes were orderly and well arranged, the rooms clean and airy. The principal of Goskurs had once been director of the Imperial Ballet and all his staff except two or three were bourgeois who had learned foreign languages from governesses and tutors. At the doorway sat the political director, an Armenian called Guzelimian. Every time I passed he examined me fiercely, as if he wished to catechize me; he had a villainous peasant face and I hurried on pretending not to notice him. One day when we were alone in the hall he beckoned me over. "When you go to England," he said, "will you get me a fishing rod?" Fumbling with his papers, he took out a picture. "Like that. I wanted to talk to you several times, but you looked so stiff I didn't dare."

The other teachers didn't talk to me but I felt an atmosphere of friendliness and goodwill. Once, when a long corridor was empty, an elderly man who had never spoken to me came up and presented me with a book. "This is my book," he said. "Don't tell anyone." He bolted before I had time to thank him. Whenever I passed him later, he pretended not to see me.

The small blue volume was an excellent Russian-English dictionary by C. K. Bojanus and V. K. Muller. Later Kolya told me that he was Professor Bojanus himself, that he intended to marry Mrs. Williamson of the mouth pictures and go with her to England, but did not want to prejudice his chances of leaving Russia by any association with foreigners.

Edmund Wilson* wrote that Bojanus was liquidated and his name taken off the title page of the dictionary, but the verb *sostavili*, "composed," was left in the plural though Muller is named as sole author. I had previously heard that he escaped and worked at the School of Slavonic Studies till he died. I reproach myself that I never enquired about this kind, good man, or sent the fishing rod to Guzelimian.

Nina Gavrilovna was against me from the start and decided that I was to blame for anything that went wrong in the flat. In Moscow I had been given a sixteenth-century icon of John the Baptist by Leonid Leonov, whose book *The Thief* I had translated, and one day I showed it to Kolya, who promptly hung it on the wall. His mother, seeing it when Kolya was out, was appalled. "What will his pupils say? It's pearls before swine." She laid the icon reverently in the laundry basket. When Kolya came back and saw the gap on the wall he marched unerringly to the laundry basket. The icon came in and out of the basket several times. Then I said to Kolya, "I'm a nuisance here. I'd better find a room elsewhere."

He flared up, "Are you not comfortable here? No one would have you except me; they would be frightened even if they had room. And at the hotel you would have to pay two pounds a day. My mother will be going to Luga soon. At the New Year I will arrange that we take a few days' holiday and go on an excursion with Lihachev and Yegunov to the South. I will arrange to get teachers' tickets."

All the same I put several advertisements in the papers and got some replies. I went round to the addresses. Nobody wanted to be paid. In fact money meant very little in Leningrad; they lost all interest in me when they heard I was not a foreign engineer paid in

*In *The New Yorker*, 20 April 1963.

valuta and entitled to meal tickets at Quisisana, the Insnab restaurant ("Insnab" meant Inostranni Snabzheniye, or Foreign Provision). One woman thought that as a foreign engineer I would be able to get her coat lined at Torgsin. One letter I did not answer. It was from a Pole called Vaishlé, who offered me a bed in his living room. His aunt used it in the daytime but she worked in the post office at night. It would be empty then and I could use it free if I would help him read an English book on geology. One day when I came back from giving Alexander Ivanitch his lesson, I found Kolya entertaining the Pole, a small, fat jolly man. He had brought his lunch and his geology book under his arm. "I thought you might be too shy to come, so I came instead." I was relieved to find that in the last resort there was someone in Leningrad eager to house me, and I offered to read some geology with him then and there. As he left, he said, "I'm in this neighbourhood once or twice a week. I'll just call round and we'll read a bit of geology and I promise to keep my aunt's bed free for you."

I agreed to this arrangement as a sort of retaining fee, and every now and then he came round. He always brought his lunch, but sometimes he came without his geology book just for a talk. Being a Pole, he was the first person I met willing to admit that I was an Irishman. He was greatly interested and told me that Daniel O'Connell's great-granddaughter was working in a large china factory on the Neva. He seemed to take it for granted at his first glance at my surroundings that for an Irishman to live in a Russian family was a chemical experiment that might or might not succeed. "How are things going?" he would ask. "Remember, my aunt's bed is always free." Once, as he left, he clasped my hand and said, "You know, Russians are Asiatics, they don't understand comfort. I advise you to come to us."

I had some £25 worth of black roubles, given me by an English sociologist who was staying at the British Embassy. He was going home and no longer needed them. So often I would ask Kolya out to lunch at one of the tourist hotels. After the season the fare was always the same. We had only one course. At the Europa there was a rich-looking pâté made of game in aspic, at the October a fish called *sudak* with sauce tartare. Except for ourselves and one waiter, the large dining rooms were usually empty. The restaurant at the October was below street level and beggars would crouch on the road outside and stretch in supplicating hands through the ventilators. Kolya came reluctantly or else refused. He was very proud. When I pressed him into coming, in order to show that he had not refused from fear of being compromised, he would talk loudly in English criticizing the Soviet regime. I think he was flattered when one day an old woman came up to us outside the October and said, "*Messieurs, votre roi est le cousin de notre empereur.*" He gave her a few kopecks. The old woman looked at them for a moment in hurt perplexity and then stuffed them quickly in her skirt.

In the end I believe it was the Pole and not hunger that prevailed upon Kolya to apply for a first-category food ticket. Though I was the cause of so much trouble, he wanted me to stay. He said one evening, "I am becoming a *naoochny rabotnik*. I have arranged that tomorrow there will be a proper English breakfast. There will be porridge and scrambled eggs." And next morning Lyubotchka produced a thin custardy substance and *grechnevaya kasha*, a sort of gruel made of buckwheat. The buckwheat lasted only a week, for, learning that Kolya was a *naoochny rabotnik*, Nadya, one of Kolya's predatory relations, made a claim on it. "There will be just scrambled eggs," he said, "but that will be a change, which is always nice." "Yes," I agreed, "but next time couldn't Nadya have the change and let us have the buckwheat?"

But he was totally indifferent to food. Once he gave up his sugar ration for a whole month so that he could buy the works of Dorothy Wordsworth, of which a consignment had reached Leningrad.

One day the first snow came and the waters in the canals moved turbidly below a film of ice. Lihachev, who had been in Armenia, was back and we talked of going to ski at Pavlovsk. Everybody became cheerful and excited, the streets were gay and sparkling, and tiny children, so tightly buttoned into leather coats called *shubas* that they looked like small sheep, pulled each other about in packing cases in the Yekaterinsky Sad. Once or twice a week we had free evenings and there were theatres and ballets and impromptu parties.

I was the only one who could buy at Torgsin, the foreign currency shop, but my black roubles were running out, so I seldom went there or to the hotels. But for our parties I got bottles of sweet Caucasian wine. I had a pupil behind the counter who helped me dodge the queues. In the markets there was always plenty of bread, and different delicacies swept over the city in waves; honey or cheese or stiff black cranberry jam crowded the shops for a few weeks and then disappeared in a night as quickly as they had come. Instead came sock suspenders or celluloid toothbrush cases and, in the window, a red cloth with a bust of Lenin on it. There were no containers for the honey and Kolya in his English mood refused to carry his jug in his hand down the Nevsky. Inevitably, Nina Gavrilovna blamed it on me that everything in his attaché case, books and lecture notes, was covered in honey.

Baroness Garatinsky came back from a visit to her son, who was imprisoned in Solovietski Island; every day for five minutes she had been allowed with all the other visitors into a long corridor, where behind an iron railing their relations were waiting to see them. So as to be heard, each tried to talk louder than his neighbour and, when it was impossible, they had to communicate by gestures. "I felt we had stopped being human and become monkeys. Perhaps we have always been monkeys."

Lihachev usually came with Yegunov, who taught English with him at the Marine Academy. He was a Greek scholar and had translated *Aethiopika*, a third-century Alexandrian novel by Heliodorus. As far as I could judge, Yegunov's translation and its ninety-page introduction would have brought him distinction in England. He was now translating Plato's *Timaeus*, also for the Academia Press, but hesitated to publish it. "Two friends of mine," he explained, "were overheard at a party setting Plato above Karl Marx and they were banished from Leningrad." "Don't risk it then," I said. "Well, it was not so bad for them," he answered doubtfully, "they were unemployed stage managers and they were sent to Orel, where, as it happened, they got jobs straightaway in a new theatre. They sneak back to Leningrad, when they can. But I could not bear to leave Leningrad." For though Leningrad is the least typical of Russian cities, its citizens love it as Parisians love Paris. They are unhappy away from its grave and charming avenues and gardens, its cold northern sunsets.

Yegunov had tuberculosis. Peter the Great built his city on a marsh for wealthy aristocrats with fur coats and servants with warming pans and stoves, or else for tough muzhiks who would warm themselves with labour and vodka. A generation ago the remnants of a well-to-do bourgeoisie lived there without fuel or fur coats to interpose between themselves and the raw and foggy winters. How could they not get tuberculosis?

Lihachev was always cheerful. His father had been a wealthy doctor who, at the outbreak of the Revolution, had invited all his relations and friends to share his two-storied house so that they need not have strangers forced on them. They had brought all their most cherished furniture with them. Two uncles had been in the consular service in Africa and had crammed the rooms with bamboo and bark and bronze and stamped leather. He told me that when they had all in the old days lived in different parts of Petrograd, they travelled long distances to quarrel with each other. "Now it's so easy, there's no sport in it."

One day in October we were eating raw herring and scrambled eggs, and having the last drop of the brandy flask I had brought from Ireland, when the telephone rang. It was a girl, in the flat above. She said she was a pupil of Kolya's at the Oriental Institute, and as they were having a party and were short of "cavaliers," would we come up and join them? Kolya said he had friends with him. "Well, bring them all," she said, so we all trooped upstairs.

The girl opened the door herself, but when she let go the door handle she slipped backwards and would have fallen if she had not clutched at Kolya. A girlfriend beside her was scarcely steadier on her feet, and when at last we got into the room, we saw the reason. It was an infinitely more luxurious flat than ours, with pre-revolutionary candelabras, family portraits and wall hangings, and a long table heaped with grapes and pineapples, every variety of wine and liqueur and plates full of appetizing food. There were men in morning coats and ladies in evening dress. It was astonishing to come from our bleak, dark and damp quarters and to discover so much light and luxury a few feet above us, and in a room the same size and shape as ours. Half dazed, I flopped into a chair beside a plump lady with enormous earrings, who poured me out some curaçao and talked to me in faultless English about Ilfracombe. Then someone told me it was a wedding, and the bridegroom came and asked me very pleasantly to bring up my curaçao and come to dance in the next room. It was very small and corresponded to one of the factory workers' rooms down below. Lihachev was fox-trotting in the tiny floor and I found a partner and joined him. It was hot and uncomfortable and I sensed that something was wrong, but I could not tell what or why. Suddenly I discovered that the tension, which I had detected, was emanating in dense waves from Kolya, who sat scowling on a sofa beside Yegunov. My partner suggested that we should stop and sample some of the delicious food and I gratefully agreed. Then I saw Kolya talking in a very haughty way to a lady, who I assumed to be the hostess and who looked embarrassed. All at once he got up and swept us along with him in a puzzled, disapproving crocodile, making it difficult for us to say any thank-yous or good-byes.

It was not until I got downstairs that I understood what had happened. The two girls, the bride and her friend, both of them Kolya's pupils and both drunk, had dared each other to ask their romantic-looking teacher to the wedding party. Brimful of hospitality and alcohol, the bride had chortled excitedly down the telephone without thinking of consulting her mama. She must have been appalled when, instead of the glittering cavaliers she expected, four frowsy intellectuals in shabby suits turned up. Lihachev was the best of us because he was still in his naval uniform. But the bride's mother, a dignified lady with grey hair, came up to Kolya and explained that there had been "a little misunderstanding": "We're not the sort of people, you know, who just ask anyone to our family functions." Kolya had snapped back loudly that it was no pleasure for him to come but the bride had been so pressing on the telephone. A stunned silence of embarrassment fell on the wedding party for two minutes and then was skilfully dispelled by a tornado of convivial noises as we trooped away down the stairs.

Once or twice my pupils invited me to birthday parties. They were mostly easy and pleasant and uneventful. Why does one remember the embarrassing occasions best? There was Olga N. and her mother, bourgeois, still only half adjusted to the new regime. Kolya and I arrived at her birthday party with a cake I had chosen with care at Torgsin, covered with crystallized cherries, and I was disappointed when Olga, not looking at it, grandly told the maid to put it with a pile of other unopened presents on the piano. She was a prize pupil of mine and prattled away in a low, quiet, self-important voice in very literary English. When we came in, the mother was saying, "Oh dear, not enough teaspoons! Where can the wretched girl have put the spoons?" Olga then said to the company in English: "My Mother had formerly four dozen teaspoons, but she was forced to sell three dozen. She is very old-fashioned and now greatly regrets the deprivation and cannot reconcile herself to the loss. Consequently she resorts to little subterfuges such as you have just heard." She herself was worried about the buttons on her blouse. The little red ornaments on them were wearing out, but, because they were enamel, couldn't be painted in, so she was getting a friend, a chemical engineer, to help. He was first of all going to scoop out the centres, and then . . .

These are the things we talked about in Leningrad in 1931: spoons, buttons, macaroni, galoshes, macaroni again. I don't believe I ever heard anyone mention Magnetogorsk or the liquidation of the kulaks or any of the remote and monstrous contemporary happenings to which by a complicated chain of causes our lifestyle and our macaroni were linked.

Communism is said to inspire a dull uniformity, but Lihachev, who was quite unpolitical, was always seeking and finding coloured variations. In his rooms I met Negro Communists and Turks, Tartars and Kirghiz, and one day he took me to the Hispano-American Society. It was held in the room of a Mexican Communist, a lady, who dreaded the Russian winter. In the autumn she had shut herself and her family into her room and sealed up the large double window and the *phortochka*, and then fought the domestic and personal smells with powerful scents. It was not yet midwinter, but it was plain to all the battle had been lost. Lilies and jasmine had been routed by an appalling primaeval smell that was neither Slav nor Latin. Lihachev said it was Aztec. The lady introduced me to a celebrated Mexican writer, but talking meant breathing, and I appeared to him to be dumb, and he went over to Lihachev. For Lihachev, as I heard long afterwards, it proved to be a disastrous meeting. The Mexican was charmed with him, and when he went home he sent his book on Communism for Lihachev to review. Unfortunately the book had Trotskyite tendencies and he was compromised by receiving it. He was dismissed from the navy and he became a literary freelance compiling anthologies of foreign poetry, always lively and occupied. In a large new sombrero, he visited all the Leningrad publishing houses and got contracts.

That was the last I heard of him, but before I left Leningrad Vera Garatinsky had told me that in a couple of years there would be enough English-speaking proletarians to replace all the bourgeois teachers and guides and translators. "That will be the end of us," she said. "It's that accursed English woman and her method. Don't let them invent any more clever methods over there, please."

My way to Goskurs lay along the Moika, the little river that ran from the Winter Palace under the Nevsky and the Vosnesensky to the Neva. It had been a very aristocratic district once. On the far side, in a pale green eighteenth-century house, Pushkin had lived and had died painfully after a fatal duel. The quays and surrounding streets were almost deserted in the winter evenings, and very quiet except for my galoshes slapping loosely on the pavements. In the marsh air the northern sunset quivered from time to time as if it was trapped between the beautiful impassive houses. In the daytime the red proletarian trimmings held the eye and the mind, but in the twilight different obsessions replaced them.

Before I went to Russia, I had been reading Dostoievsky's *The Idiot*. It is the story of passionate people pursuing each other through the streets of St. Petersburg, with love, with hate, with revolvers or bundles of roubles. Their feelings and their motives are often obscure, and Dostoievsky, standing outside his own creations, suggests different explanations of their behaviour. Through this, his characters have the freshness of reality, for mostly we only guess at other people's minds. Prince Muishkin, the Idiot, is the still centre of the hurricane, the personification of Dostoievsky's belief that "the Russian heart is more adapted to universal brotherly friendship than that of any other nation." And indeed perhaps the Russians are more perceptive and, when it is in their power, more ready than others to make allowances for the failures they perceive. The first people to give Prince Muishkin hospitality, when he arrives poor and shabby in St. Petersburg, are the Epanchins, who live in a large house on the broad bustling Sadovaya, where I caught the tram for my classes. Muishkin is at peace with himself and this, despite his simplicity, gives him a strange authority over others. To Dostoievsky he was the symbol of Russia's unconscious, unexercised power.

I do not believe that the creations of genius die without issue or that, because of a change of government, cities start to breed a different type of man. They dress differently and feed differently, and that is all.

Great writers interpret men to each other by example and analogy. The creative imagination ebbs and flows with some degree of constancy. On the one hand all men have common needs, passions, hopes, which society has to satisfy; on the other hand every man is unique and he must so manipulate society that his nature is fulfilled. The great Russian writers, Tolstoy, Dostoievsky, Chekhov, were almost always more conscious of diversity of temperament than of uniformity of needs. Then Karl Marx and the Revolution created the Economic Man, and while this wonderfully lifelike dummy is in the shopwindow, what hope is there for the genius that is kindled by human diversity? The fact that there are vast editions of the classics published and sold out keeps the flame alive but cannot fan it.

I once tried to talk about these things at Goskurs during the dangerous half-hour of free conversation, when my pupils and I, under cover of grammar, tried to find out what we were like. One of them helped me out with a cliché, "ghosts of the past," which quenched what I had to say, and instead I said that Petersburg, like Alexandria and Constantinople, had the tremendous toughness of cities that were built round an idea, not a market. Peter's "window upon Europe" had been made for autocrats and bureaucrats, but once opened it could not be shut. Marx came through as well as Dickens and Byron and George Sand and Henry George and all the strange assortment of foreign influences. Tolstoy, no less than Dostoievsky the Slavophile, had hated Petersburg and its Western culture, as the oyster hates the foreign body it turns into a pearl, but they could not ignore it. And what they had accepted and adorned, their successors could still less ignore.

The weather was getting foggy. Most Russians had sealed up their windows, but whenever I shut the *phortochka* Kolya opened it again. Fresh air was one of his cherished English traditions about which he was very sensitive. His love of England was a substitute for religion, and I knew that his welcome to me derived from it. There was a legend in Techmass about his "English reserve," but in fact there was nothing English about it. He was normally impetuous and enthusiastic but in his English mood he alternated between a cold animal torpor and a passionate misanthropy. "English dissent and socialism," I said, "are based on an accidental tepidity or, if you like, sobriety of temperament. Your emotional heterodoxy is something quite different." I would not have risked saying this but my cold was getting worse and I was scared of getting stranded in Leningrad with bronchitis. The next time I shut the *phortochka* he looked stern but left it shut.

Once, when I was sitting over my *sudak* in the October, an Oxford acquaintance, John Lane-Tuckey, and his wife, a sleek, self-satisfied university couple, came by. They were tired of crèches and clinics and wanted to see "real Russians." It seemed obvious to ask them back and Kolya was pleased. But the moment they came into the room I saw it was a mistake. John asked light ironical questions about Soviet economics—he was a sociologist. Barbara, his wife, was silent, clearly horrified by the squalor of the flat. Something in their manner and appearance turned Kolya into a pillar of Marxist orthodoxy. His open friendliness dropped and he talked to them as if he was giving copy to journalists. I took them back to their hotel. "But you can't go on living there," Barbara Lane-Tuckey said, "the smell, the dark!" She was kind and worried and pressed on me what they'd brought from England and no longer needed, a packet of lump sugar, three lemons and a bottle of hydrogen peroxide to gargle. I felt un-settled, like a child at school who has had a visit from home. I tried to come back into the flat as if it was for the first time, so as to experience what they had seen and smelt. Yes, it was unbelievable. I shut up the provisions in my trunk. Neither of us referred to the Lane-Tuckeys again.

Kolya had appalling moments of self-criticism. Soon after this he stayed up a whole night reading *A Passage to India*. Closing the book at breakfast time, he said, "I'm like Aziz. I'm an Asiatic." He was sombre the entire day, but he felt he had given himself away too much, for a little later he started to refer to Lyubotchka as "the maid" and to give her lessons in waiting at table. She was always terrified of him when he was being English. He instructed her in a cool, bitter, military voice: "All over again till you get it right, please." Lyubotchka reacted as if to electric shocks. She started to jerk and dart about like a rabbit, her eyes glazed with fear. Eating, which she had done all her life, suddenly became black magic.

When I found someone had been rummaging in my suitcase, I kept count of the lumps of sugar and chocolate, and found two or three pieces disappeared every day. They were precious as gold to me in case I got ill and couldn't go out to buy food. Nina Gavrilovna used to do all their shopping in the market, and if I asked her to go to Torgsin, the foreign currency shop, people might think she had been receiving *valuta* from abroad or hoarding jewellery.

One day a golden-haired cousin of Kolya's called, all charm and friendliness, but Kolya was nervous and abrupt. He obviously wanted her to go, but she stayed on. At last she turned to me and said, "I wonder if—?" Kolya shot up into the air and came between us, clenching his fists: "No, that I forbid you to ask him! That you shall not ask! No!" She shrugged her shoulders and left, followed by Kolya raging. The hall door slammed. After a bit the girl came back with a bottle in her hand. "I wanted to ask you if I could have a drop of peroxide for my hair?"

When Kolya came back I told him that she was welcome to my peroxide but I thought Lyubotchka was stealing things out of my trunk. He became very solemn: "The matter must be brought before the house committee." That evening the curtain flapped ceaselessly over his mother's recess. The murmur of conversation never ceased. When Kolya went out, she emerged and asked me if I wasn't ashamed, a greedy foreigner who cheated on the currency and had fine meals in the Europa, to count lumps of sugar and persecute a poor servant girl? And I had lemons in my trunk too, and chocolate.

"How did you know I had lemons in my trunk?" I couldn't stop myself asking. Oh, she crowed, she'd been digging in my trunk, had she? What would Kolya say when he heard I accused his mother of being a thief? This I could not answer. My Russian was not good enough for me to pick my way through the tangle of misunderstandings. "And Kolya has given up his translating in order to show you the way round Leningrad. You don't even pay for your lodgings."

I tried to explain the arrangement Kolya and I had come to, adding, "Perhaps he didn't fully understand?"

"So he didn't understand? He can't understand English, can he? He speaks it as well as you do, if not better. That'll be news to him he can't speak English." And then she produced her trump card. "If the GPU knew you have black roubles . . . Russians have been shot for less!"

At this moment the Pole came to the door. He was very apologetic for interrupting and sincerely anxious that we go on with our quarrel and not mind him. Nina Gavrilovna went out and he produced a slip of paper and explained to me how many weeks I had earned by my translations to use his aunt's bed. But chiefly he had come to ask me to a party. He gave a ceremonious bow. It was for the Fifteenth Anniversary of the Revolution; it was going to be a very special party. I accepted and he told me I would get a formal invitation in a day or two. I had an almost permanent cold now and I kept on wondering what would happen if either the aunt or I got ill. I wished I had paid more attention to the conducted tours round infirmaries and hospitals.

When Kolya came home that night, his mother drew him behind her curtain. Then I heard him leave. He did not come back that night or the following morning. Then the telephone started to ring as it had the first day I spent in Chernishev Pereulok, and I answered the pupils as his mother had done, "*Ne doma. Ne znaioo.*"

He came back in the evening. "I can't stay in the house with you any longer," he said. "I'm going to Lihachev's." He began to pack a suitcase.

"If you think I'm to blame, I'll go."

"You've nowhere to go."

"I'll find somewhere!" I jumped up and put on my coat and hat and, seizing my suitcase, walked out of the room.

Kolya was out of his mind. "That's my coat," he said. "I can't trust you to bring it back. You must leave your suitcase behind instead."

I threw the suitcase down and flung the coat at him too, in a rage. When I was halfway down the stairs, the door of the flat opened and his mother came running after me. "Come back," she said, "he just lost his temper. He hasn't had anything to eat all day."

"No, I won't come back."

"Please come back. If the GPU hears that Kolya turned you out, he'll get into trouble."

"They won't hear."

It was not until I was in the street that I realized I had left my passport in Kolya's coat, but nothing would have induced me to return.

Leningrad was very badly lit in the evenings and the directions hard to follow, as the new street names were usually too long to use. The Nevsky, for example, was never called its proper name, October Twenty-fifth Street. At so late an hour I hesitated to go to Yegunov, who lived nearby. He had a single room in a vast tenement house, honeycombed with arches and passages, the entries blocked with stacks of firewood and stinking rubbish heaps, and every arch and entry looked alike. The Pole's house was in the outskirts of the city in the Narva district, and I knew I would never find it.

There was a thin coat of snow in the Nevsky that flung back the light of the lamps. All the passersby had on *shubas*, except for a few beggars in the archways and the old general standing as always with his tray of transfers and celluloid toothbrush cases outside the Moscow Station. Yet in spite of the snow I was so angry and excited I did not feel cold. I walked up and down the Nevsky enquiring at all the hotels, big and small. They would none of them take me. They were full up with delegates from the provinces for the Fifteenth Anniversary. In any case, as I was registered in a private house, I would have first to get my registration cancelled at the police station, and that had closed three hours earlier. At the Gostiny Dvor, the big shopping centre between the Nevsky and the Sadovaya, I ate some piroshkis, hot cabbage pies, at a stall. There were lights in the Kazan Cathedral, where the finishing touches were being put to a historical exhibition, and outside workmen on scaffolding were nailing up strips of red cloth for the celebrations. Some others were sitting round a brazier eating food out of parcels.

Opposite the Kazan Cathedral was the British Consulate. Mr. Bullard, whom I knew, got his food from a London shop. He had deep armchairs and a roaring fire. Several times I had dropped in for a chat and a cup of tea and Huntley and Palmer chocolate biscuits.

He was friendly but did not approve, any more than the Russians did, of fraternization. Kolya told me that he had tried to take Connie Archangelsky's passport from her because she was married to a Russian. Rumour said that there was always someone lurking by the cathedral steps making a note of his visitors. He had good manners and would be able to dissemble his satisfaction at seeing somebody paid out for staying in a Russian family. He himself only met official Russians and had to go to Finland to get Russian lessons.

I could easily persuade myself that I had an official claim on him, but I loathed going to him, as I would to the GPU. I thought I had the courage and skill to treat most human problems as personal ones, but the moment I appealed to authority to help me out I was like a man on a tightrope who thinks of falling. Could I convince myself that the consul was a friend as well as an official? I hesitated and all at once the light went out in the consulate. My mind was made up.

I rang the bell on the first landing, but there was no answer. I rang again and knocked. After half an hour of waiting I came down into the street. I walked on towards the Admiralty and, sweeping aside by St. Isaac's, I tried the Astoria and finally ended up on the Neva. It was no good. When I got back to the Kazan Cathedral I was shivering with cold and the workmen round the brazier whom I intended to ask for a night's lodgings had gone. I walked back to the consulate and banged at all the doors in the building. Bullard emerged from one of them. "You were knocking at the offices, which closed at four," he explained. "The private part of the house is on this side."

I had no self-reproaches as I got into bed, for I was persuaded that I was going to be desperately ill.

The next morning I woke up feeling remarkably well. I had an English breakfast with eggs and bacon, marmalade and toast and coffee. Afterwards I went out and bought the commissar's coat with the short sleeves. The sun was shining. The palaces on the canals, freshly colour-washed in buff or pink, were framed in snow and draped with broad red banners. I felt wonderfully detached from it all. The palaces wore their banners with the patient suffering look of domestic pets wearing bows for a birthday party. About everything there was an impromptu, impermanent and almost innocent look.

It was with a feeling of insolent well-being that I returned to Chernishev Pereulok. After I had rung the bell I felt ashamed of my new coat and folded it into a bundle. Kolya was in bed. We were polite and constrained. He handed me a postcard from Vaishlé, the Pole. "Gubert Georgievitch. Congratulations on the Fifteenth Anniversary of Socialist Construction and the termination of the fourth year of the Five-Year Plan! I also invite you to my house for the latter half of tomorrow, the first day of the holidays."

The kitchen was full of smoke, for everybody in the flat was having a bath for the anniversary. No one trusted the cleanliness of the bath itself but put a stool inside and balanced a basin of hot water on the stool. Darya Andreyevna even placed in it a trough for her feet. I used to prefer to wash in the communal baths, where there was constant hot water and elderly people lashed themselves with birch twigs.

Darya Andreyevna was going to lead the procession for the theatre. Kolya was marching for the Oriental Institute. The director of Techmass had rung up to find if I would march with them, but I had been out and did not know where to meet them. Kolya, instead of being flippant as he usually was about processions, was important and treated me as if I was Lane-Tuckey. I would never be forgiven that night at the consulate. As we went out he made a stately, unfriendly apology. He had been in a Manichaean mood, he said. He insisted that I should come back that night. I agreed I would and said that I would see that his wife, Connie, in Eastbourne would get the same rent that he had to pay when he worked for the Soviet Embassy and lived in Torrington Square, but I said I must have the *phortochka* shut. We discussed the matter in a business-like way, as if Chernishev Pereulok was in fact a Bloomsbury lodging house.

As we were going down the stairs we met the Pole coming up. He had a big peony in his buttonhole with slogans stamped in gold on each petal. "I came to see if you had got my invitation," he said. "Yes, and I'm coming." "Good! And I brought you this."

It was another letter. Handing it to me, he bolted down the stairs and disappeared. When I unstuck it, a packet of roubles tumbled out with a note: "Lent for an indefinite period, in case you are short for the celebration of the Fifteenth Anniversary of Socialist Construction." I went to Torgsin and bought some bottles of wine to take to the party.

It was difficult pressing my way through the crowds in the Nevsky and, at the corner of the Sadovaya, I was brought to a halt by a fresh tributary coming in from the Neva docks and the English Quay. I had to wait there wedged against a parapet for several hours. I was told that a million men and women passed along the Nevsky that day. In each group of this endless procession two men on either flank held up a flapping red streamer with a slogan on it, or grotesque figures of European statesmen. It was fully an hour before the students' and teachers' procession passed. I wanted to see if there was anyone I knew, and how they were affected by this performance. Organized in processions, those whom we have known as complex individuals shed colour and character. Also there is some unconscious taboo that we violate every time we look at our friends in their public moments, which are often the moments of deepest privacy. The violation may be easy and pleasant, but it delays us for that split second between perceiving and observing. Kolya passed close by but not till he had gone did I realize that I had seen him. A column of sailors went by and I looked in vain for Lihachev. A little later I noticed a dislocation in the procession, people moderating their step behind and on either side of the baroness. She walked slowly enough for me to watch her. Her companions on either side, keeping step, held a pole from which a banner was stretched: WE ARE MARCHING TO-WARDS THE CONQUEST OF TECHNICAL EFFICIENCY IN A SOCIALIST WORLD. She did not look either ironical or embarrassed. It was as if she was half asleep but sufficiently awake to enjoy her dream. She did not seem conscious of her lameness, imposing her pace with confidence on those around her.

I have thought that just as half our physical lives passes in sleep, it is perhaps intended that our mental life should be equally distributed between the assertion of our uniqueness and its renunciation. If that trance-like state of submersion in a public or collective mood bears an analogy to sleep, it would reflect our individual and self-centred lives by very simple images and phrases in dream-like sequences. In such a way, the caricatures and slogans that floated above them would complement, like dreams, the intricate, logical natures of Kolya and the baroness. The slogans were the shadows of human thinking in which their thoughts merged restfully, just as their footsteps concurred in the broad beaten track upon the snow, and we do not expect faithfulness in tone or form or colour from shadows.

All I remember of the Pole's party is the food and a tall, thin guest with a bald head, a geologist like Vaishlé. As he shook hands, he said, "I am bald and thin because I think very much; my Polish friend is round and jolly because he never thinks. I have been prospecting in Turkestan and I will show you some photographs. Later still I will recite you some poems of the French poet Béranger." All happened as he predicted. As for the food, there were *golubtsi* (mince and rice wrapped in cabbage leaves and fried), hard cakes covered with stewed apple, soft cakes covered with poppy seeds, glasses of vodka mixed with lemonade and chilies. I saw the aunt and her bed, but I had decided to leave Russia, and the desperate significance they would have had for me a week before was no longer there.

The last few weeks before the schools closed I spent at Chernishev Pereulok. Kolya submerged himself in his translation of Lenin and began to take his Communism and his professional functions much more seriously. I was a foreign critic now, not a friend, and he would step coldly from argument to argument, like rungs on a ladder. His English obsession only flared up now and again, as when every Saturday he laid a neat bill on my bed for me to forward to my wife. Several times we made up parties to Sestroretsk or Pavlovsk or Gatchina. He was never unfriendly but he had become a different person, conscientious, informative and rather dull. He provoked in me all the qualities I had detested in the Lane-Tuckeys.

I took many solitary walks under the lovely alleys of lime and maple round Leningrad. Lihachev was away but sometimes Yegunov came with me. He had a big dog which was in the stud book and therefore had a ration book of its own and despite the rigours of the Five-Year Plan ate more than its master. We usually exercised it in the Kamenny Ostrov, the island in the Neva, where the wealthy merchant families, whose houses are now rest homes and hospitals, once lived. It was crisscrossed by little birch-lined canals and bridges. Sometimes I went with one or two of my pupils to the Yussupov Palace, to which as a teacher I had access. It was a Students Recreation Centre, with rooms for chess and cards and billiards. It had also a small theatre. Down in the basement in the winter of 1916 Rasputin, who was hard to kill, was beaten to death by Prince Yussupov and his companions. The vast china chandelier in the hall surely dated from those days. There were robins and canaries perched on its branches, which dripped with blue convolvulus.

For my last evening Kolya decided to have a party and, setting enough money aside for my droshki to the station, I gave him the remainder of my roubles. I was pleased when he said, "I will arrange it all," and then spent more than half on smoked fish, a favourite delicacy of his. It was like a return to ordinary humanity. Lihachev was back home again and when our guests had gone in the early morning, he and Yegunov spread their *shubas* on the floor and slept on them. My train left very early, so I did not bother to sleep. Kolya and I left without rousing the others.

At the station, the Pole and Guzelimian and Tihomirov and two of my pupils were waiting. The Pole gave me a box of liqueur chocolates, Guzelimian asked me to remember his fishing rod. Then there suddenly flashed into my mind, "My blue carriage rug!" I exclaimed aloud, and promptly Kolya said, "I'll fetch it!" and darted away. I shouted after him, "For God's sake keep it!" but I paused for one greedy moment before I said this and I was too late. The blue rug, which I had brought from Ireland, had stood between me and pneumonia; now it meant nothing to me, but it could have meant a great deal to the Archangelskys. They got it in the end, but how ungraciously.

I kept looking at the station entrance while the others were talking, because I was wondering how I could keep in touch with my Russian friends. Would it be safe to write letters to each other? Could we send newspapers? I had left all this to the last moment, for I intended to ask Kolya and hear him say, "I will arrange." But the train went out. Alexander Ivanitch and the Pole looked at the wheels, which meant, I had been told, that they wanted me to come back.

The train went through lonely swamp, thinly wooded with birch and alder. Here and there a solitary Soviet soldier guarded the line until, as we approached the frontier, the main roads slowly became cart tracks and petered out into grass and barbed-wire entanglements.

In the autumn of 1956 I went with seven other Irishmen on a "cultural delegation" to China. On the way back I parted from the others in Moscow because I wished to go to Leningrad to see if any of my old friends were alive. As the translator of Leonov's *The Thief*, I had good contacts with the Union of Writers, and when I told them my reasons for wishing to go to Leningrad, I met with understanding. They said they would look out for a guide to take me on the night train the following day. But would I in the meantime give them a talk on Irish literature? I went back to the Hotel National and spent the day in my room writing and was ready for my appointment with them in the afternoon.* There were about a dozen people there, mostly teachers and translators. They asked me searching and intelligent questions. One of them was translating O'Casey's autobiographical series and he asked me to interpret a passage in O'Casey's idiosyncratic idiom, which always seemed to me to obscure what was

---

*See above, "Irish Literature," pp. 254–59.—ed.

otherwise lucid. I did badly but recovered a little of my credit when I said that in *Sunset and Evening Star* O'Casey had written a couple of friendly pages about me and the "Insult" to the Papal Nuncio.*

As I left them I was told that my guide, Anna Shelestova, would meet me at the National late that evening and take me on the night train to Leningrad. On the train I reflected on my chances of finding any of my friends alive. There was only a thin hope. What I had heard as rumour at home had been confirmed in Moscow. In 1934, three years after I had left, Kirov, the Leningrad Party boss, whom many thought would be Stalin's successor, had been murdered. Foreign influence was suspected and many thousands of arrests were made on the flimsiest of evidence. I heard how the elderly vet who treated the German consul's dog, and the woman who sold eggs to the Polish consul, had been hauled off to prison. It was obvious that all foreign-language teachers would be under suspicion. Five years later the war had broken out, and after that came the invasion of Russia and the terrible siege of Leningrad. It was a forlorn hope.

Almost all my friends in Leningrad had had telephones, so the first thing we did when we arrived was to look up their names in the telephone book. Only one familiar name was there, the one I most wanted to see, Nikolai Mihalitch Archangelsky. He was not in Chernishev Pereulok but in the southern suburb of Narva. When Anna telephoned, a female voice said that he was out but would be back at two.

We leapt into a cab and, as Anna was a native of Leningrad, we quickly found the Archangelskys' flat. It was in a large new tenement block and No. 32 was on the third storey. When the door was opened by a big blowsy woman, there was a babel of children's voices and kitchen smells. She did not ask us in but said that if we cared to wait, Nikolai Mihalitch would be along in twenty minutes. "Does he still work at the Oriental Institute?" I asked. "No, he works at the Kirov factory." "That was the Putilov in your time," interjected Anna. "Does he write at all now?" I asked. The woman looked puzzled. "He's an engineer," she said. It took me a moment to grasp that there were two Nikolai Mihalitch Archangelskys, and that this was the wrong one. I could not stay there a second longer. "Let's at least try Chernishev Pereulok," I said to Anna. My disappointment had turned into relief, for the Nikolai Mihalitch I knew would have been miserable in such surroundings.

*See below, pp. 452ff.—ed.

I was no help to Anna in finding our way to Chernishev Pereu-lok. All the familiar landmarks had gone, and when we arrived and stopped at No. 59 I got out in perplexity. Even in the hallway it was different. The lift was working. Could these be the stairs that I had run down with Nina Gavrilovna shouting after me that night I had spent at the consul's? It was not possible. We went up in the lift all the same and stopped on the fifth floor.

Darya Andreyevna's mirror had gone and so had the mat. A stranger came to the door when I rang the bell. No, he had never heard of anyone called Nikolai Mihalitch Archangelsky, but there was a very old lady in the flat still who had been there since before the war. She might know. "Is it Darya Andreyevna?" I asked. "Yes, that's her name." I described myself and he said he would find out if she would see me. He came back and said the old lady remem-bered me—an Englishman—but she was bedridden and did not want to see a strange man; she'd see the woman who came with me. So Anna went alone. I waited for a long time on the landing till Anna came out. She said Darya Andreyevna remembered the Ar-changelskys well. The mother had died and sometime in the mid-1930s Nikolai Mihalitch had been taken away to Gorohovaia Prison for quite a short period. He had come back and after three weeks had died in the flat.

I could not leave it like that. It seemed to me that Tihomirov, as a Red Army man, was the one who was likely to have survived the purge that followed Kirov's murder. By a strange chance I had in my notebook the number of the two old women with whom he lodged, and in a moment I was talking to the one who had survived. Yes, she remembered Alexander Ivanitch talking about me, the English-man. "Poor Alexander Ivanitch! He died you know three years ago. I always told him he drank too much coffee." This seemed a very old-ladyish diagnosis, but I asked her did she remember Lihachev and Yegunov and Kolya. Indeed she did, but Alexander Ivanitch had not been seeing anything of them for a very long time before he died. "How long?" "Oh, maybe fifteen or twenty years ago. I think something may have happened to them." She was not going to tell me more and maybe she did not know. When anyone went to prison in those days, their relations used to bring them parcels, until one day they were told no more parcels were necessary. You were not informed whether they had died or been moved to another prison.

I had learned very much what I had expected to learn, which was nothing. I was sad not only for my friends but for anyone who leaves the world anonymously, surrounded by hostile or uncaring people.

Anna had done her best for me. There was still half a day. What would I like to see? I did not want to go sightseeing, and in any case most of the Intourist sights had been destroyed by the Germans. The imperial palaces in the southern environs of the city, Peterhov, Gatchina, Pavlovsk, Tsarskoye Selo, had all lain in the path of the German advance and had been looted and burned. All the trees in their parks had been cut down. "But we're restoring them," said Anna, loyal to Intourism, "and we're getting all the pictures and sculptures back again, or their equivalents. And we've replanted the trees."

In the end she took me to a hill overlooking the city and the Gulf of Finland. There was a slot-machine telescope there and with a running commentary from Anna I turned it round. To the west I saw the island of Kronstadt and the wooded coast of Finland, and Anna told me how, backed by the Finns, the Germans had flung forty-five divisions against the city. After the victory at Kingisepp, in which her brother had died, they forced their way across the Estonian frontier, confident that the city would fall to them in a couple of days, but the siege had lasted twenty-nine months and had ended in a Russian victory. Moving the telescope towards the city, I saw the Nevsky Prospekt thrusting eastwards to the Champs de Mars. The biggest fire from the incendiary bombs, Anna said, had been in the Gostiny Dvor. That was the shopping centre in the Nevsky where I had eaten piroshki the night I slept at the consulate. She told me about the famine and how her brother's family had eaten carpenter's glue and yeast with hot water, till the fierce winter of 1941–42 when they had made a road across the ice on Lake Ladoga and transported food across from the east. I traced the Neva till it veered southwards by the Finland Station and the Summer Palace. To the north I saw the islands where I had walked with Yegunov and his dog. They were now called the Kirov Islands, Anna told me, and the great highway that led to them was called Kirov Avenue. Thousands of honest men and women died because of Kirov, but their names are nowhere recorded.

I have forgotten much of what Anna told me but I am more inclined to apologize for writing about great events, which touched me not at all, than for tracing again the tiny snail track which I made myself.

Is it not obvious that when through the modern media far things are brought near, the near things must be pushed far to make room for them? Imperceptibly, we become Lilliputians wandering in a Brobdingnag of our own contrivances and persuading ourselves that through contact with greatness we ourselves become greater. Then something happens to jerk us back to thoughts and people of our own size and significance. Most of the time when I was looking through that telescope, I was thinking not of the tremendous disasters that had befallen Leningrad and all Russia, but of the small stupidities, the acts of laziness or greed I had committed myself. Why had I not given the blue rug to Kolya's mother instead of leaving it behind by mistake? Why hadn't I sent Guzelimian his fishing rod?

Mr. Pfeffer of Sarajevo

1955

It must have been in the late 1920s that the first wave of nostalgia for imperial Austria, its glamour and its grace, swept across the theatre and the screen. Later, it invaded the study and has long given a giddy twist to many serious historical researches. For very many people whose parents fought against the Hapsburgs, the assassinations at Sarajevo have come to mean the first great irruption of violence into a prosperous and orderly world, the signal for the decay of romance, colour and freedom, the prelude to the crude despotism of the bully and the statistician. In fact, there was never a time when it was harder to enter into the minds of those who saw the Sarajevo assassinations as the dawn of liberty.

But the record of the monuments on the Latinska bridge in Sarajevo shows that there was no simple struggle between poetry and prose, between tradition and anarchy. There was a duel to the death between two rival ideals; one died and the other was stricken with a mortal illness.

The large Austro-Hungarian monument to the Archduke and his wife, with its crowns, columns and marble mourners, stood on the bridge for only two years. It was smashed by the Serbs in 1918 and in the presence of an archbishop a tablet was set in its place to the memory of their assassin, Gavrilo Princip, and to the dawn of Yugoslav freedom. At the same time the bones of Princip and his fellow conspirators were collected from the prison cemeteries of Czechoslovakia and Lower Austria and given a splendid interment. The tablet stayed there for twenty-four years and then it was torn down and sent to Hitler at Berchtesgaden by one of his loyal generals. After the

Germans, Italians, Croat separatists and finally Communists held the bridge. Today Princip's romantic dreams seem scarcely more compatible with the public aspirations of his countrymen than do the ingenious political constructions of imperial Vienna. They are revered, of course, like a historic blunderbuss in a showcase, but they are not for handling.

The real tragedy of Sarajevo was never commemorated on the bridge, and yet it was more momentous than the collapse of imperialism or the rapid degradation of the nationalism which superseded it. All through the empire and through Europe there were men of liberal outlook who foresaw the fatal collision and tried in vain to prevent it. Their failure meant the disgrace and finally the extinction of liberalism. If another commemorative monument were ever to be erected on the bridge at Sarajevo it ought to be to Mr. Leo Pfeffer, the examining magistrate at the trial of the assassins; a liberal, he defended his creed as stoutly as Princip and Franz Ferdinand defended theirs, and his defeat, too, was symbolic.

It was not till 1934 that Mr. Pfeffer, a Croat and a Catholic, brought his manuscript account of the preliminary examination and his comments on it to my friend Dr. Churchin of Zagreb. Churchin was at that time editor of *Nova Europa*, the only liberal monthly of consequence published in the Balkans. He printed the manuscript in instalments and asked my help in preparing an English translation. But it was a bad time. The rise of Hitler made it hard to focus the attention of Mr. Pfeffer's scrupulous analysis of these complex distant events or to make them interesting to others. His book is still unpublished.

Mr. Pfeffer, an expert in the law of the Austro-Hungarian Empire, tried to administer it with justice and charity. He treated the assassins as what they were, men of honour and principle, who had acted deliberately and did not wish to shift the responsibility for their acts onto the shoulders of others. They resisted the bullying of the police but they were ready to cooperate with Mr. Pfeffer, with the result that we have an all but complete picture of the passage of six bombs and four revolvers from Belgrade through the Bosnian highlands to Sarajevo, of the endless variety of men and women who handled them and hid them in cow byres and in reading rooms and under pillows and in loaves of oaten bread, till finally the heir apparent lay dead on an iron bed in the governor of Bosnia's palace.

When Mr. Pfeffer had ordered the arrest of a student, Grabezh, whom he had correctly associated with the assassination, the young man, the son of an Orthodox priest near Sarajevo, was led to him, filthy and soaking and defiant. The police had tried to force him to tell them where he had hidden the bombs he had failed to throw; they had ducked him in the river and in the town drain. Mr. Pfeffer spoke to him in his usual way.

I am the examining magistrate and I am going to call you "thou," not from any lack of respect but so that we may understand each other better. I do not consider you a common criminal; you acted from political conviction and history will decide whether you were right. But the court must prosecute you for your act. It was not with my knowledge or approval that the police tortured you. If you do not tell me where the bomb was hidden it will explode and injure some innocent person.

Grabezh promptly answered: "You are the first person who has spoken to me like a human being, so I will tell you." And half an hour later the bomb was found in the earth closet of a hotel belonging to Grabezh's cousin. Another chapter was added to the story of the crime, and the chief of police liked Mr. Pfeffer even less than before.

If it was due to Mr. Pfeffer in the first place that the conspirators were detected, it is also because of him that they remain more than mere names carved in marble or woven into patriotic ballads. We know their hesitations as well as their final resolve and in them we see the reflection of an entire nation in revolt.

After the tension and the triumph of the Balkan Wars the Serbs were more proud and prickly than ever, and Mr. Pfeffer, a Croat, gives a good picture of the small mortifications that the non-German subjects of Franz Josef had to endure. Bosnia, which borders upon Serbia and has a mainly Serbian population, had been recently annexed. It was being given railways and hospitals, but every spoonful of jam had its pill and the local Austrian officials often scraped off the jam for themselves. For example, every town had its *Beamtenverein*, a small club for government clerks, but though the majority of the members were Slav, there was an unwritten law that all the committee should be German. Mr. Pfeffer tells how he and some friends managed once to canvass the voters so that the committee of the club was controlled by Slavs and its name altered. This triumph lasted for one month and then all the Slav committee members were transferred to posts in other towns. But the members elected more Slavs to the committee. Then the Germans all withdrew and formed a *Herrenklub* of their own.

If these lofty ways could exasperate a civil servant like Mr. Pfeffer, a more violent reaction can be imagined among the Serbian patriots. When the old Emperor Franz Josef came to Sarajevo in 1910, a student called Jeracic decided to kill him. But, touched by his age and frailty, he flung his bomb at the governor of Bosnia instead, missed, and then killed himself. Jeracic became a great hero, poems were written about him, declamations were made and dozens of students, including Princip himself, swore upon his grave that he would be avenged. The excitement spread to Croatia and four attempts were made upon the life of the governor in Zagreb.

Franz Ferdinand, the heir apparent, was supposed to be mildly Slavophile and to favour the creation of a triadic monarchy in which Austrians, Hungarians and Slavs had equal rights. His views made him enemies in Vienna and Budapest but no friends in Bosnia. He was a Hapsburg and that was enough.

The circumstances of his visit to Sarajevo are so strange that Mr. Pfeffer raised a doubt that has had frequent echoes and has never been satisfactorily laid to rest. Was the visit a provocation? Did the Vienna government want some incident to occur that would give an excuse for the subjugation of Serbia? Mr. Pfeffer can explain in no other way the absence of police and military from the streets (very strange when you recall that there were manoeuvres on and troops in abundance outside the town). And how was it possible for a second assassin to have another try half an hour after the first had failed? The photographs have survived, and you can see the archducal car proceeding down an almost empty street. A small boy waves his hat from the quayside while on the opposite pavement, Mr. Pfeffer tells us, six assassins were stationed at intervals (the photographer had marked one of them with a cross), but not a single policeman. Then why ever did the royal visit take place on Vidovdan, a great day of mourning for the defeat of the Serbs by the Turks in the fourteenth century, a defeat which the Serbs had just so triumphantly reversed?

But one must not oversimplify. Of course there may have been some high official who said, "The Archduke thinks he's so popular with the Serbs, let him find out for himself!" and then cynically relaxed security measures. Baron Bolfras, for example, who accompanied the Archduke, expressed that opinion in his reminiscences. But I doubt whether respectable bureaucrats often consciously plan for assassination. I think, when they want a major blunder made, they delegate authority to some naive and irreproachable subordinate.

One can imagine some minor diplomatic personage getting fuddled by the mystique of royalty and Austria's cultural mission to the Balkans. He would specially choose Vidovdan for the visit. "We must teach Serbs and Turks to forget about these ancient quarrels," he would argue, "and to bury the hatchet. We must show them how our royalty moves freely and fearlessly among its subjects. We put our trust in Providence." Then the assassination would be deemed the violation of the most sacred trust, and the ultimatum to Belgrade would seem to have been countersigned in Heaven. They could settle down to the absorption of Serbia with the easiest of consciences.

As the days passed, the mourning for the royal couple assumed a majesty that must have made it very hard for Mr. Pfeffer to keep his head. The royal corpses passed out of the hands of the doctors and the police and lay in state with a hundred tapers blazing. They travelled overland and by sea to Trieste with solemn ceremonies at every halt. Finally, at midnight, they reached Vienna; with torches and muffled drums and a cavalry escort, they were brought to the church of the Hofburg. The next day the old emperor drove up from Schönbrunn to the service while his ministers got ready for the annihilation of Serbia.

Meanwhile in Sarajevo, Mr. Pfeffer, looking out of his window, saw a procession of boys and girls issuing from the police station with a large portrait of the Archduke draped in crape. A wave of mourning was followed by a wave of indignation against the Serbs. Their shops, hotels, reading rooms were wrecked. The police knew that, provided you organize the mourning, there will always be volunteers to carry through the retribution.

Mr. Pfeffer slowly pieced together the whole of the story of the assassinations. Very many Serbs in Bosnia and outside it, as well as some Croats and Moslems, were linked in the conspiracy. The individual had set himself in a big way against the state but nothing appeared to prove the complicity of the Serbian government, which the Austrian ultimatum assumed.

There was, of course, a link between the political intrigues of Belgrade and the young Bosnian rebels, but Mr. Pfeffer, after a detailed examination of all the evidence, decided that encouragement from Serbia had been unofficial and halfhearted. Captain Tankoshitch, a hero of the Balkan Wars, had indeed got the bombs for the Bosnian students, when they had come to him in Belgrade, begging his assistance. He was a member of the Black Hand,* a Serbian or-

*There are some who now dispute Pfeffer's conclusion, e.g. Joachim Remak, an American

ganization for the liberation of the southern Slavs of the Austro-Hungarian Empire. It had seemed to him and others that the Archduke's visit and military manoeuvres in Bosnia, which as supreme commander he came to supervise, were sly preliminaries to an attack on Serbia. Possibly, they thought, a bomb or two might warn the Austrians of the resistance they would meet, though the conspirators did not seek the approval of the Serbian government, which knew nothing of their schemes. Soon after the bombs had been provided, the leaders of the Black Hand had misgivings. Not in their wildest dreams had they thought that the Archduke would be so carelessly guarded that the assassination might succeed, but the young men seemed too ingenuous to be trusted. Sharats, a theological seminarist, was sent posthaste to Sarajevo to stop the enterprise, but the bombs were already on the way, the students had made up their minds. They would not listen to him.

Mr. Pfeffer secured abundant photographs. Alone of all the conspirators, the guerrilla Tankoshitch faces the camera with dandified composure, spruce moustachios and a chest crisscrossed with bandoliers. We know the others only from prison photographs. There are about a dozen university students, a village schoolmaster, a prosperous citizen of Tuzla who had opened the first cinema, a patron of gymnastic clubs and reading rooms. There is a peasant farmer, a very handsome old man in the white tunic and gay woven girdle of the Bosnian highlands. His son, a pastoral figure from the Old Testament, appears with his hands lightly clasped. He is grave, bewildered and yet relaxed, strangely different from the tense figures of the townspeople. You can see in their eyes that their resolution was shaped by textbooks, newspapers, committees, while for the peasants the tragedy of Vidovdan was the fulfillment of old legends, ancient curses. For them the Archduke must have been a shadowy figure not easily to be distinguished from the Turkish overlords of the past. The bombs which the students brought them slipped into their broad girdles all too naturally.

These bombs must have changed hands twenty times on their way to Sarajevo. Let me describe a single episode, one of many similar ones. One June day a fortnight before the assassination, Chubrilovitch, the young teacher of a church school near the Serbian frontier, was riding beside the village priest to buy lambs. He had offered to help the priest ford a river swollen by the floods, but before

---

professor, who thinks that the whole assassination was organized by Apis (of the Black Hand) in Belgrade, but I don't believe he proves his case at all.

they reached it a ploughman came out of the woods to say that two students wanted to see the schoolmaster. As soon as the priest had gone, the students, whom the ploughman had helped across the frontier, crept into the open. They explained that in their rucksacks were bombs for the murder of the Archduke. These would somehow have to be brought to Tuzla, the market town, and left with the cinema proprietor for the next stage of their journey to Sarajevo. The schoolmaster put the bombs into the panniers of his horse and took the students to the large farmhouse of his godfather, Kerovitch. The whole family came in to discuss how to get the bombs to Tuzla. One of the sons of the house had cut his hand scything; he had to go to town to see the doctor; then he remembered that their neighbour had to take out his horse and cart to fetch a trunk belonging to a brother who was leaving his school at Tuzla. When night fell they set off, skirting the village where there were military barracks, sitting at different tables whenever they stopped at taverns, till after many adventures they reached the reading room over which the cinema proprietor had his flat.

Even so crude a summary may illustrate how the Austrian annexation of Bosnia had brought two worlds into violent collision; it shows that the assassination was not hatched in an anarchist cellar. In the wild barren mountains, which the Turk never completely subdued, the fierce spirit of independence, though it might exchange ballads for reading rooms, daggers for bombs, was scantily concealed.

Princip and Chabrinovitch, the two students who actually used the weapons on Vidovdan, were reading-room- rather than mountain-trained. Mr. Pfeffer speaks well of their courage and sincerity. When the trial was over the judge called on those prisoners who repented of their crime to stand up. They all stood up except for Princip. When interrogated, he replied that he was sorry that he had robbed some children of their parents and that he had killed the Archduchess, particularly as she was a Czech, but he was not sorry he had killed the Archduke. He had intended to do so. Then Chabrinovitch, confused and ashamed, sat down again. He had changed his mind, he said; he wasn't sorry either for what he had done.

Chabrinovitch was a nineteen-year-old printer. His evidence was heard with difficulty because the cyanide which he had tried to swallow at the moment of arrest had burned his lips. He was a more theatrical type than the others. He longed to be conspicuous and was

so unwisely talkative that the other two students, Princip and Grabezh, had separated from him on their journey across the mountains.
There had been ructions in the Chabrinovitch household the day before Vidovdan, when he had hidden the imperial standard which his
father intended to hang out of the window. He had made his prep-
arations for immortality rather elaborately, getting photographs of
himself to present to his friends, consigning his watch and his savings
to his sister. After his bomb had missed he had leaped into the river
with the cyanide between his teeth. But everything went wrong; the
river washed off the cyanide and his terrified friends destroyed his
photographs. He died in prison at the moment when Serbia had suffered her greatest defeat.

Their nationalism was of the traditional kind. Princip declared
that Serbs and Croats were one people and that Yugoslavia must be
united as Italy and Germany had been. They must throw out the
Austrians as the Italians had done. They were quite unlike the subsidized revolutionaries of later days; indeed they were always penniless. A week or two before the assassination the director of the
academy library had noticed that Princip always read on through the
lunch hour; finding that he had no money for food, he offered him
some. Princip refused but agreed to earn a few shillings by copying
out the minutes of a committee meeting. A couple of months later,
when it was discovered who had copied them, the offensive pages
were solemnly erased.

Mr. Pfeffer wrote his book at a time when the Croats were suffering as much from Serbian despotism as under Austria-Hungary.
King Alexander's police surpassed the Austrians in brutality and a
Croat might well have been tempted to regret the world of culture
and learning destroyed on Vidovdan.

But in Mr. Pfeffer's pages we see the empire fading naturally and
inevitably as a flower. It could not be saved, but the ground might
be got ready for its seeds. Mr. Pfeffer and others were doing this,
but most of the Austrian officials could not face the truth. Their
diplomacy had become a network of lies and tricks in which they
strangled as many friends as enemies. We see this happening even in
Sarajevo. The Austrians were trying to conciliate the Moslems in
Bosnia in order to counterbalance the Croats and Serbs who formed
the majority. Perhaps they had some prevision of their wartime alliance with Turkey. Their Bosnian regiments wore the fez and a
hideous Turko-Viennese town hall was erected at Sarajevo. The
authorities were therefore displeased when Mr. Pfeffer discovered

that one of the young men who waited on the quayside with a bomb for the Archduke was a Moslem. He was twice imprisoned and twice escaped with the connivance, Mr. Pfeffer was convinced, of the police. He was never brought to trial or charged.

And there were fatuous, place-hunting lies as well as mean, political ones. Contrary to custom, Mr. Pfeffer was not asked to be present at the examination of the bodies of the royal pair, but he was expected later to sign the official report testifying to facts he had not seen. He indignantly refused. Later he learned that he had not been asked in because of his grey suit. In the presence of royalty, even dead royalty, a frock coat is obligatory. Also decorations were to be awarded to all those present on that solemn occasion and his rank did not qualify him for one.

The convicted students were under twenty and therefore exempted by Austrian law from hanging. But they and most of the others died after a year's imprisonment; Mr. Pfeffer does not attribute this very strange fact to Austrian cruelty. TB can, perhaps, account for two out of a dozen. One of them went mad. Is it possible that these unsophisticated people simply sank under the gigantic consequences of what they had done? At times they may have had some intimation of the honour in which they would later be held, but more often they must have thought of the German and Austrian armies advancing everywhere and the Serbians hopelessly crushed. Night and day five soldiers watched over Princip in his cell at Theresienstadt, one in his room, two in the passage, two outside the window. He can never have learned that the empire he had challenged was collapsing.

The Austrian authorities strongly disapproved of Mr. Pfeffer, but he had done his work well and could not be dismissed. With ingenious malice the minister succeeded in transferring him to Tuzla, the home ground of so many of the conspirators whom he had brought to trial. When the war ended, the Tuzla town council pressed for his trial, but the brother of the schoolmaster, Chubrilovitch, who had been hanged, came to his defence and he was allowed to retire into private life.

He was universally detested and yet it was clear that he had acted in the only possible way that an Austrian official could honourably act. He had fixed the guilt clearly and categorically upon individuals who were ready to shoulder it. He had tried to dispel the clouds of dark suspicion and vague accusation from which wars arise. He had localized and isolated a crime at a time when the Austro-Hungarian government, with the German Empire behind it, was trying to put a whole nation in the dock.

He failed; but in honouring what was generous and self-sacrificing in a young nation which claimed its rights, he upheld better than its own ministers the honour of the doomed old empire which he served.

Epilogue

The Sarajevo conspirators were Croats, Serbs and Moslems, and they aimed at a nation in which the diverse peoples of Yugoslavia should live in free and equal union. They were mostly republicans, and the movement to which they belonged was not tainted with racialism till the new state was set up under the Serbian king. It was racialism, not nationalism, that undermined Yugoslav unity, but this vital distinction is seldom observed and when "petty nationalism" is attacked as the source of our troubles, the "petty nations" seldom defend themselves. Unlike monarchies, empires and Communist states, they have no trade union nor have they developed a common philosophy. They have few arguments to oppose to the universalists and imperialists, who believe that incompatibilities of language and culture are best ironed out by the kindly pressure of a dominant race. In fact, the small peoples often subscribe to this belief themselves. Frequently you will hear an Irish nationalist lamenting the collapse of Austria-Hungary and explaining that Yugoslavia and the other succession states were mere puppet contrivances of the League of Nations, rag-bags of racial oddments, doomed to disintegrate. He ignores that these states all have living languages and often a more distinctive culture, a longer history of independence than our own. And since the succession states owed their existence to England and France, their citizens often scoffed at Ireland's independence. The Croats used to call themselves "the Ulster of Yugoslavia" because they considered the Six Counties as progressive as themselves and in equal danger of being absorbed into the peasant economy of a more primitive people.

What then is nationalism and how can it be distinguished from racialism? Thomas Davis, being only half Irish, is probably a sounder nationalist, more immune from racialism, than Mazzini and the other Victorian apostles of the resurgent peoples. He would have said that a country belongs to the people who were born in it and intend to die there and who make its welfare their chief concern. There is no mention of "minority rights," because these were assumed. Even in Ireland not many think like that now. Read the speeches reported in the press. Where one man talks of national unity, a hundred will talk of some unity that is racial, confessional or political.

It was because nationalism lacked a philosophy that in the early 1920s it began to decay and racialism took its place. The first sign of this degeneration came in 1923, when by the Treaty of Lausanne in exchange for Turks from Europe over a million Greeks were moved from the coast of Asia Minor, where they had lived for three thousand years. This ghastly crime was committed so efficiently under the auspices of the League of Nations that it won universal applause. What Churchill was later to call "the disentanglement of populations" began to seem a sensible and modern way of solving finally an ancient problem.

The old view that men should enjoy equal rights in the land of their birth began to seem hopelessly out of date, and soon Hitler and Mussolini and Stalin were eliminating causes of friction by large and admirably organized population exchanges in the Tyrol and the Baltic states. The war had hardly started when it became obvious to all sensible Germans that, if there was ever to be world peace, all conquered peoples should be either Germanized or deported. That much-respected man Dr. Oberlander, who later became Adenauer's Minister for Refugees, said with reference to the Poles, "It is better to be harsh now than have petty warfare waged for generations." Soon the contagion of this generous realism reached the Allies, and in 1940 we find Beneš* writing in *The Nineteenth Century* that 3 million Sudeten Germans should be "amicably and under decent human conditions" expelled. When the time came they were expelled. Again, Churchill in 1944 expressed the opinion that expulsion was "the most lasting and satisfactory method" of dealing with the 7.5 million Germans of the east. They, too, were satisfactorily expelled.

When we recall such gigantic endeavours, scientifically conducted, to sort out the old ragbag nations of 1918 into homogeneous states, how petty and parochial seem the dreams of the Sarajevo conspirators, and the poor old League of Nations with its condominiums and Free Cities and minority rights! And how more than dead are Davis and Herder and their romantic insistance on Homeland and Nationhood! One has to listen hard to catch the least echo of that extinct ideology. Yet here is one from the most improbable source of all, from Germany, which once led the world in the social science of Disentanglement. It comes from the Exiles' Charter, an appeal for

---

*Edward Beneš, president of Czechoslovakia 1936–38, who resigned after the Munich agreement that validated Germany's occupation of his country—ed.

Heimatrecht published on behalf of those 7.5 million German refugees from the east.

God placed men in their homes. To drive men out of their homes spells spiritual death. We have experienced this fate. Hence we feel called upon to demand that the right to one's home be recognized as one of the basic rights given by God to man.

Carl von Ossietzky

1954

Many of the greatest martyrs and saints of modern times will never have their biographies written or their centenaries celebrated. Nobody knows when or how they died. Their lives are often a complex web of insignificant detail which few would have the patience to unravel. Often they have struggled in solitude against mass movements and it is inevitable that the mass media, through which we now obtain most of our information, should ignore them.

Lately I found a grimy old pamphlet dating from the first years of Hitler. It is called "The Case of Carl von Ossietzky" and it was the work of fifteen eminent English writers. It is an appeal to the Nobel Peace Prize Committee on behalf of Ossietzky, who was at that time in a German prison.*

They wrote: "We have all tried to do something for the cause of peace, but he has done more than any of us. He has done most of all living men to deserve this acknowledgment from his fellow-men." Because of these efforts Ossietzky did get his Nobel Prize in 1936, but a year or two later he died reclaiming marshland in Esterwegen prison camp. Nobody really knows about his death.†

Why does nobody care, either? Germans of the east and the west

---

*For the unsuccessful attempt to persuade William Butler Yeats to join this campaign in 1936, see Ethel Mannin, *Privileged Spectator* (1939).
†It is now established that he was moved on 27 May 1936 from Esterwegen to hospital in Berlin, suffering from tuberculosis, and held there under detention. In mid-November 1936 the detention order was technically rescinded, but he remained under Gestapo surveillance throughout his hospitalization, which ended with his death at the Nordend Private Clinic on 4 May 1938.

are now combing history for evidence that they resisted Hitler, but Ossietzky and his friends are seldom mentioned. Very few people talk of the large and honourable resistance to Hitler which was extinguished before the war began, before Auschwitz was thought of, and which left the German opposition leaderless. The reason for this silence is clear. History is written by survivors, and most of those who survived till 1939 had had to make many moral and political adjustments in order to do so. Inevitably they have encouraged us to believe that the best martyrs are diplomatists who balance one tyranny against another and choose (provisionally, of course) the least repugnant. Ossietzky, who did not want any tyranny at all, does not fit comfortably into this picture, and so he is honoured in neither the east nor the west. There is much competition to be numbered among those brave Germans who tried to murder Hitler because he was losing the war, but Ossietzky, who opposed Hitler because he was Hitler and war because it was war, has been almost totally forgotten.

His fifteen sponsors seem rather out-of-date figures too—Aldous Huxley, Gilbert Murray, Rose Macaulay, Norman Angell, Gerald Heard, Bertrand Russell, J. B. Priestley, Leonard and Virginia Woolf, to name a few. They all had this in common with Ossietzky: they hated the Organization Man, the mechanical dummy who does what he is told. And they believed he could be resisted. Nowadays most writers either belong to an organization themselves or else believe that the world created by the Organization Man is so obscene and ludicrous that they can only laugh at it, the bitter laughter of the defeated, of Joyce and Beckett, Albee and Genet and a hundred such others, and with a certain satisfaction reflect that this world is a Vale of Tears anyway and we should turn our minds to the next.

Ossietzky was different. He was the son of a Hamburg merchant and had fought with average ability and less than average enthusiasm in the First World War. Even then he had realized where German militarism was tending. As soon as he was demobilized he started a weekly in Hamburg whose aims he describes thus: "We who are supporters of peace have a duty and a task to point out over and over again that there is nothing heroic in war but that it brings terror and misery to mankind."

As a result of the German military collapse, there had been a great cultural revival with which the names of Einstein, Thomas and Heinrich Mann, Arnold Zweig, Gropius, Max Reinhardt, Hindemith and Bruno Walter are associated. There was springtime in the air and for a few years all Europe looked to Berlin as it had once looked to

Weimar. To Berlin Ossietzky went. He started there the *Nie Wieder Krieg* movement and became editor of the *Weltbühne*. Till the day of his last arrest it was the principal literary organ of resistance, first to the reviving German militarism and then to Hitler.

Weltbühne had been called *Schaubühne* before the war, and was an organ of the theatre. It was connected with a firm that published children's books—*Emil and the Detectives*, translations of *Dr. Dolittle* and so on. But soon it was clear that the independence of the actor, the writer, the artist, was about to be threatened and that the *Weltbühne*, the world stage, required them. The paper changed its name and its character. It became militantly anti-militarist and earned the hatred of the General Staff. For Ossietzky claimed with good reason that some of the generals were lending support to the Black Reichswehr, a secret society directed against German democracy and defending itself by what were known as the *vehme* murders. He revealed that German commercial aviation was being used as a screen for military activities. He opposed the granting of naturalization papers to Hitler. He attacked those, who, under Nazi pressure, had banned the famous anti-war film *All Quiet on the Western Front*. "Today," he wrote, "German fascism has slain a film. Tomorrow it will be something else. . . . Soon only one tune will be permitted, and every one of our steps will be carefully measured."

Ossietzky was not forced into resistance by violence like the Jews, or by political theory like the Communists. Rudolf Olden, his friend and lawyer, who was editor of the *Berliner Tageblatt*, explained him as a *Bürger*, a civilian defending the rights of civilians.

The generals were handling Hitler very gently, for they believed they could use him and had no notion how soon they would be his puppets. Ossietzky, who saw clearly what was happening, had to be silenced. In an action for slander the generals secured his arrest and imprisonment. Yet till Hitler came, a *Bürger* could still count on some justice. Over 42,000 Germans signed an appeal for his release, a brave thing to do, for it was only three weeks before Hitler came to power. When for a brief period General Schleicher took over the government Ossietzky was released.

But soon the flames of the burning Reichstag lit up unmistakably the shape of the future. His colleagues on the *Weltbühne* escaped abroad and Ossietzky's friends urged him to think of his small daughter and to follow them. But he had written: "The man who is opposing the government of his own country and who goes across the border speaks with a hollow voice."

fused to leave. The writers of my old pamphlet recall how Socrates was urged by Crito to fly to Thessaly while there was time; it was a duty to his friends, to his family; and Socrates answered: "The principles which I have hitherto honoured and revered I still honour."

The day after the Reichstag fire Ossietzky was taken to Spandau Prison and thence to Sonnenburg concentration camp. After that there were a few rumours from fellow prisoners who escaped of beatings and torture but nothing definite. We know more about Socrates.

Since Ossietzky was the principal leader of the German resistance to Hitler, why is his name so seldom mentioned when the whole German people is being charged with complicity in Hitler's crimes? I've suggested the reason already. It is because Ossietzky and his 42,000 supporters, who were eliminated with him, were absolutists. Hitler to them was an absolute evil, whereas to most of their contemporaries inside and outside Germany, he was only a relative evil. Effective German resistance collapsed with Ossietzky, for only relativists were left. Not only in Germany but all over Europe, millions of intelligent people believed that Hitler could be "handled," used effectively against the Communists and then, when his work was done, discarded. One must recall that while Ossietzky was in Sonnenburg, the British ambassador was shooting elk with General Göring, and Ribbentrop was an honoured guest with Lord Londonderry in Co. Down.

The ghost of the relativist delusion still haunts us, corrupting history as it once corrupted politics. When it is finally accepted that Hitler was wholly evil and Stalin's most effective ally, Ossietzky and the thousands who died with him will be remembered again. They were the men who would have saved us—had we supported them—not only from Hitler but from Stalin as well.

The Kagran Gruppe

1988

I believe one of the happiest times of my life was when I was working for the Austrian Jews in Vienna in 1938–39. It is strange to be happy when others are miserable, but all the people at the Freundeszentrum in the Singerstrasse were cheerful too. The reason surely is that we have always known of the immense unhappiness that all humanity has to suffer. We read of it in the newspapers and hear it on the radio but can do nothing about it.

Most people tied to a single job or profession die without exercising more than a tenth of their capacities. In the Singerstrasse for many months all my faculties were engaged and I exercised an intimate control over the lives of a great many people, and I believe I helped them.

Hitler brought into the world misery such as no man had previously conceived possible. It had to be combated. The British were slow to observe this. The Irish never did. As late as 1936 Lloyd George went to Germany and told Hitler he was the greatest German of his age. London's society hostesses flocked round Ribbentrop and received invitations to the Olympic Games, which, thanks to Goebbels, were a huge success. Predictably, the poor silly Duke and Duchess of Windsor visited the Führer.

The mood in Ireland was one of ignorant indifference. It was expressed in the Dáil in 1943 by a very pious Catholic, Oliver Flanagan. "There is one thing," he said, "that the Germans did and that was to rout the Jews out of their country." He added that we should rout them out of Ireland: "They crucified our Saviour 1,900 years ago and they have been crucifying us every day of the week." No one contradicted him.

But I was as Irish as Oliver Flanagan, and I was determined that Jewish refugees should come to Ireland. At the time of the Anschluss the Quakers were settled in the Freundeszentrum in Vienna, and through Friends' House in London I got permission to join them. The Freundeszentrum was a former nobleman's palace in the Singerstrasse, and when I got there, together with a charming and energetic young Quaker called Mary Campbell, I was put in charge of the Kagran Gruppe, a group of Viennese Jews who had banded together for collective emigration.

My first few weeks at the Freundeszentrum were spent at a desk filling in hundreds of *Bogen*, or emigration forms, for the crowds of applicants who turned up. After the usual questions about age, religion, profession, married or single, the women were asked, "Can you cook, wash, scrub, knit?" The men had a corresponding questionnaire. Almost all the questions were answered in the affirmative. At the bottom one added one's comment. I do not know what happened to the stacks and stacks of *Bogen*. Probably they were forwarded to the Friends' House in Euston Road and carefully filed. What would we have done if some instinct had told us of Auschwitz? Why was I the only non-Quaker there?

I think now it was obtuse of us not to have anticipated Auschwitz. I had walked along the Prater Strasse to the Prater, the great Viennese park where bands played and stalls sold ice cream and coffee. The street must have had a great many Jewish shopkeepers in it, because all the way down there were broken windows in front of looted shops with VERHOLUNG NACH DACHAU ("Gone for a rest cure to Dachau") scrawled over the surviving panes, and the air was full of the mindless hatred that war, which fosters all our basest passions, would inevitably make murderous.

I speak German and French, so I was shortly sent to a conference on the problem of the German Jews at Evian, by the Lake of Geneva. The League of Nations had at last got to work, and it was attended by representatives of all the countries in Europe and America. Vague gestures of goodwill were made. I talked to the two delegates from Ireland, or rather from the Irish embassies in Paris and Berne. One remarked, "Didn't we suffer like this in the Penal Days* and nobody came to our help."

*The time of the Penal Laws, dating back to at least 1657 and continuing through the late 1700s, when a series of parliamentary measures were passed in England intended to disenfranchise Irish Catholics, e.g. by denying them the right to vote, own land, or hold public office.—ed.

When I got back I visited all the embassies to get visas for the emigrating Jews. There was a kindly official at the Mexican embassy who would sign an entry visa for anyone who asked. Even though it might fail to get them into Mexico it would get them out of Austria. So many applicants arrived that he had to get his wife and family in to help him.

One day I visited the Peruvian embassy. It was a splendid building with a large map of Peru painted on the staircase. I entered a spacious room with well-filled bookcases and handsome furniture. At the far end was a small figure seated at a large desk. I assumed he was the Peruvian ambassador, though in fact it was probably the consul. After the Anschluss the ambassadors had all been transferred to Stuttgart or Berlin. I appealed to him to persuade his government to admit Viennese Jews. He looked at me doubtfully and then said, "I was wondering if you could help me. You see, I too am a Jew and want to get out as soon as possible. I've just written a letter to Churchill. Do you think that a good idea?" "It would be much better to write to Emma Cadbury," I replied. He bowed but looked too proud to be interested.

At this time the Bolivian consulate was one of the most thronged in Vienna. The report had got round that land was being given to agriculturalists on favourable terms, and that engineers and craftsmen were required. Of the many that applied only a very few were accepted. In the autumn a group of about two hundred Jews were urged to prepare immediately for the journey. While the relief organizations hurriedly helped with the official formalities, they themselves sold their possessions with desperate haste for whatever they could get for them. They kept only the barest necessities for the journey and such goods as they could carry in their trunks to their new home. A few days before the boat was due to sail, they were informed that there had been a misunderstanding between the Gestapo and the Bolivian consulate: no visas would be given for Bolivia and the expedition could not set off. The two hundred settlers, now without homes or property, had to wander round the streets looking for hospitality from their friends.

At Eichmann's trial in Jerusalem in 1961 it emerged that he personally was responsible for providing the field in which the Kagran Gruppe was trained. When he was in Vienna emissaries from Palestine had approached him for help in the illegal immigration of Jews into British-ruled Palestine. "He was polite," they said, "and even provided a farm and facilities for setting up vocational training camps for prospective immigrants. On one occasion he expelled a group of nuns from a convent to provide a training camp for young Jews."

Eichmann, like other Nazis in the early days, was sympathetic to Zionism, and this lasted till 7 November 1938, when Ernst von Rath, Third Secretary of the German embassy in Paris, ironically an anti-Nazi, was murdered by a seventeen-year-old Jewish youth, Herschel Grynzpan, whose family had been deported to Poland. This led to Kristallnacht on 9 November, when all the synagogues in Berlin went up in flames, 7,500 Jewish shopwindows were smashed and 20,000 Jews were taken off to concentration camps. This increased the tension in Vienna and ever more people joined the Kagran Gruppe.

I found a letter of that time describing the desperate atmosphere to my wife:

There was a meeting yesterday of the leading Jews. I was very much moved by their courage and seriousness and idealism and innocence, as it seemed to me. They spent about twenty minutes deciding whether they should take their mahogany sideboards and bamboo hat racks by ship or not and describing them. They have to go first to Sweden (that is to say if anything comes of the scheme at all and they can raise £14,000) and then after they've had their *Umschulung* training in agriculture there, they go off to somewhere like Paraguay or, if they are lucky, Colombia, where there is some sort of community settlement already. I said that even shipping furniture from Belgrade to Dubrovnik, as we had done, was far dearer than selling it and then buying new stuff. They looked shocked, and I realized I had said something hurtful and callous about their homes, and that to many its furniture was an intimate part of their lives. They had grown up with it and it was full of memories. "This was Papa's chair and this was Mutti's," and the more stuck in their ways and the more entrenched they are, the more terribly touching it is. However, I'm glad they did decide to bring only the most cherished pieces. This afternoon when I was alone the Controller of Foreign Currency in the biggest bank but one—quite a swell with an almost complete set of gold teeth—pleaded to be allowed to join the camp with his wife and go out with them. He produced an armful of testimonials, but how could he be any use there?

But the real time for seeing people is between nine and one-thirty. I see about ten, and by the time one has reached the tenth one is utterly drained of sympathy and ideas and resourcefulness. I just gaze at them and put a new nib in the pen and rearrange the papers on the desk. In some cases it's just a matter of advice, how to find the address of a relation in Cairo or Cincinnati or something like that. There is a tremendous drive on now to Aryanize all the

Gemeindehauser (blocks of flats) and private houses along main streets where flags have to be hung on important occasions. As a result four people who came to me yesterday have had a notice to quit by 1 August and nowhere to go. They might get taken in as tenants by a Jewish landlord, but what are they to do with their furniture? Aryans who take Jewish lodgers also are liable to lose their flats. There was one old gentleman yesterday with an ear trumpet in a state of mind about his flat. It belonged to his wife's daughter who was illegitimate and consequently happened to be Aryan, but he was terrified of disgracing her by living with her and was going to move out. Another couple had married Aryanized daughters who were very anxious to support them, but for the same reason they were frightened of embroiling them and wanted to emigrate. There was an old officer with a testimonial from his General about his bravery at the battle of Przemysl.*

It's such a relief when one comes on a really nasty one, as one does, e.g. a *Feinkost Erzeuger* (maker of delicatessen), with a horrible Aryan wife who wanted to know if the Friends' House in Philadelphia would get her an affidavit if she became a Quaker. Then there was a young police officer, very well educated, and a dark scared fanatical writer on a fashion paper, dozens and dozens of *Beamter, Buchhalter, Mechaniker, Techniker* and chauffeurs and garage proprietors. There was one young Jew who had become a Nazi and hoped to become an honorary Aryan but wasn't accepted. And yesterday at the end two women and a little girl turned up. I was so fuddled by that time I can't remember what they wanted but they suddenly quite spontaneously and untheatrically all three began to snivel.

A plump dark-haired woman, a Nazi named Baronin Rikki von Appell, was always straying into the Friends' Centre. I think her job was to keep us under observation, and she was particularly concerned about me as I was not a Quaker. She knew about Quakers and remembered the good work they had done in Vienna in 1920; the Viennese were starving, so the Quakers among other projects imported 1,500 cows from Holland to provide milk.

But what was I up to, a non-Quaker? She was puzzled and asked me to join her and a friend on a boating trip on the Danube. We started from Klosterneuburg, and I was enchanted with the unspoiled beauty, the water lilies and scarlet willows growing beside the riverbank so close to a great city. Her friend was a thin fair-haired woman with a slight limp. She told me she had been engaged to be married, but because of her limp the Nazis, for genetic reasons, re-

---

*In June 1915, German forces retook the fortress of Przemysl, which the Russians had captured nine months before.—ed.

fused to allow it. She did not seem particularly resentful. I satisfied Rikki's curiosity by telling her that, like the Quakers, I had come out to help the Jews. She said the Jews were parasites who had speculated on the dwindling value of the Austrian crown after 1918. I did not accept this but was too ignorant to comment.

If I'd been a Quaker I would have said that the Quakers would help anyone who was suffering unjustly. The Quakers helped the Social Democrats when in 1934 Chancellor Dollfuss, a so-called Christian Socialist or Fascist, had crushed them. In Emma Cadbury's brilliant account of this period, *A Three-Day War and Its Aftermath*, she wrote that this civil conflict in Austria was one of the main causes of the Second World War. The Nazi takeover of Austria without opposition from England or France had made Czechoslovakia, now surrounded on three sides, an easy victim which the great powers would hesitate to defend.

Had it not been for the Three Days' War, Austria would have been well able to defend itself against the Nazis. Democracy had been growing there as in Germany before the collapse of the two empires in 1918, and in Austria the Social Democrats (socialists) then became the dominant power in Vienna. Emma Cadbury describes all that they did for the workers' libraries, adult education, hospitals, clinics, and above all housing. Before the war 73 percent of the people had been living in two rooms or less. In 1922, 60,000 houses were built with space for trees and grass and flowers. It was a superb achievement.

"Thus," writes Emma Cadbury, "life was made easier for the proletariat and Communism found no foothold in Vienna." But the Social Democrats had their enemies. Chief among them were the Christian Socialists, who were strongly influenced by the Catholic Church. They were extremely hostile to Hitler but regarded the Social Democrats as enemies of the Church who were impoverishing the middle and upper classes by overtaxation. The Social Democrats were ready to cooperate in fighting Hitler but the Christian Socialists could not wait. On 12 February 1934, with the approval of Chancellor Dollfuss, the Austrian army with the help of the Heimwehr, the army of the Christian Socialists, and the police made an assault on the Social Democrats. They and their army, the Schutzbund, were no match for the forces allied against them. Nearly 2,000 were killed and some 5,000 wounded. Many were executed and imprisoned. The Quakers were quickly on the scene distributing food with funds that came through the International Federation of Trade Unions.

The Austrian Nazis must have taken heart when they saw this great split in the ranks of their opponents. On 25 July 1934, a group of them broke into the Chancellery and shot Dollfuss. It was thought that this might lead to an immediate Nazi takeover. But Schuschnigg managed to forestall this move, and thirteen of the assassins were hanged.

Schuschnigg was summoned to Berchtesgaden and was bullied into signing a capitulation; as he had hoped, President Miklas refused to endorse it. Then he decided to hold a plebiscite, appealing for Social Democratic support, promising to free their members from prison. The Great Day was to be 14 March 1938.

The vote would certainly have gone against the Nazis, so on 12 March, Hitler strutted into Austria. He crossed the frontier at Brau-nau and received a riotous welcome near Linz, his birthplace. Cardinal Innitzer ordered all the church bells in Austria to be rung. Schuschnigg was thrown into prison in the Gestapo headquarters and later was transferred to Dachau.

It was some months after this that I came to Vienna.

Typical of many is the story of the first Austrians I brought to Ireland. Erwin Strunz, an "Aryan" with a Jewish wife and two small children, had been a trade union secretary with promise of a career in Parliament in the Social Democratic Party till Dollfuss took over the government and routed the socialists. The Strunzes had no friends abroad, and with a small son and a newborn baby they could not cross on foot over the mountains into Switzerland.

Erwin was advised by his Jewish friend Dr. Schonfeld, president of the Austrian Atheists Association, to visit the Quaker Centre in Vienna. He had called on many Labour leaders and ecclesiastics. None of them could help. Then he remembered the work the Quakers had done in starving Vienna in 1920. With a letter from Dr. Schon-feld he visited Emma Cadbury at the Freundeszentrum. It was there I first met them at my desk and filled in their two *Bogen*. Erwin told me he was an atheist, and Lisl, who had big black eyes and a lively but firm expression, said to me, "I will be a Mohammedan if it will help my children." I entered them both as *konfessionslos* (without church), which in fact was the creed of very many Viennese Jews.

Emma Cadbury gave permission for two hundred Kagraners to meet in the Quaker Centre and discuss their plans. They begged her to help them emigrate and form an agricultural cooperative overseas. Erwin and Lisl went early every morning with little Peter and all the

others on the long tram journey to Kagran, a suburb on the left bank
of the Danube. The group worked under the supervision of armed
guards from the Gestapo who relished watching middle-aged Jews,
many of them once rich sedentary businessmen, cutting trees, digging
irrigation trenches, making a road; men who had never before held
a shovel in their hands. They worked all the summer, while Emma
Cadbury, Mary Campbell and I tried desperately to get entry permits
for them to Peru, Bolivia, Rhodesia, Colombia, Canada. As I had
already realized at Evian, nobody wanted them.

Erwin and his wife were in great danger. They slept every night
in fear of the heavy knock at 5 a.m., the hour usually chosen by the
Gestapo for the departure to Dachau. The Viennese Nazi Party
thought there might be leader material in Erwin, so the Party solicitor
offered to arrange a divorce. He would be housed, temporarily, in
the factory to avoid painful meetings with his ex-wife and children,
and a blue-eyed Nazi woman had agreed to marry him. He was told
he was lucky as she had a house of her own and some money. He
would ultimately be transferred to the synthetic-petrol factory at
Düsseldorf and allotted a car, a monoplane and a villa. He could
attend the university and later be drafted to the Party Leader School
in Nuremberg. It was a dazzling offer, so when he did not reply the
Party grew suspicious. He hurriedly took sick leave and simulated a
nervous breakdown while still digging at Kagran. The Gruppe had
seemed to be a way out of his difficulties, but now the future looked
very menacing.

On 16 September 1938 he was rung up after midnight: "Erwin.
You have forty-eight hours to get out. Your arrest and deportation
to Dachau has been decided." He recognized the voice; it was a friend
who had joined the Nazi Party but worked on behalf of the underground. (There were many such.) Erwin was thunderstruck, for
though he had anticipated trouble he had not expected it so soon.
He came to me next day in the Singerstrasse so hopeless and dispir-
ited he could hardly speak. I finally found out what had happened
and explained the situation to Emma Cadbury. After a good deal of
telephoning, somehow she obtained entry permits for England which
arrived within two hours.

The Kagran Gruppe had set aside funds for the fares of emigrants, which Hans Koch had entrusted to the treasurer, Viktor Strasser, and they were kept in a money box with two keys, of which
Koch had one; but when he went to get the fare for the Strunzes'
journey he found the box empty: Strasser had stolen it all. We were

forced to apply, as often before, to the Gildemeester Fund. (Gilde-meester was a Dutch philanthropist to whose outstanding generosity in these terrible times I have seldom seen any reference.) The Strunzes got off on the train to Ostend, and I telephoned to Peggy, my wife, to meet them at Charing Cross. After they arrived in London, owing to the strain of recent weeks Erwin had a genuine breakdown, and Peggy took them all back to her mother's home at Annaghmakerrig in Co. Monaghan.

After my own departure from Vienna I went on trying to get accommodation for the Kagran Group in Ireland and England, but Mary Campbell, who had been in charge of it with me in Vienna, was drafted by the Quakers to other work and replaced by a woman who knew nothing of Vienna or Kagran and did not speak German, so the heart went out of the idea of group emigration. She simply selected those most easy to place. In this way she was able to dispose of Hecht, the Kagran beekeeper; Kalan, one of the very few agricul-turalists; and Weinberg, our butcher, and his wife: she was delighted with herself for this achievement, particularly when she had her pic-ture in the *Daily Mirror*.

We were left with a goldsmith, seven academics, a hairdresser, an umbrella maker and many clerks, teachers and shopkeepers. It soon emerged that simply shelter and support in a friendly ambience was all that could be organized. This we achieved through the gen-erosity of various private people in Ireland such as Arland Ussher in Cappagh, Co. Waterford, and Sir John Keane at Ardmore. I went to Bunnaton, a youth hostel in Donegal that was empty in the winter months. The parish priest, Father O'Doherty, wanted to build a road from Bunnaton to Port Salon and hoped the refugees would help him. We also found places in England for three groups of Kagranners. Inevitably in Ireland the sectarian question arose, and, I believe, our Irish Refugee Committee was unwittingly to blame for this. Members of committees seem always to be chosen to represent different inter-ests, whereas they should only have one interest, in this case the defence of the persecuted.

The long peace was about to end and the fate of the Jews had not precipitated that *saeva indignatio* in the rest of Europe that would have given encouragement to the many hundreds of thousands of non-Jewish Germans who hated Hitler and, in 1944, welcomed the rising against him. Thousands must have died fighting for a Fa-therland that had betrayed them.

Lately I came across a newspaper report of 10 December 1938 which I had cut out at the time. It tells of a great meeting in the Mansion House, London, on behalf of the Jews. The Archbishop of Canterbury spoke of "the systematic persecution without parallel even in the Middle Ages" and the "incredible mental and moral torture" to which the Jews were being subjected. Cardinal Pacelli sent the following telegram:

> The Holy Father's thoughts and feelings will be correctly interpreted by declaring he looks with humane and Christian approval on every effort to show charity and give effective assistance to all those who are innocent victims in these sad times of distress.

The tone of these two communications is very different. The Archbishop is explicit, the Cardinal is vague and general, but I do not think one can argue from this that the Englishman's heart was the warmer. It is the difference between the leader of a more or less homogeneous body and the head of a worldwide and heterogeneous community of believers. The Pope had followers in every land; all the Archbishop's were in one. Our disappointment in Pius XII springs from the delusive hopes that have been placed in universalism, in ecumenism. Now we know that if Christendom were ever to speak with one official voice, it would be a mouse's squeak. There would be so many conflicting sympathies to reconcile that in the end silence might seem best.

Catholics claim the Pope was impotent, and I believe that was so. For example, it was said that the Pope saved 400,000 Jews in Hungary. But these Jews owed their lives principally to the fact that Roosevelt had followed up an ultimatum about the deportations with a tremendous bombardment of Budapest on 2 July 1944.

As it happens, we were all wrong about the 400,000. It emerged at the Eichmann trial that he had defied all the neutral nations, Roosevelt and the Pope, and deported 1,500 Hungarian Jews in mid-July, and in October the shortage of labour in Germany was so great that they asked for a further 100,000. Since trains were no longer running, they were obliged to walk. Of 800,000 Hungarian Jews, some 100,000 survived.

Some are surprised that people are not more impressed by the compliments paid to the Vatican by Jewish leaders and the fact that the Rabbi of Rome even gave up his Jewish faith. But are the few who are dragged ashore entitled to give thanks on behalf of the millions who drowned? And is it not easy to undervalue the formidable social power of the community? The Jews were penniless refugees in foreign lands. Would many countries (Ireland, for example) have accepted them readily if they had publicly claimed that the Pope or the Church had failed them in their hour of need? The Austrians who came to Ireland never even blamed Cardinal Innitzer, the Austrian Primate, who ordered all the church bells in Austria to be rung when Hitler entered Austria to forestall the plebiscite. In reply to Cardinal Pacelli's cautious telegram, they themselves sent a very grateful one from Ireland to Rome. The Jews have reason to be apprehensive, even when a non-Jew like Hochhuth criticizes the Pope on their behalf.* When *The Representative* was played in Paris, demonstrators leapt into the auditorium crying, "*A bas les Juifs!*"

It is clear that in times of stress parliaments and churches are peculiarly subject to mass pressure and one cannot expect too much from them. Nobody, whatever his faith, who had read the fulsome greeting from the leaders of the Evangelical Church in Austria to Hitler—"the Tool in the hands of the Almighty" and "the Fulfiller of the Divine Will for the Salvation of our People"—could be confident that his own church would have shown greater courage or foresight.

In the twentieth as in the first century, we find the burden of Christianity borne by solitary and often anonymous individuals.

---

*Rolf Hochhuth, a German playwright, whose *The Representative* was first staged in 1963.—ed.

The Invader Wore Slippers

1950

During the war, we in Ireland heard much of the jackboot and how we should be trampled beneath it if Britain's protection failed us. We thought we could meet this challenge as well as any other small nation, and looking into the future, our imagination, fed on the daily press, showed us a Technicolor picture of barbarity and heroism.

It never occurred to us that for 90 percent of the population the moral problems of an occupation would be small and squalid. Acting under pressure, we should often have to choose between two courses of action, both inglorious. And if there was moral integrity about our choice, it certainly would not get into the headlines.

We did not ask ourselves: "Supposing the invader wears not jackboots, but carpet slippers or patent-leather pumps, how will I behave, and the respectable X's, the patriotic Y's and the pious Z's?" How could we? The newspapers told us only about the jackboots.

The newspapers have by this time worked the subject of resistance to the Nazis to death. They have passed on to livelier issues, so it is possible to anatomize this now desiccated topic in a quite callous way. We can forget about the heroic or villainous minority or those other irreconcilables who adhered to some uncompromising political or religious creed. We can look at the ordinary people, the X's, the Y's and the Z's, about whom there is a mass of documentation. By a little careful analogy and substitution we can see ourselves, and a picture of our home under occupation emerges with moderate clarity. It is more like an X-ray photo than a war film. It is quite unglamorous and perhaps it is only by the trained mind that the darker shadows can be interpreted.

In totalitarian war human nature is reduced to its simplest terms and a skilled invader can predict with fair accuracy the behaviour of the respectable X's, the patriotic Y's, the pious Z's. Of course there are innumerable divagations but in an avalanche it is the valleys and the riverbeds that count, the hundred thousand cart tracks can be disregarded.

I know that we Irish were not more complex than anyone else and that our percentages of X's, Y's, and Z's were about average and known to every likely invader. And I dismissed as inapplicable to us the propaganda stories of the jackboot with which the Allies tried to shake our neutrality. We did not, I thought, like most of the Slav regions, belong to the area of German colonization in which extermination and spiritual enslavement would be practised. And it seemed to me that the respectable X's who told us the reverse were speaking either without reflection or with concealed motives. It was surprising when the inevitable volte-face came after the war. The people who had been threatening us with the jackboot in places where no sensible invader would dream of using it, began to applaud his restraint. Indulgent things were said of generals, even jackbooted ones like Manstein, "who simply did their duty," and Rommel's biography was widely read in those pleasant Dublin suburbs where the X's live.

It seems to me that we civilian Irish, finding indulgence where we had been led to expect violence, might easily have been tricked into easygoing collaboration. Yet small peoples should become specialists in the art of noncooperation with tyranny. It is the only role we can play when the great powers clash, and we are hopelessly untrained in it.

Careful observation of precedent and analogy is the first need. This can be done best in small circumscribed regions, whose characters are fairly homogeneous. I found three such occupied zones within my reach, where the tactics of the invader with the X's, Y's and Z's severally were displayed as on a small diagram which could be indefinitely enlarged. There were the Channel Islands, where the respectable X's were in the majority; Brittany, where the influence of the romantically patriotic Y's was strong; Croatia, where the Y's were reinforced by the fervently pious Z's.

The policy of the invader in all these places, and the response it met, is best studied in the newspapers of the Occupation. Reminiscences of course are helpful, but they are usually written by men who are exceptional for either their independence of mind or their complacency. They are edited to flatter the vanity of their compatriots, seldom to chasten it. But the newspapers show the invader at his highly skilled task of manipulating the X's and Y's and Z's. Reading between the lines you can judge of his success.

I think it was only in Zagreb that I found easy access to the files, though even there I was met with some suspicion and surprise. The reason was that in Zagreb a revolution had taken place which had, temporarily at least, undermined the natural desire of every nation to conceal its weaknesses from itself or, in the smooth phraseology of self-deception, to "let bygones be bygones." Somebody before me had been over the files in the university library with faint pencil marks, and an incriminating collection of the acta and dicta of the X's, Y's and Z's had been published.

This had certainly not been done in Rennes, the capital of Brittany. In Jersey there is an excellent museum of the Occupation, but it deals with the behaviour of the Germans and not with that of the Jersey people themselves. And in the newspaper room of the British Museum I searched in vain for the Jersey newspapers which were published all through the war and had to be content with the incomplete Guernsey file, the personal gift of a Guernsey man. This indifference of the British archivist to the history of the Channel Islands under Occupation struck me as curious and significant. Has the national mind, like its individual prototype, some Freudian censor which automatically suppresses what is shameful or embarrassing?

The public does not want a truthful account of the Occupation. It prefers to switch over from extremes of reprobation to extremes of condonation. You will see what I mean if you read the most authoritative book on the occupation of Jersey, by R. C. Maugham. The publisher appears to be about four years behind the author. On the dust cover the title, *Jersey under the Jackboot*, is illustrated by a big cruel boot crashing down on a helpless little green island, and the blurb talks of the "courage and fortitude of the islanders" and "the misery, ignominy and privations that marked the trail of the Nazi hordes across the face of Europe." But the author makes it plain that the islanders were subjected to a more subtle instrument of pressure than the jackboot. They were very liberally treated indeed. The small island parliaments and courts continued to function, provided all their measures were submitted to German sanction. It was by an ordinance of the Guernsey Royal Court that all talk against the Germans was made punishable; thus when the manager of Le Rich's stores was cheeky to a German customer, it was before the Guernsey

Court that he appeared. He got off by explaining that it was all a mistake, that the German officers had all been charming and his son-in-law was taking German lessons. Divine service with prayers for the royal family and the Empire were permitted. So were cinemas and newspapers.

In an organized society our dependence on the newspapers is abject. The readers of the *Guernsey Evening Post* were shocked and repelled no doubt to see articles by Goebbels and Lord Haw-Haw*, but not to the pitch of stopping their subscriptions. How else could they advertise their cocker spaniels and their lawn mowers or learn about the cricket results? Ultimately Haw-Haw became an accepted feature like the testimonials for digestive pills, and an edge of horror and revulsion was blunted. Here is the printed summary of events for an October day in the first year of the Occupation:

> Dog-biscuits made locally. Table-tennis League of Six Teams formed. German orders relating to measures against Jews published. Silver Wedding anniversary of Mr. and Mrs. W. J. Bird.

The news of the deportation and torture of the local shopkeepers is made more palatable by being sandwiched between sport and domestic pets and society gossip: "Lady Ozanne had passed a fairly good night." "Mr. Stephen Candon is as comfortable as can be expected." There was roller skating at St. George's Hall, and *Laugh It Off* was still retained at the Regal and "the bride looked charming in a white georgette frock." Lubricated by familiar trivialities, the mind glided over what was barbarous and terrible.

The *Herrenvolk* philosophy judiciously applied, as it was in the Channel Islands, can be swallowed easily enough if you have not too sensitive a digestion and belong to a ruling race yourself. Flowerbeds were trampled, housemaids whistled to, garden tools unceremoniously borrowed, but formal apologies, printed receipts were often forthcoming if applied for. "I must record," wrote Mr. Maugham, of the German soldiers in his garage, "they did their best to give us as little trouble as possible, were perfectly polite and grateful for any slight help which they received from us," and the Procurator of Guernsey officially declared: "The Germans behaved as good soldiers, sans peur et sans reproche."

---

*William Joyce, an American-born Irish political activist who broadcast pro-Nazi propaganda to Britain on German radio during the war, was known as "Lord Haw-Haw." He was hanged as a traitor in 1946.—ed.

Such behaviour is plainly more formidable than the jackboot; we are hypnotized by the correctness of the invader into accepting invasion itself as correct. The solidarity of our resistance is undermined by carefully graded civilities; our social and racial hierarchies are respected. For example, in Jersey there were Irish tomato pickers and Russian prisoners at whose expense German prestige was adroitly raised in British eyes. When wireless sets were confiscated, the Irish, with disdainful correctness, were paid for theirs, as they were neutrals. This punctiliousness was more repaying than jackboots since it drove a wedge of jealousy between English and Irish. When later on a feud broke out between the "correct" Occupation troops and some "incorrect" naval ratings who daubed the shop fronts of St. Helier with swastikas, the authorities blamed this breach of etiquette upon the Irish, and there were some gentlemanly headshakings between the German and English officials over these vulgar antics of an inferior breed.

I don't think the Germans on the island had a difficult task in making the Russians in Jersey detested. Some of the Russians, who were employed in the fortification of the island, were convicts liberated from prison in the German advance into Russia. They were worked hard, fed little and flogged. A whip that was used on them can be seen in the Jersey Museum. They were inadequately guarded. Almost mad with hunger, they broke loose and pillaged the neat holdings of the Jersey farmers, taking hens, pigs, cabbages, clothes from the line. These raids began through the carelessness of the guards, continued through their connivance and finally had their active encouragement. The guards indicated the eligible premises and exacted a huge percentage of the plunder. When the Jersey people asked for protection they were met with a humorous shrug from the officials. "Well, they are your allies. Must *we* protect you from them?"

It is hard for the X's to keep a balanced judgment in such circumstances. Other problems too arise. Should they acknowledge the salute of the amiable *Rittmeister* who had known their cousins at Weybridge? Should they turn the other cheek when a degenerate Mongol ally robs the hen roost? These problems are more disintegrating to the resistance of the X's than bombs or jackboots, and a competent invader will make them inescapable.

In a Zagreb newspaper of 1942, *Deutsche Zeitung in Kroatien*, I read that Ireland, with Croatia and Slovakia, was to be one of the three model "allied" states in German Europe. In other papers too there was much of flattering intent about the common loyalty of Croats and Irish to Faith and Fatherland, our similar histories, romantic temperaments and literary gifts. Irish plays continued to be played in Zagreb, when English were taboo.

All the same, I think that Brittany under the Nazis offers more profitable analogies for us in Ireland than does Croatia. In Brittany the German attempt to exploit the patriotism of the Y's and the piety of the Z's, which in Croatia had been triumphantly successful, was only halfhearted. The Nazis had no doubt of the need to disintegrate Yugoslavia; they were undecided about France. Perhaps, after defeat, France might be won over more easily if her unity was not impaired; perhaps a separatist and Celtic Brittany might slip out of German influence and look westward to Celtic Wales. Also in Brittany the Catholic Church did not support the separatist movement, as it did in Croatia. There was no wide-scale convergence of patriotism and piety. By conciliating the patriotic Y's, the Germans might risk offending the pious Z's.

For all these reasons Nazi policy in Brittany was very inconsistent. The Germans sheltered the Breton rebel leaders Mordrel and Debauvais, as they had once sheltered Roger Casement, and they, too, were invited to recruit a rebel army to fight for independence among the prisoners of war. The Breton prisoners responded in the same halfhearted way as the Irish had once done. The Germans, however, continued to support the Breton movement till France had been brought to her knees. Then they made terms with Vichy, withdrew all aid from the Breton separatists and allowed them to operate only against the Maquis. They led the Bretons the sort of dance that cannot be done in jackboots.

I think the Nazi policy in regard to Ireland would have been equally agile and ambiguous. The Celtic nationalist would, as in Brittany, have been regarded as a valuable tool for undermining a non-German hegemony, but of decidedly less value for the reconstruction of a German one. The nationalist would have been manoeuvred, not kicked, out of his privileged position.

Judging by the Breton analogy, I think the first impact of the changed policy might have been borne by the handful of single-minded German Celtophiles, who would have been entrusted with the early stages of the programme. A successfully double-faced policy requires at the start the complicity of many single-minded idealists, native and foreign.

I think when the success of the invasion had been assured, it would have emerged that the respectable X's, the Anglo-Irish *Herrenvolk* of Ulster and the Dublin suburbs, would prove the more satisfactory accomplices in establishing the German hegemony. The Jersey treatment would have been applied to them, insofar as they were civilians. There would have been a dazzling display of "correctness." It is probable that at Greystones and Newtownards, as at St. Helier and at Peterport, divine service with prayers for the king and the British Empire would continue to be permitted in the Protestant churches. Certainly the inevitable bias of German correctness would have been towards the Anglo-Saxon, towards bridge and fox hunting, and away from the Irish, from ceilidhes and hurley matches and language festivals. A master race will be at times indulgent to these regional enthusiasms but will not participate in them. Ultimately this bias would have led to a complete reversal of policy, more in keeping with the *Herrenvolk* philosophy. Lord Haw-Haw, an Irishman himself, seems to have been in closer sympathy with Mosleyites* than with Irish republicans. The British Naziphiles were romantic, traditional, imperialist. Irish separatism would have been incompatible with their Kiplingesque ideal of a merry, beer-drinking "old" England, allied with Germany, grasping once more in her strong right hand the reins of empire and dealing out firm justice to the lesser breeds. I do not see how the Irish could have raised themselves permanently into the *Herrenvolk* class from which Czechs and Poles had been excluded. Of course the Croats had arrived there. But they must have felt their position precarious, because two well-known Croatian scholars, Father Shegitch and Professor Butch, developed the theory that the Croats were really Goths who had slipped into a Slav language by some accident. Pavelitch, the "Leader" of Croatia, who had a private passion for philology, favoured the theory and brought out a Croat lexicon in which all words of Serbian origin were eliminated, a work of great ingenuity because the Serbian and Croatian languages are all but identical. We Irish would inevitably have felt uneasy. There had been in Ireland eminent German Celtic scholars who had not managed to conceal their contempt for the modern representatives of those Celtic peoples whose early history enthralled them. Nazi philosophy was permeated with race snobbery, and we are outwardly a rustic and unpretentious people. When the Nazi leader Ribbentrop visited Ireland, it was with a Unionist leader, Lord Londonderry, at Newtownards that he stayed. In the Nazi hierarchy of races the Irish would not, I think, have ranked high.

---

*Followers of Oswald Mosley (1896–1980), head of the British Union of Fascists from its inception in 1932 to its demise following the Public Order Act of 1936.—ed.

It is likely that ultimately more attention would have been paid to our piety than to our patriotism. Its pattern is universal and familiar and so more easily faked, whereas patriotism has so many regional variations that no ready-made formula could be devised to fit them all. Many of the pious Z's would have responded to skilful handling. The other day I read in an Irish newspaper the sermon of a well-known preacher. "The world," he said, "may one day come to be grateful to Hitler." He was thinking, of course, of Communism, and it was the constant preoccupation of the Nazis that the minds of the pious should always be inflamed with the fear of it. In that way charity and humanity, where they were only superficial, could be skinned away like paint under a blow lamp. But in the technique of perverting piety it was in the Independent State of Croatia that the Nazis first showed their consummate skill. Pavelitch's Croatia deserves the closest study.

When an incendiary sets a match to respectability, it smoulders malodorously, but piety, like patriotism, goes off like a rocket. The jackboot was worn by the Croats themselves and used so vigorously against the schismatic Serbs that the Germans and the Italians, who had established the little state, were amazed. Pavelitch, the regicide ruler of Croatia,* was himself the epitome, the personification, of the extraordinary alliance of religion and crime which for four years made Croatia the model for all satellite states in German Europe. He was extremely devout, attending Mass every morning with his family in a private chapel built onto his house. He received expressions of devoted loyalty from the leaders of the churches, including the Orthodox, whose murdered Metropolitan had been replaced by a subservient nominee. He gave them medals and enriched their parishes with the plundered property of the schismatics, and he applied the simple creed of One Faith, One Fatherland, with a literalness that makes the heart stand still. It was an equation which had to be solved in blood. Nearly 2 million Orthodox were offered the alternatives of death or conversion to the faith of the majority. The protests of the X's, Y's and Z's were scarcely audible.

Yet, as I read the newspaper files in Zagreb, I felt that it was not the human disaster but the damage done to honoured words and thoughts that was most irreparable. The letter and the spirit had been wrested violently apart and a whole vocabulary of Christian goodness had blown inside out like an umbrella in a thunderstorm.

---

*Ante Pavelitch masterminded the assassination in 1934 of King Alexander by the pro-Nazi Ustashe. He subsequently became leader in 1940 of the puppet state of Independent Croatia.—ed.

It is easy to illustrate this from the newspapers of a single week in spring 1941. In one Zagreb paper, for example, the king's speech on the bombing of Belgrade was published with appropriate comments on April 10:

> On the morning of Palm Sunday, while children slept their innocent sleep and the church bells were ringing for prayer to God, the German aeroplanes without warning let fall a rain of bombs on this historic town . . .

And the king went on to describe the terror of the women and children who were machine-gunned by low-flying planes as they fled from their homes.

The following day the Germans in Panzer divisions arrived in Zagreb. Flags were out in the streets to welcome them and the same paper wrote in solemn phrases:

> God's providence in concord with the resolve of our allies has brought it about that today on the eve of the resurrection of the Son of God our Independent Croatian State is also resurrected . . . all that is right and true in Christianity stands on the side of the Germans!

When Pavelitch fell, the Z's had to take a third somersault. Words had by then lost all relation to fact, and thereafter there was something schizophrenic about the exaggerations of the Croatian Z's and their sympathizers. Rather than admit their horrible inadequacy, they plunged about in contrary directions, sometimes whitewashing Pavelitch, sometimes making him blacker than life.

Many were able to turn head over heels in a quiet, gentlemanly way. For example, the Bishop of Djakovo, Dr. Akshamovitch, who received in a very friendly way the delegation from the National Peace Council of which I was a member, was a kind old man of whom we already knew a little. Under Pavelitch circulars flowed from his diocesan printing press headed "Friendly Advice," reminding the Serbs that Jesus had said there was to be one flock and one shepherd and that, as Catholics, they could stay in their homes, improve their properties and educate their children.

When Tito came to power the bishop is said to have invited the Central Committee of the Croatian Communist Party to lunch. He certainly attended a peace meeting in Belgrade. His photograph was printed in the press, as was his speech, in which warm praise was given to Tito. Should one charge him with opportunism? At this range one cannot judge him, but what is clear is that both governments valued his support and profited by it.

In future wars, if there are any, the formulae of corruption will be a little different but the principle will be the same. It may be said that the respectable X's will only be wooed by the invader if he comes from a capitalist country, but that, if he is Communist, no dangerous flirtations need be feared. I am not so sure. Acquisitive, tenacious, timidly orthodox people are not confined to any class or creed. It is a matter of temperament rather than of social standing or of politics. They have the force of inertia, which all invaders will wish to have on their side. As for piety and patriotism, whether they are deep or superficial, they are ineradicable from the human race. In the long run the modern state, East or West, will try to assimilate the X's, Y's and Z's, not to exterminate them.

Horace once wrote that the honest man, innocent of crime, could protect himself without Moorish javelins, without his bow or his quiver full of poisoned arrows. But is ordinary innocence enough nowadays or must he cultivate the unseeing eye? Must he not "mind his own business" like the professional man, or "simply do his duty and carry out orders" like the soldier, or like the tradesman "just get on with the job"? (The Channel Island papers are full of cheery synonyms for connivance!) Are we really obliged to admire the armour-plated innocence and respectability of General Rommel, that *preux chevalier* of the subscription libraries? He concentrated so fiercely on his professional duties that ten years after Hitler came to power he was still able to be ignorant of, and shocked by, the Jewish extermination policy, by gas chambers and the destruction of Warsaw. I don't think these questions can be answered unless we isolate them and study them in a small, more or less homogeneous area. It is clear that small peoples are used as guinea pigs by the great powers. Experiments are tried out on them which are later applied on a wider scale. Their suffering and their reaction to suffering are studied but only for selfish, imperialistic ends. Should not the results of these experiments be recorded now while the memory is still fresh and accuracy and candour are available? For though such knowledge will not of itself bring us the will or the courage to resist tyranny, it will prevent us from dispersing our strength in fighting against shadows. By learning from which direction the most insidious attacks are likely to come, we may acquire the skill to forestall them.

In the Adriatic

1937–78

FIUME, SUSHAK AND THE NUGENTS

Lately I have been reading Elizabeth Hickey's *Green Cockatrice* (1978), which is in part a history of the Nugents of Westmeath and in part a celebration of one of their most interesting members, the Gaelic poet William Nugent. It reminded me that nearly thirty years ago I had visited Fiume and its neighbouring town, Sushak, where the last of the Nugents, an elderly woman well remembered in the town, had recently died.

Fiume, at the head of the Adriatic where Italy and Yugoslavia meet, takes its name from the river, or *flumen*, which divides it from Sushak. This small stream was for twenty years the frontier between the Slav and Latin peoples, but now the Yugoslavs have joined the two towns with a broad flat bridge and under it the little Fiume, or Rijeka, as stream and town are now called, never very impressive, has become almost unnoticeable. The bridge is more like a big square than a bridge and is planted with rows of chestnut trees under which the citizens of Fiume and Sushak mingle and listen to the band. It is a symbolic bridge.

For D'Annunzio too the bridge, an earlier narrower bridge, had a symbolic significance. He had with his young Arditi seized the towns in 1919 from the Yugoslavs, to whom they had been awarded by the peace treaty. The Arditi were the forerunners of the Fascists and their cry "*Eja, Eja, Alala!*" with which they marched across the bridge was adopted by the Fascists. When shortly afterwards Sushak (but not Fiume) was awarded by a new treaty, once more to the

Yugoslavs, the bridge was not abandoned without a struggle, in which it was destroyed. It was photographed and widely advertised as the saddest of all the casualties.

When I was there the Italians and Croats had almost forgotten the hectic days of D'Annunzio, and I bought a history of his short reign for a few shillings. The first page was covered with a dedication in his own dashing handwriting to his glorious comrade-in-arms Attilio Bijio, and there were fifty photographs of ecstatic triumphs and processions and conquests of Dalmatian islands—all now forgotten. Or are they entirely forgotten? I was told how, a little before, a foreigner missed his wife, Eva, in a crowd at Fiume railway station. He called after her shrilly "Eva! Eva! Allo! Allo!" It was almost his last cry because he was battered by his fellow travellers with suitcases and umbrellas. They thought he had been crying "*Eja, Eja, Alala!*"

A steep rocky hill rises above Sushak. On top of it are the castle, church and village of Trsat. One tower of the castle is Roman, for there where Sushak now stands was the old Roman town of Tersatica. The rest of the castle was built by the Francopans, an ancient Italian family of unknown lineage, who claimed like Dante and Thomas Aquinas to be descended from the patrician family of Aricius, and who ruled Croatia for several generations and became more Croatian than the Croats. At the beginning of the last century it was bought by the Irish general Laval Nugent. He had left Westmeath some forty years before and taken service with the Hapsburgs. When Napoleon set up an Illyrian state in Croatia the Austrian emperor had been powerless to evict the French, so Nugent had taken the matter in hand himself. Mustering the Croats of Istria and Dalmatia he pushed the French far back into Italy. By the Austrian emperor he was later made a count and a marshal. He restored in part the old castle, built a chapel there and below it a pleasant modern house for himself.

I found a remarkable old man living in the Nugents' house, which was badly battered by bombs. He had been a *Feldwebel* in the Austrian army, then he had become an Italian, now he was a Yugoslav. He had known well the last of the Nugents, an old woman who had died aged ninety in 1941, blind and alone, and he had read and knew by heart all the history of the neighbourhood. The Yugoslav government had made him a curator of the castle.

From the square Roman tower, we looked far down on the two blue harbours of Fiume and Sushak, separated only by a spit of land and the small river. Eastwards the Croatian littoral ran past the big bare islands of Krk and Cres and Dalmatia, and behind it, gauzy grey, we could see the high Velebite Mountains that lie between Zagreb and the coast. On the west there was the rocky Istrian shore curving southwards at Abbazia, an elegant but now deserted resort. The old man pointed out the route by which Charlemagne's generals met the Croats in battle and after some reverses checked them in Istria, so that they never came into Western Europe. He sketched the campaigns of the Francopans, of Marshal Marmont and Laval Nugent. He had had none but local visitors for a long time and he was pleased to talk.

The chapel that Laval Nugent built lies above the dungeon of the Francopans. It is a big classical building, but it and one of the Francopan towers has been badly damaged by war and vandalism. There was a stack of planks lying beside it, and the old man told me that the Yugoslav government was going to spend large sums in restoring it. "Some young Communists in the village said it should all be thrown into the sea as a reminder of feudalism," he remarked, "but I told them that even the Russians respected old things. When the Finns could not pay their reparations in cash, they said, 'Then pay us in antiques.' "

A huge stone double-headed Austrian eagle perched on a coat of arms was lying on the ground. When the Italians came first they had brought a row of lorries to take anything valuable away, but the village boys had anticipated them by pulling down the eagle and hiding it in the earth. Countess Nugent liked the Italians and so they had tied her in her chair and put a handkerchief in her mouth while the digging was going on. That was during D'Annunzio's raid. In this war she had been too old to interfere and the Italians had pulled the lids off Laval Nugent's marble sarcophagus and rummaged for gold, and they had smashed holes in all the other family vaults as well. After the fall of Italy a German general arrived at Trsat. "What barbarians the Italians are!" he had exclaimed, and the Nugent bones were collected and the vaults sealed again. A modest vault, which the Italians had not bothered to break into, had the name JANE SHAW carved on it. "I wonder is she a relation of Bernard Shaw?" the old man said, and he told me that some time before the war the playwright had come to Fiume in a yacht and that he had stood on the bridge at Sushak and sung a song. "We all crowded round and laughed and were very pleased."

He brought out a big portfolio from the house and showed me photographs of the village boys grouped round the Austrian eagle in their best clothes after they had dug it up again with ceremony. Also there was a photograph of Countess Nugent talking to him on a seat. She had a mass of white hair and a cross, distinguished face. "She was very fond of reading Nietzsche," said the old man, "and knew every language but Croatian though she had lived among us for fifty years." She always called herself an Irishwoman. Her house was perpetually full of visitors, French and German and Italian and English sailors from the ships; it was only the Croats she did not like. When she grew old, she became very dirty and suspicious and would let nobody near her. Though she was stone-blind she went down every day to eat in Fiume or Abbazia and knew her way about the streets perfectly! She had not survived the war long. Her last words were "*Wo ist mein Geld?*" She had been a remarkable ascendancy type and the old man had learned much of his history from her.

When we left the castle of Trsat, church bells were ringing. One little chapel lay just below us, but as I came towards it its bell stopped and I saw there was no one inside; it was bare and small and cool with a delicious scent from a vase of Madonna lilies. Outside were two men lying on the grass on their faces. I think they had been ringing the bell in this deserted chapel of the Nugents simply to reinforce the sound from the belfry in the large church in the square towards which the crowds were streaming. Trsat village still has a feudal appearance in spite of the hammer and sickle and Communist slogans stencilled on the house walls; many of the people had the look of old retainers and their cottages were lined deferentially along the road to the castle. Their gardens were full of flowers, and oleanders were already blossoming in empty petrol cans on their windowsills.

The church of Trsat has been for centuries the focus of pilgrimages from all over Europe, and outside the door there is a cluster of beggars and a row of booths selling candles, sacred mementoes, pictures and a small book about the Blessed Virgin of Trsat written by a former priest of the parish. The story is well known, but he writes with some charm and tells many details that I have not seen elsewhere.

In 1272, as is carved on an ancient archway through which a long flight of steps descends into Sushak, the house of the Blessed Virgin at Nazareth transferred itself to Trsat; in December three years later it left again. The first to notice the strange phenomenon were some men cutting wood early one morning in March. The Adriatic below them had stormed all night but all at once it had become peaceful and still and they heard a chime of silvery bells behind them in the wood and smelled the fragrance of spring flowers. They followed the bells and came upon a small house shaped like a tiny church and, inside it, a picture of the Virgin. They went straight and told the priest, who was ill. He seemed to be expecting them for he told them he had that night had a vision in which the Blessed Virgin had appeared to him and told him what had occurred. She explained how after her death the Apostles had used her house as a church, and that was the reason for its tiny belfry. The priest recovered from his sickness and there was great excitement in the village. Count Francopan quickly took charge of the matter and sent down builders to make a fence to protect the house from cows and repair the damage that had been done in its voyage. Yet lest he be thought superstitious and trivially minded he sent a priest and two skilled engineers as a deputation to the Holy Land to bring back evidence. They took with them the precise measurements of the house in Trsat and when they got to Nazareth they had no difficulty in discovering the foundations of the house of the Virgin. They compared the two measurements, and finding that they completely coincided, they brought back the happy news to Count Francopan. Soon afterwards some Franciscans were put in charge of the chapel.

That was the start of the great fame and huge concourses of people that came to the village every year. However, in 1295 there was a sad rebuff for Trsat; one morning it was found that the Virgin's house had flown across the Adriatic to a village near Ancona. It did not stay there long but after several further flights it finally settled at Loreto, where it has remained ever since. The great stream of pilgrims was diverted from Trsat and even Croats travelled across the sea to Loreto. One day Pope Clement visited Loreto and saw a group of Croat peasants wailing with tears in their eyes, "Come back to us, Holy Mother, and bring your little house!" The Pope was touched and to console them he sent a famous miracle-working picture of the Virgin, painted, it is said, by St. Luke himself. In a very short time this picture attracted as many pilgrims as the house itself had formerly, and Trsat recovered its celebrity and has retained it ever since.

In the early eighteenth century it was decided in Rome that the Virgin of Trsat should be crowned, and there was a three-day ceremony of incredible pomp and magnificence at which a strip of gold was fixed to the Virgin's head and the picture paraded through the streets of Sushak and Fiume. Boys dressed in white sprinkled flowers before it, trumpets blew and cymbals clashed, guns from the ships in the harbour roared salvoes and there were fireworks and torchlight processions in which all the civic dignitaries of the state played a part. Unfortunately, the cardinal who was to have performed the ceremony was detained by the plague, but there was a vast number of bishops and monks, in particular Franciscans, for it was they who had charge of the picture.

If one were to study the story of the Virgin's house and its wanderings against a background of mediaeval history, much that is perplexing would become significant. Trsat may well have been, through the Franciscans, a sort of bridgehead for the Catholic advance on the Byzantine and later the Moslem world, lying as it does on the frontier of Slav and Latin cultures. When the Franciscans of Bosnia were driven out by the Turks, many of them found refuge in the monastery at Trsat and later, when they returned to Bosnia, they still seem to have kept in touch with Trsat. The part played by Franciscans in Yugoslavia in recent years has been perplexing, and anything connected with their former crusading days cannot fail to be of interest.* In Western Europe the story of the Virgin's house is treated more or less allegorically. Aviators are under the special patronage of the Virgin of Trsat and Loreto. In Ireland there is a small chapel at Baldonnel Aerodrome where she is honoured.

During the war the Franciscans of Trsat supported the Ustashe, the pro-Nazi Croats who, led by the regicide Pavelitch, crusaded to eliminate or convert to Catholicism the 2.5 million Serbian Orthodox who lived in the newly created independent state of Croatia. The Serbian Orthodox claimed that it resulted in the greatest religious massacre in the history of Christendom, and the account of the discovery of 289 mass graves at the Ustashe concentration camp of Jasenovac in Croatia, published in *The Irish Times*, 1 September 1977, seemed to bear this out. At Trsat the guardian, Father Ignacije, and three friars received minor decorations from Pavelitch "for their long and selfless toil on behalf of the Croatian people, especially at the time of the return of Sushak to her mother, Croatia, in 1943." I do not know whether they were punished for this, but though the church has "Long live Tito" written in huge letters across it there was no evidence that there had been any interference with the worship there. When I got inside, the priest with his gold cape held back on either side by two small acolytes was walking up the aisle swing-

*See below, pp. 469–71 and 480–85.—ed.

ing his thurible towards the large crowds on either side. The church is almost like a picture gallery, and I was sorry that I had not come at a time when I could look at it more carefully. In front of me was a column on which was suspended a glass case containing a big stone and a picture of a ship, the *Ban Mazuranich*. While sailing from Havana in 1897 the ship had sprung a leak which would have sunk it had not the stone fallen into the hole and miraculously stayed there. The captain, Bertini, a native of Trsat, gave the stone and the picture as a thank offering to the Virgin. There are many other pictures of ships through the church, of Austro-Hungarian merchantmen which had been saved at the last moment from imminent destruction in places as far apart as the Bristol Channel and the China Seas. In the back of the church, which I was not able to visit, is the Virgin's picture and many magnificent trophies, a silver candlestick presented by a Croat warrior to the Virgin of Trsat, who had nerved his arm to cut off a Turk's head, and a curious ornament presented by the wife of a Serbian king.

In Fiume and Sushak as in all the towns of Yugoslavia, the walls are covered with stencilled slogans, and in shopwindows and in the halls of public buildings printed exhortations to brotherhood, voluntary labour and socialism are displayed, yet I did not, as in Russia during a similar revolutionary period, see any posters deriding the Church or its practices. An Italian in Fiume told me that he believed that the Communists would try, as the Fascists had done with success, to exploit the churches in their interest. They would make no direct attack on the Christian mythology but would hope that by tact and perseverance it might be assimilated to their beliefs. He told how Mussolini had adapted Christian phrases, practices and festivals, so that those whose Christianity was one of ritual observance found an easy passage into his fold. The Fascists had had their "pilgrimages," their "martyrs," their "hierarchs." He told me how the king of Italy himself had gone on a pilgrimage to Mussolini's birthplace, and on Christmas Day that there had been a Fascist festival of "Mother's Day" which was by slow degrees to supplant it. In the same way the Christian festival once supplanted the birthday of the sun, which had been celebrated by Mithraists on 25 December.

Yugoslav Communists are often angry and insulted when accused of attacking the Church, and it is certainly possible that the more ingenious of them may be unwilling that a spiritual machinery which was of undoubted use to the Fascists and Ustashe should be sabotaged without an attempt to run it in reverse. The Communists of Yugoslavia still keep Sunday and various saints' days and foster the same cult of birthplaces, processions and martyr-doms that was once fostered by Mussolini and the Francopans be-fore them.

NAZOR, OROSCHATZ AND THE VON BERKS

At the beginning of a revolution artists and writers find themselves in a position of unaccustomed importance. Their support is eagerly canvassed, and it is very hard for them not to be flattered by these attentions. In Yugoslavia the writer must depend on a very small public, on only a fraction of the reading public, which is not large, owing to the differences of dialect within the country. Even though some writers are of outstanding merit, they have very rarely been translated, so that, when a writer parts with his country, he says goodbye, too, to his craft and his livelihood. Painters, sculptors and musicians are less tied by their medium, and a man like Mestrovich, with an international reputation, can choose his politics without ref-erence to economic considerations; a writer can't.

A French writer, when asked to explain why certain artists col-laborated in France, said "Collaborate? But in politics artists are just children, you know!" It would be truer to say that artists are pas-sionate individualists and there are certain temptations to which they succumb rather easily. They will tolerate any system which gives scope to their temperament. They are restless, discontented people in modern democracies and are unusually open-minded in regard to any change.

Pavelitch and his German patrons took very great pains to con-ciliate the artists and writers of Croatia; a novelist, Budak, was the first President, and a number of literary papers of excellent quality were produced. I do not think the artist was much molested at the start; for example, Krleza, the best-known Croatian dramatist, lived on peacefully through the Occupation in Zagreb, though a Com-munist.* In the early numbers of *Spremnost* there are constant flat-tering articles about the sculptors Mestrovich and Augustinchich, the poet Nazor and the most prominent of the Croatian painters. The articles hinted, often incorrectly, that the subjects of their praise were supporters of the government. Sometimes the artist or writer re-sponded to this flattery with an ode or a picture; sometimes he con-

*German forces occupied Yugoslavia from 1941 to 1945.—ed.

tributed something noncommittal to the papers. That was good enough. The editors felt they had netted him. They did not insist on ideological conformity, his name was what they were after, and because of that these papers of the Occupation have much admirable material in them.

There was a curious technique if the writer or artist did not respond at all to their advances. He suddenly found himself whipped off to prison for no reason he could understand . . . as suddenly he would be let out; soon after, some friendly, casual person would come up and say to him, "Oh, by the way, I'm getting up an exhibition [or bringing out a new number], I'd be awfully pleased, old man, if you'd let me have something." One artist told me that he was able to resist this technique only by pretending that his mind had been unhinged by prison. Very few said flatly, "No." But the painters had difficulty with paint or materials or found their inspiration drying up, the producers found the plays were quite impossible to cast. The mercurial artistic temperament was freely invoked, and as it was wartime, there were often plausible excuses for doing nothing. Mestrovich, after he had been in prison for some weeks, found there was only one subject to which he could do justice at the moment. He must go to the Vatican and make some busts of the mediaeval Popes. He knew Pavelitch could not refuse so praiseworthy a suggestion. On the way there he was asked to accompany the Croatian exhibition to Venice, where his sculpture was to be displayed. He did so. He then made the busts in Rome, got a visa to Switzerland through the Vatican, and never returned to Croatia.

Soon after the liberation a magazine was published in Zagreb with the intention of disconcerting the government. It published various odes and declamations, photographs, busts and pictures that had appeared under well-known names during the Occupation and in which the Ustashe and the Germans were glorified. The editor pointed out that these people were now ardent Partisans and supporters of the government. It was, I believe, the last freely critical paper published after the liberation and it was very quickly suppressed. I do not know whether the editor was making a gesture against corruption or whether he was being just malicious. What he proved, I think, was that while the power and influence of the creative mind is acknowledged, only unrepresentative governments are prepared to subsidize it. They invite writers and artists to compensate with their enthusiasm for the frigidity of the electorate.

But it was not only creative minds that the Ustashe tried to buy but also cultivated and educated minds. With the collapse of several empires in 1918 a number of men, product of the wealth and leisure of this society, found themselves deprived of the climate in which their talents developed and needed to be maintained. I suppose they were considered greenhouse plants in a society which could not afford a greenhouse, but, as it turned out, their talents, which needed artifice and privilege for their development, were missed in a thousand ways in the new states. Alexander during his dictatorship made a great use of the Russian émigrés in Belgrade, and under Pavelitch in Zagreb the remnant of the Austro-Hungarian ascendancy, which was all but moribund, began to show signs of life; they were, I think, not quite so militant, embittered and combative as the Russians, their days of glory were further in the past, but they could not forget that Zagreb and Croatia had once been a great greenhouse for the forcing of their talents and that the civilization of the Croatian towns had been given an indelible stamp by the Austro-Hungarians. Probably it was the most idealistic and disinterested of them who took part in the new Croatia; the ambitious would find more scope under Hitler in Germany or Austria.

I can think of one Austro-Hungarian poet who for the first time in his life found in Pavelitch's Croatia an outlet for his remarkable gifts. As an Austrian whose family had been connected for centuries with Croatia and Slovenia, he felt himself qualified to act as interpreter between Croat and Austrian and for three years he filled the Zagreb newspapers with remarkable poetry and prose. The new Croatia was as indulgent as it dared to the old ascendancy—its temper was romantic and pseudo-mediaeval—but as all the Croatian aristocracy had disappeared or been absorbed generations earlier into the Austro-Hungarian upper classes, much compromise and connivance was essential. Poets, if they can't be anarchists, are susceptible to the romance of aristocracy, and I think it must have been this spurious pretence of aristocracy, with its bogus titles and resurrected pomps, ceremonies and traditions, that seduced for a time some of the better Croatian writers.

I am told that the great poet Nazor was induced at the beginning to write praises of the new regime, but though I found many articles in the Occupation papers praising his work, I could not find anything written by him. After a year he had had enough and in the New Year of 1943 the Partisans sent a car to Zagreb for him to fetch him "to the woods." He was an old man in poor health, and victory for the Partisans was still a long way out of sight, so his courage in leaving his comfortable home in Zagreb and a devoted sister in order to undertake this arduous journey across the frozen rivers and through trackless mountains of Bosnia will not be forgotten. The Partisans on their side paid a fine tribute to his fame and to poetry in undertaking the task of transporting, often by stretcher, this distinguished old gentleman with eczema and digestive troubles. He had his reward when he became vice president of the Federal Republic of Croatia and was the first to address in Zagreb the liberated citizens.

If it is true that romance and poetry disappeared under the Communist government in Yugoslavia, there was an abundance of both in the Partisan warfare. There cannot be many wartime descriptions to equal Nazor's; it is not ordinary reporting . . . the enchantment of the Bosnian woods in the early morning and the hallucinations that the interlacing branches and mists weave in the mind of a sick old man recall Turgenev. The hero worship and the comradeship of the woods was the real kind; not till it was transferred to the streets and newspapers and the election platform did the metamorphosis begin. The process is, I think, inevitable. Nazor prints in his book the poems that his comrades wrote, often about Tito; they are monotonous and uninventive as the song of the blackbird, but in the woods they have their own appropriateness. Tito is their Achilles, he has the head of a young lion, says Nazor, and like the heroes of Homer he is only partly real; he becomes the symbol of what men admire in each other, and everything he does and says becomes charged with significance. It is not till the symbol has to appear on the election platform that some spell is broken. "Tito with us and we with Tito" they scribble on all the walls. But it is not the same. Some appalling catastrophe happens which should be explained in terms not of politics but of social psychology.

Nazor's diary has great documentary interest.* As an old, bourgeois poet campaigning with young revolutionaries, his elderly attempts to share their thoughts as well as their hardships are sometimes embarrassing, but the reader gets the feeling that he is trying sincerely to interpret the virtues of the old world in which he grew up in terms of the new, and that he is trying to save a good many venerable but discredited idols from the first fury of the iconoclasts.

A staff officer, Major Moma Djurich, looked after him and saw

---

*Vladimir Nazor, *Partizanska Knjiga, 1943–1944* (Zagreb, 1949).

that he had very quiet horses and refused to allow him to carry arms. In a rebellious mood Nazor wrote him a poem:

> When will you give to me, Commandant Moma,
> Rifle and horse, not a broken old screw?
> Did you forget how Nestor of Homer
> Was older than I but a warrior too?
>
> Did you forget how, when Doichen was dying,
> They strapped on his harness? Come harness me well,
> And set me on horseback! I'm weary of lying.
> I too would be after the black infidel!

One day they arrived at a castle in Bosnia where Tito had his headquarters. It had been built in 1902 with turrets and battlements by a romantic landowner, Frau Isabella von Berks. She herself was of Croatian descent, but her husband's family came originally from England to Austria during a time of religious persecution under James I. They had been Earls of Berkshire but had been deprived of their estates, and that may have influenced her in spending her dowry on erecting this imitation Anglo-Norman castle on the banks of the stormy river Una. Inside it was furnished with four-posters and rich canopies, with carved Gothic presses and cabinets and refectory tables, no doubt in polished pitch pine. The long gloomy passages were hung with trophies of the chase, there were mirrors in heavy gilt surrounds, and ranks of ancestors in the dining room. The library was full of ancient tomes in lofty bookcases, German and French and Italian, but there was not a single book in the Croatian or any other Slav tongue. There was literally nothing in the whole castle, said Nazor, to indicate the country in which it was built. It was as if the owner had deliberately set out to ignore the people of whose blood she was. The castle had been ransacked by all the armies which had passed through it in the last year, Italian and German and Ustashe, as well as Moslem fugitives, and insults about the von Berks family were scribbled in Italian on the walls. Now it was the temporary headquarters of Marshal Tito and Nazor describes the speed and vigour with which water and electricity and telephones were installed by the Partisans and Tito. "May he do as well," he cried, "when they come into possession of the derelict and plundered castle which is Croatia!" Outside there was deep snow, so that the burnt and deserted villages, the unburied corpses, were hidden from view, the stumps of the plantations along the Una which the Italians had cut down no longer offended, even the rocks gleamed like silver in the sunlight. On the wireless the news came through of the victories of the Partisans in the Lika, of the Russian armies by Rostov. It was easy to believe, in this castle, that the worst was past.

In the night Nazor was restless with his illness and could not sleep, so he got up and wandered round the castle. There was no one about except two guards on watch outside the little room where Tito was still writing up his despatches. In the dining room the bright snow outside the window made such a lovely light in the rooms that he found his way around without lighting his torch. He was looking for a ghost, the inevitable tenant of an English castle, and what ghost was he more likely to see than Isabella von Berks? If she was ever to appear it would be now, when "barbarians" were desecrating this creation of her romantic soul. There was no ghost, and he did not know which of the portraits was Isabella, but he persuaded himself that if he flashed his torch into their faces, one after the other, the proud owner would surely move in her frame, if only to turn her back on him. He had an obsession that one day he would meet her and know more about her; he would find her perhaps sitting at the head of the dining table, reproachful and indignant, waiting for him. He felt that he understood her, for he too had a nostalgia for the past. He had lived for twenty years on his Dalmatian island in the shadow of a tower, and wherever he had moved to afterwards, conscious of being ridiculous, he had built himself a tower. He went back to bed disappointed but confident that all the same he would somehow get to know her.

The next day the doctor would not allow him to move, and while Tito and his men were ranging the countryside, Nazor was confined to the castle watching from the large window the snow thudding and slipping down from the evergreens and tossed off irritably, like premature flowers, from the bare and spindly twigs of the lilac. There was a slight thaw. The Una was black between its snowy banks, and the devastation on either bank was revealed. Where were the woods in which the animals whose heads hung in the dining room had ranged? Where was the bridge and little mill? When Isabella lived here and sat on the terrace the hills must have been clothed in greenery and filled with songbirds. (Now there is nothing but bleakness and in the distance the minarets of a mosque.) The voices of the villagers and servants must have come up to her. What a place for an old person to live and forget the past!

Every day, as they did repairs, something came to light in the castle; a muffin dish from behind the panelling, some candelabra from a hole in the wall, silver fruit dishes from the roof; but the Partisans had not time for a thorough investigation. Only Nazor had the leisure to explore, but that was not the sort of research in which he was interested. He wanted to re-create the life of Isabella.

He had luck, for Lisica, the wife of the caretaker, a sly and lazy person, still lived in the castle, and she took Nazor to see Isabella's room, and showed him an old photograph of Isabella, an unpretentious-looking woman in a white blouse and Edwardian coiffure. Lisica told him she was tall with blue eyes, did not talk much, and as a mistress was kind but firm.

Isabella sent him a second messenger, a Serbian in Tito's entourage called Tsrni, who had lived in Soviet Russia and spoke and read Russian and French, a hard, dry but prompt and resourceful man. Somewhere or other he discovered the *Stammbuch* of the von Berks, one of those monstrous, illuminated books, all gold and azure and crimson, compiled at the end of the last century to please the parvenu wives or unmarried sisters of the Austro-Hungarian nobility. He also found two packets of letters from Isabella to her son written in 1922 and 1923.

From these letters Nazor learned that Isabella's last years had been spent in struggles and difficulties, not peacefully and romantically in the castle of Oroschatz. Her son was looking after it for her; his own house in Slavonia had been burnt by the Communists (that is what he called them but probably they were Serbian nationalists) in 1918, and she was living with a married daughter and nine grandchildren in Germany. It was the inflation time and they were in great poverty and wretchedness. But she wrote with patience and courage and an utter absence of that pride and self-dramatization which Nazor had anticipated; she seemed to have given up her dreams about the castle, there was nothing left of her romantic fantasies. "She had only her Croatian mother's heart," said Nazor, "the cold misty romanticism of the foreigners from the North had been purged and chastened on the day of wrath, and it had given way to our Slavonic sensitiveness, warm, plebeian, creative."

Isabella was not buried here, said Nazor, and it was useless to look for her ghost, but if the hopes of Tito were realized and the castle was turned into a holiday home for poor children or for veterans, perhaps her kind shade would appear under the roof.

It seemed to Nazor that she had not spent her dowry in vain. "Build!" he exclaimed, as he ended this entry in his diary. "Build!

Even though you do not know for whom or for what you are building!"

I read all this with interest because I had stayed with Isabella's son, to whom the letters had been written, at his house in the village of Podgorac in Slavonia. I had come as a friend of his children's tutor, Christopher Cooper, whom I had met in Zagreb. Von Berks had been murdered early after the invasion of Yugoslavia, I suppose by the same people who had burned his house thirty years before and whom he called, with more justification than then, "Communists." They were probably just his neighbours and employees. He and such neighbours as he considered his equals were living precariously and resentfully on the edge of the abyss into which they were shortly to plunge. If he had been told that he would be murdered and his wife and sons have to fly, and his daughter, to whom he was devoted, could save herself only by marrying a village Communist, what would he have done? I think he could have done very little, except juggle a bit more with his and his wife's investments and see that his sons got a good English education.

They all of them refused to see anything inevitable about their fate; they had a personal grievance against Destiny which had permitted them, intelligent, educated, fastidious and honourable people, to be ordered about by people of low breeding and semi-barbarous culture. Yet when I read Nazor's diary it seems to me that there is nothing inevitable about ruthlessness, that it comes from a misuse of words; that it is the business of men of education to keep words flexible and rich in significance and to keep them free of crude antitheses. Mr. von Berks and most of his friends indulged freely in antitheses. There were good people and bad people, Communists and democrats, educated and uneducated, Slav and Teuton, us and them.

Mr. von Berks had none of his mother's romantic nature nor was he a snob; he valued wealth and privilege for the power they conferred, not for prestige. He had been in a bank in America after the collapse of Austria-Hungary and he had a superstitious belief in science. This did not interfere with his support of the Church, which he thought exercised a stabilizing influence on those incapable of independent reflection and without scientific training. Archbishop Stepinac* was an honoured guest at his table, but when the parish

---

*The Catholic leader of Croatia, in 1946 tried and convicted of collaboration with the Germans. See below, pp. 431ff.

priest came to meals this polyglot family used to joke about him in different languages, and their superior education showed itself not in the power to deflect or soften the impact of cultural difference but in giving the contrast extra pungency and force, which they did with eloquence and skill. International politics entertained him, local politics hardly at all. I think that he derived his extraordinary arrogance less from his pride of birth than from scientific enlightenment and American bumptiousness.

When the mayor's daughter in Podgorac was married Mr. von Berks asked me and Christopher to the interminable banquet in the village hall. He enjoyed himself on equal terms, arguing, quarrelling, drinking in the most convivial way with his red-faced sweating neighbours. He knew all their failings, just as they knew his, but there was not a trace of real comradeship in this reciprocal knowledge. He was an individualist more than a democrat. I don't think he had any confidence such as his mother had in the glamour and prestige of his ancestors. What he admired was science and power and American nationalism, which he mistook for internationalism. He regarded small nations as nonsense and was humiliated by the imputation that he now belonged to one. It was degrading to have to ask permission of Belgrade to travel though the land of the former Austro-Hungarian Empire, so he had provided himself with a special stamp and ink eraser so that he could organize his own passport and travel to Budapest or Vienna without ridiculous formalities.

I think his generation, Americanized and internationalized, was less easily assimilated than even his mother's. They were of more common fibre: they could capitulate or dominate but not live on equal terms, and with the disappearance of the feudal relationship with all its vague reciprocal obligations, the stark antitheses of wealth and poverty, pretension and powerlessness, became more pronounced than ever before.

The von Berks lived in an ugly mansion at the end of the main street of Podgorac. It had been rebuilt after the Yugoslav nationalists had burned it in 1918, as splendidly as was consistent with comfort and practical good sense. The grandeur had been laid on afterwards on the side that faced the street. At the back was a straggling garden with a large rickety greenhouse which did not look as if it were much used. Paprikas and tomatoes drying on the edge had stuck to the woodwork. There were aubergines there, some like polished ebony but most had gone a dirty brown. Obviously the von Berks took no interest in their garden.

The second day I was there a local magnate, the Count, came to lunch. I had met him at the wedding banquet and had found him a very congenial person. After we had eaten we all four walked up the street together. It was October and the broad flat fields round Podgorac were full of dried stumps of maize stalks with golden pumpkins crawling around them, some of them pale green, some frosted and rotten. Four Podolian oxen were dragging a one-furrow plough across one of the fields. The ploughman shouted at them as they reached the headland and they trudged round as if in a trance, dark-eyed and blue-grey. "How beautiful," said the Count. "Horses would do this quicker," said the steward, "oxen for harrowing."

I never learned the Count's name or saw his house, but the fields at the eastern end of the village must have been his, as he showed us his wine cellar under a mound in the Turkish cemetery. "I won't have much wine this year, I'm afraid, as I've had lumbago and I could not go round and see that the vines were properly sprayed."

I think that, unlike von Berks, the Count was proud to be Yugoslav. He spoke Croatian, not German, to the steward. He had been born an Austro-Hungarian citizen but remained proud of his Croat nationality. Many such had cherished the Yugoslav ideal and, when the empire collapsed in 1918, had given their support to it. The man who had earlier pioneered the Croatian revival, Lyudevit Gai, had been half German. It often happens like that. In an empire subject peoples are ashamed of their language till someone of the imperial blood urges them to value it. That was the story of Douglas Hyde and the Gaelic League, of Yeats and Synge and the Irish Literary Renaissance. They were all Anglo-Irishmen.

As elsewhere in the formerly Hungarian parts of Yugoslavia, each cottage had a strip of land behind it. In the Austro-Hungarian days the landlord ruled the village and had the right of life and death over the villagers and kept a certain routine going, which still partially survived. At four o'clock on summer mornings the cow boy blew a horn under the priest's window and the cows went off to their grazing. The broad street was crisscrossed with the tracks of the cows. It is very muddy in the autumn but there is space enough for the traffic to use one half of the road till the other half has time to dry.

Podgorac on my last day seemed amazingly tranquil and beautiful. Turkeys and geese strutted down the street. There were maize cobs stuck away for the winter under the tiles. There was a short, rather noisy interruption. The fire-brigade band, having got out their uniforms and instruments for the wedding, marched up and down a couple of times extra before they put them away. The second time they collided with the cows coming back from the pastures. Each cow knew its own home and made for it, but they were wildly alarmed by the drumming and trumpeting, and for a few moments man and beast were helplessly interlocked.

Before I left, the Count insisted on my visiting the village school. There were little boys with books and little girls with embroidery crouched round the central stove. They must have had an imaginative teacher. He had helped them make a map of the country round Podgorac and another map of the Dravska Banovina, the province through which their river, the Drava, flows. It was constructed out of coloured matches, powdered paint and little bits of a sponge dyed green for trees. They were growing cherry trees from cherry stones and later were going to learn to graft them. The Count had given them a drawer full of oddities from his home and also an "orrery" to show the movements of the planets round the sun. And there were two large coloured posters on the wall, one to illustrate the growth of a lobster, the other the formation of a molehill. The children all looked lively and interested. I complimented the Count from my heart for what he had done for the school. I thought that, as he trotted away behind his white pony, he looked pleased.

Years later, when I heard what had happened to the von Berks, I wondered how the Count had fared when the Partisans arrived in Podgorac. Is it true, as a Roman poet thought, that the good man is his own protection? "He does not need Moorish javelins and poisoned arrows." I doubt if that applies in the post–von Berks world, where one is judged not by one's temperament but by one's presumed politics.

THE RUSSIAN CONSUL

On a night journey to Split in 1946, the other berth in my compartment was taken by a solid, youngish-looking man whom the wagon-lit attendant told me sotto voce was the Russian consul at Split. After we had shown our passports to the next official, the Russian told me that he had never met an Irishman before, though he had read about our agricultural problems in Engels. He was the first Russian I had seen after three weeks in Yugoslavia, though I had been told they would be ubiquitous, so we were both of us ready to be talkative. He discovered a catch in the window frame which released a small table and in a remarkably short time he had it covered with bottles of wine and beer and mineral water and two tumblers.

He disposed quickly of Engels and Ireland and then he asked, "What do they say of us in your country? Do they say we are savage illiterate muzhiks?"

"No, not exactly that," I lied, "but they are convinced that you are trying to get control of Eastern Europe."

"They're always saying that but it's not us, it's the people in these countries themselves. In the old days democrats used to look for their models to England or America or France; nowadays Communists look to us, as we are the only Communist nation. Is that not natural enough? As for the propaganda, look at this country! We have only fifteen representatives here, the British have about thirty. Look at the English reading rooms and clubs and the British Council. Do you know in Belgrade there's a French and an American and a Czech and a Polish and two British reading rooms, but not a single Russian one? And look at the other towns too, Zagreb, Maribor, Dubrovnik and the rest!"

I knew he was right about Belgrade and Zagreb, but I also knew that English people would say that Russian influence travels through unofficial channels and is applied through direct and sometimes violent measures. The Russians, they say, can dispense with reading rooms. But I had only started to mention this when the consul began about American intervention in Turkey and Greece, which I had to counter with remarks about Russian penetration in Hungary. I realized we were launched on one of those barren newspaper arguments from which there is no exit but silence and ill-temper.

"You see," he said, "we have never forgotten that Churchill and the Western powers intervened against us after our Revolution in 1917; we know that they'd like to do it again now. Why should we trust them?"

I was not sure how to reply to this, because in Trieste I had met many Yugoslav émigrés and their British sympathizers and I had heard the cry raised a score of times: "England and America must fight Russia now, while she is weak; in ten years' time it will be too late."

I could only repeat to the consul the platitude "Because everybody knows that the next war will be the end of civilization," but I was not convinced myself. I had read its refutation in the eyes of the Triestan émigrés: "We must all die soon anyway, and if civilization dies with us our personal tragedy will be, if anything, less anguishing."

There are numbers of broken and frustrated people with no great love of life or expectations from it who look forward to Armageddon with an almost religious excitement. Communists, on the other hand, never developed a mystique about war as a cataclysm that purges and sanctifies and, at the worst, releases. That kind of thinking is a disease of the West. Communists only like wars which they win or profit by. It is the saving grace of materialism.

The consul told me how much he and his family were longing to get back to Moscow. Split was nice enough—and he made a few deferential remarks about its antiquities—but it was not like home. His wife found Split women standoffish and unfriendly. Though he had only been a year in Croatia, he spoke Croatian fluently, so similar is it to the Russian language. Yet he seemed to feel himself almost as much a foreigner in this country as I did. Croatia is honeycombed with ancient prejudices and idiosyncrasies, and a Soviet citizen, used to the size and shapelessness of Russia, soon loses patience. He finds himself constantly obliged to move circuitously around some venerable taboo.

The consul's father had been an illiterate Moscow factory worker, and he spoke with immense pride of the campaign against "analphabetism." Soon there would be no illiterates left in the Russian army.

When I asked him about the devastated areas of the Ukraine he had the usual inhibitions. Sympathetic enquiries are always treated as attempts to spy out the nakedness of the land. He said quickly that in spite of Russia's vast sufferings she would in two years, because of her gigantic efforts, be stronger than ever before.

We spent a large part of the night talking like this, never entirely frank but always affable. The light was coming in under the blinds and the wine had been of the stimulating not the soporific kind. When I lay down in my berth, I knew I could not sleep, so I tried to give some shape to the ideas left by his conversation and my experience of Russian influences in Zagreb and Belgrade.

The competition for cultural influences is one of the newest and nastiest features of international relationships and so far the Russians, preoccupied with economics, have played rather a small part in it. Pan-Slavs were associated with reaction and Communists have not yet abandoned their belief that genius is international. Yet there are signs in Slav countries that they might modify this creed in the interests of a reformed Pan-Slavism. At the Zagreb fair in June, for instance, much honour was paid in the Soviet pavilion by means of busts and books, pictures and articles to the great Russian writers, even those who, like Dostoievsky, have been considered reactionary.

Undoubtedly this Pan-Slavism was inflamed by the German and Italian assault upon Slav culture; it might be still further stimulated by the cultural competitiveness of the Western democracies. When in the course of a friendly article in *The Manchester Guardian* on Yugoslavia A. J. P. Taylor wrote quite accurately that Croatia had always had closer cultural ties with the West than with Russia, he was venomously attacked in the Moscow papers.

How can this Russian distrust be overcome? In their contacts with the West it is impossible for Russians to make those admissions of insufficiency or indebtedness which as individuals they will make so generously. I found circulating in Zagreb a well-written article on the corruption of the British press. It was only by accident that I discovered that the Russian writer had drawn most of his material without acknowledgment from a book by Wickham Stead. A comparable analysis by a Russian of the Russian papers would at present be impossible. I see only one way in which a breach might be made in the wall of Russian suspicion, and that is by demonstrating constantly that other communities can criticize themselves and flourish; also by emphasizing always the cultural interdependence of nations and the international character of genius. Communists in theory believe this too, and opportunities for cultural collaboration in small ways might open up.

Unfortunately the Western powers in their official contacts are much more concerned with prestige than with candour or real cultural reciprocity. There is a kind of self-advertisement that many British mistake for self-criticism. "We may be slow-witted," say writers like Mr. Arthur Bryant, "but somehow we 'muddle through' in the end, thanks to our glorious . . ." etc., or again, "Maybe we attach too little importance to book learning, too much to what we English call character . . ." Only very ingenuous foreigners mistake this for the real thing. Handed out by the British Council in liberal doses, it acts as an emetic or perhaps I should call it a virus, because it induces something akin to rabies in the sensitive foreigner who comes into contact with it.

Leaving all the prestige business aside, an attempt should be made to show how extensive is the literature of criticism and revolt in Western countries and how closely interrelated and what deep roots Communism has in Western thought. It could be shown that

Western revolutionary theory is still developing and that Communism is only one of its offshoots. In England, for example, Wells, Shaw, Russell, the Huxleys, Orwell and Koestler are the legitimate heirs of the revolutionaries.

Yet such ideas have made little headway. They were not reflected in the collection of English books displayed by the British Council last June in Belgrade and Zagreb, nor in the small present of books given by the United Nations to Zagreb University. Typical of the nine or ten dozen presented, I found *The Life of Charlotte M. Yonge, The Later Life and Letters of Sir Henry Newbolt*, Vols. II and VI of Ben Jonson's *Plays* and a mass of belles lettres by Alfred Austen, etc. The idea behind this choice was probably a kindly one. "The patient is in a nervous state; give bromides!" An alternative possibility would be that there was no idea at all.

At present there is little organized resistance to Western cultural propaganda. The British reading rooms in Yugoslavia are always crowded, the exhibitions of British books had a huge attendance and a couple of Yugoslav ministers at the opening. A large shop in Ilica now stocks a big collection of British books, and the demand is not only for bromides. A professor of Zagreb University has just translated *The Years* by Virginia Woolf: five thousand copies have been published and are likely to be sold. In the universities there are five or six times as many students of English as of the Russian language. All this does not suggest a severe censorship or a cultural subordination to Russia. Yet such a subordination is so constant a theme in American and English circles that it is impossible not to believe that it derives from pique that any other cultural influences besides their own should be admitted. The constant marching about of children with flags and songs is regarded as a direct import from the Soviets, but actually the embarrassed godfather of marching, singing, over-confident children was Baden-Powell. As for sport, English influence is still supreme with Futbalkup, Boksmech, Dirt-track, Fiskultur, Ping-Pong. Only the earnestness with which they are regarded comes from Russia, as does the enthusiasm for chess. (There are special chess-match excursion trains.)

I am sure that the strongest foreign cultural influence still comes directly or indirectly from Hollywood, and though an attempt has been made to counter it with French, Russian and homemade films, it has not been successful. A good Russian film like *Alexander Nevski* would not even today draw as big a crowd as a million-dollar American production.

Russian example is no doubt responsible for the new state book-shops in Zagreb and Belgrade. There are a great many, and in structure and display they are a vast improvement on what preceded them. The books are largely political pamphlets, but there are foreign classics as well. Dickens, of course, is the favourite English author, Upton Sinclair, Steinbeck, etc., among Americans. Of the Russians the great writers are all represented. A window in one shop was given entirely to Lermontov.

The Zagreb Theatre, which is being very lavishly subsidized, is certainly not under exclusive Communist control. While I was there *Othello*, as well as *A Midsummer Night's Dream*, was staged, a Molière, an Ostrovski and two Croatian classics. In Fiume, Shaw's *Widowers' Houses* was showing. Owing to the advent of a left-wing government, the greatest of Yugoslav dramatists, Krleza, a revolutionary, has after a generation of suppression come into his own: in three months his chief play, *The Glembays*, has been staged more frequently than in the previous two decades.

Unquestionably there will be an increase of Russian cultural influence, but it is as likely to be exercised through the Russian classics as through their Soviet successors, and in view of the affinity of language and race it will be natural enough. Unless there is pressure from other nations it will not inevitably be chauvinistic. Yugoslavia should be regarded not as a cultural battlefield in which Russian influence must at all costs be defeated, but as a meeting ground in which propaganda might take a rest and friendly reciprocity begin.

After Ogulin the train passed through the Lika and I drew the blind up cautiously to see, if I could, that savage country of massacre and reprisal which Father Chok had described. The tiled houses were more substantial than I had remembered but they were scattered in lonely clusters around these forbidding mountains. Round each settlement were maize fields and cow byres and well-tended lettuce beds. Here and there a settlement was scorched and roofless. These were the crimes of neighbours, not of enemy bombers, and that much the more horrifying.

The blind slipped from my hand with a snap and woke the consul. We talked again till Split, where he was met by a lively and charming family. When he said goodbye the consul added with warmth: "I do not see why two different systems cannot exist side by side in friendliness." In print this reads easy and meaningless; as he said it, it carried conviction. A sociable and inquisitive people, the

Russians do not enjoy the isolation into which a conflict of principle has forced them.

IN DALMATIA*

The most sensational way to approach Dalmatia is from inland, for the small train that winds through an infinity of tunnels from Serbia across Bosnia and Herzegovina to Dubrovnik takes you in one March night from deep winter to mild spring. One day in Macedonia I saw a policeman and his wife laboriously cutting their way onto a main road through a bank of snow seven feet high. Our bus was stuck on the main road and we needed spades and tools, but for all the help the policeman could offer us he might have been a hundred miles, not a hundred yards, away. Not very many hours later and in bright sunlight, we saw Dalmatian women washing their clothes in the Adriatic, plum trees in blossom, hills covered with narcissus and wild hyacinths, mimosa and almond flowers already faded and families sitting under magnolia trees sipping wine and complaining of the weather. In the meantime, I had crossed the great barrier of karst that separates central Yugoslavia from the Adriatic and which accounts for the extraordinary divergence in the climate. Herzegovina, which I saw by moonlight in the early morning, must be one of the most desolate and barren districts in Europe. For miles, the only houses are the ruined cottages of the workmen and engineers who built the railway; here and there a cabbage patch has been formed by collecting earth into a pocket and protecting it with boulders from the goats. The cabbages bear tiny leathery heads on tall fat stalks; they are as high as the Herzegovinian oak trees, which the goats and the rocks have kept to the size of pot plants. Yugoslavs say that the Venetians cut down the original forests for the piles on which Venice was built and later rains and storms washed away the soil. It is hard to replant, for in the summer the hot sun sets fire to the parched conifers. But to reafforest the karst is one of the great ambitions of Yugoslavia and, in the summer, schoolchildren can be seen planting and watering young spruces in the mountains near their village.

For a long way, the line clung to a ledge of rock that hung over a black, winding lake which dries up in the summer and is planted with maize. As we descended almost vertically towards the sea, the tunnels and twists became more frequent, and sometimes we saw the

*This essay was composed in 1937.—ed.

engine coming from the mouth of tunnels we had not yet entered ourselves. A final bend, and the creeks of the Ombla and the islands opposite Dubrovnik appeared, and we were climbing down through myrtle and arbutus, yellow spurge and heather, into an almost tropical luxuriance of vegetation. This band of barren rock which runs from Fiume to Kotor separates the whole Dalmatian coast from central Yugoslavia. The barren hinterland has given the coast its unique character and history and has forced Dalmatians to look to the sea, rather than to the land, for their livelihood. From these districts the Yugoslav navy recruits its best sailors, as did the Austrian navy before the war. Dubrovnik (or Ragusa), Split, Kotor, Trogir, Sibenik and Zara, not merely from Greek and Roman traditions, but also by geography, were forced to become seafaring city-states, repelling raids from the hungry hinterland and keeping their independence by intriguing alternately with one or other of their powerful, predatory neighbours, with Venice or Turkey, France, Spain or Hungary, the Serbian or Bulgarian empires. Dubrovnik alone was completely successful in this. There is no breach in the walls which surround the town; it must be, with Rhodes, the most compact and beautiful and unchanged of mediaeval cities. Till Napoleon conquered it and made it a part of the Republic of Illyria and created Marmont Duke of Ragusa, it had been governed by its own aristocratic council for a thousand years. It is true its rector was for many centuries a Venetian, but this was a device worthy of Mr. de Valera for making him a nobody; not he but the native half-Slav, half-Latin aristocratic families were to be the real rulers; but to prevent rivalries it was necessary to have a nominal figurehead, whom nobody could envy and everybody would distrust. Characteristically, the Republic of Ragusa offered Machiavelli a seat on its council.

On the way from Dubrovnik to Split, most ships call at the islands of Korcula and Hvar, and there is just time to race round the little towns before the steward summons one back with his bell. They are all walled against pirates; flights of narrow ramshackle stone steps run past old houses with the coats of arms of Venetian noble families over the doorways. Above the towns there is nothing but rocks and olives and hens scratching among tins. Korcula is the loveliest but has a more pretentious seafront, with palm trees and local beaux and belles lined up to watch the steamer come in. They owe their prosperous appearance to sardines and rosemary, from which a special essence is made, and later on in the spring the tourists begin to come. In this season, most of the travellers are businessmen. There was a French agent for Bordeaux from Fiume, a Russian shipping agent and an American engineer who had been visiting his parents in Herzegovina. He was earning seven dollars a day, so had to stay not with them but at the hotel. He was shocked to find that his sisters wore "silly clothes" and he had spoiled all his four suits in the mud on his father's farm. This can only have been a stage in his social development, because the same day a Cunarder had landed in Ragusa, and its passengers had ransacked the town for "silly clothes," which, in Ragusa, it has already become profitable to fake.

We passed the island of Brač, which provided Diocletian with limestone for his palace at Split, and soon along the seafront we could distinguish vast Roman walls and Corinthian columns embedded in a long line of hotels and shops and restaurants. For Diocletian's palace has been preserved by being absorbed. The greater part of the old town is squeezed between its immense ramparts. The mausoleum, except for an ugly tower for which an English architect is responsible and a Renaissance chapel, survives almost intact as a Catholic church, while round it, except for a line of columns and the narrow lean-to roof, the peristyle stands almost as it did. Diocletian, who resigned his imperial powers in Nicomedia, had this palace, as large in itself as a small garrison town, built rapidly in ten years for his old age. As at Dedinie, King Alexander's residence near Belgrade, the royal quarters must have been a modest appendage to a vast military establishment. When the barbarians captured and laid waste Salona, the great Roman seaport a few miles away, twice the size of modern Split, the survivors took refuge in the palace, and, till the Slav invasion, it was never taken. They dug themselves houses out of the thick walls, and even now fragments of columns, of tablets and Roman archways, can be seen buried in the walls of the squat stone houses.

As for the great city of Salona, till a few years ago not a trace of it could be seen. When the Dalmatian coast (all but Ragusa) came under Venice, Venetian officials were encouraged to carry away the masonry and build from it the palaces in Venice. Sometimes they got masonry in part payment of their salaries. From the mountain above, the town debris slowly slid down but was held back by the city walls. Now it is on the higher level outside the ramparts that the most interesting discoveries have been made. A long line of sarcophagi stretches around the outer edge of the cemetery, each of them with a neat round hole bored in its massive lid, through which the Avars extracted everything of value. They left only one tomb for the museum officials to rifle. Attilia Varia, a civil servant's wife, was buried with a pair of gold brooches shaped like cockles—un-Roman, un-Illyrian. Soon after Diocletian's death Christianity became the religion of the Roman Empire, and his body was flung out from his mausoleum. A couple of centuries more and his birthplace, Salona, had been sacked by the barbarians. Illyria was lost to Rome.

Soon, generations later, a pope, by birth an Illyrian, collected funds and sent a mission to help Roman citizens who still survived in the devastated land. They came back with the bones of the martyrs of Salona, and there still exists in Rome an altarpiece he had painted in their honour: four Roman soldiers carrying their martyrs' crowns and four martyred high officials of the Church surround the pious organizers of the expedition.

Trogir is only a few miles from Split. It is the most perfect of all the little Venetian towns of the coast. Two years ago, Mussolini declared in a resounding oration that wherever there was a lion of St. Mark's, there was Venice; wherever was Venice there was Italy. The patriotic youths took up the challenge and one night at 1 a.m., armed with stones and mallets, they smashed all the Venetian lions in Trogir. One vast lion, half disembowelled, still wags his tail upon a bastion too high and large to be easily destroyed. Two were removed in time to the safekeeping of the museum; a third still survives in Trogir because the courtyard where it stands is always locked. This lion is the most insulting of them all, because the Bible on which he props his paw is closed; the text which the Venetian lion usually examines is one of peace, but there could be no peace with the Slavs of Dalmatia. The lion at Trogir had to be always ready to spring.

There is one town on the Dalmatian coast, Zara, that was given to Italy by the peace treaty. But in Dalmatia as a whole the population is overwhelmingly Croat, at most 5 or 6 percent are Italians. Italy can, therefore, base her claim to Dalmatia only on sentiment and history. Zara and Fiume are sufficiently expensive tributes to sentiment, for the port of Fiume, severed from its hinterland, is dead and Zara must buy its food from Yugoslavia and have its numerous officials paid from Italy. There was a rumour in Split that a result of the new friendly relations between Italy and Yugoslavia might be the return of Zara to Yugoslavia in exchange for concessions to Fiume, by which she might recover some of the shipping which has been diverted to Sushak, Fiume's Yugoslav suburb. But in modern Italy glory is more important than gain and the rumour has been sceptically received.

The cruising habit has led to the discovery of the more famous

Dalmatian ports, such as Split and Dubrovnik. How long will it be before Sibenik and Rab, Crikvenica, Herzegnovi and all the enchanting towns and islands that line the coast from Fiume to Montenegro become well known to British tourists? Those who like hotels that are good and cheap and life that is simple and unspoilt must go now, before commercial tourism has turned Dalmatia into a second Côte d'Azur.

The Last Izmirenje

1947

For three days the rain had fallen steadily. When we arrived in Kotor, the top of Lovćen was invisible, and festoons of moist cloud swam across the mountains behind us. Nonetheless, there was a band to meet the boat and a great crowd, and on an iron mooring post a youth was arranging salvoes of welcome. Every now and then there was an enormous bang and he disappeared in thick white smoke, for explosions are the Dalmatians' favourite way of celebrating great occasions, and today was a feast day in both the Catholic and Greek churches. It was Easter Day for the Orthodox, while for the Catholics it was the feast of St. Hosanna, a nun whose mummified body lies below an altar in one of the Kotor churches.

I pushed my way through the crowd, and asked the first likely person I met where the monastery of Grbalj was, and what time the *izmirenje* was to be. Nobody knew, though I had heard about it in Belgrade three hundred miles away, while here it was only half an hour's drive by car. It was not till I had searched the town for information that I found, at last, that I was a day too early. I was rather relieved; perhaps the next day the rain clouds would have lifted.

In the afternoon, with two others, I made a halfhearted attempt to drive to Cetinje, but soon after we had passed the old Austrian customs house at the frontier of Dalmatia and Montenegro, we were in dense fog and the whole panorama of Kotor Bay, which must be one of the loveliest in the world, had disappeared, and we were shivering with cold and damp. We went back; that evening, when I was having tea in one of the old houses at Dobrota, I was told the story of the Montenegrin blood feud by a lady who had studied law and had attended the trial of Stevo Orlovich in an official capacity.

The Orloviches and the Bauks were two families living some fifteen miles from Kotor, not in Montenegro itself, but observing the old Montenegrin customs. Two years ago the Orloviches had made enquiries and learned that Stjepo Bauk, whose father was dead, would let his sister accept a proposal from Stevo Orlovich. Stevo, thereupon, set out with a group of his relations to make a formal offer, carrying firearms, as was the custom, so as to celebrate the betrothal with the usual explosions. When they reached the Bauks' house, they were told that the offer was refused.

It appeared that an old uncle of the Bauks had been greatly insulted that his permission had not been asked. He had made a row, and Stjepo had given in to him. Stevo Orlovich was outraged and indignant, and whipping out his gun he fired at Stjepo Bauk and hit him in the leg. Bauk fired back and injured Orlovich—there was a scuffle and the Orloviches took to their heels. A few days later, Stjepo Bauk's leg had to be amputated, and he died. The case was tried in the courts, and Stevo Orlovich was sentenced to three years' imprisonment.

But the Bauks were not in the least pacified by this; they held to the old Montenegrin tradition that blood should be avenged by blood, and the Orloviches continued to feel uneasy. Near Podgorica, in Montenegro, just such a murder had taken place in 1930, and since then thirty murders have followed it in alternate families, the last one six months ago. It has been impossible for the courts to collect satisfactory evidence; though the relations of the victim in most cases knew the murderer, they would scorn to hand him over to justice. Revenge is a private, not a public, responsibility. But there was a way out, and this the Orloviches took.

Some ten months ago, when Stevo Orlovich had had the rest of his sentence remitted for good behaviour, twenty-four "good men" of the Orloviches called on the Bauks, and asked them to agree to the *izmirenje* ceremony. The Bauks refused. Five months later, the Orloviches appealed again, and this time they were granted a day's armistice for every member of the deputation, that is to say, twenty-four. After that they came a third time, and at last the Bauks granted their request. It would be the first *izmirenje* celebrated in the neighbourhood for more than a generation, and it was this ceremony that I had come to Kotor to see.

"Of course," my friend said, "it won't be nearly as elaborate an affair as it used to be. In the old days the murderer had to crawl on his hands and knees and beg forgiveness; and then he must give a gun to the head of the other family as a token. And then there were the babies at the breast. Seven women of the murderer's family had to come with their seven babies in cradles, and ask the head of the family of the murdered man to be the *kum*, or godfather, and he was obliged to accept.

"That shows what size the families were," she added. "Today, in all Dobrota, you couldn't find seven babies at the breast, far less in one family."

The birds were singing next morning at six o'clock, and the fog seemed to have lifted completely from Lovćen. It looked as if the day was to be fine. I was told to be ready on the quay at 7 a.m., and was to share a car with the two judges who had sentenced Orlovich, two local correspondents of a Belgrade paper and one of the hundred guests invited by Orlovich. This guest was so confident that the ceremony would wait for him that we were an hour late in starting. To get to the monastery of Grbalj you must climb up the slope of Lovćen out of the Boka, and then down again towards Budva on the open sea. Most of the district is a *polje*, or flat space between the mountains, and relatively fertile; the peasant houses are placed for the most part on the rocky, barren slopes where nothing grows except scrub or wild pomegranates and stunted oak; their farms lie below them in the *polje*, full of vines, fig trees, beans and potatoes, market crops that they can sell in Kotor.

The people of Grbalj were always an enterprising community from the time of the great mediaeval Tsar of Serbia, Dushan; they had their own laws; and the Venetians, when they occupied the Boka and its surroundings, respected the Grbalj Statute, which was abolished only when Dalmatia was seized by Austria after the Napoleonic Wars.

We soon saw the monastery perched on a hill on the left—an unexpectedly small, insignificant building, its courtyard black with moving people. The larger half was completely new.

"The old building was raided and burned by the Montenegrins themselves during the war," the judge told me. "They say the Austrians were using it as a store for ammunition. It was rebuilt, and they opened it again last year. There are some twelfth-century frescoes in the end of the chapel, but they're badly damaged by damp, as it was roofless for so long."

Behind us, a mile or two away, but plainly visible as it lay open on the rocky face of the mountain over against the monastery, was the cluster of houses where the Bauks and the Orloviches lived. They were large red-tiled farmhouses two or three storeys high, with big windows and several annexes. The Bauks' house was the bigger of the two.

"The Bauks have a dozen families scattered over the place," said the judge, "but the Orloviches have only two, so I don't know how they'll pay for the dinner; you see, they must bring a hundred of their supporters and the Bauks must bring a hundred of theirs: the Bauks will be the hosts, but the Orloviches must pay for it all. It may run them into a couple of thousand dinars. If either side brings more or less than a hundred, it's a gross insult, and they'll have to start the whole business over again."

The hundred Orlovich guests were already there when we arrived; outside the wall of the churchyard a group of women and neighbours, whom neither side had invited, were leaning watching. The women, in Montenegrin fashion, had their thick black hair wound across their foreheads in heavy plaits; black lace veils fell from behind to their shoulders.

There were two long tables stretched out in the courtyard covered with brown paper, but the Orloviches were most of them sitting upon the wall. The six "good men" who headed the Orlovich deputation were in the vestry when we arrived, drinking Turkish coffee. One was a fat, pleasant-looking priest in a grey soutane from a neighbouring parish. Two seemed prosperous town relations in smart overcoats, clean-shaven, with gold teeth and Homburg hats; two were well-to-do farmers in full Montenegrin dress, round caps with red crowns embroidered in gold and the black bands that all Montenegrins wear in mourning for the battle of Kossovo, when the Serbians were defeated by the Turks in 1399. They had red waistcoats with heavy gold embroidery, orange sashes and blue breeches with thick white woollen stockings and string shoes. The other ninety-four Orloviches had compromised about their clothes; they nearly all had the caps and some had either the breeches or the waistcoat, but they mostly had an ordinary Sunday coat on top. They all had black moustaches, and held either a heavy stick or an umbrella in their hands. I saw one or two men who had both.

One of the journalists from Kotor beckoned me into the church, and introduced me to the priest and a small dark man with terrified eyes who stood beside him.

"That's the murderer," he told me. "You are the murderer, Stevo Orlovich, aren't you?" he asked to make certain.

"Yes"—and we shook hands.

We shook hands with his brother, too, an older, solid-looking man. He, too, had received a bullet wound in the leg as he was running away from the Bauks' house. Stevo Orlovich shrank away behind the chapel walls as soon as he could; he was very slightly built, and had black bristly hair and a small Charlie Chaplin moustache; he wore a neat but worn black suit, with a fountain pen clipped in the breast pocket. He was evidently in an agony of shame and embarrassment about the ceremony he was going to have to go through. But he was sufficiently collected to make it clear that he wasn't pleased to see us.

All at once a boy began to toll the three small bells of the chapel, and five or six people went in to hear the priest celebrate the short Easter Mass according to the Greek rite. I saw the correspondent of the Belgrade *Politika* standing beside them leading the responses in a booming voice.

"Christ is risen!"

"Lord, have mercy on us!"

The priest was swinging a censer vigorously, and the whole courtyard was filled with sound and the smell of incense.

It lasted a quarter of an hour. When I came out of the church one of the Orloviches who was sitting on the seat cried out, "Hello, boy!" and I went and sat down beside him. He had been at the copper mines at Butte, Montana, and said that at least ten others present had been there, too. I complimented him on his gorgeous embroidered waistcoat, but he said it was nothing to what they used to have. Times were bad . . .

"Montenegrin mans should do like Irishmans," he said, "raise hell, holler!"

Evidently, a good deal of information about Ireland had filtered via Butte, Montana, to Grbalj, because he had a muttered conversation with his neighbour about de Valera and the Lord Mayor, who had died after a seventy-day hunger strike.

"I was telling him about the Liberty Irish State," he said.

The six good men walked out of the churchyard and he said. "You see that bunch? They go fetch the otha bunch!"

But the six Orloviches returned alone and another hour passed before, down the mountain slope, the procession of the Bauks, a long black line like a school crocodile, issued slowly from behind a little wood. They were a long way off still. From the terrace of the priest's house I watched them going down a small lane through an olive grove into the main road, crossing the wooden bridge over a very swift stream, then climbing up the hill towards the monastery.

A man came out of the monastery with a big basket of bread and he was followed surprisingly by a sailor with some paper table napkins. Carafes of *rakkia* were planted at intervals along the table. . . . The Orloviches got up and walked leisurely towards one side of the churchyard; they formed themselves in a long row, fifty abreast, two deep. In the back row towards the end I saw the murderer flatten himself against the wall. He was fingering his fountain pen nervously. His brother was beside him.

The little priest in the grey soutane came bustling out of the church. "Take off your hats," he said, and we all did so.

Then the Bauks came in, headed by two handsome elderly priests with black beards, then four other good men. They lined themselves opposite the Orloviches, exactly a hundred, with their hats still firmly on, facing a hundred with bare heads. It was like Sir Roger de Coverley.

There was a long silence and then one of the Bauk "good men," a professor from Kotor, came out into the middle and in a loud voice read the sentence. This is a slightly abbreviated version of what he read:

In the name of Christ the Saviour Who is eternal peace between men.

Today, when the Ascension is near at hand, in the year of Our Lord 1937 in the monastery of the Blessed Virgin of Grbalj good men have met together and pleaded with the families of Bauk and Orlovich to lay aside their blood feud which arose in the month of February 1935.

In the name of God from Whom all true justice proceeds and after long cognition, they pronounced this sentence which shall be executed on the third day of Easter, 1937, in the monastery of the Blessed Virgin of Grbalj.

Seeing that God's justice fell upon the wounds of Stjepo Bauk, the son of Vuk and Stevo Orlovich, the son of Lazo, who remained alive after wounds received, and seeing that Mirko Bauk valiantly forgave the murder of his brother Stjepo and reconciled himself through God and St. John with the Orloviches, we declare this sentence:

1. That the brothers Orlovich wait with a hundred of their people on the Bauks with a hundred of theirs.
2. That the Orloviches humbly, according to custom (but not carrying firearms), shall approach the Bauks, who shall embrace them in this order.

Mirko Bauk, the son of Vuk, shall kiss Stevo Orlovich, the son of Lazo.

Vaso Bauk, the son of Rado, shall kiss Ilya Orlovich, the son of Lazo.

3. That at the first baptism of a child of theirs the Orloviches shall ask Bauk to be godfather and he shall accept.
4. That from this reconciliation everlasting friendship and mutual respect for their mutual honour in word and deed shall proceed and that this blood feud shall be ended for all time.

Each family must receive a copy of this sentence and one must be preserved in the archives of the monastery where this reconciliation was made.

Drawn up by the undersigned

[Here follow the signatures of the six good men of the Bauks and the six good men of the Orloviches.]

The professor stepped back into the Bauk ranks and put the sentence back into his leather portfolio.

Then one of the Orlovich good men cried out in a voice breaking with emotion: "Stevo Orlovich!"

The murderer folded his arms across his breast and, bending down from the waist, he darted forward from the wall. He was like someone in a trance. He did not see where he was going and butted his bowed head into a man in front. It was a second before he had disentangled himself from the overcoat and was heading once more for the Bauks. Mirko Bauk, a fat young man with fair hair and moustache, all in black except for the red crown of his Montenegrin cap, stepped out and raised him up.

"Forgive me!" said Orlovich.

"I forgive you my brother's blood," Bauk answered and they kissed each other on both cheeks. I heard people sobbing behind me. Then Vaso Bauk, who was small and puny, embraced Ilya Orlovich and finally all the hundred Bauks stepped forward and shook hands and greeted the hundred Orloviches. Then they all took their seats at the table, the Orloviches sitting at one table, the Bauks at another. Stevo Orlovich did not appear but stayed in the monastery with his brother.

I and the four men from Kotor were preparing to go home but the Bauk professor pressed us to stay.

"The Orloviches would like to ask you," he said, "but they have to be so humble today—it isn't the custom—so we invite you."

A table was brought out from the vestry and a red tablecloth and we sat by ourselves in the other side of the courtyard.

Before we started to feed, the Bauk priest got up and began an Easter hymn . . . and once more the journalist's big voice filled the courtyard.

A lot of forks arrived and a platter heaped with boiled beef. Someone else explained to me that when the monastery had been rededicated last year, there had been six hundred guests and each had a knife for himself and also a tumbler; but today it was different—it was custom. So there were no tumblers and we pushed round from mouth to mouth first a big bottle of *rakkia*, then a big flask of an excellent red wine.

"Please you thank you, Mister!" the journalist with the big voice said every time he gave the flask a shove in my direction.

He then muttered very rapidly into my ear a couple of verses of a poem beginning:

> My 'ome iz zy ocean
> My 'arth iz ze ship!

The meal was quite good and the platters were constantly replenished by the sailor and two men running backward and forward with white napkins held in their teeth. After the beef came boiled ham. Except at our table nobody talked very much. There seemed to be no fraternization between the Bauks and the Orloviches. First came forgiveness; a little later, perhaps, friendship would follow.

They must have had an extraordinary capacity for keeping the practical and the emotional side of their lives distant, for on the slope of the hill their two houses seemed only a few hundred yards apart. Their sheep must graze the same mountains, they must use the same tracks. How had they managed to pass two years so close without lending things and without borrowing things?

There could be no doubt, anyway, that the quarrel had at last been settled. The sentences of the law courts usually leave bitterness and dissatisfaction behind, but the ceremony at Grbalj, so impressive and deeply moving, aimed at something far higher. Did it achieve it? I thought so, but couldn't be sure. Did Mirko perhaps look a bit too self-righteous? Does one ever feel very friendly towards people who force on one too abject an apology or towards one's relations who watch it? I think Stevo may go to Butte, Montana.

Most European law is based on compensation and punishment; justice is important, but it is also impersonal. Montenegrin custom on the other hand takes into account forgiveness, which English justice ignores, and because of that, when *izmirenje* passes away, as pass it must, an important element of justice will have gone with it.

The journalist borrowed the copy of the sentence from the monastery archives. "Meet me in the café at Kotor," he said to me, "and I'll let you have a read of it."

And we crammed in, eleven of us, for some of the Orlovich friends came too, into the car. . . . There was some angry tooting behind us and a lemon-coloured sports car thrust past, containing the professor and two of the Bauk "good men." A moment later we were on the main highway to Cetinje, negotiating the hairpin bends of that incredible road. Every now and then we passed policemen with fixed bayonets and we dodged a charabanc full of German tourists. Below us at Kotor a yacht lay at anchor by the quays; a procession of soldiers was marching through the streets, which were green with acacia trees. The grimness of the mountains lay behind us and we were in the twentieth century again.

"It's beautiful," I said to one of the judges.

"Yes," he replied, "but you should have seen it when the King and Mrs. Simpson were here. The evening they arrived all the bay from Tivat to Kotor was illuminated—bonfires and petrol. It was wonderful. One of the bonfires set alight to some dry grass where there were some young trees. Not much damage done, but it made a wonderful blaze!"

By the time our car had drawn up at the Town Kafana, the *izmirenje* at Grbalj was like something that happened in a dream. Will there ever be another one in Montenegro? I can hardly believe it. The "good men" in the Homburg hats were getting self-conscious about it and I am convinced I heard the murderer and his brother grumbling about the journalists behind the chapel wall. I was glad he didn't know that someone had suggested bringing a film apparatus. Nowadays, too, one can always interrupt blood feuds by going to Butte, Montana.

Report on Yugoslavia[*]

1947

I spent a part of last summer in Yugoslavia, which I knew well before the war, because I was a teacher in Zagreb and held a travelling scholarship from the School of Slavonic Studies. The Yugoslavs are, like my own nation the Irish, among the least pacifist people in Europe, and at the best of times it would not be easy to persuade them that liberty could be won or maintained except by fighting. They have good historical arguments for this view. Serbia, for example, became free after repeated insurrections against the Turks, and the other Slav provinces—Croatia, Slovenia, Bosnia and Herzegovina, and Montenegro—were added to the Yugoslav state only as a result of the Great War. You might argue that Austria-Hungary through the growth of liberal ideas and Turkey through indolence were in any case relaxing their grip on their subjects. You might say that the Yugoslavs could have obtained their freedom by obstructiveness that stopped short of killing, by the development of cultural institutions, by passive resistance and political manoeuvres. You might argue quite plausibly on those lines, but I'm afraid you would argue in vain. On the whole, history, as it is ordinarily interpreted, is against the pacifist in the Balkans. He must depend on faith, on the belief that by following his conscience he will ultimately be justified, even though the facts of everyday life contradict him. Only by great personal courage and high intelligence would a pacifist in Ireland or Yugoslavia win any

*A report submitted at a conference of the Quaker-inspired War Resisters International at Shrewsbury, England, August 1947.—ed.

respect. If he depended on the ordinary arguments of expediency, it would simply be supposed that he was a coward or a traitor who was anxious to shirk his responsibility to his nation.

I was not surprised to find in Yugoslavia that the small group of people who had been associated with the War Resisters International and other international movements of the kind had more or less dissolved. They had not actually been suppressed but had been voted away as superfluous by extremists within the groups themselves. These had urged their incorporation ("to prevent overlapping" is the usual excuse for this kind of cannibalism) in the officially sponsored societies, the various anti-Fascist leagues, cultural, economic, male and female. I did not find that they had been persecuted so much as rendered powerless. I talked to several men and women who before the war had been active internationally minded people, who visited conferences all over Europe and America, who were used to lecturing and writing. I think I seemed to them, as would anybody else from our islands, a figure from the past, stirring very sad memories that had scarcely any bearing on the life they were leading. The business of living from one day to the next was absorbing all their energies. They had often lost their jobs or their incomes and had no surplus leisure for thinking of abstract problems or international movements. All their efforts were bent on securing some sort of future for their children or elderly relatives. "We are tired of living," one of them told me very sadly. Most of these people were liberals by temperament, left-wing rather than right-, so that their extinction by the Communists is a cruel tragedy. But none of those to whom I talked had gone back on their principles or come to believe in reactionary politics; they still valued individual liberty, the freedom to think and act in the light of reason. Simply, they had been robbed of all power to advance their views. I think that an external pacifist organization can make very few demands on these people. Even by communicating with us they come under the suspicion of giving information to foreigners.

You have, I am sure, heard of the trial of Jehovah's Witnesses which took place recently in Zagreb. The principal defendants were sentenced to death, the others to long terms of imprisonment. Owing, it is thought, to petitions from abroad, those sentences were in some cases revised, but there is no doubt the Witnesses had exasperated the Yugoslav government both by their pacifism and by their contact with fellow believers in other countries. To quote the official report:

They engaged in oral and written propaganda against the People's Republic and harmed the military power and defensive capacity of the country by persuading citizens to shirk conscription. They collected false information on the political and general situation, which they sent abroad, thus presenting a false picture of the state of affairs in Yugoslavia.

The Public Prosecutor declared that these reports of persecutions were sent abroad at the time when Archbishop Stepinac was discussing "intervention." In this way the Jehovah's Witnesses were linked up with the Roman Catholic Church as collaborators in an attempt to defame and overthrow the Yugoslav government. Anyone who is aware of the relations of the Catholic Church and Jehovah's Witnesses will be amused as well as bewildered by this suggestion. The Jehovah's Witnesses defended themselves with great courage and made no attempt to disguise their views. In the words of the official report of the trial:

They called themselves faithful servants of Christ, to whom earthly life was of no concern. They said that they would not take up arms in case their country was threatened. At the time of the most intensive work for the rehabilitation of their country, they preached utter passivity. Their pacifism benefits international reactionaries whose agents they are.

The Yugoslav Witnesses were principally simple people, shoemakers, sanitary inspectors, mechanics, and they had a simple and fervent creed based on a literal acceptance of the Bible. There is no doubt that it was their simple faith with its rigid rules and curious dogma about the future that has enabled them to keep alive Christian pacifism in Eastern Europe. They are, I believe, almost alone in this field. Not many of us share or could ever share the views of the witnesses, and we have to ask ourselves how, without their convictions, we can imitate their courage. Like them, we reject all the sophistries by which war is justified by leaders in political and religious life. I think we can do something by the fearless and incessant exposure of these sophistries. Stripped of them, Christianity might recover some of the vigour and universality which it has lost.

When I was in Zagreb I spent several days in the public library looking up the old files of the newspapers that were issued in the Occupation period, particularly Church papers. I wanted to see what resistance, if any, was made by organized Christianity to the ruthless militarism of the Croat national leader Pavelitch, and his German and Italian patrons; I am afraid the results were disheartening. I did not expect to find outspoken criticism or condemnation in the Church papers because, if it had been published, the papers would certainly have been suppressed. But I was wholly unprepared for the gush of hysterical adulation which was poured forth by almost all the leading clergy upon Pavelitch, who was probably the vilest of all war criminals. He was their saviour against Bolshevism, their champion against the Serb, Eastern barbarian and heretic; he was the restorer of their nation and the Christian faith, a veritable hero of olden time.

As I believe that the Christian idiom is still the best in which peace and goodwill can be preached, I found this profoundly disturbing. I doubt now whether it is even wise for us to use the language of Christianity to the Yugoslav till all the vile things which were said and done in the name of Christ have been acknowledged and atoned for. I think the bitter hatred which is felt for the churches in Yugoslavia is inflamed by all the lies and dissimulation about these things, by the refusal to admit that the Christian Church during the war connived at unspeakable crimes and departed very far from the teaching of Christ. The principal church in Croatia is of course the Catholic Church, but I don't think the Christian failure there is attributable to any specifically Catholic disease. There was also a small Protestant community whose published utterances make as horrifying reading today as anything in the Catholic papers. Their disgrace is smaller only because there were fewer of them. The mistake they all made was that they believed that the survival of Christianity depended on the survival of their churches, and they were prepared to sacrifice truth and charity to an almost unlimited degree if they felt they could forward the interests of their particular confession. Instead of resisting absolutely the rise of nationalist hysteria and hatred, they thought they could guide it into sectarian channels, they believed and said that Hitler and Mussolini and Pavelitch were instruments in the hands of God for the establishment of His kingdom. Unsatisfactory instruments, perhaps, they might admit among themselves, but God has power to turn Evil into Good. In fact, as one reads through these extraordinary papers it becomes clear there was nothing they could not justify by the adroit use of ecclesiastical language. You will not misunderstand me if I say that after reading those papers for several days, certain phrases seemed to be defiled for ever by the use to which they had been put. If we are to make a Christian approach to Yugoslavia, we shall have to eschew ecclesiastical phraseology.

You may think I am exaggerating, so I will explain what I mean.

You know about Pavelitch probably. I have heard him described as a guerrilla leader and the whole Croatian struggle has been made to appear a wild Balkan affray which does not concern civilized people. It was not so at all. Pavelitch was a professional man of respectable standing in Zagreb, the writer of a couple of books, the editor of newspapers in Austria and Berlin; he considered himself the champion of Western as against Eastern values; and his object was to withdraw Croatia from the Yugoslav state and from what the Nazis called *Balkanismus*. His heroes and patrons were Hitler and Mussolini, and the cruelty which he practised was copied from Western models—the concentration camps, gas chambers, the Aryan laws, the racialism and wholesale evictions—and much of it came under direct Nazi guidance. Yet he surpassed his teachers. It was a horrible blend of sophistication and savagery. You can imagine what was said of him by the Yugoslavs and you can discount some of it, but even his Fascist allies thought his cruelty in bad taste. Count Ciano,* who was not a particularly fastidious person, describes him and his following, in his diary, as "a gang of cutthroats." Another Italian diplomat, Curzio Malaparte, in his book *Kaputt* describes how he visited him and found in his study what he took to be a basket of shelled oysters; Pavelitch explained that they were forty pounds of human eyes sent to him by his soldiers, who were crusading among the Serbs. There are many similar stories, some of them probably exaggerated, but taken all in all we have a picture of a man and a regime for which no apology can be made.

Unfortunately they had their apologists, fervent ones, and where you would least expect to find them, in the Christian churches. This will not be forgotten within our lifetime in Yugoslavia. When Pavelitch first entered Zagreb in 1941, church bells rang and Te Deums were proclaimed by the Primate. When he left in 1945, driven out by the Partisans, it was under the floor in the Franciscan monastery in Zagreb that the state treasure was hidden, in the hope of a victorious return. It included boxes of jewellery and gold watches and gold teeth stripped off the victims of the concentration camps. He had managed to gain Church support by saying that Croatia was the *Antemurale Christianitatis*, once more the bastion of Christianity against the heathen, and whenever he visited a monastery or a convent he was received with enthusiasm and extraordinary reverence. The compliments and speeches which were exchanged on those oc-

*Ciano was Mussolini's Foreign Minister.—ed.

casions have been collected and published by the Yugoslav government, but they can be verified, as I did myself in many cases, in the back files of the newspapers in which they were always reported. For Pavelitch was very proud that his work should always be blessed in this way. The most remarkable of all these ovations was a twenty-six-verse ode by the Archbishop of Bosnia, Monsignor Sharitch, which was published in several papers in his own diocese and in that of Monsignor Stepinac, at Zagreb.

Sharitch described how he met and embraced the great Pavelitch in the Cathedral of St. Peter's at Rome, and he compared him to Leonidas, the man who never gave way:

> Each of thy days contains a sacrifice and is full of holiest work.
> As the sun thou art pure and radiant . . .
> And the freedom is dear to thee as thine own mother.
> For her thou didst stand forth like a giant
> Against all brigands [i.e., the Serbs]
> And against the Jews, who had all the money,
> Who wanted to sell our souls,
> Who built a prison round our name,
> The miserable traitors.
> Thou art the first standard bearer of our country
> And thou keepest our lives free
> From that hellish Paradise, Marxism,
> From Bolshevism.

And he told how, like King David, he went forth into a strange world, where enemies lay in wait for his soul, yet God protected him:

> God has sent thee strength in foreign parts
> God has crowned thy faith with laurel
> Which will never wither, Hero of Fortune! . . .
> Doctor Ante Pavelitch, the dear name!
> Croatia has in thee a treasure from Heaven.
> May the King of Heaven accompany thee,
> Our Golden Leader!

Pavelitch's terrible campaign of compulsory conversion of Orthodox Christians resulted in some of the worst religious massacres that have ever happened in European history. The churches have denied that the Croatian hierarchy had any responsibility for all this, but unfortunately the complicity of many leading churchmen is put beyond a doubt by their own printed utterances in their diocesan magazines and religious journals. As you have just heard, Monsignor Sharitch applauded Pavelitch's appalling measures against the Jews. As far as I know he got no official reprimand for his behaviour from his superiors. He is in exile and is referred to in the religious press as a victim of Yugoslav and Communist slander and intolerance.

You cannot go very far in Yugoslavia today without coming across traces of these fearful days. I had an introduction from Grace Beaton to a sympathizer with the WRI, a very intelligent barrister. He told me that his three brothers had been murdered in Bosnia in the course of the conversion campaign. His sister had accepted conversion.

The Church still enjoys immense prestige in Yugoslavia, because it is regarded as the defender of Croatian nationalism and of the bourgeoisie, and it is in fact one of the few channels through which dissatisfaction with the present regime can be expressed with relative impunity. Croatia, though she entered the Yugoslav state joyfully and of her own free will in 1919, did not receive fair treatment from the Serbs and for twenty years was discontented. Many now support the churches for reasons which have nothing to do with Christianity. There is therefore very little likelihood that the Communist Party will risk a direct attack on the Catholic Church. It will try to assimilate it by degrees, as it has already tried with some success with the Orthodox Church. In Bulgaria, for example, the head of the Orthodox Church makes frequent complimentary references to the Soviet armies. For some curious reason the churches in all countries have been much more ready to applaud Soviet soldiers than Soviet civilians. Full use will be made by the Soviets of this strange ecclesiastical partiality.

How will the churches react to Soviet advances? I think that they will be, on the whole, conciliatory. We can discount the cries of indignation against Communism that are raised in the churches of Western Europe. There is as yet no need for them to be accommodating. More significant is the attitude of Monsignor Rittig, rector of St. Mark's, Zagreb, and next to Monsignor Stepinac the most prominent prelate in the diocese. He holds a portfolio in the Communist government of Croatia, and he gave me a signed statement about the relations of the Communist Party and the Catholic Church. This declaration is very sympathetic to the efforts of the Communists to reach an ecclesiastical settlement. Monsignor Rittig has not been disowned or disorientated by the Vatican, and therefore I must assume that his policy of trying to work with the Communists and obtain from them what concessions he can has the approval of Rome.

So, whether the Church defeats Communism or is assimilated by it, it has a strong hope of survival as an institution. The Church has been called by Marxists "the opiate of the people." The hardships and discontent of many subjects of the Soviets are very great, and it may well appear to their rulers that an opiate against the sufferings of this world, if it is administered by a state church, might forestall an outbreak of rebellion. Therefore the Church is not likely to jeopardize its hope of recognition by espousing views which, like those of the pacifists, are equally unpopular with Communists and anti-Communists. Because of this, the prospects of disseminating pacifist opinions in Yugoslavia by direct methods are poor. You can only act through individuals or through groups. The individual pacifists, as I have shown, are hopelessly crushed, and the smallest gesture on their part towards international pacifism would be regarded as sabotaging the war potential and entertaining relations with foreign reactionaries. On the other hand, the only independent institutions are the churches, and they are likely to irritate the Communists by aiding pacifism. On this subject, I had an interesting talk with Herr Franz Zücher, the secretary of Jehovah's Witnesses at Berne, where is the international centre to which the reports about the persecution of Christians are said to have been sent. He informed me that the trial of the Witnesses had been the result of a pact between the Catholic Church and the Communists, and if you read the Jehovah's Witnesses' *Year Books*, you will find the same extraordinary allegations made about their misfortunes in Soviet Russia and Poland.

Is one to believe these things? I don't know. All we know is that great institutions fighting for their lives fight quite blindly, and they are able to ignore all those truths and scruples which an individual finds obvious and inescapable. In Ireland, though we have almost no Communists, there is a vigorous campaign against Communism. Possibly the object of this campaign is to invigorate the Church, by proclaiming a common platform on which Protestant and Catholic and all the divided branches of the Church may stand together. Anyway, at the time of the trial of the Jehovah's Witnesses and their death sentences, full publicity was given in our press to this instance of Soviet brutality. Very shortly afterward the Witnesses began campaigning in southern Ireland and the tables were promptly turned. It was put about that so far from being the victims of Communism, the Witnesses were Communists or crypto-Communists themselves. A few weeks ago *The Irish Times* quoted on its front page from an address by the Catholic Bishop of Cork, denouncing the Witnesses on these grounds and suggesting that the police should take notice of them. *The Irish Times* is the paper of the Protestant minority, and so I wrote to explain the situation, quoting from the Public Prosecutor's speech in the Zagreb trial about the reactionary associations of the Witnesses and the grave damage they were doing to the Communist cause, damage so serious that only death could atone for it. *The Irish Times* refused to print this, nor have the Protestant churches of Ireland done anything to protect this small group. Calm relations between Protestant and Catholic in southern Ireland are highly precarious and it may have appeared that it would be unwise to endanger them by telling the truth about an unimportant body like the Witnesses. This tacit collusion between old enemies in Ireland at the expense of the Witnesses makes it appear possible to me that the same thing happened in Yugoslavia, and that Herr Zücher may not have been far wrong in thinking that Catholics and Communists were at one in regard to this brutal trial.

If there are no direct ways of doing propaganda for resistance to war in Yugoslavia, are there indirect ways? Serbs and Croats approach the problem of peace very differently. The Serbs, like the Russians and the Bulgars, tend to be extremists. When they become pacifists they often renounce not only war but all the other vanities of the world; they withdraw into some closed religious community with which it is hard for outsiders to make contact. It is interesting, all the same, that these groups with their extreme and fixed opinions often get recognition from the government, whereas an individual of more moderate opinions is persecuted. I believe that the small Tolstoyan community near Plovdiv in Bulgaria is still in existence and is tolerated by the Communist government. Yet, on the whole, it is among the Croats rather than among the Serbs that the international pacifist outlook, as we know it in the West, is most likely to be understood.

This sounds a paradox, because the Croats were known as great fighters and formed like the Irish Wild Geese a specially devoted corps famous for their loyalty to the emperor of Austria-Hungary. In spite of that, I would say that militarism is wholly alien to the Croat character, which is supple and imaginative. If anything, they are too docile, acquiescing from indolence or curiosity in ways of life which their intellect rejects. How was it possible that this clever subtle people tolerated Pavelitch and the Nazis so patiently? Perhaps for a time all the small pomps and ceremonies of the Independent State of Croatia appealed to them, but very soon they saw how ridiculous it was. They are cynics by temperament, certainly they no longer believe in war since it has brought them nothing but unhappiness. I think that many of them vaguely hope, though, that the Americans and the atom bomb will bring them some sort of painless liberation from their enemies and that they will not be obliged to fight themselves. This opium dream of miraculous release from Communism will prevent them forming any plans for escaping service in the Communist armies or thinking out pacifist ideas. Yet there have been in the past many distinguished Croats who have been pacifist as well as nationalist. They believed in peaceful evolution and feared the contradictions and absurdities into which the military policy of their leaders might lead them.

The career of Archbishop Stepinac is a wonderful illustration of the twists and turns which an ambitious, rather conventionally minded Croat has had to make in recent years if he was to keep pace with history. His life seems to have been spent in *reductio ad absurdum* of militarism and its first cousin, militant ecclesiasticism. He is a Croat by birth but born an Austro-Hungarian subject. In the First World War he was conscripted into the Hungarian army and fought against the Italians, allies of the Serbs. He fought loyally and well and was twice awarded the Medal of Valour. He was taken prisoner with other Croats; he changed sides, joined the Yugoslav Legion and fought for the Serbs against the Austro-Hungarians. Again he fought loyally and well and was awarded the coveted Karageorge Star. Some years later, he became a priest and very soon with the king's favour Archbishop of Zagreb. On the eve of the collapse of the Yugoslav kingdom he remained loyal to the king, issuing an appeal to the Croats to stand by the young King Peter. A few days later Yugoslavia collapsed and he ordered a Te Deum in all the churches to celebrate the establishment by Pavelitch of the Independent State of Croatia. He was loyal to Pavelitch, praying for his victory against the Serbs and the remnant of the Yugoslav army, and was awarded by him the Grand Cross of the Order of King Zvonimir with a star "for exposing both at home and abroad the rebels from the territory of the Independent State of Croatia," that is to say, the Yugoslavs. Pavelitch fell and the Partisans came in and established the Federal Republic.

Then, his biographer Count O'Brien tells us, he became a loyal subject of the Communist government. O'Brien angrily declares that the suggestion that he remained a loyal subject of the previous government was purest calumny, and in his book he prints a photograph of the Archbishop watching a military parade beside the military commander of Zagreb, the Soviet military attaché and the Communist premier of Croatia. In spite of all this, it is curious to find the following anecdote to illustrate the Archbishop's humanity and courage. At the height of the religious massacres, he is said to have burst into Pavelitch's room and cried out, "It is God's command! Thou shalt not kill!" and without another word, says Count O'Brien, he left the Quisling's palace. Almost all these facts are drawn from the official biography of Monsignor Stepinac which was published in Ireland and which Cardinal Spellman laid in a bronze box on the foundation stone of the new Stepinac Institute in America. Therefore we are expected to admire these swiftly adjustable loyalties and not observe any inconsistencies. Monsignor Stepinac was certainly a brave man, but his guiding principle was loyalty to the established authority and its armies. These changed four times during his life, and he, too, was obliged to change. I do not know what he meant when he said, "Thou shalt not kill!" I think he really meant: "Thou shalt not kill too much!" or "Thou shalt not kill except when thou art in uniform and thy victim is, too," or something of the kind. I do not think that qualified advice like this is ever very impressive, and I am sure that Pavelitch must have wondered what the Archbishop meant.

It is easy to see how Christianity became so popular in Yugoslavia. I see only two ways in which it can recover its prestige—a bad, safe way and a good, dangerous one. The bad, safe way gains privileges in exchange for unqualified support of the state in its wars and political adventures. That is to say, there will be army chaplains attached to Communist regiments, there will be prayers and thanksgivings for victory in return for the right to hold certain views about the next world and the preparation for it, and about sex relations. This development is particularly probable. In the Orthodox Christian regions of the Balkans, it has already taken shape.

The good, dangerous way is so unlikely to be adopted that perhaps you will think me naïve even to mention it: It is that the churches should become pacifist again as they were in the first centuries of Christianity, that they should no longer demand from the Communists the privileges which come to those who bless armies and pray for victory. Could this mean that they would meet with the fate of Jehovah's Witnesses? There is always that danger, but it has not deterred the Witnesses. Why should it deter the older Christian communities?

I have heard it argued that it would have eased the lot of pacifists in Yugoslavia and given them status if Christian pacifists in our countries, at the time of the Stepinac trial or earlier, had pressed not for the Archbishop's acquittal, as did many churches, but for his withdrawal from Yugoslavia by the Pope. The Yugoslav government had promised not to prosecute if this withdrawal took place. It would have meant the Archbishop's freedom and some relaxation of tension. But the Vatican, for reasons of prestige, refused to withdraw him. I think that this prestige has been maintained at too great a cost, and that a great part of the cost is being borne by those who are not Catholics and have nothing to gain and everything to lose by the advertisement which has been given to the Archbishop's views through this unnecessary martyrdom. Undoubtedly it has deepened the hatred and misunderstanding between East and West. In my country, I have heard the trial described by people who took their opinions from the newspapers as a legitimate *casus belli*. Anyone who gave this issue any serious attention was looked on as a Communist. Yet surely, without in any way disputing the Archbishop's courage or sincerity, we here today must regret that he should be regarded as a leading representative of Christian views or a champion of Christendom. He stands surely for the principle of a state-controlled church, with its army of chaplains and its readiness to support the state, whatever that state may be, in all its military adventures with prayers and *ovatio* and offerings of money and labour. In fact, he stands for all those things to which we here are most strongly opposed. Those who resist this idea of a state church with its army chaplains will today no doubt be regarded as little better than Communists, but now that the Communists have succeeded in assimilating some of the churches, opinion will begin to change. If the unspeakable Pavelitch was able to obtain the prayers of the churches and chaplains for his regiments of brigands, need we suppose that Communist generals will fail to conciliate the churches when they wish? I am sure they will not fail.

I am afraid I have told you very little that is encouraging about pacifism in Yugoslavia, yet I believe that there is no nation in the world that longs so ardently for peace. It is still a Christian country, but I think that its churches will provoke wars rather than avert them till they become pacifist. That would be a big revolution, but whenever it happened, whether in the East or the West, it would quickly spread. I believe that there is no people with a greater understanding of Christian pacifism than the Slav people if their enemies and their leaders allowed them to adopt it.

Yugoslavia:
The Cultural Background

1947

Some years ago a Yugoslav professor came to lecture on his country in Ireland. The Central European intellectual has a passion for information and, even before he reached our shores, he was an expert on the Language Question, the Annuities and the Northern Education Act. He returned home with so many anecdotes and opinions that he decided to give a lecture on Ireland in the Dalmatian port where he was employed. It was well attended and rather feverishly applauded. As he left the hall, he was accosted by two members of the secret police and marched away to the police station, where he was sharply cross-examined. That was an old dodge, they told him. Clearly he was a Croat separatist and his audience understood that "Ulster" meant "Croatia." Was he advocating partition for Yugoslavia or wasn't he? He was not released till he had produced a copy of *The Irish Independent* with a report of his Dublin lecture. It was found, on translation, to contain no heresies. He proved that he did not like partition either in Ireland or in Yugoslavia.

The Yugoslav intellectual has, in fact, a keener sense of the common interest of small nations than has his Irish counterpart. He is used to foreign analogies, and the story of the Anglo-Irish struggle has often been studied as a textbook of rebellion, much as Arthur Griffith studied the manoeuvres of Hungarians against the Hapsburgs.* Even in peacetime a drastic censorship accustoms him to the oblique approach. The most celebrated comic paper in Yugoslavia

---

*Arthur Griffith (1871–1922) was a Founder of Sinn Féin and president of the Dáil in 1922. His book *The Resurrection of Hungary: A Parallel for Ireland* appeared in 1904.—ed.

was called *Brijani Yezh* (*The Shaven Hedgehog*); in this ingenious journal words never bore their obvious meaning and innocent expressions like "Eire" might be charged with subversive innuendo.

Unfortunately there is no trade union of the oppressed. The brave little Hungary which inspired Sinn Féin by its nimble resistance to the Austrian oppressor used its new freedom to oppress the Croats even more than before. This was not surprising. In the centre of Zagreb, the Croatian capital, stands the statue of the Croatian general who fought against the Hungarian patriots for his Austrian overlord. To the Croats the resurrection of Hungary and the Magyar aristocracy had a different message to that which it held for the leaders of Sinn Féin.

Griffith was right, all the same, in seeing that all small nations are menaced by similar forces. The great powers have been able to obscure this fact by the manipulation of local rivalries. Centuries of Austrian diplomacy lie behind the failure of the "Succession States" to achieve solidarity in themselves or friendliness with each other. Yet except through collaboration there is no future for the small national state.

During the war a mayoress of Dublin asserted that Czechoslovakia was an English invention. There is more than ignorance behind this remarkable statement. A genteel snobbism has often kept oppressed nations apart and attracted them to the oppressors of others. Many Czechs and Serbs still think of the Irish as an obscure cross-breed of the liberal and cultured English. The Irish have, in the same way, always rated the Austrian above his uncouth Slavonic subjects, and for centuries the Irish Wild Geese assisted the Hapsburgs in oppressing them. The mayoress was true to type.

Still, we cannot deny that in each of the new states the same pattern recurs. In Yugoslavia a simple and indigenous society appears to have defeated a sophisticated one that was privileged and antinational. Yet both societies are equally moribund and more akin to each other than to the mechanized and impersonal civilization which is likely to succeed them. The cultural conflict has more significance than any other, but to follow its development in Yugoslavia a little knowledge of the political background is necessary.

In 1918 the small kingdom of Serbia became a great state by the accession of six historic Slav regions—Croatia, Slovenia, Montenegro, Bosnia, Herzegovina and Dalmatia, as well as territory in Macedonia and in the northern plains. Of these provinces Austria, Hungary and Italy had formerly been dominant in the north, Turkey in the south, including Serbia itself. Montenegro alone has resisted every oppressor and most external influences. The common bond between all these peoples is the Serbo-Croatian language with its Slovene and Macedonian dialects. It is a very frail bond but without it Yugoslavia would certainly fall apart. That much must be conceded to the language enthusiast.

The kingdom of Serbia is chiefly responsible for the liberation of all these peoples. For generations all their energies have been directed to this end, and after two Balkan wars and the first German war, it was finally achieved in our century. Unlike the Slovenes and Croats, the Serbs had little time or opportunity for culture and education, nor are they noted for diplomacy. Courage and cunning were more valuable weapons against the Turk.

The history of Yugoslavia since 1918 has been a struggle between the Serbian "racial" conception of nationalism and the mellower, more cosmopolitan nationalism of the northwest. One might say that the latter is based on regional sentiment and, as such, is uncongenial to the more unsophisticated Slav, who still has nomadism in his blood. In moments of tension the Quisling with his myth of cultural superiority appears in the north, the chauvinist among the Serbs; and a familiar pattern repeats itself.

In 1929 King Alexander attempted to create a new Yugoslav patriotism by an attack on regional sentiment, replacing with modern departments the old historic territories. He drew upon himself the hatred of the Croats. In 1934 he was murdered at the instigation of Pavelitch, a Zagreb lawyer. The complicity of the Italian and Hungarian governments was suspected.

On the collapse of Yugoslavia in 1940 Pavelitch was appointed *Poglavnik* of the puppet state of Croatia, which was given an Italian king, the Duke of Aosta. Many prominent Croats were collaborationists, for example Stepinac, Primate of Croatia, and Sharitch, Archbishop of Bosnia, and many industrialists and former landowners. The evidence for this comes from anti-Communist sources. We must think of Zagreb and Belgrade as much farther apart in sentiment than Dublin and Belfast. Only a very little manoeuvring of religious and cultural antipathies by a great power is necessary to set hatred ablaze.

I heard the news of the surrender of Yugoslavia from the German-controlled station of Belgrade on a Yugoslav boat moored on the Liffey. The crew sat round listening. They were friendly with each other and seemed united in their grief. At the end they divided up into two groups, Croats and Serbs. One walked off to the German legation and the other to the UK office to learn their destinies. So easy is it to divide a people whom only a common language unites.

Will it be possible to consolidate the diverse elements of Yugoslavia into one people without spectacular abdications at both ends of the scale of civilization? As we go north from Montenegro to Slovenia, we pass from primitive and traditional communities to a sensitive and highly civilized society where racial loyalties are qualified by more sophisticated pieties. All the northern districts of Yugoslavia are still irradiated by the sun of Vienna, which has not yet set. Zagreb is a charming and civilized city with theatre, opera, ballet and art gallery. In addition it has one of the best folk museums in Southern Europe. It was to cosmopolitan Trieste, in Slovene territory, that James Joyce withdrew to write his epic of Dublin. From Trieste to Macedonia and Montenegro an immense gulf of cultural experience is spanned by the frail bridge of a common language. The formula for spiritual unity has not yet been discovered, for the cultural elements, which must be reconciled, are seldom analyzed.

Starting from the south, Montenegro is the Gaeltacht of Yugoslavia, where the last traces of a southern Slav culture survive. We find communities so self-contained that Western civilization encroaching on every side has not yet decomposed them. Yet the mountains which protected them so long from the Turk are no longer a barrier to subtler agents of destruction. The patriarchal society of Montenegro is doomed as surely as is the Gaeltacht, and yet something perhaps can be salvaged. Before the war two codes of justice, Montenegrin, which was personal, and Yugoslav, which was abstract, ran concurrently. The last *izmirenje*, or reconciliation ceremony, took place at the monastery of Grbalj in 1935.*

Dalmatia, which stretches along the Adriatic Sea from Montenegro to Slovenia, is another of Yugoslavia's problems. Except as a tourist resort, there seems to be no future for these lovely barren shores, but tourism raises difficulties. Here is the shopwindow that Yugoslavia presents to the enquiring West, and it is unfortunate that, though all the salesmen except 2 percent are Croats, the goods displayed are, despite the labels, unmistakably Italian. The great palaces that fringe the shores of Kotor and Gruz were built when Venice controlled the carrying trade of the East. Her wealth filled the churches with gold vessels and fabulous vestments. The lion of St.

*See above, "The Last *Izmirenje*."—ed.

Mark prances over town gates and on castle doorways. But Yugoslavia is fortunate to possess in Mestrovich a great European sculptor. The fine plaque of King Peter of Serbia over the town gate of Dubrovnik, the Racic Mausoleum at Cavtat, the striking statue of Bishop Gregory, too aggressively placed in the ruins of Diocletian's Palace, are evidence that Italy has no monopoly of culture along the Adriatic coast.

The Yugoslav patriot is morbidly sensitive, and in Dalmatia his feelings are constantly bruised. He has no status with the tourist of the luxury cruise. To the average American all the territory from the Carpathians to Corfu is inhabited by "Hunkies" and little has been done to glamorize them. No one has edited them for the shilling seats, as Mr. Bert Feldmann edited the Irish with "Tipperary" and "When Irish Eyes Are Smiling." The Yugoslav must blow his own trumpet and he does it without skill. When some years ago an American company proposed to film Dalmatia, the Belgrade government eagerly collaborated, even putting the navy at their disposal. A final polish by a publicity expert had to be given to the film in America. He knew his job. The uncouth Croatian names and terms were exchanged for melodious Italian ones, familiar to the filmgoer's ear: Antonio instead of Zvonko, Spalato for Split. It was inevitable but sad.

At the head of the Adriatic lies Trieste, which will be a focus of discord for some years. Roughly speaking, it is about as Yugoslav as Belfast is Irish, and no Italian, Austrian or Slovene can discuss its future calmly. Once a powerful race interferes with a weaker one, it is hard for it to withdraw when a milder mood prevails. Too many hostages must remain behind. Trieste was built on the site of a Slovene fishing village by a Rhineland Baron Bruck as a port for the Austro-Hungarian Empire. It became the harbour for the greater part of Central Europe as well as for the Slovenian hinterland. Austria-Hungary, a polyglot imperial state, made no attempt to impose a German culture upon it. Italy was weak and divided before the Risorgimento, and the Hapsburgs, to keep an equilibrium in their empire, used to favour minority cultures. In Trieste, as in Dalmatia, there were very few Italians, but, indulged by Austria, it rapidly became a city of Italians and Italianized Slovenes in the middle of a Slovene countryside. On the building of the port of Trieste, Austria-Hungary sunk more than a hundred million pounds. The railway which she made opened up the whole of Slovenia and increased its prosperity enormously. Blasted through the Julian Alps, it can be rivalled as an engineering feat only by the vital mountain railway that the Austrians built from the Sava Valley to the coast. An immense amount of Austrian wealth, enterprise and talent has been sunk into Yugoslavia. After the defeat of Austria in 1918 Italy was awarded Istria with Trieste, and half a million Croats and Slovenes passed under her control. Italy, unlike Austro-Hungary, was a fiercely nationalist state. She determined that Istria and Trieste should be unmistakably Italian. All Slovene schools were closed, newspapers and books banned, and the public use of the language prohibited. Slovene-speaking clergy and doctors were expelled. An Italian doctor, who was told that his patients could not explain their symptoms to him, replied, "Nor can the cow explain her symptoms to the vet." When the Abyssinian War broke out the Fascist government conscripted the Slovenes among the first. A clear Italian majority was ultimately secured. In the dispute now raging the voice of Austria will not be raised, but the Italian and Yugoslav arguments are of a type so familiar to us in Ireland that they need not be repeated.

There is no solution of this problem so long as cultural nationalism is identified with political and economic nationalism. Marshal Tito is probably an internationalist who, in claiming Trieste for Yugoslavia, finds it opportune to use a nationalist argument; but an internationalism which tries to reconcile divergent peoples by ignoring the sources of their culture can bring no permanent pacification. Nor are the histories of Fiume and Danzig so encouraging that another Free City at Trieste could be risked. Trieste will probably be granted to Yugoslavia, and in this, at the worst, there will be a certain retributive justice.

Trieste is a danger point because it lies upon a frontier, but in fact there is hardly a town in northern Yugoslavia about whose nature a similar dispute might not be raised. Yugoslavs, like Irish, are not by temperament originators of towns, railways, factories. It was as employees and colleagues of Austrians and Venetians that they gathered into the cities. Where they have lived relatively undisturbed by the foreigner, as in Montenegro, the pattern of their lives is based upon the rural community. The Turk, who unlike the Austrian was purely predatory, without the power to assimilate, sometimes left this primitive pattern intact. The *Zadruga* of the Serbian countryside is a family cooperative society, which is dying only because all village communities are everywhere dying beneath the impact of urban civilization. The forward-looking Serbian peasant, no longer able to emigrate, looks to the city for advancement. Torn from his own social traditions, he jibs at new ones. He is so little hampered by the sense of civic responsibility that his economic progress is often as rapid as his moral decline. It is not unusual to find a peasant who can neither read nor write the proprietor of a block of up-to-date flats in Belgrade. How does he manage it? Possibly there are not yet enough hereditary go-getters to block the path of the enthusiastic amateur. Immense power has fallen into the hands of wealthy and ignorant peasants, and to this, in part, is due the naïve egoism and corruption of the Belgrade politician, which has often alienated Croats and Slovenes to the pitch of sedition.

"Innocent" is sometimes a better word than "ignorant" to apply to the ruling classes of Balkan lands. Ignorance implies vulgarity, but the flats built by illiterate peasants are often full of the same taste and refinement that their own homes display. For centuries they have made their own clothes and their own furniture; the larger farmers have made their own pottery. Their natural taste for colour and form does not desert them as quickly as their morals. At present only the established middle classes have access to the mass-produced commonplaces of Germany and America. No doubt this restraint about domestic architecture is a transient phenomenon and would speedily be corrected by the opening of Yugoslavia to the West, but it is so striking that it deserves comment.

In such a society the word "Communism," so freely used and abused, needs careful interpretation. It is not in the first place greatly assisted by Pan-Slav sentiment, which so long favoured church and state. Both King Alexander and Prince Paul, the one by education the other by marriage, were closely associated with Tsarist Russia. On the collapse of White resistance, a horde of generals and ex-landowners and former administrators with large treasury chests descended on Belgrade. It was natural that they should be asked to assist in the government of the young and inexperienced state, natural also that they should raise a hue and cry about Communism. Unfortunately they thought they were dealing with muzhiks speaking a Slav patois, who could be made to understand Russian if spoken to in peremptory tones. Every Serb, on the other hand, knows that he belongs to a race of heroes which fought for centuries against the Turk and ultimately won, and in our century fought against German, Austrian, Hungarian and Bulgar, and also won. Russian superciliousness was resented. Except among Montenegrins ("We and the Russians are 170 millions!"), Serbian royalty and a handful of Croatian illuminati, Pan-Slav sentiment has had little influence. Romantic nationalism, patriarchal traditions and peasant proprietorship may retard the spread of Communism. Yet obviously there is a very strong possibility that the Balkan states, Slav and non-Slav, will pass under Russian influence and that Communist Quislings will replace Fascist ones.

Clearly the churches can do much to bring to the Balkans a unity based on brotherly love rather than on economics, but so far their contribution has been meagre and disrupting. The Catholic Church is accused of having played the Fascist and Italian game in Slovenia and Croatia and, by its clamour for privileges and concordats, of jeopardizing that brotherhood of southern Slavs which is the keystone of Yugoslav unity. The Orthodox Church still retains its prestige because it rallied the Serb against the Turk, but it is an easygoing community, more notable for its feast days than for its doctrine or its discipline. At the time of the concordat the faithful rallied round it with fervour,* but without the halo of persecution it cannot long retain its hold over the flock. Except for an understandable assault on the Moslem at the time of the liberation from the Turk, the southern Slav believes in religious toleration: *"Brat je mio, koje vere bio"* ("He is my brother whatever his faith").

There remains the old aristocracy. Though they are negligible in numbers and power, I believe that much depends on them if Yugoslavia is ever to become a cultured European state. Their loyalty has, like that of their Anglo-Irish counterpart, often been qualified, yet where it has been given it has been of inestimable value. They derive mostly from the old Austro-Hungarian provinces of Yugoslavia and are of hybrid Croatian and Austrian blood, for the Turk prevented the development of an aristocracy in the south. Such princely families as survived in Serbia owed their authority, like the royal dynasties of Karageorge and Obrenovitch, to military prowess. They united the virtues of the patriarch and the courage of the bandit. The Croatian nobility stands at the opposite pole; they are sometimes called over-civilized and useless, but some blame must rest with the inexperienced state which failed to use them. Many of them are highly educated and cosmopolitan, thinking in three languages, often witty, intelligent, liberal. Of Slav descent and Viennese culture, they should be the natural interpreters between Yugoslavia and Western Europe. Though they have long ago lost property and estates, from fastidi-

---

*A concordat with the Vatican was signed in July 1935 granting the Catholics in Yugoslavia wider privileges. When Orthodox groups objected, the project was dropped.—ed.

ousness and snobbery they have, many of them, held aloof from the Nazis and the Quislings. It is among the professional middle classes of Croatia, solicitors, doctors, auctioneers, that the doctrine of race superiority and disdain for the Serb has flourished most, small men who have to feed their self-esteem on contempt for others. There are scores of their brothers in the smarter Dublin suburbs. Foreign cultural bodies such as the British Council and its opposite number, the Deutsches Haus, made converts among this class, but at the expense of Yugoslavia. Only an educated minority, whose patriotism is reinforced by sensibility or pride, has the power to assimilate foreign culture without being overwhelmed or corrupted by it.

Like every hybrid aristocracy the Croatian nobility has had its rebel minority which has inspired the subject peoples with the dream of liberty and rallied them to its attainment. In the Austrian provinces the Yugoslav ideal was first fostered by the great Bishop Strossmayer, an aristocrat of Austrian descent. He was an amazing personality, as fervent as Thomas Davis, as practical as Horace Plunkett, as lavish and eccentric as the Earl Bishop of Derry. He revived the national spirit of the Croats and shaped their demands for independence.

I shall describe one of these hybrid families, typical except in one particular. They are doubly alien in descent. Like the Nugents and Kavanaghs of Slovenia, they are of Irish ancestry and name. This, however, is only of historical significance. German is their mother tongue and they have the dark mobile features of the Croat. Their ancestor, an Irish Catholic, forfeited his estates under Oliver Cromwell and took service with the Hapsburgs in the regiment of Irish Dragoons, quartered at Prague. He rose to be a general and was granted estates in Croatia by the emperor, for it was the habit of the Hapsburgs to award their foreign subjects with land in the Slav marches where they could be trusted to keep order without partiality. He must have married into Schloss Pischatz, the vast castle where his descendants lived, because it is far older than the seventeenth century. It is surrounded by acres of dark pine forest which the von Buttlar Moscons still own, though, by the ingenuity of the tax collector they derive nothing from it but firewood. Outside the castle gates is a village or rather one long broad street of farmhouses. Rudi, the elder Count, showed me the spot where, a century ago, the gallows stood on which his great-grandfather strung up insubordinate villagers. "They bore us no ill-will," he said. "In 1918 after the liberation, when they burnt Perovitch's house, they did not molest us at all." The Moscons dislike Perovitch. He is very up-to-date. He worked in

America before he inherited his family home, and acquired there a lot of go-ahead ideas, none of them, strange to say, either democratic or original. A specimen remark would be "What these chaps want is a Hitler to wake them up." He is certainly a Nazi. With a small adjustment of vocabulary and opportunity, he is to be found among the philistine ruling classes of every country.

The old Count von Moscon was a Minister of Franz Josef and they lived all the year in Vienna, except for a month of summer holiday at Schloss Krnica. Therefore they never bothered about the plumbing. Servants carried water all over the castle. On the collapse of the Central Powers they found themselves all at once Yugoslav citizens with Krnica their only property, and no water and no servants. Dick, the elder son, who was in the Austrian navy, transferred to the Yugoslav navy; Rudi, who was gay and expensive, recoiled from so dowdy a destiny. After a search through the family archives, he wrote to the representatives of the Moscons in Ireland and asked them to get him a commission in the Free State Army. In Ireland only one branch of the family had emerged from the forfeitures of Cromwell and it had long ago made its peace with authority. The Irish army seemed to them as comical as the Yugoslav army. They sent Rudi £2 c/o Thomas Cook, Stefansplatz, and put his letter into the curio table. In despair Rudi took a job in the First Croatian Savings Bank in Zagreb.

It was their sister, the Countess Wanda, who had the brains of the family. After dealing with the family finances so that Krnica could pay its way, she took a job in an American shipping office. Simultaneously the queen made her a lady-in-waiting, for decorative and honorary jobs were still at the disposal of the old nobility. She was worried about her brothers, though. Dick was unhappy in the navy. He had rather elaborate manners and his new shipmates thought he was putting on airs. She got him a job dubbing gangster films in Belgrade and he left the navy. He liked the work but did not do it very well. Though he spoke Serbo-Croatian fluently, he could not write it well. He had been brought up to consider it a language in which one gave orders to servants. His sister had to assist him. Meanwhile Rudi found the bank insupportable and he left for Vienna. There was a theory that he intended to marry a rich Viennese commoner. Anyway he became an Austrian citizen and asked for his share of the family property. Wanda had for years been working unsuccessfully to have Krnica taken over as a national monument. Now the furniture, which was the only thing realizable, would have to be sold and the proceeds divided. This was a difficult as well as a sad task. In the days of Maria Theresa a celebrated Italian cabinet-maker had travelled round Croatia and Slovenia, staying a few years in each castle, building magnificent furniture from the local timber. In the salon at Krnica there were priceless wardrobes and chests, so vast that without dismemberment they could not be brought down the narrow winding stairs unless a breach were made in the salon walls. The breach was made. Rudi, abandoning Yugoslavia for good, refused to pay his share for the repair. "Let them use the castle for road material, if they choose, the ignorant boors! I, thank God, am an Austrian." He became a Nazi and put his knowledge of Yugoslavia at the service of its enemies. He was a very ordinary person. The challenge presented to him by the young state was crude and unimaginative, and so was his response. Their failure to be reconciled was disastrous to them both.

Dick was not ordinary. He did not sell his furniture but had it brought by lorry to Belgrade. It was to him a symbol that he was a Croatian gentleman and not a mere Austrian colonist. The problem of adjusting his furniture to a tiny labour-saving flat had a spiritual counterpart. The framework of the new Yugoslav society is crude, without the dignity of the peasant or the culture of the nobleman. Dick was good and loyal; he had that rare perceptiveness and candour which sometimes develops behind a shelter of security and privilege. He was constantly misquoted and distrusted. He did not fit in. A small group of pushy Croat businessmen cultivated him and imperceptibly he too drifted into the ranks of Yugoslavia's enemies. They were Croat separatists and the brand of Slavophile Fascism which they preached was not at all crude. Ljutic, their philosopher, was a mystic and Dostoievsky was his prophet. The contacts with Italy and with the White Russians seemed to be on a spiritual plane, the political pledges were ingeniously disguised. If it had not been for Wanda's good sense Dick would have committed himself irrevocably. His fine gifts have been wasted by his country but not used against it.

This unimportant family history is a parable applicable to any new national state with an unassimilated minority. Minorities which from some scruple of pride or cultural superiority refuse to assimilate often accept with resignation the choice of two destinies, exile or extinction; a handful attempts to survive by becoming Quislings. The upper classes of Yugoslavia and the other Succession States are not merging; they are disappearing. This would not matter if they left behind them the rich and fertile civilization which they acquired through generations of privilege as mediators between Slav and Teuton. Rightly this hybrid culture belongs to Yugoslavia and should be claimed by it. Otherwise it will be appropriated by Vienna. With every fresh access of educated émigrés from the new states, the cultural magnetism of Vienna, so long irresistible in Eastern Europe, will be reinforced. This magnetism has possibly even been increased by political decay. Attracting unappreciated talent from all the border countries, Vienna has, like London, been able to disturb the consolidation of new civilizations politically beyond her control. Only by the free crystallization of all cultural elements, old and new, can these new civilizations become strong enough to hold their own.

I have shown how the old southern Slav way of life, as exemplified by the *izmirenje*, is inevitably doomed. The survivors of it are not sufficiently sophisticated to resist the encroachments of middle-class Western civilization, nor, except in the educated classes, is there any real cultural toughness and integrity to form the basis of a distinctive Yugoslav civilization. Even though the new intelligentsia may appear to take their politics from Moscow, it is probable that, as in the past, they will take their culture from Vienna. Typical examples of this inevitable Austro-Yugoslav culture are the Zagreb Communist playwright Krleza, and Mestrovich, the Dalmatian peasant boy who made contact with Rodin and the sculptors of the West in the Viennese art schools. The remnant of the ruling classes, if they can be won over, are far better qualified by hereditary fastidiousness to select and transmit these external influences than is the more easily deluded middle-class majority.

For there is no such thing as a pure national culture. In the monasteries of Pec and Decani and Gracanica there is evidence of a lofty Serbian art, inspired by Byzantium, yet the promise of a greater future was destroyed by the Turk as catastrophically as were even greater Irish hopes by the Norman. A few frescoes and ballads and some rapidly dying social traditions are all that the Serb chauvinist has to build on, and he is building badly after the cheapest standards of the West, scorning the assistance of those who understand the West. A common language survives, it is true, and a language unites men, so long as you can close the frontiers, mental and physical, but it cannot give the spiritual unity from which great cultures develop. If you looked before the war in the popular bookshops or in the cinemas in Zagreb or Belgrade, you would see that men follow the same fashions, dubbed and adapted, as in Dublin or Cardiff. Despite all the talk of national culture, Edgar Wallace and Garbo and their Viennese counterparts have a more potent educational influence on the average Serb and Irishman than Decani or Cormac's Chapel.

I have scarcely mentioned Mihailovitch and Tito, and the unbelievable cruelties and heroisms which in Yugoslavia have for four years usurped the place of normal development. At the moment of writing the political foreground is blurred, but I have tried to give some account of the constant forces, social and cultural, with which any Yugoslav government, of whatever complexion, will have ultimately to reckon.

Yugoslav Papers:
The Church and Its Opponents

1947

It was surprising to find in Communist Yugoslavia how elementary and almost perfunctory was the criticism of the Christian churches. It seemed to be based almost exclusively on Charles Darwin and certain clerical misdemeanours of recent date. I suggested to a friend who was a translator that it might be a good plan if the works of some freethinkers, like Bertrand Russell or Arthur Weigall, who are Christians and humanists as well as distinguished scholars, were translated. He told me, however, that there would be no demand for such work. The policy of both the Church and its opponents in Yugoslavia was "all or nothing," and no attempt to salvage Christian conduct from the mythology in which, in the view of many, it had become entangled would be countenanced. The baby, in fact, must be drowned in its bathwater or thrown out with it.

It is a very tragic situation, which might, I think, be relieved by extreme candour and truthfulness on behalf of the churches. They would have to avow more explicitly than hitherto that Christian virtues existed and could exist outside their ranks, and that, in fact, the representatives of the churches had, in Yugoslavia, done a disservice to the Christian way of life by claiming to be its unique exponents. Their weakness and subservience had compromised fatally those in their flock, or outside it, who were neither weak nor subservient.

In Ireland interest has focused itself disproportionately on Archbishop Stepinac, whose trial* was only a small episode in a struggle

---

*In 1946, on charges of collaborating with the enemy. He was convicted in September.—ed.

for Christian values which lasted for four or five years and in which the churches were as deeply divided as any other branch of society. At the very start the Protestant Church, which was very small, accepted the Nazis with enthusiasm, as did the Evangelical Church in Austria. The ecstatic welcome given to Hitler by the Viennese Evangelical clergy is recorded in the Dean of Chichester's *Struggle for Religious Freedom in Germany* (1938). But some effort has been made to prove that the Catholic Church in Yugoslavia was the backbone of the resistance to totalitarianism. Such an extraordinary notion could scarcely have gone unchallenged if it had not been feared that any admission of guilt would help the Communists. To do this would seem to be a greater crime than falsehood.

A large volume was published in Zagreb in 1946, *Dokumenti O Protonarodnom Radu* (*Documents about the Anti-national Activities and Crimes of a Part of the Catholic Clergy*). Some of the innumerable documents contained in it were used in the controversy. By most churchmen they were held to be spurious; the Communist Yugoslav government was accused of faking the evidence. When I was in Zagreb I looked up ten or twelve of the most significant passages in the back number of papers published during the Occupation. They are stored in the University Library and many other libraries easily accessible. I found them all, without exception, accurately recorded. Moreover, I found that the Yugoslav government had not used a tenth of the material at its disposal. The Catholic Church in Yugoslavia for the most part received the invaders not with resignation but with transports of joy, and many of its prominent priests and friars had been preparing the way for them for many years.

Archbishop Stepinac, by his many brave sermons in defence of Jew and Orthodox, did something to redeem the welcome which he had given to Pavelitch on his arrival and the appeal which he broadcast to his clergy for submission. (I saw his appeal, which has been called a fake, both in the diocesan paper of Zagreb and in two other papers.) But unquestionably his conciliatory attitude influenced others who were not capable of his restraint. So it happened that the man who organized the murder of King Alexander and was later responsible for the attempted extermination of the Serbs as well as the Jews in Croatia, was received with rapture in convents and monasteries and ecclesiastical seminaries, as well as being idolized in the Catholic press. Here is an account in a Church paper of a visit of 140 Zagreb theological students to the *Poglavnik* (Leader, or Duce):

And then He entered. Himself, He opened the door of His room and stood before us. A kingly face, He raised His arm and greeted us with His wonderful deep voice, commanding and fatherly.

"*Za Dom!*" ("For Fatherland!") "*Spremni!*" ("Alert!") [This corresponds to the Nazi greeting "*Heil Hitler!*"]

A roar from 140 youthful throats, and then there stepped before Him the president of the Council of Young Clerics, Stephen Krisovitch, and addressed Him.

While He spoke our eyes rested on the heir of the great Croat heroes of the past, on Ante Pavelitch! We try to watch the meaning in every feature of His face, every flicker of His eyes. And He—our sovereign—stands before us, wonderful in His simplicity. His was the holy calm of the grotto.

The president finished his speech and handed to the Poglavnik our gift, five Roman missals in the Croatian tongue, and the Poglavnik enfolding us in His glance exclaimed: "Brothers!" We held our breath from excitement and a strange exhalation seemed to flow towards us from the Poglavnik. His words sketched out a new page, the loveliest and most precious of all in the history of the Seminary Youth of Croatia.*

Then they sang to him the Ustashe hymn and there was a further exchange of heartfelt cordiality and they went away.

As you see, capital letters are used throughout in the pronouns referring to Pavelitch. There is a photograph of Pavelitch in the midst of the 140 students. They look mild and submissive young men and I do not think they would have ventured on this demonstration if it had been displeasing to their ecclesiastical superiors or likely to prejudice their careers in the Church.

The following month there was a solemn gathering in honour of Pavelitch at the archiepiscopal church of Sarajevo, at which a choir sang Ustashe hymns and Archbishop Sharitch's "Ode to the Poglavnik" was recited; also, a young cleric recited a declamation on the Poglavnik's heroic deeds in the "Barbarous East." At that time the mass slaughter of the Serbs in Bosnia was in progress with the Poglavnik's approval, so the young man's reference to the Barbarous East was highly topical.

The pages of the papers published during the Occupation are full of such astonishing stories. Many of them are illustrated, because the Poglavnik, who claimed to be religious, obtained great advertisement for himself by his association with ecclesiastics and there was

*From *Nedjelja*, 17 May 1942.

usually a photographer nearby. And so he is seen as a sturdy, strutting figure surrounded by gentle nuns or eager theological students inhaling his loving-kindness with eager smiles.

I have quoted hitherto the more serious papers of Yugoslavia. There are also innumerable smaller papers, like *The Messenger of the Heart of Jesus, The Guardian Angel, St. Joseph's Herald,* etc., etc., which reached a less literate public. One and all they have photographs of the Poglavnik in strange proximity to angels, doves, lambs, little girls, and poems and prayers of sickly piety extolling his virtues.

It would be wrong to deride the simplicity of these people, whose fault lay in believing what they were told, if it had not had terrible consequences. We read in *St. Antony's Messenger,* June 1941, the calm announcement: "There are too many Jews in Zagreb with their aims of world domination and their perfidy and destructiveness. The Poglavnik has decided that the Jewish question must be radically solved." A few weeks later an announcement of an anti-Jewish exhibition and an article that might have been inspired by Streicher appeared. Almost the whole of the Jewish populations of Zagreb was, in fact, in those days plundered and taken to the camps of Jasenovac and executed. I believe that in spite of the Christian papers, the population regarded their fate with horror and revulsion. In the diocesan magazine of Bosnia and Slavonia for June 1941 parish clerks are notified of an important new decision: "Today it is the solemn duty of every citizen to show proof of his Aryan parentage."

It has been said that these papers were forced to print these articles under threat of suppression. But a healthy Christianity could only have been invigorated by the suppression of *St. Antony's Messenger* or, when it became a travesty of Christian principles, would have prevented its circulation. Nor do I think that "political" pressure is a sufficient excuse. Those who read *Katolicki List* will find that the editorship of the paper did not change at the time of the invasion. Its new policy was merely an inflamed and exaggerated development of tendencies which had been evident before.

It is true that Archbishop Stepinac many times spoke against racial discrimination. Yet he must have been aware that such laws would follow quickly on the establishment of that government to which he had given his sanction and support. He seems to have had a curious detachment from the laws of cause and effect and to have believed that any crime committed against Russia could be overlooked. He seems to have been scarcely aware of the crimes committed on a wide scale in the name of the Church and the connivance and condonation of which many of its leaders were guilty. It is not possible that the Church leaders were ignorant of the wild and murderous excesses of hundreds and perhaps thousands of fanatical priests and monks in Yugoslavia. Yet in their statement of 8 March 1945 there is one solitary reference to these misdeeds: "When in exceptional cases a mad priest has assailed his neighbours' rights, we have not hesitated to lay a church punishment on him, and even to take away his priestly orders"!

In September the bishops also declared: "There were isolated cases of priests blinded by national and party passion who committed offences against the law and had to be put on trial before a secular court." In the same circular they tell how all the friars of Shiroki Brieg* were executed without trial by the Partisans, but they weakened their case against this brutal act by saying what is not true, that almost all the friars were known for their "opposition to Fascist ideology." In the diocesan papers of Bosnia there are reports of ecstatic celebrations at Shiroki Brieg on the Poglavnik's birthday and other Ustashe festivals similar to that I have described. Many of the most prominent of the Ustashe leaders had been educated at Shiroki Brieg.

If the Church leaders had shown some penitence and cared about the wrongs they had done to unoffending people they might expect a more candid examination of the wrongs done to them and others in the name of Communism.

---

*A Franciscan monastery in Herzegovina that was a center for Catholic hostilities to the Serbs during the war. See below, pp. 480–85.

The Sub-Prefect Should Have Held His Tongue

1956

In countries where the old beliefs are dying, it is the custom for educated people to handle them with nostalgic reverence. It is thought crude and undignified for a sophisticated man to take sides in a religious squabble, and it often happens that, the less he believes in himself, the more indulgent he is to the time-honoured beliefs of others. I have been reproached several times by sincere and civilized unbelievers for my efforts to find out the details of the vast campaign in Croatia in 1941 to convert 2.5 million Orthodox to Catholicism. "Why not let bygones be bygones?" they say. "If we rake these things up we'll merely start trouble at home and play into the hands of the Communists. And anyway, they are always killing each other in the Balkans." I once heard an ambassador in Belgrade argue like that, and indeed I have never heard a British or American official abroad argue in any other way. When in 1946 I went to Zagreb and looked up the files of the wartime newspapers of Croatia in which the whole story was to be read, it was obvious that no foreign inquirer had handled them before, and the library clerks regarded me with wonder and suspicion.

Yet it seemed to me that for a man as for a community, too high a price can be paid for tranquillity. If you suppress a fact because it is awkward, you will next be asked to contradict it. And so it happened to me when I got back to Ireland and gave a talk about Yugoslavia, the country and its people, on Radio Éireann. I did not mention the Communist war on the Church, or Archbishop Stepinac, who had just been sentenced to imprisonment for collaboration with Pavelitch, the Quisling ruler of Croatia, and for conniving at the

forced conversion campaign. I could not refer to the Communist persecution of religion without mentioning the more terrible Catholic
persecution which had preceded it, so I thought silence was best. But
silence did not help me. In the following week our leading Roman
Catholic weekly, *The Standard*, published a long editorial diatribe
against me and against Radio Éireann. I had not, it declared, said a
word about the sufferings of the Church and its ministers under Tito,
and by sponsoring me, Radio Éireann had connived at a vile piece
of subversive propaganda. The officials of Radio Éireann, knowing I
was no Communist, supported me, and finally *The Standard*, under
pressure from my solicitor, agreed to print a long reply from me. I
received the proof sheets, corrected and returned them, but the reply
never appeared. Months later, a muddled, amiable explanation
reached me, and my friends said "Let bygones be bygones." I did.
That is the way things happen in Ireland.

But it became increasingly difficult to be silent. The foreign editor of *The Standard*, Count O'Brien of Thomond, had published a
little book about Archbishop Stepinac; it had an introduction by the
Archbishop of Dublin and commendation on the dust cover from a
couple of cardinals, Canadian and English, and half a dozen bishops
and archbishops.* Cardinal Spellman had laid a copy on the foundation stone of the new Stepinac Institute in New York City, and
told 1,700 schoolgirls, drawn up on a polo ground in the form of a
rosary, what they were to think about Croatian ecclesiastical history.
Yet it seemed to me that there was a major error of fact or interpretation, or a significant omission, on almost every page of this book.
Meanwhile all the county councils and corporations in Ireland met
and passed resolutions. Extracts from Count O'Brien's book were
hurled about, and fiery telegrams despatched to parliaments and ambassadors.† But the climax of my discomfort was reached when our
Minister for Agriculture, Mr. Dillon, addressing some law students,
advised them to model themselves on Mindzenty, Stepinac and Pavelitch, who had "so gallantly defended freedom of thought and freedom of conscience." Those who knew Yugoslavia were aghast, for
Pavelitch, one of the major war criminals, was the Yugoslav counterpart of Himmler, and it was under his rule that the gas chamber

---

*A. H. O'Brien, *Archbishop Stepinac: The Man and His Case* (London, 1947).
†In my own country town, Kilkenny, a muddled but enthusiastic alderman insisted that
Tito was in Dublin in the capacity of Yugoslav ambassador, and proposed at the Corpo-
ration meeting that he should be told, "Get out, Tito!"

and the concentration camp were introduced into Yugoslavia and the forced conversion campaign initiated. Clearly Mr. Dillon was speaking in ignorance, not in bigotry, but ignorance rampaging with such assurance and harnessed to religious enthusiasm is like a runaway horse and cart. It must be stopped before serious mischief results.

I felt that the honour of the small Protestant community in southern Ireland would be compromised if those of us who had investigated the facts remained silent about what we had discovered. In many Roman Catholic pulpits the sufferings of the Catholics under Tito were being compared to the long martyrdom of Catholic Ireland under Protestant rule. "Yesterday and today Herod abides." If we agree that history should be falsified in Croatia in the interests of Catholic piety, how could we protest when our own history was similarly distorted?

In letters to the newspapers I had replied to Mr. Dillon and many others who had expressed similar opinions. A well-known Irish Jesuit, Father Devane, assuming a Slav name, Mihajlo Dvornik, to lend force to his accuracy, solemnly declared that there had been no forced religious conversions in Croatia, but I could find no one ready to argue the details. Mostly they quoted at me passages from Count O'Brien or, on a priori grounds, accused me of vile slander. "The Catholic Church had always insisted that conversion must be from the heart. *Ad amplexandam fidem Catholicam nemo invitus cogatur.*" I was alleging the impossible.

Soon afterwards it was announced that Tito was to visit London, and in Ireland as in England various anti-Yugoslav demonstrations were arranged. My friend Owen Sheehy-Skeffington, a lecturer in Trinity College and now a member of the Irish Senate, invited me to a meeting of the Foreign Affairs Association, at which the editor of *The Standard* was to read a paper: "Yugoslavia—the Pattern of Persecution." The Association had been modelled on Chatham House* as an international fact-finding society and Arnold Toynbee himself had come over to give his blessing to the first meeting. In the *Survey of International Affairs* of 1955 he was later to express himself as strongly as I had about the persecution of the Orthodox. This is an undenominational society with a tradition of free speech. The lecturer had never been to Yugoslavia, and I believe that all the others on the platform were in the same position, though one of them said that on a cruise down the Dalmatian coast he had met members of a Yu-

---

*Headquarters, in London, of the Royal Institute of International Affairs.—ed.

goslav football team. I decided that at the end of his paper I would try to make those points which he had failed, despite his promise, to publish for me. I would try to show how variegated was the pattern of persecution in Yugoslavia, and how misleading our crude simplifications would be. What followed has been told by Paul Blanshard, whom I met for the first time that evening, in his book *The Irish and Catholic Power*. It is enough to say here that the chairman's attempt to close the meeting at the end of the paper was ruled out, on a vote, as unconstitutional. I got up, holding in my hand *The Martyrdom of the Serbs*, a book published by the exiled Serbian Orthodox Church in Chicago, in case anything I said required authoritative corroboration. It had been given me by Archpriest Nicolitch, the head of the Serbian Orthodox Church in England. But I had spoken only a few sentences when a stately figure rose from among the audience and walked out. It was the Papal Nuncio, of whose presence I had been unaware. The chairman instantly closed the meeting, and there was an appalled silence, followed by a rush of reporters in my direction. They had understood nothing in the confusion. There was, consequently, some lively reporting, and two leading dailies quoted me as saying that the Orthodox Church, not the Communists, had initiated the persecution of Catholics in Yugoslavia. In gigantic letters in the *Sunday Express* (Irish edition) I read: "Pope's Envoy Walks Out. Government to Discuss Insult to Nuncio."

Blanshard has described the measures taken against Skeffington in Dublin and myself in Kilkenny. The persecution was of a familiar pattern, and I try to see in it not a personal hard-luck story, but material for a study in the modern indifference to evidence, but I think both of us knew that had we been less fortunate in our backgrounds we would have been ruined. Skeffington, the son of a father executed by the British in 1916—or, to be more accurate, murdered at the orders of a hysterical British officer—is at his happiest when he is fighting, and shortly afterwards he fought his way into the Irish Senate. For myself, I am grateful for the few inherited acres which helped me to survive the disapproval of my neighbours. All the local government bodies of the city and county held special meetings to condemn the "Insult." There were speeches from mayors, ex-mayors, aldermen, creamery managers. The county council expelled me from one of its subcommittees, and I was obliged to resign from another committee. Although my friends put up a fight, I was forced to give up the honorary secretaryship of the Kilkenny Archaeological Society, which I had myself revived and guided through seven difficult years. My opponents hoped that my liquidation would be decorous and quickly forgotten, but my friends and I were little inclined to oblige them, and for a time our small society enjoyed in the metropolitan press a blaze of publicity which its archaeological activities had never won for it.

I decided that before I resigned I would tell our two or three hundred members something about the forced conversion campaign in Yugoslavia. Much of the evidence, including the utterances of the Orthodox Church and its bishops, and Archbishop Sharitch's "Ode to the Poglavnik," with its sonorous denunciations of Serbs and Jews, I put aside, because I was certain that it would not be believed. Finally, I decided to publish the long letter written by Stepinac to Pavelitch on the subject of the forced conversions. I had translated it from a typescript in Zagreb in 1946, and it seems to me a document of vast importance which deserves a prominent place in the annals of religious history. Its reception was disappointing. Many were confused by the outlandish names and inextricably complicated series of events, and I was taken aback when one friendly disposed reader congratulated me on "my interesting article on Czechoslavia."

There is in Ireland a historic loathing of proselytism. The well-meaning Protestants who plied the starving peasants of the west with soup and Bibles after the famine of 1846 had never been forgiven. Religious apprehensions as strong as these survive in Yugoslavia, and I had hoped that some of my neighbours would be capable of the necessary mental adjustment and would see the parallel. Surely it would be obvious to them from the Stepinac letter that the Croatian bishops, while denouncing the use of force, were delighted with the opportunities for mass conversion which the chaos and defeat of Yugoslavia afforded them. There was, for example, Dr. Mishitch, Bishop of Mostar and the kindliest of mortals, whom even the Communists have praised for his clemency. He too had made quite plain the hopes which he had entertained at the beginning of Pavelitch's regime:

By the mercy of God [he wrote] there was never such a good occasion as now for us to help Croatia to save the countless souls, people of good will, well-disposed peasants, who live side by side with Catholics. . . . Conversion would be appropriate and easy. Unfortunately the authorities in their narrow views are involuntarily hindering the Croatian and Catholic cause. In many parishes of [my] diocese . . . very honest peasants of the Orthodox faith have registered in the Catholic Church. . . . But then outsiders take things in hand. While the newly converted are at Mass they seize them, old and young, men and women, and hunt them like slaves. From Mostar and Chapljina the railway carried six wagons full of mothers, girls, and children under eight to the station of Surmanci, where they were taken out of the wagons, brought into the hills and thrown alive, mothers and children, into deep ravines. In the parish of Klepca seven hundred schismatics from the neighbouring villages were slaughtered. The Sub-Prefect of Mostar, Mr. Bajitch, a Moslem, publicly declared (as a state employé he should have held his tongue) that in Ljubina alone 700 schismatics have been thrown into one pit.

Elsewhere in his letter the bishop wrote:

At one time there was a likelihood that a great number of schismatics would be united to the Catholic Church. If God had given to those in authority the understanding and the good sense to deal effectively with conversion, so that it could have been carried through more ably, more smoothly and by degrees, the number of Catholics might have been increased by at least five or six hundred thousand. Such a number is required in Bosnia and Herzegovina, if there is to be an increase from 700,000 to 1,300,000.

The other three bishops whose letters Stepinac quoted all took the normal human view that it is inadvisable in the name of religion to throw wagonloads of schismatics over cliffs; they were critical of the conversion campaign, but they did not find the occasion for it unseasonable. Had there been no cruelty, and if possible a little soup, they would have welcomed it. But compared with Monsignor Mishitch's letters theirs are cold, calculating and self-righteous. Archbishop Sharitch opined that the town council of Sarajevo was imposing too high a tax on the Bosnian Orthodox for their change of religion. The Bishop of Kotor, Dr. Butorac, declared that missionaries to the Serbs must be wisely selected. "We must not entrust the problem," he wrote, "to monks or priests who have no tact at all and who would be much better suited to carry a revolver in their hands than a cross." And he expressed the fear that if the Serbs were driven too hard they might, out of defiance, pass over in a body to Islam.

I must confess that I find Monsignor Stepinac's comments on these letters and the situation that provoked them curiously narrow and thin-lipped. He scolds the miserable, hunted Orthodox for their terrible errors, deriving, he declares, from "hatred and schism," and he blames them for the Russian Revolution, just as he blames the crimes of Pavelitch and his gang on the Chetniks—that is, followers of Mihailovitch—the Communists, and the Royal Yugoslav Government. He considers that the best way to convert the Orthodox might often be found through the medium of the Greek Catholic Church, which recognizes the authority of the Pope while preserving its Orthodox ritual. He ends his letter, as he began it, by exonerating Pavelitch from all blame in the crimes that had been committed.

Yet Count O'Brien told us in his little book that at this time, in defence of the Orthodox, the Archbishop had swept into Pavelitch's office. " 'It is God's command!' he said, 'Thou shalt not kill!' and without another word he left the Quisling's palace."

Stepinac's long and respectful letter to Pavelitch at this date proves the anecdote to be a hagiographical fabrication. Yet it was quoted at me several times in the press of Kilkenny and Dublin. The letter was obviously the longest and most important that Stepinac had ever written, and it struck me as odd that though I had published it twice in Ireland—for my critics in Kilkenny and also in *The Church of Ireland Gazette*—nobody in the British Isles, at a time when so much was written and said about the imprisoned Archbishop, ever commented on it, quoted from it, or wrote to me to enquire how I had secured it. Three years later, however, Richard Pattee published a lengthy book in defence of Stepinac, and among his documents the letter belatedly appeared.* Yet I believe that my translation is the more accurate of the two. Mr. Pattee has thought it best to omit a sentence or two here and there. He leaves out, for instance, Monsignor Mishitch's calculations of the number of conversions required in Bosnia and Herzegovina. Again, wherever the word "conversion" appears in the text Mr. Pattee reads it as "legitimate conversion," thus adding an epithet which I could not trace in the original. Stepinac's admiring description of the Bishop of Banja Luka as "that old Croatian warrior" likewise disappears, presumably because Mr. Pattee does not wish his readers to infer that the bishops were Croatian separatists trying to ingratiate themselves with Pavelitch.

About the same time Mr. Michael Derrick published in *The Tablet* a paragraph or two from Mishitch's letter, but he attributed it to Stepinac, and he omitted the extraordinary parenthesis about the sub-prefect who told of barbarities inflicted upon the Orthodox, and the bishop's comment that "as a state employé he should have held his tongue." In the succeeding issue of *The Sword*, Mr. Derrick published my translation of Stepinac's *The Regulations for Conversion*

---

*Richard Pattee, *The Case of Cardinal Aloysius Stepinac* (London and Milwaukee, 1953).

without acknowledgment! Anybody who read these regulations with an open mind, and particularly an Irish Catholic with his inherited horror of "souperism," would have to admit that they bore every trace, except soup, of *illegitimate* conversion. For instance, Clause XI, an appeal that the Orthodox be granted full civic rights, has been much applauded, but it begins: "A psychological basis for conversion must be created among the Greek Orthodox inhabitants." If still in doubt as to the bearing of these regulations, one would have only to read the manifesto of Dr. Shimrak, editor of the leading Catholic daily and chosen by Stepinac as one of his two colleagues in the supervision of conversion:

Every priest must have before his eyes that historic days have come for our mission. Now we must put into practice that which we have spoken of in theory throughout the centuries. In the matter of conversion we have done very little up to this, simply because we were irresolute and dreaded the small reproaches and censure of men. Every great task has its opponents, but we must not be downcast on that account, because it is a question of a holy union, the salvation of souls and the eternal glory of the Lord Christ. Our work is legal in the light of the ruling of the Holy See . . . also in the light of the ruling of the Holy Congregation of Cardinals for the Eastern Church . . . and finally in the light of the circular sent by the Government of Independent Croatia, 30 July 1941, whose intention it is that the Orthodox should be converted to the Catholic faith.*

Count O'Brien, an Austrian of Irish descent, had been until he came to Ireland after the war the editor of an important Viennese paper, and he claimed in his book to have known Shimrak intimately for twenty years. He also wrote that all the Croat bishops had opposed Pavelitch's "evil plan" for the forced conversion of the Orthodox. This seemed in such strong conflict with Shimrak's declaration that long before the "Insult" I visited Count O'Brien to ask for an explanation. An explanation was forthcoming. The Count replied at once that Shimrak had not been a bishop at the time, but only an administrator. It appeared from his reply that it was actually after he had proved himself in sympathy with Pavelitch's plan that Shimrak was appointed to the bishopric and to Stepinac's committee for regulating conversion. I then asked how it came about that, if all the bishops were hostile to Pavelitch and his plans, Archbishop Sharitch of Bosnia, one of the greatest of them, had been able to print his

Diocesan Magazine of Krizhevtsi, No. 2 (1942), pp. 10–11.

"Ode to the Poglavnik" in the ecclesiastical papers of his own arch-diocese and that of Zagreb. I had made a translation of his ode in twenty-six verses, describing his meeting with Pavelitch at St. Peter's in Rome, and I now ventured to remind Count O'Brien of a few lines:

> Embracing thee was precious to the poet
> as embracing our beloved Homeland.
> For God himself was at thy side, thou good and strong one,
> so that thou mightest perform thy deeds for the Homeland . . .
> And against the Jews, who had all the money,
> who wanted to sell our souls,
> who built a prison round our name,
> the miserable traitors. . . .
> Doctor Ante Pavelitch! the dear name!
> Croatia has in thee a treasure from Heaven.
> May the King of Heaven accompany thee,
> Our Golden Leader!

Count O'Brien had an explanation for that, too. He said, "The Arch-bishop was an abnormal man, very emotional. He was always em-bracing people. Whenever we met, he used to kiss me on both cheeks. He can't be taken seriously."

These replies made me feel very helpless, since they could not have been made if venal indifference had not reigned around us. When I went home I was feeling as emotional as the Archbishop, and I remember that I wrote a poem myself on the Massacre of the Orthodox, though I must admit that it was the massacre of the truth that really outraged me.

> Milton, if you were living at this hour,
> they'd make you trim your sonnet to appease
> the triple tyrant and the Piedmontese.
> "Why for some peasants vex a friendly power?
> We'd like to print it, but Sir Tottenham Bauer
> and half the Board would blame us. Colleen Cheese
> would stop its full-page ad. They're strong RCs.
> It's old stuff now, and truth, deferred, goes sour.
> So cut those lines about 'the stocks and stones'
> and 'slaughtered saints,' or keep for private ears
> that fell crusade, for even in undertones,
> it breeds disunion and the Kremlin hears.

Say nothing rash or rude, for it is right
that all the godly (west of Kiel), unite!"

I thought my poem almost as good as the Archbishop's, but I had some difficulty in getting it published. In the end it appeared in a pacifist weekly, but very inconspicuously and in very small print. The Archbishop had been luckier. His had appeared in *Katolicki Tjednik* (*The Catholic Weekly*) on Christmas Day, with a signed portrait of Pavelitch and a decorative border of Christmas tree candles and little silver bells.

I suppose that the small community in which I live has about the same significance for the world as the community of Mr. Bjitch, who as a state employé "should have held his tongue" about the massacres, so I need not apologize for returning to it. My friends and neighbours were memorably kind and supporting; for they knew that I had not intended to insult anybody. But others were puzzled. I was not, like Mr. Bjitch, a state employé, and some found it difficult to make their disapproval materially felt. This problem would not have baffled them for long had it not been for the courtesy and good sense of the local Catholic clergy. I was most vulnerable through the Kilkenny Archaeological Society. This had been a famous Victorian institution, with the Prince Consort as patron and the Marquess of Ormonde as president, but it has shifted to Dublin as an All-Ireland society, and when I revived it in Kilkenny in 1945 it had been dead there for half a century. In a couple of years the new Society became a real bridge between Protestant and Catholic, Anglo-Irishman and Celt. The friendliness which it created was perhaps our main achievement, but we did other things, too. Mr. O. G. S. Crawford made for us a photographic survey of old Kilkenny such as no other Irish provincial town possesses; Dr. Bersu, the director of the Institute of Archaeology in Frankfurt, made his principal Irish excavation on a hill fort outside Kilkenny and reported it in our journal; we had a centenary celebration of the old society in Kilkenny Castle; and the National Museum cooperated in a very successful Kilkenny Exhibition. But I think I was proudest of having organized a week's visit from the principal archaeological society in Northern Ireland, for cultural fraternizations between North and South are as rare as they are valuable. I feared that all this work would be wasted, so I decided to appeal to a certain Stephen Brown, a Jesuit, who had attended meetings of our Society. He had escorted the Nuncio to the fateful meeting and afterwards in *The Irish Independent* had defended the Croatian hierarchy against the charges of illegitimate proselytism, with copious quotations from Count O'Brien but, as it seemed to me, with a total ignorance of Yugoslav conditions. Father Brown received me warmly. He said he was satisfied that I had not intended to insult the Nuncio, that he strongly disapproved the introduction of the incident into the affairs of an archaeological society, and that in any case the Nuncio had visited the meeting by mistake under the impression that he was bound for a meeting of a Catholic society with a similar name. Father Brown said that he would send me a letter making these three points, and that I might publish it in any paper I chose. The letter never arrived. It seemed, however, that a compromise had been reached in the matter, for a few days later a paragraph appeared in *The Standard* under the heading "Mr. Butler Rebuked." After commending all the denunciations by public bodies, the passage ended:

It is well that such repudiation should be known. But we doubt if any good purpose would have been served by the proposed step by which Mr. Butler would have been deprived of office in, say, the Kilkenny Archaeological Society, of which he is presumably an efficient functionary, and into which he can scarcely introduce sectarian issues. If he has any regard for public opinion he must know by now that his action met with not alone local but national disapproval. That is sufficient.

It was difficult for me to return as a presumably efficient functionary to a Society which I had myself founded, so I never after attended a meeting, but my friends, both Catholic and Protestant, still support the Society and I am glad today that it continues.

I hope I have not appeared to diagnose in my Catholic countrymen a unique susceptibility to a disease with which we are all of us more or less infected. Speed of communications has increased, and we are expected to have strong feelings about an infinite series of remote events. But our powers of understanding and sympathy have not correspondingly increased. In an atmosphere of artificially heated emotionalism truth simply dissolves into expediency. This shifting current of expediency may be illustrated by a chronicle of the changing attitudes to Pavelitch in the past ten years. In Croatia, upheld by the victorious Germans, he had for four years been regarded as a great Christian gentleman and patriot. All the Catholic bishops and the Evangelical bishops were among his panegyrists and received decorations from him. Then the Nazis collapsed, and Pavelitch was regarded by the outer world as one of the basest of war criminals, while in Croatia all the dignitaries hastened to disavow the compliments they had paid him. A former Italian Fascist, Malaparte, has described how, as correspondent of *Corriere Della Sera*, he visited Pavelitch in his office in 1942 and saw behind him what appeared to be a basket of shelled oysters. "Are these Dalmatian oysters?" Malaparte asked. "No," Pavelitch replied, "that's forty pounds of human eyes, a present from my loyal Ustashe in Bosnia"—eyes, that is to say, of Serbian Orthodox. I am ready to believe that this story is an invention, like Stepinac's visit to "the Quisling's Palace," and that stories like this were repeated by ex-Fascists who thought that if they made the whole world black their own shade of dirty grey would be less conspicuous. But in 1948 no one told Malaparte that he was a liar. Indeed, writing in *The Irish Times*, Mr. Kees van Hoek, biographer of the Pope, said that Malaparte was "the most accurate observer and reliable witness."

That was the universal Western view of Pavelitch seven or eight years ago—a monster of iniquity, an ogre out of a fairy tale. But since then Pavelitch has become more respectable, and if he was wanted again in a campaign against Communism in the Balkans, it is possible that he and his friends would be used. He now lives in South America and two or three papers and journals are published in his interest. Five years ago he issued postage stamps commemorating the tenth anniversary of Independent Croatia, and he has cashed in very effectively on the Stepinac legend, since one of his Ustashe clubs in Argentina is called after the famous Cardinal. Archbishop Sharitch, the devoted admirer of both Pavelitch and Stepinac, lives in Madrid, but still publishes his odes (rather modified), as well as ecstatic reminiscences of Stepinac, in *Hrvatska Revija*, a Croatian separatist quarterly of Buenos Aires. I once visited Monsignor Stepinac in prison and found him a gentle and serious man who obviously acted as he thought was right. Surely it must be one of the hardest blows that fate has dealt him that both Pavelitch and Sharitch speak well of him?

In one way or another the memory of a terrible crime against humanity is being confused and effaced, so that many people believe that it never happened at all or that it has been monstrously exaggerated. I have seen Pavelitch compared in Irish papers with Roger Casement and Patrick Pearse, as a simple-hearted patriot who merely did his best for his country in difficult circumstances. In October 1952 he was interviewed for an Italian picture paper, *Epoca* of Milan. He was photographed basking in the South American sun with his wife and family, stroking a pet dog. He told how he had escaped from Croatia through the Allied lines, how he had paused for weeks at a time in Naples, the Vatican City, and Castel Gandolfo. He was to be considered a romantic fellow, the carefree immunity which he enjoyed no more than his due.

How had all this happened? Three centuries ago Milton gave undying notoriety to the massacre and forced conversion of the Waldenses, and Cromwell sent out emissaries to collect information about the sufferings of this tiny Alpine community. We are mostly now immune from the religious fanaticism which once intensified racial antipathies and to which Cromwell himself was no stranger; why has it become unwise to censure or even to take notice of an explosion of those ancient passions fifty times more devastating than that which Milton observed? There were scarcely ten thousand Waldenses to be persecuted in Piedmont, while the decrees of Pavelitch were launched against more than 2 million Orthodox, and 240,000 were forcibly converted.

Looking for a reason, I can only conclude that science has enormously extended the sphere of our responsibilities, while our consciences have remained the same size. Parochially minded people neglect their parishes to pronounce ignorantly about the universe, while the universalists are so conscious of the worldwide struggles of opposing philosophies that the rights and wrongs of any regional conflict dwindle to insignificance against a cosmic panorama. They feel that truth is in some way relative to orientation, and falsehood no more than a wrong adjustment, so that they can never say unequivocally, "That is a lie!" Like the needle of a compass at the North Pole, their moral judgment spins round and round, overwhelming them with information and telling them nothing at all.

The Artukovitch File

1970

REFLECTIONS ON A CROATIAN CRUSADE

Some years after I had written "The Sub-Prefect Should Have Held His Tongue," I was in New York and read how the Yugoslav government was urging that Artukovitch, Pavelitch's Minister of the Interior, who was living in California, should be extradited. I went to the Yugoslav consulate to enquire about this and was handed a fat yellow booklet called *Artukovitch, the Himmler of Yugoslavia* by three New Yorkers called Gaffney, Starchevitch and McHugh.

Artukovitch first won notoriety in October 1934. He had gone to England at the time of King Alexander's murder at Marseilles. After his visit to Paris, the king had intended to see his son, Crown Prince Peter, at Sandroyd School, so, in case the Marseilles attempt failed, Artukovitch had been deputed to arrange for the king's assassination in England. It did not fail, so Artukovitch waited in Czechoslovakia and Hungary till the Nazi invasion of Yugoslavia. He then returned with them and held various ministerial posts under Pavelitch from 1944 to 1945 in Independent Croatia. Very few people have heard of him, yet if his story were told with remorseless candour, we would have a picture not only of Croatia forty years ago, but of all Christendom in our century. Everything that the New Yorkers relate was already known to me except for one startling paragraph, an extract from a memoir by Artukovitch himself. After describing how he escaped to Austria and Switzerland in 1945, he goes on:

I stayed in Switzerland until July 1947. Then with the knowledge of the Swiss Ministry of Justice I obtained personal documents for myself and my family, which enabled us to travel to Ireland. Using the name of Anitch, we stayed there until 15 July 1948. When our Swiss documents expired, the Irish issued new papers and under Irish papers we obtained a visa for entry into the USA.

So evidently we in Ireland had sheltered this notable man for a whole year. He was not, like Eichmann, a humble executive, but himself a maker of history, dedicated to the extermination not of Jews alone but also of his fellow Christians the Serbian Orthodox. He was a member of the government which in the spring of 1941 introduced laws that expelled them from Zagreb, confiscated their property and imposed the death penalty on those who sheltered them. Some twenty concentration camps were established in which they were exterminated. Why do we know so little about his sojourn among us? Did he stay in a villa at Foxrock or in lodgings at Bundoran or in some secluded midland cloister? And who looked after him? The Red Cross? And did we cherish him because he presented himself to us as a Christian refugee from godless Communism? That seems to me rather likely.

Nowadays we usually estimate cruelty by statistics, and Gaffney and Co. use the figures normally recorded for Croatia by Jewish and Orthodox writers, that is to say, 30,000 Jews and 750,000 Orthodox massacred, 240,000 Orthodox forcibly converted to Catholicism. Even if these figures are exaggerated, it was the most bloodthirsty religio-racial crusade in history, far surpassing anything achieved by Cromwell or the Spanish Inquisitors. I am sorry that Gaffney and Co. give so many photographs of headless babies, of disembowelled shopkeepers, of burning beards soaked in kerosene, for Artukovitch was, like Himmler, a "desk murderer," who deplored the disorderly and sadistic way in which his instructions were carried out. He was respectable, and it is the correlation of respectability and crime that nowadays has to be so carefully investigated.

The three writers tell Artukovitch's story with much emotion, because, as is plain, they want him to be extradited and hanged. But in itself the story is of the highest importance, for no earlier crusade has been so richly documented. If the abundant material were coolly and carefully studied, how much could we learn about human weakness and hypocrisy! We could observe how adroitly religion can be used in the service of crime. When Pavelitch and Artukovitch and their armies retreated, they were sure that, on the defeat of Germany,

England and America would turn upon Russia and they could return to Zagreb. Therefore nothing was destroyed, the state documents were stored in the Archiepiscopal Palace, the gold (dentures, wrist-watches and all) was hidden below the deaf-and-dumb confessional in the Franciscan monastery and cemented over by the friars themselves. The newspapers of the time, secular and ecclesiastical, are still to be seen in the Municipal Library, but this huge pile of documents, the Rosetta Stone of Christian corruption, has not yet been effectively deciphered.

These terrible Church papers, 1941– 45, should destroy forever our faith in those diplomatic prelates, often good and kindly men, who believe that at all costs the ecclesiastical fabric, its schools and rules, its ancient privileges and powers, should be preserved. The clerical editors published the Aryan laws, the accounts of the forced conversions, without protest, the endless photographs of Pavelitch's visits to seminaries and convents and the ecstatic speeches of welcome with which he was greeted. Turn, for example, to *Katolicki Tjednik* (*The Catholic Weekly*), Christmas 1941, and read the twenty-six-verse ode in which Archbishop Sharitch praises Pavelitch for his measures against Serbs and Jews. Examine the Protestant papers and you will find the same story. Is it not clear that in times like those the Church doors should be shut, the Church newspapers closed down, and Christians, who believe that we should love our neighbours as ourselves, should go underground and try to build up a new faith in the catacombs?

Why did our professional historians not deal with all this long ago? They seem to wait till history is dead before they dare to touch it. But does a good surgeon operate only on corpses? They have wholly misinterpreted their functions, for it is their duty to expose the liar before his contagion has spread. While Artukovitch was on his way to Ireland, a Dublin publication told us authoritatively that the massacre of the Serbian Orthodox had never happened. In Count O'Brien's book on Monsignor Stepinac, to which I have already referred, we read:

They [the Orthodox] were offered by Pavelitch the choice between conversion to the Catholic faith or death. . . . But the Catholic Church as a whole, all her bishops and the overwhelming majority of her priests, led by the Archbishop of Zagreb, made this evil plan impossible.

Some of the correspondence between Artukovitch and Stepinac was published in English by Richard Pattee and, collating with Gaff-

468 : *Hubert Butler*

ney, we see how Stepinac, a brave and merciful though very simple man, was hopelessly compromised by his official connection with the state. It was only his own flock whom he could help, and even them very little. For example, he appealed to Artukovitch on behalf of one of his priests, Father Rihar, who had defied Pavelitch. His failure was absolute, for this is how Artukovitch replied:

Zagreb. 17 November 1942. In connection with your esteemed request of 2 November 1942 . . . notice is hereby given that Francis Rihar by the decree of this office of 20 April 1942, No. 26417/1942, was sentenced to forced detention in the concentration camp at Jasenovac for a period of three years . . . because as pastor at Gornja Stubica he did not celebrate a Solemn High Mass on the anniversary of the founding of the Independent State of Croatia . . . nor did he consent to sing the psalm Te Deum Laudamus, saying that it was nowhere prescribed in ecclesiastical usage. . . .

Stepinac appealed again, but Rihar had been already three months at Jasenovac and, therefore, according to the rules of this camp, he was killed.

How, anyway, could Stepinac defend Father Rihar with any authority, since he himself had done what Rihar refused to do? Gaffney and Co., on page 42, reproduced seven photographs of the celebration of Pavelitch's birthday on 15 June 1942 and a letter from the Archbishop exhorting his clergy to hold a Te Deum after High Mass the following Sunday, 17 June, because of "Our Glorious Leader."

Since Pattee omitted this very relevant letter, it is strange that he printed Stepinac's correspondence with Artukovitch about the Jews, for this makes it clear that in acknowledging the authority of Pavelitch, the Archbishop, for diplomatic reasons, felt obliged to accept the terminology of the anti-Semites and their human classifications. For example, on 30 May 1941 he urged Artukovitch "to separate the Catholic non-Aryans from non-Christian non-Aryans in relation to their social position and in the manner of treating them."

Much has been written about Communist distortions of history, but only recently has our own inability, as Christians, to report facts honestly been closely investigated. Now, after twenty years, the dam has burst and the truth, a turbid stream, is inundating our self-complacency and irrigating our self-knowledge. Catholic scholars are leading the way. For example, Professor Gordon Zahn has shown how selective is the documentation on which the biographies of Christian heroes of the resistance are based. Their sermons and speeches were pruned of all the compliments they paid to Hitler and his New Order and no row of dots in the text marks the excision of these now-embarrassing ecstasies.

In the long run, remorseless truth-telling is the best basis for ecumenical harmony. Hitler once explained to Hermann Rauschning how he intended to use the churches as his propagandists. "Why should we quarrel? They will swallow anything provided they can keep their material advantages." Yet Hitler never succeeded in corrupting the churches as effectively as did Pavelitch and Artukovitch, who professed to be Christians. We shall not be able to estimate the extent of their success and how it might have been resisted, while a single fact is diplomatically "forgotten." It is well known that those who suppress history have to relive it.

How did Artukovitch (alias Anitch) get to Ireland? I wrote to Yugoslavia, to America, France, Germany, and questioned Yugoslavs in Dublin and London. The Yugoslavs, both Communist and anti-Communist, had no information. A friend in London, who had been to Trinity College, Dublin, remembered someone saying, "I'd like you to meet a very interesting chap called Anitch," but the meeting had never happened. In the end Branko Miljus, a former minister of the prewar government in Belgrade who now lives in Paris, got some news for me from a friend in Switzerland. If I seem to give too many names and details, it is so that his story can be checked and completed.

The first stage of the journey is fairly well known. Pavelitch and Artukovitch escaped to Austria when the Croatian state collapsed. They seem to have been arrested by the British in Salzburg and, after "a mysterious intervention," released, and there was an interval of hiding in monasteries at Sankt Gilgen and Bad Ischl. The Yugoslavs were in hot pursuit, so Pavelitch fled to Rome disguised as a Spanish priest called Gomez. Artukovitch stayed on till November 1946, when he met the learned Dr. Draganovitch, professor of theology at Zagreb, who was touring the internment camps with a Vatican passport. He had secured the release of many hundreds of Croat priests who had fled with Pavelitch. Now he obtained for Artukovitch papers under the name Alois Anitch and put some money for him in a Swiss bank. Two other priests, Fathers Manditch and Juretitch, also came to his aid. The former, the treasurer to the Franciscan order, controlled a printing press at the Italian camp of Fermo and assisted the Ustashe refugees with funds and propaganda. Juretitch had been sent on a mission to Fribourg by Archbishop Stepinac, so he and

Manditch, both former students of Fribourg University, were able to secure a welcome there for Artukovitch. Archbishop Sharitch, Pavelitch's poet-champion, had got there ahead of him. Both Draganovitch and Juretitch had been appointed by Monsignor Stepinac to the Commission of Five for the Conversion of the Orthodox in November 1941. These three were important people to have as sponsors. The ecclesiastics of Fribourg must have been impressed. They recommended Artukovitch to the police, who got him a *permis de séjour*. There were other difficulties, which, according to report, Artukovitch smoothed out by the gift of a Persian carpet to an influential official.

But meanwhile the Federal Police had learned that Anitch was the war criminal Artukovitch. They told him he had two weeks in which to leave Switzerland. Once more the Franciscans came to his aid. The prior of the Maison Marianum at Fribourg recommended him to the Irish consulate at Berne. And so it happened that in July 1947 Artukovitch landed with his family on the Isle of Saints, sponsored by the disciples of that saint, who had prayed:

> Lord, make me an instrument of Thy peace!
> Where there is hatred let me sow love,
> Where there is sadness, joy!

I do not know where Artukovitch spent his Irish year, but one day, as a matter of history, and perhaps of religion, we shall have to know. If Artukovitch had to be carried halfway round the earth on the wings of Christian charity, simply because he favoured the Church, then Christianity is dying. And if now, for ecumenical or other reasons, we are supposed to ask no questions about him, then it is already dead.

On 15 July 1948 Artukovitch with an Irish identity card left Ireland for the United States, where he settled as a bookkeeper, near his wealthy brother in California, still under the name of Anitch. It was over two years before his true identity was discovered. The Serbian Orthodox were slow to move. Oppressed by the Communists at home, dispersed as refugees abroad, they still managed to publish the facts in books and papers in London, Chicago, Paris. In 1950 Branko Miljus and two other prominent monarchist politicians in exile sent a memorandum to the Fifth Assembly of the United Nations urging it to implement its resolution of December 1946, which had branded genocide as a crime against international law. They asked that its member states should take into custody, till a commission be appointed to try them, some 120 Croat nationals, who had taken refuge among them. On the long list appended, the names of Artukovitch, Archbishop Sharitch, Fathers Draganovitch and Juretitch and many Franciscans were mentioned, and some of the scarcely credible Franciscan story was related. It is stated that a Franciscan had been commandant of Jasenovac, the worst and biggest of the concentration camps for Serbs and Jews (he had personally taken part in murdering the prisoners, and Draganovitch, with the rank of lieutenant colonel, had been the chaplain). The memorandum relates how the focal centre for the forced conversions and the massacres had been the Franciscan monastery of Shiroki Brieg in Herzegovina (Artukovitch had been educated there), and how in 1942 a young man who was a law student at the college and a member of the Crusaders, a catholic organization, had won a prize in a competition for the slaughter of the Orthodox by cutting the throats of 1,360 Serbs with a special knife. The prize had been a gold watch, a silver service, a roast suckling pig and some wine.

How can this be true? One recalls a great hero of Auschwitz, the Polish Franciscan Father Kolbe. But it *was* true and rumours of it had reached Rome. Rushinovitch, Pavelitch's representative at the Vatican, reported to his Foreign Minister in Zagreb the remarks of Cardinal Tisserant, with whom he had an audience on 5 March 1942:

I know for sure that even the Franciscans of Bosnia-Herzegovina behaved atrociously. Father Shimitch, with a revolver in his hand, led an armed gang and destroyed Orthodox churches. No civilized and cultured man, let alone a priest, can behave like that.

Tisserant had probably got some of his information from the Italian general of the Sassari division at Knin, who reported that Shimitch had come to him as local representative of the Croatian government and had told him that he had orders to kill all the Serbs. The general had had instructions not to interfere in local politics, so he could only protest. The killing, under Franciscan leadership, had begun. The following year the Superior of the Franciscan monastery in Knin was decorated by Pavelitch for his military activities with the order of King Zvonimir III.

The Croat bishops themselves were aware of what was happening. The Bishop of Kotor, Dr. Butorac, while agreeing that the moment was propitious for mass conversion, wrote to Monsignor Stepinac (4 November 1941) that the wrong type of missionaries were being sent—"priests in whose hands revolvers might better be placed than a crucifix."

In parenthesis, I should say, how fascinating are Rushinovitch's accounts of his audiences in Rome with Pius XII, with Cardinals Tardini, Maglione, Sigismondi and Spellman. Only Tisserant and to a lesser extent Monsignor Montini, the present Pope, appear to have fully grasped what was happening in Croatia. In Cardinal Ruffini the Ustashe had a firm supporter.

The memorandum made little impression on the United Nations, since it had no member state behind it. It had accused Tito's government, which *was* a member state, of sheltering many Croat criminals and using them to break down the anti-Communist resistance of the Serbs. However, in 1952 Tito appealed to the United States for the extradition of Artukovitch. The California courts to whom the case was referred argued that the extradition treaty of 1901 between the United States and Serbia had never been renewed and that therefore Artukovitch could not be handed over to Yugoslavia. Six years later the Supreme Court rejected this view (by 7 to 1) and decreed that the case must be tried again in California. In the meantime Artukovitch had become a member of the Knights of Columbus and a much-respected figure who gave lectures to institutes and interviews on television. When he was arrested again 50,000 Knights sent petitions on his behalf to Congress, and the West Pennsylvania Lodges of the Croatian Catholic Union forwarded a resolution that "his only crime is his ceaseless fight against Communism" and that he was a champion of the rights and freedoms of all the peoples of the world.

That was the way his counsel, O'Connors and Reynolds, presented him, too; and Father Manditch, who had helped him in Switzerland, was once more by his side, in charge of another printing press and now Superior of the Franciscan monastery on Drexel Boulevard, Chicago. His papers *Nasha Nada* and *Danica* (Our Hope and Morning Star) not only supported him but in their issues of 7 May 1958 urged their readers to send subscriptions for the Ustashe refugee fund to Artukovitch at his address in Surfside, California.

Another very useful ally was Cardinal Stepinac's secretary, Father Lackovitch, who had sought asylum at Youngstown, Ohio. In Europe, Stepinac had been almost beatified for his implacable hostility to Pavelitch and Artukovitch, but now *The Mirror News* of Los Angeles (24 January 1958) reported Lackovitch as saying that he had seen Artukovitch almost daily and that he had been "the leading Catholic layman of Croatia and the lay spokesman of Cardinal Stepinac and had consulted him on the moral aspect of every action he took." The murderers of the Old World had become the martyrs of the New.

The American public was so ill-informed that it was possible to get away with almost anything. Pattee prints a statement that 200,000 of the converts from Orthodoxy were returning "with a right intention" to a Church, which "for political reasons" they had been forced to abandon. In fact, of course, the Serbian Orthodox had been in schism for some three centuries before the Protestant Reformation. Cardinal Tisserant, who had a rare tolerance of disagreeable truths, denounced Rushinovitch vigorously when he tried out this argument on him:

I am well acquainted with the history of Christianity and to my knowledge Catholics of Roman rite never became Orthodox. . . . The Germans helped you kill all the priests and you got rid of 350,000 Serbs before you set up the Croatian Orthodox Church. What right have you to accuse others and keep on telling us that you are guardians of culture and the faith? In the war with the Turks the Serbs did just as much for Catholicism as you did and perhaps more. But it was the Croats, all the same, who got the title of *Antemurale Christianitatis*.

When I was in California, I went to see Father Mrvicin of the Serbian Orthodox Cathedral at West Garvey, near Los Angeles, and asked him why the Orthodox and the Jews of California had tolerated so many lies. He told me that at the time of the extradition trial he had circularized close on a thousand Serbs who must have known well about Artukovitch, urging them to give evidence, but very few had replied. Life in the United States was hard for them as refugees, they did not want to affront a powerful community, McCarthyism was not yet dead and they were shy of associating themselves with an appeal that came from a Communist country. A naturalized American who took the matter up died violently and mysteriously.

As for the Jews, though 30,000 with their forty-seven rabbis had been murdered in Croatia, Croatia was far away, and many who had escaped to America had owed their safety to holding their tongues. Even so, the Jewish War Veterans of California, *The Valley Jewish News* and some Gentile papers like *The Daily Signal* of California came out against Artukovitch. But most Americans felt for the unknown refugee and his five children the easy charity of indifference. Finally the Yugoslav government did some profitable deals with the United States and became indifferent, too. It is now interested only in proving that Artukovitch was a helpless stooge of the Nazis and that therefore the Bonn government should pay compensation to Yugoslavia for the damage that he and the Ustashe had done.

The other day I came across a *History of Croatia*, published by the New York Philosophical Library. The author, Mr. Preveden, acknowledges various "inspiring messages of commendation and encouragement." One of them comes from "Dr. Andrija Artukovitch of Los Angeles." He is quite a public figure. He may have changed his address but his telephone number used to be Plymouth 5-1147.

Now many people want him hanged but there would not be much point in it. He was an insignificant man, who got his chance because there had been a great breakdown in the machinery of Christianity and he was able to pose as its protector. Why did this breakdown occur? Can it be repaired and, if so, how? So long as we are obliged to pretend that the breakdown did not happen, we shall never find out.

Postscript
1971

There has since been an easing of tension between Communism and Christianity, most notably in Yugoslavia, where diplomatic relations with the Vatican have been resumed and there has been friendship between Catholic and Orthodox. For example, in a Christmas message, Bishop Pichler begged forgiveness of the Orthodox Church and their Serbian brothers for all the wrongs done to them, and funds have been raised by Catholics to restore the destroyed Orthodox churches.

Some of the leading Orthodox are not wholly happy about all this. Is it spontaneous or government-inspired? Is it possible that Tito fears the deep-rooted and passionate nationalism of the Orthodox more than Catholic universalism, which can be manipulated by external arrangements? Under the amnesty to political offenders, many Ustashe have returned home, notably Father Draganovitch, one of the five "regulators" of the forced conversions, who escorted Pavelitch and Artukovitch to safety. He is in a monastery near Sarajevo editing the *Schematismus*, a sort of ecclesiastical yearbook whose publication has been suspended since 1939. Some of his returned colleagues are more active politically.

There is, of course, everything to be said for peace and conciliation, but the brotherly love that is brought about by diplomatic manoeuvres is often a little suspect.

IN SEARCH OF A PROFESSOR OF HISTORY
1985

I could not get it out of my head that Artukovitch had stayed for a year in Ireland. How had he come here? Who had sheltered him and where? In the spring of 1966 I was in Dublin for a week and I decided to find out. I was convinced that only some highly organized international body could have brought a wanted man so secretly and efficiently across Europe, and since the Franciscans had been so closely associated with the Ustashe in Croatia and had many international links, I was confident that it was they who had brought him. I have never heard anything but good of Irish Franciscans, but they were an institutionalized body and as such able and anxious to protect their members who get into trouble abroad.

There were a dozen Franciscan Houses in Ireland and I wrote to the Provincial in Merchants' Quay, Dublin, and also to four or five other houses, which, because of their remoteness, I thought were likely. Most of them answered with polite negative replies. The Provincial told me there had been a Croat Franciscan at their Galway house for some time but his name, Brother Ivanditch, was on the list of their order and they had no doubt of his identity.

It was not till Branko Miljus sent me his copy of *The Mirror News* of Los Angeles that I made any progress. Artukovitch had been interviewed by the reporter Henry Frank, who for the photograph had arranged him at a piano, grouping his wife and five handsome children round him. The Rev. Robert Ross of the Blessed Sacrament Church was there, too, as a friend and advocate. He told Frank how, as Minister of the Interior, Artukovitch had helped the Jews and been a formidable foe to the Communists.

"Artukovitch listened gravely and said with quiet dignity, " 'I put my faith in God.' "

Frank spoke of Artukovitch's "strong, seamed face" and his "modest well-lived-in living room." He told how his daughter Zorica had won an essay competition in Orange County High School and his nine-year-old son, Radoslav, had been born in Ireland.

Here was a clue. The children had been exploited sentimentally to mask the truth, so they could be used to rediscover it. I went to the Customs House and after prolonged search I found Radoslav

Anitch's birth certificate (A.164, No. 75). He was born on 1 June 1948 at the Prague House Nursing Home, 28 Terenure Road East; he was the son of Alois Anitch, professor of history, of 6 Zion Road, Rathgar.

On the strength of this discovery, I sent a letter to all the Dublin dailies, explaining that I was writing an account of the Independent State of Croatia (1941–45) and that I wished information about the former Minister of the Interior, Andrija Artukovitch (alias Alois Anitch), who had lived at 6 Zion Road, Rathgar, in 1947. Only *The Irish Times* printed my letter, turning him into a lady called Audrey.

In the meantime I visited the two houses, which were close to each other. No. 6 Zion Road is a two-storeyed house of red brick with an ivy-tangled sycamore and an overgrown privet hedge, but it had changed hands so often that it told me nothing about Artukovitch's Irish sponsors. No. 28 Terenure Road, a tall building of red and white brick with much ornamental ironwork, has ceased for some years to be a nursing home. Nobody knew where the former owner had gone, and it was not till I had paid two visits to the Guards Barracks at Terenure that someone recalled where she now lived. It was not far off at 7 Greenmount Road and I went there immediately. The matron was a charming and intelligent woman, and after eighteen years she remembered the Anitches perfectly. She had found them a pleasant and pathetic couple. He had spoken little English, Mrs. Anitch had spoken fluently, and because of that, she had asked that he should have lunch with her in the nursing home. "He is my baby," Mrs. Anitch had said, "he wouldn't know how to get lunch without me." They had two little girls who were at the Sacred Heart Convent, in Drumcondra Road, and now they wanted a boy. "If it's a girl," said Mrs. Anitch, "don't call him till the evening." But when on the morning of 1 June Radoslav had been born, she was so delighted that she said her husband must be called at once. Anitch came and in his joy he had embraced the matron, much to her embarrassment. The Anitches had behaved nicely, paying all their debts with money from America. After they had gone some months Mrs. Anitch had written a grateful letter, which the matron showed me.

Only one person besides her husband had visited Mrs. Anitch in the nursing home. He was a Franciscan who had been in Croatia, but the matron was not clear whether or not he was a foreigner. The Anitches had told her that the Communists had been particularly vindictive against the Franciscans.

My anticipation that the Franciscans had helped Artukovitch in

Ireland had now been confirmed, so I went to see the Provincial at Merchants' Quay. This time he agreed with me that the friar at the nursing home must have been the Croat at the Galway house. His name, he said, was Ivanditch. He was a supporter of Pavelitch and had often gone from Galway to Dublin.

Yet a Croat friar could not have made all these arrangements without powerful Irish assistance. Where had it come from?

The process by which a great persecutor is turned into a martyr is surely an interesting one that needs the closest investigation. I had only four days left in Dublin, so I could not follow up all the clues, but I made some progress.

First I went to the Sacred Heart Convent, 40 Drumcondra Road, a big red building on the left-hand side of the street. I was shown into a little waiting room and was received by a charming and friendly nun. I told her I was trying to trace the family of two little girls called Zorica and Vishnya Anitch, who had been at the convent in 1947 when they were four and five years old. She went away to look them up in her register, and I sat for a very long time contemplating the plate of wax fruit and the little figurine of St. Anthony. Then the nun returned and told me that the two little girls (but they were called Katerina and Aurea Anitch) had been admitted on 9 August 1947. Their parents had lived at 7 Tower Avenue, Rathgar, and had taken the children to America on 15 July 1948. She did not recall them herself but suggested that I ring up an older nun, Sister Agnes, who would certainly remember them. She was at St. Vincent's Convent, North William Street. I rang Sister Agnes, who remembered them all vividly. The little girls were sweet and she had found the two parents "a lovely pair" and Dr. Anitch was "a marvellous musician." She did not remember that anybody came to visit the children except their parents, but a Franciscan monk, a nephew of Dr. Anitch's, who had escaped with them from Croatia, was with them and had helped them to find lodgings.

Next I visited 7 Tower Avenue and was directed to a previous tenant, who worked in an ironmongery in D'Olier Street. He said he did remember having a lodger with a name like Anitch. He added, "He was black, you know." I tried other houses in Tower Avenue. Everybody was helpful and interested but I got no further clues.

After this I returned to Mrs. O'Donoghue in Greenmount Road and found she had been keenly interested in what I had told her and herself had been trying to find out who had been the landlord in 6

Zion Road when the Anitches had lived there. She said I should get in touch with Patrick Lawlor, 32 Hazelbrook Road, who had sold the house to some woman in 1947.

I wrote to him and the next day he rang me up. He said it was so long ago that he could not remember the woman's name, but the auctioneer might know. After that I made some dozen visits and twenty telephone calls. They would be boring to relate but I found them exhilarating, as each clue led to another clue. I telephoned the doctor who had delivered Radoslav and examined the parish registers in Terenure and Rathgar for christenings. I went to the Valuation Office and telephoned the Voters Register, the Irish Red Cross, the Aliens Office and the International Office of Refugees. I enquired at the city hall about corporation rates. In the end I got onto the solicitor who had acted both for Mr. Lawlor and for the woman to whom he had sold 6 Zion Road. His clerk made an unsuccessful search for her name and then suggested, "Why not call on Thom's Directory?"

I went there the next day and the secretary took down from a shelf the directories for 1947 and 1948 and found Patrick Lawlor's name in both. "But that's impossible," I protested. "He sold the house to a woman in 1947." "Yes, but there might have been a delay in publishing after we collected the information." She took down the directory for 1949. "The woman's name was Kathleen Murphy," she said. I was off like a shot to a telephone box.

There were three Miss K. Murphys in the directory and five Mrs. Kathleen Murphys and several K. Murphys, who might be either male or female. It was a lengthy business, for some were out and I was asked to ring later, and some were testy at being catechised by a stranger. The fifth answered very suspiciously. "Who are you? Why do you want to know? Yes, I was at 6 Zion Road, but if you want to know more you must come down. I remember the Anitches and, if you're friends of theirs, I'd be glad to see you. Do you know them?" I said I did not but that a friend of mine in Paris, M. Miljus, would like to get in touch with them.

So we drove down to 6 Barnhill Road, Dalkey, a fine broad street with handsome villas. My wife waited outside in the car writing letters, while Mrs. Murphy, a friendly middle-aged woman, talked to me in her drawing room. A friend of hers was just leaving when I came in, an Ulsterwoman with a nice downright manner whose husband had been a bank manager in Kilkenny. She remembered us straight off when I said my name. "Yes, I know who you are. I read your letters and articles in *The Irish Times*. I remember you got into a row with the Nuncio, Dr. O'Hara, and it was on the head of you he got the boot!" She and Peggy talked together while I was with Mrs. Murphy, who I could see had a powerful affection for this foreign family who had lodged with her. In particular she admired "Dr. Anish," whom she connected with "Czechoslavia." This confusion is not very surprising. Artukovitch would not have mentioned Yugoslavia, which did not exist for him, and not much was known in Ireland of Croatia, though one of those who were kind to him in Dublin said he came from Craishe. In general he was befriended as a foreign refugee from Communism, and hitherto I have found no trace of sinister international intrigue among those who gave him hospitality.

Mrs. Murphy reproached herself repeatedly for not having kept in touch with the "Anishes" in California. Several times they had written charming letters. What a delightful family they were! "They made a wonderful impression all round," she said. "I'd like to show you some snaps I have of them." Mrs. Murphy took down a photograph album with a large bundle of snaps in the middle. She rummaged through them all the time we were talking but never found what she was looking for. I explained to her that some time after Dr. Anitch had got to California he had been the subject of bitter controversy and I showed her the picture of the family in *The Mirror News*. "Ah, how old he has got to look, poor man! And that big girl must be Katerina and that one Aurea. And goodness me that young chap must be Radoslav! How time flies!" When I told her what his enemies were saying she shook her head indignantly. "People will say anything! I don't think he thought of politics at all. All he cared about was his family. He was a wonderful father and husband! He was a very good man you know. He was rather like President Kennedy. He wanted justice for everybody. And he loved the Church. They were daily communicants."

Then I asked her how she had met him in the first place and she said she thought it had been at some party. Maybe some priest had introduced them. She became a little vague on the whole in this pregnant conversation. I was being the sly one, she the candid one. I asked did she meet a Franciscan with him and she said, "Oh, yes, there was one came to lunch a couple of times. But the Anishes lived very quietly. They hardly saw anyone. You see, he was a very retiring scholarly man. He once or twice gave a lecture at UCD,* but oth-

*University College, Dublin.—ed.

erwise they just thought of the children." I subsequently made enquiries about those lectures at UCD but with no success.

Then I told her what remorseless enemies he had and explained something of the collapse of Yugoslavia. I showed her *Artukovitch, the Himmler of Yugoslavia*, turning the pages rapidly so as to reach some not too emotive pictures of him in the days of his glory. There he was giving the Nazi salute to a German general and there again greeting Hitler's envoy at the head of his Security Police, and there with his wife at a cocktail party in the Hungarian embassy. I skipped some horror pages, headed with heavy irony ANDRIJA ARTUKO-VITCH'S HEROIC DEEDS and including a picture of a soldier scissoring off the head of a seated peasant with some shears. Except for their attribution, such photographs are probably genuine. As I have said, Artukovitch was probably a desk murderer only. Mrs. Murphy must have caught a glimpse of the scissored head, for she stiffened and started to fumble again in her album for her friendly snapshots.

"Everybody in Dublin seems to have liked him," I said, "but why did he come here with a false name?"

"Probably he was forced to. Lots of people are. He couldn't have been a Nazi, though he may have been forced to take that side. I'm a good judge of character. I've travelled in sixteen countries and know a good man when I see one."

"But he signed all those laws against the Jews." (I thought it would be too complicated to talk about the Orthodox; she might not know who they were.)

"Well, look what the Jews are doing to other people!" (I suppose she was thinking of the Arabs.)

Then we said goodbye. As I left, she repeated, "They just lived for their children. They thought the world of them."

The next place I had to visit was the Franciscan House in Galway from which Dr. Anitch's nephew, Brother Ivanditch, paid visits to Dublin to see him.

When we reached Galway I went round to the Franciscan House, which is a few streets away from Eyre Square. Beside the big church I saw a small private door through which some travelling clerics with suitcases were being hospitably ushered. I waited till they had all been welcomed before I went in and, after a few moments, the Father Superior appeared. Though he was preoccupied with his visitors he received me kindly. Seeing my attaché case, he thought I was a commercial traveller, but when I explained I had come as a historian interested to find out about a Croat friar called Ivanditch, who was in Galway in 1947, he said, "I'm afraid I don't know the good man. I'm only here three years, but if you come tomorrow, when we've a bit more time, I'll get Brother Bede onto you. He was here in 1947."

The following day I went round to the Franciscan House at eleven-thirty and Brother Bede received me. Yes. He remembered Brother Ivanditch well and had looked him up in the *Schematismus* of the Order. He was from the Province of Bosnia, near Sarajevo. He was a very striking-looking chap and must have been over six feet. He was born in 1913. "He wasn't here but at our hostel, St. Anthony's College along the Moycullen Road, so I didn't see much of him. But they say he spent all his time at the wireless listening to the news in German, French, Italian, Spanish; he was a very intelligent fellow, learned English quickly. But he was broody, reserved and melancholy. All soul, you might say."

Brother Bede had spent the war years in Rome. In the Franciscan headquarters the Croats had been more prominent than any other Slav group. Apart from Father Manditch, the treasurer of the Order, there was Father Jelachitch, a great canon lawyer, and Brother Balitch, an eminent palaeographer who had written about Duns Scotus. "You've no idea what confusion there was in Rome at that time. As for us, we put all the Slavs in one basket, a terribly passionate lot. We couldn't unscramble them."

"Who sent him here? Oh, I suppose it was the General of our Order in Rome. I think it was Schaaf at that time, but I could look that one up. It was a question of obedience, you know."

I told him that the Ustashe ambassador to Rome, Rushinovitch, had been given audiences by many cardinals and had sent his impressions of them back to Zagreb. It was obvious that not only the Irish but all the clerics at Rome had been highly confused by what was happening in Croatia. Only Cardinal Tisserant, I said, had a clear idea. On the other hand, Cardinal Ruffini was a vigorous supporter and protector of the Ustashe!

"Ruffini!" Brother Bede laughed. "Yes, indeed. He was a Sicilian, a great nationalist! They are as excitable as the Slavs. We took everything they said with a pinch of salt."

As for Ivanditch, he had stayed for about a year in Galway and then gone to Canada. But there was a rumour that he was in Valencia, Spain, now. He was still alive or he wouldn't be in the *Schematismus*.

Brother Bede did not think I would get much more information from St. Anthony's College, as they were always changing their staff there, but there was a Brother David who might remember him. "Worth trying anyway. Cross the salmon-weir bridge and along the Moycullen Road till you come to a long grey building on the left."

They were widening the road and the surface was terrible, so it must have been very close to the Brothers' dinnertime when I got to St. Anthony's. The most pleasant thing about the building was the fine stone wall, a new one, that surrounded it. Most of the Galway walls are still excellently built and of stone, as unlike as possible to the new walls of the midlands, which, maybe because of the rich stoneless soil, are built of concrete, which submits itself readily to many vulgar and modish fancies.

I waited in a very clean and polished parlour under a picture of Jesus meditating on the Mount of Olives, till Brother David came along. He and his colleague, Brother Edmond, remembered Ivanditch well, and Brother David showed me a photograph of himself and Brother Ivanditch and a Galway lady, Mrs. O'Halloran. They were a handsome group. Ivanditch, whose religious name was Brother Louis (Croatian Luji), was dark, clean-shaven, spectacled. A pleasant serious person he looked in his long brown habit with its white cord.

"But he was very hysterical," Brother David said. "He'd been sentenced to death by the Communists and he spent all his time listening to the ups and downs of Communism on the wireless. He was with us about a year, sent here by the General at Rome, waiting for instructions where to go. He was a professor of dogmatic theology. According to what he said, he was second-in-command to the Provincial at Zagreb. He had been given the seal of the Province of Croatia—he had it with him here—when the Provincial was imprisoned."

I asked him if Artukovich (Anitch) had ever been to visit him. "No, he had no visitors at all, though once or twice he went to Dublin. He brooded the whole time. He said the only hope for us was to have a third world war immediately. He thought us a very weak lot. There was a milk strike in Galway at the time and he could not understand why we did not settle it straight away by shooting the milkmen. And we should invade the six counties and settle that matter, too, *immediately*."

"What amazed us about him," Brother Edmond said, "was the way he ate jam for breakfast . . . sometimes nearly a whole pot, and without any bread, just with a spoon. And though he got to know English very well, he used some very funny expressions. When we used to ask him if he would like another helping of anything, he would say, 'Thank you, no, I am fed up!' But he made a great friend in the town who could tell you more about him than I can, Joe O'Halloran of the Corrib printing works. He was working in O'Gorman's bookshop in those days and he and Brother Louis used to see a lot of each other. Joe is the son of Mrs. O'Halloran you saw in the snapshot."

It was difficult to believe that the Galway Brothers belonged to the same order as the Ustashe Franciscans. What was nearest to Brother Edmond's heart was a scheme for building houses for the homeless by voluntary groups. He had been considering this idea while he was with the Order in Louvain.

Joe O'Halloran was in a white coat working at the Corrib printers when I called. He asked for a few moments to change and then he joined me at the Imperial Hotel and we had vodka and orange together. He had only been eighteen when Brother Ivanditch was in Galway, and he had been hugely impressed by this glamorous and passionate foreigner who had fled from his country under sentence of death, who had seen his Provincial sentenced to five years' penal servitude and his Primate, a world-famous cardinal, condemned to sixteen years' imprisonment by a Communist government. They had spent every Sunday together, and Joe's parents had been equally captivated by this engaging person, who bore with him the seals of the Franciscan Order in Croatia and the responsibility to make its sorrows known to the world. It was his dream to establish a Croatian Seminary in Dublin. Ireland must know what Croatia had suffered and was still suffering in the name of Christ. She must know that the fate that had befallen Croatia awaited all Europe. They must be prepared.

Brother Luji counted on Joe O'Halloran's support in this sacred cause. But after a year the orders came from Rome for him to cross the Atlantic. He sailed from Liverpool to Montreal and Joe O'Halloran saw him off in Dublin. But though he had left Joe in charge of a sort of crusade, he had not replied at all regularly to his letters and slowly they had lost touch with each other. Joe learned, though, that Brother Luji had been appointed chaplain to the Croat workers at Windsor, Ontario, on the Canadian side of the Detroit River. They worked in the Ford factory at Dearborn and Brother Luji built for them the Chapel of St. Joseph. Later on he had heard that he had been secularized and had left the Franciscan Order, and it now occurred to Joe O'Halloran that this might have been because the

French-Canadian Franciscans did not like Ivanditch's Croatian politics, which a few years later resulted in the murder of the Yugoslav consul in Stockholm and a curious entente with the Communists.

I asked about Artukovitch-Anitch and also about Count O'Brien, but Joe knew nothing of them. The only layman in Galway that Ivanditch saw was Mr. O'Flynn, the county manager, who invited him to tea because his niece had once taught in Zagreb. Ivanditch had, however, told Joe that he had an uncle in Dublin who had been a minister in the government of Croatia. Joe O'Halloran stressed that Ivanditch had totally failed to inflame the Franciscans in Galway and was very much disappointed in the Irish. He had been in Galway when the Republic was proclaimed in Eyre Square, and he was amazed that the government had tolerated an opposition for so long. Why had not they just shot them?

In the past eighteen years Joe had changed. Ivanditch, were he to return, would no longer have the intoxicating effect which he had had on him as a very young man. In those days he had been puzzled that his elders should be so apathetic. For example, Father Felim O'Brien, a well-known Franciscan, had been lecturing in Galway and had treated very coolly Ivanditch's passionate appeals for a crusade. O'Brien was known all over Ireland for his dislike of "liberalism." Two or three years later, in 1950, he engaged Owen Sheehy-Skeffington in a long controversy in *The Irish Times* later published as a pamphlet, *The Liberal Ethic*. I had contributed to this controversy, so I have kept some records of it. O'Brien had maintained that in Ireland we owe our freedom of expression more to the clerics than to the liberal doctrine of tolerance, and that in Europe the Catholic clergy are the chief champions of liberty.

We got back late from Galway and it was a day before I was able to look up Ivanditch in my books. I found only one reference to him. He was referred to on page 20 in the report of the Stepinac trial, *Sudenje Lisaku, Stepincu, Salicu I Druzini*, in connection with the trial of the Provincial of the Franciscan Order, Father Modesto Martinchitch. The Provincial is said to have given Brother Luji (Ivanditch), an Ustashe, a large sum of money to enable him to escape abroad. Brother Luji was not one of the five friars who helped the Provincial bury the thirty-four trunks of Ustashe treasure under the confessional in the Franciscan church in May 1945, and I find no record of any activities that in Communist eyes were criminal. I think

that when he claimed to have been sentenced to death by the Communists, Ivanditch was trying to make himself more glamorous. He
seems to have escaped early on with an ample travel allowance and
the seals of the province. Whether or not Artukovitch was really his
uncle, it may have been his task to escort him abroad in safety.

Since Brother Bede had mentioned Dr. Balitch, the eminent palaeographer, at the Vatican, I looked him up in the vast book *Mag-
num Crimen* by Professor Victor Novak of Belgrade, not expecting
to find anyone so scholarly and remote in this record of horror. But
there he was on page 900. "Brother Doctor Karlo Balitch, professor
at the Franciscan University at Rome." His offence seems to have
been slight but significant. When Marshal Kvaternik, commander of
the Ustashe forces, had arrived in Rome and visited the Institute of
St. Jerome in February 1942, Balitch had been there to receive him,
together with several other distinguished Croatian clerics and the
whole staff of the Institute. Dr. Balitch seems to have listened appre-
ciatively while Dr. Madjerec, the Rector, praised Kvaternik and the
leader Pavelitch for their illustrious deeds in the cause of Christ.

The St. Jerome Society was a very old and established Croat
institution with headquarters at Rome. Every year, even when Novak
published his book in 1948, there were celebrations there in honour
of Pavelitch's birthday, attended by Croat Jesuits, Dominicans, Ca-
puchins, Benedictines. When Marshal Kvaternik addressed the Institute praising its work for the Ustashe, there was loud and prolonged
applause. This was in Rome, yet we have been told repeatedly that
it was only under the strongest pressure that in Croatia itself the
hierarchy lent their support to Pavelitch.

After the St. Jerome Society had been suppressed in Croatia by
Tito, Monsignor Stepinac declared in his speech of defence: "The St.
Jerome Society has ceased to exist. Its suppression is a grave offence
against the whole people." But surely it was rightly suppressed. In
an authoritarian community, when there is hypocrisy and connivance
at the centre, the ripples from them spread outwards to the remote
circumference: "In vain do they worship me, teaching as their doctrines the precepts of men."

In 1985 there is news of Dr. Draganovitch, who helped Artukovitch
to escape. I have been reading Tom Bower's story of Barbie, "the
Butcher of Lyons," who eluded French justice after the war in 1951
by the "Rat Line," an escape route which the Americans set up for
people who were valuable to the Central Intelligence Agency. They

were equipped with fake passports and identity cards, but a contact was needed in Genoa, the port of embarkation, to supply the Rats with immigration papers for South America. Draganovitch, who had helped so many Ustashe escape to Argentina, was obviously the man for the job. His fees for the Rat Line, according to Tom Bower, were $1,000 for adults, half price for children and $1,400 for VIP treatment.

Surprisingly, though his services to the escaping Ustashe were well known and though he had been on the infamous Committee of Five for the conversion of the Orthodox, he was permitted legally to return to Yugoslavia. Is it possible that just as Barbie had useful information to give the Americans about the Communists, so Draganovitch had useful information to give the Communists about the Americans?

Artukovitch himself is still in California and, as I have related, sometime in the 1960s the Yugoslav government tired of asking for his extradition. Among other reasons, maybe, they thought that a sensational state trial in Zagreb might revive animosities between Serb and Croat.

However, in July 1981, the U.S. Board of Immigration Appeals, in view of a 1979 ruling of Congress, ordered that Artukovitch be deported. This was followed by further legal proceedings, appeals, counter-appeals, hearings and rehearings. The Justice Department acted on a legal reform excluding "Nazi collaborators" from seeking refuge, and on 14 November 1984, "three carloads of federal marshals, guns drawn," burst into Artukovitch's house at Seal Beach and took him into custody.* He is now eighty-five and, according to his Dublin-born son Radoslav, he has Parkinson's disease, a congestive heart condition, and is also blind and suffering from delusional paranoia. It is uncertain whether he will be competent to take part in an extradition hearing and its sequel, deportation to Yugoslavia and a show trial at Zagreb.

Postscript
24 September 1986

Artukovitch was finally extradited to Yugoslavia on 12 February 1986. On 15 May, after a four-week trial, death sentence was pronounced. Twenty-six witnesses were called, evidence of much bru-

*Sunday Times, 12 January 1985.

tality given. Yet Artukovitch maintained that he was innocent and his duties chiefly administrative: "I have always acted according to my conscience and the teachings of the Catholic Church." Security for the trial was tight; policemen patrolled neighbouring streets with machine guns and muzzled dogs. There has been no word of Artukovitch's execution. I believe he is still alive.

In Russia and China

1956–57

A VISIT TO YASNAYA POLYANA

Yasnaya Polyana is one of the famous homes of Europe, like Voltaire's house at Ferney, Goethe's at Weimar, Rousseau's near Chambéry, and our own Edgeworthstown. It survives by a mere chance, for it was occupied by the Nazis for forty-five days, and after their withdrawal orders came from the High Command that it was to be destroyed. Some motorcyclists arrived to do the job, but time was short, and the Russians pressing on their heels. Though it was set alight in three places, only a couple of armchairs, some doors, floorboards and a bookcase were burned before Russian fire hoses were turned upon the house. Though about a hundred articles were looted, the loss was not a serious one, for at the time of the German invasion all the major treasures had been removed to Tomsk, in Siberia, and they have now been replaced.

The house and property have had a complex history since the Revolution in 1917. The early years of the struggle for its preservation have been described with great candour and detail by Tolstoy's youngest daughter, Alexandra, who for five years dedicated herself to the task of preserving Tolstoy's home, defending his reputation, his ideals and social and educational enterprises, and securing the continued publication of his works.

Her book ends in defeat, for she gave up the Russian part of the struggle in 1922 and left for Japan and America. Yet her story is mainly concerned with personal disappointments and betrayals and day-to-day frustrations. The Tolstoy family could not today be wholly dissatisfied with the course of events. Tolstoy's position as the greatest and most widely read of Russian novelists seems to be firmly established and, though Tolstoyanism as a creed is dead in Russia, it was moribund long before the Revolution. It is impossible to believe that so great a genius as Tolstoy does not still exercise a powerful influence in unexpected ways and places.

Certainly I have never seen a national shrine preserved with greater taste and reverence than Tolstoy's two homes, his town house in Moscow and this country house near Tula, two hundred kilometres south of Moscow. In both cases the caretakers are enthusiasts; one of them, Mr. Loshchinin, has written a book about Tolstoy's early life. As far as the dead can speak through the books they read, the houses they built and furnished, the trees they planted, the places they loved, Tolstoy and his family are allowed to say their say without any tendentious interruptions.

Yasnaya Polyana is not as large or grand a country house as one might have expected. In the 1850s there was a big central block with two wings, but when Tolstoy was soldiering in the Crimea he wrote home to his brother-in-law, who was minding the estate, that he wanted funds to start a soldiers' magazine. "Sell something, please, to raise about five thousand pounds!" So without more ado the brother-in-law sold the central block and a neighbouring landowner carted away stones and woodwork to his estate. Tolstoy heard of this surprising decision with dismay. He had not even the soldiers' magazine to console him, for the government forbade its publication. Tolstoy erected a commemorative stone on the site and planted elm trees round it. As an old man he would sometimes point out one of the upper branches to his guests: "I was born up there in those twigs." As his family grew up he twice enlarged one of the wings, and the house is now as it was when he died.

Apart from the final outrage, the Germans seem to have behaved with moderate propriety. The trees were not cut, and an ancient elm called the Tree of the Poor (because the peasants used to come there to tell Tolstoy of their troubles) still stands outside the front door; the old iron bell which summoned the Tolstoys to their meals is now half embedded in its trunk. Tolstoy's grave, in a far corner of the woods, was not desecrated except insofar as the Germans buried their dead beside him. (The indignant Russians have disinterred them.)

The continuity of tradition has scarcely been interrupted. Here, for example, is the room, an old storeroom with hooks for hanging hams on which Tolstoy converted into a study, where he started *War and Peace* and completed *Resurrection*. And it was in an upstairs room that he finished *War and Peace*, as always weaving into his stories many of the familiar features of his home. It was under one of the big oaks in a grove behind the house that Kitty and Levin shelter from a thunderstorm, and the Prospekt, the avenue that runs from the village to the house, is the same Prospekt that occurs in the novel. It was the occasion of an unfortunate misunderstanding between the steward and his employer, the old prince, who shared the peculiar autocratic-democratic views of Tolstoy's grandfather, Prince Volkonsky, and indeed of Tolstoy himself. One day the prince remarked to the steward that the Prospekt had been cleared of snow. The steward, gratified that the prince had observed it, explained with modest self-satisfaction that he had cleared it because one of the Tsar's ministers was coming to dinner. "What!" the prince had exclaimed. "You will not clear the snow for my wife and daughters, but you will clear it for a minister? What do I care about ministers? Put the snow back again!" And the snow was put back on the Prospekt.

We were shown the hut below the orchard and the Wedge Grove (so called because paths radiate from the centre, dividing it into eight wedge-shaped segments) where the coachman lived. He had been roused up that October evening in 1910 to drive Tolstoy, accompanied by his doctor and close friend Makovitzky, to escape for ever from that aristocratic existence that had become intolerable to him. Surely it was the most ill-timed and uncomfortable act of literary escapism that has ever happened. They did not get farther than the railway station, and a couple of weeks later Tolstoy's body was brought back to Yasnaya Polyana and given, as he wished, a pauper's burial.

The second wing of the old house was used by Tolstoy and his daughter as a school, and is now a museum with many fascinating family portraits and photographs. I saw there the photographs of Tolstoy's funeral, which was attended by all the peasants for miles around. All the birch trees round the grave were black with boys and men, perched in the branches to see the burial.

There is an upper room in which the old man lay ill for a long period. There is a striped armchair, and on the iron bed a gaudy bedspread embroidered by Countess Tolstoy. Above it is a photograph of Tolstoy sitting on the same bedspread, on the same bed, talking to Dr. Makovitzky, who is sitting in the same striped armchair. Beside it is another extant memorial of the past, a frightful leather cushion presented by the municipality of Tula and stamped with its compliments in gilt; it has survived the Revolution and the Nazi Occupation.

When we left, Mr. Loshchinin gave us each a green Antonovsky apple from the orchard, but he scrupulously disclaimed for it an unblemished Tolstoyan heredity. The Antonovskys which Tolstoy had planted had died in the frost of 1948, and these were replacements. The great birch trees on the Prospekt had also died and been replaced, regrettably enough, by gloomy conifers.

I expect Mr. Loshchinin's Antonovskys taste much the same as Tolstoy's, but the flavour of Tolstoyanism and the circumstances which produced it are harder to recapture. Yet Mr. Loshchinin and his colleagues (I was told that Tolstoy's last secretary still works in the museum, but he was absent when I was there) have done their best. And if one is to believe that the past can ever be satisfactorily potted for posterity, it can seldom have been done with greater care and conscientiousness than at Yasnaya Polyana.

SIBERIAN JOURNEY

Though it is more accessible than it has ever been, Siberia has never been so little known to us. Forty years ago it was liberally sprinkled with governesses from the West, and reports came back to English rectories and Scottish manses about their remote and snowbound lives. At the time of the Bolshevik Revolution an excitable French minister who wanted Allied intervention from Vladivostok reported the murder of some fifty French governesses at Irkutsk, a frontier town on the edges of Mongolia. Unfortunately for his plans the governesses had not been murdered at all, and perhaps he had exaggerated their numbers also; as the French are reluctant travellers it would be sufficiently extraordinary if even ten French governesses had ever reached the pink shores of Lake Baikal. In the struggle for cultural supremacy, English, Irish, Scottish governesses pressed hard upon the French, and had the Revolution not happened it is likely that English rather than French would have become the drawing-room language of the Russian upper classes. There must have been many English teachers in Siberia.

Nowadays few of us see anything of Siberia but its airports; we accomplish in a couple of days vast journeys which up till recently took several weeks, and as we grumble a good deal about sleepless nights it is wholesome to read of Anton Chekhov's journey across

Siberia in 1890. We passed great cities without noticing them, while in his mind small villages were to be indelibly engraved. Here he spent the night in the ferryman's hut waiting for the storm to abate so that he could cross the Irtish; his sodden felt boots were turning to gelatine on the stove. Here his buggy crashed into the post wagon and he was hurled onto the ground with his portmanteau on top. But there were no such landmarks for our journey. Even the airports are inextricably confused. Was it at Sverdlovsk that we ordered omelette and got fried eggs, and was Sverdlovsk the new name for Ekaterinburg, where the imperial family were murdered in 1918? Yes, I think it was, and I know it was at Omsk that mud prevented us reaching the airport buildings and some peasants told us that it was the centre of vast state-owned farms as distinct from collectives. But I cannot be sure whether it was at Novosibirsk, the greatest city in Siberia, that we saw the jet plane that is to do the journey from Moscow to Peking in eight hours and the little garden of frostbitten asters encircling a marble Lenin sitting on a marble sofa and patting paternally the marble shoulders of Stalin. In general one Brobdingnagian air palace was much like the next; heavy plush curtains divided the saloons, and the cavities between the Corinthian columns were draped and decorated with epic gentility. There were chrysanthemums girdled with paper lace, tubs of castor-oil plants swathed in velour—even the wooden chairs had canvas covers. There were pictures five feet by ten feet of local heroes of the Revolution, of dying horses, wild duck and melons. At Kazan one big wall had a mural of Lenin, the boy from Simbirsk, heading a students' rebellion at Kazan University.

I regretted that so few now try to penetrate behind these imposing facades. Life could hardly be drearier for a teacher of English in Novosibirsk than it was for these Edwardian rectory girls whom fate had stranded in some isolated manor house beside the Kama or the Ob, but we are more poor-spirited than they were. It would not be necessary to be a Communist to have such a job and one would learn something of these formidable people who present such a challenge to us and whom we fear so much.

Sometimes a traveller, after poking his nose into one of these teeming cities, brings back a report of dreariness, overwork, dowdiness, provincialism. But it tells us nothing because it has always been like that. Chekhov sent back just such reports, but horror was blended with love. Of Siberia he wrote:

The people here would make you shudder. They have high cheekbones, pro-truding foreheads, tiny eyes, gigantic fists. They are born in the local iron foun-dries; it's a mechanic, not a midwife, who officiates. . . . The cabs are inconceivably squalid, damp, filthy, springless and the horses' hooves are stuck onto their spindly front feet in an astounding way. Here, I'll draw it for you. . . . And, O Lord, that sausage in Tyumen! When you stuck your teeth into it, it lets out a fearful puff, just as if you went into the stable when the coachman was unwinding his puttees. And when you began to chew it, it was like sticking your teeth into a tar-smeared dog's tail.

But another day he writes:

My God! How rich Russia is in good people! If it were not for the cold which deprives Siberia of summer, and were it not for the officials who corrupt the peasants and exiles, Siberia would be the very richest and happiest of lands.

At Irkutsk on the return journey fog delayed the plane for eight hours, and at last the opportunity arrived for pushing through the plush curtains into Siberia. We were a long way from the town and a taxi was impossibly expensive, so we considered hitchhiking. One of us got a lift from some workmen carrying sand to a great Ortho-dox monastery which is now a cinema. They stood him a drink and exchanged friendly remarks in sign language. We two who remained were overtaken by an official from the airport who offered to help us with a difficult bus route to the town. It was a crowded factory workers' bus. The first frost had come and the passengers were swol-len to twice their normal size with sheepskin *shubas* and padded jackets. At every pothole those who stood collapsed into their neigh-bours' laps with cheerful cries of dismay.

Irkutsk is a town of 300,000 inhabitants, and if my description is depressing I have to record that though the town and the river Angara which traverses it and the grey sky might all have been made in corrugated asbestos sheeting at the foundry, the people were hu-man and friendly. A great deal should be forgiven to those who have to live in Irkutsk, and I record as a fact, not an accusation, that all the women who have graduated (and it is not, I think, unconnected with a university degree) from being female bundles in gum boots, head scarves and padded bodices like life belts, all wore vertical tam-o'-shanters with a small feather in them. You will meet this hat all the way from the Pacific to the Ural Mountains and beyond.

There was a touch of the iron foundry about our airport friend Mr. Kardin. He wanted to impress us with the progressiveness of

Irkutsk, and those who lagged behind schedule—the ancient female bundle, for example, who was moving leaves about with a broom and did not leap out of our way nimbly enough—got a good hammering. But he indulged our less progressive tastes in a friendly way. He showed us the bronze plaque of Chekhov, bearded and pince-nezed, which still decorates the wall of the hotel he stayed in. He showed us the theatre where classical plays are acted: Lermontov, Ostrovsky and Sheridan were billed. "Sheridan was an Irishman," I said. "Oh yes, we know quite a lot about Ireland in Irkutsk," he answered. "We do Irish history after the fifth class. We had two Irish films here lately. One was called *The Road to Freedom*, the other *The School of Hatred*." I had not heard of either of them, but the first sounded as if it was about the Desmond Rising,* the second— was it Russian, English, American?—was "about an Irish boy who was taught in an English school to hate Ireland." These themes seemed unsuitable enough for Irkutsk, but were they more so than Sheridan's eighteenth-century gallantries, than Lermontov's Byronic tragedies—than Ostrovsky, who wrote about the amours of wealthy Moscow merchants?

"We must hurry," said Mr. Kardin, "or the football match between Irkutsk and Angarsk will be over."

On our way to the football ground we passed the bleak-looking Park of the Paris Commune, and down by the cold grey Angara we saw the baroque palace of the former governor of Irkutsk. It has a placard to commemorate a famous siege, when a group of local Bolsheviks had held it against some White generals in the first years of the Revolution. In the same street there was a row of low and charming houses made of elaborately carved wood. Mr. Kardin could not share our admiration for them, and said they were shortly to be replaced by fine modern flats. But he had no prejudice against the past, and confessed that he greatly admired a gorgeous cocoa-coloured villa with turrets and gazebos—a vision from the Arabian Nights, which a timber salesman of the last century had built himself and which is now an old people's home.

The many-tiered gateway to the football ground was also vaguely Arabian and had halfhearted minarets from which the grey paint was flaking off. The short avenue that led to it was lined with framed posters praising the cult of the body and urging application

---

*In 1597, when the Earl of Desmond was among the leaders of a rebellion against the English.—ed.

to sport. One of them was a quotation from Lenin, who was not noted for athletic powers. The soccer match was already half over when we reached the playing field, but there was only a handful of middle-aged peasants and factory workers watching the game from some wooden benches. Nobody cheered or exclaimed, and on the opposite side of the field twenty or thirty young men and women in shorts actually had their backs to what was going on. They were working their arms and legs rhythmically up and down and sideways, and were obviously addicts of some rival cult of the body.

Behind them a tall row of buildings closed in the field. Reading from left to right, Mr. Kardin told us they were the morgue, the boiler house for a vast block of flats and a technological institute. Of Angarsk, from which the visiting team had come, he told us that six years ago it had been a wooded valley on either side of the Angara, but now it has a population of 120,000. Petrol is made from coal there, and nearby, at Bratsk, is the largest hydroelectric factory in the world. The match went cheerlessly on, and it seemed to us that the players were as bored as we were. If it was Dr. Arnold of Rugby who invented compulsory games, I could not wish a better punishment for him than to be an everlasting spectator of the match between Irkutsk and Angarsk.

Some way off I saw the bulbous dome of a cathedral on a hill and I suggested to Mr. Kardin that we should visit it. He smiled at this strange caprice but came with us willingly enough up the rough cobbled road that led to it. It was closed and empty except for the inevitable old woman with the broom who pottered about in the porch. Mr. Kardin gave her a few brisk words of command and she trotted off to look for the key. She soon came back with a group of excited women. They were touchingly pleased to show us the church and led us through chamber after chamber, gorgeous with icons and murals and candlesticks. It was all in good order and there was a fine iconostasis. Our admiration obviously gave pleasure and one of the younger women asked with gentle patronage, "Haven't you any churches where you come from?" They told us that the evening service was just over and that on Sundays the large church was full.

I can well believe this because, on the way from Moscow to Yasnaya Polyana, I had stopped one Sunday morning to see the church in Lopasna, which is now called Chekhov because Anton Chekhov lived a few miles east of it at Melikhovo. The church had been so full that I could scarcely get beyond the door. There, too, the congregation was mainly of women and older men; it is hard to make deductions about the survival of Christianity in Russia because one does not know how many former parishes each church now has to serve. In Irkutsk, apart from the large church which was used as a cinema, the large monastery church which dominates the town from the crest of a hill is now used as a planetarium.

I regretted that I had not been able to visit Melikhovo, because Chekhov, though he was an unorthodox Christian and called himself a "materialist," had given to the local church a gleaming spire which could be seen for miles around. I would like to have seen it if it still survived and if reference was made to it in the Chekhov museum at Melikhovo. About Christianity in Russia there is great need for an unemotional record such as Chekhov made of the convict island of Sakhalin. For he not only made a census of the inhabitants but interviewed many hundreds of officials and peasants. Listening to their life stories, he had to reckon the part which fear, dishonesty, simplicity and ambition had played in what they told him. No one had believed that the Tsar's government would permit such a survey to be made by a humanist of unorthodox views. But the unbelievable happened; he had been allowed.

On our way back to the bus Mr. Kardin lingered with pride through the main square of Irkutsk, which is like an iron founder's dream of a university campus. A huge square of scraggy grass is surrounded by vast academies and institutes of scientific research. They wear on their pediments, carved in stone, abrupt, congested titles such as Vostsibugol, which is short for the Eastern Siberian Coal Research Institute. Among them is a colossal library, a museum, students' hostels. They are vast factories of learning, where muzhiks are smelted and hammered into scientists. As on an endless conveyor belt a stream of geologists, mineralogists and plant physicists passes through these buildings and falls, in a thin spray of professors and engineers, over backward and thinly populated regions of Russia.

The province of Irkutsk is one of the great centres of industrial development in Russia and perhaps in Europe. Every conceivable mineral lies beneath its soil and only the men and machines for mining it and converting it to some higher purpose are absent. More and more of the experts are now bred locally, but the working-class populations to fill the great new cities are drafted in from all the regions of Russia.

Sir Eric Ashby, Vice-Chancellor of Queen's University, Belfast, once gave formidable statistics about this great drive for scientific education in Russia. From a population which was 75 percent illiterate in 1918, so many science teachers and experts are now being trained that they not only satisfy Russia's present needs but can be lent to the backward countries of Asia. In 1954, 250,000 science teachers were working in Russia as against 20,000 in Britain.

Walking with Mr. Kardin through Irkutsk, one could easily persuade oneself that all this was very regrettable and alarming. Vostsibugol soars above the decaying villas and ugly tenement houses like some sinister intellectual forcing house from the Brave New World of 1984, that vision of the future with which two disillusioned Etonians have clouded our judgments. But had one seen Irkutsk as Chekhov saw it in 1890, surely one would judge it less harshly? To the grandson of the ferryman who sheltered the writer on the banks of the Irtish, Vostsibugol must seem the gateway into a world of unimagined opportunity; it must offer to his young heart the same glamorous illusions of emancipation that Christchurch or King's holds out to the middle-class youth of England.

Perhaps if one were to spend several months in Irkutsk one might be able to make some sense of this extraordinary jumble of colossal enterprises and mean economies, of generous ambitions and spiritual poverty, of desperate ignorance and brilliant speculation. On the credit side, one would have to note the complete absence of one kind of vulgarity, advertisement hoardings, beauty queens, comics and film stars, and to analyze the new negative vulgarities which are replacing the old.

Without sharing the lives of these people, one could make no guess where they are going. Is all this vast activity merely a stage on the way to war and universal annihilation or is it a short step towards that world which the heroes of Chekhov so often predicted, when, after two hundred or three hundred years of weary intellectual and spiritual struggle, life will at last be "unspeakably, amazingly lovely"?

SMALL FEET AND BIG NOSES

In the old days a visit to China was a relatively simple affair and you were not expected, after a month's sojourn, to have formed any private opinions. Uncle Fred was in the Shanghai Police, Cousin Harold was in a bank in Canton and Aunt Alice was in Fukien Province teaching in a mission school. They were all strongly opinionated people and would have been very snubbing to any relative who started, after a few casual meetings with Chinese, to have independent views.

The idea of a cultural delegation to China would have seemed to them preposterous.

They are all gone now and an easy, if at times unreliable, channel of communication is blocked for ever. We have to form our own opinions without any friends, relations, compatriots to help us, and we are definitely expected to express them. I took with me the *Marlborough Chinese Word Book* (1914) in the hope that it would at least help me to break a small hole in the language barrier. But a glance at it showed that even that was written for Uncle Fred, Cousin Harold and Aunt Alice, and by no means for us. There are no fewer than eighteen pages for Uncle Fred: Charge! Eyes Right! Defaulters' Drill! Reveille, Rations, Right Wheel! There are twelve pages for Cousin Harold: Affidavit, Arrears, Assets, Demurrage, Dividend, Double Entry. There are seven pages for Aunt Alice: Offertory Box, Parable, Sunday School, Temperance, Temptation, Wickedness. But I looked in vain for a single page to help a cultural delegation. Pictures, Plays, Pagodas, Poetry, Publishers—such things can never have been a topic of Anglo-Chinese conversation.

For an analogous reason, the editor is hopelessly misleading about the five tones of the Chinese language. He says that if you get the idiom right you need not bother about the tones: the chances are you'll be understood. But in fact the tones are as impenetrable a barrier to mutual understanding as the character writing, and only one or two of our delegation tried to leap it. In the early hours before breakfast you could hear them going through their scales with a teacher: "Má, Má, Má, MA," their voices rising and falling; for only one of these Ma's means "Mother." The others mean "hemp," "horse," "curse," or an exclamation of surprise; and a single fault will fuse a whole sentence.

There is very little English of any kind, or indeed of any other European language, spoken in China today. It has become once more a land of mystery, as in the days of Marco Polo. But there is a difference. Everyone is friendly and interested, and we were treated as equals and brothers. Only a few generations ago the Emperor of China had written to George III forbidding all social intercourse. He realized, he said, that later on a visit to the Celestial Empire might possibly be of moral value to the Western barbarians, but he did not think that they had as yet reached a cultural level to profit by it. The average educated Chinaman disliked the Big Noses, thinking they smelt unpleasantly and finding something sinister in their round eyes, irregular pigmentation and hairy cheeks; and, of course, they were keenly and justifiably frightened of the Pink Peril. Till Sir Henry Pottinger brought his warships up the Yangtse in 1842 there was very little intercourse and no diplomatic relations between China and the West.

The intimacy, started in such an unpropitious way, was never cordial. At the time of the Boxer Rebellion the last Empress ordered a massacre of all the Europeans; and there was continuous constraint and suspicion. No doubt today, too, a spark would set the old passions flaming, but we certainly were only aware of friendliness and courtesy. It was not the old ceremonial courtesy of the imperial China of the London music halls ("My humble doorstep is not worthy that your honourable shadow should fall on it") but an imaginative and unobtrusive sympathy and solicitude. This was not laid on for our benefit, for we met it also as we wandered on our own round the streets shopping or sightseeing.

Once or twice we were mistaken for Russians; but it was not because of Stalin's big nose and Marx's beard which decorated so many clubrooms and lecture halls that our Western idiosyncrasies were smiled upon. Such few Russians as we saw were as little acclimatized as ourselves. They held together, sightseeing in depressed busloads and poking mournfully with their chopsticks at Chinese delicacies. "When you get to Canton," one of them said to me, sadistically and quite incorrectly, "you'll have to eat cat-and-snake pie."

How much of the fascination that we found in Peking was a relic of the imperial or bourgeois past which will disappear in a few years? Much of it, I suppose. Peking is a city of trees and gardens, because the Emperor liked an uninterrupted view from the imperial palace and two-storeyed houses were forbidden. The middle and upper classes expanded sideways, so that their homes usually consisted of a group of low buildings of brick and glass and latticework, set lightly like summerhouses round quadrangles filled in September with Michaelmas daisies and tubs of lotus. The father and mother lived in one of them, the grandmother, perhaps, in another, a married son in another. There might be seven or eight separate establishments, and one could picture them living a willow-pattern existence, walking across rustic bridges to take tea with each other and composing ironical couplets in the shade of a magnolia tree.

These houses took up an immense amount of space and presupposed a life of leisure which is not now possible. Yet an elderly clergyman with whom I took tea contemplated with equanimity the ultimate disappearance of his home. He was not being hustled, he said, change was inevitable; he had left one of the summerhouses to the Church. Nor was he frightened of the materialism of the age. A materialist philosophy had prevailed in the Sung dynasty, yet the arts had flourished. The Chinese peasant was not a primitive person. And if he was emancipated, he too would display creative talents. Each dynasty had ended like this in social revolution.

Listening to him, one could believe that the Chinese were the most rational and practically minded people in the world. If they occasionally ate cat-and-snake pie, it was because they had been experimenting with the material world for three thousand years and had shed all vulgar prejudices. For example, he said, modern medical science in China is now justifying and exploiting the empirical observations of the Chinese herbalists.

I could take most of this. The Chinese can make something exquisite and refined out of the most unappetizing spiritual and material ingredients. But, of course, every now and then something happened to shake this belief in Chinese common sense. Occasionally one heard behind one a small patter of two feet and a stick, and an elderly lady with her hair screwed back in a serious sensible bun hobbled past on small doll's feet fitted into triangular pockets of leather. Instantly all that I had read of bound feet and infanticide came back to me; perhaps it was true, as a sailor had told me twenty years ago, that he had seen the weirs in the Yangtse choked with the bodies of unwanted female infants. We saw women as young as thirty with bound feet. Plainly, long after the practice had been officially forbidden, upper-class parents must have crippled their children deliberately so as to give them an aristocratic helplessness.

To the passing stranger Chinese children are certainly enchanting. If you get up early in the morning you may see them rolling by in their school pedicabs, glass boxes like greenhouses on wheels drawn by bicyclists in coolie hats. Behind the panes seven or eight tiny scholars are fidgeting and chattering like sparrows. We never heard a child cry, except one who was seen having a surgical operation in a barber's shop, and they seem without shyness. Once at a crèche we were mobbed by thirty or forty infants. They left their playpens and their educational toys and swarmed round us thrusting their arms stiffly into the air, pleading for picky-backs.

But once up in the air they focussed all their attention on the mysterious un-Chinese growths of hair on our faces, exploring them with speculative fingers. One of us who was hairier than the others had babies hanging all over him in clusters, like leeches, insatiably curious.

How can one reconcile these happy children with the cruel traditions of their ancestors? It is not sufficient to say that those customs have been abolished. How could they have survived so long in a highly civilized people? That is one of those questions which we had to leave unsolved.

TEMPLES AND CHURCHES

One of us developed the dubious theory that the Chinese language is descriptive, not informative, and that place names are not meant to locate but to explain. Certainly if you asked the name of a hill or a lake, there was always the greatest difficulty. One day we stood with a Chinaman on a sacred island, looking at the marble slab on which its name was written in flowing characters. "You want its name?" he answered doubtfully. "Well, it's rather hard to translate. There was a king, you see, and he saw the shadow of the moon falling between two Tangs."

"What is a Tang?"

"Those are Tangs, those stone things sticking out of the lake. When it has a stone cap on it, it's a tomb, otherwise it's just a monument. They were made in the Tang dynasty."

"Is that why they are called Tangs?"

"Oh, no, that's quite different. I said Tang, not Tang! Ho, ho, ho! Ha, ha, ha!" (A lot could be written about Chinese laughter. It comes from lower down the throat than ours and is an immensely warm and sociable noise. It is seldom derisive, but often used to cover up the traces of someone else's embarrassing stupidity.)

"Yes, but what is the *name* of the island?"

"Please, I am telling you now. Ho, ho! You see, this king had a dream . . ."

Another temple's name was a very long story about a tiger, another was concerned with some blue clouds. Large crowds reached it by bus, so plainly the Chinese have some device for telescoping these anecdotes for the purpose of a bus ticket, but they had difficulty in sharing it with us.

The Chinese are expert acrobats and jugglers, and I think they can keep as many contradictory ideas dancing about in their mind as they can plates, parasols, eggs and coconuts. Otherwise the government's curious attitude to these temples and the Buddhism to which they are dedicated is hard to explain. Buddhism, at least in its material manifestations, is in violent conflict not only with Marxism but with all the ideals of the West. Yet our path crossed several times that of a world Buddhist organization which was touring China. Draped in robes of orange, lemon and saffron, bald-headed, spectacled, they were to be seen trooping in and out of taxis, hotel lifts, museums, in Hangchow, Peking, Shanghai. They were always delighted. "The government is doing wonders for Buddhism and spending large sums on its temples."

We saw evidence of this ourselves. The repair of a Buddhist temple is not a matter of an odd coat of paint. Scores of dragons, lotus buds, whales, phoenixes, camels, souls in agony, six-headed cows, as well as Buddha in several manifestations with his many attendants, have all to be carefully redecorated. Swallows' nests have to be taken from the intricate woodwork under the eaves and the protective wire netting carefully reinstated. Real hair whiskers have to be replaced on gilded demons and acres of porcelain tiling, camphor-wood columns and carved stone pillars have to be renovated.

There are many possible explanations for this energy, some of them credible, some not. Cynics say that the government is still wooing the Tibetans, the most religious people in the world (a third of their male population are monks), who are still imperfectly assimilated to China. But Buddhist temples are usually charmingly situated, surrounded by groves and streams and carefully tended gardens. Fat carp, orange and dun-coloured, swim about in sacred tanks, and from the tops of the temples you look down on doves nesting in lime trees. Or perhaps a very small bird is perching in an ornamental cherry tree, and a holidaymaker is stalking it with an air gun. These places will always have a secular appeal, and that is maybe why a secular government can afford to spend so much money on them.

Many of the large Buddhist temples north of Peking are in excellent repair, but we visited one near Hangchow which was being rebuilt from the beginning. (Its collapse was attributed to Chiang Kai-shek, but I expect that time and disbelief were the real offenders.) While still some way off we could hear the whirr of saws and the hammer of mallets, and inside the temple we found scores of craftsmen chiselling dragons round stone pedestals, shaping wooden columns or painting arabesques upon altars. The back of the temple was completed and, passing a score or more of half-finished gods and goddesses three times life size, we came to a screen sixty feet high of painted wood and plaster.

I do not know whether it was an apocalyptic vision of Heaven or Hell, but it left us speechless. We had never in our lives seen such a profusion of intricate and horrific detail. Let me describe one corner where there is a sort of vertical cavalcade. Surrounded by jellyfish and snakes, a naked man is riding a sea monster, which is vomiting onto an umbrella, which is carried by a demon, who is riding a griffin, which is swallowing . . . but no description can do justice to these strange works of art, and nobody could tell us what they meant.

"Who is that man roaring and stamping his feet?"

"He is a god."

"But why is he beating the naked woman with his guitar, and why has he two eyes in the soles of his feet?"

"Because he is an angry god."

Nobody could be blamed for not knowing, for only a specialist could unravel these complex mysteries. But it was very puzzling to witness the elaborate reconstruction of a symbolism in which, it would appear, very few now believe.

Possibly the Communists argue that popular Buddhism is innocuous and politically moribund. In the old days the landlords used to have an annual feast in the temple of the City God, and he may have seemed to some "a symbol of feudalism"; but these feasts have long been discontinued and the City God is worshipped for himself alone. The God of Shanghai and his temple have been for a long time completely swallowed up in the market. To buy cabbages or peanuts you must go through the innermost sanctuary and pass his four gigantic guardian gods; in front of the City God himself is a bowl in which some joss sticks are smouldering, a box of matches, a dishcloth and a copy of the *Shanghai Daily News*. There is no evidence of disrespect, but none of awe, either, and for the simple surely awe is an essential part of Buddhism.

But perhaps I have no right to argue infidelity from absence of fervour. The Chinese have always been a sceptical people—"Worship the gods," said Confucius, "as if they existed"—and it is possible that their Communism will be as individual as their religious beliefs, and as liable to be submerged in ornamental accretions.

We visited also a Taoist temple. Taoism used to be a deeply spiritual faith, but, like the others, it has through the centuries become encrusted with a gorgeous and fantastic mythology. In the central shrine we found the usual pop-eyed divinities with bared teeth and furious tomato faces, but in the rear was a very benign god, Tao's father, the creator of the world. He had a black wedge-shaped hat upon a knob of hair. Some attempt has evidently been made to modernize his worship, for he is said to have appeared in the sky over Peking one day in June 1927, and just below him there is a framed and enlarged photograph of his apparition. The clouds have parted over the tops of trees and roofs of houses to reveal him. There is his wedge-shaped hat right enough, and the very same benign smile.

There were still five priests in the temple, gentle creatures, one of them quite young, busying themselves laying out on plates in front of the gods little pyramids of buns and apples. But they have had to let a part of the monastic premises to some workers' families and ten or a dozen small children gazed at us from behind the latticed windows.

Confucianism is perhaps at present more discouraged than the other ancient religions, because Chiang Kai-shek, who was in fact a Methodist, tried to base a new social order on its revival. It is an ethic rather than a faith, but it has shaped Chinese life for so many generations that it is unlikely that its influence will ever disappear.

What has happened, and what will happen, to the Christian churches in China? This is a vastly important question for us; to the Chinese it does not appear so, since only an infinitesimal percentage of the population has ever been Christian. Two or three of us heard much about the churches and saw many clergy, but what we heard and what we conjectured were sometimes in conflict.

Everybody knows how hard it has been for the Christian churches in China to dissociate themselves from the political and commercial aspirations of the Western powers, and how often they have failed. Toleration of missionary effort was grudgingly granted after humiliating defeat in the Opium War, and, now that the concessions then extorted have been withdrawn, it would be very strange if the old suspicions did not revive, taking their colour from Marxism rather than from the moribund creeds of imperial China.

Must it be a case of war to the death? I can only quote a distinguished Chinese Christian scholar of Peking. He told me that the government is not hostile to Christianity, but it is challenging, and that the future of the churches in China depends on the Christian answer to that challenge.

THE BRIDGE OF RU KO CHOW

When you are a guest in a foreign country and like it very much, a wholesome corrective to any excessive infatuation is to visit some

European embassy. You will usually find there some very knowing, disapproving person who will puncture your naive enthusiasms and explain how far you have been led up the garden path. He will sometimes hint that your judgment has been warped by caviar and civic receptions. To those of us who loathe caviar, these insinuations can be irritating, but I am glad that some of us took the the risk of visiting two foreign embassies in Peking, that of a large democracy and that of a small one.

We had been told things that we found it very hard to believe; a resident who was also an outsider might be able to help us. Was there some catch in the tremendous slum clearances we had seen in Shanghai? Was it true that the war on dirt and disease had improved the general health? And if it had, were they as little worried about overpopulation as they claimed to be? Then we had just seen the Peking gaol. Was it really true that 1,800 prisoners went to bed every night in unlocked cells, that the warders were unarmed (or rather that there were no warders, but only teachers, cooks, experts in the manufacture of socks and textiles, etc.), and that the only guard was a military one outside the walls? Had we been shown special cells suitable for visiting delegations, or were they all as airy and clean, with gay wall decoration and Chinese lanterns in the corridor? Had they all cotton counterpanes printed with tractors in a ring of rose-buds? What about brainwashing and mob trials?

We got the expected douche of cold water from the great democracy, but administered with intelligence and charity. From the small one we got a less guarded approval of the social achievements of the Chinese government. We had not been deceived on these points. The cells were not locked, but the prison we saw, where two-thirds of the prisoners were political, was not the only one in Peking. There was another one where "re-education" often took the form of interminable cross-examination. But there was nothing secret about this prison or its methods; it had been frequently visited by foreign correspondents; we could have seen it had we asked.

And indeed, to a large extent we made our own programme, visiting whom we chose; and had we, as a cultural delegation, refused to see any "non-cultural" spectacles, our wishes would, I think, have been indulged, if not approved. But naturally we were interested in the future of China as well as its past. For the middle-aged and set in their ways, the future certainly did not look rosy. Or rather, among the rosebuds there was always a tractor. The willow-pattern world of leisure and cultivated conversation had gone for ever. One of us visited a banker friend who had remained behind in Shanghai to "wind up" as best as he could the last tangled shreds of his Shanghai bank. He was thirsting to be gone. Every day's delay was torture. "It's all right for the Chinese. What they have done to clean up Shanghai is beyond belief. They have checked corruption and disease, but they have made life intolerable for Europeans."

That was more or less what we had heard, too, in the embassies. For generations the Chinaman had been considered a backward, ridiculous fellow, who for his own good must be forced into the main streams of Western progress. The Chinese put up a feeble but persistent resistance to Westernization. They clung to their old traditions, building tombs for their ancestors and solving all social, moral and political questions by reference to the teaching of Confucius. Western pressure became stronger and stronger, and by the end of the last century it seemed almost certain that China would be carved up, like Africa, among the European powers. Only their mutual jealousy prevented this from happening. The Chinese had watched Japan becoming in a few generations a great power, able to challenge successfully the Russian Empire. She had done this by adopting Western civilization. It was plain that for China, too, Beelzebub had to be thrown out by Beelzebub.

The Europeans were so securely planted in China that it was more or less inevitable that the Chinese should choose the most explosive of Western philosophies to dislodge them. Long before Mao Tse-tung, Chiang Kai-shek had applied to Moscow for assistance in the shaping of the Kuomintang, and Borodin had been sent as an adviser for a few years. But the opposition leaders considered that a bigger charge of Marxist dynamite was needed. In 1949 there was a gigantic explosion; not only were the Westerners thrown out, but the old China was blown sky high.

In so tremendous a cataclysm it is difficult to count the casualties or to estimate how soon, if ever, the new energy which has been released can repair the damage which has been done. Whole classes have disappeared—landlords, bankers, scholars, civil servants, priests; and such things do not happen without appalling wastage and suffering. Obviously there must have been peaceful ways in which the same force could have been generated; but who was likely to find them? Certainly not the Europeans, to whose interests it had been that China should remain weak and divided.

All that is clear is that the energy *has* been generated. For good or evil, China has become a force to be reckoned with; she is more united than she has been for a century. And even the most unsympathetic visitor could not fail to be aware that the air was charged with excitement and enthusiasm. Dreams were not, as in other countries, divorced from reality, but were being realized daily. What right had a Westerner to complain that they were mainly Western dreams, and were being fulfilled in ferroconcrete and not in jade and camphor wood and marble? A vast bridge, one of the greatest in the world, was being built across the Yangtse, and every province had its own schemes for factories, power stations, irrigation projects.

But, of course, we did complain. The old China was being swept away, and the energy for these achievements was being diverted from those pursuits which we had come out to observe. Probably as much manpower, skill and enthusiasm had been applied to the Ru Ko Chow bridge near Peking as has gone to spanning the Yangste, but it will never be applied in that way again. The balustrades are sustained on either side by a hundred stone lions and supported at either end by stone elephants. Each lion is slightly different; they seem to have their hearts (or are they heart-shaped lockets?) round their necks, and their cubs are chewing them. Nobody, of course, could tell us why.

There are thousands of such monuments all over China, most of them betraying high craftsmanship. There is a replica of Ru Ko Chow bridge in the grounds of the Summer Palace built thirty or forty years ago, but already it bears traces of the Age of Progress and the detail is slipshod and inferior. The Summer Palace itself was burned by the English in 1860. A cultural defeat can often be as serious as a military one. Those who rebuilt it, decorated it and furnished it had obviously caught the contagion of the Great Exhibition and of Balmoral Castle, and the portrait of the Empress Dowager in the vestibule bears a striking likeness to Queen Victoria.

It was plain that the museums were admirably kept, the temples and palaces were being restored; there were galleries and cultural institutes where none had been before. But all that was a matter of maintenance and organization, not of creation. It is probable that the creative impulse has shifted away from the arts. The best painter, Chi Bai She, is well over ninety, and did not seem to have any obvious successors. He spent his life not in movements and revolutions, but watching the shape and colour of a jackdaw's tail feathers, the tendrils of the vine, the veins in a maple leaf. And that is the tradition of old China, an intense concentration on small things. A Chinese took as much pain in writing his name as in painting a flower, and his signature is an integral part of the picture. Can this delicacy of perception be carried over into a hydroelectric proletarian civilization? It is not, of course, a Chinese problem only, but our artists and sculptors did not appear to get much encouragement for its solution from China. Looking at exhibitions of contemporary art, they found abundance of skill, unsurpassed mastery of technique, but something, perhaps the proud independence of the artist, was missing. Where Chinese art became the accomplice of contemporary politics, appalling outrages were often committed.

On a lower plane, the Chinese decorative sense seemed infallible. At the mid-September Moon Festival in Canton, every lantern was a triumph of inventiveness. They were shaped like dragons, griffins, camels, elephants. It was easy to fall into the old trap and to mistake the unknown for the magnificent. The Canton moon, the guest of the evening, seemed far larger and brighter than ours, and if we could have seen the gay and ubiquitous Chinese script as words and not as pictures, possibly we should have been disillusioned. Someone asked the meaning of a gay arabesque that ran round the brim of a coolie hat. It meant: "We must hit the bull's-eye on the target of productivity."

THE BIRD CHING-WEI

*"The bird Ching-wei carried small twigs
in her unshakeable determination
to fill up the Eastern Sea."*

I am not certain whether the poet was here making fun of Ching-wei, but in her patience, optimism and industry Ching-wei was a very Chinese bird. In Russia one hears only of Five-Year Plans, but in China Hundred-Year Plans are discussed. Time is of no importance.

If the Chinese had wished to dazzle us with the speed of their accomplishments rather than to exhibit the problems to which a solution had to be found, they would not have taken us to that collective farm near Peking. It was a very large one, containing 2,443 families, 94 more or less absorbed and assimilated ex-landowners, 560 pigs, 494 mules and donkeys, nine schools, two lorries, 33,000 library books. They grew wheat and cotton and maize and millet, peanuts, kaoliang and sweet potatoes.

I would consider that I had made a mistake about those two lorries if I had not seen some collectivized peasants engaged in old-style farming on their own private allotment. An old donkey with some blue cotton pants over his eyes was walking round a millstone, pulling a roller which was crushing some maize. As the maize scattered outwards to the edge of the stone a little girl pressed it back under the roller with her fingers. From time to time the little girl gave some handfuls of crushed grain to her mother, who sat on the ground beside her and sieved it in a bowl through a coarse-meshed sieve. When she had filled a bowl, she went across to a kitchen colander and resieved it all into a cardboard box. There were some pans of wheat and millet waiting to be done in this way, too.

The collective threshing of the soya bean was scarcely more up-to-date. The dry haulms were stacked on some square yards of trampled mud and lashed about with forks. Then they were tossed to one side and the grain was swept up with brooms. Twenty of the thinnest pigs I have ever seen looked on from their sties at this process; to reach them we had to paddle across a small channel of disinfectant.

I dare say that, apart from the little stream of disinfectant, in itself a cultural revolution, things were much the same in the days of the ninety-four landowners. The old donkey looked as if he and his ancestors had been walking round the millstone for thousands of years, and as if his children—but, I think, not his grandchildren—would follow in his footsteps. Behind one of the barns a vast stone tombstone lay on its side and beside it the stone tortoise, the symbol of longevity or enduring memory, on which it had been reared. No doubt the Chinese characters recorded the rank and virtues of a former landlord, but no one could tell us much. "It's just a tombstone."

"What are you going to do with it?"

"Nothing. It's no use."

Apart from the splendid tombstone, there was no trace of former parks and gardens and architectural splendours. Aristocratic families were large, and the properties divided or shared among innumerable descendants; so it is likely that the ninety-four landlords were quite simple people, extravagant only in their devotion to their ancestors. It was against the ancestors as much as against the landlords that the revolution was directed, and there had been friction for some generations between them and the agricultural experts. All the way from Peking to Canton the fields had been dotted with grave mounds like large ant heaps; sometimes a marrow or a pumpkin had been planted on top of them, but usually they were bleak islands in a sea of rice or soya bean. In the spring the descendants used to come out and, laying an embroidered cloth on the grave and seating themselves on crimson satin cushions, have a commemorative picnic.

Only occasionally did one notice a concentration of these graves, where they clustered round a triumphal arch or two stone columns with stone clouds, the symbol of eternity, projecting from the summit. In the office of the collective farm there was a poster of some fresh-faced, productivity-increasing pioneers tackling some tombstones with spades and pickaxes. It was inscribed: "The dead must not stand in the way of the living." But after seven years of Communism the paddy fields are still speckled with millions of graves. The bird Ching-wei is in no hurry. It has not occurred to her to use a bulldozer.

Yet the mechanical revolution is on its way. When it comes, it will surely transform society as much as it transforms the countryside. Can it fail to bring with it the usual problems of overpopulation and unemployment? The contrast with the empty plains of Siberia, where there often seemed to be as many tractors as men, was startling. Looking out of the railway carriage windows, we seemed to see every few yards a Chinaman in a large hat hoeing or transplanting rice seedlings, steering a tub across a pond to collect water chestnuts, stripping the foliage of hemp or soaking the long hemp skeins in tanks, working a long-armed wooden pump to irrigate the rice fields. Only the ox and the buffalo and the mule were there to lighten their labours. There were not many horses, but sometimes we saw one drawing a wagon with basket sides like an old-fashioned governess cart, loaded with sacks of lime or piles of bamboo. A donkey, as often as not, trots beside the horse; he does not seem to be pulling very hard, but he is said to have a pacifying and encouraging effect on his big brother. Some wear eye shields, but others have been blinded by the dust and lime.

What will be the ultimate effect of mechanization on unemployment? In so vast and enigmatic a land as China perhaps one man's guess is as good as another's. In one of the great courtyards of the Forbidden City a long blue tide of crouching Chinese was creeping slowly across the cobblestones. They were rooting out weeds from the crevices with knives and putting them in tins.

"You could do the whole thing with a couple of gallons of weedkiller," I said to Mr. Pu, but he replied, "We want to save our foreign credit for really vital imports."

"Surely," I said, "the real reason is that you would not know what to do with all these people if you used weedkiller?" But Mr. Pu would not agree that there is or ever could be an unemployment problem. "And why not a garden hose for all those flower beds and lotus tubs, instead of those old men dropping roped buckets into the lily pond?" Same answer.

The Nazi solution for unemployment was intensive militarization, but I think only fear for its frontiers could shake China out of the old Confucian prejudice that the soldier ranked lowest in the order of society. It was because of that prejudice that Messrs. Jardine and Matheson were able to build and defend with force their commercial empire in China.*

Though frequently exploited, I don't think the prejudice is extinct. Yet one would hesitate now to presume on it. On 1 October, National Day, we stood for five hours at the Gateway of Heavenly Peace watching many thousands of soldiers and sailors march past in the pouring rain. Their legs moved like pistons, their white gloves like bobbins in a weaving machine. There was not a solitary mistake or misadventure to relieve the awful tedium, but every hour or so there was a frivolous interlude, a procession of dragons or a van load of cardboard vegetable marrows, each the size of a horse, or all at once the sky was full of multicoloured balloons.

The evening ended auspiciously in superb fireworks, and we recalled the old tradition that gunpowder had been known in China centuries before it reached Europe, but that this sensible people had used it only for social and religious purposes, pyrotechnics at parties, ceremonial salvoes and squibs to scare away demons. It will be of painful interest to us to discover how much of this common sense has survived Confucianism.

JOURNEY TO SHANGHAI

Chinese railway journeys are usually immensely long and begin with ceremony. As the doors slam, the railway porters stand to attention and the vendors of roast chicken and water chestnuts fall in beside them in a wobbly, courteous line.

The engine gets up speed and the music starts, an exceedingly squeaky and alien sound with a gay refrain that jingles round and round with the wheels. After a time it breaks off, and a female voice, squeaky like the music, pronounces: "Comrades! This train is yours. Keep it clean. Put your cigarette stubs in the ashtray. Leave the toilet

---

*The British firm of Jardine, Matheson expanded their activities from opium to shipping, banking and textiles in late-nineteenth- and early-twentieth-century China.—ed.

as you would wish to find it. Make sure you have your tickets. Dinner is served at seven."

Then the music starts again, sad, nostalgic, gay, round and round, like the nursery musical box. Surely we are not just a delegation going to see the slums of Shanghai, but Gullivers off to visit some socialized Land of Prester John where golden apples are graded for export and red lacquer dragons give a record yield of brimstone.

Every twenty minutes a smiling Lilliputian comes in with a large watering can of boiling water with which he fills and refills our tea mugs. As the last flush of colour fades from the tea we speculate whether by jamming the lid on tight we can keep it warm till we are ready to shave, for in this beardless land shaving is attended with difficulties.

Once or twice a day an attendant, with a cotton pad over mouth and nose, grins us out into the corridor, souses our compartment with disinfectant and brushes out the floor. This is a part of the great and successful crusade which is purging China of flies, mice, sparrows, germs. The waiters in the dining car also wear pads, but my waiter has not quite caught the spirit of the crusade, for he has his thumb in the fruit salad, just as he might at home in Ireland.

At the opposite table two students are spitting their chicken bones onto the tablecloth. This is quite normal good manners, though, for a Chinese chicken is sliced up whole into small pieces that can be handled by chopsticks, and the bones, which are thought to give an indispensable flavour, are not extracted. The disintegrated chicken sits on a single plate between the two students, who demolish it with chopsticks from opposite sides. The tablecloth, which always returns freshly laundered, is meant to be spat on.

At Shanghai we decided that in all that really matters the Chinese must be among the cleanest people on earth. In the slum district of Drug Lane there are 18,000 inhabitants; the streets are cobbled and so narrow and crowded with washtubs, Primus stoves (they cook out of doors), vegetable stalls and babies that only a man-drawn pedicab could pass down it, and pedicabs are now disappearing as "degrading to human dignity."

Imagine the symphony of smells that would arise from such a street on a hot day in Naples! There were no smells at all in Drug Lane, except such as are appropriate to a summer afternoon. Many of the residents had made their own houses out of bamboo, wood and bricks, thatched them and whitewashed them. They are small and crumbling, and till not long ago all their water had to come from the canal; the Kuomintang gave them twelve taps and now they have thirty-two.

One of the cottages has been made an office, and there the secretary holds meetings of the six welfare committees of the neighbourhood. The only one of them that seemed convincingly Chinese was the reconciliation committee. Looking at the passersby in the street, we could see that the committee would have to reconcile not only squabbling neighbours but whole epochs of civilization. Two small boys passed by with cotton pads over their noses; they grabbed them off and grinned at us in case we should think they had some terrible disease.

Behind them came an elderly sage in a black skullcap, a wisp of white hair projecting from his chin; he wore a lilac dressing gown, and a scarlet umbrella slung across his shoulder in a case. After him came a little girl swinging in her hand a willow twig to which two large grasshoppers were tethered. Her skull was shaven bald except for three pigtails, plaited tightly with red ribbon. We were told she was probably a dearly loved only child and that she had pigtails so that her parents could hold on to her.

A great deal of Chinese superstition is an elaborate kind of ancient fun like this. In Peking the old streets sometimes had a sharp bend, so that if you were chased by a demon you could dodge him by an abrupt swerve.

I do not know if there is any place for this ancient fun in the new suburb into which 6,370 families from Drug Lane have been transferred. It has broad roads and savings banks, fifteen buses in a row, hot and cold communal taps, television aerials and a tall painted tower to carry slogans about cleanliness, flies, productivity, Formosa. Apart from the tower and the hot-water taps, it is indistinguishable from a million workers' suburbs in Western Europe.

It is too easy for the travellers to repine for pigtails and pedicabs and to say that good plumbing and well-built roads do not lead to contentment. But what Western government has discovered a better route?

The "cleaning up" of Shanghai is one of the most remarkable achievements of the Communist regime. The Chinese, when they decide on a moral objective, are frighteningly wholehearted. Lowes Dickinson, who travelled in China after Sun Yat-sen's revolution, relates how in the campaign against opium, smokers were flogged and beheaded, and in Hunan seventy farmers who resisted the destruction of their poppy crops were shut up in a temple and burnt alive.

I do not know the method by which vice was suppressed in Shanghai, but few can dispute its success. We visited one of the famous haunts of sin in the city, formerly called the Great World, and found it transformed into a People's Recreation Palace. It contained fourteen theatres as well as clubrooms for table tennis and chess and many other blameless games and hobbies.

You can see acrobats and opera, puppet shows, tragedies, comedies, ballet. It is a gay but noisy place, for the Chinese like to beat gongs behind the scenes to emphasize the emotional crises on the stage; these make a furious barking sound, as though one of those enraged bronze animals that decorate the terraces of the imperial palaces were suddenly to find a tongue. It is the most characteristic of all the many Chinese noises.

On my way out I passed through a reading room where a number of elderly people were sitting round a pile of small fat books three inches square. These books are the Chinese equivalent of comics, but better than ours. I looked over the shoulders of a serious spectacled man, expecting to see that his comic would be about Stakhanovites or spacemen, but judging from illustrations it was about a wicked magician who had swallowed his own evil potion by mistake. His nose had grown ten feet long and was coiling round his ankles.

Perhaps the Chinese endure their revolutions so calmly, because, despite their four thousand years of civilization, they have retained the lively imaginations of childhood. No catastrophe, either natural or supernatural, can really surprise them.

The Children of Drancy

1968*

Lately I was comparing three versions of the story of the Children of Drancy, and it occurred to me that we mostly have more detailed information, more curiosity, about remote and now irrelevant events like the murder of the two little princes in the Tower in the summer of 1483 or the death of 123 English people in the Black Hole of Calcutta on 19 June 1756. Two of the writers I consulted said it was in July, a third said it was in August 1942 that 4,051 children were sent off to be killed in Poland from the transit camp at Drancy, north of Paris. Were they French Jews or foreigners? Were they girls or boys? It is usually said boys, but suburban residents on the outskirts of Paris who heard them wailing at night say they were little girls, and there is a story of a bleeding ear torn by a harried police inspector as he removed an earring.

They spent four days without food at the Vélodrome d'Hiver (the winter cycle-racing stadium) before their mothers were taken from them; then they were loaded three or four hundred at a time into cattle trains at the Gare d'Austerlitz and taken to Auschwitz. It was related at Nuremberg that an order came from Berlin that deportees from Vichy France should be mingled discreetly with the children to make them look like family groups. Was this done? It is not as though dubious legend has grown up around these children as it has around King Herod's far smaller enterprise in Bethlehem. The facts are bleak and few. It should not be hard to

*This essay was first composed in 1968 but subsequently revised in 1978 and 1988.—ed.

find more and to iron out discrepancies. But no one seems interested.

I believe we are bored because the scale is so large that the children seem to belong to sociology and statistics. We cannot visualize them reading Babar books, having their teeth straightened, arranging dolls' tea parties. Their sufferings are too great and protracted to be imagined, and the range of human sympathy is narrowly restricted.

Had four or five children only been killed and burned, and had it happened outside the booking office at the Gare d'Austerlitz, we would have responded emotionally, and probably their names and their fate would have been carved on a marble tablet like that which commemorates the victims of the Black Hole outside the post office in Calcutta. And the names of their murderers would be remembered for ever. But to kill and burn 4,051 children after transporting them to Poland was a huge cooperative endeavour in which thousands of French and German policemen, typists, railway officials, gas fitters and electricians were engaged. It was composite villainy, and when you try to break it down there are no villains, just functionaries as neutral and characterless as the clusters of ink blobs of which a press photograph is composed. The officials who handled the children were, we are told, deeply affected. Even the Vichy Commissioner for Jewish Affairs, Louis Darquier, who deported Jews in the thousands from France, had suggested that the children be transferred to a French orphanage, but he did nothing about it. Though Pierre Laval, the French Premier, was enthusiastic about the deportation of all foreign Jews, even those under sixteen, neither he nor Pétain realized that they were not going to be "settled" in the East but killed there.

Even at the peak of the organizational pyramid one finds duty, routine, idealism of a kind more often than sadism as the motive power; in the interests of a more glorious future the tender impulses had to be suppressed. At the Jerusalem trial even the most hostile witnesses failed to prove that Eichmann, an exemplary husband and father, had ever been guilty of wanton cruelty. These people were really what they claimed to be, idealists, whose seedy ideals would never have germinated and pullulated in any other century but ours.

However confident we may be of the facts, there are irreconcilable divergences when we come to their interpretation. "Too much science," say some. "Too much literary scorn for science," say others. François Mauriac, who was in Paris at the time, wrote some twenty years later:

Nothing I had seen during those sombre years of the Occupation had left so deep a mark on me as those trainloads of Jewish children standing at the Gare d'Austerlitz. Yet I did not even see them myself. My wife described them to me, her voice still filled with horror. At that time we knew nothing of Nazi methods of extermination. And who could have imagined them? Yet the way these lambs had been torn from their mothers in itself exceeded anything we had so far thought possible. I believe that on that day I touched upon the mystery of iniquity whose revelation was to mark the end of one era and the beginning of another. The dream which Western man conceived in the eighteenth century, whose dawn he thought he saw in 1789, and which, until 2 August 1914, had grown stronger with the process of enlightenment and the discoveries of science—this dream vanished finally for me before those trainloads of little children. And yet I was still thousands of miles away from thinking that they were to be fuel for the gas chamber and crematorium.

Yet even at the time few thought like that. It is easier to forget about the Children of Drancy than to liberate ourselves from the increasing control that science has over our lives. The year after Mauriac wrote what I have quoted, Charles Snow delivered at Cambridge his famous lecture on the "Two Cultures" in which he claimed the traditional culture of the past, and science, the culture of the future, should make peace with one another. Charles Snow, a novelist himself, addressed his lecture mainly to the "traditional" man of letters, scolding him for being ignorant of elementary scientific knowledge like molecular biology and the Second Law of Thermodynamics. He quoted with approval someone he referred to as "a distinguished scientist":

Why do most writers take on social opinions which would have been thought uncivilized at the time of the Plantagenets? Wasn't that true of most of the famous writers of the twentieth century—Yeats, Pound, Wyndham Lewis—nine out of ten of those who have dominated literary sensitivity in our time? Weren't they not only politically silly, but politically wicked? Didn't the influence of all they represent bring Auschwitz that much nearer?

Snow scolds Ruskin, William Morris, Thoreau, Emerson and D. H. Lawrence for their rebellion against the Age of Science: "They tried various fancies, which were not in effect more than screams of horror."

I dislike quoting Snow when he talks nonsense or endorses other people's nonsense. (When I was younger I enjoyed his novels and in 1941 wrote a rave review of *The Masters* in *The Bell*.) As an Irishman

who knew Yeats, I can only gasp when the great Irish poet is linked
with Auschwitz.

Snow's lecture caused tremendous interest. It was published and
many times reprinted. There was a three-week-long correspondence
in *The Spectator*, most of it favourable to Snow. He was thinking on
popular lines. When he wrote his novels he was Charles Snow, then
he became Sir Charles, and finally Lord Snow.

Only F. R. Leavis, professor of English literature at Cambridge,
reacted violently. He delivered and later printed a lecture furiously
attacking Snow, denouncing him as few leading writers had been
denounced before. He, too, was printed in *The Spectator* and there
was much comment, most of it hostile.

Snow [writes Leavis] takes inertly the characteristic and disastrous confusion of
the civilization he is trying to instruct.

He is intellectually as undistinguished as it is possible to be.

He thinks he has literary culture and scientific culture. In fact he has neither.

He rides on an advancing swell of cliché without a glimmer of what creative
literature is or what it signifies.

Who will assert that the average member of a modern society is more fully
human or alive than an Indian peasant?

As a novelist he doesn't exist. He can't be said to know what a novel is.

Leavis is an ardent champion of D. H. Lawrence, and, possibly, compared to Lawrence, Snow as a novelist is negligible.

Leavis mentions the Indian because Snow had a detailed plan
for rescuing the poorer peoples of the world by means of a scientific
revolution. He thought, for instance, that the United States and Britain should educate ten or twenty thousand scientific specialists "to
the level of Part 1 Natural Science or Mechanized Science Tripos"
and send them to India, Africa and Southeast Asia to help industrialize the inhabitants and lever them out of their pre-scientific stagnation.

How could Snow fail to see that the transportation of 6 million
Jews to the camps was, like the atom bomb, among the most sensational of science's achievements and that, in the international field,
science is more often used as an instrument of hatred than of neighbourly love? Think of the export of arms to Iran and to the Contras
in Nicaragua, and indeed of the great build-up of armaments all over
the globe.

He was surely driven to entertain these visions, more fantastic than the dreams of William Morris, by his knowledge that science was in fact irresistible and had enormous potentialities for good and evil, which only the men of traditional culture, if they accepted it and understood it a little, might be able to control. If they know a little about genetics, for example, they might be able to monitor and arrest the appalling experiments of the geneticists, which now only religious leaders with the wisdom and authority of the pre-scientific centuries behind them can forbid. They might have persuaded the Americans to industrialize Vietnam (if the Vietnamese wanted to be industrialized) rather than devastate it. But at present the average man of letters knows nothing of science and most scientists are culturally illiterate. Snow says that the average scientist, when one tries to probe what books he'd read, would modestly confess, "Well, I've tried a bit of Dickens." Snow himself must have guessed that the gulf between the Two Cultures is unbridgeable.

Has any decade seen so much sophisticated science-promoted violence as the 1980s? All over the world, in small countries and large ones, men who could not invent a popgun themselves have access to the newest and most lethal weapons. In Ireland the IRA get their arms from Libya and pay for them by kidnapping the owners of supermarkets (the ransom is always paid and then lied about). Where do the Libyans get their arms from? Who knows? A brisk trade goes on all round the world and the great powers are helpless to end it.

For Mauriac, the eighteenth-century dream of a future enlightened by the discoveries of science died at Drancy. In England, Aldous Huxley and George Orwell had earlier predicted all sorts of horrors. In his book *The Revolt of the Masses* (1932) the Spaniard Ortega y Gasset had analyzed what was happening much more accurately: "Technicism, in combination with liberal democracy, had engendered the Mass Man. . . . Modern science has handed over the command of public life to the intellectually commonplace." Observe the calibre of the world leaders of 1987.

Snow would have none of this. "The scientific edifice of the physical world is in its intellectual depth, complexity and articulation the most beautiful and wonderful work of the mind of man." In fact beauty is in the eye of the beholder. A primrose by the river's brim is just as likely to dazzle it as the structure of the haemoglobin molecule. All nature can be seen as beautiful.

According to Snow, let the Two Cultures but unite and educate those twenty thousand Mechanical Science Tripos men, and the gap between the rich and the poor will be bridged, overpopulation checked and the atomic war averted.

Most thinking men stand midway between the despair of Orwell and Mauriac, from which only the grace of God can rescue us, and the twenty thousand Tripos men, but believe that God and the Tripos men are slowly converging. Though they might express themselves differently, they would concur with the prayer which Major Cooper, the heroic astronaut, composed on his seventeenth orbit round the earth; it ends:

Help us in future space endeavours to show the world that democracy really can compete and still is able to do things in a big way and is able to do research development and conduct new scientific and technical programmes.

Be with all our families. Give us guidance and encouragement and let them know that everything will be okay. We ask in Thy name. Amen.

Though the joint session of Congress to which this prayer was read approved of it, a Hindu about to be industrialized might complain that life is more complex than Major Cooper and Charles Snow believed. A certain intellectual simplicity is the price that has to be paid for irrigation and tractors and freedom from famine and disease. An idea that has to travel far by modern means and circulate freely among alien people must, like an air passenger's luggage, be very meagre indeed.

In spite of that, most men would sooner believe in the healing powers of scientific research and technology than accept François Mauriac's counsel of despair.

But the true answer of the scientific optimist to Mauriac will not, I think, be found by Major Cooper in outer space or by those twenty thousand Tripos men. Should one not consider the question of size and whether we really have "to do things in a big way"?

Anti-Semitism, the idea which killed the Children of Drancy, was small and old and had existed for centuries in small pockets all over Europe. If humane ideals had been cultivated as assiduously as technical ones it would long ago have died without issue in some Lithuanian village. But science gave it wings and swept it by aeroplane and wireless and octuple rotary machines all over Europe and even lodged it in Paris, the cultural capital.

No one likes thinking on these lines. Yet observe how even pity can become helpless and sometimes destructive when it is divorced from deep personal concern and becomes a public matter. Public pity forms committees, sends tinned meat, secures entry visas, but the beating of its collective heart can be heard from miles away and it is easily eluded. Those in charge of the children eluded it by taking them to Auschwitz. It was to dodge public pity that the children were torn from their mothers and travelled alone or with doomed strangers. The mothers, when their future first became known, preferring death for their children to the lonely fate they foresaw for them, had started to throw them down from the tops of buildings. They would have continued to do this from the railway carriage windows and the dead or dying bodies might have roused some dormant committee into action in France or Germany or Poland.

Something similar was happening in Free Europe. As the funds of the refugee committees swelled, the price of liberty for a Jew went higher and higher. The compassion of the Allies, turned into cash, could be used against them. In 1944 Allied pity could have saved a million Jews in return for 100,000 trucks, but the trucks would have been used against Russia and so divided the Allies and resuscitated the latent anti-Semitism of the Russians. Looking at the matter in the large way it was better even for Jewry as a whole that a further million Jews should die.

Because of these complexities the Children of Drancy will always remain shadowy figures, and as nursery symbols of the vast cruelty of the world we shall go on using Herod and the little princes and the Black Hole. These stories are educative because they are about wicked men who can be punished or at least reviled, and not about that Faceless and Mysterious Collective Iniquity against which we are powerless. It is not a satisfactory choice, all the same, because historians now think that Herod never massacred the Innocents and that Richard Crookback never smothered the princes and that Surajah Dowlah thought the Black Hole was properly ventilated, whereas no one denies what happened to the Children of Drancy.

It is because we do things in the big way that the Wicked Man has now become so elusive and almost an abstraction. The chain of responsibility lengthens every day; we can think of it as an immense row of Part 1 Science Tripos graduates holding hands across the earth and linking together the triumphs of civilization to a depth of savage misery which the Aztecs, because they never discovered the wheel, could not inflict upon their victims. Snow mentions with approval a prototype of these Tripos men, a Prussian called Siemens, a pioneer in electrical engineering over a hundred years ago. I prepared this paper by the light of electricity that was brought from the great dam at Ardnacrusha on the river Shannon by Messrs. Siemens a generation ago; each bulb had "Siemens, made in Germany" printed on it. In this way Siemens helped to modernize Ireland, but Ireland was only one link in a long chain. In November 1932 Karl von Siemens used his wealth and influence to bring Hitler to power, and later his firm installed the electricity at Auschwitz, where of course it was not used just for reading lamps and making toast. There too, as at Lublin, Siemens set up factories for the employment of slave labour, while for their factory at Berlin Haselhorst they bought seven hundred women from the SS at Ravensbrück at four to six marks a head. The directors of Siemens were on the American list of German industrialists to be prosecuted at Nuremberg, but probably they were all humane and agreeable men belonging to the upper, beneficent end of the long chain; anyway, the charges against them were dropped. On the other hand, Ezra Pound, who had, on his own responsibility and not as a link in a chain, given much foolish praise to the Fascists, was punished and arraigned. Yet he had never killed or enslaved anybody.

It will always be so. A mischievous poet is like a thorn in the finger. He can be pulled out. But the mischief that results from a concentration of Tripos men is like disseminated sclerosis. And that is another reason why we talk so little about the Children of Drancy.

Charles Snow was surely right when he said that most literary intellectuals are "natural Luddites." I think he meant that they continue to worry when worry is useless. Ruskin, Morris, Thoreau, Lawrence, all repudiated the new world to which engineer Siemens was devoting his genius, but even a century ago it was hard already to contract out while now it is all but impossible. Should I read by candlelight because the firm that gave me electricity illuminated also the last agony of the Children of Drancy? I don't think so. I am less frightened of science than I am of that doctrine of the Mystery of Iniquity, which is to many the only consolation left now that there is no traffic on the road to Brook Farm, and New Harmony is sealed off. The Mystery of Iniquity has its roots in despair, but wickedness would no longer be mysterious if the chains of responsibility were shorter and science, which lengthened those chains, must be forced to go into reverse and shorten them.

Fortunately there are still small communities where the Wicked Man is not yet woven so scientifically into the fabric of society that he cannot be extracted without stopping the trains and fusing the electric light. It is not a coincidence that two small countries, Denmark and Bulgaria, stemmed the flow to Auschwitz better than any of their more powerful neighbours on the continent. Apart from size the two countries have nothing in common. The Bulgars are primitive, the Danes a highly sophisticated people. They are no doubt individually as wicked as the rest of us, but wickedness still has a name and an address and a face. When the rumour, a false one, went round Sofia that the government intended to deport its Jews, the citizens demonstrated outside the Palace and blocked the roads to the railway station. In Denmark on the night of 1 October 1943, when the Jews heard they were to be rounded up, each family knew which Danish family was prepared to hide them. Very few were caught. At the Gare d'Austerlitz the Children of Drancy were surrounded by the most civilized and humane people in Europe, but they were scarcely less isolated and abandoned than when they queued up naked for their "shower bath" in the Polish forest.

But I must answer the charge made by Snow's scientist that W. B. Yeats "brought Auschwitz nearer," because by focussing his mind on distant horizons Snow failed to see what was under his nose. Yeats deliberately chose the small community, moving his heart and his body and as much as he could of his mind from London to Ireland, his birthplace. For him and a dozen other well-known Irish writers Ireland had been a larger Brook Farm, a refuge whose walls were built not by some transcendental theory but by history and geography. For a few years our most parochial period became also our most creative. If there was in Yeats a Fascist streak it derived from his disillusionment with the drab unheroic Ireland in which the dreams of the visionaries of 1916 had ended. He complained that "men of letters lived like outlaws in their own country." When he saw that Irish Fascism promised to be as drab and demagogic as Irish democracy, he rapidly backpedalled and rewrote the song he had composed for the Blue Shirts, making it so fantastic that no political party could sing it. He led the campaign against the Irish censorship and in everything he did and said he was a champion of intellectual and moral and social freedom.

In all this he was an isolated figure and even in Ireland the range of his influence was very small. But in my opinion personal and parochial efforts like his did form a real obstruction on the road to Auschwitz, whereas its traffic was never once interrupted by conventional weapons.

The courage of the astronauts, the talents of the twenty thousand Tripos men are needed, but they must break down, link by link, those long chains of atomized guilt with which the Children of Drancy were strangled.

Postscript

The Children of Drancy were not totally forgotten in France. On 5 November 1978 a programme on the last days of Marshal Pétain was to be screened. It was abruptly withdrawn and a film on the Renaissance Pope Clement VII was substituted. The reason was that there had been a remarkable national re-examination of conscience in France due to an interview published in *L'Express* with the eighty-year-old Darquier, the Vichy government's Commissioner for Jewish Affairs, whom I have mentioned already. Despite the kindly intentions towards the Children of Drancy with which he has been credited, he had deported 75,721 French Jews to German concentration camps, including the Children. He was so virulent an anti-Semite that even the Germans were surprised by his zeal. He escaped to Spain and was condemned to death in his absence but this was soon forgotten. After a pause he changed his name to d'Arquier de Pellepoix* and, an elegant figure with a monocle, he became a welcome guest in the cocktail circles of Franco's Spain. It was here that the enterprising correspondent of *L'Express* contacted him thirty-three years after the war was over. He was a sick man crippled by hardening of the arteries, but he still enjoyed the protection of many leading figures, military and political, and he met the correspondent's enquiries with amused condescension. The 6 million concentration-camp deaths, he declared, were a Jewish invention. "They were all of them exported to new homes in Central Europe," he said. "The only victims of the Auschwitz gas ovens," he added, "were fleas." (I suppose he meant that their clothes were fumigated in preparation for their new life.) He refused to look at the photographs of the piles of gas-chamber victims. "Jewish fakes!" he exclaimed.

The whole of France was moved by the new revelations. President Giscard d'Estaing and Prime Minister Barre warned about the treatment of their Nazi past on the television screen and the press. Simone Weil, the Minister of Health, was profoundly stirred. She had been deported to Auschwitz with her family at the age of fourteen. "It is the first time since the war," she said in the National Assembly,

---

*He did not have to do even this much. Max Ophuls's documentary film *Le Chagrin et la Pitié* shows him in 1940, proudly greeting General von Streicher under his full name.

"that anyone has dared to go so far." There were pictures of Auschwitz and the other death camps shown on television and in the press. There was a clamour to have Darquier extradited. There was much indignation that French television refused to acquire the American series *Holocaust*. "Too expensive," one network said, and an artist, Marek Halter, opened a fund for private donations to contribute to the cost.

Then the public prosecutor, acting on orders from the Minister of Justice, opened a new case against Darquier for "defence of war crimes and incitement to racial hatred." But Spain has never extradited political offenders to France, and time had run out under the twenty-year statute of limitations.

The Writer as
Independent Spirit[*]

1966

The theme of the recent PEN Congress at New York was "The Writer as Independent Spirit." Differently expressed, that has been the theme or subtheme of many of its congresses. PEN was started in 1921 by a literary lady from Cornwall, one of those serious provincials whom the salaried broiler-fowl of letters often call culture vultures. She interested Galsworthy and he interested H. G. Wells and Anatole France, and many writers were recruited from the small new nations who felt that their emerging cultures were threatened. Wells himself was a militant crusader, and as the war approached, the congresses assumed an international importance. More and more delegates walked out of more and more meetings, and Wells himself was turned out of Australia for speaking disrespectfully about "the head of a great and friendly power." (It was in this way that Premier Lyons described Adolf Hitler.)

It was not long before imitations of PEN with quite contrary aims sprang up everywhere and sapped its strength. To match the Institut Français, the Russians had VOKS, the Germans had the Deutsches Haus, the British had the British Council and so on. Money and prestige and ready-made audiences were to be had for the asking, and many writers who had supported PEN defaulted to the BBC or the British Council or their continental equivalents. H. G. Wells attacked these renegades at a PEN meeting in Stockholm, much as Julien Benda had done before him.

---

*An essay written after Butler's participation in the International PEN Club Congress, New York, June 1966.—ed.

I'll be damned if I lend myself to any government propaganda. Some of the writers who succumb are fascinated by the idea of effective intrigue; some are bribed by simple flattery and the importance of semi-official touring; some are simpletons and believe that what they say will be noted, respected and honoured. But the reality of the case is that any writer, artist or teacher of repute who allows himself to be put on a wire and dangled in this fashion, according to the narrow ideas of some Director of Propaganda, Herr Goebbels, Lord Perth, Lord Lloyd or what not, fails to grasp his real significance in the world. He is getting into low company. He is falling short of the essential aristocracy of his profession.

Since then no writer has dominated letters as Wells did in the 1920s and 1930s or would dare to speak in the same way. We have travelled very far from Wells in forty years, but has it been in the right direction? When I first met PEN some twenty years ago, it seemed to me a very timid and opportunist organization. When the International Meeting was held in Dublin, I suggested that Dr. Churchin of Zagreb be invited. A friend of Galsworthy and Wells, he had been a great liberal editor and one of the earliest supporters of PEN. He had visited Horace Plunkett in Dublin. Surely he was an obvious choice. No, he could not be invited; he came from a Communist country.

Yet PEN is now anything but moribund. There were many lively rows in New York, many angry but fruitful confrontations, many startling diagnoses of our present literary paralysis. There was much friendliness and sociability.

In 1966 the greatest threat to the "independent spirit" no longer seems to come from totalitarian governments. It is true that there were Catalan and Ukrainian delegates with long lists of imprisoned and persecuted writers and convincing evidence that Madrid and Moscow are trying to destroy their language and their literature. But these are external wounds. The disease that may prove mortal is internal, and Arthur Miller, Saul Bellow, Elmer Rice and many others tried to diagnose it.

Much that they said we have all heard before. Unlike generals and clergymen, writers have no set forms of words, litanies or exhortations by which they can remind each other of unchanging difficulties and duties. When one writer says something the others already know, they yawn and often shout him down. So I missed most of what Elmer Rice had to say about the commercial exploitation of the writer, his subjection to the administrator, the editor, the talks director. It was detailed and factual, but when I asked a leading member of PEN why he was forced back to his seat clutching a half-read manuscript, she replied, "It's true enough but he said it all fourteen years ago." There may have been another cause for irritation. Many writers have been forced to sell their "independent spirit" at a good price, and the well-fed slave does not like to be reminded of his slavery.

Saul Bellow offered a more original diagnosis and was listened to with rapture. He said that the prophets of the 1920s who had believed that under mass culture we were approaching an era of unrelieved stupidity, had proved to be wrong. Intellectuals had not been liquidated. On the contrary, millions of college graduates "have been exposed to high culture":

We have at present a large literary community and something we can call, *faute de mieux*, a literary culture, in my opinion a very bad one. Modern literature is not scorned as it used to be, but taught, and in this way more effectively sterilized. There are clear signs that the university intellectuals are trying to appropriate literature for themselves, taking it away from the writers. They talk about it, they make careers out of it, they become an elite of it. It is their capital, their material. . . . They seem to have it both ways. Our most respected men of letters have adopted the *Wasteland* outlook and share the distaste of modern classic writers for Western civilization. They think themselves the only heirs of the lonely and struggling pioneers, the Joyces, the Rimbauds, the Lawrences. But they are very well off. They have money, influence, dental care for their children, jet holidays in Europe, even yachts.

Yachts? I think these yachting cognoscenti must be a special American phenomenon, for the Americans on the platform looked delighted.

Arthur Miller in his presidential address also stressed the huge price the intellectual now pays for the esteem in which he is held: "It is because they are important that so many people work to regulate them. That is why in just about every country there is censorship and book burning. PEN's Writers in Prison Committee rarely lacks customers."

One morning was devoted to the relatively cheerful theories of Marshall McLuhan. Recent inventions are undermining mass culture and may replace it by the culture of the group. By means of Xerox, for example, men may become their own publishers. Megalopolitan bureaucracy will disintegrate and mankind will be "retribalized." The audience was entertained but not convinced.

In the meantime it is clear that the propaganda value of writers is appreciated. The representatives of Eastern Europe may have paid for their tickets to New York but only satisfactory ones will have got visas. What about the delegates from South Korea? As many came as from Spain and Italy combined, and they brought with them two fine literary journals in the English language. Had they come from North Korea, someone would have accused China of exploiting the PEN Club for political purposes. As it was, no one said anything that might offend our kind and hospitable hosts. And in any case it is better to have a delegate dangling on a wire than no delegate at all. Six dull-sounding men had agreed to come from the U.S.S.R. and then, with a unanimity rare in writers, had all changed their minds. Why? Some said it was because David Carver, the International Secretary, had been to Moscow to appeal for André Sinyavsky and Yuli Daniel* and had incited many branches to send protests to the Union of Writers in Moscow. Others said it was because Valery Tarsis had been invited.

Tarsis is an enigmatic man. In the U.S.S.R. he had been a vociferous critic of Communism, and when he started publishing his work across the frontier, he had been shut up in an asylum in Russia. Then he was let out again at the very moment when Sinyavsky and Daniel were being persecuted. Now here he was in New York bawling to the PEN Club at the top of his voice against the Soviets. He attacked the Nobel Prize committee for its award to the Soviet writer Sholokhov, he attacked the Chilean delegate, Pablo Neruda, who was a Communist. He screamed that he wanted not a cold war against Russia but a hot war! At this point there were signs of embarrassment, and he asked the chairman to explain that he was only speaking figuratively. He caused a bad impression, for everyone had liked Neruda, a great poet who had given a modest and stimulating address. A Bulgarian, Mme. Mileva, and a Hungarian, M. Boldizsar, replied to Tarsis in an incisive and well-mannered way. Some suggested that Tarsis is a Soviet agent, but the evidence is that he is a sincere and courageous man and that he owes his liberty to the fact that he is so hysterical no one is likely to believe him.

One evening we abandoned the official programme and went to a Joyce symposium on the West Side. It seemed to confirm the worst of Bellow's forebodings. A delegate from Brazil read an extract from

---

*In February 1966 the writers Sinyavsky and Daniel had been sentenced to several years' hard labor for having willingly allowed their "anti-Soviet" literary works to be published abroad. The appeals against this were fruitless.—ed.

his translation of *Finnegans Wake* into Portuguese and a university graduate gave a discourse of appalling aridity on the paper, the print, the folios, editions and textual alterations of *Ulysses*. Joyce has become an institution, of course, a source of "dental care for the children of professors." *Finnegans Wake* is a cry of despair made melodious, for Joyce had the genius to extract music from the smashing of crockery, the squeals of a rabbit caught in a trap. He is the least international of writers, the least capable of being translated into Brazilian Portuguese. The American student read some lines from the end of *Finnegans Wake* about, I think, the wanderings of the Liffey for "moyles and moyles." Involuntarily I thought of "Silent, O Moyle . . ." and a moment later Padraic Colum remarked, "It just occurred to me that Joyce was thinking of 'Silent, O Moyle, be the roar of thy waters!' " Yes, of course, he was. The book is built up from the spongy sediment of an Irish upbringing, from echoes of things we all heard or half heard when we were growing. "Moyles and moyles" can never be translated into Portuguese, and the main international significance of *Finnegans Wake* is that a great writer, caught like the rest of us in a trap, gave up shouting for help and hummed to himself euphoniously instead.

How Joyce would have despised the PEN Club and H. G. Wells, who believed in shouting. And Sinyavsky, if free, would also have been, I think, an abstainer. For he believes, like Beckett, that a sense of the grotesque, the absurd, the fantastic will bring us closer to truth than science and reason can. All the same, there is a rumour that next year, to celebrate the fiftieth anniversary of the Revolution, Sinyavsky and Daniel will be released from prison. If this happens, the PEN Club can take a small but honourable part of the credit.

Little K

1967

Preface
1988

I wrote this in 1967 under the impact of a tragedy that was still fresh in my mind. My opinions have not changed and, though more people share them, it has not become easier to express them. I have only once seen my granddaughter and, as she lives the other side of the Atlantic, I am unlikely to see her again. She has passed from infancy to childhood, to adolescence, to maturity. Her body has changed but her mental age remains the same. She is one of nature's mistakes and left to herself nature might have taken her away, but though often disastrous experiments to improve on nature are made, we seldom trust her to do the best for us.

Yet there seems to have been an unexpected change of policy in the United States. Baby Jane Doe, the three-year-old child of Long Island parents, was born severely retarded with many physical handicaps. Spinal surgery would prolong her life but would not correct her retardation. Her parents, after consulting doctors, clergy and social workers, rejected the operation. Thereupon a Vermont lawyer, a right-to-life activist, took the child's parents to court to force an operation. The Court of Appeals denounced his suit as offensive and supported Baby Jane's parents.

The Reagan administration then took up the cause, but in June 1985 the Supreme Court rejected its appeal. There will be very few parents of such children who will not rejoice at the rebuff to the administration.

A further decision of the Supreme Court invalidated a 1982 federal rule which required that hospitals which received federal money should post up notices urging staff members to report any denial of treatment to handicapped newborns. On behalf of the majority in the Supreme Court, Justice Stevens declared that the reason why newborns, such as Baby Jane Doe, do not always get special medical treatment is not because hospitals discriminate against them but because their families do not want them to have that treatment. Federal law, he held, does not require hospitals to treat handicapped children without parental consent or require parents to give it.

It was suggested that there should be hospital-based infant care review committees, on which there should be clergy and community representatives as well as legal and medical experts to review such cases. *The New York Times* ended its report succinctly: "That puts the problem where it belongs: out of Big Brother's hands and into those of concerned committees."

The Supreme Court has in this way many times proved itself to be the protector of the rights of the citizen against the state, the one against the many. The Reagan administration thrives on broad generalizations: Soviet Russia is an evil empire, Libya a terrorist state, Nicaragua a Communist threat to her neighbours. If we look at a very small map of the earth and interpret it by the very big headlines in the daily press, this is quite a normal view of the world. But 99 percent of its inhabitants live out of reach of the headlines, and their deepest feelings, their strongest convictions, are often incommunicable till someone appears like the parents of Baby Jane Doe with the will and the skill to articulate them and present them to the Supreme Court. It has often struck down callous and cruel decisions of the Reagan Justice Department, which, inspired perhaps by Southern fundamentalists, tried to legislate in the spheres which the Founding Fathers held to be the province of private judgment.

LITTLE K

In order to treat this subject objectively I had thought of calling them A, B, C, D and E. C, D and E would be my three granddaughters, A and B their parents, but I find I cannot reach such heights of detachment and that I must call them by their true initials, J, D, C, S and K.

I do not see them very often, for they live in America. C is five years old and rather serious. She does not say very much, preferring to nod for "Yes" and shake her head for "No," but the whole time she is remembering and judging. I have an idea that when she grows up she will reject a great deal that most people accept. I feel very close to her and wish I could be beside her when the time comes for her to make decisions. S, who is still only two, is very different. She accepts everything and everybody and flings herself laughing and chattering into the arms of those she knows. C and S both remember K, my youngest granddaughter, of course, but there is always so much happening that they do not often ask about her. C liked to be photographed holding her but K went away when she was two months old and they will, I think, soon accept her absence as permanent. [So little happens to K that once at least I shall give her her real name, Katherine Synolda (1987).]

On my way to see K this morning, I walked through the park at Yonkers and tried unsuccessfully to find the Doric temple from which you are supposed to see the broad sweep of the Hudson River and the Palisades beyond. The park is laid out so as to make you forget that the largest city in the world stretches all around it. I walked down woodland paths, where wild copses of acacia and fir were choked and bent with their burdens of honeysuckle, and I came at last to a romantically ruined manor house with sagging roof and rotting window frames. The park is a place in which to relax, to tear yourself away from the complex and sophisticated problems of the city, where everything is pulled down before it has time to grow old, and plastic flowers outnumber real ones a hundredfold. So nature is allowed to half strangle the shrubberies and tear the manor house apart. But, in fact, you cannot walk very far without being reminded of the well-organized sorrows and joys of the city. At one end there is a Cardiac Centre and the jungle slides away from it deferentially towards the river; the rough paths compose themselves into gentle gradients suitable for wheeled chairs and cautiously shuffling heart cases. There is a smooth lawn with rectangular panels of salvia and petunia as neat and tended as temperature charts.

At the other, merrier end of the park, the derelict manor house, embedded in kalmia and rhododendron, has a notice on it: NO WEDDING PHOTOGRAPHS TO BE TAKEN HERE.

If you find relaxation here, it is by withdrawing and pretending; it is that fragile sort of peace which the gravely disturbed find in barbiturates.

East of the park and higher still above the Hudson is the long, low white house where K lives. I met D there and together we went to her room. She is with ten other babies and she has her name on her cot. She has a sweet baby mouth and chin and large blue eyes and above it a high domed forehead, which would have been lovely too were it not for the sharp ridge that runs down it from her skull. She has, I am told, agenesis of the corpus callosum. That is to say the central part of her brain has not developed and, therefore, the optic nerve too is defective. The whites of those beautiful eyes are tinged with blue and she is all but blind.

"But look," said a kind nurse, "she blinks when I wave my hand. I think she can focus a little too."

K did indeed blink, but it seemed to me that she just felt the draught of the nurse's hand.

D unclasped her hand, which was folded up like a bud, and showed me the palm.

"That's the simian line going straight across. You meet it in mongols. But it's not a sure test, as she isn't a mongol. I showed it to an obstetrician and he just held up *his* hand at me. He has the simian line too. All the other children here are mongols. Look at their lower eyelids! Look at the way their ears are set—very low!"

The nurse leant over and touched a small tin box attached to the cot and a tiny tinkle came from it.

"She loves her little musical box," she said.

There was a pause while we watched for a sign that K was loving it but none came. The nurse closed it by saying, "She never cries. She's so good." (Later D told me that, when K was born, she did not cry, like other babies, but was unnaturally quiet.)

"Will she ever be able to walk?" I asked.

"Oh, why not? Of course!" she replied encouragingly.

"And talk?"

"Oh, I expect so. But you must ask the doctor." She was embarrassed and broke off to greet a little boy who trotted into the room.

"Hello, Sammy! Back again?" and to us she said, "Sammy is the brightest of our little mongols."

I asked to see the older children and she took us into a sunny courtyard, where ten or twelve of them were playing. The swings were soaring up and down and a big ball was rolling about. A tall, almost handsome boy in a jersey with BEATLE printed on it rushed up to us jabbing his left shoulder and shouting something. It sounded like "Resident! Resident!" "No, we're not residents here," D said, "we're just here on a visit." "Resident! Whi How!" the boy bawled on, and we grasped that he was saying that he was the President of the United States. A girl of twenty with a broad blue band round her head, which was flopping from side to side, charged up to us. A swollen tongue stuck out of her mouth and she barked at us something we could not understand.

"Do they ever quarrel?" I asked the nurse.

"Oh, indeed they do!" She smiled at the innocence of my question. Then we went to the room of the totally unmanageable. "Don't you come!" I said to D but he insisted on going with me. These children cannot be given toys, because they destroy them. Some were incontinent and some had limbs that were frenetically askew. Television was on non-stop. ("They love their television," said the nurse.) Many of them had dreary commonplace delusions like the Beatle boy, taken from television or secondhand from the newspapers. One or two had some droll hallucination which two months ago I would have found touching and even entertaining.

As we went down the passage we passed the open door of a small room and in it I saw a charming-looking woman with greying hair. Her husband was with her and they were talking to a young defective. ("He gets fits," explained the nurse, "that's why he has the black eye.") As the mother saw us she turned to the boy with a gay and loving laugh. He looked unresponsively back and I knew that her animation was directed at us rather than at him. She was telling us that she was ready to do her part in trying to lift the great curtain of sadness that hung over us all.

When we reached the hall two merry little girls dashed past us, with their parents behind. "I know who you've come to see!" said the nurse, bending down to them. "Yes, Lucy! Lucy!" they shouted, and tore ahead. The nurse smiled at us as though to say, "You see, it's not all sadness. Children take it quite as a matter of course."

But I think it is all sadness, unnecessary sadness, from which the world has piously averted its eyes. The realities are concealed from us by a labyrinth of platitude as specious and unnatural as the honeysuckle jungle at Yonkers. There is not a child in that large establishment whose parents have not at one time thought what they dare not articulate: "I wish that my child would die!" And many, perhaps most, are still thinking it and secretly praying for it.

MME. VANDEPUT AND THE NINE CATHOLICS

As we drove home, D told me that one in ten of all the children in the United States is defective. I thought he must be exaggerating but when I got back I turned to the appendix of the book about the trial at Liège of Suzanne Vandeput, who killed her armless "thalidomide baby." The nine gently disapproving Catholic authors of this book, doctors and priests, give statistics of the mental defectives in France. They are about 7 percent of the population. How many of these, I thought, can be as well cared for as our little K, surrounded from babyhood with toys and paint boxes and swings, with practised smiles and laughter that is innocent or lovingly simulated?

The nine French Catholics are thinking of that too. Their book is learned, tender, imaginative. Not in one sentence do they denounce Suzanne; she was wrong, of course, they say, but they see her sin against a dark background of callousness, stupidity and smugness, and they recognize that science has transformed the human scene and totally changed the nature of our problems: "The new drugs," writes Father Roy, "can be as dangerous as they are salutary. The number of abnormal children is increasing; the doctors are opposing the process of natural selection by allowing beings to exist which are in no way human."

They are aware that the support that Suzanne Vandeput received from press and public in Liège and beyond was not only sentimental and unreflecting but scholarly as well. Father Roy quotes, with bafflement and sadness rather than horror, two French doctors, Barrère and Lalou, who present a humanist point of view:

Our age has effected so many transformations on man that the moral problems raised can no longer be answered by the ancient formulae. It is almost a new reality that we must learn to accept and mankind will need many years to construct a new humanism founded on the new man. Euthanasia seems to be one of the keystones of this future edifice.

The fact that this is quoted without horror shows that the nine writers are aware how unresponsive we have mostly become to the ecclesiastical anathemas of the past. With the advent of totalitarian and nuclear war the old Christian taboos on killing have fallen into such confusion that one moral argument has now to support itself with ten practical ones. Most of their arguments are therefore addressed to the humane and farsighted rather than to the devout.

(1) Only one writer, Father Roy, uses an argument that a sceptic or a Protestant might find offensive, for he links the euthanasia of the defective with divorce as a source of bad examples. Divorce, he says, is not only a disaster for the children of broken marriages but it also influences others to part, who without this way of escape might have "risen above their selfishness" and "attained to a richer

marital understanding and love." But a non-Catholic could argue that divorce has brought as much relief as tension, as much joy as sadness, and that this is no argument at all.

(2) Father Beirnaert, S.J., predicts "personality disturbances" for the child whom Mme. Vandeput said she was going to bear in order to replace the armless child that she killed. It is right that we should reflect on such indirect psychological effects, but they are unpredictable. How can we judge their importance? One of the nine, Dr. Eck, speaks frankly of the marriages that were broken because of a defective birth, and the jealousy that normal children, brothers and sisters, sometimes feel because of the special love which a good mother will sometimes give to her defective child. All these things may happen. But love and wisdom can sometimes solve these problems, sometimes must recognize that they are insoluble.

(3) Dr. de Paillerets asks how can one decide that one malformation will justify infanticide, while another will not? How can we decide who will be unhappy, who not? Healthy people may be miserable and severely handicapped people may be cheerful.

(4) He asks how can we be sure that cures will not be discovered for defects that now seem irremediable?

(5) He says, if doctors, even in exceptional cases, were to become the auxiliaries of death rather than of life, would they not certainly lose the confidence of their patients? "Without this confidence medicine cannot exist." And he says that, since the time of Hippocrates in the fifth century B.C., this "unconditional respect for human life" has been obligatory. He quotes the Hippocratic oath, which all doctors are still obliged to swear.

(6) The sixth argument is very odd:

Infanticide [he says] puts a curb on the enthusiasm of those who through their research contribute to the increase of our knowledge, and on the enthusiasm of those who, devoting themselves to the care of the unfortunate children, now find that we are equivalently disowning them and regarding their work as unnecessary. Medicine needs support from all of us if it is to keep its essential dynamism.

It is possible that one day some instrument will be invented which will register human sympathy, warmth of feeling. Surely, if it was attached to Dr. de Paillerets as he wrote this, it would register zero. How otherwise can he think of a parent's agony in connection with the progress of medicine and the nursing profession? It rouses instantly the suspicion that it may be in the interests of geriatrics and allied studies that men are sometimes forced by doctors to live on beyond their natural span.

(7) The seventh argument also betrays a curious professional egoism, disguised as modesty. Dr. de Paillerets dreads the possibility of some kind of medical commission entrusted with the task of selecting infants for death. "What a terrible temptation is this for us to accept such a right over the life and death of others."

But what parents would ever grant to doctors such a right? It is a right that only those who love the child and are close to it could claim and exercise. The doctors' function should be a minor one. It should be little more than that which, under pressure, the Catholic bishops of Nazi Germany permitted when they decreed that Catholic doctors and social workers could report to the authorities those afflicted with ills calling for sterilization, provided they did not at the same time order or authorize sterilization. The operation was performed in scorn rather than love, and permission was granted with casuistry, but it is not impossible to imagine that religious men and doctors could, without casuistry and without scorn, help a parent in a sad decision.

Most of these seven arguments deal with problems that we meet every day and that are solved rightly or wrongly according to our instincts and knowledge. There are stresses and strains in family life which we can palliate but seldom elude. A great sadness will produce other sadness whatever we do. It seems to me that when Dr. de Paillerets considers these practical arguments against infanticide he has already despaired of defending the only absolutely compelling argument, which is that all killing is a mortal sin. He may have reflected that public opinion, like war, sometimes has the power to modify the most uncompromising dogma and that there was an absolute and peremptory quality about the support which the people of Liège gave to Mme. Vandeput.

PALLIATIVES

In our time there has been so much ecclesiastically condoned and sanctified killing that few clerics would nowadays have the effrontery to bring up again, without diffidence or qualification, that dishonoured and bamboozled old commandment, THOU SHALT NOT KILL. Father Roy condemns the doctor who simply repeats it and concerns himself not at all with the tragic situation of those who must cherish the helpless being which medical science has preserved for them. Left to herself nature would often have borne away the malformed child in a miscarriage or by some ordinary illness like measles to which, without inoculation, the often feeble defective child could have succumbed. The doctors feel a greater responsibility towards their profession than towards their patients. When a friend of mine with a defective child asked that it should not be inoculated he was told that he must not "tie the hands of the doctor."

The nine French priests and doctors are fully aware what a burden of responsibility they bear for what is happening. For the doctors save and prolong lives that are useless and unhappy and the priests mount guard over them with moral precepts. They urge upon their colleagues, in recompense, a devotion, a dedicated study, a depth of understanding, which is far beyond the reach of most men.

Dr. de Paillerets writes of the meagre, badly supported research which is being done on encephalopaths. In Paris it is often many years before the defective child can even be received into a specialized establishment. "It is our duty as doctors," he writes, "to expose this scandal. . . . The Liège trial has occurred but the real trial is yet to come and, if we do not act in this matter, our place will be in the first row of the accused."

And Father Roy, stressing the urgency, asks if we are prepared to postpone the laying down of new major roads till the specialized homes are provided. This question carries its own answer with it. No, we are not.

The nine Frenchmen also urge that the parents of the afflicted should form associations to discuss their common problems and share the burden. And Father Roy distinguishes between the "pity," a negative, egoistic thing which men are ready to show, and the "compassion" which is demanded of them and which forces them to share the sufferings of the afflicted and to act. He quotes Bernanos: "Modern man has a hard heart and tender guts." He weeps for the sufferings of others and winces at the thought of being involved in them.

Is there any likelihood that these generous ideals will ever be fulfilled? The next day, in search of enlightenment, I went uptown to see Dr. S, the obstetrician who had delivered K. He confirmed what I had suspected. There is no reality in these dreams of Father Roy. Dr. S is a kind and brilliant man but his talents have made him much sought after and there is no likelihood that he will ever desert his other patients in order to show more than perfunctory sympathy with the parents of defective children. Nor, as far as I know, has there been any "dedicated study," any researches into the origin of K's misfortune which might be helpful to others.

Then there is the question of parents' association. I learnt from one of the nurses in the home where K is that Dr. S himself has a mongol child there. Yet he never told J or D about him, though he, as a doctor, frequently handling our problems both in his home and in his profession, could have forwarded such an association more than anyone else. About this I do not feel I have any right to reproach him. We are all of us preternaturally sensitive about our defective children. For educated people they may represent a private anguish that is well nigh unshareable. This intense "privatization" of our problem (to use an American word) belongs to the Age of Scientific Organization, as does the increase in the number of abnormal children. The bourgeois, for the most part, live in small labour-saving flats and it is usually obvious, if not obligatory, that the defective child should go to an institution where he can receive "proper care." Though it may well be that the parents think of their child every hour of the day, they do not have to talk about him or constantly plan for him. Only rarely will talking help them. About this I understand Dr. S.

It was very different when I was a child. Our rector had a mongol daughter and the neighbours frequently took charge of her. (Father Roy would say that it was not half frequently enough.) She is looked after by her relations and I still see her sometimes, a woman of fifty. It is possible that our rare gestures of true "compassion" were largely neutralized by our chattering "pity." But even such small efforts as we made would now be difficult and unwanted. The compassion which Father Roy demands is not compatible with professionalism. Doctors, nurses and social workers must take their courses, earn salaries, go where they are told, and so must the clergy. Their lives are too full, too controlled for them to have any time for that total imaginative involvement which is compassion. There is no reality in these dreams of Father Roy. The revolution in men's behaviour which he desires cannot happen in a scientifically organized society. The position which he is trying to defend is based upon moral precepts which have lost their validity. The relief which he promised will never come.

I asked Dr. S what he thought of euthanasia and he said that Mme. Vandeput was wholly wrong. All life is better than all death. He was coming to believe that only in rare cases was even abortion justifiable.

"Are your objections religious?"

"If you mean am I a Catholic, the answer is no, but I believe in God."

He was surprised that I should know about his little boy and he told me that he had often longed for him to die but he no longer did so. He had wondered too whether he had been wrong in sending him to an institution.

I did not ask him why he had not told J that he was a fellow sufferer, as this might have comforted her a little. I now regret my shyness, as I believe his answer would have shown that our attitude towards the defective is now one of absolute negation. No trace remains of the old belief that they are in some way the special children of God.* They are just genetic mistakes which, since we cannot, like the Greeks, extinguish them, we must relegate to some place where they are no nuisance to society.

Dr. S's God is different from mine. Churchmen are now ready to admit into their ranks those who reject all historical certainties and see God and his son Christ as constructions of the mind by which the human imagination tries to express its revelation of the divine. This revelation varies from man to man. To me God is the assurance that the world of men is not purposeless or evil and that we can trust ourselves to it and that, when old laws lose their significance, new ones will slowly shape themselves to take their place. As for Christ, he is the assurance that a man can learn when and how to free himself from the power of the law, however strongly it may be reinforced with venerable traditions and popular approval. The show bread may have to be eaten, the sabbath profaned, the prostitute exalted. "GOD" is the promise that out of this disorder a better order will ultimately ensue.

---

*A friend of mine claims that this is untrue and that here in Ireland the Steiner movement is represented in the village communities at Duffcarrig and Ballaghtobin and other places. I have visited Ballaghtobin, which is in Co. Kilkenny, and know how dedicated men and women have devoted themselves to improving the lives of the handicapped adults. They think of the mentally defective as fellow individual spirits who have slipped sideways on the evolutionary ladder, but who command innate respect, dignity and potential. Some of the villagers among whom they live accept this and conclude that mongols, to whom in particular the movement addresses itself, are in the world to teach their busy "sane" fellow travellers the true value of brotherhood, love, acceptance. Hence they view them as "special" and inherit the children-of-God outlook. I appreciate but do not share this sentiment. [1988]

NATURAL LAW AND THE GREEKS

M y mention of the Greeks recalls to me that I have not answered one of the arguments (no. 5) used against Mme. Vandeput. It is medical rather than religious but seems to suggest, as the clergy do, that there is some sort of Natural Law at issue, which we neglect at our peril.

Dr. de Paillerets quotes the Hippocratic oath which doctors have considered binding upon them since the fifth century B.C.

I shall not give a homicidal drug to anyone, no matter who may ask me to do so, nor shall I initiate the suggestion that it be given.

. . . The least exception to the unconditional respect for human life would place the doctor in a position which he could not accept. It would curb the enthusiasm which is the prerequisite of progress in medical knowledge. Furthermore, it would destroy the confidence of the patients, without which there can be no Medicine.

But surely the oath is greatly misinterpreted and the historical foundations of medicine strangely misunderstood. The Hippocratic oath mainly concerned the Greek habit of administering poison to those condemned to death. Hippocrates considered it beneath the dignity of a doctor to become a paid executioner. Moreover the world in which Hippocrates practised gave a limited authority to the doctor in the matter of life and death. His duty was to cure those who wished to be cured, but he did not interfere with ancient practices. In his day and for a century or two afterwards, in all the city-states except Thebes, deformed or sickly children were exposed. Aristotle, a great admirer and younger contemporary of Hippocrates, thought the custom should be made law, for he writes: "With respect to the exposing or bringing up of children, let it be a law that nothing imperfect or maimed should be brought up." Plato gives the same advice to the lawgivers in his ideal republic. Is there any evidence that Hippocrates opposed what was a universal custom?

The Greek father could decide whether a child was to live or die, for the infant did not become "a member of the family" till he was formally presented some days after birth. Infanticide was not eugenic, though Plato and Aristotle would have treated it as such, for the father had a right to eliminate even a healthy infant whom he did not wish to rear, and this was freely exercised in the case of girl infants whose dowry might present a problem. The unwanted infant was placed in a cradle or pot and put in the corner of the marketplace, in the temple or wrestling ground. It might be picked up and reared by a stranger, so sometimes some objects of value were wrapped up with it. But the father had the right later to claim it after it had been reared, so the infant was usually left to die.

Only at Sparta was the absolute right of the parent over his children disputed, for the state would sometimes weed out, for eugenic or military reasons, sickly infants whom the parents had spared.

All this is very shocking to Christians, if Christians have not forfeited their right to be shocked at such things by their connivance at Auschwitz and Hiroshima, but some great classical scholars have shown sympathy. Of Greek infanticide Zimmern writes:

The Athenian had a traditional horror of violence and interfered, when he could, on behalf of the helpless. If he consented to exercise his immemorial right over his own offspring, he did so with regret for the sake of the city and his other children, because it was more merciful in the long run. We have no right to cast stones either at him or his fellows.

And Bernard Bosanquet writes in his *Companion to Plato's Republic*:

The high mortality of young children today suggests that we are superior to the ancients more in theory than in practice. . . . Can any race safely arrest selection? It is quite conceivable that the actual infant mortality on the ancient system might be less than ours at present.

Plato and Aristotle both had the pragmatic, society-centred religion of most modern scientists. They did not see in the eugenic infanticide, which they preached, anything incompatible with orthodoxy. After a sentence or two about infanticide Aristotle returns to the subject of childbirth and urges that for the sake of exercise and the tranquillity of mind which is favourable to successful parturition, the pregnant woman should walk to the temple every day and offer prayers to the gods who preside over matrimony.

All this has a callous, calculating sound. In our society our leading thinkers are more humane and imaginative, but Greek society itself was less cruel and impersonal and we have discovered new forms of physical agony and lonely introverted misery of mind of which the Greeks were incapable. The gulf between Plato or Aristotle and daily life at Athens was large, but not so large as that between, say, D. H. Lawrence and daily life at Nottingham, or the Bloomsbury group and Bloomsbury (it would be easy to discover some more modern and apposite antithesis), and I do not feel perverse or paradoxical in suggesting that there has been a real deterioration.

What are the principal forces that have drawn us away from the Greeks? First there is "science," which, looking for conformity in men, tends to impose it. It classifies all living things by their shared characteristics. It pares down those distinctions upon which personality is built and which defy classification. It achieves its best results by treating men as statistical units rather than as individual persons. Such methods are damaging to that flexibility of conduct on which Greek ethics is based.

Secondly there is professionalism, which claims exclusively for itself spheres of authority, fields of investigation and experiment, which were once open to ordinary men, parents, neighbours, friends.

Thirdly there is universal democracy, which aspires to offer to the whole multiracial, heterogeneous world laws which all will accept. That means boiling down into a simple code of Dos and Don'ts a vast complex of interlocking moralities deriving from very varied traditions and customs.

The Greek moralist or lawgiver always had in mind the small community in which public opinion could sometimes enforce the law, sometimes replace it. So occasionally Aristotle, instead of saying, "Let there be a law that . . . ," says instead, "Let it be held in utter detestation that . . ."

Today public opinion, manipulated by pressmen and politicians, has become so ignoble a thing that we distrust it and put our faith instead in the law. Its chief defect, its inflexibility, becomes in our sad circumstances a merit.

Finally there is Christian theology, which has shaped the law, so that even those who reject its dogma are still bound by it. Bosanquet, for example, argues that our respect for human life has been deepened by religious doctrines, even discredited ones, such as that concerning the fate of unbaptized children in the world to come.

Modern churchmen are evasive about the future world, its penalties and prizes, and tend to judge our actions in accordance with their conformity to something they call "Natural Law." But it seems to me that Greek custom was closer to nature than we are and that it is not "natural" for a doctor to insist on prolonging, by drugs and inoculations, the life of a defective child against the wishes of its parents. Bosanquet is surely justified in writing of the "immemorial right which a parent has over his own offspring."

In regard to infanticide I ought to add that the Greek practice had been inherited from primitive times. It can be traced among such primitive peoples as the anthropologists have investigated and it is usually linked with religion or food. The Aruntas of Australia suckle their infant children for several years and a new child whom the mother thinks she will be unable to rear is killed at birth. It is thought that the child's spirit goes back whence it came and can be born again. Twins are thought to be unnatural and are immediately killed.

Among the Todas of South India twins are also regarded with dismay and one of them is killed. Newborn female babies are sometimes laid in the mud for buffaloes to trample on. These practices are most prevalent among the priestly caste in the Nilgiri Hills where Western influence is weakest. Margaret Mead describes them as "the desperate expedients to which a simple people have to resort to fit their survival rate to their social structure. These practices are dying out but so are the Todas." She tells much the same story about the South Seas and the Far North, where the Eskimos practise female infanticide. And there is much in our own social history which is seldom remembered and is never written. An Irish friend of mine, herself the mother of a loved and cherished defective child, remembers as a girl being told how in her country neighbourhood a malformed infant was usually put at the end of the bed and left there unfed and untended till God, in his good time, should take it. I have never heard of this elsewhere or read of it but I believe it to be true.

No sensible person, of course, considers that primitive people can give us directives as to how to behave. We are not qualified to learn much from them or they from us. Yet there is a tendency to argue from the "natural law" which we are supposed to have inherited from the remote past. There is no such thing. The most that a traditionalist might claim is that in all times, lands, peoples, we can trace, however faintly, one constant passion, the distaste for cruelty, injustice, waste. It is sometimes a minority sentiment but, when held with tenacity, it invariably prevails.

Surely today any deeply concerned parent, grandparent, or friend would agree that we have to retreat from many strongly held convictions which we have inherited from the past, and that "desperate expedients" may have to be contemplated, if slowly and laboriously a new ethic and a new morality are to be built around our new convictions. How widely are these convictions shared? Am I just dreaming when I think that almost all those who have the same cause for sadness think as I do?

In *Le Dossier Confidentiel de l'Euthanasie*, Barrère and Lalou endorse what I have said about the attitudes of Greeks and Romans with quotations from Epicurus and Seneca. To them a man was the master of his own body and had a right to leave it when it could no longer give shelter and sustenance to his faculties. It was not till St. Augustine that suicide and euthanasia became the crimes which Christians hold them to be today. And even in Christian times devout men could think differently. St. Thomas More in the Second Book of *Utopia* wrote that when an Utopian was dying in incurable anguish, the priests and the magistrates exhorted him

Either to dispatche himselfe out of that payneful lyffe as out of a prison or a racke of tormente or elles suffer himselfe wyllinglye to be rydde oute of it by other . . . But they cause none suche to dye agaynste his wyll . . . He that killeth himselfe before that the pryestes and the counsel have allowed the cause of his deathe, him an unworthy they caste unburied into some stinkinge marrish.

And Francis Bacon had similar ideas.

As for the present state of the law in various countries I must depend as others have done on R. Raymond Charles's *Peut On Admettre l'Euthanasie?* The laws of Spain, Holland, Hungary, Italy, Poland, Norway, Denmark, Brazil treat with leniency those who kill from pity with the consent of their victim. Peru and Uruguay go further, for they permit the judge to grant exemption from all penalty where no selfish motive can be discovered. In Europe the Penal Code of Czechoslovakia arrives more cautiously at the same conclusion.

In the United States and the U.S.S.R the law has advanced and retreated. In 1906 the Ohio legislature passed the first reading of a law permitting a man who was dying painfully to summon a commission of four to judge his right to end his life. A few months later Iowa voted for a law of still greater latitude, for it embraced defective children and idiots. However, when Congress had to pronounce at Washington, its verdict was wholly hostile.

In the U.S.S.R. a law of 1922 which abolished the penalty for homicide whose motive was pity was repealed a few months later because of evidence that it was being abused.

Sometimes the law seems to nourish itself on its own vitals, developing without relation to what happens around it. In Nazi Germany in 1944, when the slaughter at Auschwitz was at its peak, a law was passed which prescribed the full legal penalties for those who from pity kill the incurable and the mentally deficient.

How then does it happen that in France and Britain, countries with long humanist traditions, no special exemption for those who kill from pity is embodied in the law? Is it perhaps that in these sophisticated countries there is an awareness that in human relationships there are zones in which a man may make his own terms with the Source of Law, whether he deems this to be God or the Natural Order, and that such a man needs no intermediary? Certainly in France, at least, euthanasia trials, despite the law, have usually ended with an acquittal or token punishment for those whose integrity is manifest.

CHRISTIANITY AND KILLING

Was there ever before so much mental confusion about the killing of men by men?

When does human life begin? There is the widest dispute. When does it end? Even that is not so clear as it once was. Granted that a man may kill in self-defence, is he also obliged to? And, if so, how many others is he obliged to defend by killing as well as himself? His family, his friends, his neighbours, his fellow citizens, his nation? And has he to kill on behalf of the friends of his friends and on behalf of the nations who are allies of his nation? And should he practise preventative killing? Should he in this way defend himself or his friends or his nation when they think they are threatened? Or might be threatened? And has he to kill people in order to bring about justice in the world, in the way that his elected representatives think best?

Wherever his duty may lie, what actually happens is always the same. The individual, till a man rushes at him with knife or gun, can kill nobody, not even himself. The state can force him to kill anybody, though his whole soul rebels against the killing, and the churches, because for their survival they have made their own pacts with the state, can give him no support in his rebellion. On the contrary they will support the state against him and often bring to bear all their supernatural sanctions against the individual, so it seems to him that he will be damned in the next world as well as in this if he does not kill those whom he neither fears nor dislikes.

Their clergy are kindly sensible men, anxious to preserve the venerable institutions which they serve and whose future is precarious. Therefore almost without exception they have interpreted the commandment THOU SHALT NOT KILL in the way that is most pleasing to secular authority. They have given their blessing to those that kill from fear and hatred, and they have condemned as sinners those who kill from love.

When I was thinking of this, *The New York Times* came in and I read of a seventeen-year-old boy in Detroit who had tried to kill himself with a stick of dynamite rather than go out to kill people of whom he knew nothing in Vietnam. In the adjoining paragraph I read how five hundred rabbis, American and Canadian, assembled in Toronto, had by a majority vote censured the Vietnam War and insinuated that its roots were largely commercial. Later on I read how other denominations had also debated the war, and, except for the Orthodox of America, had also by a majority censured it. In fact there can never again be a war whose "justice" is uncontested by religious men. It is a measure of their helplessness, their cowardice or their confusion of thought that they still continue to sanction war. They will still censure a bewildered boy for killing himself rather than become a killer. Should we censure them? I think not. They are caught, as we are, in a trap from which it is very hard to escape.

Yet the churches still consider themselves to be the unflinching champions of the rights of the individual and the family, of the sacredness of human life; there is an ostentatious straining at gnats by those who have swallowed camels.

Even the nine Catholic authors, though they write so modestly and perceptively, sometimes appear to picture themselves as representatives of an austere tribunal from whose unbending judgment the timid layman shrinks away. Father Beirnaert, S.J., for example, says that a merciful doctor will sometimes in disregard of Christian principles suppress a defective child "because he finds the morality of the Church too severe."

On the contrary, it is not its severity that is repugnant but its extreme flexibility. The churches make absolute judgments, but they qualify them for the powerful and only enforce them against the weak.

Father Roy, for example, says, "The affirmation of respect for human life must therefore be absolute and universal—that is, categorically binding all mankind—if we are not to founder in multiple disasters." This covers Mme. Vandeput but not Hitler, for conscience obliges Father Roy to add a footnote about the right to kill in war. He makes a distinction between "human life," which must be absolutely respected, and "biological life," which we can destroy in self-defence, or in "a just war." And he says that the Church, while tolerating killing in war, has "never given formal approval to it."

Surely this distinction between "human life" and "biological life" is a dishonest one? Does a man's life become biological rather than human when he puts on a uniform? The only true distinction is that between views that it is politic to hold or "tolerate" and those that are not. Father Roy's Church, a vast multiracial organization which is unpopular with many, cannot afford to assert unequivocally against everybody the sacredness of life, as it was asserted in the first two centuries of Christianity. In those days there was no conscription and all that the Christian expected from the state was to escape its attention. The distortions and compromises which we accept as inevitable had not yet been forced upon him.

Can we still accept them? I think not. There has been a great change. Long after other historic events are forgotten the name Auschwitz will recall the most stupendous crime in history. And, linked to it enduringly is the greatest non-event, the Silence of Pius XII, more terrible now that his apologists have argued that prudence and Christian charity demanded it. For this argument shifts the guilt of impotence from one man to the whole of Christendom and justifies a billion meaner connivances.

The gospels say that a darkness fell upon the earth when Christ was crucified and when a new era began. Surely the Silence of Pius has the same symbolic quality. It was mysterious and ominous, like the silence of woods and fields that precedes a total eclipse of the sun. It must herald some great change, either the final collapse of Christianity or its rebirth in some new and unforeseen shape.

In fact, if there is a rebirth, I believe that the ancient law THOU SHALT NOT KILL will have to be interpreted with greater severity and not less. And, if it is to be qualified at all, those who kill from loving compassion will seem to us far more forgivable than those millions of conscripted killers whom the churches forgive and even exalt.

The problem of "unnatural death," that is to say death which is not due to accident or bodily decay, is a unitary one. The hastened death of the defective baby and the incurable adult to whom life is only useless pain is linked to the involuntary death of the criminal and the conscript soldier and allied to all other assaults which we make upon human life, to birth control, sterilization and abortion. We shall never be able to face the problem of the useless, the unwanted, the criminal, the hostile, the unendurable life with courage and understanding, so long as our laws compel the innocent to kill the innocent against his will. So long as the churches condone it, the taint of expediency must colour everything they say. Nothing can change till the leaders of the Church dare to say once more, "Those that take the sword shall perish by the sword."

This would be a lightning flash, dazzling and destructive, that would shake the world. Many venerable establishments would crumble, but the dark unvisited places which breed ugliness would be illuminated. All the things that we do or fail to do in the antechambers of life or at its exit would be seen in their proper perspective, birth control, sterilization, abortion, euthanasia. Our judgment, no longer clouded and crippled by the great betrayal, the stupendous fallacy, would be free to act. Our little K's life, a frosted bud that will never open and bear fruit, would be allowed to drop.

CHURCHES UNDER PRESSURE

The ideal does not become more remote when the real is closely examined. The man who intends to escape must know each stone of his prison walls as though he loved it.

The narrow territory on the verges of life and death, which is now almost all that remains of the once vast spiritual dominion of the churches, is constantly under dispute. Let us observe how its Christian defenders behave when they are under attack. If most of my information is about Catholics, that is because in recent years they have excelled others in self-scrutiny. Let us watch how they acted when the Nazis tried to interrupt the cycle of man's life at its generation, in its prime and in its decay. We shall see that in general the churches capitulated to the powerful and compensated themselves for their defeat by tyrannizing over the defenceless.

Maybe this is just a law of life. If you have to draw sound from an instrument whose principal chords are dumb, you must strike those that remain all the harder. As their power to enforce laws that are binding on peoples and governments declines, the churches enforce them with special vigour in those spheres where men are solitary and amenable to persuasion. In all that concerns childbirth and sex and marrying and the death of relations, we are so much alone as to be almost grateful for public interest and hence ready to be counselled, cajoled and coerced. The warrior defeated in the field finds consolation in being a tyrant at home.

In Germany, which sometimes calls itself "the Heartland of Europe," ideas which are current elsewhere are often acted out so boldly and dramatically that, like the details in an enlarged photograph, we can see universal human behaviour most clearly in a German context.

There were three stages in the attack on the sacredness of human life, and corresponding to them two great ecclesiastical and one partial triumph. The Nazi sterilization laws attacked the unborn; the euthanasia campaign was directed in the first place against life in its decay; genocide, which was an attack on life in all its stages, was little more than an extension of the "just war" which the Nazis claimed to be waging.

It was to the question of procreation that the Nazis attended first. In May 1933 Hitler laid before the German bishops the draft of a law providing for voluntary sterilization. The Catholic bishops rejected it as a violation of the encyclical *Casti Conubii*, 1930, but the concordat with Hitler was about to be signed and the day after the signing a law for forcible sterilization of the diseased was approved. Catholic resistance was strong but, National Socialism having been accepted, the encyclical had ultimately to be set aside. Finally even in Rome compromises were made, and in 1940 the Sacred Congregation ruled that Catholic nurses in state-run hospitals might under certain circumstances assist at sterilization operations. It was argued that, if a recalcitrant nurse were dismissed, she might be replaced by an anti-religious person who would withhold the sacraments from those in danger of death. And, though it remained sinful for a Catholic physician to apply for the sterilization of any patient, he was allowed to report to the authorities the names of those afflicted with ills calling for sterilization.

The relationship of Church and state followed this familiar pattern of quibble and counter-quibble; when the Church was forced to some shameful capitulation, it invariably tried to make good its losses by some tiny usurpation in the domestic sphere. And thus it was that the German hierarchy forbade the marriage of sterilized persons, since "by natural law the main purpose of marriage is procreation." However, in the first three years of the decree 170,000 people had been sterilized and the Catholics among them made a formidable body. So even the Church was forced to retreat and to withdraw its veto.

Then followed the euthanasia campaign and a Church–state war of great significance, for in it the Church proved its power and influence and demonstrated that it was unwilling to use them except when public opinion was favourable. On 1 September 1939 Hitler decreed that all those with incurable diseases should be killed and before the end of the year establishments for the shooting and premises for the gassing of victims were opened in Württemberg and Hesse. As soon as rumours of this reached the clergy there were furious protests and after the campaign had lasted two years and 70,000 patients had been killed, there was an abrupt change of policy. The principal credit for this must go to Bishop Galen of Münster, who delivered a famous sermon demanding that those who had done the killing should be prosecuted for murder. He warned them that human life was sacred except in the case of self-defence or a just war, and that invalids and seriously wounded soldiers would be next on the list. Some of the Nazi leaders wanted Galen hanged but they dared not do so, so great was his popularity in Münster and in all Westphalia. Instead, the campaign of euthanasia was called off.

This great Church triumph was significant in several ways. It showed that in our frailty we are strengthened by being able to appeal, beyond our conscience, to infallible dogma. In other words it is easier for us to say: "That is forbidden by the encyclical *Casti Conubii*, 1930," than to protest: "That revolts me to the bottom of my soul!" But the disadvantage is that if we wait for the august and infallible Voice to proclaim the truth and the Voice is silent, we are more helpless than those who have treated their consciences as primary and not secondary sources of enlightenment. For the testing time for Christians in Germany came not when the government began to kill their crippled and defective kinsmen. It came when the Nazis began to kill their innocent and helpless neighbours the Jews. When the Voice was silent and the priest and the Levite passed by, it was inevitable that the ordinary man should consider it no concern of his and that the cold and cruel heart should be sanctified.

At that time the ecclesiastical opposition to euthanasia, successful as it was, showed that the bishops knew about gas chambers before the Jews did. They knew that they were built for the elimination of the "unproductive" and that Jews were officially declared "unproductive" and that many clergy had endorsed this view. They knew that they had been deported to the east—the bishops were not mentally deficient—and they had heard rumours.

If the purpose of religion is to arouse our conscience and to sharpen our sensibilities to the perception of evil, the churches had failed disastrously. What they offered was not a stimulant but a drug. In the matter of euthanasia we must turn aside and listen to the voice of our own conscience.

There is abundant evidence that the bishops' minds had been befogged by the theory of the just war and the image that it had printed indelibly on their imaginations of the conscript soldier as a knight-errant and even, in the fight against Bolshevism, as a soldier of Christ. In a fog of crusading holiness Auschwitz was hard to distinguish from an air raid, one of those sad events which it is necessary to endure and to inflict if, in our imperfect world, justice is to prevail. In order to preserve morale one must not say too much about specific cruelties and injustices of the war—in fact, better say nothing at all. So that Guenter Lewy in his magnificent book *The Catholic Church and Nazi Germany* writes: "While thousands of anti-Nazis were beaten to pulp in the concentration camps, the Church talked of supporting the moral renewal brought about by the Hitler government." And Gordon Zahn, in *German Catholics and Hitler's Wars*, declares that after exhaustive research he could only find a record of four German Catholics who had openly refused military service. He attributes the "near unanimity of support" for the war from German Catholics to "the external pressure exerted by leading Church officials" and the spiritual influence that their words and examples were bound to have on their flock.

For years after the true character of the war had revealed itself the clergy went on proclaiming it a just war and denouncing those brave men who refused to serve. For example, when the Austrian peasant Jägestätter chose to be beheaded rather than to take part in what he deemed an unjust war, his bishop reprimanded him severely for his disloyalty. They were all of them deceiving themselves in the interests of ecclesiastical survival.

Years later the President of West Germany, Lübke, said in a memorial address, "No one who was not completely blinded or wholly naive could be completely free of the pressing awareness that this war was not a just war."

That is to say that much innocent blood was shed, often by innocent men, because of the Church's failure to follow its own teaching. Lewy believes that had the leaders of German Catholicism opposed Hitler from the start, they would have made the home front so unreliable that he "might not have dared going to war and literally millions of lives would have been saved." But once a war has started it is not easy to see how the Church, with its intricate relationship with the government of every state, would be able to oppose it. When nations are engaged in combat it is already too late to ask where justice lies and to urge soldiers to desert.

I hope I have shown how vacillating the Christian approach to those problems has been. The encyclical about sterilization was only scrupulously observed so long as observance was not likely to injure the faithful seriously and damage the prestige and authority of the Church and alienate its disciples. The euthanasia of the innocent was only vigorously denounced when it concerned people of the same race as the denouncing ecclesiastics. The problem of the "just" or "unjust" war was never seriously considered. I believe that there is not a bishop in Germany or in all Europe and America who would now dare publicly to assert that Hitler's war was a just one. Yet when they were already in full possession of all the facts, thousands of bishops, and not only in Germany, asserted this.

PUBLIC AND PRIVATE KILLING

I see only one path through this moral chaos. The Church sometimes claims to be a higher court attending to those spiritual needs of mankind which governments, concerned for its material welfare, must ignore. If that is so, could she not insist that a man is the master of his own life and that he cannot be obliged to offer it or preserve it against his will? The community may try to educate him in the use of this right but cannot deprive him of it. If he should abuse it, no doubt we might suffer "multiple disasters," but not so many as we suffer through denying that that right exists.

In the matter of killing in self-defence, which the Church tolerates and often commands, this new code of ethics might work more justly and effectively than the old one. Science allied to bureaucracy concentrates power in the hands of the few; a genius in a laboratory conceives an idea and shares it with a governing minority. As a result great cities crumble, army corps collapse, empires capitulate. The only antidote to the captive genius and his captors is the free man's passionate conviction. He normally operates single-handed and is trusted by neither Church nor state. All the honours, all the blessings, go to the conscript armies. These armies are composed of a few men who identify themselves with the aims of the government and are prepared to kill for them, a few more who are convinced that it is their duty to suppress all private judgment and to kill as they are ordered, and finally vast hordes of ignorant or innocent or deeply reluctant conscripts. If there is often or ever a clear-cut antithesis of good and evil, the last place to look for it would be in the opposition of rival armies. This is an old story which we have come to accept as inevitable. What we should not accept, what is obscene and intolerable, is that the churches should bless this arrangement and continue to preach as Father Roy does that "respect for human life must be absolute and universal and that it must be categorically binding on all mankind."

Only a Quaker or one of the other pacifist sects can talk like that without the grossest hypocrisy.

Yet if the Quakers are wrong and we have to kill in defence of innocence and justice, how best can it be done? In scientific warfare the innocent and the just who are conscripted and forced to use modern weapons will be as indiscriminatingly murderous as their fellows and must be resisted with the same mechanical ruthlessness. There is only one way in which death can be dealt out selectively and that is by assassination, a form of private enterprise on which the Church has always frowned. Those who took part in the 20 July attack on Hitler are now recognized as great heroes who, had they succeeded, would have ended the war and preserved the unity of Germany. Yet at the time they received nothing but discouragement from even those of the Church leaders who had opposed the Nazis. Cardinal Faulhaber, for example, when questioned by the Gestapo after the plot had failed, is said to have expressed the most vigorous condemnation of the attempt and to have affirmed his loyalty to Hitler.

Yet it is obvious that assassination, when a man chooses his victim of his own free will and, risking his life, takes upon himself the complete responsibility for his acts, can have a nobility that must always be lacking in the mass slaughter of conscripts by conscripts. And after the event the successful assassin will certainly get the blessing of the Church. It has been said that Bishop Preising, who had been informed in advance of the 20 July plot, was to have replaced the pro-Nazi Orsenigo as Papal Nuncio to the government of assassins. Whether or not this is true it is certain that Archbishop Stepinac cordially welcomed the government of Pavelitch, whose members had been involved in the assassination of King Alexander. All the Croatian bishops extolled Pavelitch, who was himself received in audience by Pope Pius XII.

If the Church were to accept assassination as a form of resistance, which, however deplorable, was preferable to conscript warfare, it might be able to judge it by some subtler criterion than success. In that case it would surely condemn Pavelitch and Stepinac and praise Stauffenberg and Preising.

But could the Church ever show greater indulgence to the assassin than to the soldier? Not as she now is. Being herself a social organization, she is always disposed in a time of crisis to ingratiate herself with the great political aggregations to which she is affiliated. Though she often claims to be the defender of the individual conscience, she usually concedes that when mankind organizes itself into powerful national groupings, it can legitimately dodge the impact of those "absolute and universal laws" which are "categorically binding" on the individual. In the matter of killing, the churches will therefore line up with the worst of governments till it is defeated, rather than with the best of assassins before he succeeds.

I have written sympathetically of assassins without recalling any particular one of whom one could unreservedly approve. The German heroes of 20 July seem to have plotted to destroy Hitler principally because he was losing the war. Bonhoeffer, who excites interest and was executed for his complicity, does not seem to have been deeply implicated. Pavelitch was a bloodthirsty fanatic. Perhaps I have most sympathy for Princip and Chubrilovitch, the assassins of Sarajevo, who, as many think (not I), precipitated the First World War. Why are assassins mad or simple or discredited people, or else like Princip have a fatal illness? I think it is because public opinion is conditioned to abhor what they do and only the most desperate conviction and courage will induce a man to risk a healthy life for it. He knows that a conscript who mindlessly kills a hundred other equally harmless conscripts will be criticized by nobody, while a brave and resolute man who rids the world of a tyrant is staking his honour and his reputation as well as his life.

How trivial my problem seems compared to his, yet I have linked them together because law and religion have already done so. I too ask more than orthodoxy could ever concede. I am claiming much more than the right over my own life, which in the long run no one can permanently withhold from me. I believe that love can give us the right of life and death over those who are helpless and dependent on us. And that when circumstances are desperate we must snatch it, as did those parents who flung their children from the trains transporting them to Auschwitz. It is a right that can never be confirmed by any legislature, for the essence of law is impartiality and detachment, and those who are detached cannot judge the depth of love and the urgency of despair.

THE NORMALITY OF LOVE AND THE LAW

It is not healthy to live alone for long periods with dreams which you cannot realize, for it is certain that little K's parents can never claim their rights and it is improbable that I will. But you can obtain relief from a particular problem by generalizing it, observing its impact upon others and preparing for its solution by posterity. So I took the subway downtown to East 57th Street, New York, where the Euthanasia Society of America has its headquarters, and there I came to my senses. The secretary told me that there is no likelihood that in our lifetime euthanasia for defective children will be legalized. "You see," she said, "religion is very powerful in America. Even to work for legalization might be unwise. We have to approach our objective step by step, and the first step concerns the elderly and hopelessly diseased who wish to die." She showed me an article in *Harper's Magazine* of October 1960, "The Patient's Right to Die" by Joseph Fletcher, who has a chair in ethics and moral theology at Cambridge, Mass.

This article is very illuminating but confirms what the secretary said. It is the problem of the old who wish to die which occupies the mind of these reformers. He tells the familiar story well. He describes how we have altered the whole pattern of life and death; men live far longer than they used to do and die painfully and slowly as their faculties decay. "The classical deathbed scene with its loving partings and solemn last words is practically a thing of the past. In its stead is a sedated, comatose, betubed object manipulated and subconscious, if not subhuman."

The doctor who from worthy motives refuses to prolong this indecency must first be protected by the law; the next to be championed is the doctor who deliberately curtails it. The case of little K is something quite other; it cannot even be considered.

Evidently modern medicine has caused us to invert the thinking of the Greeks, for whom old people, whose lives were never artificially prolonged, presented no problem, since if they were not reasonably healthy they soon died. Not even Aristotle or Plato, who favoured the killing of defective children, required that old people should be helped into the tomb.

Reading Mr. Fletcher I have come to think that in fact the Greeks understood better than we do the nature of the affections. We stress the "sacredness of life" but a Greek would consider that life becomes sacred but is not born so. The reverence which we feel for the young is woven out of memories and hopes and gathers in complexity as they grow older. But where there are no memories and no hopes the Greeks would only see "biological life," to use a phrase of Father Roy in a way which he would greatly dislike.

"Biological life" is something that we spare and cherish from biological instinct, and instinct will perhaps only slowly develop into love. Where there are no hopes, we may come to feel resentment or even hatred towards the life which instinct bids us cherish.

There is indeed in general estimation nothing sacred about the instincts. We defer to them perhaps even less than we should do, inhibiting all those that are incompatible with social order. The sexual and philoprogenitive instincts, the instinct of self-preservation and many others, are subordinated to the needs of the state. Even the maternal instinct submits to control.

Joseph Fletcher talks of a new "morality of love," which he also calls "the morality of human freedom and dignity." He does not define it, but he seems to think that it is something that the law could be brought to tolerate. Could it? To me, this morality of love will always be apart from, and sometimes in conflict with, the law. For as the law extends its scope wider and wider over men of all creeds and races, it will concern itself less with the intimate relations of men and more with their public communications. Its goal will be to avoid social collisions. The only support that the morality of love could offer to a man in conflict with the law would be the assurance that he was doing right.

A pamphlet which I was given by the Euthanasia Society, combined with Fletcher's plans for a graduated reform of the law, made me wonder whether I even wanted the legislation of what he calls "the morality of love." Attached to the pamphlet is a specimen application form which the seeker after death would have to send to "the authorities" (in this case not GOD but some medical-legal committee). Can death safely be made something you apply for like a widow's pension, a traveller's visa, a set of false teeth, filling in details about your age, your illness, the degree of your pain? Is it some tenderness of guts that makes me squeamish? I should like to ask permission to die from those I love, for they alone can judge whether it is time for me to go. I would prefer that old laws should be generously applied than that new ones should be made. Otherwise in a bureaucracy one application form begets another. It might happen that when the Society had won its cause, the application form for dying would breed as its legitimate heir an application form for living. Even if this did not happen, the pressure on useless people to make them feel unwanted is intensifying. There used always to be room for an old grandfather by the chimney corner but now there is a waiting list for every bed in the hospital.

Father Roy was talking sense when he said that "this principle, the suppression of abnormal children, first announced as a right, is in danger of being insensibly transformed into a duty," and that "war is being prepared against the feeble and the abnormal."

This danger is a real one and if infanticide were left to the medical services it might become a branch of eugenics and under government control. This would be an outrage upon the "morality of love, of freedom and dignity." For what we have to assert is that a man has a right over his own life and a shared right, in certain cases, over the lives of those that are dear to him. We cannot define these rights, but love, which is not transitory, has duties and powers and will define them according as we acknowledge its authority. I believe that it would define them unmistakably for those that love little K.

Because of this, it might be better to take a life in defiance of the laws of the state and to be called a murderer than to arrange a legal death, if by so doing we allowed it to appear that the state had any right over the lives of the innocent. Though we might come to claim that even an adult belongs to those that love him, we could never admit that he belonged to such random collectivities as the state, the people, the nation, the race.

In another respect I feel myself in sympathy with the nine Catholic writers. Fletcher links artificial insemination with birth control, sterilization and abortion as "a medically discovered way of fulfilling and protecting human values and hopes in spite of nature's failures or foolishnesses."

Now artificial insemination seems to me to belong to a different category from these others. It is a prim suburban device for replenishing the nursery without the illicit pleasures of adultery or the illegal obligations of polygamy. It is anti-social and anti-historical, and an affront to those who believe in the ties of kinship and are ready to be bound by them. It undermines the solicitude that a man must feel for his offspring. The most carefree adulterer cannot free himself from concern for the child he has begotten, even though it may be hard for him to express it. A "donor" on the other hand releases his child into the unknown and will never think of him again.

And artificial insemination is only the first of the scientific marvels by which the family is liable to be transformed. It is now possible for a woman, through the transplantation of fertilized ova, to bear children unrelated to her own family as well as to her husband's.

Would Fletcher consider such devices as ways, like artificial insemination, of "protecting human values and hopes"? I think that they violate them and that though they may be legal, they should "be held in utter detestation."

How can artificial insemination be integrated into a "morality of love," since to love the real father of one's child instead of his assumed father would bring fresh complications to an already complicated situation? If Fletcher does not see how fraudulent and furtive such arrangements are, he has not understood the true nature of family love, how it develops out of ties of blood, out of shared memories and associations, responsibilities. He does not see what a huge part the sense of continuity plays in the love we bear for our children and their children. I think of my little K as carrying with her till she dies the rudiments of tastes, qualities, talents, features, prejudices which I and her father and mother have seen in those akin to us or observed in ourselves. Because of this sense of continuity she is called, like many others of my family, after an ancestress who lived centuries ago and of whom we know nothing but without whom we should none of us exist. Because of her affliction she will never be able to coordinate her inheritance or develop it. She is starting on a long and hopeless journey in more or less the same direction as we and ours are travelling and have travelled. She may be travelling it alone when we, who brought her into the world, are no longer there to shield and love her. Is this conviction that her destinies and ours are interwoven a necessary part of family love or something that can be detached from it and quite irrelevant? I can only say that it is not irrelevant for me and mine. And sometimes when I have been thinking up arguments for the legalization of infanticide, I pull myself up with the reflection: "What business is it of theirs anyway, the doctors, the police, the judge, the jury, the hangman?" Little K is ours, irrevocably ours, in virtue of our deep involvement and I abandon myself to a vision of the future that is more like a Chinese puzzle than a dream, for even as I construct it I see all its intricate improbabilities. Yet there is no other way, at present, in which "human values and hopes" can be protected.

ORDER AND CHAOS

There is very small chance that any widespread change of opinion about these things will occur during peaceful times. Not till something desperate happens will parents of defective children dare to articulate the knowledge which they have found in their hearts, or look to others to endorse it. The average man is unconcerned. Since death and decay await us all, he might take a remote interest in euthanasia for the old and sick but he will be more likely to dodge the law when his time comes than to try to change it in advance. I cannot see that even for the elderly or diseased who wish to die, there is any likelihood of a change in the legal or religious position till the graver problem of the conscript killer has been faced. A reconsideration of this by Church or state might cause a revolution in the structure of society, as Christianity did in its first centuries. In the rebuilding of a new order, a man might recover the rights which he once abdicated to the state.

Certainly the desire for a revolution, a rebirth, is there but no one knows in which direction to look for it or how to prepare for its coming.

The state seems to wish to renounce its right to kill or to expose its citizens to be killed for causes they do not approve. Capital punishment has gone and the rights of the conscientious objector are acknowledged though not widely acclaimed.

Can it go further without laying itself open to internal decay and external assault?

In the Church, too, there are signs that under pressure of science and public opinion some of its most sacred taboos are being relaxed. If birth control is permitted, a very ancient and fundamental belief about the human soul will have been abandoned. At the other end of life, science has pushed back the frontiers so far that most people can outlive their faculties. This means that the preservation of life, which was once a sacred duty, no longer appears so.

Therefore Pius XII has said that, when life is ebbing hopelessly, doctors need not try to reanimate their patient but "may permit him, already virtually dead, to pass on in peace." And Dr. Lang, the Archbishop of Canterbury, wrote that "cases arise in which some means of shortening life may be justified." There are clergymen on the committees of euthanasia societies.

Yet in these directions Church and state, with their survival at stake, must move so slowly and cautiously that frequently their leaders have to appear as the enemies of the causes in which they believe. A great prelate may find it impossible to exhibit in public the rebellious wisdom and gentleness of his nature. Whatever his private views might be, he could not give public comfort to the conscript who felt no hate and refused to kill, or to the men and women who killed because they wished to spare suffering to those they loved. That is the price he pays to the people for the platform from which he is permitted to address his message *urbi et orbi* or to his nation.

The pyramidal structure of a great state or a great Church imposes prudence. By his exalted position at the apex a prince of religion is exposed to pressure which obscurer men can dodge, and, as with a general who capitulates, his surrender forces submission on men still capable of resistance. Pius XII, for well-known reasons, lagged very far behind the most enlightened of his bishops in his defence of the innocent. The bishops on their part, crippled by the weight of bonds and bargains by which their relations with the state were regulated, passed on to their priests the responsibility of protesting. The priests passed it on to the laymen. And, equally fearful of damaging the Church, the laymen passed it on to those outside the Church. Was there in all Germany a Christian who resisted Hitler as promptly, unreservedly, heroically, as the non-Christian Ossietzky? But the clerics were justified in their prudence. The pyramid still stands, a massive monument to the advantages of discretion.

But even now its security would be endangered by any serious squabble with the state. So it is unlikely that leading churchmen will ever support aggressively the rights of conscience or question unbecomingly the justice of any war in which their government is engaged. Until something happens to interrupt the easy tenor of events, this prudence is obligatory. For if the government were to grant to each citizen the right to decide who his enemy was and whether he should be killed (a right which many savages enjoy), not only would armies be in danger of disintegration but so would states and churches. There would be chaos of a kind.

But what kind? We have been conditioned to think that even war is better than chaos or disorder. Though we do not, like many great Victorians, actually value war (Ruskin said it was "the foundation of all the arts, all the high virtues and faculties of man"), many see it as the mother of invention, of better aircraft and nuclear discovery. And a huge number of respectable people find in it great enjoyment and liberation of spirit. In contrast few social opportunities and interesting assignations are to be offered by the disorder that results when some conflict of principle, normally inhibited, flares up into violent civil discord. And everybody condemns it. Yet the free human spirit is less enslaved by the worst kinds of social disorder than by the best kind of war. The most dreadful crimes of the century have been committed by orderly people subordinating themselves to the commonweal. When the Czechs unburied the corpses of the thousands who had been massacred at Theresienstadt, they were able to give each victim an individual tombstone, for a number had been attached to his or her big toe which corresponded to a name and an address in a carefully kept register. It was not brutal people who did this, but hundreds of selfless and dedicated morticians and stenographers. The massacres which were conducted chaotically, as in the Balkan countries, were not nearly so comprehensive. The killers often tired or felt queasy or amorous or compassionate or accepted bribes. Nature was able to assert itself. And nature is not evil till we make it so.

In fact fruitful ideas are often nourished by what the Organization Man calls disorder. They grow like ferns in the interstices of crumbling walls. You cannot say, as some do, that the ferns are pulling down the wall, for unless it was already collapsing the ferns would not have a foothold there.

Today, in the huge discrepancies between official belief and private behaviour, almost any revolutionary idea could comfortably take root and slowly dislodge a stone or two from the established certainties. Half of Europe is officially dedicated to the belief, which shows no sign of being fulfilled, that the state will one day "wither away," its mission accomplished. Would it matter if the other half also came to think of states and governments as provisional, as methods of collective administration concerned with the problems that arise when men meet each other impersonally in large numbers, with traffic, that is to say, rather than with ethic? Such a view might be more congenial to us than it is to the Russians who preach it. Things would move slowly but by degrees problems of morality and ethic, of punishment and penance, might be released, finger by finger, from the palsied and uncertain grasp of the Church and the state, and settled quietly by men who knew each other.

Maybe the right to kill is the last that the state will relinquish, but the pattern of society is changing rapidly. Consider Charles Whitman, the psychopath, who killed his mother and his wife and then climbed to the top of a tower in the University of Texas and killed or injured forty passersby before he was himself killed by the police. Friends, relations, neighbours, all knew what he was like and might have foreseen and forestalled what happened. Do we not need dreams, ideas and plans that will strengthen the authority of those who are fond of us, or at least interested in us, and weaken the power of the remote, indifferent people who are normally appointed to judge us?

This is fantasy, of course. But the world of Auschwitz was a fantastic one, built upon evil dreams, which no one except the dreamers thought could be realized. The ordinary familiar methods failed to disperse them. We might do better with what is extraordinary and unheard of.

THE SMALL COMMUNITY

So it appears that for me and mine the situation is hopeless for many years to come. Legalism becomes increasingly more powerful than love, and religion sanctions it. The secret ways of ending life are carefully guarded by the specialist. Only a doctor can defy the law and terminate an unwanted life without being detected. Frequently, of course, he will refrain from "respirating" a malformed infant. But in this he cannot be said to be animated by love but by certain scientific classifications.

Even in that kindly book about the Liège trial, the nine religious writers print an appendix in which the retarded are divided into four grades according to their IQ percentages. Little K belongs, I believe, because she has only two-thirds of a brain, to the lowest group of the four, and Hitler's doctors would have given her a high priority for the gas chamber. But by these physiological groupings we distort the problem and make it likely that a categorical "No" will one day lead to a categorical "Yes." Science has, in fact, by reducing the significance of the individual human life, disintegrated love and impaired the rights which a man has over his own life and his child's. Almost everybody today would agree that the doctor, the judge, the clergyman and the geneticist should have greater authority over the life and death of a baby than those who begot him and bore him.

The nine French authors, dreaming of fresh fields opening up for the compassionate heart, the dedicated volunteer, have exiled themselves from reality, as I do when I speculate how I can end little K's life, which can bring only suffering to her parents and to herself. Measuring our convictions, we may be ready to believe that present reality will change more easily than they will. In the meantime I see that I cannot follow my conscience without causing complications for everybody and in particular for those I wish to help, and so I put all my proudest hopes into reverse. Because I cannot take life I become anti-life, and I pray that little K will have a sort of vegetable apathy and that she will never be so conscious of her inadequacies as to suffer for them.

But how can one wish that anyone one loves should be as stupid and helpless as possible? That is a sin of course far worse than the act which I accept as right but cannot perform, yet I am driven to it by a society which refuses to recognize the rights of love.

Moreover, I am forced to admit that till the whole structure of society changes, there are excellent reasons for this refusal. In an acquisitive society, where property is accumulated and inherited and men advertise themselves by their offspring, where labour has to be mobile and families move from place to place, it would be very easy for prudence to pass itself off as love, and for respectable people to engage in a covert war against all physical and mental non-conformity. It would be very difficult to establish that kind of community in which the fraud would be detected and "held in utter detestation." In an open society love is easy to simulate. One cannot trust it, and even when one can, one could not allow our social institutions to be shaped by such a trust. As democracy widens its scope and we reach towards a universal government with uniform laws, it is less and less safe to judge a man's acts by the purity of his motives. We have to be impartial, which means impersonal. In a mass society news of our actions reaches far beyond the small circle which they directly affect, so we must be punished not for what we do but also for things that are done by those unknown people who imitate us. That is to say that if we do what we know to be right, it may be something that society is forced to condemn.

Will this always be so? Can there ever be a society in which the rights of love are recognized and even the law bends before them? If so, it will necessarily be a small society. It will differ I think from the kind of society in which Aristotle preached and Hippocrates practised, because Aristotle thought it was a matter of law, not of love, that defective children should be killed. One may suspect that such laws, where they were enforced, were very loosely administered. The city-state grew up as an aggregate of many families and was itself a vastly inflated family, and its laws must have been flexible enough. Despite Aristotle, natural affection probably played a larger part in their application than eugenics. It was not the state but the parents themselves who exposed their infants on the mountainsides. All the same, good citizenship and not love was the criterion by which behaviour was judged, and if Aristotle had his way the state would have usurped the rights of the parents and made the exposure of defective children the concern of the city not of the family.

But even if we wished to, we could not re-create the city-states. Where else can we look? In our loose and inchoate society are there any traces of a submerged or nascent community in which the rule of love is observed and to whose collective judgment we could refer? There are many; but they crystallize round some specific problem and evaporate as soon as it is solved. And of course there are our families, more permanent in their mutual dependence but seldom acting as a

566 : Hubert Butler

unit. If they had the confidence and assumed the authority, it seems to me that my family and D's could judge more wisely about what concerns them intimately than any government could. And, if we considered, too, the judgment of those friends to whom we are bound as closely as by ties of blood, we should have a community as capable of deciding its own affairs as, say, Megara or Sicyon ever claimed to be.

In such a community the weight of the decision would bear most heavily on those that love most, but concern would travel outward from the centre, the focus of agony, to the periphery, and authority to endorse or dissent would be proportionate to love. If such a community were to coalesce out of chaos, I would trust it to decide wisely about little K or to form a loving background for such a decision.

But it has not coalesced and there is as yet no sign that it will. And, even if it did coalesce, how could it ever acquire legal status? This question can be illuminated by another question. How would it be possible to withhold legal status from the offspring of scientific marriages, the children of sperm-filled capsules and transplanted ovaries? The answer to these questions is that the law in both cases is helpless. These matters are outside the law, and men and women must decide for themselves.

Before there is any change we shall have to live through this period of remote and impersonal control and, in the meantime, for the sake of future freedom, a greater burden than ever before will fall upon the man who refuses to conform. Politically, socially, domestically, the individual may have to make in solitude great and tragic decisions and carry them through in the teeth of a hostile and mechanical officialdom. Ossietzky and Stauffenberg, Sinyavsky, Daniel and Djilas are well-known names, but they owe their deserved celebrity, at least in part, to the publicity services of their country's enemies. In other spheres thousands of men and women will have to fling themselves fruitlessly against the barriers before they collapse. Their names will be known only to a very few, and by the time they are due to be honoured they will be forgotten.

Joseph Fletcher says that we are at the end of the theological era and that those who do not believe in personal survival after death do not fear it as much as those that do. Certainly this is true of me. As it approaches, I seldom look forward but often backward, thinking of the things I have never done, the faculties that are likely to decay before they have been used.

When I do look forward, I see a faint line becoming fainter as I draw closer to it. Beyond it I will live for a certain period in the thoughts of those I love or have influenced. This measured immortality belongs to almost everybody, but for little K the dividing line is dim and blurred. The emptiness beyond can scarcely be more empty than that through which she is passing now. Maybe in ten or twenty years, as little K, climbing very slowly, has reached the highest rung she will ever reach, she will meet me there descending much more rapidly. If that were so, she would be the companion that I would choose above all others to travel back with me into nothingness.

Note on Sources

The essays in *Independent Spirit* were drawn from the following four books. In the cases where the works had been originally published elsewhere, the additional bibliographical data are so indicated.

Escape from the Anthill
1985

Introduction

Henry and Frances   *The Dublin Magazine*, April 1950

Beside the Nore   *Ireland of the Welcomes*, under the title "Nore and Barrow"

The Deserted Sun Palace   Under the title "Anglo-Irish Twilight, the Last Ormonde War," *Journal of the Butler Society*, 1978–79

A Visit to Hesse and Some Thoughts about Princes   *The Irish Times*, 20 September 1968, and *Journal of the Butler Society*, 1978–79

The Bell: An Anglo-Irish View   *Irish University Review*, Spring 1976

Divided Loyalties   Revised from an earlier version in *An Cosantoir, The Irish Army Journal*, August 1979

New Geneva in Waterford   *Journal of the Royal Society of Antiquaries of Ireland*, December 1947

Three Friends   The comments on O'Mahony in *The Irish Times*, 21 February 1970

Boycott Village   *The Twentieth Century*, January 1958

The Eggman and the Fairies   *The Twentieth Century*, July 1960

Two Critics   *The Bell*, March 1952

Peter's Window   Robert Greacen, ed., *Irish Harvest* (New Frontiers Press, 1946), under the title "The Teaching Brigade," then revised and expanded

Mr. Pfeffer of Sarajevo   *Nonplus*, Winter 1960

The Invader Wore Slippers   *The Bell*, November 1950
The Last *Izmirenje*   *The Irish Press*, 28 February 1947
The Sub-Prefect Should Have Held His Tongue   *The Twentieth Century*, June
    1956
The Artukovitch File   Reflections on a Croatian Crusade in *New Blackfriars*,
    February 1971

The Children of Drancy
1988

A Fragment of Autobiography
Aunt Harriet
Saints, Scholars and Civil Servants   *The Bell*, November 1954
Boucher de Perthes: The Father of Prehistory   *Social Biology and Human
    Affairs*, 1986
Influenza in Aran
Maria Edgeworth   Radio Éireann Thomas Davis Lecture, January 1954
Ernest Renan: The Statue and the Cavalry   *The Listener*, 31 August 1950,
    then expanded
Riga Strand in 1930
Carl von Ossietzky   *The Irish Times*, 6 June 1954
The Kagran Gruppe
In the Adriatic   "The Russian Consul," BBC Third Programme, 17 October
    1957, under the title "A Journey to Split"
In Russia and China   The sections on Russia in *The Irish Times*,
    6 November 1956 and 7–8 January 1957; the sections on China in *The
    Irish Times*, 16, 19–21 November 1956, and *Peace News*, 30 August
    1957
The Children of Drancy   *The Irish Review*, Spring 1988
Little K

Grandmother and Wolfe Tone
1990

The Auction
Crossing the Border
Grandmother and Wolfe Tone   *The Kilkenny Magazine*, Spring and Autumn
    1963
Abortion
The Decay of Archaeology
Yugoslavia: The Cultural Background
Yugoslav Papers: The Church and Its Opponents

In the Land of Nod
1996

Wolfe Tone and the Common Name of Irishman   Lilliput Pamphlet 5, 1985

Down the Parade

Irish Literature

Topical Thoughts on Shaw   Parts of this essay appeared in *The Irish Times*
    8 January 1976

Leavis on Lawrence   *The Irish Times*, 4 September 1976

Peter and Paul   *The Irish Times* 1 May 1976

Materialism Without Marx: A Study of Chekhov   Compiled from three
    typescript drafts of articles published in *Envoy*, August 1950, December
    1950, and January 1951. One was marked, "Broadcast BBC 1 January
    1949. Both talks repeated on Third Programme a month later."

Leonid Leonov   A version of this essay appeared in *The Irish Times* (n.d.)
    and *Manchester Guardian Weekly*, 15–22 May, 1946

Report on Yugoslavia

The Writer as Independent Spirit

Index